THE SHAPING OF AMERICA

THE SHAPING OF AMERICA

Volume 1
Atlantic America, 1492–1800 (1986)

Volume 2
Continental America, 1800–1867 (1993)

Volume 3
Transcontinental America, 1850–1915 (in preparation)

Volume 4
Global America, 1915–1992

THE SHAPING OF AMERICA

A GEOGRAPHICAL PERSPECTIVE ON 500 YEARS OF HISTORY

Volume 2
Continental America
1800–1867

D. W. MEINIG

Yale University Press
New Haven and London

Published with assistance from the foundation established in memory of Philip Hamilton McMillan of the Class of 1894, Yale College.

Set in Goudy Old Style type by The Composing Room of Michigan, Inc. Printed in the United States of America by Vail-Ballou Press, Binghamton, N.Y.

Library of Congress Cataloging-in-Publication Data
(Revised for vol. 2)

Meinig, D. W. (Donald William), 1924–
    The shaping of America
    Includes indexes.
    Includes bibliographical references.
    Contents: v. 1. Atlantic America, 1492–1800—v. 2. Continental America, 1800–1867.
    1. United States—History.   2. United States—Historical geography.
E178.M57   1986   973   85-17962
ISBN 0-300-03548-9 (v. 1 : cloth)
       0-300-03882-8 (v. 1 : pbk.)
       0-300-05658-3 (v. 2 : cloth)
       0-300-06290-7 (v. 2 : pbk.)

A catalogue record for this book is available from the British Library.

The paper in this book meets the guidelines for permanence and durability of the Committee on Production Guidelines for Book Longevity of the Council on Library Resources.

10   9   8   7   6   5   4   3   2

for
Lee

Think of the past as space expanding infinitely beyond our vision. . . . Then we choose a prospect. The higher it is, the wider and hazier our view. Now we map what we see, marking some features, ignoring others, altering an unknown territory . . . into a finite collection of landmarks made meaningful through their connections. History is not the past, but a map of the past drawn from a particular point of view to be useful to the modern traveler.

Henry Glassie

CONTENTS

PART THREE
TENSION:
THE SUNDERING OF
A FEDERATION

PART FOUR
CONTEXT:
THE UNITED STATES IN
NORTH AMERICA CIRCA 1867

ILLUSTRATIONS

PREFACE

Continental America offers a rather different way of looking at a period of enormous expansion, development, and crisis in the career of the United States. Although it stands as a discrete, coherent work, it is best understood as a continuation of the special kind of description and assessment set forth in *Atlantic America, 1492–1800*, the opening volume of this geographic interpretation.

I must acknowledge that *Continental America* covers only half of the span originally announced for Volume II. Once I was immersed in the writing it became apparent that the amount of basic geographic change was simply more than could be conveniently contained within a single book without sacrificing too much pertinent detail. Thus, *The Shaping of America* is now projected to be four volumes. Volume III, *Transcontinental America, 1850–1915*, now in preparation, will begin at midcentury, overlapping the coverage of Volume II so as to give proper attention to the several regions of the American Far West, which in the present book have merely been brought into the framework of the United States as the western realm of empire. In that way the treatment of their fuller development and incorporation into the body of the nation and federation will become an uninterrupted theme in the formation of a genuinely transcontinental republic. Several other important topics only touched on in *Continental America*, such as the emergence of a more stable regional structure within the United States as a whole, immigration and the changing sociocultural composition of the population, and continuing cultural connections with Europe, will also receive more attention in this next volume.

A succinct statement of my views on the nature of geography and history, relationships between these fields, and a few basic geographic principles that inform this entire project can be found in the Preface of *Atlantic America* and will not be repeated here. I would reemphasize, however, that these volumes are intended as both a complement to and a critique of more common versions of American history. As for the first, they make no attempt to deal with many topics central to the concerns of historians and therefore are not offered as a substitute for more orthodox treatments; on the other hand, they do seek to demonstrate that a broader geographic context and far greater concern for the character and significance of place and location, for geographic structures, systems, and change, are fundamental to a better understanding of what the United States is like and how it got to be that way.

I must also emphasize again how very limited my treatment is within my own field. *The Shaping of America* is not environmental history, nor a close study of colonization and the development of resources, and certainly not an analysis of the changing spatial economy of the nation. Such themes are important facets of historical geography. I make no claim for the superiority of my particular emphases over these, or any others, but neither do I make any apology for what I have done and left undone. It will be obvious to any specialist in American history that despite the size of these volumes they can provide no more than a sketch of even these selected patterns and developments of such a huge and complex subject. Yet it is not a rough or simple sketch, it has been drawn with much thought and care, it offers a coherent picture within its own terms, and it aspires to limn a likeness that will be at once recognizable and appreciated as a fresh way of looking at something familiar and important.

My main focus is on the emergence and continuing development of the United States, and I have followed the common usage of the term *American* to refer to features pertaining to this country, however illogical, ambiguous, or annoying to other people on the same continent this universal practice may be. That the term occasionally is used in some broader sense should be clear from the context. I must also try to make clear how I have dealt with several rather more difficult problems of terminology in this human geography. I have used *Indian* as the collective term for the descendants of the aboriginal inhabitants of North America because I see no better alternative. *Native American* is too ambiguous, especially for nineteenth-century history, wherein American-born citizens might well use that reference or some variant to differentiate themselves from new immigrants. As for specific Indian groups, I have tried to use names now in general use, but one cannot overcome a good deal of complexity and controversy in these matters. So, too, with such generic terms as *confederation, nation, tribe,* and *band;* these European concepts are prickly with connotations about relative status and often grossly misleading as to actual sociopolitical structures. I have tended to use them to convey some sense of scale of the relative size of groups, but one must recognize that there is no way of achieving clarity or certainty with any of these widely employed—imposed—shorthand terms.

The descendants of Africans in America pose even more intractable problems. One wants to be sensitive to the preferences of the referent people themselves, but these, too, are varied, nuanced, and unstable. I have chosen to stick with *Afro-*

American and *Black* as two interchangeable terms of general reference. "Negro" and "colored" appear only in quotations or where directly tied to some historical use by government or society. Readers will note that throughout these books *Black* and *White* are capitalized. That is a deliberate attempt to emphasize that race is an abstraction, a social construct that has little relation to colors of ordinary reference: after all, most American "blacks" are not black, "whites" are certainly not white, and there is no objective way of separating the one group from the other on such a basis. That such words can engender heated disagreements, be expressions of pride and instruments of hate, underscores the long-festering and most fundamental problem of American society and, ironically, the continuing need to use them in any discussion of that relentless reality.

Similarly, one wants to be sensitive to the sexism embedded in common language, but there is no obvious guide to appropriate usage. Here, too, the text often reflects the social practice of the times under study and, as well, my own tendency to resist radical—and clumsy—alterations and restrictions on our venerable tongue. In a work of this scale one is talking more of "populations" and "peoples" than of specific communities or smaller groups, and unless otherwise specified one may assume that all such collective terms routinely include both men and women, without implication as to proportions or status.

Finally, I would call attention to some common words central to this geographic interpretation that are little less complex and laden with meanings even if they might seem, at the moment, to be much less provocative. *Empire, nation, culture, region,* and other terms related to them do not refer to fixed and readily defined entities. Such words are an essential, generalized shorthand for elusive formations that are continuously under construction and alteration. I have tried to use them with care. Indeed, a major purpose of this project is to help us understand them a little more clearly in their special application to America and Americans.

D. W. Meinig
Syracuse, New York

ACKNOWLEDGMENTS

My greatest debt continues to be to those many scholars, mostly historians, who have produced the detailed studies and informed assessments that make this kind of synthetic overview possible. The range of my reading is detailed in the Bibliography. Some indication of more specific debts may be inferred from the sources of quotations appended, but because *The Shaping of America* is offered as a fresh interpretation rather than as a closely argued response to current propositions about American developments, I have not larded every page with footnotes. Although I have tried to be accurate, I cannot pretend to be an "authority" on all these topics, and my contribution lies not in an assessment of specialist literature but in a way of looking at some important topics—a perspective developed over a lifetime of thinking as a geographer.

I feel very fortunate to have these volumes issued by Yale University Press. I am grateful to John Ryden, director, and Judy Metro, my editor, for their patient and unstinting support of such a large and prolonged project and to the many others who have had a hand in it for the quality and care that has marked every phase of publication. The gentle touch of my manuscript editor, Laura Jones Dooley, has improved every page, and Nancy Ovedovitz has continued her fine work on design.

A generous fellowship from the National Endowment for the Humanities allowed an uninterrupted year of writing. I also acknowledge, somewhat belatedly, a Faculty Enrichment Grant from the Canadian embassy in Washington, D.C., that supported two months of study and reconnaissance of eastern Canada. I am even more indebted to the consistent support of Syracuse University in many forms. My departmental chairmen, Robert G. Jensen and John Mercer, and the deans of the Maxwell School, Guthrie S. Birkhead and John L. Palmer, have covered all the costs of manuscript preparation and most of the cartographic services, provided extra travel funds (support for a month-long exploration of the Border South was especially important), reduced teaching loads, and, most recently, arranged for me to devote full time to this project.

Kay Steinmetz not only transformed my handwriting into type but scrutinized every line with a keen editorial eye and a sensitivity to language, and I gratefully acknowledge her many contributions. She also helped prepare the index. Cynthia A. Miller served as my graduate research assistant for a year, and her familiarity with government documents was especially valuable on such topics as transportation programs, new states, and secession. A journalist reviewing Volume I commended "the plethora of maps which broaden and sweeten the text," and Marcia Harrington continues her ameliorative work in this one, transforming my sketches into maps and charts. Michael Kirchoff, director of the Cartographic Laboratory, was, as always, an efficient helper with all sorts of problems with illustrations.

John Reps, with his usual generosity, allowed me to select whatever I wanted from his wonderful store of historic maps, plans, and views. Many persons assisted in the search for illustrations or provided information about those in hand. Even though not every search was successful nor could every item found be used, my hearty thanks to the following for their readiness to help: Ronald Grim, Andrew Modelski, and Richard Stephenson of the Library of Congress; Richard Smith, the National Archives; Rachel D. Bliven, history consultant, Troy, N.Y.; Janice K. Broderick, curator, A. G. Edwards and Sons, St. Louis; Craig Colten, Illinois State Museum; Helen Deroia, National Archives of Canada; Susan Familia and James G. Ward, Passaic County Historical Society; Jeanne Frantz and Jesse Matz, Yale University Press; Charlene Gill, Alton Museum of History and Art; Katherine R. Goodwin, University of Texas at Arlington; Judith M. Jacobi, University of Tennessee, Knoxville; Linda Leazer, Virginia Historical Society; Brian Osborne, Queen's University, Kingston; Richard Pillsbury, Georgia State University; Sandra Stetts, Pennsylvania State University; Susan Sutton, Indiana Historical Society; David Tatum, Syracuse University; Mark Weimer, Syracuse University. I thank Boomer Kennedy-Raisz for permission to use portions of Erwin Raisz's great map of Landforms of the United States.

Portions of the manuscript were read by Peirce F. Lewis, James Roger Sharp, Stephen Saunders Webb, and John Western, and I thank them for their critiques and their encouragement.

Twenty years ago I corresponded with Rodman W. Paul, then professor of history at the California Institute of Technology, about our mutual interest in the American West. His strong support of my published attempts at historical geographic interpretation helped embolden me to apply my approach to the entire country, and I am very sorry that he did not live to see this project unfold to this point and to receive my public recognition of his encouragement. More recently, I only belatedly learned just how decisive has been the help from another fellow student of the American West, Howard R. Lamar of Yale University. He strongly endorsed my original prospectus, reviewed the entire manuscript of *Atlantic America*, and has long been supportive of my work, and I wish to express a special thanks for his generosity. Such endorsements from historians are especially important to one who tries to apply a different set of tools to some of their well-cultivated ground.

This book, like its predecessor, is dedicated with deepest thanks to the one who has lived it with me day by day.

PART ONE
EXTENSION: THE CREATION OF A CONTINENTAL EMPIRE

History abhors determinism but cannot tolerate chance. Why did we become what we are and not something else? . . . Why does the United States consist of just the land area the map now shows: why are there not two or more nations in that area, why does it not include parts or all of Mexico? . . . I do not know how powerful a force, absolutely or relative, our continentalism has been [but] . . . American history . . . could not be written at all if that experience were left out of account.

Bernard DeVoto

Prologue

The United States began in a spacious frame—the world's largest republic, obviously rich in potential if as yet modest in development. And just twenty years after its formal independence, it was, at a single stroke, *doubled* in area. During the next fifty years an even greater expanse of territory was added so that by midcentury the United States was more than *three times* its original size.

The creation of the outer framework of the Republic is a geographic topic worthy of close analysis and speculative reflection. However "natural" and matter-of-fact this broad, compact, almost symmetrical transcontinental belt of territory must seem after all these years, no one ever envisioned exactly that extent and shape for the nation during this era of expansion; no far-sighted statesman ever sketched that geographical design on the map as the objective of national policy.

We are concerned with the various geographical designs that were put forth during each episode and stage of that history, with what the territorial issues were, what alternatives were considered, and why the United States did come to have the particular outline it eventually obtained. We are also concerned not simply with the setting of exact boundaries but with the creation of broad borderlands. While a sequence of gigantic extensions shifted the western limits of the United States from the Great River to the crest of the Great Mountains to the shores of the Great Ocean, we will be dealing not simply with the Westward Movement, so famous in our national history and mythology, but, more accurately, with a powerful Outward Movement that ramified deeply into every neighboring society. And while we will not, in this part, focus closely on the actual expansion of the "American" people, we will pay attention to those other peoples who got caught in the path of that expansion through these successive extensions of American jurisdiction. Having established the outer bounds of the United States, we will then be ready to look more closely at the momentous geographical changes taking place within this expanding structure during these years.

1. Doubling the National Territory: Louisiana

In 1800 the United States was one of the world's largest states. Extending broadly inland from the Atlantic, spanning the Appalachians and fronting upon nearly the entire length of the Mississippi, its boundaries (as yet uncertain in some sectors) encompassed about 900,000 square miles (fig. 1). Few Old World empires exceeded it in size; no single nation or kingdom rivaled its extent. In simplest geographic terms, apparent to all at the time, it was a country divided into two grand parts: east and west, seaboard and interior, old and new. The American people were eagerly expanding into the newly opened and nearly empty lands of that western interior, and the prospects for national growth and enrichment seemed unlimited in a country blessed "with room enough," as Thomas Jefferson said in an inaugural flourish, "for all descend^{ts} to the 1,000th & 1,000th generation."

And yet there was another side to this grand scale and geographic situation that was a cause of concern for many of its leaders and citizens. For size alone, no matter how rich the lands, does not necessarily bestow strength and security and advantage to the state. The United States was in fact huge in extent but strained in coherence and constricted and unsatisfied in geographic position. Three great geographic problems confronted its leaders:

1. How to bind together the East and the West, divided as they were by such a broad corrugation of mountains and so divergent in their alignments on the grand waterways of nature;
2. How to secure geographic positions deemed essential to the development of its territories, especially unrestricted use of the Mississippi River, upon which the traffic of the western half of the nation must move; and
3. How to maintain the delicate geopolitical balances of federation as the spreading population became formed into an array of new western states.

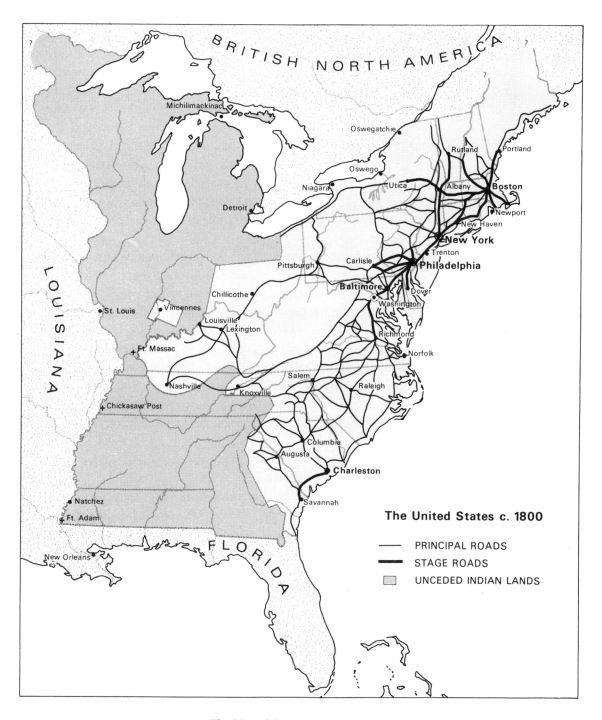

BRITISH NORTH AMERICA

Michilimackinac

Oswegatchie

Rutland

Portland

Oswego

Niagara

Utica

Albany

Boston

Detroit

Newport

New Haven

New York

Pittsburgh

Carlisle

Trenton

Philadelphia

Chillicothe

Baltimore

Dover

St. Louis

Vincennes

Washington

Louisville

Lexington

Richmond

Ft. Massac

Norfolk

Nashville

Salem

Knoxville

Raleigh

Chickasaw Post

Columbia

Augusta

Charleston

Natchez

Savannah

Ft. Adam

The United States c. 1800

PRINCIPAL ROADS

STAGE ROADS

UNCEDED INDIAN LANDS

New Orleans

FLORIDA

LOUISIANA

1. The United States, c. 1800.

No one appreciated these national problems more than the Virginian philosopher, scientist, and geopolitician who assumed the presidency in 1801. From the
time he began service as Secretary of State in 1790, Thomas Jefferson had given
extraordinary attention in particular to the second of these matters, focusing on
New Orleans and American access to the Gulf of Mexico. In August of that year he
had drawn a memorandum rehearsing a variety of possibilities for solving the
problem. The basic assumptions, boldly stated, were that the United States "by
Nature" and "by Treaty" have "a *right* to the navigation of the Mississippi"; "it is
necessary to us," and therefore must be obtained, preferably by negotiation, but if
necessary by force. This said, there followed a rationale as to why it would be in
Spain's best interests to accede in some significant way to American desires for full
and free use of the lower Mississippi.

So long as they had only to deal with Spain, Americans seemed confident of
eventual success. Spain might not wish to give up New Orleans, but Louisiana was
a huge and distant province thinly settled and feebly held, whereas in the adjacent
American territory, as the Spanish governor of Louisiana warned his superiors, "a
new and vigorous people, hostile to all subjection, [were] advancing and multiplying . . . with prodigious rapidity." Both parties knew that if the Americans were
determined to seize control of the Mississippi it would be impossible, in the long
run, to stop them. The Treaty of San Lorenzo (Pinckney's Treaty) in 1795 was an
attempt to stabilize the situation. It favored the Americans by setting their boundary with West Florida as far south as 31° North latitude, by recognizing American
rights of navigation on the entire Mississippi, and by specifying their privileges of
deposit (landing and transfer of cargoes without payment of customs) under Spanish jurisdiction at New Orleans.

Subsequently there was a great increase in American traffic on the river, reflecting the rapid growth of settlement in the Ohio Valley. Each year more flatboats
descended upon New Orleans, where the waterfront was crowded with American
shipping and American merchants played a predominant role. But such commercial growth only aggravated American political feelings, for all was at the sufferance of Spanish officials. In spite of provisions of the deposit, many activities
required Spanish licenses, papers, fees, inspections, and essential services (such as
river pilotage), and the aggressive, restless Americans found it increasingly galling
that the vital trade of their western territories should have to run this foreign
gauntlet. Such concerns were not merely local or even regional, for the Mississippi
trade had become part of a rapidly emerging national, continental pattern. Because movement upstream was so difficult and tedious, settlers in the Ohio Valley
imported their needs across the mountains from the leading commercial centers on
the seaboard. By 1800 mercantile houses in Philadelphia, Baltimore, and New
York (but not Boston) had become heavily involved in this western trade and

thereby "the Hudson, not the Potomac, was now the northern boundary of the 'Mississippi interest.'"

Decisive action on the "Mississippi problem," however, was prompted not so much by these operational aggravations as by larger and ominous geopolitical concerns. The whole matter was beclouded and intensified by political turmoil in Europe, where a renewal of the great struggle between France and Great Britain threatened to subordinate Spain to one or the other and make the mouth of the Mississippi a tempting prize in new imperial strategies. From 1795 on, rumors that Spain had secretly agreed to cede Louisiana back to France fueled American fears. Furthermore, throughout these years there were schemes and rumors of schemes, homegrown or fostered from afar, powered by political ambition and land specula-tion and involving a number of prominent Americans, that envisioned some sort of new geopolitical creature carved out of the western territories and Louisiana—a Mississippi Valley republic fitted more to nature's frame rather than attenuated across the mountains or artificially divided along the grand trunk stream itself. In all this swirl of aspirations and intrigue the only certainty seemed to be a general feeling that the existing pattern of boundaries and sovereignties in this important but largely undeveloped sector of North America was unlikely to endure.

Jefferson came to the presidency determined somehow to remake that pattern more to America's liking. We shall not try to follow all the nuances of domestic and international politics leading up to the astonishing solution of the problem. It will be useful, however, to bring into focus the basic geographical dimensions of this Mississippi Question and the range of alternatives Jefferson considered during his years of attention to the matter. These can be arranged from minimal to maximal in terms of the amount of change required in the existing political geography.

The most minimal alternative in fact involved no territorial change at all, for at one point when Jefferson was seeking to calm the rising American alarm over Spanish interference, he opined that "the United States could, in case of necessity, make itself independent of New Orleans by developing the rival port of Natchez." This town, poised where the looping river cut into the high loessial bluffs 200 miles above New Orleans, came under American control only in 1798. It was booming from its own productive hinterland as well as from the traffic coming down the Mississippi, and in 1802 ocean vessels began to come all the way up to load cotton. But that was a long, slow run, and it was obvious that Natchez could serve as no more than a "worst case" alternative and did not constitute a satisfactory long-term solution (fig. 2).

The most limited change was one Jefferson suggested in the early 1790s, when the possibility of any major cession from Spain seemed dim. He urged the necessity of obtaining at least a separate American entrepôt near the mouth of the Mis-sissippi at some "convenient spot placed under our exclusive occupation, & ex-

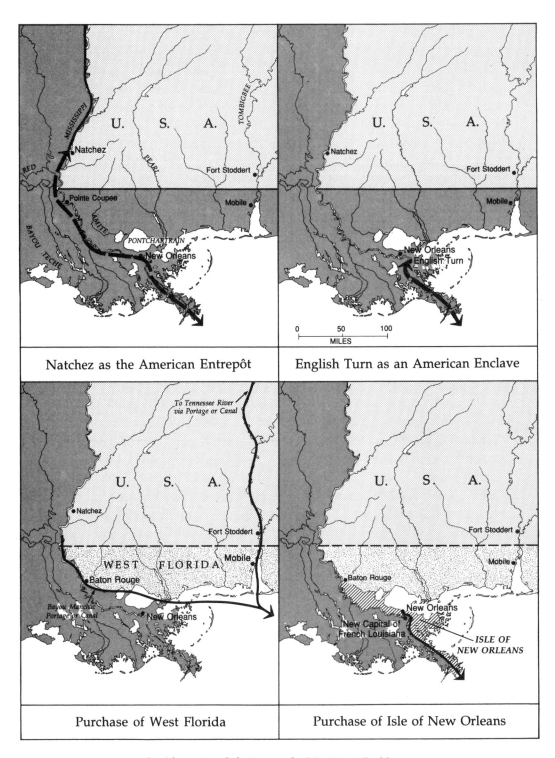

Natchez as the American Entrepôt

English Turn as an American Enclave

Purchase of West Florida

Purchase of Isle of New Orleans

2. Alternative Solutions to the Mississippi Problem.

empted from the jurisdiction & police of their government." Such an extraterritorial enclave would separate the two peoples and put an end to those "eternal altercations" that "keep us in ill humour with each other." With typical thoroughness, he specified the desired spot: at the Detour aux Anglais, or English Turn, about eighteen miles downriver from New Orleans, "the only lands below the town, not subject to inundation." But this, too, was far short of the ideal and could only be a step toward the eventual solution that was in fact already entirely clear in his mind. What was required was "a well-defined separation" of Spanish and American territories and an ample American position on the lower Mississippi. Fortunately, in his view,

> Nature has decided what shall be the geography of that in the end, whatever it might be in the beginning, by cutting off from the adjacent countries of Florida and Louisiana, and enclosing between two of [the Mississippi] channels, a long narrow slip of land called the Island of New Orleans. . . . A disinterested eye, looking on a map, will remark how conveniently this tongue of land is formed for the purpose; the Iberville and Amit channel offering a good boundary and convenient outlet, on the one side, for Florida, and the main channel an equally good boundary and outlet, on the other side, for Louisiana; while the slip of land between, is almost entirely morass or sandbank; the whole of it lower than the water of the river, in its highest floods, and only its western margins (which is the highest ground) secured by banks and inhabited.

That inhabited margin happened to contain New Orleans, the capital and commercial center "with about ten thousand white inhabitants," and Jefferson understood that the idea of handing that city over to the Americans would be "too disagreeable at first view," but he thought that "reason and events" would "by little and little" bring the Spanish to such a consideration.

Ten years later reason and events emboldened Jefferson, now president, to move to obtain exactly that piece of ground. Actually, there were two steps in his move. In 1801, when the transfer of Louisiana back to France was still a rumor in America, Jefferson instructed his newly appointed ambassador to Paris, Robert Livingston, to find out if the rumor were true and if it were to suggest that France consider ceding West Florida (assuming it to be part of Louisiana) to the United States as a simple means of lessening inherent frictions in the area. Such a change would give the United States Baton Rouge and bring its border to the old Manchac-Iberville-Pontchartrain route and, farther east, to the gulf itself. There was more to the American interest in West Florida than in the obvious advantage of controlling the mouths of the several streams reaching into Mississippi Territory. One of the more fervent speculative schemes of the day was that of the Yazoo Company, led by William Blount of Knoxville, which envisioned a colony and commercial center at Muscle Shoals (a stretch of rapids on the southerly swing of the Tennessee River) and a canal from that point connecting to the upper waters of the Tombigbee from which a moderately deep channel led directly south to Mobile. The whole project foundered in political scandal, but the concept of an all-American waterway that might drain the traffic of a huge area and compete in some degree with the Mississippi was not unrealistic, given the technology of the time (pre-steamboat) and assuming the continued political partition of the Mississippi Valley. (The idea was, in fact, finally accomplished in the Tennessee-Tombigbee Waterway, completed in 1985—and regarded by its opponents as one of the greatest porkbarrel projects in congressional history.)

Before Livingston could broach this idea, confirmation of the retrocession was received and emboldened Jefferson to move more decisively. He now declared the reappearance of powerful France in this vital part of North America to be a crisis for the United States: "There is on the globe one single spot, the possessor of which is our natural and habitual enemy. It is New Orleans, through which the produce of three-eighths of our territory must pass to market, and from its [the West] fertility it will ere long yield more than half of our whole produce and contain more than half our inhabitants." Whereas Spain was feeble and might be pressured to accede to American interests, it was "impossible that France and the U.S. can continue long friends when they meet in so irritable a position." Therefore in April 1802, he instructed Livingston to enlarge his proposal and inquire about the purchase of "the island of New Orleans and the Floridas." Later that year a Spanish imperial official abruptly suspended the American privilege of deposit at New Orleans. This action infuriated the Americans and greatly intensified pressures for a radical resolution of the problem. In response Jefferson sent his fellow Virginian, James Monroe, to Paris as an envoy extraordinary to join with Livingston in the urgent task of persuading the French (and if necessary the Spanish, for the formal retrocession had not yet taken place) to yield on this vital matter. After many delays, Livingston finally had a chance to make his proposal, modified to fit his own assessment of the bargaining possibilities. He suggested that in return for some negotiable sum France cede to the United States

> so much of Louisiana as lay above the mouth of the river Arkansas. By this, a barrier will be placed between the colony of France and Canada from which she may otherwise be attacked. . . .
>
> Let her retain the country lying on the west of the Mississippi and below the Arkansas river—a country capable of supporting fifteen millions of inhabitants. By this she will place a barrier between the United States and Mexico. . . .
>
> Let her possess East Florida as far as the river Perdido, with all the ports on the Gulf, and cede West Florida, New Orleans, and the territory on the west bank of the Mississippi [above the Arkansas] to the United States.

Livingston excluded East Florida from his offer because it seemed clear that

France in fact had no claim on that territory, it having never been part of Louisiana. That he sought all of Louisiana north of the Arkansas was unprecedented in Jefferson's formulations and may be seen as a bargaining ploy, one made credible by the very slight European hold on that remote ground and the near impossibility of shielding it from American infiltration. The key area was of course the Island of (New) Orleans, and Livingston elaborated at some length why France should not be overly concerned about giving up that famous colonial outpost: "It may be supposed that New Orleans is a place of some moment; it will be so to the United States, but not to France, because Fort Leon, on the opposite bank, affords a much more advantageous station; has equal advantages as a harbor; is higher, healthier, and more defensible; and, as the great bulk of the settlements must necessarily be on that side, the capital must be transplanted there even if France continued in possession of New Orleans." New Orleans was there, on the wrong bank, he explained, because the whole region had been first approached and settled from the east, along the sheltered passageway hugging the coast west from Biloxi via Lake Pontchartrain. But once the Mississippi became the great avenue, the west bank must be preferred. Here was an interesting vision of two capitals as twin cities astride the great river serving the two halves, French and American, of the Mississippi Valley.

That these two sovereignties would in fact continue to face each other in this strategic sector seemed a reasonable assumption even to the best informed and most hopeful. Jefferson confessed privately more than once during these months that he was "not sanguine in obtaining a cession of New Orleans for money," but he was convinced that an attempt at peaceful negotiation for territory that the United States must eventually obtain by whatever means was the appropriate move at this time. In April 1803 the Spanish government restored the deposit at New Orleans and invited negotiations to select an alternative location for such privileges. The American administration proceeded in the hope that France, once it got formal control, might sell a small enclave for a new American entrepôt. That would not be a lasting solution, but it would ease the pressures and probably avoid war.

In that same month of 1803 the French foreign minister startled Livingston by asking if the United States would like to buy the whole of Louisiana. In retrospect, historians have offered plausible explanations for Napoleon's sudden shift of plans and attitudes, but the prospect of obtaining the whole vast province in one simple transaction exceeded all expectations. There could be no hesitation on such a remarkable opportunity, and a deal was soon worked out. The signing of the treaty was made known to Jefferson on July 3 and announced to the public on the following day, the twenty-seventh anniversary of the Declaration of Independence.

The Louisiana Purchase was an unprecedented and exhilarating event. At the stroke of a pen and for what even then seemed a trifling cost, the world's largest republic was doubled in size. Its landward border was shifted hundreds of miles to the as-yet-unexplored crest of the continent, the western rim of the immense basin of the Mississippi system. Uncertainties over these new limits precluded any exact calculation, but the national territory now approached two million square miles, including a thousand million acres of incalculable potential. And all this was a bonus to the original objective of removing the galling geopolitical constriction on American commerce on the Mississippi. And not only was that issue dissolved but the nation's security was immeasurably enhanced. North America was once more freed of the imperial presence of France, the world's most powerful military state; the Spanish hold receded to Texas and the Floridas—and the boundaries of these colonies were uncertain and immediately placed under pressure by American claims.

This sudden enormous geographical augmentation of the state must have had a tremendous impact on the whole citizenry and society: enlarging visions, whetting appetites, swelling national pride, bolstering American self-confidence, elevating the West into even greater prominence, and confirming a genuine continental destiny for the young republic. There was, however, another, more sobering side to the matter, arising from the scale and content of Louisiana. If one of the great geopolitical issues had been dissolved, the other two had been magnified and joined by further complications.

There was the immediate question, deeply troubling to Jefferson, of the legality, the constitutionality, of such an addition to the federal republic. Could the executive, even with the consent of Congress, simply expand in such a way what was basically a compact among states? Included in this was the difficult and potentially embarrassing question as to whether the people of Louisiana could simply be purchased and annexed without their consent. And once brought under American sovereignty, just how should this non-English-speaking population with its French and Spanish institutions and legal codes be incorporated into the federal structure? Beyond those immediate issues lay a host of matters pertaining to the management and development of such an enormous territory of unknown qualities. Could such an expanse be effectively bound up with the older states? Would not the acquisition of the whole Mississippi Basin magnify the physical divergence between the Atlantic seaboard states and the gulf-oriented interior and eventually force the nation to yield to the power of "natural law"? Should Louisiana be reserved for Indians, including those to be pressured out of lands east of the Mississippi, or opened for colonization by Whites, like the rest of the United States was or would eventually be? And once settled, how many states and what portion of the national population would these new western lands contain, and what would such an immense amount of geographical change do to the delicate balances and harmonies of a

fragile federal structure? Such questions necessarily received a good deal of attention in the opening years of the new century; some of them would not be answered
until much later in that century.

Not everyone was delighted with the acquisition of "this new, immense, unbounded world." In Congress, Senator Samuel White of Delaware declared that
Louisiana's incorporation into the Union would be "the greatest curse that could at
present befall us." He dismissed any plan to keep all west of the Mississippi an
Indian reserve: "You had as well pretend to inhibit the fish from swimming in the
sea" as to prevent "the adventurous, roving, and enterprising" Americans from
populating that country. And once that happens, White warned,

> our citizens will be removed to the immense distance of two or three thousand miles
> from the capital of the Union, where they will scarcely ever feel the rays of the
> General Government; their affections will become alienated; they will gradually
> begin to view us as strangers; they will form other commercial connexions, and our
> interests will become distinct.
>
> These, with other causes that human wisdom may not now forsee, will in time
> effect a separation, and I fear our bounds will be fixed nearer to our houses than the
> waters of the Mississippi. We have already territory enough.

But such fears for the future were a feeble parry against the virtual gift of one-third
of a continent and visions of a far greater republic. Senator John Breckenridge of
Kentucky scornfully dismissed the geographical principle implied in White's argument: Louisiana too great an extension?

> I would ask, sir, what is his standard extent for a Republic? How does he come at that
> standard? Our boundary is already extensive. Would his standard extent be violated
> by including the island of Orleans and the Floridas? I presume not, as all parties seem
> to think their acquisition, in part or in whole, essential. Why not then acquire
> territory on the west, as well as on the east side of the Mississippi? Is the Goddess of
> Liberty restrained by water courses? Is she governed by geographical limits? Is her
> dominion on this continent confined to the east side of the Mississippi? So far from
> believing in the doctrine that a Republic ought to be confined within narrow limits, I
> believe, on the contrary, that the more extensive its dominion the more safe and
> more durable it will be. In proportion to the number of hands you intrust the precious
> blessings of free government to, in the same proportion do you multiply the chances
> for their preservation. I entertain, therefore, no fears for the Confederacy on account
> of its extent.

Whatever uncertainties and uneasiness there may have been about such an unprecedented issue—and one must be wary of taking these political orations at full
face value, for such debates were enmeshed in more personal and party struggles—
there was never the slightest doubt about congressional as well as popular approval

of the Louisiana Purchase. It was an enormous triumph for Jefferson and his fellow Republicans. More than all else it ensured their reelection, and the president's comment on the topic in his second inaugural address was a temperate affirmation of Breckenridge's argument:

> I know that the acquisition of Louisiana has been disapproved by some, from a candid apprehension that the enlargement of our territory would endanger its union. But who can limit the extent to which the federative principle may operate effectively? The larger our association, the less it will be shaken by local passions; and in any view, is it not better that the opposite bank of the Mississippi should be settled by our own brethren and children, than by strangers of another family? With which shall we be most likely to live in harmony and friendly intercourse?

The annexation of Louisiana was a triumph of nationalism over regionalism. But it created new and in part unexpected regional issues. Few shared Jefferson's deep concerns for the constitutionality of this executive acquisition of territory, and he was reluctantly convinced not to insist on a constitutional amendment as a prerequisite to ratification of the treaty. But if territory could be added to a federation without the direct consent of the member states, could it be legally or ethically annexed without obtaining the consent of its citizens? That issue was debated in Congress as one of political principle rather than possible contention in Louisiana, for it was generally assumed and repeatedly asserted that "the inhabitants would readily agree to the proposed transfer of their allegiance," for none could "be so unwise as to prefer being the colonists of a distant European Power, to being members of this immense Empire, with all the privileges of American citizens" (although the question of just how such persons actually might become citizens was not readily apparent). It was soon revealed that few congressmen agreed with John Quincy Adams that "we ought to have applied to the inhabitants of Louisiana to recognize our right to govern them." Most believed it was quite enough, and salutary, that the treaty declared that "the inhabitants of the ceded territory shall be incorporated in the Union of the United States, and admitted as soon as possible, according to the principles of the Federal Constitution, to the enjoyment of the rights, advantages and immunities of citizens of the United States; and in the meantime they shall be maintained and protected in the free enjoyment of their liberty, property, and the religion which they profess."

In fact, Jefferson envisioned neither statehood nor cultural integrity for this Louisiana community. His first thought was to annex the settled region of Lower Louisiana to Mississippi Territory so as to amalgamate the people "with such a body of Americans as may take the lead in legislation and government." He soon gave that up as impracticable and set about devising a special interim territorial status for the former French colony. The Louisiana Purchase was immediately divided in two at 33° North latitude. All land north of that arbitrary line was designated the District of Louisiana and placed under the administration of the Territory of Indiana, seated at Vincennes. Jefferson's intent was to lock that huge area up as an Indian reserve for the time being. The remainder, south of 33°N, containing an estimated 50,000 mostly French-speaking inhabitants, was set up as the Territory of Orleans. Jefferson had originally assumed that the upriver boundary should be drawn near Pointe Coupee, at the northern margins of settlement along the Mississippi. But that would have excluded Natchitoches, an important outpost and border station to the northwest, and it seems clear that the boundary was set so far north to enclose about as much country above the French settlement along the Mississippi as below and that this configuration was directly related to Jefferson's design for the eventual incorporation of this foreign body into the Union.

Louisiana was an imperial colony of alien people—this all American leaders recognized, though they differed as to how comfortable they were with that fact and what means should be taken to "Americanize" this sudden addition. Jefferson, and apparently most others, assumed some combination of pressured acculturation and dilution of numbers as appropriate and essential to the task. Louisianians, in the eyes of these Americans, were a people speaking a foreign tongue and steeped in foreign ways, exhibiting unusual and even questionable values and behavior (festivals and frolics on Sundays!), used to authoritarian government, unlettered in representative institutions, following strange legal customs and laws. They must therefore be ruled firmly by an American governor under close supervision of federal authorities, assisted by an "Assembly of Notables" selected by the governor to give some voice to the people but with a majority of strong Anglo-Americans, and their laws and courts must be quickly remolded to the American system. To hasten and broaden the processes of culture change as well as to ensure the political allegiance of this strategic border territory, a rapid immigration of Americans into this part of Louisiana should be induced, and Jefferson strongly supported a bill designed to do just that:

> I propose . . . enlisting 30,000 volunteers, Americans by birth, to be carried at the public expense, & settled immediately on a bounty of 160 acres of land each, on the west side of the Mississippi, on the condition of giving two years of military service, if that country should be attacked within 7 years. The defence of the country would thus be placed on the spot, and the additional number would entitle the territory to become a State, would make the majority American, & make it an American instead of a French State. This would not sweeten the pill to the French; but in making that acquisition we had some view to our own good as well as theirs, and I believe the greatest good of both will be promoted by whatever will amalgamate us together.

Certainly there was a strategic urgency in his mind. Lower Louisiana was nearly surrounded by potentially hostile forces, and its borders were in serious dispute. The Spanish still held West Florida, with gunboats on Pontchartrain and Fort San Carlos overlooking the Mississippi at Baton Rouge, and they were expanding and reinforcing their positions in Texas. A bill to induce such a migration passed the Senate but stalled in the House, more from a perceived threat to competing land speculations in older territories than from any lack of conviction about Jefferson's concept, although the military provision also gave some members pause.

The president's reference to "sweeten the pill" acknowledges that in fact the French were not overjoyed about the sudden blessings of American rule. There was much unease and a good deal of social conflict, and in the first year a delegation of Louisiana's leaders traveled to Washington to plead for immediate statehood on terms that would provide equality of treatment with other states but at the same time ensure the integrity of Louisiana laws and customs. They saw themselves as being under the thumb of a governor who could neither read nor speak French, with a council stacked seven to six in favor of the Anglo-Americans (even though they were no more than one in twelve of the population), forced to transact governmental business in English, and threatened with alarming changes with respect to their laws, rights, and property. A major grievance was the arbitrary embargo on the importation of slaves into Louisiana, even though the states were free to augment their labor force with slaves until the constitutional prohibition went into effect in 1808. The most tangible response was a new bill, approved in 1805, that generally brought Louisiana into line with the territorial provisions of the Northwest Ordinance as it applied to the territorial process toward statehood. A more representative council was authorized, and the bill specified the continuation in force of local Louisiana law for the time being.

The matter of laws, of legal philosophies, codes, and procedures, was the most intense and explicit difficulty facing the incorporation of Louisiana into the Union. The American legal system was based on English Common Law, that of Louisiana on French and Spanish civil law. Americans assumed not only the need for uniformity within the Union but generally the superiority of their system as basic to their unprecedented freedoms and protections; French Louisianians saw no such superiority, regarded the Americans and their system as offensively litigious, and were deeply alarmed by the disruptive potential of any general change. The differences were fundamental, touching every dimension of life. With regard to domestic affairs, for example, the French system emphasized family interests, in contrast to the American emphasis on individuals and especially males; the French recognized husband and wife as contractual partners, put limitations on disinheritance, and provided for the legitimatization of bastards; whereas the Americans merged the couple under the husband's authority, allowed complete disregard of family heirs, and had no provision for legitimatizing bastard offspring. In Louisiana free persons of whatever color had all the rights of citizens, whereas American common law allowed an almost complete denial of human rights to persons defined as having even a fraction of "colored" blood. As George Dargo has detailed, illustrations of such differences can be drawn from throughout the laws of obligation, property, and commerce.

The one feature of American law Louisianians readily adopted was trial by jury in *criminal* cases. They welcomed such personal protection after the arbitrary authority they had experienced under Spain. But they assiduously resisted all attempts to supplant their civil code and in 1808 achieved a major triumph when the United States formally recognized the Digest of the Civil Laws, modeled on the Code Napoléon and printed in French and English (with French as the authoritative language). Thus, as Dargo has put it, the territory of Louisiana became "a civil law island in a sea of common law," a notable Jeffersonian concession "in an otherwise heavy-handed effort to bring about some kind of adjustment between America and its first subject people."

This compromise came in the wake of other developments that had eased American attitudes toward this alien people they had annexed. Most important, perhaps, was the fact that the French Louisianians were in no way implicated in the complicated intrigues of the so-called Burr Conspiracy, which had seemed, momentarily, to pose great dangers to the integrity of the United States in the Mississippi Valley. It was the allegiance of Americans, not the French, that was the cause for concern, and the volatile potential of these Western societies spurred Congress to incorporate them more firmly into the Union. In 1809 bills approving Louisiana's preparation for statehood were introduced in Congress. The debate reopened the constitutional question of whether by action of Congress new member states could be carved out of territories that were not part of the original United States. A number of northern legislators spoke strongly against the validity of such additions to the federation. Debate reached an ominous point when Josiah Quincy of Massachusetts spoke fervently against such a "great usurpation" engineered by "the slave vote" to add to the weight of their section "the mixed, though . . . respectable race of Anglo-Hispano-Gallo-Americans who bask on the sands at the mouth of the Mississippi." If this be approved, he argued, it would be but the first in a relentless sequence of such additions whose cumulative effect would be such a grotesque distortion of the original compact as to be the "death-blow to the Constitution" and force the dissolution of the Union. Quincy's fellow New Englanders endorsed his principle, though not necessarily his threat, but their amendment to require the unanimous consent of each state or a constitutional amendment was defeated by a vote of eighteen to ten. After much further debate Louisiana statehood was approved in 1811 by two-to-one majorities in both houses.

Approval was granted even though the census of 1810 counted just 34,311 free Whites among the population of 76,556, whereas the Northwest Ordinance prescribed a minimum of 60,000 such persons as a prerequisite of statehood (the Louisiana bill denied the franchise to the 7,585 "free coloreds"). There was, however, a further body of people that might readily be added to Louisiana. From the first discussions of its great acquisition the United States claimed that West Florida, reaching east to the Perdido River, was part of Louisiana and therefore included in the purchase. Spain strongly denied that interpretation, and France refused to specify, so the issue remained in dispute. The Spanish hold was meager, at Mobile and a few coastal and waterway points along the route to Baton Rouge, and the backcountry began to fill with Anglo-Americans, especially in the west, a spreading out from the thriving Natchez hinterland. In 1804 a local Anglo attempt to seize Baton Rouge failed. In the same year Congress authorized the creation of a district and port of entry on the waters of the Mobile. Spain protested this act; the United States reasserted its claims but set up its customs station at Fort Stoddert, just upriver within the Mississippi Territory. In the years following, various plans were laid for the purchase or, if need be, seizure of West Florida. The matter came to a head in 1810, when Spain was struggling against Napoleonic domination and revolt was beginning to well up in various parts of Spanish America. Anglo settlers now took control of Baton Rouge and sought annexation to the United States. When the American government delayed, not wanting to provoke Spain unduly, the settlers proclaimed a "Republic of Florida" and set about forming a government. However, unwilling to foster this ambiguous state on its borders, the United States soon ordered the governor of Louisiana to occupy the area as far east as the Pearl River and organize it under his jurisdiction. This block of territory between the Mississippi and the Pearl, known ever after as the Florida Parishes, was not included in the Louisiana statehood bill, primarily because of uncertainties about the American legal title to it. Louisiana's French leaders strongly opposed the addition of the Florida Parishes because it would augment the Anglo-American population by several thousands. Under American pressure, however, the first act of the legislature of the new state in 1812 approved this annexation. Only with this seemingly minor addition did the United States achieve full control from source to mouth over both banks of the Mississippi.

The character of Louisiana as an imperial colony remained vividly apparent even as immigrations and economic developments altered the patterns and proportions of its peoples. Common perception and reference viewed it as being divided between two peoples, the "Americans" and the "French," or "Creoles," although such terms masked a considerable variety in each case (creole, especially, had many shades of meaning in local usage). The cultural geography of the state evolved not simply out of an influx of Americans upon a residual Creole society, for the French population was expanding, too, not only by a high rate of natural increase but also by immigration. For many years émigrés trickled in from recurrent upheavals in France. More important was the fact that animosities arising from the Napoleonic occupation of Spain reverberated in the Spanish Empire and sent thousands of St. Domingue French who had earlier fled to Cuba on to a new refuge in Louisiana. By 1810, 7,000–8,000, including many wealthy planters with retinues of slaves as well as many free Blacks and mulattos, had arrived, to the discomfort of the American governor, who both wished to enforce the law forbidding the importation of slaves and feared the free "coloreds." He relented out of recognition of the exigencies of political exile and the near impossibility of controlling the influx.

These new planters, like those who had come to Louisiana after the first phases of the Afro-American revolution in Santo Domingo, played a major role in the rapidly developing sugar industry, thickening settlement along the lower river and spreading west and north from Bayou Teche. Newcomers added to the factionalism within French Louisiana, the Santo Domingan planters being regarded as a particularly haughty and aggressive group, but they also significantly augmented the wealth and leadership of the whole. That "whole," meaning the non-Anglo-American population, was in fact hard to define internally, for in addition to the great variety that had accumulated during the century of French and Spanish rule, there was a continual drifting in along all the tropical sealanes: French, Spanish, Portuguese, Italians, and a wide sprinkling of others; White and Black and all shades in between; seamen, fishermen, trappers, smugglers, pirates, traders, artisans, farmers; having in common only a niche somewhere in the watery labyrinth of the Delta or the downriver suburbs of New Orleans, a convergence toward a common creole tongue, and a strong sense of distinction from the Americans, who regarded them all with a degree of disdain.

Meanwhile the Americans came flocking in, spreading over the Florida Parishes, sprinkled through the northern districts along the Ouachita and Red rivers, extending the sugar and cotton plantation country northward along the Mississippi, and edging into the older districts at many points. The general divide between an American north Louisiana and a Creole south, with French outliers at Alexandria and Natchitoches, emerged within the territory and became fixed in common perceptions within a few years. These Americans were also of several types and sources: southern backcountry pioneer hunters, stockmen, farmers; Carolina planters with their Black slaves; traders and speculators from the American West; Kentucky rivermen; merchants and agents, lawyers and other professional classes from Baltimore, Philadelphia, and New York. To these may be added many European immigrants, ranging from people of means to poor Irish laborers, all of whom reinforced the English-speaking sector of society.

New Orleans was of course the great meeting point, the fulcrum of Louisiana society. There had been Anglo-Americans there before the purchase, prominent as merchants and agents in the burgeoning trade of the Mississippi Valley. Such persons necessarily had close associations with Spanish and French merchants and officials; most were at least bilingual, and some had married into prominent Creole families. During the troubled years of transition toward American statehood some of these Anglos, as well as some later arrivals, aligned themselves with the Creoles in seeking special concessions to the cultural distinctiveness of Louisiana. The emergence of such intermediaries, whether arising from cultural attraction, ethical persuasion, personal and political advantage, or most probably some complex mixture of such motives, is a common feature in imperial colonies.

Certainly for the great majority of the population, American and Creole alike, there was a strong sense of separation between the two peoples and this the physical and social patterns of a rapidly expanding New Orleans prominently displayed. The first steamboat came downriver from the Ohio in 1812 and such vessels became a famous symbol of the boom that ensued. Soon there were scores, then hundreds, and by the 1830s a thousand such boats on the Mississippi system, as New Orleans became what it had long seemed destined to be: the emporium for half of North America. The city was quickly expanded in form as speculators platted wedges of streets extending back from the curving riverfront (fig. 3). Laid out on either side of the original French grid, these extensions gathered distinctly different peoples. Americans were arrayed in all their variety on the upriver side above the Vieux Carré (as the old French town was now known) in thriving commercial blocks along the river, handsome residences of merchants and planters in the Faubourg St. Mary, and shacktowns of riverfolk, drifters, and free coloreds in the backswamps. Downriver was Faubourg Marigny, designed by its wealthy French promoter to attract the Creole elite but filling instead with a miscellany of lesser folk of all colors—French, Spanish, and West Indians—who were drawn to this thriving center. These three sectors of the city were clearly apparent, set apart by broad avenues and esplanades. There was of course a good deal of interaction among many of these people and especially along the busy riverfront, the "main street of the world." The newspapers were bilingual, and many civic affairs brought Americans and Creoles together. But there was much antagonism and chronic tension as well, so much so that in 1836 the state withdrew the city's charter and reissued one that divided it into three municipalities, each with its elected aldermen, with a single mayor and council over the whole. That was a formal geopolitical expression of the continuing, even intensifying, geocultural reality of New Orleans as the capital of an imperial colony.

By then the city had perhaps 50,000 inhabitants, and the Creole/American ratio had been reduced from 7:1 to 2:1. In Louisiana as a whole the population had doubled between 1810 and 1820 (to 153,000) and reached 216,000 ten years later.

3. Plan of New Orleans, 1815.

This well-known engraving, based on the work of Jacques Tanesse, city surveyor, depicts the famous ninety-year-old city in its first phase of expansion following the American takeover. The walls of the original bastide have been replaced by broad boulevards (with one remnant bastion on the downriver corner), and newly platted suburbs— Faubourg Ste. Marie on the left, Faubourg Marigny on the right— extend the city along its narrow natural levee between the river and the swamp behind. Note the north arrow on the compass rose in the middle of the river showing that the original grid, oriented to the river, is at 45° angles from the cardinal directions. The border display of public buildings, including church, hospital, almshouse, convent, college, theatre, barracks, and customshouse, emphasizes the strong institutional presence typical of a French colonial capital. (Courtesy of John W. Reps, from the Geography and Map Division, Library of Congress)

Such decennial growth masked the deadly punctuations of yellow fever. This infamous feature of the Louisiana environment was an annual menace, killing hundreds and sometimes thousands; epidemics were especially severe in the late 1820s, and that of 1832–33 is estimated to have taken a toll of about 10,000. Newcomers from the northern states and Europe were more vulnerable than those from the south and the tropics, and Whites more than Blacks. That is one important reason why, as measured by the census and its categories, Whites remained a minority through all these years. In 1830 the "colored" population constituted more that 58 percent of the total, up from 55 percent in 1810. A more important change was the fact that the "free colored" had declined from 18 percent to 13 percent of these totals. We should not rely on these as exact figures, but we may well note the processes of "Americanization" implied. In their census taking as in their laws, the Americans attempted to impose a rigid categorization and separation of Blacks and Whites, lumping all those subtle gradations of color, so important in the actual pattern of Louisiana social life, into a simple category of people who were forbidden (as specified in a law of 1806) "to ever consider themselves the equal of whites." Louisiana Whites were understandably haunted by the specter of Santo Domingo. The large number and prominent role of the free coloreds, especially in New Orleans, was regarded by Americans as a chronic menace. Laws were passed to make it harder for masters to free their slaves; regulation after regulation attempted to control the movements of Blacks and to prohibit the assembly of, indeed any contact between, free Blacks and slaves. But the older patterns of Creole Louisiana prevailed. Free Blacks could own property—some of them owned slaves—they resisted adoption of those patterns of deference so viciously enforced elsewhere in America, and they continued to play diverse and important roles in the local scene. In fact, despite all laws and pressures local color lines blurred; there was in places and at times much contact among all these many peoples. Most free coloreds were mulattos, whose very existence and expansion testified to intimate contacts of great social importance. This variegated vibrancy of Afro-American Creole Louisiana and the range and rituals and unusual openness of associations between White and Black, as much as anything else, made New Orleans, this American "colonial city," such a self-conscious and famous place.

Not all Americans were comfortable with such a colorful and anomalous place. From statehood in 1812 onward there were repeated attempts by the Americans to shift Louisiana's capital from this cosmopolitan turbulent city to some quieter town nearer to the cultural border, such as Baton Rouge or St. Francisville. In 1829 legislators voted to move the seat of government to Donaldsonville, eighty miles upriver, but a couple of sessions in that rural retreat drove them back to the comforts and pleasures of New Orleans.

Louisiana thus had a special and surprising meaning for the young republic. The

United States purchased the western half of the Mississippi Valley to obtain an outlet for the eastern half; it took over the whole of Louisiana to obtain the one small part it considered essential to the nation's security and prosperity. That small part proved to have a significance quite beyond such simple geopolitical calculations. Louisiana was a remarkable case of expansion without conquest (although the threat of conquest, by overt war or covert infiltration, was surely a major factor in Napoleon's decision to sell) but it was nonetheless an imperial acquisition—imperial in the sense of the aggressive encroachment of one people upon the territory of another, resulting in the subjugation of that people to alien rule. The Louisianans were suddenly annexed to the United States without the slightest gesture of interest on the part of either America or France as to how they might feel about it. If they did not take up arms to resist annexation (as American leaders feared they might), they openly resisted absorption and insisted on official recognition of their cultural identity and differences from the national body. The Constitution had no provision for such an acquisition; it spelled out no special terms for such a disparate case. Louisiana therefore became an unexpected experiment in empire; in subtle, as yet little appreciated, ways, it challenged Americans' views of themselves as well as of others, and it began to give the word *empire* another and not altogether comfortable connotation for America: not just a rhetorical term for a republic grand in scale and rich in possibilities, nor that wonderful new thing of Jeffersonian vision, "an empire for liberty," but an America that included a bloc of captive peoples of foreign culture who had not chosen to be Americans. Of course, the American Indians were exactly that, too, but had long been relegated to a special, primitive category that eased the American conscience about such matters.

2. Pressures on the Borders: Southward

The Louisiana Purchase gave the United States its first territorial frontage on the Gulf of Mexico. Narrow at first, little wider than the Mississippi, it was a position immediately broadened in claim and soon made broader still in common readings of its geopolitical implications.

With the extension of the country's borders to this tropical sea, a whole circuit of coasts—Florida, Cuba, Yucatán, Mexico, Texas—suddenly took on new meaning for Americans, and before long such places were being declared to be of compelling national interest. For the Gulf of Mexico was an inner compartment, "a Mediterranean with two outlets," as the geographer Alexander von Humboldt put it, guarded by Havana, an American Gibraltar "strongly defended by nature and still more strongly fortified by art." Unlike its European counterpart, one could not sail outward past this bastion directly into the Atlantic but had to skirt a broad and a dangerous archipelago to the north and east or pass the whole length of Cuba and other large islands extending a thousand miles to the south and east before reaching the open sea. So it was necessary also to bring the Bahamas, Jamaica, Hispaniola, and Puerto Rico into this new American view (fig. 4).

This was not a tranquil prospect. Through Louisiana the United States stepped directly into an arena that had been the scene of intense European imperial activities and immense geographical changes for 300 years. The young republic immediately asserted claim to a major role in that theater and found itself participating in a tumultuous drama involving three European powers and a dozen American peoples. We need not enter very far into the bewildering complexities of diplomatic, political, and military history during the first two or three decades of the new century. We do need, however, to get a clear picture of the geopolitical context and pay special attention to some details of the changing human geography of this complicated American arena. Our concern is not so much with the political drama as with some regional patterns during a critical phase in the formation of one of the world's great cultural border zones.

For 300 years the central strategic feature of these tropical seas was the trunk line of empire connecting Spain and Mexico, a trafficway anchored on Vera Cruz (the sole authorized port of New Spain), secured by pivotal Havana (with a branch line to Panama and Peru), and with outposts guarding the eastern channels at St. Augustine, Santo Domingo, and San Juan. For a long time such bases made the Gulf of Mexico a Spanish sea without need of imposing control upon the whole littoral. The French first appeared through a back door, coming down the Mississippi from Canada. Failing to secure what gradually began to emerge as the key position on the northern shore, the Spanish hastened to broaden their defenses of the great riches of Mexico by creating the province of Texas to bar any encroachment westward from the Mississippi Valley. There followed a century of intrusions and intrigues, of recurrent warfare and tradings of territories by treaty among Spain, France, and Britain, but persisting through it all was the basic Spanish concern for this lifeline of empire.

FLORIDA

In this perspective, the American purchase of Louisiana was more than a change of control over a foothold in the gulf. It represented a thrust from the interior, powered by growth within the continent. Further, it superimposed an American trunk line through the Florida Straits that connected the two grand halves of the nation. The Florida peninsula, always of concern to the Spanish but never of primary interest to its European rivals (the British traded it back in 1783 after twenty years of control), thus now took on a new importance for the United States. The simple conformation of the continent had invited American interest, and in

4. Southern Borderlands.

1802 Jefferson had set out to purchase the Floridas along with New Orleans. At that time his agent was instructed to consider the Floridas one-fourth the value of the Island of New Orleans, and East Florida one-half the value of West Florida. Such valuations of course reflect the main purpose of obtaining for the Mississippi Valley direct access to the Gulf of Mexico. The congressional committee investigating the issue noted that whereas East Florida was not essential it was nonetheless desirable for several reasons: "The southern point . . . is not more than one hundred miles distant from the Havana, and the possession of it may be beneficial to us in relation to our trade with the West Indies. It would likewise make our whole territory compact, would add considerably to our seacoast, and by giving us the Gulf of Mexico for our southern boundary, would render us less liable to attack, in what is now deemed the most vulnerable part of the Union." The danger was not from the Spanish in Florida but from France or Britain taking advantage of the weakness of Spain to appropriate Florida or Cuba. There was good reason to be concerned about the British intriguing from their base in the Bahamas with the Creeks and other Indians against the United States, and their powerful navy could put any but the most stoutly defended seacoast at hazard.

Although views of the value and significance of Florida varied, there was a fairly consistent assumption among the American leadership that the whole territory should and would be obtained, sooner or later, in one way or another. As we have noted, Jefferson quickly asserted a claim to West Florida as being part of Louisiana, and in 1805 he made overtures to Spain to purchase the remainder and to resolve the disputed boundary on the west with Texas. Spain disdained to respond to the aggressive claims of the Americans, but the Louisiana-Texas border was stabilized in that year by the actions of local authorities in the field, and the United States soon began to pick away at the lean, attenuated body of Florida. The territory west of the Pearl River was occupied in 1810 and soon annexed to Louisiana, following a local coup.

Spain itself was then in turmoil; a popular uprising against Napoleonic occupation had sent a strong tremor of republicanism to the Spanish colonies. In response to such uncertainties, Congress, by a secret act in 1811, authorized the president to take possession of the Floridas under any of a number of specified circumstances that might develop. An attempt to generate one of those circumstances soon followed as a group of Georgia filibusters, conniving with a few Americans resident in Florida, gathered at St. Mary's to proclaim a "Republic of Florida," crossed the border, and captured the frontier (and notorious smuggling) station of Fernandina, and, now joined by American troops, moved south to lay siege to St. Augustine. Such a blatant attempt to steal East Florida caused a political storm in Washington and Europe. Eventually the United States apologized to Spain and withdrew the militia, but not before the Americans, regulars and irregulars, had laid waste every settlement within reach. Meanwhile, in support of the standing American claim to all west of the Perdido as part of the Louisiana Purchase, an American army occupied Mobile in 1813, an action further justified as a need to keep it out of the hands of Great Britain, with which the United States was at war.

Spanish Florida did become a theater of that war, a minor one with respect to the overall contest but with major implications for the future of the region. Both British and American forces invaded Florida, showing little respect for Spanish sovereignty (each briefly occupied Pensacola), but there were no great confrontations between them before the American slaughter of the British army in the belated finale of New Orleans. The critical feature of the contest in this sector was the situation and role of the Creeks and Seminoles.

The Creek Nation, which had so long dominated much of the southern coastal plain, was a loose and unstable confederation of Indians long experienced in coping with competitive and acquisitive imperialisms. The Creeks had dealt with the Spanish, the French, the British, and, most recently, the Americans, through the trading systems reaching inland from Charleston, Augusta, Pensacola, and Mobile. Such protracted encounters had brought many social and economic changes, called forth generations of skilled intermediaries, and produced many "mixed-blood" offspring of the various peoples involved—European, Indian, African—some of whom became important leaders in the confederation. Through it all the Creeks had held their ground and in some ways prospered. In 1800 about 15,000 Creeks were living in more than thirty towns in the core of their homeland along the Alabama-Coosa-Tallapoosa (Upper Creeks) and the Chattahoochee (Lower Creeks). Tukabatchee and Coweta, serving as capitals of these major groups, were seats of power, conference centers to which not only the Creeks but occasionally delegations from bordering tribes gathered. There was also a major nucleus in the savannas and canebrakes of the lower Alabama and Mobile, settlements of the complex "Muskogee" métis stockraisers closer in culture and commerce to Euro-Americans but under their own leadership. The Seminoles were an independent group, perhaps largely of Creek origin with remnants of other tribes, now living to the southeast extending into northern Florida.

After the turn of the century American pressures on this large area increased ominously. Georgians, emboldened by a federal commitment to the eventual extinction of Indian title to their lands, were especially aggressive. By 1804 all land east of the Okmulgee had been given to them in payment of ostensible debts, and in the following year the federal government extracted the right to establish a road for the mail, serviced by ferries and inns, cutting across the heart of Creek lands from Georgia via Coweta to Fort Stoddert. As many chiefs had feared, traffic and trouble grew together along this swath, and when American agents, without full Indian approval, began to explore for a north-south road between Tennessee and

Mobile, the Creek confederation was plunged into crisis over the proper response. The problem, faced sooner or later by every American Indian people, was basic: how to survive in the face of such relentless pressures. The response was also common: two irreconcilable factions, the "nativists," who opposed any concession and wanted to root out European influences that had so permeated the culture, versus the "civilizationists," who saw extensive but controlled adaptation to European ways and submission to United States polity as the only hope for survival. When in 1812 the civilizationists executed some nativists who had taken revenge on some Whites, civil war erupted among the Creeks.

The first action was an attack upon the métis, culminating in the killing of several hundred who had taken shelter at Fort Mims, one of the many stockaded settlements scattered along the Alabama. At the first news of warfare Americans in the bordering territories jumped to the conclusion that the whole Creek Nation was on the warpath against all Americans, and they further assumed "the Creek troubles as originating in British machinations and encouraged by covert Spanish aid." Militias from Georgia and Mississippi and an army from Tennessee under Andrew Jackson, assisted by some groups of Cherokees and friendly Creeks, invaded the Creek heartland, fought a series of bloody battles in which several thousand Indians were killed, laid waste villages, fields, and herds, and when it was over, forced the Creek Nation, friend and foe alike, to hand over more than half its lands. Jackson designed these cessions so as to ring them about with American territories and separate the Creeks from the Choctaws in the west, leaving the Creeks only the land between the Coosa and Okmulgee. Peace was soon followed by American pressures to remove the Creeks altogether from this remnant territory to lands west of the Mississippi.

Having defeated and despoiled the Creeks, Jackson moved on to Pensacola. The British, who had landed there and armed Indian and Black militias, withdrew with these associates eastward to the Apalachicola. After the war with Britain was formally over, Jackson asked the Spanish governor to dismantle the fort left by the British on the Apalachicola, return all runaway slaves to American authorities, and disperse the largely Black settlement that had gathered around the fort. When the governor refused, Jackson sent a force to destroy this outpost, killing most of the inhabitants. Further mutual depredations between Americans and Seminoles and continued shipments of arms from Nassau traders to Indians and Blacks led to yet another American invasion of Florida in 1818. This time the Americans and their Lower Creek allies, under Jackson, destroyed virtually all the Indian and Black villages in the Apalachee and Suwanee districts and captured and executed Indian leaders and two British traders. In the prelude to this campaign Jackson had written to President James Monroe saying, "Let it be signified to me through any channel . . . that the possession of the Floridas would be desirable to the United

States, and in sixty days it will be accomplished." He had already virtually done so; he had held Spanish officials at Pensacola and St. Marks captive while American forces roamed at will. Whether he had received the kind of signal he had suggested was debatable, and his actions, especially the execution of British citizens on Spanish soil, caused an uproar in Congress, but these were rationalized by the president, widely applauded by the American public, and only mildly rebuked by an investigating committee. Negotiations that had been underway between the United States and Spain over disputed borders now received a sudden stimulus. Obviously unable to defend Florida against American aggression, Spain ceded it to the United States in return for definition of an exact boundary of Louisiana on the west that left all of Texas as a Spanish buffer for essential Mexico.

Americans generally justified these invasions and destructions as necessary in view of Spain's inability to control its own people and police its borders, as a legitimate response to unbearable provocations. In the language of the time (and in most American accounts thereafter), Florida was the lair of "murderous Indians," "runaway Negroes," "white renegades," "villainous outcasts," "foreign adventurers." In the words of John Quincy Adams during the negotiations with Spain, the whole province was "a derelict, open to the occupancy of every enemy, civilized or savage, of the United States, and serving no other earthly purpose than as a post of annoyance to them." A good deal of evidence was cited in support of such fervent characterizations. But there is another way of interpreting such evidence and the larger affair. Despite a long history of turbulence on this old border zone, for the past twenty years the Americans had played the leading roles in this drama. They were the most numerous, varied, and aggressive participants, openly seeking major changes in the human geography of the region. One could view the problems cited and the responses undertaken as being primarily the result not of Spanish but of American disorder: the forays of American slavehunters, the wanton violence against Indians, the unwillingness of American governments to honor treaties, the open defiance of courts and federal policies by state officials, the blatant attempts to provoke rebellion against Spanish authorities. Clearly, the United States made little attempt to control its borders in the interest of good neighborly relations. To some extent, certainly, runaways, renegades, and refugees in Spanish Florida were products of American society.

It is not our purpose to try to weigh rights and wrongs and apportion blame in such matters. But it is important to get a reasonably clear picture of what happened to the peoples of this region and how such changes fit into the broader panorama of historical geography. Spanish Florida was a regional entity, albeit a fragile and attenuated one, sparsely developed and sporadically governed. It was a multiracial, multicultural colony with Europeans, Indians, Africans, and various blends of these three living in contact, though not everywhere in close association, with one another. In addition to the Spanish garrisons and officials at St. Augustine, Pensacola, and St. Marks, there was a small civilian population of Spanish Creoles, Minorcans, French Creoles (at Pensacola), and a miscellany of other Whites and mestizos, including a number of British planters along the St. Johns, some of whom had returned to Florida after disappointing results in the Bahamas. The plantations were largely worked by Black slaves, but there was also a considerable population of free Blacks in the towns, as well as in their own villages inland from St. Augustine. Like the Whites, these Blacks were varied in origin and status as Floridians: some had been there for several generations; others had come during the turbulence of the American Revolution, when British officials had actively encouraged slave defections from rebel owners; some had been left behind after the British evacuation in 1784; others had come from Cuba with the Spanish reoccupation; a good many were recent runaways from cotton planters on the expanding Georgia frontier. Many Blacks and mulattos also lived with the Seminoles, sometimes as slaves but commonly in a client relationship of mutual advantage. Blacks were important as agriculturalists, artisans, interpreters, and advisers to the Seminoles, and there was considerable intermarriage. In 1800 the Seminoles occupied a scattering of districts across northern Florida and overlapping the unsurveyed boundary into southwestern Georgia. The Atlantic end of that border, well away from these Indian areas, was much the most troublesome area. St. Mary's and Fernandina were the sort of volatile settlements common to such political outposts, and the United States had legitimate concerns about Amelia Island as a smuggler's base. But Spanish Florida as a whole was neither a chaotic colony nor a body of oppressed people longing for liberation. Away from the American border it was a relatively tranquil society, and for some peoples it was obviously an attractive refuge from more brutal conditions to the north. That it was so was not because the Spanish Empire was an intrinsically benign and tolerant system—a long and violent history belied any such notion—but because Florida was a marginal holding in a system that had long since lost its expansive vigor. Florida had never held many attractions for European colonists, and the Spanish occupance in 1800 was less extensive than it had been a century earlier.

American actions and official rationale show that it was this very character of Florida that made it necessary to take the colony over. Its very existence was intolerable to influential American interests. For such Americans, Florida was a "backcountry" out of control: its Black villages were a standing enticement to American slaves; its Black militia (not uncommon in Spanish colonial services) were an open inflammatory threat to the order and safety of American society; its Indians, who harbored refugees from American attacks and occasionally retaliated for American trespass and murder on their lands, were a savage enemy hiding under a foreign flag. That the British supplied such people with arms and Spanish officials sought to impede the intrusion of Americans seeking to retrieve runaway slaves or to punish retaliating Indians was undeniable, but whereas Americans read such arming and officiating as intolerable threats and affronts to the United States, and the British were certainly interested in stirring up as much trouble for the Americans as possible, Floridians had good reason to regard such actions as desperately defensive measures against their American enemies. Surely the likelihood that free Blacks would leave their precarious sanctuary in Florida and risk death, torture, and reenslavement to go raiding extensively into Georgia seems limited indeed.

The most insistent drive for American annexation of Spanish Florida thus was generated and sustained not so much as a national response to British machinations, the possible disintegration of the Spanish Empire, or larger geopolitical considerations, as from those who wanted to control, crush, even utterly destroy some specific peoples of Florida who were considered to pose a danger to immediate regional interests. The real pressure on this order came directly out of the frontiers and plantations of Georgia and Tennessee from people who regarded free Blacks and Creeks and Seminoles as anathema. The Americans had made considerable headway in remaking the human geography of this borderland well before annexation. The invasion of 1812 ravaged Indian and Black settlements in the Alachua; the war against the Creeks reduced them in number and territory; and the flight of resisters into Florida provided an excuse for the invasion of 1816, which wiped out most of the Blacks on the Apalachicola and drove the remainder eastward to the Suwanee, from where they and their Seminole hosts along with others in the Alachua prairies were pushed further into the watery wilderness of the peninsula. One small group of about 200 Seminole Blacks put to sea in their long dugouts, families packed in with a few provisions and seeds for planting, and crossed the Straits of Florida to refuge on Andros Island—a "boat people" fleeing the relentless tyranny from the north.

Unlike Louisiana, the acquisition of Florida was essentially an expansion by conquest. Like Louisiana, the United States thereby captured some populations that had no desire to be included in the Republic. Because of the precedence of Louisiana, annexation of the largely French Creole settlers of Biloxi, Pascagoula, Mobile, and the Tensaw was not regarded as a serious problem. This Creole coast was attached to Mississippi Territory, which was soon subdivided to create Alabama Territory in such a manner as to give both access to the gulf. The Creole population remained locally important but was soon a tiny minority in these large and rapidly developing units, and no special provision was made for them. The rest of Spanish Florida, all east of the Perdido, was organized as a single territory, with Andrew Jackson its first governor. The total population was probably less than 20,000, including about 5,000 Seminoles. Territorial officials moved quickly to pressure the Indians into a more constricted inland reserve on unwanted lands on the peninsula, south of Ocala, and the federal government established Fort Brooke on Tampa Bay to keep an eye on them and to prevent any shipments of arms or other traffic with Cuba, the Bahamas, or elsewhere. In 1824 a new capital was located at Tallahassee, and the attractive cotton lands of Middle Florida (a new juridical designation for the area between the Apalachicola and the Suwanee rivers) were readied for sale. Meanwhile, Georgia planters came in search of runaways, Florida statutes provided death penalties for slave stealing or assistance to fugitives, and the free Blacks now found themselves part of a society in which they were considered to be an anomalous and dangerous people.

CUBA

This American obsession with a small number of free Blacks was of course grounded in the latent fear of slave revolt, a worry magnified during this formative period of Florida by the sensational conspiracy of Denmark Vesey in South Carolina but more deeply sustained by the ominous example of French Santo Domingo. In any new American view southward, Black Haiti loomed in the distance; with the acquisition of Florida, only Cuba lay between. With this extension of the Republic's national borders to encompass the southeastern corner of the continent and the rapid expansion of the American slave economy westward across the cotton lands of the coastal plain, Cuba began to take on a new and important meaning for American policies and aspirations.

In Thomas Jefferson's mind Florida and Cuba were readily coupled. When contemplating reprisals against Spain in 1807 he remarked that an American force could easily take Florida and "probably Cuba will add itself to our confederation." Two years later he was assuring his successor, James Madison, that given the French conquest of Spain and the incipient disintegration of the Spanish Empire "the Floridas and Cuba . . . will offer themselves to you." In 1810 Madison sent a consul to Havana with instructions to make it known that the United States would not allow any other power to take over Cuba, and to sound out Cubans about annexation to the United States. The agent eventually reported that annexation would be favored only as an alternative to a drastic internal change: the abolition of slavery in the Spanish Empire. Such a response might suggest that Jefferson was mistaken about Cuba and that it was in fact a colony critically different in kind from Spanish Florida.

In the early 1800s Cuba was no mere husk of a moribund empire; rather, it was a prosperous colony growing in population and production, which had been invigorated by the recession or collapse of empire elsewhere. Indeed, the beginning of this unusually thriving era could be traced directly to the influx of thousands of planters fleeing the French disaster in Santo Domingo. Within a few years the sugar and coffee industries were expanding vigorously. The arc of deep red limestone soils back of Havana reaching east to Güines and Matanzas was beginning to display the basis of its later fame as one of the world's finest sugarcane environments.

Havana itself was thriving not only on the productions of its hinterland but from the relaxation of Spanish controls on its commerce begun during the exigencies of the various wars and blockades. The 1810 census enumeration of 96,114 inhabitants made it almost exactly the size of New York City, and that total did not include several thousand military, members of religious orders, and foreign transients. It did include the suburbs around the bay, which Humboldt, visiting a few years later, found especially attractive, noting that the "light and elegant" country houses there "are ordered from the United States, as one would order any piece of furniture." In 1817 the population of the island was reported as 572,363, more than double what it had been in 1792. Of these 45 percent were listed as White, 35 percent as slaves, and 20 percent as free Blacks and mulattos. Throughout this period there were important additions from immigration as well as from natural growth. Imports of slaves continued. When, under pressure from Britain, Spain signed a treaty in 1817 to end the slave trade by 1820, nearly 60,000 slaves were brought in during those final three years, and in fact the treaty was ignored and imports continued at a high rate for decades. And there were important influxes of Whites, in addition to the Santo Domingan refugees. As we have noted, some of these French planters moved on to Louisiana in response to strong anti-French feelings during the Napoleonic occupation. But Cuba also received most of the Spanish citizens and soldiery evacuated from Louisiana and the Floridas. Much more important was the fact that the first upwellings of revolt against the empire in 1810 brought in a trickle of royalists from Mexico, and by the time the revolution had engulfed the mainland perhaps 20,000 such emigrants had taken refuge in Cuba. In 1817 the Spanish government undertook a program to encourage foreign immigration. Cienfuegos was begun as a French colony, and a number of other new towns were founded in this period to foster the development of districts well away from Havana. The selective infusion of so many royalists strengthened the ties of Cuba to Spain, and as Ferdinand VII gained firm control over the motherland in the 1820s, annulling the work of the liberal *Cortes*, Cuba and Puerto Rico were increasingly treated as privileged preserves, bases for the eventual reconquest of the empire.

Despite this invigoration and reinforcement the fate of Cuba remained uncertain because other forces were contending for its control. On the inside no colony could be wholly immune to the independence and republican movements that were dissolving the Spanish Empire. On the outside other powers hovered. Spain rejected a British proposal to take over eastern Cuba. A British squadron patrolled the northern Cuban coast to suppress piracy so that the United States would not have an excuse to occupy Cuba as it had Florida. And just as the United States was receiving formal title to Florida it was faced with what to do about its new neighbor across the narrow seas, for in 1821 a Cuban group openly sought American sympathy and material support for revolution against the Spanish regime. President Monroe referred the matter to his cabinet. Secretary of War John C. Calhoun, of South Carolina, urged immediate annexation of Cuba to the United States. Secretary of State John Quincy Adams argued that American interests would be best served by the continuance of Spanish imperial rule. Two major concerns dominated the discussion: the fear that a liberal revolution would inevitably lead to a massive slave revolt, and the possibility that Great Britain would seize all or part of Cuba. The first would produce the alarming situation of another Haiti adjacent to the American South; the second would put the Gibraltar of the American Mediterranean in the control of the world's greatest naval power (a base far superior to that of Nassau in the niggardly Bahamas and much more strategically positioned than Jamaica, islands Britain had long held). The Adams position prevailed because it was judged to be the best response to both concerns. Thus American policy gave tacit support to the continuation of Spanish rule, Creole planter dominance, and slavery, because an imperial autocratic society seemed to offer the best hope for political and social stability in a region of new strategic significance to the United States.

In a letter to the U.S. minister in Madrid in 1823 Adams looked beyond this temporizing policy and spelled out his geopolitical views and expectations at some length:

> It may be taken for granted that the dominion of Spain upon the American continents, north and south, is irrevocably gone. But the islands of Cuba and Porto Rico still remain nominally, and so far really dependent upon her, that she yet possesses the power of transferring her own dominion over them, together with the possession of them, to others. These islands, from their local position, are natural appendages to the North American continent, and one of them, Cuba, almost in sight of our shores, from a multitude of considerations has become an object of transcendent importance to the commercial and political interests of our Union. Its commanding position with reference to the Gulf of Mexico and the West India seas; the character of its population, its situation midway between our southern coast and the island of San Domingo; its safe and capacious harbor of the Havana, fronting a long line of our shores destitute of the same advantage; the nature of its productions and of its wants, furnishing the supplies and needing the returns of a commerce immensely profitable and mutually beneficial; give it an importance in the sum of our national interests with which that of no other foreign territory can be compared, and little inferior to that which binds the different members of this Union together.
>
> Such indeed are, between the interests of that island and of this country, the geographical, commercial, moral and political relations formed by nature, gathering

in the process of time, and even now verging to maturity, that in looking forward to the probable course of events from a short period of half a century, it is scarcely possible to resist the conviction that the annexation of Cuba to our federal republic will be indispensable to the continuance and integrity of the Union itself. It is obvious however that for this event we are not yet prepared. Numerous and formidable objections to the extension of our territorial dominions beyond the sea present themselves to the first contemplation of the subject. Obstacles to the system of policy by which it alone can be compared and maintained are to be foreseen and surmounted, both from at home and abroad. But there are laws of political as well as physical gravitation; and if an apple severed by the tempest from its native tree cannot choose but to fall to the ground, Cuba, forcibly disjoined from its own unnatural connection with Spain, and incapable of self-support, can gravitate only towards the North American Union, which by the same law of nature cannot cast her off from her bosom.

The "no-transfer" part of this policy was promulgated later that year in the Monroe Doctrine. It obviously applied to Puerto Rico as well as to Cuba, and American support for continued Spanish rule of the smaller island followed the same rationale as with Cuba. In 1822 a small expedition of revolutionaries fitted out in New York and Philadelphia set off to free Puerto Rico and establish the "Republic of Boriqua." This meager attempt became diverted and thwarted before it reached the island, but the fact that its leaders had been conspiring with Blacks in Puerto Rico and intended to abolish slavery was a cause of alarm to island and mainland planters alike. The role of sugar and slavery was less important within this more mountainous island than in Cuba, and whether Puerto Rico was another fruit that would eventually ripen and fall to the bosom of the United States was not of such moment, but its fate seemed likely to be connected to that of the larger and nearer island.

Thus the Hispanic islands and the North American mainland became bound together in important ways. Underneath the larger geopolitical concern to keep the greater European powers away from positions of strategic importance was a fundamental feature shared by Cuba, Puerto Rico, and the southern United States: these societies constituted one of the last flourishing sectors of the centuries-old American institution of Black slavery (Brazil was another). Vigorous agricultural expansion, based primarily on sugar in the one case and cotton in the other, reinforced this traditional tropical system of labor in both areas. In 1808 the American constitutional prohibition of further slave importation went into effect, and it had been proscribed within the British Empire in the previous years. But it remained tacitly open in the Spanish colonies, and the merchants of Havana and Santiago de Cuba began sending large vessels (mostly built especially for this trade in Baltimore and usually captained and manned by Americans) across the Atlantic, taking over a trade long dominated by the British, Dutch, and French. More than 400,000 Africans were brought to Cuba in the forty years after 1820; Blacks soon exceeded the number of Whites, and slaves accounted for more than a third of the population. Cuba and Puerto Rico thus became the last great entryways through which Africa continued directly to replenish the northern sector of the deep-rooted and expanding Afro-American world. Cuba thereby became the chief source of illegal imports into the United States, and a prospering Cuba increasingly important to southern American statesmen and planters as a society allied in basic interests.

Elsewhere, the world of slavery was collapsing. Abolition in some form was a basic tenet of all the new Hispanic American republics, and in 1833 a program of staged emancipation (involving a transitional period of indenture) was begun in the British Empire. The Royal Navy took the lead in suppression of the slave trade. Cargoes seized on the high seas were freed, and many of these (about 4,000 by 1838) were taken to Nassau and eventually given small plots of land in the Bahamas.

MEXICO

This variegated extension of American involvement southeastward into the tropical seas had been obtained in some degree, at least in formal diplomatic terms, by the relinquishment of claims and the establishment of an exact boundary to the United States on the southwest toward Mexico. Events in that sector and the developing human geography of Texas itself, however, suggested that American interests would not be so simply contained.

Shortly after the purchase of Louisiana, Jefferson laid claim to the Rio Grande as its western boundary, an obvious bargaining ploy of little substance, since the Spanish had colonized San Antonio in 1718 and founded twenty towns along the lower Rio Grande in the 1750s. In their attempts to gain the Floridas, American negotiators soon backed down to the Colorado River, debouching into Matagorda Bay, as a more feasible claim. But that, too, was a line well west of the Spanish nucleus at Nacogdoches, and the local military forces sent by the Spanish and by the Americans to assert their claims soon agreed to settle in at the old outposts of Los Adais and Natchitoches, respectively, reaffirming the de facto bounds of Spanish Texas and French Louisiana, with a narrow neutral strip between.

When formal negotiations were resumed in 1816, the United States again laid claim to the Colorado River, but the American delegate was instructed to back down to the Sabine if that would be necessary to obtain Florida. By 1819, John Quincy Adams, the American negotiator, was quite willing to accept that more easterly stream with a geometric extension north to the Red River (Rio Roxo) as a southwestern boundary for Louisiana because he had obtained formal agreement to set a northern limit to Spanish claims all the way from this boundary to the Pacific

Ocean (via the Red, the Arkansas, and the Forty-second parallel). Thus the long-sought cession of Florida to the United States, extending the American border around the southeastern corner of the continent, included formal declaration of a transcontinental United States with claim to a broad frontage on the northwestern coast of North America.

Spanish officials were well aware of all this while also aware of the need to strengthen their hold on Texas. In 1805 they approved a program to establish settlements at each of the main river crossings along the road between San Antonio and Nacogdoches, but, as had always been the case with this distant frontier, it was next to impossible to find appropriate colonists. A few stockmen from San Antonio and La Bahia (Goliad) formed the nucleus of San Marcos on an upper branch of the Guadalupe, and a miscellany of people displaced from Spanish Louisiana were brought together at Salcedo on the Trinity, but in 1809 the governor could report only about 3,500 people plus 1,000 soldiers in all the settlements of Spanish Texas. The problem was that the only people attracted to the piney woods of East Texas were the wrong kind, the kind that had been infiltrating for some years: traders, squatters, drifters, adventurers, smugglers, conspirators—people attracted by the possibilities of a ill-policed border zone and minimal civic authority.

The more conservative of Spanish strategists advocated giving up East Texas and withdrawing to the only part of Texas worth living in, the fine ranching country anchored on the old San Antonio nucleus. But others insisted on holding to the Sabine River line to create a substantial buffer against American pressures and retain influence with the Caddo Indians.

Several episodes rather more dramatic than the usual border infiltrations made the dangers here all too apparent. In 1812 in the aftermath of the abortive Hidalgo revolt in Mexico, a cosmopolitan filibuster group of Mexicans and Americans marched in from Louisiana, defeated a Spanish troop, captured San Antonio, and declared an independent "State of Texas," only to mire in dissension and be annihilated by a Spanish counterattack. In 1818 the Spanish had to drive off a band of Napoleonic exiles who tried to form an unauthorized colony along the lower Trinity. In the following year another group of American filibusters seized control of Nacogdoches. And during most of this time pirates had used Galveston Island as a base for preying upon Spanish vessels. In response to such affronts the Spanish government did decide to alter its age-old policy and open its territories to colonization for foreigners under a carefully defined program (as it had done in Cuba). Before anything could be accomplished, however, the independence movement led by Colonel Agustin de Iturbide had effectively severed Mexico from Spanish authority.

The new Mexican state inherited the problems and the program and soon fostered important changes in this border region. Much the most significant was the Austin Colony, originally authorized by the Spanish to Moses Austin, a Connecticut-born entrepreneur who had long resided in Missouri, been a citizen of Spanish Louisiana, and had extensive dealings with Spanish officials, and after his death reconfirmed to his son. Stephen F. Austin thereby became *empresario* of a huge block of country in the Brazos and Colorado basins, bounded on the north by the main road across Texas and on the south by a coastal strip from which Mexico wished to exclude foreign colonists. It was thus central within the spare framework of Texas and included a rich mixture of prairies, woodlands, and especially bottomlands attractive to Anglo-American settlers. Further, it could be had in munificent amounts, for in keeping with common Spanish practice it was allocated in ranch-size units of a square league (about 4,428 acres) to each family. Land could thereby be obtained in Texas in far larger amounts at far less cost than in the United States (where the Panic of 1819 had put great strain on overextended farmers and speculators), and eager applicants began to arrive from the western frontiers of the United States even before Austin could lay out his capital town of San Felipe on the lower Brazos. As empresario, Austin was accountable to the Mexican government for the selection of settlers, allocation of lands, and imposition of regulations relating to citizenship. By 1830 he had settled more than 5,000 Americans on his lands, including many slaves (the importation of which was technically forbidden by Mexico but tacitly allowed). In time he received additional grants, including the bordering coastal strip, and other empresarios developed similar holdings on either side. Austin was an unusually conscientious agent, and his colony gave no serious trouble to the Mexican state in these early years. But in districts to the east toward the Louisiana border there were conflicts between new American grantees and the scattering of older settlers, uncertainties and unrest over the boundary in the northeast, and continual problems with squatters, smugglers, and speculators. Increasingly alarmed at the scale and temper of the Anglo-American influx, in 1830 Mexico halted further immigration from the United States and imposed customs duties in an attempt to redirect Texas commerce from American to Mexican ports. Texas was reorganized into three departments (Bexar, Brazoria, Nacogdoches), several new garrisons (bearing famous Mexican-Indian names: Anahuac, Lipantitlan, Tenoxtitlan) were established, and a program to recruit Mexican and European colonists was drawn up. By this time at least three-quarters of the 25,000–30,000 people in Texas (excluding Indians) were Anglo-American (including Black slaves). However, throughout this time the Mexican government had kept Texas bound to Coahuila, with officials at San Antonio generally subordinate to those in Saltillo. In this larger grouping, the Anglo-Americans' preponderance in central and eastern Texas was more than offset by the Hispanic populations of Bexar and Coahuila, but such would not long be the case if recent trends continued.

The newly independent and unstable Republic of Mexico was thus in serious difficulty on its most critical frontier. Nacogdoches was the only district along the length of its vast and vague continental bounds facing directly on an organized state and an expanding people. In 1805 when the Spanish and the Americans had defined a neutral zone between them at Los Adais-Natchitoches it was an appropriate demarcation, concordant with the human geography and reasonable claims of the two peoples; when the boundary was shifted slightly westward to the Sabine and formalized in 1819, such separations had become more blurred but not deeply altered. By the 1830s, however, the situation was fundamentally different. The dynamics of American frontier expansion, aided by Mexico's own calculated program, had produced a major discordance between political and cultural boundaries. The western margins of Anglo-America were now beyond the Colorado (that limit American statesmen had so long claimed on so little substance), 250 miles west of the Sabine, lapping against the old Hispanic areas of Bexar. Of course, by law and by intent of the empresario program all colonists were to become Mexican citizens and accept the basic rules and patterns of a Spanish-speaking, Catholic society. In one sense, this was not an unreasonable expectation by the new Mexican state. After all, foreign colonists were nothing new in the American world. Acculturation would lead to assimilation, or at least to some kind of tolerable incorporation of such immigrants and their descendants into the body of the larger receiving society. Perhaps there could be special recognition of certain Anglo-American customs, as in the neighboring example of the Creole Louisianians in the United States. And in fact the Coahuila y Texas legislature did respond in 1835 to Anglo-American petitions for special concessions, guaranteeing religious toleration, allowing the use of English in official documents, extending local government, and offering a number of other reforms. The plea to make Texas a separate state was rejected, but Texans were given an increase in representation in the legislature.

But the Anglo-American presence in Texas was not really analogous to that of the French in Louisiana. These were new colonists, not hapless victims of impulsive territorial trades concluded in distant capitals, and they were but one part of a much broader westward migration of Anglo-Americans into new lands. We can never know how many of these immigrants sincerely intended to become loyal citizens of Mexico (as Stephen Austin demonstrably did); we should note that most of them came out of the western frontiers of the United States, where the reshaping of geopolitical territories, the formation of new local and state governments, and contentious political agitations were concomitant with pioneering. Had the relative power and internal stability of Mexico and the United States been more alike, the results might have been very different. As it was, the efforts of a rapid succession of insecure Mexican administrations to control and contain this new population and ensure the integrity of the national state only heightened the discontent of that population and turned it toward alternatives. By the 1830s an autonomous Texas, an independent Texas, the annexation of Texas had become common topics in this far frontier, and all the while unwelcomed overtures from United States representatives in Mexico City to purchase Texas strengthened Mexican fears of American intentions.

This uneasy relationship was quickly transformed in late 1835, when as so easily happens in such a situation, a minor dispute with local customs officials flared into a wider defiance of Mexican authority, attempts to exercise that authority met armed resistance, and conflict soon escalated into open warfare. Started by a few extremists, expanding despite the efforts of many Anglo-Texans to dampen it, the revolt quickly engulfed the region in a bitter struggle between the Anglo-Americans and the military power of the Mexican state. On March 1, 1836, while the Alamo was under siege, Anglo-American leaders gathered at Washington-on-the-Brazos in the midst of the Austin Colony to declare an independent Republic of Texas, an aspiration that hardly seemed assured until the defeat of the Mexican army at San Jacinto seven weeks later.

In their first general election Texan voters almost unanimously endorsed annexation to the United States, and a formal proposal was made to the American government in 1837. But the idea proved highly controversial in the United States, and after a long, humiliating delay Texas firmly withdrew the offer, its leaders turning more fully to the daunting task of asserting control and developing this new republic that claimed the whole course of the Rio Grande as its southern and western bounds.

The Louisiana Purchase thus had powerful ramifications southward. It was more than a portal on the gulf, the other half of the Mississippi Valley, and a vast opening to the west. Louisiana was like a wedge, inserted at New Orleans, driven by repeated American hammerings to expand until, piece by piece, it broke the Spanish off the mainland on the one side and created such heavy pressures and fracture lines as to leave the loose piece of Texas hanging uncertainly on the other. The great cultural border zone of the Americas was thereby extended and altered in important ways. The French Creoles of Louisiana and West Florida were encompassed and incorporated into the Anglo-American state, retaining some measure of identity. The Hispanic presence in northern Florida was removed and the political border shifted to the Florida Straits, leaving the Seminoles and the jungly waterlands of the peninsula as a precarious buffer between the vigorous slave-based planter societies of the American South and Hispanic Cuba. On the southwest Anglo-Americans had expanded to the Guadalupe, held the small residual Hispanic population of Bexar captive, and laid claim to all north of the Rio Grande as within the bounds of a new Anglo-American republic. And by their policies and performance, by public discussions and popular agitations with reference to Cuba and Mexico and related areas, the governments of the United States and Texas and their Anglo-American citizens were declaring that both the political and the cultural borders between Anglo-America and Hispanic America remained open to further and perhaps major alterations.

3. Pressures on the Borders: Northward

In 1800 the boundary between the United States and British North America extended halfway across the continent. It was a varied and indirect line, traced most of the way along rivers and watersheds and broad looping bi-sections of the Great Lakes for more than 2,700 miles between the Bay of Fundy and Lake of the Woods. And it was an uncertain line in several sectors, for complications arising from inaccurate maps and ambiguous identity of streams in treaty definitions had yet to be resolved. More important for our purposes was the varied human geography of this elongated zone and the significance such a line was accorded by those living on either side. Even a glance will make clear that this political divide, created in 1783 following the dramatic disruption and disintegration of an encompassing British America, was no barrier to commerce or migration, and, with certain important exceptions, was not generally perceived as a sharp separation of peoples or prospects in the development of North America.

The principal exceptions to this generalization were to be found in those settled districts on the British side that had been created for and by Loyalists fleeing the Republic: around Passamaquoddy Bay, along the upper St. Lawrence, around the Bay of Quinte, and at Niagara. In such places a self-conscious "Britishness" was kept alive, nurtured especially by local elites and by colonial officials—appointees of the Crown—of New Brunswick and Upper Canada. But such feelings had not been intensified by any strong American pressure, or even presence, in relation to these areas. The forts at Niagara and Oswego were barely manned by American troops. Samuel Ogden had laid out a town at the site of the old Canadian outpost on the Oswegatchie, but the lands along these borders of New York and Maine had as yet scarcely felt the touch of American frontier development (fig. 5).

West of Niagara there was little relation between the political boundary and the respective fields of activity of the British and the Americans. The whole country tributary to Lakes Huron, Michigan, and Superior had been an unchallengeable part of Montreal's hinterland ever since French explorers had penetrated the area a century or more earlier, and the freedom of the British and the Indians (as well as the Americans) to "pass and repass by land or inland navigation" and to carry on commerce across this boundary had prevailed since the Revolution and been explicitly confirmed in Jay's Treaty of 1795. In 1800 the few Americans who had come to the ostensible border posts of Detroit and Michilimackinac found them-

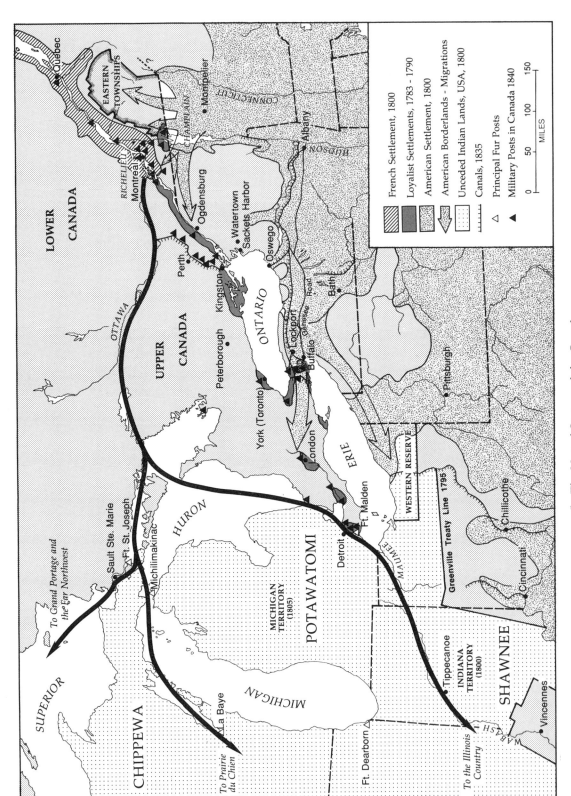

5. The United States and the Canadas.

selves deep within a vast region of British activity. Each post was in fact a pivotal point within long-established networks comprehending the Great Lakes and reaching westward to the Mississippi. Detroit was the forward base on the old Maumee-Wabash route to the Illinois Country, a hinterland much diminished in profits but magnified in its political significance for Indian relations. Michilimackinac was similarly situated with reference to the Green Bay-Fox-Wisconsin route, leading to the old French outpost and Indian rendezvous at Prairie du Chien on the upper Mississippi. Thus the whole northwest corner of the United States was under American sovereignty but quite untouched by American power or influence. The Indians were clients of the Montreal traders, the thin scattering of settlements was wholly French Canadian and métis, with a few British traders. Both Detroit and Michilimackinac had been diminished by recent British evacuations to nearby sites on Canadian soil. They were establishing Fort Malden downriver on the Detroit and had shifted to St. Joseph Island near the Sault Sainte Marie in the north, and these now became the great centers of contact between the British and the Indians of the Great Lakes region.

A further blurring of the boundary in quite a different way took place during the early years of the nineteenth century in two important areas. In the aftermath of the Revolution it was the policy of British governors of Quebec to keep Loyalists and other Americans out of the strategic border zone south and east of Montreal. In the 1790s, however, the governor of the newly designated territory of Lower Canada sought to fill that very area with English-speaking colonists, in part as a counterweight to the French Canadians. The Eastern Townships were surveyed and put on the market, and Yankee landseekers, who by 1800 were finding little left worth taking in adjacent Vermont and New Hampshire, came flooding in. Much of the land was granted in township units to leaders acting for a body of settlers, a practice well suited to New England traditions of colonization. Because this northward thrust was simultaneous with one to the west of Vermont into northern New York, a common pattern of life and landscape, bisected by the international boundary, was quickly spread over a broad area between the Adirondacks and the St. Lawrence. The pace of development quickened markedly from 1807 onward as blockades and embargoes incident to the Napoleonic Wars turned Britain to Canada for vital shiptimbers and naval stores. Much of the timber exported from Montreal and Quebec actually originated in New York and Vermont, as did a growing share of the potash and flour, and with the expansion in facilities and prosperity Montreal merchants began to import consumer goods more and more by way of New York City and Albany-Troy. By 1810 many of those merchants were American immigrants, as were almost all the millers, mechanics, storekeepers, innkeepers, schoolmasters, and ministers, and the majority of the farmers and lumbermen in these borderland districts of Lower Canada. These Americans had been lured by economic opportunities: by land in large amounts on better terms than in New England or New York, by commercial possibilities in a suddenly thriving Laurentian system, of which, by the avenues of nature, the whole Champlain area was an integral part. Any sense of American nationality was weak. In spite of differences in the structure of government, English laws and institutions prevailed in both countries, and allegiances were not deeply rooted. After all, Vermonters in particular had lived in ambiguity for years before their state had belatedly become a formal member of the American federation in 1791. In these expansive years, then, not only was the international boundary essentially "non-existent in the routine affairs of daily life," but it had "all but disappeared from the consciousness" of Vermonters and a good many—but not all—Canadians in this area.

A similar development took place west of Niagara in the long peninsula of land between Lakes Erie and Huron. The first governor of Upper Canada had laid out a framework for colonization as well as military defense and calculatingly sought to lure experienced American farmers, believing that he could nurture them into loyal British subjects. The first contingents coming in response to his advertisements were known as "late loyalists," being in many cases relatives, friends, or former neighbors of original Loyalist refugees or, as in the case of various Quaker and German pietist groups, people who had reason to feel uncomfortable in the rather bellicose and disorderly new American republic. After 1800, as western New York was being settled and the Genesee Road was extended to Niagara, more and more landseekers ferried the river and ranged on farther over well-established military roads into the western districts of Upper Canada. The land there was generally excellent by any comparison familiar to these Americans, and it was more accessible and could be had on better terms than lands in the Western Reserve or other tracts in Ohio. Further, although there were Indians along the Grand River, they were friendly Indians, Iroquois allies of the government, and there seemed to be little reason to fear the kind of bloody preludes to colonization so widespread in the United States. Thus in broader view a swelling vanguard of westward-moving pioneers bifurcated around Lake Erie, submerging the political border under layers of uniformities: the same kinds of people from the same source regions, spreading at the same time upon the same kinds of lands to domesticate and develop them in similar ways. By 1812 probably 80 percent of the people of Upper Canada were Americans; 20 percent of these were Loyalists and their children, but the rest were immigrants of the last few years and such people were a large majority in the lands west of Niagara. As A. L. Burt has noted, the "American" character of this movement should not be emphasized, "for it was primarily North American. It was land these people were after. Few seemed to care whether they lived under the American or the British flag." Differences in formal government, land surveys, taxes, and militias became mere details within the larger pattern of a single region of settlement.

To leaders of Upper Canada who were striving to ensure the continuance of a *British* North America, that kind of indifference was, of course, a cause of some concern, and there was a growing unease about the magnitude and character of this influx. But even for that vocal and influential minority the political border was not a sharp line of separation. The Loyalists among that group had, after all, once resided in America, and almost all had left friends and relatives behind, maintaining regular contact with them by letters and visits and travelers' reports. Commercial relations flourished; news of the larger world came more regularly by way of New York and New England than by Montreal and Halifax. And, "far from rejecting all things American, many Upper Canadians . . . consciously used the United States as both a positive and a negative point of reference by which to gauge their own development." Such persons found much to admire in American economic progress and some of its institutions, while at the same time they "watched apprehensively as the fragile stability of American society" seemed "threatened by the influence of unruly democracy." In this they found allies and interpreters in the Federalists of adjacent New York and New England, whose "critique of American democracy and of republican France together with . . . enthusiasm for 'peace, order and good government' naturally struck a responsive chord with Upper Canadian loyalist leaders." And the same might be said of the leadership of New Brunswick and, to a lesser degree, of Lower Canada as well. Thus, when relationships between the United States and Great Britain deteriorated rapidly after 1807 it began to appear to some North Americans that there were greater differences— geopolitical differences—*within* the United States than between the northern states and their northern neighbors.

One spot along this lengthy border, however, became a festering sore between the two sovereignties. Fort Malden, at the westernmost point of the Ontario peninsula, was the critical link between British officials and Indian nations of the western lakes. And that link became a focus of American agitation as the Indians intensified their resistance to powerful American pressures on their homelands in the opening decade of the nineteenth century. We shall look more closely at those pressures in a later section. Suffice it to note here that these were generated by a deep-rooted expansionism that was intensified after the acquisition of Louisiana by Jefferson's idea of removing all Indians to a western sanctuary beyond the Mississippi (leaving behind only those who agreed to settle on small agricultural reserves). The principal agent of this policy in the northwest was William Henry Harrison, seated at Vincennes as governor of the recently created (1800) Indiana Territory. Through aggressive use of threats, trickery, and bribery, creating and capitalizing on tribal dissensions, Harrison, in treaty after treaty, gained the cession of millions of acres of Indian lands, clearing the way for the creation of Michigan (1805) and Illinois (1809) territories. The establishment of such frontier governments further intensified American pressures, as officials and land speculators sought to maximize the development of their territories. The Indians' deepening fears and resentments were brought into focus by two charismatic Shawnee leaders, Tecumseh and his brother, The Prophet. Tecumseh visited Fort Malden to seek British support for organized resistance against further American expansion. British officials tried to follow a policy delicately balanced between befriending the Indians as allies and restraining them from attacking the Americans. Although British traders wanted to preserve their dominance over the Upper Lakes (and there was still talk about a formal Indian buffer state and even an eventual revision of the international boundary), the principal British motive was defensive: to protect the precarious attenuated inland and border colony of Upper Canada from American aggression. Americans in contrast, understandably regarded any British contact with these Indians as a brazen interference in American domestic affairs. In geopolitical terms, conflict arose as the opening phases of the American frontier process (Indian treaties, territorial formation, land speculation) moved in upon a de facto British imperial protectorate on American soil.

In 1810, having failed to get a retraction from Harrison of his latest land-grab, Tecumseh called for Indian attacks on American frontier settlements. Harrison's counterattack at Tippecanoe dispersed a major Indian force along the Wabash frontier, and although not an unqualified victory, it confirmed American suspicions that the Indians were making extensive use of British arms, and that led to a mounting cry from western interests for the conquest of Canada and elimination of Britain from North America. If this issue was not the main cause of the War of 1812, it was an important contributor, constituting a strong pressure upon the beleaguered president of a deeply divided nation, and it made Detroit-Fort Malden the initial focus of international conflict on the mainland.

The War of 1812 is a curious, complex, and controversial topic in American history. It was a war generated primarily by maritime policies and practices so remote from modern behavior as to be difficult to comprehend; it was declared and fought by a United States so deeply divided on the very idea of such a war as to generate not only internal resistance but considerable support for the enemy; and it was concluded by a treaty formally recognizing that nothing had been changed in the basic relationship between the two belligerents. Like most wars, it had unforeseen results, not least of which were those relating to the international boundary between the United States and British North America, a geographical line left unchanged in position but profoundly altered in meaning.

In general, the U.S. plan for the war was utterly simple: defend American coasts and seize Canada. Canada was understood to have a special importance for Britain as well as for the United States. Whereas spokesmen for the American West were obsessed with the need to "cut off the communication between foreign nations and the Indians on our frontiers and in our own territory," President Madison had come to see the conquest of Canada more as a means of pressuring Britain to stop interfering with American oceanic shipping by severing it from a vital resource, for he understood that the British navy and merchant shipping, having been shut out of the Baltic for several years, had become critically dependent on North American timbers. Canada thus was more than a convenient hostage in the American plan to force Britain into negotiation of the festering issues between them.

And it was a strategy widely regarded as not only obvious but easily executed. Thomas Jefferson in a letter written shortly after the American declaration of war (and subsequently famous as a succinct expression of American illusions), declared: "The acquisition of Canada this year, as far as the neighborhood of Quebec, will be a mere matter of marching, and will give us experience for the attack of Halifax the next, and the final expulsion of England from the American continent. Halifax once taken, every cock-boat of hers must return to England for repairs." Upper Canada, inland, beyond the support of the British fleet, adjacent, "defended by only a few regular soldiers, and containing a predominantly American population that would presumably welcome the invaders as liberators" seemed to be "a plum ready for the picking." A quick thrust to seize Montreal and simultaneous invasions from Niagara and Detroit were expected to do the job in short order.

It did not work out quite that way. In fact, the United States was utterly unprepared for war. It had almost no regular army, no system to support and no leadership competent to undertake such extensive operations; most important, the country was deeply divided over the very idea of waging war. New York and New England, the American areas most critical for operations against British North America, refused to support the national administration. There was no quick invasion to seize Montreal because it proved impossible to raise volunteers and militia in those states willing to undertake the task, and the general placed in charge of that sector became instead preoccupied with the "Tory revolt"— meaning the Federalist opposition in that populous corner of the nation. In simple terms, that opposition arose from an intense divergence between the commercial interests of the North and Republican agrarian interests of the South and West. Having been dragged into the war, Americans in these northeastern border zones were willing to take up defensive positions but were quite unwilling to invade their neighbors, with whom they had no grievance and with whom they were, in some degree, kin. They would, in fact, continue to trade across these borders, even to the point where, in the late stages of the war, the commander of the by-then-sizable British forces poised for the invasion of the United States reported that two-thirds of his army "were eating beef provided by American contractors, drawn principally from the States of Vermont and New York."

Unable to mount an attack upon the "trunk" of British power on the St.

Lawrence, the Americans flailed away at "the leaves and branches" with feeble incursions at Detroit and Niagara. The results were disastrous. The British repelled these intrusions and counterattacked, seizing Detroit and Michilimackinac and, with their Indian allies, clamping a hold upon Prairie du Chien and the Northwest. These surprising successes transformed the conflict. Whereas the American declaration of war had produced much consternation and even despair among the people of Upper Canada, who saw themselves as vulnerable innocents (British commanders also had a hard time organizing local militias, even for defense), these initial British victories gave them hope and a mounting pride in having defied America's gratuitous assaults and arrogant assumptions.

From these opening salvos the war on this northern front developed into an intermittent set of local military engagements on land and on the lakes with first one side, then the other, victorious, but neither able to bring the other to bay. The Americans were unable to conquer Canada, the British were unable to invade and threaten any vital part of the United States. But even though the war was in a larger sense a stalemate—on this border and as a whole—two and a half years of hostilities affected, often severely, many localities along the border. Detroit, the Thames River Valley, the Niagara frontier, Sacket's Harbor, the St. Lawrence below Prescott-Ogdensburg, and Châteauguay and the northerly margins of Lake Champlain were battle zones. Homes and farmsteads, orchards, crops, and livestock, public buildings and whole towns had been ravaged, pillaged, burned, blown up. An American force had sailed across Lake Ontario, captured York (Toronto), and spent four days looting and burning, including the parliament and other public buildings of the capital of Upper Canada; some months later the British did the same to Joseph Ellicott's rising New Amsterdam at Buffalo (and more pointedly and powerfully, on the Atlantic front the British sailed up the Chesapeake in 1814 and seized and burned the Capitol, the president's house, and other buildings in Washington in direct retaliation for York). These were the experiences that produced the most important results. The Treaty of Ghent, ending the war, specified restoration of the *status quo antebellum*—nothing to be changed in the territorial relations of the United States and British North America; those several areas never exactly defined in 1783 to be settled by amicable negotiation. But there was no way the people of this northern border could undo history, could forget what had happened to them in these anxious years, what they had done to one another in this unwanted war.

Actually, the two parties at Ghent had begun their negotiations with major geopolitical alterations in mind. The British opened with an insistence on the creation of a permanent Indian buffer territory encompassing a huge area (nearly all west of the 1795 Greenville Treaty line) to be jointly guaranteed by Great Britain and the United States, and they had up their sleeve demands for cessions of

Michilimackinac, the Niagara corridor, and a large part of Maine (British forces had taken firm hold of Castine, Bangor, and all east of the Penobscot). Some members of the American delegation had come to Europe a year earlier (hoping for Russian help in securing an armistice) and had in the meantime received instructions to do their best to obtain British cession of Upper and Lower Canada. But the peace negotiations, like the war, were a stalemate from the start, dragging on for months until the two governments, each too insecure at home to be confident of obtaining the resources to pressure the other to an advantageous conclusion, decided to get out of it with what was in effect an armistice and withdrawal to their sovereign boundaries.

In the United States the war was proclaimed a victory; there was general satisfaction and considerable pride in the fact that the Americans had stood up to and in the end yielded nothing to the world's most powerful imperial state, the very state that in that same year had emerged triumphant in the vast convulsions of Napoleonic Europe (and would yet again, at Waterloo, in the summer of 1815). Jackson's victory at New Orleans provided a resounding response to the humiliation of the burning of Washington. The Federalist opposition was discredited and the movement toward New England secession brought to an abrupt halt by a surge of national feeling. Canada faded from view as Americans again fixed their gaze westward.

In British North America the Canadians, too, could proclaim victory. They could take considerable pride in the fact that scarcely half a million British Americans had stood up to seven and three-quarter million Americans; if it was pointed out that it was really the British army and navy and treasury that made the balance, they could take great satisfaction in the proven vitality of that connection. They could also breathe a great sigh of relief that they had not been conquered and forcibly incorporated into the body of their aggressive, volatile, republican neighbor. But there were disappointments as well, especially in the fact that London had once again reneged on its promises to its Indian allies and again given up the western lakes country wherein the Americans had never been more than marginally present. But, perhaps more important than any of these, was the bitterness that Canadians, and especially Upper Canadians, now harbored. These people had had no quarrel with Americans, had not so far as they could see, given any offense whatever (those few British officials and traders at Fort Malden were operating in a specialized and remote world), yet they had been attacked and made to suffer. One might respond by saying that they were victims of geography: they had been attacked simply because they were near at hand, and, of course, they were attacked simply because they were British, for in such circumstances this connection was a liability as well as an asset. This much could be readily understood by Americans and Canadians alike. But if one seeks to understand the consequences, one must go further and note that many Canadians felt they had been attacked because they were considered weak and vulnerable, that they had been victimized by the predatory opportunism on the part of a bullying neighbor, that there had been intent to seize them and never let them go. Once people survive that kind of experience, they do not readily forget—or forgive. They learn not to trust the expressed goodwill of such a neighbor, and they take steps to be in a stronger position should it ever happen again. The War of 1812, so quickly forgotten by succeeding generations of Americans, would become a pivotal event in a developing Canadian nationalism.

And so although the international boundary might remain unchanged, the relationships between the peoples on either side were deeply altered. Some commerce continued to follow natural avenues, but it was reduced by imposts and in a decade or so redirected by the Erie and Champlain canals. And people might continue to move across these borders, but no longer in such numbers, and no longer from the United States into Canada with the welcome or indifference of prewar days. There was now a greatly heightened sense of two sovereignties. The war had produced a quick sorting. For the original Loyalists and those nurtured in loyalism it was a dreaded reopening of a wound; for the thousands of Americans who had recently settled in Canada it was essentially a North American civil war that suddenly forced them to make agonizing decisions about oaths of allegiance, service in militias, staying or leaving. We have no reliable count of such movements, but apparently most stayed put, hoping to hang on to land or business and preserve life and limb while staying as neutral as possible. Brebner notes that "loyalty and willingness to fight on the part of the Canadian militia increased in a sort of progression from the Americanized west to the loyalist east of Upper Canada. French Canadians fought valiantly in defence of Lower Canada." Such exodus and forced commitment together with the whole experience of war sharply accentuated the Britishness of Canada, and officials set about to strengthen that trend. In January 1815 the governor received authorization to refuse grants of land to Americans, to prevent them from entering Canada if he wished, and to place special restrictions on those allowed to come. This policy was not favored by local commercial interests, but its effects were meant to be offset by a corresponding encouragement of British immigration. It was some time before immigration made much of an impact, but the governor was still insisting ten years later that "the speedy settlement of the Colony however desirable is a secondary object compared to its settlement in such a manner as shall best secure its attachment to British Laws and Government." Various subsidy schemes implanted a few thousand Scots and Irish in backcountry townships, as at Perth and Peterborough, and in 1826 the Canada Company began development of its million-acre Huron Tract, but the western districts expanded mainly through the unassisted migration of thousands of poor—Irish, English, and Scots, Catholic and Protestant—who provided a profitable return cargo for the timber ships working out of Quebec. Numbers increased rapidly in the late 1820s: the population of Upper Canada doubled to 321,000 in the ten years after 1825; by 1842 it was nearing half a million.

But it was simply not possible to erase all American influences. Relatively few migrants now came from the United States (whereas many immigrants to Canada soon moved south across the border to what they thought were better opportunities), but their impact was not to be measured by members. Some twenty years after the war most of the ministers and preachers of the many Protestant denominations and sects in Upper Canada were American. Methodist circuit riders were particularly influential, entering as an extension of the Genesee Conference of western New York and maintaining full formal connection with the American church (founded and headquartered in Baltimore) until 1828. British Wesleyan ministers provided a potential counterweight, but for some years they agreed to confine their work to Lower Canada. All the while the politically powerful Anglican leadership asserted the prerogatives of an established church but provided little service to rural communities. What few schools existed were thus also mostly staffed by Americans, to the dismay of many a British visitor. Thomas Rolph, who toured the province in 1833, found it a really "melancholy" experience to visit the common schools:

> You find a herd of children instructed by some anti-British adventurer instilling into the young . . . mind sentiments hostile to the parent state; false accounts of the late war . . . geographies setting forth [American] cities as the largest and finest in the world; historical reading books describing the American population as the most free and enlightened under heaven and American spelling-books, dictionaries and grammar teaching them an anti-British dialect and idiom.

In the following year American immigrant teachers were specifically required to become citizens, but that by itself could not solve the problem. Indeed, there had been a bitter debate a few years earlier over who constituted the legitimate citizens of Upper Canada, wherein the Tories had sought to force a protracted naturalization process on all American-born settlers who had arrived after 1783. In face of an outcry that such a law would disenfranchise and categorize as alien large numbers who had been loyal through the late war and spent much of their life building up the colony, the decisive date was shifted to 1820. But the special concern remained. Canada was feeling, as it would ever after, the cultural pressures of propinquity with a powerful neighbor with which it had much in common and was deeply entwined. Only by extraordinary self-conscious efforts could it nurture effective distinctions—beyond the obvious differences in government—as it began to do in education, under the leadership of Egerton Ryerson, John Strachan, and others in the 1830s and 1840s.

The British government meanwhile undertook a program to provide stronger defenses for all its North American colonies, and especially for Montreal and Upper Canada. The most notable and costly was the Rideau Canal, a 130-mile link opened in 1832, from the foot of Lake Ontario to the Ottawa River, designed to be a strategic route bypassing the American border along the St. Lawrence. The old Loyalist town of Kingston thereby became a major pivot in the defense system, its economy and sociopolitical status enhanced by the naval dockyard and Fort Henry.

Far more important commercially was the Welland Canal across the Niagara isthmus, initiated by a private entrepreneur (with about half the funds provided by American investors) and completed in 1833. Widely touted as a Canadian answer to the Erie Canal, it in fact functioned in considerable part as simply an alternative route within the Erie system as both Canadian and American shippers made use of it, Lake Ontario, and the Oswego Canal to connect with the Erie Canal at Syracuse. The Welland was not more effective as a Canadian instrument because of shipping limitations on the St. Lawrence above Montreal, where programs for navigation improvements foundered in political controversy. And indeed the whole Laurentian commercial system, now tapping a rapidly developing agricultural hinterland, came under severe pressure from American competition. The Champlain Canal, connecting that lake to the Hudson, had ended the ambiguities of Vermont and turned it firmly away from Lower Canada, and the Oswego and Erie canals brought similar New York competition to bear on the most fertile districts of Upper Canada.

In Montreal, the great entrepôt of this Laurentian system, there was acute awareness of this American commercial pressure but less concern than in Kingston and Toronto (as York had been officially named in 1834) over the threat of American cultural influences. Here at the de facto hinge of the two Canadas, "English" stood in opposition to "French," and the obsessive issue was not "americanization" but "anglicization." Central to nearly all development—"the heart of the country, and from it circulates the life blood of Canada"—the city had passed Quebec in population ten years after the war, and surpassed 40,000 inhabitants by 1840. Most important was the fact that the British population was now greater than the French. English-speakers dominated commerce and industry and had put their unmistakable imprint on the landscape of the growing city: their Georgian and Greek Revival mansions climbing the flanks of Mount Royal, their neoclassical banks on St. James Street, their English-style churches, and their gray granite public buildings were all "conscious symbols of British Protestant authority."

Yet for all this obvious display of prosperity and power, English Montreal remained embedded locally and provincially within French Canada. The British governors sent over from London resided not in Montreal but on the citadel at Quebec, where they could never forget the presence of and their responsibilities to the nearly half a million French of Lower Canada. Through all these years, there-fore, Montreal commercial interests sought ways to extricate themselves from what they considered to be the stifling constrictions of a backward, rural, anti-progressive, priest-ridden entity. They fervently backed a British proposal of 1822 to unite the two Canadas, a scheme designed to anglicize the French and nullify any tendencies toward American republicanism. The matter proved to be highly controversial; fiercely opposed by French Canadians and no more than gingerly supported in Upper Canada, the bill was defeated in the House of Commons. Within a few years these same Montreal merchants were pushing hard for the annexation of the island of Montreal (and intervening seigneurie) to Upper Canada. Such a modest geopolitical change would, in their view, "liberate" a large portion of the English-speaking population of Lower Canada; provide Upper Canada with a seaport and direct control over customs receipts (a critical source of governmental income); consolidate under one government all those deeply con-cerned with improvements in the St. Lawrence trafficway; and bring Upper Canada out of its inland seclusion and more effectively into the British orbit and away from American influences. As Gerald M. Craig has remarked: "It was a dazzling conception, and the conservative and commercial leaders of Upper Canada could never fully understand why everyone concerned did not endorse it with enthusiasm." Of course, the very idea of losing control of such a famous and vital part of la patrie was anathema to the French, however much they resented the grip of these Montreal English on so much of the vitals of their province. Failing to achieve this intercolonial annexation, these Montrealers sent a delegation to the Colonial Office in London to propose a more radical change: to place the St. Lawrence waterway directly under imperial control, removing it from the politics of both Canadas. But in this, too, they got nowhere.

These issues (and they were entangled in many others) suggest the profound difficulties that faced political leaders in British North America. There was a general concern to magnify the separation from the United States, to insist on the importance of the connection to Britain. This common theme was widely accepted (although the public seemed at times exasperatingly lax and indifferent to all the nuances of the matter), yet there appeared to be insuperable difficulties in binding the two Canadas, Upper and Lower, English and French, together in some work-able way, a linkage that seemed to be demanded by the physical and economic realities of the St. Lawrence Valley and system. In the late 1830s a set of dramatic political crises within the two colonies provided the impetus for a bold new experi-ment.

As the Panic of 1837 plunged the Atlantic trading world into severe depression, long-smoldering political grievances in the two Canadas burst into flames. In simple terms, disaffections arose from deadlocked struggles between elected assemblies and entrenched oligarchical executives. In both colonies impassioned critics fomented extreme actions: rallies led to brawls, to clashes with police and militia, to bloodshed, and finally to quick defeat and dispersion. The leaders and many of their followers fled to sanctuary in the United States, where they found considerable popular sympathy in border districts. There followed a season of intense activity in such places as Detroit, Buffalo, Lockport, Watertown, Ogdensburg, and Montpelier, as Canadian rebels and American supporters, adventurers, and mercenaries organized secret societies and plotted invasion and the final expulsion of British monarchical tyranny from North America. Half a dozen raids on Canadian soil, however, found no support for such radicals; their meager forces were quickly captured or repulsed, and these impulsive movements soon subsided. The unplanned involvement of these uprisings with America and Americans deepened the separation between the two countries. For the most part, the federal government and bordering state governments did their best to avoid actions that might be deemed interference in Canadian affairs. But inevitably there were antagonisms and misunderstandings on both sides, and although the whole affair could be quickly dismissed in the United States as a distinctly minor flurry on the fringe, it could not but magnify old suspicions and bitterness among Canadians, who saw themselves once again attacked from American soil. In fact, the military implications seemed serious enough to cause both Great Britain and the United States to give renewed attention to their frontier fortifications.

Shortly after the rebellions of 1837 the British government appointed John George Lambton, earl of Durham, as governor-general with orders to investigate and propose a solution for the festering problems of government in the Canadas. His penetrating and eloquent report, published in 1839, was greeted with alarm or suspicion by many Canadian interests, but his fundamental geopolitical recommendation, union of the two colonies under a single legislature, was adopted by the British government in the next year. In 1841 the assembly of the new United Province of Canada, with forty-two members from Canada East (Lower Canada) and forty-two from Canada West (Upper) gathered for its first session in Kingston, that "sober, granite town," the most Loyalist of places, "true-blue and free of the taint of rebellion."

This bold new design was based on one critical, precarious, assumption, however: that the British dimension of Canada would so expand in extent, prosperity, and power, as to pressure the French (in the words of the Durham Report) to "abandon their vain hopes of nationality" and acquiesce to integration and assimilation into an English-speaking and English-dominated society. It was a goal long espoused by British Canadians but now featured in an unusually forthright manner. Lord Durham was uncompromising on the matter:

If the British Government intends to maintain its hold of the Canadas, it can rely on the English population alone. . . . The French Canadians . . . are but the remains of an ancient colonization, and are and ever must be isolated in the midst of an Anglo-Saxon world. . . . There can hardly be conceived a nationality more destitute of all that can invigorate and elevate a people, than that which is exhibited by the descendants of the French in Lower Canada, owing to their retaining their peculiar language and manners. They are a people with no history, and no literature.

Such comments infuriated the French Canadians, as did the stipulation in the new design that English would be the only language used in the Assembly and the allocation of an equal number of seats to the two colonies when Canada East contained 60 percent of the more than one million people in the United Province. How such talk and concepts and actions could ameliorate "the deadly animosity" that Lord Durham had, to his surprise, found separating "the inhabitants of Lower Canada into the hostile divisions of French and English" could only be grasped, one is tempted to assume, by those as imperious, arrogant, and optimistic, as imbued with confidence in the new liberal industrial order, as English—or almost—as Durham himself. But it must also be emphasized that it was quite explicitly a view shaped by what were widely understood to be North American realities. His rationale for assimilating the French was based on the apparent hopelessness of their survival as a nationality on a continent so obviously destined to be completely dominated by the English "race." Even if set apart in a province of their own (he had considered taking the Eastern Townships and Montreal away to form parts of a third, intermediate Canada) they would soon become impoverished by their increase in numbers and their inability to compete in the modern commercial and industrial world. "It is to elevate them from that inferiority that I desire to give to the [French] Canadians our English character"; the way to give them that character was to immerse them in an English province, and, he argued at some length, the way to do that "without disorder or oppression, and with little more than the ordinary animosities of party in a free country" was "memorably exemplified in the history of the state of Louisiana, the laws and population of which were French at the time of its cession to the America Union." Durham acknowledged that at the outset there had inevitably been deep divisions, jealousies, and rivalries between the French and the Americans, but these were easing from the simple and obvious fact that "the French of Louisiana . . . were incorporated into a great nation, of which they constituted an extremely small part." Therefore, in politics, in commerce, and in every other progressive dimension of life, the object of any aspiring man was "to merge his French, and adopt completely an American nationality." Louisiana had by then been a state for twenty-six years; Durham thought that it would be "no long time" before the French language and manners there would "pass away like the Dutch peculiarities of New York." He recognized that the bloc of 450,000 French in Lower Canada might be less easily or quickly digested, but the example of Louisiana as well as the experience of the two unions in the British Isles (with Scotland and with Ireland) showed how effectively "refractory" populations could be made to acquiesce in their fate.

The Durham Report became a great landmark in Canadian history not by such a misreading of the future of the French in Canada (or of the Irish in the British Isles) but because Durham's presentation of the need for fundamental structural changes did lead directly to "responsible government" in British North America. Such a move was compelled not only by the equity of the case and the recent disorders but by the attractive power of the American example with regard to popular government and concomitant land policies (Durham noted that in the 1830s probably 60 percent of the British emigrants to Upper Canada soon moved on to the United States).

Of course, this new British program for the Canadas was heartily supported by the British commercial establishment in Montreal and Upper Canada. Along with a promised infusion of British funds, it gave hope of stimulating development, rationalizing the Laurentian system (Durham had emphasized the unity demanded by "the great natural channel of the St. Lawrence"), and making Canadian merchants more competitive with the Americans. Even so, there were reservations. As Donald Creighton, a famous historian of that system, has noted: "Experience had proven that the two provinces could not live economically apart and instinct warned that they could not live politically together." In 1841 it was impossible to define just what this ambiguity of two Canadas United meant.

One thing that was much clearer in general, even if also not easy to define, was the fact that what had been a border zone across half the width of northern America had, in forty years' time, become much more sharply defined as a boundary, a line of separation, a division between cultures as well as sovereignties. It was not a readily visible line. For that, one needed to go to one of the marked discordances between political and cultural geography created early in this era, such as could readily be seen southeast of Montreal at Granby and St. Nom-de-Marie or Farnham and St.-Jean; to see, in other words, where Yankee settlers in the Eastern Townships had spread up against French settlements in the seigneurial lands of the Richelieu; to see how "two totally different traditions of vernacular architecture contributed to one of the most visible breaks in the cultural landscape of northeastern North America." That vivid line was a Canadian-American boundary in an older, deeper historical sense: a recent juxtaposition of two of the earliest European-founded societies in North America. But that lay wholly within the body of Lower Canada, and there was nothing like it to be found along the actual political boundary between the United States and Canada. There the separations were in the attitudes and allegiances of two peoples whom visitors from abroad had a hard time telling apart.

American pressure had been applied northward as it had been southward into the Hispanic borderlands. In this northern zone, however, the one brief phase of hard hammering had forced open the light British grip on a large piece of American territory in the northwest but had failed to break off any expanse of British ground. What the War of 1812 had done, quite undesignedly, was harden the existing boundary, fixing it in place as a far more decisive factor in the lives of the peoples on either side. Viewed more broadly from the standpoint of the two countries, the effects were quite asymmetrical. By 1840, Americans in general, as a people or as a government, were not much concerned with their northern border, at least in this long sector, for they had far more compelling opportunities and problems else-where. The people and government of Canada, quite the contrary, were now highly conscious of their southern border and of the society and polity that loomed so large beyond. It was a danger zone. Twice they had been called upon to defend that line by arms. And the dangers were not simply, or even mainly, military or political; they were far broader, more relentless, and more insidious than that—and, as might be expected, no one had put the case more clearly than Durham:

> The influence of the United States surrounds [the Canadian] on every side, and is for ever present. It extends itself as population augments and intercourse increases; it penetrates every portion of the continent into which the restless spirit of American speculation impels the settler or trader; it is felt in all the transactions of commerce, from the important operations of the monetary system down to the minor details of ordinary traffic; it stamps, on all the habits and opinions of the surrounding coun-tries, the common characteristics of the thoughts, feelings and customs of the Ameri-can people. Such is necessarily the influence which a great nation exercises on the small communities which surround it. Its thoughts and manners subjugate them, even when nominally independent of its authority.

During this period, clearly, Canadians had become well aware of this power of geographical propinquity and were determined to resist it, at least in terms of its political implications. Harsh experiences, the allegiances called for in times of emergency, and the selective sortings of migrations had all worked toward the fact that "there was nowhere any substantial group which favoured acceptance of the standing invitation to become part of the United States." Canadian nationhood was as yet feeble and unfocused except in this negative way: by now, as ever after, the fundamental feature of Canadian nationhood "was the determination not to be American." What the positive side of nationality might be was only beginning to be argued. The English-speaking population, faced with American expansionism, responded by persuading themselves "that they were more British than they actu-ally were." Much of the internal crisis of these times, especially in Upper Canada, was bound up with the fact that by emphasizing this Britannic connection Cana-dians were, as David Bell comments, cultivating a paradox: clinging "to the sym-bols of colonial status to serve as symbols of national status." Lord Durham, of course, had something to say about that matter, too: "If we wish to prevent the extension of this [American] influence, it can only be done by raising up for the North American colonist some nationality of his own; by elevating these small and unimportant communities into a society having some objects of a national importance; and by thus giving their inhabitants a country which they will be unwilling to see absorbed even into one more powerful." Here Durham was arguing in favor of a federation of all the British North American colonies, an idea first promulgated by a governor just after the drastic revisions of 1783 but one that neither these colonies nor the British government were as yet ready to try.

It has been said that "the American Revolution created not one country, but two: a nation and a non-nation." Half a century later there was a growing awareness within the non-nation that if it were to continue to share the continent with its powerful neighbor it might have to turn itself into something more nearly like a nation. For Canadians the political boundary between the two countries had become a hard edge against which they defined themselves. The United Province of Canada was a new framework within which its designers sought to build something more positive and substantial. It was a thoroughly British creation, and its larger geocultural premise of an encompassing, assimilating British North America would, as was understood to some degree then, have to cope not only with the enormous ever-pressing neighbor to the south but with an existing nation within: the original Canada for which *la survivance* was hardly a new concept. In their struggles to cope simultaneously, experimentally, reluctantly, with these two great realities of their historical human geography, British North Americans would gradually become Canadians.

4. The Reach Westward: To circa 1830

When Thomas Jefferson made his wonderful announcement of the Louisiana Purchase on the Fourth of July, 1803, neither he nor anyone else knew just what had been obtained. None of the parties involved—least of all the Americans—knew of its bounds or much about its character. Uncertainty over its extent was not just because of inevitable disputes as to where such lines should be drawn but because no one had a map of the features relevant to their placement. Europeans had been vigorously probing, measuring, and appraising their New World for more than 300 years, but a large portion of western North America was still undefined. Characteristically, Jefferson, already the best geographically informed American, immediately undertook to gather and collate as much information as possible in preparation for congressional deliberations. But when this official "Account of Louisiana" was made available that November, it contained a good deal of information about New Orleans and the lower Mississippi Valley but admitted that the geography of the greater portion of this enormous new domain remained "but little known."

The historical geographer John Logan Allen has likened this level of American knowledge to "a basin, surrounded by ridges of better knowledge and grading into a vast, flat surface of pure conjecture, broken here and there by a peak of better understanding." One of those "ridges" arched across the map at higher latitudes where the fur traders had been sorting out the intricate northern river systems of British America. Publication in 1801 of Alexander Mackenzie's account of his recent explorations began to show the relation of these Hudson Bay- and Arctic-flowing networks to the Pacific Slope, but only tentatively, for no one had yet been able to confirm the intrepid Scot's assumption that he had touched the upper waters of the Columbia in his difficult detour to the ocean.

Another "ridge of knowledge" extended narrowly along the entire Pacific margin of the continent, where the vague coastline and a few named headlands had become defined in much greater detail by a flurry of activities in the late 1700s. The Spanish had staked out their hold on the new province of Alta California as far north as San Francisco Bay; and in an intensely competitive series of strategic, scientific, and commercial explorations, Spanish, British, Russian, and American seafarers had charted the intricate shorelines of the maze of islands and deeply serrated mainland in the rain-soaked, densely forested northwest coast.

Beyond the mountainous horizon occasionally visible through the fog and cloud, however, virtually nothing was known of the western side of the continent. A great river, long rumored, then confidently inferred from offshore evidence, had finally been confirmed, entered, and named in 1792, and its lower course became fixed on the maps. The Columbia River thereafter seemed the obvious corridor inland, but no European knew where, how far, or into what kind of country it led. To the south, Alta California was a strategic frontier of state and church confined to a string of presidios and missions within a narrow coastal belt. Concerned with fending off seaborne encroachment, the Spanish remained comfortably ignorant of all that lay beyond the broad emptiness of the Great Valley. The Spanish claim, of course, included all that unknown interior, and far to the east, Santa Fe and the remote nucleus of New Mexico stood out on contemporary maps as a "peak of better understanding."

Along the eastern edge of Louisiana the great sequence of rivers flowing in from the west were known and named and reasonably well placed on the maps, but their upper reaches lay in that "vast, flat surface of pure conjecture"—as did, indeed, the source of the mighty Mississippi itself.

In 1803, then, the Americans, British, and Spanish (with the Russians pushing in from the far northwest) were variously positioned for the exploration, exploitation, and eventual partition of this vast, vague remainder of the continent. We need to bring into focus some important centers or districts on this perimeter and fields of activity emanating from them.

For the Americans, St. Louis, the forty-year-old town that fell to them fortuitously in the purchase, was the obvious base. As New Orleans was the key to the Mississippi, so St. Louis was the key to westward expansion, the natural entryway into Greater Louisiana. Its site on a low limestone rise a short distance below the mouths of the Missouri and Illinois rivers had been chosen with exactly that in mind by Pierre Laclede, a New Orleans merchant who had obtained a franchise for the Indian trade. By the time his stepson, Auguste Chouteau, was laying out the town, all east of the Mississippi had been given to Great Britain, and so the new trading post became an instant town as some French from Kaskaskia, Cahokia, and other Illinois settlements moved across the river to stay on French soil—only to find, in December 1764, that Louisiana had been transferred to Spain. Local merchants prospered on trade with the Osage, Kansa, and lesser local tribes but were unable to lure upriver Indians from the hold of British traders. In the 1790s several major efforts extended contacts up the Missouri as far as the Mandan Villages but failed to halt what officials regarded as blatant British trespass on Spanish soil. In 1803, St. Louis was a town of perhaps 200 houses and fewer than 1,000 inhabitants, but it was clearly the civic and commercial center of a major frontier region and the portal to far greater possibilities. As nearly all its people stayed on under yet another change of flag, new American interests had access to invaluable regional expertise.

The transfer of Louisiana to the United States magnified a chronic worry of Spanish officials in North America. They had always been obsessed with shielding the great riches of Mexico, the heart of the empire, from foreign attack or any kind of penetration. During their forty-year tenure of Louisiana they had regarded it primarily as a buffer against British and American encroachment. They were so concerned with defense that they had detached all the northern provinces from the direct jurisdiction of Mexico City and placed them under the Commandancia General de las Provincias Internas. This military governor, seated in Chihuahua, was ostensibly charged with defending the entire frontier from coastal California to Texas. Within such a scheme New Mexico appeared as the great forward base for securing interior North America, but it was so remote, its imperial resources were so limited, and the extent of territory was so great as to be an impossible task (fig. 6).

Santa Fe was the capital of a substantial colony. By 1800 there were nearly 30,000 inhabitants in the upper Rio Grande Valley, two-thirds of whom were indigenous Hispanic mestizos living in little villages and on farms amid the general area of the Pueblo Indians, who were much reduced in number and extent. Beyond this nuclear region the Spanish situation had been affected by the emergence of

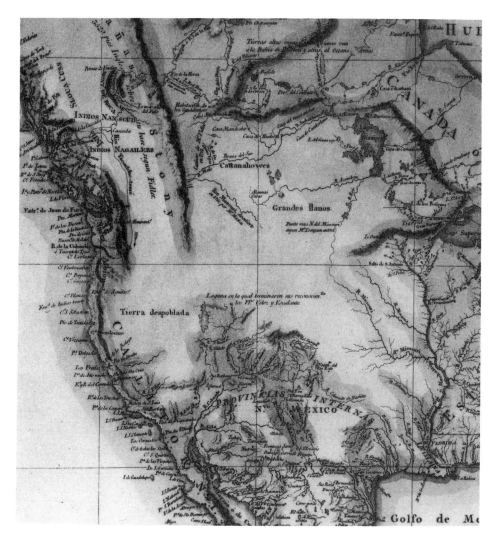

6. A View of North America, 1802.

Shown is a major portion of a map of "La America Septentrional," prepared by Isidro de Antillón y Marzo to accompany his course in geography and printed in Madrid. Warren L. Cook brought it to the attention of modern readers in his *Flood Tide of Empire* to display "a graphic idea of the concepts being taught to young Spanish noblemen and officers about Madrid's claims in western North America." He notes how "astonishingly well proportioned and complete" it is. In comparison with a good many other maps of the day one might well emphasize how "honestly *incomplete*" it is, unafraid to leave unknown areas blank rather than full of mythical mountains and hypothetical rivers. Mackenzie's conjecture about the upper Columbia is appropriately tentative, and the limits of Spanish knowledge about Louisiana are starkly apparent. (Courtesy of the New York Public Library, Astor, Lenox, and Tilden Foundations) armed and mounted Indian societies on all sides. These dangerous neighbors required careful diplomatic attention, and New Mexican governors recurrently dispatched emissaries and gifts to cultivate the friendship of the Ute, Arapaho, Kiowa, Pawnee, and especially the Comanche (powerful newcomers to the southern plains). Meanwhile, traders working out of frontier villages beyond easy surveillance, such as Abiquiu and Taos, carried on a minor traffic in furs and skins, ranging as far afield as the Green and Platte rivers. There had been occasional efforts to search out pathways across the plains to connect Santa Fe with San Antonio, Natchitoches, and St. Louis (most notably in the expeditions of Pedro Vial), but local interest in the commercial possibilities of such routes as alternatives to the costly tedium of the only authorized connection by way of Chihuahua and Vera Cruz was countered by bureaucratic caution. More common were the patrols sent out to intercept foreign trespassers, to keep the "Grande llanos" as a desolate and dangerous barrier between the Mississippi Valley and the vital regions of the empire. News of the transfer of Louisiana to the United States produced no immediate alteration of policies. Spain did not accept American definitions of the area purchased and was prepared to insist on its claim to the upper Missouri country. When French traders carrying stocks of merchandise arrived overland from St. Louis early in 1804, Santa Fe officials detained them and sent them off to Chihuahua for interrogation. At the same time, the general in command of the Provincias Internas directed the governor in Santa Fe to hasten a force into the field to intercept an American expedition reported to be headed up the Missouri.

Meanwhile, 700 miles to the north of St. Louis a region of new strategic and economic importance was emerging within the British sector. It was centered on a distinctive kind of country: a parkland mixture of woods and meadows and open grasslands, an obvious transition between the great wilderness of forest and rock to the north and east and the vast plains opening out in a rising succession of broad steps to the south and west. It was a land where the streams flowed slowly northward across the lacustrine plain, easing into the swampy margins of broad sheets of water that extended for 200 miles or more before draining off in rivers that tumbled jaggedly across the Shield into the shallow saucer of Hudson Bay. The richest fur country lay much farther to the north and west, in Athabasca, but its exploitation was becoming dependent on food from the plains. Pemmican (shredded dried buffalo meat mixed with tallow, flavored with berries, and packed in buffalo-skin bags of about ninety pounds each) had become the staple food of the fur trade in this great northern interior and its preparation part of the great annual ritual of the peoples of the parkland. The system was still evolving. Hunting buffalo was presumably as ancient as people in America, but hunting on horseback was a complex trait that had spread from the margins of Spanish America northward over the plains and was only becoming integrated into the routines of the Assiniboin (northernmost of the Siouan people) and Plains Cree (a western Algonkian people) toward the end of the eighteenth century. By this time, also, the use of guns (diffusing southward from Hudson Bay) had largely replaced bows and arrows in the hunt. The regularization of this new economic relationship was associated with the emergence of the métis as a distinct regional society. A mixed-blood population had of course begun to appear from the first sustained encounters between Europeans and Indians long ago, and such people were to be found throughout the fur trade system. By 1800 an increasing number of métis were congregating in the parklands as an autonomous group specializing in buffalo hunting and the preparation of pemmican.

At this time a competition between the great fur trade companies whose strategies intersected in this general region intensified for several reasons: wars in Europe, which affected prices and policies; the contest for Athabasca and the reach toward the Pacific; the influx of people out of Michilimackinac, Prairie du Chien, and other posts south of the American border following Jay's Treaty; the intrusion of aggressive new partnerships directly into this zone of rivalry. During these years the North West Company abandoned Grand Portage (now on American soil), worked over the Kaministiquia route as an alternative between Lake Superior and Rainy Lake, and built Fort William as its main base of operations in the west (fig. 7). In 1804 the company absorbed a new rival (which had been organized mainly by former Nor'westers, including Alexander Mackenzie) and began to press even more vigorously into new districts. Meanwhile, the Hudson's Bay Company built Norway House (the name coming from a group of Norwegian boat builders brought in to improve the transport system) near the foot of Lake Winnipeg, a pivotal position selected to serve the new aggressive policy by the old conservative company to follow the example of its great Montreal rival in binding "the plains rich in meat to the forests rich in fur." Both companies had outposts in the parklands and prairies, but there was as yet no major center, no civic focus, not even an official name for the area. Today we conveniently refer to the Winnipeg basin or, more narrowly, the Red River country; in 1800 it was more commonly known as Assiniboia.

The Northwest Coast was another area of intense competition, with vigorous Indian participants, but it was a maritime rivalry narrowly confined to the sheltered anchorages in the fjordlands north of the Strait of Juan de Fuca, a region apparently walled off from the interior by a solid mass of high mountains. Nootka Sound on the west side of Vancouver Island was the main focus, a rendezvous for ships plying rapidly extending Pacific circuits. A clash there between the Spanish and the English led to a diplomatic settlement that forced Spain to abandon its Nootka outpost and insistent claim to the area. By 1800 the Americans ("Boston Men") had taken advantage of their rivals' preoccupation with European upheavals to

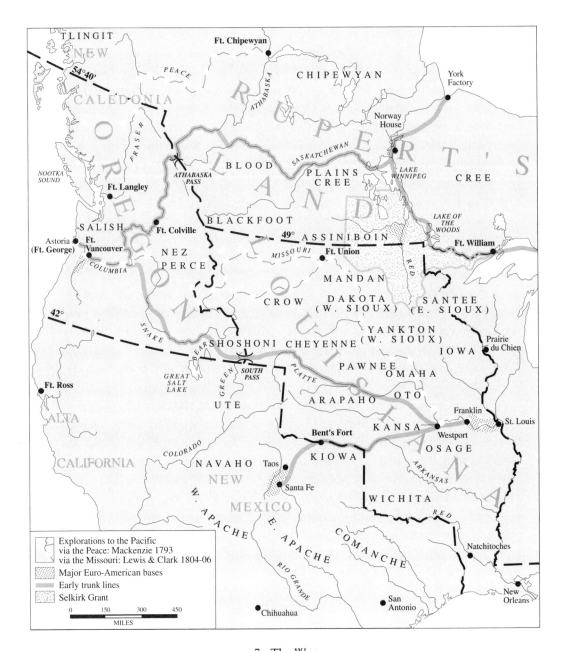

7. The West.
Only a selection of Indian nations is shown, relating to the
activities noted in this section of the book.

become dominant in the sensationally rich trade in sea otters. Meanwhile, the Russians had extended their Aleutian-Alaskan system to New Archangel (Sitka) on Baranof Island, the threshold of some of the richest waters (and most dangerous Indians, the Tlingit, who soon sacked and burned this outpost; it was rebuilt in 1804).

At this moment in North American history a remarkable geopolitical anomaly was discernible in this remote coastland: a field of intense competition but none of it directed to the Columbia River, a known feature of incomparable strategic value, specified as the key to Mackenzie's transcontinental program as it was in Jefferson's vision of an American version of the same thing. But such views were projections from the East, extensions from existing operations anchored in Montreal or New York. They were longer-term corporate strategies. As yet, no one had set about to build a Pacific terminus for a commerce that did not exist. That must await demonstration of a feasible route across the continent.

It is well-documented that Thomas Jefferson nurtured the idea of a transcontinental traverse for many years (probably since boyhood). In 1793 he had been the leading sponsor of a scheme to send the French naturalist André Michaux, "to find the shortest and most convenient route of communication between the U.S. & the Pacific ocean, within the temperate latitudes." In a letter to Michaux he noted that the latest maps made it seem "as if a river called Oregon interlocked with the Missouri for a considerable distance" (cautioning, however, that "these maps are not to be trusted"). The Michaux effort was stillborn but Jefferson never gave up. Ten years later, during his first term as president and before there could be any thought of purchasing the whole of Louisiana, he asked Congress in a confidential message (for it would involve travel through foreign and disputed lands) for a modest appropriation to pay for an expedition up the Missouri and across to the western ocean. Having obtained such support, preparations were soon under way, and so it was that Meriwether Lewis and William Clark could begin their actual traverse of Louisiana only a few weeks after the official transfer of sovereignty in the spring of 1804. Their main interest was in those "interlocked" rivers. That was the compelling concept, as it had been, broadly speaking, for centuries: a route to the Indies, a Northwest Passage. Jefferson's instructions made that clear: "The object of your mission is to explore the Missouri river, & such principal stream of it, as, by its course and communication with the waters of the Pacific ocean, whether the Columbia, Oregon, Colorado or any other river may offer the most direct & practicable water communication across this continent for the purposes of commerce."

Twenty-eight months later the expedition arrived back in St. Louis and Meriwether Lewis had the great pleasure of reporting by letter to his president: "In obedience to your orders we have penitrated the Continent of North America to the Pacific Ocean, and sufficiently explored the interior of the country to affirm with confidence that we have discovered the most practicable rout which dose exist across the continent by means of the navigable branches of the Missouri and Columbia Rivers." As a human effort the entire affair was a triumph, appropriately recognized at the time and ever after as one the great explorations. As a result of their "penitration" American sovereignty was asserted across the ridgepole of the continent to connect with the earlier American claim to the Columbia, and American maps could detail the river and mountain systems of a broad swath of country from sea to sea.

In terms of the declared objective, of practical commercial strategies, the results were less clear. Only publication of the journals of the expedition, some years later, could reveal what a gloss on their actual experiences Lewis's initial summation was. He did admit that the Rocky Mountains were "a most formidable barrier," and rather than an interlocking of streams there was a land passage of 340 miles between the navigable portions of the Missouri and Columbia systems, 140 miles of which was over "tremendious mountains." Nevertheless, summer passage was feasible, as they had demonstrated, and the difficulties of the portage were offset by the availability of horses "in immence numbers and for the most trivial considerations" from the Indians of the plains country on either side of the mountains. Thus he confirmed that such a route would afford "immence advantages to the fur trade," but not quite in the pattern envisioned. Whereas Jefferson had assumed a reorientation of the Pacific coast fur trade eastward across the continent to American ports, Lewis suggested the opposite. The furs of the upper Missouri ("richer in beaver and otter than any country on earth") and even of the Assiniboine and Red rivers (served by British establishments) could be sent westward to the lower Columbia and thence directly to Canton, a leading world mart. In return, certain kinds of East Indies goods ("articles not bulky brittle nor of a very perishable nature") could be brought to the Columbia and thence forwarded across to the United States. Because the season of mountain travel was short Lewis suggested an inland depot on the Clearwater River at the western base of the Rockies as the principal point of exchange for such shipments.

An American response to such possibilities was soon under way. In the opening years of the nineteenth century John Jacob Astor, a wealthy German-born New York merchant, was seeking to dominate the fur trade of North America. Working out of Michilimackinac, his American Fur Company soon brought such pressure on the British in the Great Lakes region that a division of territories was negotiated. He tried but failed to lure the North West Company to join in creating a transcontinental system and therefore set about doing so himself (with the help of some disgruntled Nor'westers he enticed to staff his organization). His scheme was a close variant of that outlined by Meriwether Lewis: a Pacific headquarters and depot on the Columbia estuary; an annual shipment of trade goods and essential supplies from New York via Cape Horn; the collection of furs through outposts in the Columbia interior and vessels trading up and down the coast; and the export of furs to the Canton market to be exchanged for Chinese goods that would be conveyed to Europe and America. An overland route with protective forts and facilities would be established between New York and the Columbia primarily as a line of more rapid movement of messages and personnel. Working parties to initiate this program were sent out by sea and by land.

Thus in the spring of 1811, Astoria, the first American outpost on the Pacific Slope, began to take shape at a deepwater anchorage on the south side of the Columbia estuary. During the next two years inland posts were set up, arrangements with various Indian tribes negotiated, and trading relations with the Russians in Alaska initiated. A feasible route across the continent had also been discovered, after some delay and difficulty. The original westbound land party had intended to follow the Missouri route of Lewis and Clark, but news of deadly opposition from the Blackfeet (generated in part by the one mortal clash the famous American expedition had with Indians en route) diverted them more directly westward, and they barely survived a six-month struggle across terribly difficult country. The search for an overland passage was renewed in 1812, when Robert Stuart and six companions went up the Columbia from Astoria to the Walla Walla River, then veered across the Blue Mountains to the Snake River Plain, around several short ranges into the open country of the Wyoming Basin, passing over the continental divide at (or near) South Pass, from where they followed the Platte River to the Missouri and on to St. Louis. There were no "interlocking" rivers on this route either, but neither were there any forbidding obstacles, a fact emphasized in a St. Louis paper (and widely reprinted): "By information received from these gentlemen, it appears that a journey across the continent of N. America, might be performed with a waggon, there being no obstruction in the whole route that any person would dare call a mountain in addition to its being much the most direct and short one to go from this place to the mouth of the Columbia river." Thereby not only the route but the concept of an Oregon trail was set forth.

While the Astorians were preparing for their first expedition into the Columbia interior in the summer of 1811, they were surprised by the arrival of David Thompson, who had come down the Columbia in a large cedar canoe. From him they learned that the North West Company already had several posts on the Pacific Slope and that he was in the last stages of his assignment to sort out the baffling geography of Pacific streams and determine the best route across the continent. On his return journey from Astoria he concluded that Athabasca Pass, a steep, short pathway connecting the Athabasca with the northernmost bend of the Columbia, would serve.

As a result of these two great efforts there was the prospect of parallel transcontinental systems and head-on competition between the British and the Americans in the far northwest (their posts stood within sight of one another at Spokane and Kamloops). This nascent rivalry was abruptly ended, however, by a distant reverberation of the War of 1812. In 1813 the Americans at Astoria received word of the impending arrival of a British warship, and since they were already under passive siege from an encampment of North West Company personnel who had come downriver from inland posts, they decided to sell out to the rival company rather than risk what appeared to be certain capture and possible destruction. Thus the only tangible American hold on the Columbia country was abandoned, the British claim to the whole area was reaffirmed, Astoria was renamed Fort George, and a disappointed John Jacob Astor turned his attention once again to the Great Lakes (where having repelled the British he now set about to drive the official United States fur trade "factories" out of business).

Even before this strategic triumph the North West Company had decided that costs would force it to imitate the Astorians and work from a Pacific coast base rather than ship furs and supplies across the continent. The two systems were soon integrated, and the British company undertook vigorous exploitation of a thousand-mile span of the Pacific interior, reaching from the upper waters of the Fraser River (New Caledonia) to the southeastern headwaters of the Columbia system (the Snake Country), as well as trade with the Russians in Alaska and the Spanish in California, all brought into periodic focus at Fort George.

This British system soon underwent one more major mutation. East of the Rocky Mountains the rivalry between the North West Company and the Hudson's Bay Company reached a climax. Here, too, there were duplicate posts and competition for the allegiance of the same Indians, as well as some new tactics. The Montreal company, suffering from the strains of an extremely attenuated trunk line, laid plans for a legal challenge to the de facto monopoly of its rival over the Hudson Bay route. At the same time, the London-based Hudson's Bay Company decided to consolidate its position in a critical region by planting an agricultural colony in Assiniboia. This latter program was organized as a personal proprietorship of the earl of Selkirk, a prominent stockholder and philanthropist who had been involved in a number of schemes (Prince Edward Island, Upper Canada, western New York) to relieve the plight of Scottish and Irish crofters being cleared off their homelands. Selkirk was given a huge grant (five times the size of Scotland), "the bounds drawn with . . . magnificent freehand embraced a great natural province, the central basin of the northern mid-continent." He began sending colonists to Red River in 1812, and eventually came himself to supervise. Selkirk had tried in vain to gain approval of his program from the North West Company, but the Montreal firm and its métis allies felt threatened by the whole concept and deeply resented the intrusion of immigrant colonists into such a vital area. There followed a tumultuous period of harassments and property destruction that culminated in a clash between two militias, killing the local Selkirk governor and twenty-one settlers. While the ensuing political and legal battles dragged on, a sick and disillusioned Lord Selkirk (who had hurried in from Montreal to restore peace) returned to Britain and soon died, but he left behind a new nucleus of major regional significance: a small colony of farmers rooted in the rich black soil of the Red River Settlement. The contest for Assiniboia was merely one phase of a struggle that became so ruinous and politicized that these two great British companies merged in 1821, thus ending the ancient rivalry between the St. Lawrence and Hudson Bay in the contest for northern America. As the surviving entity, the Hudson's Bay Company now had a monopoly over the fur trade of British North America.

The Hudson's Bay Company was a striking exhibit of a special British mode of empire. It was a powerful commercial enterprise run by a corporate body of stockholders, but it was also a surrogate government. In return for its License for Exclusive Trade it administered all British territories west of Upper Canada, with responsibility for law and order, local justice, and the proper treatment of Indians—an instrument of imperial control. Under the energetic leadership of George Simpson, who soon became resident governor of all American operations, the entire system was rationalized with a keen eye for maximizing profits, geographic advantage, and British dominion. The old Montreal–Great Lakes network of the Nor'westers was set apart as the Southern Department, a depleted minor component. The main transcontinental line connected Hudson Bay to the lower Columbia by way of Athabasca Pass. East of the Rockies all was focused on York Factory, where the London ships called during the few ice-free weeks of late summer. Assiniboia was expanded as the critical source of provisions. Relations between colonists and the métis eased, and the métis became increasingly involved in stock raising and even farming while retaining their great role in buffalo hunting and pemmican production. The Red River Settlement remained a rather attenuated and informal affair, its narrow river lots strung out for 100 miles along the Red and Assiniboine rivers; but farming, after many setbacks, began to prosper, there were new colonists (most notably French from Lower Canada) and several churches and schools, and the cluster of facilities near the river junction—Fort Garry, the company experimental farm, St. Boniface Cathedral (Roman Catholic) and St. John's (Anglican)—gave a semblance of civic focus. On the Pacific Slope, Fort George (Astoria) was replaced by a new and much larger post, Fort Vancouver, ninety miles upriver across from the mouth of the Willamette Valley. Like Colvile on the upper Columbia (replacing Spokane) and Langley on the lower Fraser, it was a site selected with an eye to agriculture as well as to the fur trade as part of

Simpson's policy to reduce costly imports of food. Through the use of packhorses New Caledonia was bound to the Columbia system, and Simpson expanded upon the North West Company practice of sending out large trapping parties into the Snake Country. These forays reached California, the Great Basin, the Great Salt Lake, and east into the headwaters of the Colorado and Missouri river systems. Such expeditions were designed to exhaust the resources of a vast borderland, to create a "fur desert" as a barrier to American expansion. Similarly, Simpson expanded earlier coastal ventures, hoping to blunt the Russian advance southward, remain on good terms with the Spanish, and so undersell the Boston Men as to send American vessels off to other seas in search of gain. By 1830 the British were essentially unchallenged on the Pacific Slope. The "Oregon territory" of the Americans was, operationally, the Columbia Department of the Hudson's Bay Company. While St. Louis trappers and New England traders pecked at the edges of his domain and American expansionists called for the occupation of Oregon, Governor Simpson could assure his London superiors that "we have little to apprehend from Settlers in this quarter, and from Indian traders nothing."

The Americans had set out to challenge the British in areas closer to home as well. On his return, Meriwether Lewis reinforced a general feeling that American interests must move "firmly and speedily" against British dominance of the upper Missouri country. In the very next year Manuel Lisa, a long-experienced St. Louis trader, led a large party upriver, and the returns over this and the next few seasons were so encouraging that a group of St. Louis men (including Lisa, William Clark, and the Chouteau brothers) formed the Missouri Fur Company to create an extensive system of operations reaching into the Rocky Mountains. But it was an unstable, undercapitalized organization and soon faced ruinous competition from the British and murderous opposition from the Blackfeet. The Americans were never wholly closed out of the upper Missouri country, but for years trade proved so dangerous and disappointing as to preclude extensive exploitation. A few major attempts were made to stake out a firm American position; but Major Stephen Long's ponderous government-sponsored Yellowstone Expedition of 1818–19, with all its troops and tonnage and half a dozen steamboats, never got above Council Bluffs, and William Henry Ashley's large commercial party bound for the same sites a few years later was turned back by Indian attacks. Some success eventually came through the resources and connections of John Jacob Astor, who in the late 1820s bought into the Missouri fur business, put an old experienced Nor'wester, Kenneth McKenzie, in charge, and through McKenzie's long friendship with the Blackfeet, paved the way for the erection of Fort Union at the mouth of the Yellowstone and some redirection of trade.

Meanwhile, attention had been concentrated on the middle reaches of the Missouri, where trappers worked out from the broad terraces of the main stream up the White, Cheyenne, and other tributaries into the higher broken country and the crumbling crenellations of the badlands (the *mauvaises terres* of early Canadian explorers). This was the territory of the Sioux, a loose association of peoples who had been spreading westward on these plains for decades and whose friendship had been cultivated (in line with Jefferson's instructions to Lewis) "because of their immense power." Like most horse-mounted Indians, they disdained spending their lives trapping for furs but were superb buffalo hunters, and as steamboats began to ascend the Missouri, bales of buffalo robes soon became a major export.

The most important American development was a derivation from these Missouri operations. When Ashley's upriver expedition was thwarted in 1822, he sent Jedediah Smith to reconnoiter directly westward into the central Rockies. Smith rediscovered Stuart's South Pass–Platte route, and his report resulted in a new direction and design for the American trade. It was a system of annual caravans of trading goods, tobacco, and whiskey sent out from St. Louis to some designated place within the mountain country, where the trappers who had wintered in the wilderness and the Indians from a wide radius would meet to exchange goods and celebrate. As Billington notes, it was a great success because it avoided the overhead costs, rigidities, and overt intrusions of permanent posts and responded to Indian traditions of periodic intertribal meetings, elevating "trading from a purely commercial to a social function." As a result of this "rendezvous system," by the late 1820s the main axis of the American fur trade was not the upper Missouri but the trail—soon widened into a road—from the lower Missouri, up the North Platte, across the low saddle at South Pass into the Wyoming Basin and the various sites in the recesses and high parks of the Wind River, Teton, Wasatch, and Uinta ranges—the famous "holes" of the mountain men in the headwaters of the Green, Snake, and Bear rivers. The profits were great, and other outfits quickly moved in. Astor's company had barely gotten started in the Blackfeet country before it was sending trappers southward up the Big Horn, and in 1832 it sent a caravan to compete at the annual rendezvous. The open, volatile character of the American system tended toward a ravage of resources and chaos in Indian relations, and it was increasingly understood at the time that it was a destructive, ephemeral economy. What, if anything, might succeed it in such distant and difficult regions was not at all clear.

In the southerly sectors of Louisiana, developments took on quite a different pattern. At the outset Jefferson was active here as well, squeezing small appropriations out of Congress to finance explorations of the Red and Arkansas rivers, but none of these actually got very far. Much more notable was a reconnaissance that in some sense got too far: that of Lieutenant Zebulon M. Pike, who was sent out with a small party from St. Louis in 1806 to cultivate good relations with the Indians on the plains and explore the western margins of Louisiana. Pike followed the upper

Arkansas well into the Rockies, but suffering from winter privations he turned southward and crossed over the divide into the San Luis Valley of the upper Rio Grande. There he was arrested by a Spanish patrol, taken to Santa Fe, sent on to Chihuahua, and eventually escorted back to the United States via Texas and Natchitoches. Pike's experience did not in itself deter other Americans, but there was insufficient inducement to support much activity. Traders from St. Louis had long been active with the Osage and occasionally ventured onto the open plains, but it was a bleak and dangerous country. Spanish patrols sent out by nervous New Mexican governors deflated recurrent rumors in Santa Fe of major American intrusions and arrested an occasional small party of hunters and trappers.

The decisive changes were geopolitical: first, the Adams-Onis Treaty of 1819, which erased Spanish claims to the Missouri country and fixed the boundary of Louisiana along portions of the Red River and the Arkansas; second, the end of Spanish rule and its rigid exclusions and control over imperial commerce. In 1821 Mexicans came across several small parties of Americans working the margins of New Mexico and invited them to come on to Santa Fe and trade. News of this revolutionary openness, avid interest, and financial success generated an immediate response in St. Louis. The first caravan set out the next year, and within three years the whole system of the Santa Fe Trail was becoming routine. New towns upriver from St. Louis, first Franklin, later Independence and Westport, became the "jumping-off places" where the wagon trains were formed; Council Grove usually served as the last staging ground before the long trek across the open plains; the Cimarron cut-off became an alternate, though risky, route, avoiding the longer, heavier haul over Raton Pass; San Miguel del Bado was the customs station and portal to New Mexico. The Santa Fe Trail was a two-way street, a connection of mutual interest. American agents and merchants were soon resident in Santa Fe and Taos, and in time Mexicans began to take caravans eastward and to maintain a consul in St. Louis. It was an international link of commercial and cultural importance. In 1828 three veteran Missouri plainsmen built Bent's Fort where the trail turned southwesterly from the Arkansas toward Santa Fe. A formidable adobe structure built by Taos laborers, it was a telling symbol of the new borderland. Taos meanwhile became a favorite wintering place for American trappers working the southern Rockies, and some of them began to range on through the Navaho country to the west and across the rugged rimlands into the desert basins. Here, as in New Mexico, they were drawing into Anglo-American experience lands long familiar to Hispano-Americans.

Through all these probings and connections, the "vast, flat surface of conjecture" gave way to the delineation of the gross geographic features of western North America. By the 1830s the general patterns of plains and mountains, rivers and valleys, of a great salt lake and sinks and a broad barren interior basin where the rivers faded into the desert (a concept foreign to American geography in 1800) were becoming reasonably clear, as well as more detailed knowledge of various traverses and districts. There was of course a gap between the mental maps of mountain men who knew all the nooks and crannies of favorite territories and the maps available to officials and the public, but there were also some very direct connections between fur traders and cartographers, most notably in the person of David Thompson (who with his sextant, chronometer, and barometer impressed the Astorians as "more like a geographer than a fur trader"). Having sorted out the Columbia system, the North West Company gave him leave to prepare a detailed chart of the river systems of northern America. Although that great map long remained on the wall at Fort William, much of its content, as well as information from other British explorers, was soon incorporated into the maps of Aaron Arrowsmith, a leading London publisher, and such information was rapidly diffused through the Atlantic world (several American firms published in partnership with Arrowsmith). The most famous American contribution was the map drawn by William Clark. As it was not readied for publication until 1810 (and not printed until 1814), Clark was able to incorporate the results of some later explorations with his own. Pike's charts of "the Internal Part of Louisiana," published in 1810, provided the first American coverage of the southern plains and mountains, and these were accompanied by a map of Mexico apparently plagiarized from Alexander von Humboldt, whose *Atlas of New Spain,* based on his travels and research in Mexico, was published in the following year. The famed German geographer had been eagerly welcomed to Washington by Jefferson and others on his way home from Mexico in the summer of 1804, and his reports, books, and maps long remained a main source of information about large sectors of the American West.

Mapping was generally cumulative, a business of progressive extensions and refinements (with occasional lapses and aberrations) impressing an ever-greater mental control upon territory. The imprints of commerce and politics were less secure. Strong initial projections and claims might not be sustained by firm incorporation into the main body of economic and political systems. During the twenty-five years following the sudden addition of Louisiana, American officials and private entrepreneurs were variously involved in binding that huge area to the nation and reaching beyond into even more distant lands, but the results were mixed and remained uncertain in some important sectors.

The main geopolitical accomplishment of the United States was the establishment of an international definition of Louisiana and a transcontinental claim to a Pacific frontage. It took about fifteen years to fix some formal limits upon the "new, immense, unbounded world" of Louisiana. In the Adams-Onis Treaty settlement with Spain over the Floridas, the United States obtained formal definition of its boundary with the Spanish Empire all the way from the Gulf of Mexico to the

Pacific Ocean. This boundary line was drawn across the southern plains so as to skirt New Mexico and thence across the continent along the Forty-second parallel. Such a line represented a large recession of Spanish claims but no serious infringement on its settlement regions (this entire boundary was later reaffirmed by Mexico).

After the War of 1812 the United States and Great Britain agreed to negotiate amicably all territorial disputes. A commission was charged with establishing a division west of Lake of the Woods. During all the long imperial rivalries for North America no official boundary had ever been drawn across the northern plains. There were precedents for asserting hydrographic definitions: the Americans (in succession to the French) to a Louisiana encompassing the western Mississippi basin; the British to a Rupert's Land including all the territory that drained into Hudson Bay. However, the latter claim had been compromised by the Hudson's Bay Company long ago (1719) when, fearful of the French thrust west from Lake Superior, the company had requested official British recognition of the Forty-ninth parallel as the southern boundary of its monopoly territory. No such formal response was ever given, and in its later actions the company did not observe any such limitation (for example, the Selkirk Grant), but such a line had shown up on maps frequently enough to provide a ready basis for an American claim, and in 1818 it was accepted as the boundary without serious challenge. It was a geometric line approximating the natural divide between the waters draining to Hudson Bay and those draining to the Gulf of Mexico, with the major exception of the northward-flowing Red River, which arose 200 miles south of the boundary. The decision thereby cut off a large portion of the Selkirk Grant (and led to cession of those lands by the Selkirk estate) but placed only one small outpost and settlement, at Pembina (just south of the line), within the United States.

"Westward of the Stony Mountains" (as the Rockies were still often called), however, no division could be agreed upon, and the negotiations concluded with a declaration that the country would be "free and open" to the "vessels, citizens, and subjects of the two Powers" for a period of ten years without prejudice to the claims of either side. The two powers were soon reminded that a third country claimed a share of northwest America. The Russians had been competitors in explorations and trade for many years and continued to extend their activities. A plan of 1807 to establish settlements at the mouth of the Columbia and in California and Hawaii foundered in shipwreck, but soon thereafter the Russian-American Company was working near the Golden Gate, sending its Aleut hunters after the seals on the Farallon Islands (they even sneaked into San Francisco Bay). In 1812 they set up a supply base seventy miles to the north at Fort Ross (Rossiya) and shortly thereafter one on Kauai (from which they were soon expelled by the Hawaiians). In 1821 the czar claimed exclusive rights for Russian hunters as far south as 51°N (just above the north end of Vancouver Island). Great Britain and the United Stated challenged this assertion, and in subsequent (separate) treaties they got Russian America (east of Mount St. Elias) limited to a narrow coastal fringe extending only to 54°40′N. That was a marked recession, but the Russians were feeling overextended, they had nearly exhausted the California sealery, and they were turning more to other Alaskan districts.

In 1827, after sparring over a boundary settlement, the United States and Great Britain agreed to extend their joint arrangement on the Pacific Slope for an indefinite period. The creation and continuance of this formal geopolitical status may be considered a diplomatic triumph for the United States. Although Gray, Lewis and Clark, and the Astorians had provided a basis for claim to some part of this distant territory, there had been no substantial American presence anywhere on the Pacific Slope since the collapse of the Astorian effort. Throughout the 1820s there were agitations in Congress to reestablish an American hold upon Oregon. Lengthy reports were compiled, strategies devised, and bills debated, but no program was undertaken. The topic was suffused with a mixture of motives: the fur trade, whaling, Pacific commerce, support of American rights, the need to oust the British from their overbearing position. Near the end of the decade the impassioned debate over a bill to establish a military post at the mouth of the Columbia exposed such conflicting evidence and such a paucity of reliable information about Oregon that an amendment was proposed to "cause an exploring expedition to be organized and executed, to consist of not more than eighty persons, including a corps of geographers and topographers for the purpose of collecting information in regard to the climate, soil, natural productions, civil and political conditions, harbors, and inhabitants, of the territory of the United States west of the Rocky Mountains." In the end, neither the amendment nor the bill was passed. Twenty-five years after Jefferson's bold initiative, Americans chafed for some further expedition to find out what it was that Lewis and Clark had given them a claim to on the Pacific Slope.

Such was not the case with Louisiana. It had been not only pretty well fixed in place but extensively described by a sequence of firsthand observers. The broad physiographic character of this huge territory was becoming common knowledge. Attention was focused on the new kind of country that lay beyond the familiar woodlands of the Mississippi Valley. There was general agreement as to a westward sequence of a land opening out from the forest margins to an expanse of gently rolling prairies, grading on to higher, drier plains of short grass—or little grass at all—extending to the base of the great mountains. But if the existence of these "immense plains" as a great "natural region" of the continent was commonly understood, there remained a good deal of imprecision and uncertainty. As Ralph H. Brown noted, explorers and geographers from the East could routinely employ their compasses and surveying instruments but found "that most sensitive of instruments, the language, did not fit the new land so well."

The term *Great Plains* had begun to appear on British maps, applied to the northernmost sector of the famous modern physical province, as early as the 1770s, but it did not take hold as a formal geographical designation until much later. *Plains* was clear enough as a descriptive term; and by the 1800s *prairie* was becoming rapidly absorbed into the American language. Attesting to the French role in exploration of so much of interior North America, and applied routinely at first to much smaller—but extensive by any European standard—openings in the eastern forest, the word was still often translated or explained as *meadow*; but that very English word must have increasingly seemed so inadequate for the scale and sense of the American scene (as in "Extensive Meadowes ful of Buffaloes," on the famous Mitchell Map of 1755) that the foreign word was welcomed as a useful addition (even though its original French meaning was more or less equivalent to the English term). Widely applied to the eastern and northern portions of the open country and most commonly first encountered by travelers in springtime, when it presented a lush carpet of grass and flowers, with woods along the streams and the whole landscape teeming with wildlife, this "prairie" belt rarely failed to excite admiration as a fertile, well-watered country "perfectly susceptible of cultivation," as Lewis and Clark put it.

But the higher plains farther west were another matter. Wood was rare or nonexistent ("not a stick of timber"), water scarce, and the experience of the heat and dust and distance of a midsummer crossing left powerful impressions of difficulties and dangers. Zebulon Pike's prediction that "these vast plains of the western hemisphere, may become in time equally celebrated as the sandy deserts of Africa" was brought closer to reality after Major Stephen Long, leader of the next official exploration (an offshoot of his ill-fated Yellowstone Expedition), inscribed "GREAT DESERT" boldly across his map, and in the official report his geographer, Edwin James, stated: "In regard to this extensive section of country, I do not hesitate in giving the opinion, that it is almost wholly unfit for cultivation, and of course, uninhabitable by a people depending upon agriculture for their subsistence. Although tracts of fertile land considerably extensive are occasionally to be met with, yet the scarcity of wood and water, almost uniformly prevalent, will prove an insuperable obstacle in the way of settling the country." It was an opinion widely reported, endorsed by other travelers, repeated in some form in various accounts for decades thereafter—and it continues as a controversial issue in the historiography of the Great Plains. Problems of interpretation were manifest at the time, for if *desert* gave rise to visions based on the "sandy wastes" of Africa or Arabia, such descriptions of the country almost always included statements about "Innumerable Herds of Buffaloes" (as inscribed on Pike's map just above "not a stick of timber").

For this high, dry country could also teem with life, and these vast herds were by now a famous feature of the American scene. Whatever *desert* might imply, it could hardly be taken here to refer to a truly sterile wasteland.

The most pertinent feature in these early reports was the general conclusion that much of the plains could never become a "settled country" by an agricultural people. "This Great Desert is frequented by roving bands of Indians who have no fixed place of residence but roam from place to place in quest of game," wrote Major Long on his maps, and he and Pike and many others agreed that much of Louisiana was best left to the "wandering and uncivilized aborigines of the country." This general characterization of these Indians was true enough, and it pointed to an important feature in the human geography of North America. Here roughly along the prairie margins of the higher plains was a cultural boundary separating the agricultural societies on the east from the nonagricultural societies on the west. Tribes such as the Osage, Kansa, Oto, and Omaha (and the outlying Arikara and Mandan) represented the inland edge of an agricultural system to be found throughout the Eastern Woodlands, whereas their neighbors to the west, such as the Comanche, Kiowa, Arapaho, and Western Sioux, were hunters and gatherers dependent upon the buffalo for their mainstay (to the southwest, the Pueblo Indians were the northernmost representatives of an agricultural system that extended deep into Mexico).

To refer to this basic difference in human ecologies as a "boundary" or an "edge," however, risks a wrong impression. There was no such line to be seen on the ground. Indian farming along the Missouri was a scattering of small fields and gardens around widely separated semipermanent villages, as it was in much of the eastern United States. There was much land of the same quality lying untilled, and that, too, was an important feature. In the common view of Americans, the whole vast region was essentially *empty*. They had long ago convinced themselves that all Indians, even the largest of the agricultural societies, were no more than casual occupiers of territory, a people with little attachment to the soil. Certainly there seemed to be plenty of room for more people of the same sort in these western lands. And so it was that a great geopolitical decision in 1830 designated these great prairie plains of North America as the receiving ground for all of the Indians then living in the organized area of the United States. A line would be laid down approximately along the eastern edge of the prairies, and every tribe to the east of it would be removed, under federal supervision, to an allotment of lands to the west of it. It was a national program to reshape the human geography of the nation, to provide a clear and curative separation of the two peoples. This decision to establish an Indian America and a White America was the enactment of an idea set in motion at the very inception of an American Louisiana.

5. Shoving the Indians Out of the Way

Thomas Jefferson, in a letter accepting congratulations on the Louisiana Purchase, emphasized that this wonderful addition to the Republic ("not inferior to the old in soil, climate, productions & important communications") could become "the means of tempting all our Indians on the East side of the Mississippi to remove to the West." Suddenly, quite unexpectedly, there appeared to be a way out of a vexing national problem.

Like his predecessors, the third president of the United States had been struggling to formulate an effective Indian policy. On that topic, American leaders were confronted with a deep dilemma: how to have "expansion with honor"; that is, how to dispossess the Indians of their lands with a clear conscience, how to get such people out of the way without affronting the moral opinion of mankind. There was little disagreement among officials or the general public about the basic objective or justification of the matter. Whether one appealed to history, theology, logic, or common sense, Americans came to the same conclusion: one could not leave the continent to wandering bands of savages. Europeans had heeded the biblical injunction to "be fruitful, and multiply, and replenish the earth"; history had shown that the hunter and the casual tiller who camp for a season must give way to the farmer fixed upon the soil. When that consummate frontier spokesman, John Sevier ("reputed the handsomest man and best Indian fighter in Tennessee"), stated that "by the law of nations, it is agreed that no people shall be entitled to more land than they can cultivate," he was merely echoing centuries of European rationale. In Thomas More's famous *Utopia* (1516, first published in English in 1551), seizing the territory of a people who "holdeth a piece of grounde voyde and vacaunt to no good or profitable use" was "the most just cause of warre" undertaken by an expanding nation.

Such a succession had of course been taking place on the North American seaboard over a period of 200 years, and the inevitability, rightness, and continuing progress of that triumph of "civilization over savagery" was taken for granted. It was equally understood that there was an ugly and dangerous—and some would add poignant—side to this grand drama, and it was generally agreed that a clear geographic separation of Indians from Whites should be a basic tenet of national Indian policy. That idea and practice were as old as English America. Put into effect with the defeat and expulsion of Indians from the Lower Neck of Virginia after 1644, separation assumed a continental scale in the famous imperial Proclamation Line of 1763, which was, in turn, reaffirmed in principle by George Washington at the very beginning of the Republic, when he stated that the Indians should be told that "the Country, is large enough to contain us all, . . . we will . . . establish a boundary line between them and us beyond which we will *endeavor* to retain our people."

It was of course clear from all that history that such boundaries were not immutable. They were not intended to be; they were understood by those who imposed them to be geopolitical devices to effect orderly change, a means, so it was always argued, to allow the reasonable expansion of the one people without the destruction of the other. Nevertheless, in any reflective mind these recurrent shifts westward gave rise to a nagging conundrum: What, eventually, would become of the Indian? The Louisiana Purchase seemed to offer a great release from the inexorable logic of that sequence. Suddenly, by a single stroke of diplomacy, those "illimitable regions of the west," which had eased George Washington's conscience in 1783, had miraculously reappeared; despite twenty years of massive White expansion, the country once again seemed "large enough to contain us all."

It is not at all surprising therefore that Jefferson would envision removal and separation on a grand scale as a means of resolving the destructive consequences of this inexorable collision between two unequal peoples. In the first flush of exhilaration he even proposed that the Constitution be amended to confirm the Indians' right of occupancy and self-government under the protection of the United States in lands west of the Mississippi. But he found little support among his colleagues for that kind of commitment and rigidity. The pressure of events relating to the purchase made it expedient to avoid constitutional deliberations, and Jefferson was soon talking, as he had before, more about the need for rapid acculturation and eventual assimilation than about such a comprehensive removal (although he instructed Meriwether Lewis, while Lewis was in St. Louis preparing for his expedition across the continent, to ascertain how the White residents of upper Louisiana might respond to inducements to remove to the east side of the Mississippi so as to clear the area for eastern Indians).

Like most Americans who voiced any concern for the Indians, it seemed obvious to Jefferson that they must be pressured "to abandon hunting, to apply to the raising of stock, to agriculture and to domestic manufacture, and thereby prove to themselves that less land and labor will maintain them . . . better than in their former mode of living." That kind of intensification of their economy would allow them, indeed induce them willingly, to release their excess lands. Thus, to the extent that any possibility of the Indians' remaining in their homelands was offered, it became the standard American proposition that Indians must conform to the common American rural pattern: that is, for each family to reside on a farm laid out within the federal rectangular survey (allotments of 640 acres per head of household, plus additional acreage for each child became common offerings), which land would be held in fee simple and the Indians become individual citizens subject to the laws of the state of residence. Unlike many Americans, Jefferson went further and accepted forthrightly the intrinsic equality of the Indians as human beings. He regarded them simply as victims of history, people in a primitive stage overwhelmed by "the stream of overflowing population" from civilization across the sea. He therefore advocated not only acculturation to European ways but assimilation with European peoples (in this, too, he could have taken his cue from More). He was quite ready to prescribe this course to the Indians themselves, as for example in his statement to a delegation of chiefs from the Northwest in 1809:

> I repeat that we will never do an unjust act towards you—On the contrary we wish you to live in peace, to increase in numbers, to learn to labor as we do and furnish food for your ever increasing numbers, when the game shall have left you. We wish to see you possessed of property and protecting it by regular laws. In time you will be as we are: you will become one people with us; your blood will mix with ours: and will spread with ours over this great island.

Under Jefferson the national administration took an increasingly active role in fostering culture change among the Indians. In 1796 the government had established two trading posts ("factories") to provide the Cherokees and the Creeks with manufactured goods at reasonable cost and a regularized market for furs and skins. It was hoped that such installations would lure the Indians away from whiskey dealers and foreign traders and, more broadly, promote their amity and allegiance to the United States. This system was subsequently expanded to serve all the major Indian tribes, and the factors at such posts were encouraged to provide agricultural implements and blacksmiths and other craftsmen to assist the Indians in adapting to a settled, productive life. By 1822, when Congress yielded to pressures from private trading interests and abolished this factory system, twenty-two posts had been established, although no more than thirteen were in operation at any one time. But even shorn of this specific commercial dimension, Indian agents remaining at these and other locations were charged with doing all they could "to promote civilization among friendly Indian tribes." Furthermore, in 1815 an aggressive new superintendent of Indian Affairs began to foster a system of regular schools, operated by various Protestant missionaries. In so doing, the government enlisted willing allies and resources in a task Congress would never support with adequate funds. As Francis Paul Prucha has noted, this was accepted as a natural and necessary partnership: "It was quietly understood, by government officials as well as by church leaders, that the American civilization offered to the Indians was *Christian* civilization, that Christianity was a component of civilization and could not and should not be separated from it."

By the early 1820s there were about thirty schools in operation, partially subsidized by the government, and their number soon increased as the enthusiasm for and urgency of the task mounted.

These ostensibly benign institutions of commerce and philanthropy were not the principal instruments of official American presence and pressure. They existed within the framework and often within the very shadow of frontier military posts, and the pattern and power of these reflected major changes in Indian-White relationships. After the wars of 1812–18 there could no longer be any doubt about the ability of the United States to dominate its own national territory. The devastation of the Creeks and Seminoles and expulsion of foreign traders from the southern mainland, and the defeat of Tecumseh and the failure of the British to further their designs upon the Northwest marked an obvious and decisive shift in what had been an uncertain balance of power. The Indians had been dispossessed of huge portions of their lands, but the pressures for more were unrelenting. In his first annual message to Congress, in 1817, President James Monroe reaffirmed the age-old aggressor's principle that "no tribe or people have a right to withhold from the wants of others more than is necessary for their support and comfort," and the idea of comprehensive government-sponsored displacement now came strongly to the fore in discussions of Indian policy. In this, too, the government and religious leaders were closely associated, as especially notable in the work of the geographer-clergyman Jedediah Morse and of the Baptist missionary Isaac McCoy, each of whom undertook an extensive reconnaissance of Indian tribes and western lands and presented elaborate proposals to federal officials.

In December 1824, twenty-one years after Jefferson had envisioned it, President Monroe put before Congress a formal proposal for the removal of Indians to a western sanctuary, together with a program to help them respond to the demands of the modern world:

> Between the limits of our present states and territories, and the Rocky Mountains and Mexico, there is a vast territory to which they might be invited, with inducements which might be successful. It is thought, if that territory should be divided into districts, by previous agreement with the tribes now residing there, and civil governments be established in each, with schools for every branch of instruction in literature, and in the arts of civilized life, that all the tribes now within our limits might be drawn there.

The superintendent of Indian Affairs reported that about 130,000 Indians were then residing within the organized states and territories, distributed among sixty-four tribes or remnants of tribes (his enumerations are now generally considered to be somewhat short of the actual populations, but there remains much disagreement about specific cases). Those long encapsulated on tiny reserves in the eastern states were of little concern, but even the smallest groups west of the mountains were considered to be candidates for relocation.

By this time the Mississippi River was no longer the obvious divide for such a separation of peoples. The State of Missouri (1821) and the Territory of Arkansas (1819) had been created west of the river. North of Missouri all was still Indian Country, and so, in effect, was much of the area east of the Mississippi. Although placed within the bounds of a vast Michigan Territory in 1818, most of the lands west of Lake Huron and Lake Michigan contained no American settlers, and the idea of creating a formal Indian protectorate in this northwest region was now seriously advocated by various interests, governmental and private, Indian and White. Now that the foreign threat in this sector seemed eliminated (British traders were excluded and American fur companies had taken over all commerce and contact), these northern woods seemed an obvious possibility for an Indian refuge. Jedediah Morse strongly urged it, following his extensive tour of 1820. He envisioned the area studded with small communities of Indians under the care of "Education Families." Each settlement would have its own church, school, and industries under the tutelage of dedicated missionaries, teachers, and agents. Eventually there would be a "great central college" to serve the needs of an Indian state. His concept has been likened to that of the Spanish missions; he must have been directly influenced by the ready examples of the Stockbridge and the Oneida Indians. The Stockbridge, made up of remnants of the Mahicans and others devastated in colonial and intertribal wars and long under Christian acculturation, had left their western Massachusetts village in 1783 and come to the Oneidas in central New York. In 1818 most of them had moved on to Wisconsin, having negotiated with the Winnebagos and Menominees for a tract near Green Bay. Soon a faction of the Oneidas, under the influence of a strong Episcopalian lay missioner, was preparing to do the same. Thus by the voluntary action of the Indians themselves, the Northwest was already serving in a small way as a refuge area, and in his bill detailing Monroe's general proposal, Secretary of War John Calhoun formalized it as such. Calhoun's successor, James Barbour, did the same in the following year, specifying most of Michigan Territory west of Lake Huron as an area as yet unsought and not likely to be strongly desired by White settlers.

Aside from a few remnants of Delawares and Wyandots in Ohio, the Indians considered most obviously appropriate for removal to such a Northwest protectorate were those who still hung on to attractive lands along the southern margins of that large region. The Ohio Valley had been cleared of Indian tenure in the years just before 1812. After the war (and Tecumseh's death) American pressures were strongly reasserted, and by 1821 most of Indiana and Illinois and a large part of Michigan had been ceded. That left the Potawatomi, on the St. Joseph and Kankakee rivers along the southern end of Lake Michigan, and the Sauk, anchored on the Rock River just to the west, as the obvious targets for the next phase of American expansionism, to which may be added small reserves of the Miami Indians along the Wabash and two bands of the Kickapoo who had ceded, but not wholly departed from, locales along the Wabash and the Sangamon. These were Algonkian tribes of generally similar economy and society. They lived by summer agriculture and winter hunting, supplemented by fishing, fowling, and gathering, shifting with the seasons from their substantial villages along the rivers to temporary hunting camps, making use of forest and prairie and open woodlands. In good years the yields from such an economy could be more than adequate, and surplus maize and other foods as well as furs and skins might be traded to nearby Whites. All lived in active connection with the American economy, dependent upon traders for tools, arms, cloth, and other supplies. And all were intent upon remaining Indian and sustaining their specific identity, even though every tribe was deeply divided as to how best to do so. There were extreme nativists and extreme civilizationists and many gradations in between, as well as special kinds of responses, such as the emergence of charismatic religious leaders who preached new moral codes and special destinies. Several decades of pressures and harassments had already produced what would become a characteristic Algonkian adaptation among the Shawnees and Kickapoo (and soon to be apparent among the Sauk, Fox, and the Siouan Winnebago): a propensity to move, often long distances and necessitating severe economic and social adjustments, not just under direct White coercion but on their own volition in order to keep "out of the meshes of the settled life, where Americans dominated, . . . [to be] able to pick and choose what they wanted to add to their way of life." (The sketch of Kickapoo displacements in figure 8 shows only the more prominent relocations within a much more complex, far-ranging sequence of movements by a people unusually resistant to American incorporation.)

The succession of proposals to create a Northwest Indian Territory never got through Congress (although Calhoun's bill passed the Senate), and the fate of the Indians in this region was decided in the usual American way: by uncontrolled encounter, bloodshed, and coercion. The lead deposits in the Driftless Area (an "island" of rugged hill country that escaped the tremendous smoothing forces of the continental glacier) along the upper Mississippi, long known and casually worked, suddenly became the scene of intense activity in the 1820s. This had followed hard upon the opening of most of Illinois to land seekers and the well-advertised success of a Kentucky promoter who had arrived in 1822 with a large retinue of miners and slaves. The town of Galena, perched steeply on the terraces of the Fever River with steamboat connections to St. Louis, became the main focus of a surge of fortune seekers. Indian agents worked intently to gain cessions and arrange for the removal of tribes to lands west of the Mississippi, but they could not clear the way fast enough to avert collision. The situation was complicated by the return from Iowa of one faction of the Sauk to their old homeland along the Rock River. By 1830, some 10,000 Whites had swarmed into the district; unrestrained by any territorial or national force, they trespassed widely on Indian lands and so wantonly pillaged villages and fields as to drive these Sauk into retaliation, which action dragged on into what was called the Black Hawk War, resulting in the killing of several hundred Whites and the near annihilation of that large part of the Sauk tribe. By the time this bloody mess was over an Indian Removal Bill had passed Congress,

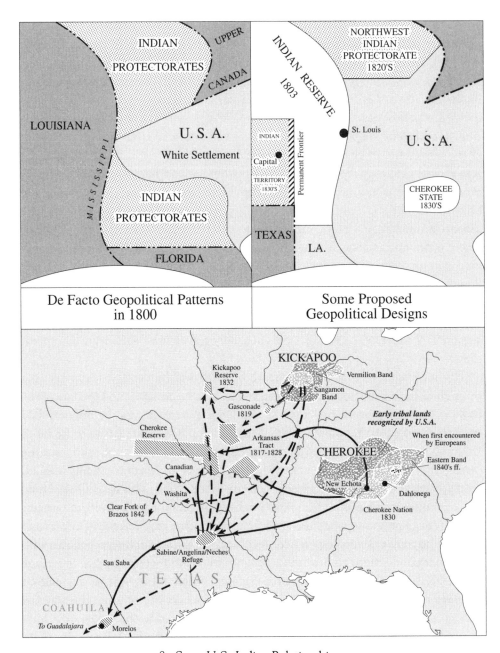

8. Some U.S.-Indian Relationships.

and all the tribes of the Northwest were pressured into a series of large cessions that culminated, after a long holdout, in the ousting of the Winnebago from central Wisconsin. With that, two small enclaves negotiated by the Oneidas and the Munsees and a scattering of Chippewa bands in the remote northern woods were all that remained of the large de facto Indian territory and the prospective Northwest Indian protectorate of twenty years earlier.

In the Southwest (as the Georgia-Mississippi area was often still called) the situation, sequence, and results of American-Indian relations were broadly similar but with important differences in detail. Most of the some 60,000 Indians here were long experienced in dealing with Whites. They had been initiated by de Soto's brutal foray through their territories in the 1540s; they had been participants, willing or unwilling, in the complicated European rivalries for position and control on the Gulf Coast; they had been in sustained contact with White traders for at least 150 years. Inevitably, they had been deeply affected by such experiences: they had incorporated many European items—plants, animals, tools, trifles, clothing, words, concepts—into their lives; their economies had been critically altered and in various degrees bound into the Euro-American system; they had received many European persons (as well as runaway Africans) into their society, and the offspring of such racial mixtures were often prominent leaders, members, and sometimes whole factions of these nineteenth-century nations. They were the "Civilized Tribes," a name bestowed upon them in recognition of their native sophistication as well as their "progressive" response to European contact; it was also implicit recognition that in spite of all that contact and change they remained implacably Indian societies and formidable adversaries.

The decisive prelude to removal was the Creek wars of 1812–14, which shattered the largest confederation and forced great cessions of lands from all the main tribes. But other antecedents also influenced the idea and geography of relocation. In the aftermath of the American Revolution, a few small bands of Indians who had fought against the rebels had sought refuge across the Mississippi in Spanish Louisiana. In 1808 a delegation of Cherokee leaders had visited Jefferson, and one conservative group (opposed to the cultural adaptation program then vigorously underway) had received the president's strong encouragement (and subsidy) to inspect lands between the Arkansas and White rivers. No concerted removal followed immediately, but a trickle began to flow west, and ten years later there were 2,000–3,000 in what became known as the Western Cherokee band in Arkansas Territory. Following the Creek wars, the United States and the State of Georgia renewed pressures and inducements to get the entire Cherokee nation to move to Arkansas, where a tract was now formally set aside for them. The great majority firmly refused, but some accepted American subsidies and went west. During these same years some of those in Arkansas grew dissatisfied with turbulent conditions there and moved on southwesterly into Spanish Texas. Such shiftings and scatterings were of course nothing new, they were simply further reverberations of the kind that had been rumbling westward from the first violent encounters between Europeans and Indians in Atlantic America.

By the early 1820s the great Indian nations remaining in the Old Southwest had been reduced to a hard core of tribal territories: two in the east, the Creeks in the Piedmont country east of the Coosa and the Cherokees just above in the southern Appalachians; and two in the west, the Choctaws in the rolling red lands of central Mississippi and the Chickasaws on the loessial blufflands just to the north. These were ancient homelands, with intensive agricultural plots and sprawling villages in some of the same valleys, terraces, and open woodlands where de Soto had found them nearly 300 years before. Just such continuity in place undergirded the Indians' argument against removal. When in 1823 the federal government, at Georgia's prodding, tried to open negotiations once again about moving to a trans-Mississippi sanctuary, Cherokee chiefs responded that "it is the fixed and unalterable determination of this nation never again to cede *one foot* of land." That rebuff brought a warning from Secretary of War Calhoun: "You must be sensible that it will be impossible for you to remain, for any length of time, in your present situation, as a distinct society or nation, within the limits of Georgia, or any other State." To which the Cherokee leadership forthrightly replied:

> Sir, . . . we beg leave to observe, and to remind you, that the Cherokees are not foreigners, but original inhabitants of America; and that they now inhabit and stand on the soil of their own territory; and that the limits of their territory are defined by the treaties which they have made with the Government of the United States; and that the States by which they are now surrounded have been created out of lands which were once theirs; and that they cannot recognize the sovereignty of any State within the limits of their territory.

Such an exchange pointed to the fundamental issue in what was a three-party dispute involving the Cherokees, the State of Georgia, and the United States. In 1802, in order to resolve a long drawn-out conflict over Georgia's western land claims, the United States had agreed to extinguish the Indian title to all lands within the state "as early as the same can be peaceably obtained on reasonable terms." Such a pact was open to conflicting interpretations. The Cherokees had made it clear that they were not willing to give up title to their lands "peaceably . . . on reasonable terms." Georgia insisted that they be expelled, accusing the central government of negligence and overt discrimination against a member state of the federal union in not pressing, as required by the agreement, to end formal Indian control over any part of Georgia territory. Federal officials were caught in between, and indeed, the whole nation became caught up in the controversy. The expulsion of these southern Indians and especially the Cherokees, became a political and moral issue of intense debate in the national press, as well as in party and sectional politics, and it seriously strained relations among the executive, legislative, and judicial branches of the federal government, as well as between Washington and the states.

Central to this complex issue was the character and response of the Cherokees during this time of stress. Until well after the American Revolution the Cherokees had adhered as best they could to a policy of insulation from White societies. They did not hold themselves aloof from all contact but tried to be selective of traders, unwelcoming to missionaries, and to fend off officials who sought to lure their support in extraneous political and military causes. They were not wholly successful; they had suffered serious defeat from Carolina forces in the 1760s, but they long remained a substantial force lodged in a mountainous country under no serious threat from Indian neighbors and at some distance from European societies on the seaboard. Eventually, of course, American speculators and settlers, armed and aggressive, pressed in upon their borderlands from the east and north, and the Cherokees had slowly, grudgingly, given ground, shifting south and west. Only in the early 1800s did they establish numerous villages in northwestern Georgia (although that area had been part of their hunting ground for centuries). As this pressure intensified and the power of the federal and state governments became ever more apparent, the Cherokees made a conscious collective effort to alter their tactics and try to remodel their economy, society, and polity in such a way as to survive intact within the body of the American republic.

There followed a remarkable cultural florescence in response to this stimulus of pressures and contact. The Cherokees, like all these southern Indians, had long been relatively intensive agriculturists with a diet and domestic economy richly supplemented by hunting and gathering (fishing was minor compared with their neighbors on the coastal plain). To this indigenous complex they had readily added European and African crops (such as watermelons, peas, sweet potatoes, and peaches) and, more slowly, animals (hogs and, less extensively, horses and cattle). They now began to incorporate new products and activities: plows, drawn by oxen or horses; cotton, with gins, household looms, and spinning wheels; gristmills, sawmills, and smithies. These were accompanied by alterations in labor practices, with males joining females in farming and industry and the extensive use of Black slaves, and by some modification of traditional concepts of wealth and property (capitalism had seeped into Cherokee society 100 years before as a response to the Charleston market for deerskins and Indian slaves). Programmed changes in social and political organization and operations followed. Missionaries were invited to set up schools, and Cherokee leaders soon took advantage of the remarkable syllabary, created on his own initiative by Sequoyah, to spread literacy in Cherokee as well as in English. The political structure was radically reorganized. A long trend toward greater centralization of power was accelerated; the National Council was strengthened in 1817, a constitution modeled on that of the United States was later adopted, laws were codified and elections held, and a new national capital was laid out at New Echota. Such features were not simple imitations; there was an attempt to adapt them to use within a polity still suffused with Indian values, to operate as much as possible on a basis of harmony, consensus, and community with a distaste for hierarchy and individual power.

The Cherokees were living refutations of all those deeply ingrained and widely propagated European and American ideas of Indians as primitives, savages, foot-loose hunters—wild people. Their domestic economy was certainly equal, and probably superior, to that of most southern White pioneers; their society, though factionalized, was more orderly and less volatile; their official behavior sought to be scrupulously legal according to American standards. Many federal officials and congressmen supported the Cherokees in their insistence that they could not be removed without their consent. But a quick sequence of events decisively altered the situation. First came the election of Andrew Jackson as president, soon fol-lowed by the rush into the Dahlonega goldfields within the Cherokee lands, and the extension of Georgia law over all Georgia territory, with specific provision to exclude all Indians and their properties from its protection. Whereas John Quincy Adams had warned the State of Georgia not to press its jurisdiction upon Cherokee lands in violation of federal treaties with the Indians, Jackson was an open advo-cate of removal, by coercion if necessary, dismissing such treaties as no more than a temporizing action now made obsolete by the strength of the United States. The Indian tribes east of the Mississippi, he stated forthrightly, "are a conquered & dependent people," and the federal principle required that the central government sustain any state in the exercise of its right to regulate civil affairs within its own limits. With such encouragement, Georgia proceeded to exercise such rights, and the clash of authorities together with the ensuing rush into the goldfields produced chaos. Amid this crisis (and extreme pressures upon the other large southern tribes as well), Congress, after one of the most impassioned debates in its forty years, passed (barely) the Indian Removal Bill in May 1830. Although that bill made no mention of coercion, it was clear that the Jackson administration would use what-ever means necessary to expel the Indians from the bounds of the southern states and territories.

The subsequent history is not one that most Americans, then or thereafter, have cared to think about too closely. The Cherokees appealed to the United States Supreme Court, to no avail. It was ruled that the Indians were "domestic depen-dent nations" and had no legal right to bring suit for injunction against Georgia laws; in a subsequent case it was decided that the Cherokees were indeed a nation, "a people distinct from others," and were protected by federal treaties from uncon-stitutional infringements by Georgia, but Jackson refused to enforce the court's ruling. The result of this testing of forces and wills was widespread plunder and seizure of Cherokee villages, farms, and lands by local Whites, a splintering of Cherokee resistance, a treaty of cession of all Cherokee lands extracted by federal officials from a small minority group, rejection of that treaty and continued refusal to move by the great majority, and eventual removal by the U.S. Army of this main body of the Cherokee nation to a western reserve. "Removal" was in detail a series of forced expulsions and migrations over a period of several years, under harrowing circumstances that cost several thousand Cherokee lives, a melancholy drama that became fixed in Indian—and more recently, American—history as the Trail of Tears. A few Cherokees fled into the mountains and escaped military patrols and eventually settled down among the sixty or so families that had accepted individual allotments in ceded lands under the laws of North Carolina and were thereby exempt from the expulsion order. This remnant, a markedly conservative group long marginal to the main body, became the nucleus of the Eastern Band of the Cherokees that eventually secured a small reservation in the Great Smokies. In the west, three leaders who had signed the removal treaty were soon assassinated and the bitter factionalism would smolder for generations.

The Cherokee case was the most notorious of the time and region, made so by the unusual qualities and drama of that nation's attempts to adapt and resist, and its failure and heavy human cost, but the pressures and results were not generally dissimilar in the cases of the Creeks, Choctaws, and Chickasaws. These nations, too, claimed to be distinct bodies of peoples with formal treaty guarantees from the United States and not subject to the laws of the states of Mississippi or Alabama; they, too, rejected removal but soon found themselves under intolerable pressures, deliberately unprotected by the states, factionalized by intolerable choices. The Chickasaws fared better than most by accepting temporary allotments in place and then selling out and moving west a few years later. The Choctaw experience was more like that of the Cherokees. They were skilled negotiators in Washington but unable to stem the local forces arrayed against them. About a third of this relatively large nation (20,000 or so people) chose to accept a treaty offer of local allotments but were largely defrauded of these by the local agent and other speculators. Eventually about two-thirds of the Choctaws were pressured out (and suffered severely from unseasonable weather en route west), and the thousands who remained scattered into the swamps, canebrakes, and backcountry in search of refuge.

The experience of the Seminoles was significantly different. They had already been "removed" once, having been driven from northern Florida in 1816–18 into an official reserve in the center of the peninsula on lands of little attraction to Whites and shut off from the coast so as to preclude foreign contact. That proved to be such a niggardly environment and the plight of the Indians was so severe that in response to their pleas the United States twice modified the northern boundary to give them a bit of cultivable land. There could be no pretense about a primitive people holding valuable ground "to no good nor profitable use." Nevertheless, passage of the Indian Removal Bill brought immediate pressure on the Seminoles to cede these lands and move west. For the national government such action was simply a logical part of a comprehensive program for "solving" the "Indian problem" with the added advantage of clearing Florida of such dissident peoples, for Florida was bordered by British and Spanish waters, and as a federal Indian agent remarked, "it was a misfortune to Florida as a frontier Territory and with her maritime exposure to have any Indians within her boundaries." As elsewhere, of course, the main pressure was local, from those who wanted not only to get rid of all Indians but, in this case particularly, "to gain possession of the blacks among them and to close off Florida as a place to which their own slaves could escape and find refuge." Forays by Whites to retrieve runaways had been a chronic source of irritation with the Seminoles.

The Seminoles repudiated a fraudulent treaty of cession in 1832. Two years later the immediate threat of forced removal induced them to kill a federal agent and ambush a company of U.S. troops, and there ensued a guerrilla war in the thickets and swamps that lasted seven years, costing from battle, disease, and privation the lives of 1,500 American soldiers and probably that many Seminoles, at an expense to the United States of at least $20 million (some say $30 million or more, but a staggering sum, whatever—more than the cost of Louisiana, several times the cost of Florida). The Seminole War became a national embarrassment, and to many Americans a national tragedy. After two years of frustration the American general in charge in the field concluded that removal was impracticable and the war a useless waste: "We have committed the error of attempting to remove them when their lands were not required for agricultural purposes; when they were not in the way of white inhabitants; and when the greater portion of their country was an unexplored wilderness, of the interior of which we were as ignorant as of the interior of China."

But the secretary of War replied that the treaty (ratified, as usual, under duress by a tiny minority) was the law of the land and no authorization for the Seminoles to remain in Florida could be made. That general was soon replaced by another, but none of his successors could really finish the job. The war never clearly ended (although in 1842 the U.S. Army declared that it had); it simply petered out as the resolute remnant of a few hundred Indians faded into the labyrinth of hammocks, jungles, and swamps of the southern peninsula (a truce signed with the descendants of that defiant group in 1934 was hailed as the official close of hostilities—100 years after they had begun). The result of this protracted campaign was the capture, in total, of about 3,200 Seminoles, groups of whom were from time to time shipped off to a concentration camp in New Orleans, and eventually upriver to Little Rock and on to an assigned tract in the west.

This dribble of Seminole deportees was part of the last phase of government-sponsored removal of Indians from lands east of the Mississippi. The intent of Jefferson's vision of "tempting all our Indians . . . to the West," formalized in Monroe's proposal of 1824, had been ruthlessly carried out by Jackson and his successor Van Buren in the 1830s. In such a sequence the election of the aged William Henry Harrison, famed warrior of Tippecanoe, to the American presidency in 1840, could be seen as a fitting finale to a great national project (even though he was the figurehead of a new anti-Jacksonian party).

Removal was of course only half of this immense project. There had to be a resettlement of those removed—or, more exactly, of those that survived the exodus, the deadly "middle passage" across the American states and territories. The citizens of Missouri and Arkansas deplored the idea of adding more Indians to their western frontier but were eager to clear their own territories. Thus the first negotiated removals undertaken by the federal government involved eastern Indians already west of the Mississippi who had crossed the river years earlier (such as the Cape Girardeau Shawnees). At the same time the federal government pressured the Kansa and Osage tribes into further large cessions of their traditional lands in order to make space for such relocations. The western boundary of Missouri had been drawn along a meridian passing through the mouth of the Kansas River. In 1828 the western boundary of Arkansas was shifted east and brought into an approximate continuation of that line. The original plan called for a longitudinal "neutral zone" five miles wide between this western edge of Missouri and Arkansas and the "Permanent Indian Frontier," to be maintained as a buffer and patrol path in which settlement by either Whites or Indians would be prohibited. That concept was soon abandoned as unworkable. The change in the western limits of Arkansas was made in conjunction with the creation of a large reserve into which the Western Cherokees, coming under heavy pressure from Whites filling in the Arkansas Valley west of Little Rock (some of whom had been squatters there before the Cherokees had been given rights to the area), would remove altogether from Arkansas territory (fig. 9).

By the time the general Indian Removal Bill had been enacted, therefore, a large sanctuary and program for resettlement had been defined and in some degree tested. In general terms there was to be latitudinal continuity: tribes from north of the Ohio River were to be relocated on tracts north of the Osage reserve and those from south of the Ohio on tracts lying between the Osages and the Red River boundary with Texas. There was an obvious broadly deduced and often implied environmental logic underlying this, but in fact the decisive factor was the insistence by Northern congressmen that Cherokees and Choctaws and other slaveholding southern tribes be confined to the southern sector of this new western protectorate (though such tribes were not in fact held south of the 36°30′N line designated in the perilous national compromise of 1820).

The qualities of this extensive range of western country were much discussed during the fervent debates over removal, and the proposed exodus made biblical allusions irresistible: "It is true," said Mr. Vinton of Ohio (a leading spokesman for the opposition) that "the children of Israel were led out of the wilderness, into a land flowing with milk and honey; but, contrary to the Divine example, we propose to lead a whole People, nay, more, the remnants of forty different nations of men, out of a land of plenty, into the wilderness."

Such metaphors beclouded understanding. Although the exiled Indians could hardly be expected to regard their new lands as an equivalent of their old, these western tracts were far from being an unknown wilderness. Many traders and travelers were familiar with them, Isaac McCoy filed reports, and the federal government gathered information from various sources. In 1832 the War Department dispatched a special commission to "examine the country set apart for the emigrating Indians" with an eye to locating them all "in as favorable positions as possible, in districts sufficiently fertile, salubrious, and extensive, and with boundaries, either natural or artificial, so clearly defined as to preclude the possibility of dispute." Their report in 1834 was accompanied by a new "Map of the Western Territory," prepared by Lieutenant Hood of the Topographic Bureau, on which a "Western boundary of habitable land" was laid down (on the basis of McCoy's assessments) delimiting a longitudinal belt about 200 miles wide between the Platte River on the north and the Red River on the south. It was widely agreed that this strip of well-watered country, grading out from woodlands and tall prairies on the east through scattered groves and valley strips to open rolling prairie was eminently suitable for settlement. The only deficiency, voiced by some, was the scarcity of timber in its western reaches. That the eastern Indians could survive on the resources of such country without severe adjustment seemed apparent from the economies of the Osage, Kansa, Oto, and Omaha resident there. Indeed, some of these Siouan tribes had themselves once lived well to the east in the wetter and more wooded environments of the Ohio and Mississippi valleys. An important difference in subsistence patterns was the dependence of these Indians on seasonal buffalo hunts, and by dividing this belt into latitudinal territories similar access to the buffalo range could be given to the newly relocated Indians.

In the 1830s, therefore, the United States formalized a large sector of its western borderlands in unprecedented ways. A broad belt of country between the Platte and the Red River was set apart as the "Indian Territory" or "Western Territory" (a congressional denomination of "Neosho" for the whole area did not reach enactment) and subdivided into a set of territorial allotments to accommodate a great variety of Indian groups. These peoples were divided into two basic categories: "indigenous village" tribes and "emigrant" tribes. The former included the Osage, Kansa, and Oto; the latter, by 1840, included about two dozen tribes removed from

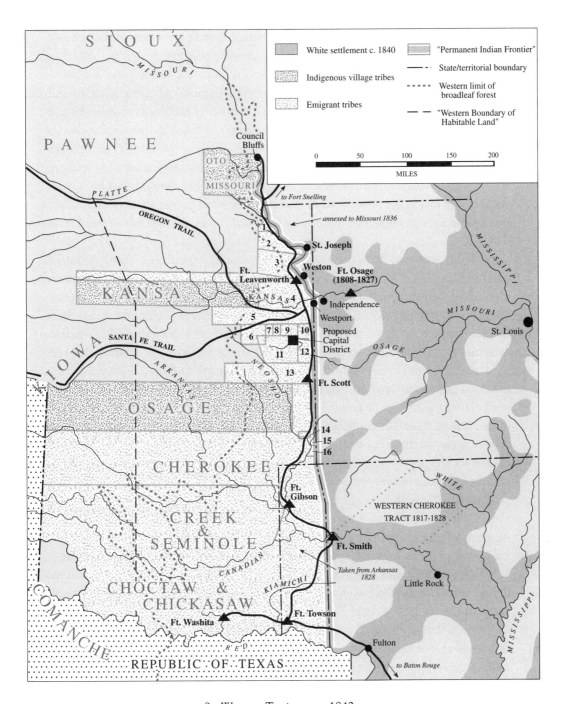

9. Western Territory, c. 1840.
The numbers in the smaller areas refer to the Indians so identified in table 1.

lands to the east. All of these allotments were anchored on the eastern margins of this belt, giving rise to a series of loose settlement clusters along the Nemaha, Kansas, upper Osage, middle Neosho, lower Neosho, Canadian, and Kiamichi rivers. Each district was in a subagency serving one or more tribes, each had one or more licensed trading posts, mission schools, and other facilities provided by the various removal and reduction treaties. The larger of these reserves extended in long, narrow strips westward into buffalo country. There on the high open ranges lived the "Plains Tribes," notably the Comanche, Kiowa, Cheyenne, Arapahoe, and Pawnee, with whom the United States was only beginning to make official contact and had as yet negotiated no territorial cessions (other than an agreement by the Pawnees to withdraw, except for seasonal hunts, from south of the Platte River).

Such a drastic and intricate alteration of human geography obviously required extensive oversight by the managing power. In this, too, beginnings had been made some years before the formal removal program. In 1808, Fort Osage had been established up the Missouri 200 miles directly west from St. Louis. For ten years it was the farthest American outpost and a focal point of diversifying White-Indian activities. In time, similar outposts were set up to the south on the Arkansas and on the Red River, and farther up the Missouri to the north at Council Bluffs. As the idea of a permanent Indian frontier began to emerge, two substantial new posts were established: Fort Leavenworth on the Missouri (replacing Fort Osage and Council Bluffs), and Fort Gibson, near the head of steamboat navigation on the Arkansas (replacing Fort Smith). In the 1830s these became the principal imperial centers for the northern and southern sectors of the newly defined Indian territory, and they thereby became pivotal posts within any larger strategic design (fig. 10).

The need for such a design was generated by this unprecedented frontier situation. In the succession of proposals for expansion and rationalization of the entire western defense system (which heretofore had been developed in piecemeal fashion), two quite different concepts emerged. One was essentially longitudinal, calling for a cordon of posts from the border of Texas to the upper Mississippi, connected by a good road to provide for routine patrols in the policing of the border between the Indians and the Whites and the swift shifting of troops to any imperiled sector. The competing concept was primarily latitudinal in design, stressing the need to connect a series of outposts by military road and steamboats (or railroads, as proposed by one percipient strategist of 1838) with larger garrisons and depots secure within the body of the nation at St. Louis, Memphis, and Baton Rouge. Out of a welter of discussions by various congressional committees and War Department administrations something of both of these designs was adopted. By the early 1840s a military road from Fort Towson on the border of Texas to Fort Snelling had been completed, with Fort Scott positioned about midway between

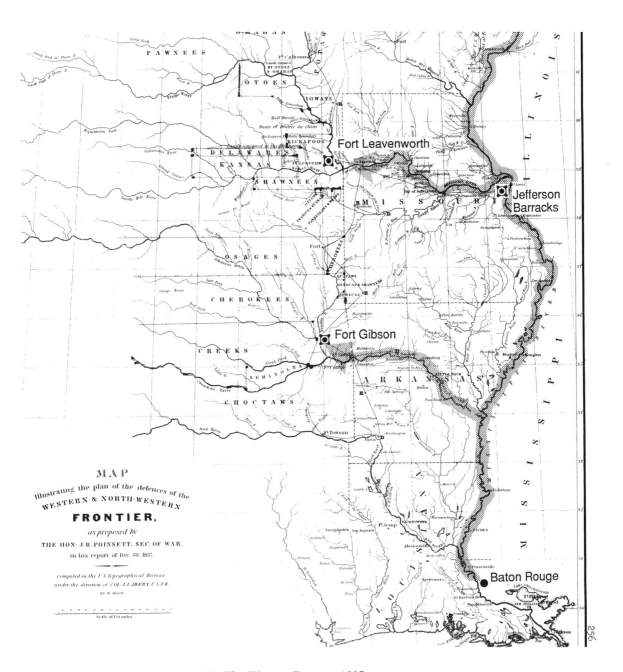

10. The Western Frontier, 1837.

We have enhanced the main routes, posts, and political borders on this portion of a map prepared by Lieutenant W. Hood to illustrate "the plan of the defences of the Western & North-Western Frontier, as proposed by The Hon. J. R. Poinsett, Sec. of War" and published in Senate Document 65, 25th Cong., 2d sess., 1837–38.

Fort Gibson and Fort Leavenworth pivotal to the two sectors of the new Indian territory. But the system operated primarily from a national axis reaching westward from Jefferson Barracks near St. Louis to Fort Leavenworth, from where dragoons (mounted troops, first deployed on this frontier in 1832) made periodic expeditions through the western country as a show of force. There were similar operations out of Fort Gibson, and in 1842 a new outpost near the Texas border (Fort Washita) was established in an attempt to protect the Chickasaws from the Kiowas and Comanches.

Arguments over strategies were enmeshed in disagreements over purpose: Was the main task of the U.S. Army to protect the Whites from the Indians? to protect the Indians from the Whites? to protect the Indian tribes from one another? Such questions were intrinsic to the removal program. It was taken for granted that the primary purpose of the army was to protect White settlers from "inroades and depredations" from the "numerous hordes" of "Savages" hovering on their borders (to use language common in frontier newspapers and petitions). No federal, state, or territorial administration could ever demur from that basic political reality even if the behavior of its frontier citizens might occasionally tempt officials to do so. And every treaty in some way solemnly declared that the United States would protect the Indians from interruptions, intrusions, or any form of encroachment by Whites in these lands that had been set apart for the free and unmolested use of the Indians forever. As for intertribal disputes, the central government had long tried to stay clear of those often bewildering and dangerous affairs but had felt it necessary to intervene in the protracted harassments and bloodshed that ensued after the Cherokees had begun to move into the Arkansas lands of the Osage. The program of comprehensive removal inevitably multiplied such problems, and from 1834 on the United States routinely committed itself by formal treaties to the formidable job of preventing "intestine wars between the several tribes" in the new Western Territory. And so, however complicated or even contradictory these tasks might be, the army found itself charged with all three—and given resources inadequate to perform any one.

That this new Indian territory was a formal protectorate within the body of the United States was clear enough, but just how it was to be governed and what its geopolitical future might be was a matter of recurrent and often heated debate. For the time being, it was under the jurisdiction of the commissioner of Indian Affairs in a subdivision of the War Department. Nearly all proposals envisioned a progressive transformation from tribal authority to some sort of "enlightened system . . . formed on the principles of our own" (to use Calhoun's phrasing of 1825). Discussions tended toward regularizing this new entity as part of the existing territorial system. But ordinary territories were assumed to be states in embryo, and although the idea of an exclusively Indian state as an eventual member of the Union had flickered through the decades of treaty negotiations and committee discussions, it was a prospect too controversial for congressional endorsement. The original bill of 1834 formalizing the new Western Territory specified exactly that as the eventual goal, but such words were deleted from the final act. Renewed attempts in 1837 and 1839 to form a territorial government (one of the bills included Isaac McCoy's selection of a seven-mile-square district on the upper Osage River for the capital) were approved by the Senate but stalled in the House. And so this new area remained anomalous, a formal conglomerate of tribal territories under the regional superintendency of St. Louis and military supervision of the commandants of Fort Leavenworth and Fort Gibson.

It is important to understand that all this debate was among Whites. Indian leaders had occasionally proposed that their homelands be organized as territories looking toward eventual admission to the Union, but never in accordance with the standard pattern, for each territory was to remain under its own tribal government. Indian leaders vigorously resisted pressures toward confederation, amalgamation, dissolution, or any other compromise of tribal autonomy and identity. Their formal relationships with the United States were by treaty, as nations, and they insisted (to use language typical in such documents) that "the United States guarantee" that the western lands allocated to them "shall never be within the bounds of any State or territory, nor subject to the laws thereof."

In 1845 the commissioner of Indian Affairs reported that the current western population of the tribes "wholly or partially removed" surpassed 82,000 (table 1). There remained several thousand more in the east scheduled for removal (not all in the right-hand column of table 1 were so included). And of course the resettlement of these emigrant Indians deeply affected the thousands of indigenous village Indians, forcing them to relinquish lands and adjust to lesser, geometrically defined homelands. By the commissioner's account, therefore, approximately 100,000 Indians were directly involved in the formation of this new Western Territory. But such figures are inadequate to assess the impact of this program. The reported tribal figures varied considerably in source, date (1841–45), and reliability, as might be expected in such a scattered swirl of activity, and virtually everything tended toward undercounts. More important, such totals say little or nothing directly about the number who over the years had scattered into the countryside, or fled to Texas or Mexico, or been killed or died in the roundup or exodus or during the often horrendous first year or two in the new lands. Even without taking into account the further impact of the declines in births attributable to such disruption (a recent calculation of the full "demographic devastation" of the Cherokee concluded that 10,000 additional Cherokees would have been alive in 1840 had removal not occurred), the number of Indians affected was surely some tens of thousands more than these published figures suggested.

Table 1   Indian Populations, Western Borderlands
(adapted from Report of the Commissioner of Indian Affairs, 1845)

Tribe (Numbers refer to map of Western Territory)	Plains Indians, adjacent & unconfined	Indigenous village tribes assigned to reserves	Emigrant Indians in West	Number of these staying in East
Assiniboines	7,000			
Sioux	25,000			
Poncas		777		
Pawnees	12,500			
Cheyennes	2,000			
Iowas		470		
Omahas(1)		1,301		
Otoes and Missourias		931		
Sacs and Foxes of Missouri(2)			414	
Kickapoos(3)			516	
Delawares, Wyandots, Stockbridges, Munsees(4)			1,862	652
Shawnees(5)			929	
Kansas		1,607		
Arapahos	2,500			
Sacs and Foxes of Mississippi(6)			2,200	
Chippewa(7), Ottawa(8) and Potawatomi(11)			4,360	14,963
Peoria and Kaskaskia(9)			150	
Weas and Piankeshaws(10)			274	30
Miamis(12)			(no data)	650
New York Indians(13)			(no data)	3,293
Kiowa	1,800			
Osage		4,102		
Quapaw(14)		247		
Shawnees and Senecas(15)			241	
Senecas of Sandusky(16)			153	
Cherokees			25,911	1,220
Creeks			24,594	160
Seminoles			3,136	(est.) 100
Choctaws			13,592	5,800
Chickasaws			4,211	
Comanches	19,200			
Total	70,000	9,435	82,543	26,868

There is a further complication to this story: this new western protectorate of the United States became a refuge for an uncertain number of the several thousand Cherokees, Shawnees, Caddos, and others driven from the Republic of Texas. Such action was not the result of a policy of assisted resettlement but was expulsion, by direct military assault, an undertaking instigated after Sam Houston, the famous honorary Cherokee and friend of the Indians, had been succeeded as president by Mirabeau Lamar as part of a leadership that declared all Indians to be a subversive population favoring Mexican reconquest and therefore enemies to be extirpated.

All advocates of this immense American project insisted that it was not intended to be simply another stage in the miserable sequence of dispossession. Certainly it was the vision, the hope however qualified, of a genuine solution to the problem of Indian-White relations that rallied many avowed friends of the Indians to support removal as a national policy. Such persons were vital to formulations of a program unprecedented in scale, comprehensiveness, and purpose. The gross difference between the promise and the performance in the matter is of course one of the great scandals in American history, but we should not let that becloud the character and magnitude of what was ostensibly undertaken. It was a program never spelled out in a single definitive document; it took form only in the separate treaties with these many tribes. These agreements varied considerably in detail, but a review of them reveals the federal government committing itself to a process involving cessions of eastern lands in return for compensation for improvements thereon and for cattle left behind, annuities to various leaders, cash payments (derived from the sale of their relinquished lands) to a tribal fund, and allocation of equivalent lands in the west; payment of the cost of, and assistance in, the movement to these new lands, including advance reconnaissance (for example, "a deputation of six chiefs or headmen"), issuance of basic equipment (such as rifles and ammunition, axes, iron kettles, and blankets), provision of daily subsistence for each emigrant, procurement of shipping and transport facilities, and protection and care en route; cessions of lands from indigenous Indians to provide ample space for resettlement ("a tract of country . . . sufficient in extent, and adapted to their habits and wants"), including survey and demarcation (and the expense of an Indian observer of such preparations); and once arrived in these new homelands "a sufficiency of good and wholesome provisions" (corn, pork, beef) for one year, an adequate supply of farming and domestic implements (plows and hoes, sets of horse gear, yokes and chains, wagons and carts, axes, saws, cornmills, looms, reels, and wool cards), a resupply of livestock (cows, calves, and bulls, working cattle, sheep, breeding hogs), assistance in breaking up and fencing in the ground, the services of a blacksmith together with his house, shop, tools, and an annual supply of iron and steel (for sixteen years in the case of the Choctaw), gristmills and sawmills and millers for each; schools and teachers, vaccines and the services of a physician, an interpreter, and a resident agent who would see that an adequate supply of trading goods was always available, prohibit whiskey peddling, and in general provide liaison with the federal government. No particular treaty contained every one of these provisions, but several contained most of them, and all removal agreements covered this general process.

Of course the entire affair was awash in deceit and cynicism, regarded by many—probably most—Americans as simply an expedient to pry the Indians out of their eastern lands and shove them out of sight. But there is no reason to doubt that some public officials and concerned citizens were deeply committed to the official rationale: removal as an act of rescue, resettlement as an impetus for cultural change, the whole project a national attempt at a kind of geographical social engineering. That the Indians formally agreed to all these provisions, actually requested and specified many of the tools and teachers they were to be supplied with, must not be taken as representing general agreement within any one tribe or nation as to the desirability, direction, or pace of culture change. Here the benign language of treaties masks the ambivalence and factionalism, the pain and despair of captive peoples under relentless pressures to make themselves into something that seemed to contradict all that they had ever been.

Thus the western margins of the American nation had been greatly altered in position and character. Here, too, was a great cultural border zone, but unlike those on the south and the north, this one lay wholly within the bounds of the United States and was being shaped by domestic rather than international policies and actions. The Louisiana Purchase had opened up the possibility for drastic geographical change on a grand scale. That narrow wedge of settlement thrusting westward in the Ohio Valley of 1803 had by the 1840s been advanced and broadened into a thousand-mile front bending from Green Bay to the corner of Texas. The early idea of using all of this new western half of the United States primarily as a place to store Indians had long since vanished; the Indian-White boundary had been pushed to the edge of the great prairies, half a million Whites now resided west of the Mississippi, and half a dozen tongues of settlement were advancing across the rolling countrysides of Iowa and Missouri. The human surface of the vast area east of that separation line had been radically changed. It was (if we may be pardoned an anachronism) as if a gigantic bulldozer had scraped the Indians off the land and piled them up on the farther edge of Arkansas and Missouri, leaving behind only tiny shreds and fragments caught upon some bit of uneven ground—a swamp, a mountain cove, a rocky waste—or dislodged but escaping from the mass carried forward, as in the obscure scatterings of Indians into the backwoods of Alabama, Mississippi, and the Northwest; here and there were widely spaced clumps marked for the next pass of the blade.

To carry the image further, a succession of shuntings kept changing the edge of Indian country in the Northwest, for no "permanent frontier" had been fixed in that sector. Between Council Bluffs and Lake Superior lay a shatter zone of displaced and indigenous tribes, all under mounting pressures for further cessions and relocations. Potawatomies and Sauks and Foxes had been moved across the Mississippi in the 1830s. For a time, a forty-mile neutral zone provided a buffer between them and the Dakota Sioux, but that tract was later given to the Winnebago. The plains of the upper Missouri had long been an unstable zone of rival Indian societies, differing in languages and economies, disturbed by the spread of guns from the north and horses from the south, entangled in the competitions of British and American traders. Disease had recurrently taken a grim toll, but nothing to equal the estimated 17,200 deaths from the smallpox epidemic of 1837, which drastically altered the relative and absolute strength of every tribe. In the following year the entire area between the Mississippi and the Missouri and north of the State of Missouri was formed into the Territory of Iowa, and further adjustments of the Indian-White boundary were implicit. In 1842 troops were sent to Council Bluffs to protect the Potawatomi from the Dakota, and shortly thereafter negotiations were under way to relocate all these emigrant Indians somewhere further afield and to open another broad swath of lands to White settlement.

It must be emphasized that this long boundary, which "in common parlance" was now referred to as "the Frontier," was never a clear and simple separation of peoples, however well defined it might be in some sectors. It had political and legal meaning, but as always in North America, the vast Indian country lying beyond the cordon of military posts was variously penetrated year after year by traders, explorers, missionaries, adventurers, and others (after 1834 passports were no longer required of American citizens who wished to enter Indian country). And of course, some of the Indian nations therein had been routine participants in American and European commercial systems for generations. In the 1830s St. Louis traders had begun to operate steamboats with some seasonal regularity as far up as the mouth of the Yellowstone. The Santa Fe Trail was a well-worn track across the southwestern plains before this Indian territory had been established. For years trading expeditions had taken the Platte route across the central plains to the Rockies. In the 1830s a number of traders and missionaries had gone on to Oregon, and a growing body of reports and promotions prompted the first emigrant train to set out for that far northwestern corner in 1841. That was apparently only the opening trickle of a swelling stream, because two years later nearly 1,000 people headed across the continent, new towns were laid out farther up the Missouri at Weston and St. Joseph (by Joseph Robidoux, long involved in the Missouri fur trade), seeking the advantage of a more forward position for what seemed to be the American thrust to the Pacific so long advocated.

Even before the removal phase of the national program was completed, there-fore, it was becoming clear that any idea that this new western Indian territory could provide separation and sanctuary was becoming seriously compromised. Its most central, strategic locale was becoming a thoroughfare. Even though formal approval of these main routeways had been negotiated with the Indians of that area, the ramifications of such traffic—thousands of Whites, with their wagons, oxen, and horses, their herds of cattle and mules foraging over a broadening belt of country, cleaving the buffalo range, disrupting the hunting patterns, and endan-gering the relationships with and among a dozen Indian nations—could hardly reassure anyone with a serious concern for the future of America's original inhabi-tants. By the 1840s what had once so dramatically loomed as the "new, immense, unbounded world" of Louisiana was no longer really new nor unbounded (nor called Louisiana); it was still immense and as yet unorganized over much of its extent, but it was increasingly perceived that this vast acquisition was not to be the western half of the United States but only an intervening region serving to bind together the Atlantic and Pacific coasts of a truly transcontinental nation.

The pressure for further geopolitical change rapidly increased. The migrations to Oregon became a "fever," thousands of Mormon refugees camped for months on lands of the Otoes and Missouris across from Council Bluffs and later began to move west along the north bank of the Platte through unopened country. The Gold Rush brought not only many thousands more but also smallpox, which devastated the Pawnee and spread on north and northwest. In 1849 Fort Kearny was reinforced and the government purchased and garrisoned the old trading posts of Fort Laramie and Fort Hall. Two years later, at a great convocation at Fort Laramie, treaties with a dozen Plains tribes cleared a corridor for the passage to Oregon, Utah, and California.

But the greatest forces were focused on the immediate trans-Missouri margins of the Plains, and the real "Indian barrier," the complete belt of reserves between the Platte and the upper Neosho, began to crumble under the assault of squatters, townsite and railroad speculators, and politicians. Prominent spokesmen, such as Thomas Hart Benton, used false maps and contrived legalisms to suggest that unassigned lands in the Indian Territory were open to White squatters. Indian commissioners began to talk of creating two "Indian colonies," one to the north and one to the south, in order to "open a wide sweep of country . . . for the expansion and egress of our white population westward," and to discount the generally optimistic reports from agents in the field about the agricultural progress of the emigrant Indians and declare that the great "experiment" of this transplant-ing of Indians to a bountiful land ("an emanation of the purest benevolence") had "measurably failed." In 1848 the Kansa and Potawatomi were pressured into a drastic diminution of their reserves, but it was the frenzy generated by the Gold

Rush that actually broke down the barrier. Squatters swarmed into the area, and before any further negotiations with the Indians had been undertaken, before any land was legally open to Whites, Congress took all of the land north of 37°N between the Missouri and the Continental Divide and created Kansas and Nebraska territories. The immediate result was anarchy: a lawless scramble for lands, bloody competition between organized groups (that between pro-slavery and free-soil settlers being the only part commonly featured in American histories), and relentless despoliation of Indians and their properties. Amid this disaster, treaties of removal, drastic reduction, or individual allotment were forced upon every tribe north of the Neosho. By the time federally surveyed land was actually put on the market in late 1856 there were tens of thousands of White residents, a dozen substantial towns, and a major settlement district extending as far west as the new army post of Fort Riley at the head of navigation on the Kaw.

And so the basic concept of the West as a designated geopolitical territory for the "Preservation and Civilization of the Indians" was shattered. The Indian titles to these lands in the West were even less substantial than they had been in the East because they "had no foundation in antiquity. The Government gave them and, when it so pleased, defied them. As a consequence, before the primary removals had all taken place, the secondary had begun, and the land that was to belong to the Indian in perpetuity was in the white man's market." This Indian Territory was a formal official protectorate (or, more accurately, a set of protectorates), but the United States refused to uphold its part of the treaty obligations. It was a deliberate dereliction. When the Indian commissioner and his agents pleaded for help in stemming the turmoil, the secretary of the Interior (to whose department the Indian Office had been transferred in 1849) advised President Franklin Pierce that it was not appropriate to use the military forces at Fort Leavenworth to expel squatters and trespassers because such action would be "discordant to the feelings of the people of the United States."

6. Assertion and Division: Oregon and the Northern Boundary

In 1830 an eighty-page booklet entitled *A Geographical Sketch of that Part of North America Called Oregon* appeared in Boston bookshops. As the title might suggest, it dealt with an area uncertain in name or nature to Americans. The booklet was a propaganda tract by Hall Jackson Kelley, a Massachusetts schoolman who had become obsessed with the topic of Oregon. Its descriptions were crafted for use in fervent discussions and agitations, and it helped confirm that name as well as assert American claims to the Northwest Coast.

The word *Oregon* was of obscure, apparently Indian, origin. Although it had appeared occasionally in some form, it had remained unfamiliar to the general public until it resounded in William Cullen Bryant's poem *Thanatopsis* in 1817 (the very year Hall Kelley first read Lewis and Clark and underwent a change of life). Thereafter it began to emerge as the preferred American term for this large, ambiguous area. Congressman John Floyd's bill in 1822 had proposed the creation of a "Territory of Origon." A few years later William Darby included notice of the "Basin of Columbia, or Territory of Oregon" in his *View of the United States, Historical, Geographical, and Statistical* (1828)—but gave it only 4 of his 634 pages because "that imperfectly explored territory . . . appears at present as if on another planet." The name continued to be applied to the river (as in *Thanatopsis*) as well as the region, but the American designation "Columbia" was more generally accepted in Europe and America for the famous River of the West. However, the main settlement of that territory asserted, quite by design (and to Kelley's alarm), another presence: Fort *Vancouver*—so named, as the governor of the Hudson's Bay Company put it, "to identify our Claim to the Soil and Trade with Lt. Broughton's [of Captain George Vancouver's expedition] discovery and Survey." In the 1830s this expanding cluster of facilities and fields overlooking the Columbia (and over-looked from either side by the towering snow-capped peaks bearing other pres-tigious British names: *St. Helens* [after the ambassador to Madrid] and *Hood* [Lord of the Admiralty]—Kelley tried to get these renamed for American presidents) would become a major focus of the geopolitical competition implicit in this regional toponymy.

The founding of Fort Vancouver marked a change in regional strategies. The initial focus had been upon the obvious: the mouth of the Columbia River. That seemed the key point for competitive continental programs, as Astoria–Fort George and repeated calls in Congress for a military post there attested. But experience in that locale and expanding knowledge of the Pacific Slope brought a shift to a site upriver. The important difference was not in the river itself but in climate and countryside. It was a change from the beclouded, rain-soaked, densely forested, coastal region (Lewis and Clark had reported at length on their miserable winter there) to the great lowland in the lee of that rugged margin, a region with half the rainfall and considerably more sunshine, yet still shielded by the even greater mountain wall to the east from the drier, hotter, and colder conditions of the continental interior. This lowland area was part of the remarkably mild mar-itime zone blessed with "that surprising difference between the climates on the western and eastern sides of the continent"; this northwest coast, it soon became common to observe, had "a climate much like England" (two centuries earlier, Western Europeans had been surprised—shocked—at the harshness of climate they had found on the *eastern* side of North America). This moderation of climate was accompanied by a more attractive landscape, intermediate in kind between the almost impenetrable rain forests of the coastal margins and the extensive deserts and grasslands east of the Cascade Range, and best exhibited in the *Willamette Valley* (Kelley's *Multnomah* valley: the two names, both Indian in origin, were used interchangeably for several decades), a broad lowland extending 100 miles south from Fort Vancouver. The mountains bounding the valley were luxuriantly covered in fir, spruce, and cedar, but its floodplain and valley floor, isolated buttes, and gentle foothills carried a mixture of oak woodlands and open prairies, laced with many streams and offering a variety of soils. The Willamette Valley was the southern section of a great structural trough between the Coast Range and the Cascade Range. To the north the wetter, more forested and gravelly Cowlitz Plains led to the deepened and largely drowned glaciated lowlands of Puget Sound, which was itself the southerly compartment of the spectacular landscapes of deep water, towering forests, and mountain walls extending northward to Alaska (fig. 11).

Fort Vancouver was located, therefore, at the intersection of the two great natural axes of the Oregon country: where the mighty Columbia flowing westward through the mountains to the sea crossed the north-south lowland trough—and, more exactly, a location almost opposite the junction of the Willamette and Columbia rivers. By the mid-1830s, a decade after its founding, many of the virtues of this district were apparent in the considerable complex spread along the north bank of the Columbia. The main post was a large stockaded rectangle enclosing offices, stores, workshops, and residences of company officers. Nearby were the workers' cabins aligned on broad streets ("the whole looks like a very neat and beautiful village"), more workshops, barns, and a boathouse, and farther out a busy sawmill (with mainly Hawaiian laborers). About 1,000 acres were under cultivation, yielding grain, peas, potatoes, garden and orchard produce; 2,000 more were enclosed for livestock. Twenty miles to the south, at the Falls of the Willamette, a gristmill and sawmill had been set up, and farther on, where the valley suddenly broadens, was an informal settlement of French Canadians—retired employees of the Hudson's Bay Company. In total nearly 1,000 people resided in and around this primary focus of the Northwest Coast, the center of a geographic system gathering produce from much of the Pacific Slope, trading with Alaska, California, and Hawaii, and maintaining annual contact with London, York Factory, and Montreal (Governor Simpson's winter residence).

Fort Vancouver was an impressive, thriving nucleus, the capital of an immense region, but it is important to understand that it was also something else: it was a company town, not a rooted colony (fig. 12). It was the creation of private enterprise, its purpose was profit, its people were intended to be sojourners not settlers, personnel on assignment who were subject to recall and reassignment to other stations. The thriving farms and mills were a branch of the fur business, designed to

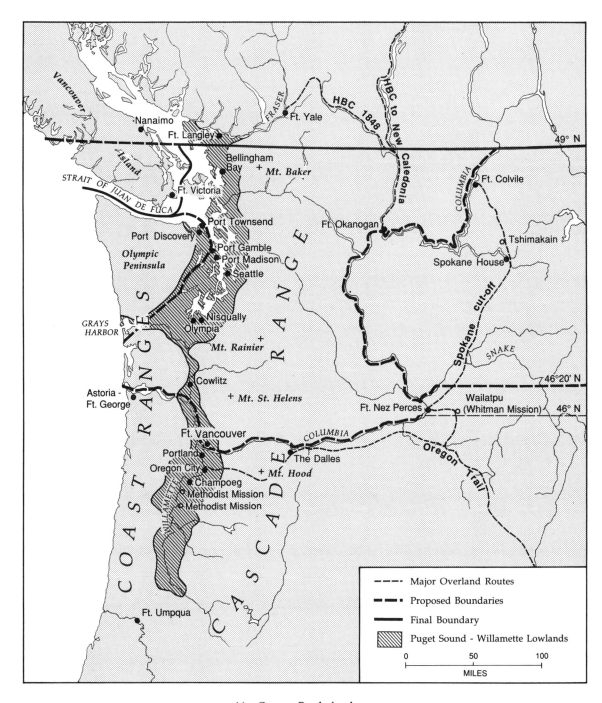

Vancouver

Island

STRAIT OF JUAN DE FUCA

Olympic
Peninsula

GRAYS
HARBOR

COAST RANGES

CASCADE RANGE

Nanaimo

Ft. Langley

FRASER

Ft. Yale

HBC 1846

HBC to New Caledonia

49° N

Bellingham
Bay

+ Mt. Baker

Ft. Victoria

Port Townsend

Port Discovery

Port Gamble
Port Madison
Seattle

Ft. Okanogan

COLUMBIA

Ft. Colvile

Tshimakain

Spokane House

Nisqually

Olympia

+ Mt. Rainier

Spokane cut-off

SNAKE

46°20' N

Cowlitz

+ Mt. St. Helens

Astoria -
Ft. George

Ft. Nez Perces

Wailatpu
(Whitman Mission)

46° N

Ft. Vancouver

COLUMBIA

Portland
Oregon City

The Dalles

Oregon Trail

+ Mt. Hood

WILLAMETTE

Champoeg
Methodist Mission
Methodist Mission

Ft. Umpqua

- - - - - Major Overland Routes

- ▪ - ▪ - Proposed Boundaries

——————— Final Boundary

Puget Sound - Willamette Lowlands

0   50   100

MILES

11. Oregon Borderlands.

reduce the costs of the main enterprise. The settlement up the Willamette was a reluctant answer to a social problem: what to do with retired employees and their Indian wives and mixed-blood children. Setting them up on farms in the valley was not calculated to initiate a colony in a strategic area; it was designed to remove them far enough away so as not to be a nuisance around the main base of operations. That Fort Vancouver and its Willamette outliers might be transformed into something more permanent, that indeed it was becoming more and more like a commercial town and colonial nucleus, that, given the quasi-governmental role of the Hudson's Bay Company, there was a good deal of the symbol and substance of

12. Fort Vancouver.

About 1845 an unknown artist painted this portrait of the headquarters of the Columbia Department at the peak of its development. The view is from the higher terrace on the north (where the U.S. Army would later establish Vancouver Barracks) overlooking the majestic Columbia. The Willamette, running along the foot of the low mountains in the background, converges with the main river about four miles downstream to the right. In the foreground are two common sights of this British North American system: a high-wheeled Red River cart, and an Indian or metis man on horseback with his woman following on foot. (Courtesy of the Beinecke Rare Book and Manuscript Library, Yale University)

empire about it, that such a British nucleus must have some bearing upon an eventual partition of Oregon were matters of which the Hudson's Bay Company leaders were well aware and increasingly concerned. In 1838 the governor and committee summoned George Simpson, governor of American operations, and John McLoughlin, chief factor at Fort Vancouver, to London for consultation on geopolitical strategies to cope with impending problems in their Columbia Department.

At that time there were probably fewer than forty Americans—men, women, and children—in all of Oregon, none of whom had been there for more than three or four years. Out of such a meager presence was an American pressure generated. Indeed, one might say that American success in the competition for Oregon came very directly out of apparent American failures—even an interrelated set of failures.

One of these notable and pertinent failures was Hall Jackson Kelley, the man who worked so relentlessly for an American Oregon. He had prospered enough from the writing of school textbooks to devote his attention to the cause. He lobbied in Washington for government aid in establishing a colony, organized the American Society for Encouraging the Settlement of the Oregon Territory, and shortly after publication of his *Geographical Sketch* issued "A General Circular to all Persons of good character who wish to Emigrate . . . ," inviting them to join him in forming a settlement "to be commenced in the Spring of 1832, on the delightful and fertile banks of the Columbia River." But no government aid was forthcoming, and his attempts to form an expedition were unsuccessful; Kelley himself got there after a dispiriting journey of two years by way of New Orleans, Mexico, and California, yet he was considered by those in charge at Fort Vancouver to be as sick in mind as he obviously was in body, and after four strained months they shipped him back to Boston.

But Kelley had a direct influence upon a fellow Yankee of different talents and temperament: Nathaniel Wyeth, a prosperous young Cambridge entrepreneur (his ingenuity had helped create an extensive export ice business). Wyeth became interested in Oregon through Kelley but soon gave up on him as an expedition leader, organized his own company, raised capital, and set out in 1832 to engage in the fur business. He joined the annual caravan to the Rocky Mountain rendezvous, and with the help of some experienced trappers, he and a few companions eventually arrived at Fort Vancouver, only to find that the supply ship he had sent out from Boston had been lost. Wyeth spent several months in Oregon and saw enough to induce him to return to Boston, reorganize, and set out again in 1834 with a larger company that included two eminent scientists (a botanist and an ornithologist) and five Methodist missionaries. Unable to sell a load of trade goods to the American company at the rendezvous, as he had expected, Wyeth built his own post, Fort Hall, on the upper Snake River. Moving on to the Columbia, he constructed Fort William on an island at the mouth of the Willamette (six miles from Fort Vancouver) and set about developing a salmon fishery and a sawmill. Wyeth soon found that although he was hospitably received and given some assistance by the chief factor, he was dogged with difficulties (seventeen of his men died from disease or accidents) and quite unable to compete in the fur trade or sustain his other enterprises, and in 1836 he gave up, sold out to the British company, and returned home. As a commercial challenge, Wyeth's adventure had been no more effective than other occasional American interlopers' forays into Hudson's Bay Company territories.

The Rev. Jason Lee and his Methodist brethren who attached themselves to the Wyeth expedition were intending to establish a mission in the upper Columbia country. They were responding to what had been interpreted and widely publicized as a call from some Flathead Indians for Christian teachers, but after a stay at Fort Vancouver they decided for various reasons to begin their work in the Willamette Valley near a small Calapooya Indian village on the edge of French Prairie, the Canadian retiree settlement. There were in fact few Indians left in the valley or lower Columbia following devastating epidemics in 1829–32 (McLoughlin estimated that nine out of ten had died); and in terms of Christianizing the native population, this Methodist effort, as well as that of several other Protestant missions soon initiated east of the Cascades, was a failure. But these mission stations were intended to support the missionaries as well as to teach the arts of Christian civilization to the Indians, and as agricultural settlements those in the Willamette Valley were not only successful, they were soon famous as such.

Despite its failures, the second Wyeth expedition may be seen as a telling display of the range of American interests in Oregon: fur trade, salmon fishery, lumbering, Pacific commerce, farming, science, Christian philanthropy, and all of this in some degree suffused with an American national purpose so shrilly proclaimed by Hall Kelley and other expansionists. Because of the national attention they attracted, these unsuccessful private initiatives helped mightily to impel the kind of American reach for Oregon that Congress had so far failed to undertake. Wyeth's testimony as to the character of Oregon was drawn upon by various congressional committees, and it was more reliable than most. He offered a reasonable appraisal of its regional qualities, emphasized the power of the Hudson's Bay Company, and stated bluntly that insofar as relations with the Indians were concerned, "the Americans are unknown as a nation, and, as individuals, their power is despised by the natives of the land." In late 1835 President Jackson, responding in part to the returned Kelley's cries about British tyrannical domination, commissioned William Slacum as his personal agent to inquire about the settlements on the "Oregon or Columbia river." Slacum arrived there by ship in December 1836 and stayed just three weeks, but he was thereby able to testify about the "extraordinary mildness of the climate" and richness of the pastures even in winter, as well as the thriving activities in and around Fort Vancouver. The missionaries wrote many letters and reports that were widely reprinted in eastern papers and thereby greatly magnified public interest in, and information about, Oregon. In 1838 Jason Lee returned East for an extensive lecture tour and lured reinforcements for the Methodist program as well as a small party of settlers from Illinois. By then it was becoming clear that the Oregon mission had evolved into an American agricultural colony. The settlers themselves had no doubt about what they were creating; as their petition to Congress seeking the extension of American laws and courts phrased it: "We flatter ourselves that we are the germe of a great State." Senator Lewis Linn of Missouri had already begun a major push in Congress to assure them of that, with a bill calling for the formal establishment of Oregon Territory, a port of entry, and military occupation.

The Hudson's Bay Company thus had good reason to reassess its position on the Northwest Coast. The fur resources of the Columbia country were no longer of great value (and changes in fashion were depressing the market for beaver), but the Columbia River remained the trunk line of operations on the Pacific Slope, Fort Vancouver the key location (and a major investment), and the sustained British presence a powerful claim to territory. If there was no way the company could stem the influx of emigrants from the United States who were responding to "the overcharged pictures of [Oregon's] fertility and commercial importance," there was a reasonable hope of holding the Americans south of the Columbia. To do so the British position north of the river would need to be substantially augmented. Accordingly, the Puget Sound Agricultural Company was organized as a subsidiary to develop a large livestock operation at Nisqually (an earlier outpost near the southern end of the sound) and a colony of farmer-settlers in the lowland corridor at Cowlitz. There was a new economic rationale for this program, for the Hudson's Bay Company had signed a contract with the Russian American Company to provide subsistence for the latter's Alaskan operations. But the main concern was geopolitical, as the directors reaffirmed in a letter to McLoughlin: "We consider it of the utmost importance for various reasons, but especially in a political point of view to form a large settlement at the Cowlitz portage as early as possible, as the fact of a numerous British agricultural population being actually in possession there would operate strongly in favor of our claims to the territory on the Northern bank of the Columbia River." Their first thought was to bring in colonists from Scotland and England, but they soon turned to a more ready source of experienced North American farmers: the Red River Settlement. The first contingent (21 families, 116 persons) arrived overland from Assiniboia in 1841 and was apportioned between Nisqually and Cowlitz. At the same time, two Roman Catholic priests sent out earlier from Red River were called upon to help induce the retired employees in the Willamette Valley to move north to the Cowlitz colony.

Thus, thirty years after the brief encounter between the Astorians and Nor'westers a new confrontation in the Columbia country was apparent. The ventures of a miscellany of Americans in the British company's monopoly territory had turned into competitive colonizations—and Christianizations, for the Protestant and Roman Catholic missionaries had a keen competitive, national, geostrategic view of their tasks. Rather suddenly, momentarily, there seemed to be a balance of forces and an obvious basis for geographical partition (fig. 13). Two notable visitors to Oregon in that year, 1841, were important representatives of these contending powers. Sir George Simpson arrived overland from Montreal and paused to assess the state of affairs in the Columbia Department en route to inspect new company trading posts in Alaska and California (San Francisco Bay). At Fort Vancouver he encountered Lieutenant Charles Wilkes and various members of the United States Exploring Expedition. Wilkes was the naval commander of this American undertaking modeled on the great geographic expeditions of James Cook and the comte de La Pérouse. Carrying an impressive array of natural scientists, topographers, and artists, it was a conscious assertion of national power and pride. Authorized by President Jackson in 1836, the fleet of six ships had sailed from Norfolk in 1838, made extensive surveys of Antarctica, the South Pacific, and the Sandwich Islands (Hawaii), and was now carrying out its orders "to direct your course to the Northwest Coast of America" and make a careful examination of "the territory of the United States on the seaboard, and of the Columbia River." Simpson and Wilkes were both strong, assertive personalities, and they had little time for each other, but they exchanged some views, and the very presence of such an official American party making an extensive reconnaissance of Oregon (several detachments ranged into the interior east of the mountains), together with the growing American presence in the Willamette, had an effect upon Simpson. He was not ready to yield on the Columbia as the appropriate boundary between the two sovereignties, but he was now less confident, and as a precautionary measure, he urged that an alternative base be set up on Vancouver Island. That idea had been proposed as early as 1839 when it became apparent that "the influx of strangers to the Columbia" might endanger the company's operations even if the river did become the boundary. Wilkes, on the other hand, while not a forceful advocate for the American colonists (having received the hospitality and assistance of the British company at every post, he thought the settlers' complaints were petty or unfounded), was outspoken in his view that the United States must never give up Puget Sound, an opinion based on the expedition's confirmation of its magnificent harbors and the experience of losing a ship trying to enter the Columbia ("mere description can give little idea of the terrors of the bar of the

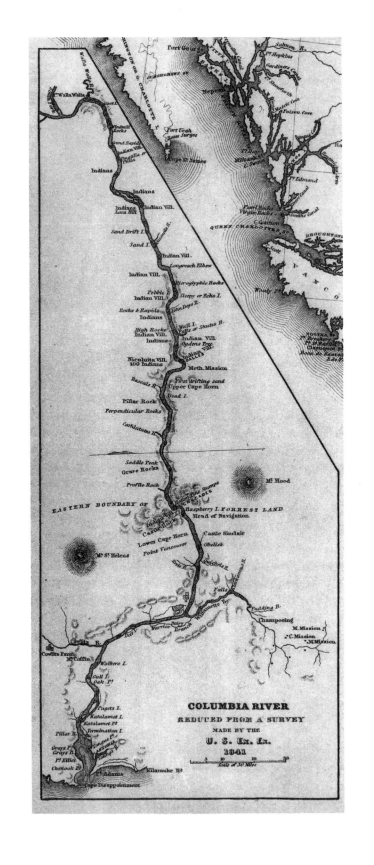

COLUMBIA RIVER

REDUCED FROM A SURVEY

MADE BY THE

U. S. Ex. Ex.

1841

Scale of 30 Miles

Columbia"). Thus the British expert turned to a strategy of retreat from positions long held, while the American ófficial asserted the national necessity of lands never occupied by its citizens.

From this point, developments in Oregon, in national politics, and in diplomatic relations between the two powers rapidly brought the issue to a decision. The trickle of American farmer-emigrants became a flood. A party of a hundred or so arrived in 1842, getting wagons as far as Fort Hall. Some were dissatisfied with what they found and left for California, but that fall the St. Louis newspapers reported that much larger emigrations "to that celebrated region" were being organized, and throughout the western states "the Oregon fever" was raging. In 1843 the first "great migration"—nearly 1,000 people—took place (getting their wagons, for the first time, as far as The Dalles, from where they were floated downriver), in the following year 1,000 more arrived, and in the next, perhaps 3,000 (by several routes, and getting at least some of their wagons across the Cascades). By 1845 American settlers occupied attractive sites for sixty miles above the Falls of the Willamette. The original Methodist mission had been relocated and redirected entirely to serve the American settlement: "there was no mission in Oregon at all; there was only a replica of frontier Methodism complete with itinerants and a church"—and, it may be added, with a gristmill, sawmill, school, and plans for a town. Furthermore, the attractions of the Willamette Valley lured more than Americans; they completely subverted the Hudson's Bay Company's "counterimmigration" north of the Columbia, for the Red River emigrants, dissatisfied with their lands and chafing under the company's restrictions (leaseholds and rents), soon packed up and moved south to join their compatriots in and around French Prairie (none of whom had been induced by the company to resettle in the Cowlitz).

The Americans had also taken the lead in forming a government. When the

---

13. The Lower Columbia River.
Those "beautifully conspicuous" volcanic cones towering over the lower Columbia are cartographically conspicuous on this map of the great artery downriver from Walla Walla (at the top of the map—the view is straight east) that was included as an inset on the "Map of Oregon Territory," in volume 4 of Lieutenant Wilkes's *Narrative of the United States Exploring Expedition.* What is curiously missing is the name Fort Vancouver, even though it is prominent on the main map and its location is clearly shown here in the set of squares just above the mouth of the Willamette. By this time a number of other settlements have appeared, including three Methodist missions, a Catholic mission (at French Prairie), and the HBC Cowlitz Farm. Note the absence of Indian villages below the Cascades ("Head of Navigation") and the cluster of them around prime salmon fishing sites upriver, especially at The Dalles. (Courtesy of the George Arents Research Library, Syracuse University)

Linn bill to establish an Oregon Territory failed in Congress, the settlers, concerned about law and order and especially about titles to their lands, held a mass meeting at Champoeg ("Champooing" on the Wilkes map), the river landing at French Prairie, which led to the drawing up of a constitution and legal code, and to the delimitation of a set of counties for "Oregon Territory" to be in force until the U.S. government extended jurisdiction. The French métis and Hudson's Bay Company officials were wary but did not dare ignore completely or resist directly for fear of endangering their rights and properties. In response to these obvious differences in allegiance, the agreement was carefully worded so that participation would be construed as being consistent with the duties of a citizen of the United States or of a subject of Great Britain. In 1845 this compact was further elaborated with the creation of the office of governor and designation of Oregon City (at the falls) as the capital.

By 1844 Oregon had become a major issue in American national politics. Extreme expansionists called for the annexation of all of Oregon and Texas. President James Polk, in his inaugural address, declared that the American title to "the country [he didn't say the 'whole'] of the Oregon is clear and unquestionable." Such, of course, was not at all the case. The British were adamant that the United States had no claim at all on a large part of Oregon. Actually each country had strong claims only to part of the region, and the expectation of a division of the whole had been present from the earliest discussions of the matter. The issue, therefore, was where to draw the line: the United States insisted on an extension of the Forty-ninth parallel boundary from the Rocky Mountains to the sea; Great Britain insisted on the lower Columbia River as the appropriate division. The territorial dispute therefore was centered on the 200-mile strip between those lines, which included the whole of Puget Sound.

The United States advanced the idea of the Forty-ninth parallel without any extensive rationale. Some Americans evidently believed that such a boundary was implicit in early spheres of influence; it had actually appeared on some United States maps as early as 1806; John Melish imprinted it on his first map of 1816 as the presumed ultimate arrangement even though "towards the Pacific Ocean, we have no very correct data for forming an opinion as to the boundaries." But there was no historical precedent nor American activity on which to base a strong claim, and the American case rested on simple concepts of "extension," "contiguity," or the old colonial precedent of latitudinal sea-to-sea charters. In the 1820s some Americans began to specify the hazards of the Columbia Bar as a reason why that river was unacceptable as a boundary. But that was a controversial topic even among Americans who knew something about it. The Columbia entrance could be dangerous, but it could also be managed at other times without problem, and the possibilities for improvement through lighthouses, dredging, and breakwaters were argued.

Those who emphasized the inadequacies pointed to the need for harbors on the Strait of Juan de Fuca (and thus the Forty-ninth parallel boundary). In an extensive series of articles, a knowledgeable Bostonian strongly recommended Port Discovery as the best place for a naval station. This concern for American harbors was argued not on the need for an alternative entrance into, nor colonization of, the Oregon country, but on the need to provide a haven for American whaling and shipping in the Pacific and, in some accounts, to keep the Russians and the British from closing the Americans out of the Northwest Coast. At the time such views were not incongruent with the conviction of many persons (and especially New Englanders) that this remote Pacific seaboard could never become an integral part of the American nation.

In 1826 the British offered the United States just what such American spokesmen had called for: Port Discovery with a five-mile radius of territory. When that was summarily rejected, they offered the whole of the Olympic Peninsula, giving the Americans the southern shore of Juan de Fuca and the western harbors of Puget Sound. But the United States refused to consider any such enclave and became increasingly insistent on the entire contiguous block of territory. In 1837 Slacum declared Puget Sound to be "of the highest importance to the United States" from "a military point of view," and Wilkes obviously concurred, declaring that "the entrance to the Columbia is impracticable for two-thirds of the year."

Great Britain never pressed for any territory south of the lower Columbia. In 1823–24 it explicitly offered a boundary along 49°N from the Rocky Mountains to the Columbia and down that river to the sea. In the next year George Simpson was in London, following his first assessment of the Columbia Department as part of the company's strategic system, and British diplomats were urged to reopen negotiations in order to obtain a boundary drawn from the Continental Divide at the point of Lewis and Clark's crossing (thought to be 46°20′N) west to the Snake River (at the junction with the Clearwater River) and downriver to the sea. Such a line would preserve the Flathead and Spokane countries (where the British had outposts before the Astorians) and, more important, would preserve (with slight adjustment) the overland trail between Fort Nez Perces (which could be shifted to the north bank) and Fort Colvile on the upper Columbia. Inbound brigades used that trail, and the procurement of hundreds of horses annually from the Cayuse and Nez Perces Indians in the Walla Walla and lower Snake areas was fundamental to the operation of the whole interior system. In the very last stages of boundary negotiations, when the company was asked for a list of alternatives, Simpson again nominated this line as the first choice. But having already offered the 49°N–Columbia line, British negotiators were in no position to insist on a boundary less favorable to the Americans, and so an argument based on routine British occupation and use of this large block of territory was foreclosed.

During these recurrent deadlocked negotiations the United States offered two modest concessions: freedom of navigation on the Columbia, and the termination of the Forty-ninth parallel line at the Strait of Georgia and extension of the boundary through the Strait of Juan de Fuca. The original American insistence on 49°N to "the sea" could be interpreted to mean extending that line across Vancouver Island to the open ocean. This modification would leave that island entirely to the British and Juan de Fuca open to both parties. Other alternatives were discussed privately. In 1842 Daniel Webster, then the principal American negotiator, was of the opinion that a boundary drawn east through Juan de Fuca, south through Puget Sound, and on to the lower Columbia would adequately serve American interests (close to the British proposal of 1826), but he made no such official offer (turning instead toward trying to gain British help in securing San Francisco Bay from Mexico) and it is unlikely he could have gained approval to do so (he was in disfavor with expansionists for having "given away" part of Maine).

By 1844 the British government, for a variety of reasons having little to do with Oregon directly, was ready to settle this festering dispute. The great domestic issue was free trade (repeal of the Corn Laws); new economic theories were being intensely debated, and an important faction of leaders was persuaded that Britain would be better served by a widening of trade and a contraction of empire; over the ensuing months there were fears of rebellion in famished Ireland and memories of rebellions in the troublesome Canadas; the Americans would go to war with Mexico and become alarmingly bellicose over Oregon (loud cries of "Fifty-four forty or fight!"); war with France was a chronic concern. The British public had slight interest in this distant affair, and the particular British diplomats then in charge of the matter had no great sympathy for the monopolistic privileges of the Hudson's Bay Company; at the same time, the company's directors, while clearly preferring a Columbia boundary, no longer argued that the Forty-ninth parallel would be disastrous to its operations or its profits. Thus, a partition along 49°N to the Strait of Georgia and the mid-channel of the Strait of Juan de Fuca (a dispute over the connecting line through the maze of islands separating these points would flare up later), together with specification of navigation privileges on the Columbia for the Hudson's Bay Company (but not British subjects in general) and protection of its "possessory rights" within the territory awarded to the United States, was offered by the British, quickly accepted by the American administration, and ratified by a generous margin in the Senate in June 1846.

As a large body of historical studies makes clear, settlement of the Oregon dispute was more the result of particular persons and parties working within the context of other national and international issues than of the actual historical geography of exploration, exploitation, and occupation of that vast territory by the contending nations. It is true that the basic geographic character of Oregon was much better known in the 1840s than when the agitations began in the 1820s, and such knowledge was drawn upon in every debate, discussion, and oration. The particular natural features most pertinent to the boundary question were the Columbia River, the bar at its mouth, the Strait of Juan de Fuca, and Puget Sound, together with various harbors therein. As for the human geography, Fort Vancouver and Astoria were central, but other British posts and the overall system were rarely brought into focus, and references to them were usually incomplete and inaccurate. The Willamette Valley and its settlements were usually mentioned, often at length, but since these did not lie within the primary disputed territory, they were directly pertinent only in terms of a perceived threat to Fort Vancouver and British use of the Columbia. As for more general regional qualities, extensive accounts were often given, but opinions differed sharply, and most of the descriptions and assessments in the American literature were polemical. One must conclude that momentous geopolitical decisions on Oregon, as with so many other parts of North America, were made with limited understanding of, and even limited concern about, its geography.

It is common—and surely appropriate—to commend the peaceful resolution of this dispute during a very bellicose time; it is also common for American historians to suggest, sometimes explicitly, that in the end it was an almost matter-of-fact, obvious, and equitable compromise in which each side got approximately half of the whole. Frederick Merk, one of the most distinguished American specialists on the matter, concluded that the Forty-ninth parallel was the most reasonable basis of settlement; indeed, that line, he said forthrightly, "was the boundary that the finger of nature and the finger of history pointed out for the partition of the Oregon area." As for the first, it is difficult for a geographer to discern "the finger of nature" (Merk took the term from John Quincy Adams) in a geometric line drawn straight across great mountains and rivers and across the human systems adapted to those gross lineaments of nature. As for "the finger of history," it is true that the United States kept its "finger" pointed firmly along the Forty-ninth parallel, but it must also be concluded that it thereby achieved a geopolitical victory that its historical geographical position could hardly justify; this "compromise" resulted in Great Britain losing the entire area in serious dispute. Perhaps we should interpret "the finger of history" as pointing to the basic difference in character of the British and American positions in the human geography of Oregon: the one created and maintained by a commercial company, the other by a spontaneous folk movement; the one a network of widely dispersed stations staffed by assigned agents, the other an organic colony of settlers. That is a telling difference in kind but has little to do with the line of partition, for there were not two dozen Americans north of the Columbia River in 1845–46. We should recognize that the Hudson's Bay Company regarded colonization within its own territories as being a costly complication and infringement upon the fur business, and only reluctantly undertook it as an implied obligation to win renewal of its charter from politicians with larger British interests in Oregon. In retrospect, the 1841 counterimmigration appears to have been fatally handicapped from its inception. But lest we slip into the easy assumption that there could have been no hope that British colonization could have competed with American colonization in Oregon, it might be interesting to reflect on the fact that at the very time Hall Jackson Kelley was whipping up attention with his *Geographical Sketch* and schemes for the colonization of Oregon, Edward Gibbon Wakefield (a man at least as obsessed, capricious, vain, and difficult as Kelley) was avidly promoting his National Colonization Society in London. Suppose that in his search for a distant place to try out his theories Wakefield had fixed his eye on the northwest coast of North America instead of the southern coasts of Australasia—and suppose the Evangelicals in England had done the same. The idea is not wildly implausible. While Kelley was trying to organize his Oregon expedition, Wakefield and associates had formed the South Australian Association; and just as Nathaniel Wyeth was reluctantly allowing Jason Lee and his fellow Methodists to tag along, George Fife Angas was paving the way for Wesleyans and other dissenters to stamp their imprint on the only nonpenal colony in Australia. The pertinent point is that overseas emigration, the results of recent colonizations, and how to improve on them were lively topics in England all through the 1830s. Wakefield's theories were controversial and, insofar as they were tested, not wholly practical; nevertheless he had a major influence on several successful undertakings. If we are going to refer to "the finger of history" we might think about the one that pointed him first to Australia and New Zealand rather than to North America (to which he in fact did come, to the Canadas as an associate of Lord Durham, for whom he composed the appendix on Crown Lands and Emigration for the famous report).

The purpose of this digression from what did happen is to help us guard against simple assumptions that colonization had become a peculiarly American talent and American expansion inevitable and irresistible. Ultimately it seems most reasonable, perhaps, simply to conclude that the United States gained a major geopolitical victory because Oregon became a more important issue in its national politics and it gave the impression that it was willing to risk more in support of its demands than was the case with Great Britain.

The boundary settlement produced no immediate American expansion or British withdrawal. The Hudson's Bay Company's properties and operations were ostensibly protected by the treaty, and American emigrants continued to choose the Willamette Valley. Two dramatic events, however, one within the region and one nearby, impelled important changes. The first was the massacre at the Whitman mission in the Walla Walla Valley in late 1847. An explosion from long-smoldering grievances, it was not an uncommon type of event in American history. The Oregon Trail led directly across the territory of the Cayuse Indians; tensions grew with the annually increasing traffic and erupted in the aftermath of scarlet fever and measles epidemics that devastated the Cayuse; the retaliation was directed at the missionary who had ministered as a physician to Indians and Whites alike for many years. There were important repercussions: Indian-White relations were endangered throughout the interior country, the Protestant mission system was dissolved, American army units were sent to Fort Vancouver and The Dalles, and the Hudson's Bay Company diverted its interior brigades away from the Columbia Plain to the lower Fraser.

The California Gold Rush reverberated around the world, and its impact upon adjacent Oregon was immediate. Large numbers left the Willamette for the gold-fields, and most of the overland emigrants from the East now diverged toward the Sacramento Valley. But the impact was not all negative. More than fifty vessels came up the Columbia in 1849 seeking Oregon produce for this sudden new market. The Donation Land Act of 1850 provided unusually liberal allotments (640 acres to a husband and wife), and a good many among the now much larger numbers of American emigrants decided that an Oregon farm was a better way to wealth than the frenzied scramble in Sierra Nevada streambeds. The census of 1850 recorded nearly 12,000 persons (excluding Indians) in the Territory of Oregon (created in 1849). Oregon City, the capital and milling center at the falls, and Portland, the largest among several rival ports, had become thriving intermediaries between the Willamette Valley and Pacific commerce.

North of the Columbia, activity was less intense and less focused. Fort Vancouver was included within a U.S. military reserve; squatters encroached on the Hudson's Bay Company's various lands; American customs stations, Indian agents, and territorial officials impinged on the company's operations; and the company held on south of the border only in the hope of some reasonable liquidation of its assets (a process that took more than twenty years). A sprinkling of land claims were filed along the road leading north to Puget Sound, but it was not very attractive country to farmer-colonists. The main lure of this newly acquired area was the towering forests rising above deepwater anchorages on Puget Sound. California provided a market, Yankee ships a link with New England lumbermen, and in the early 1850s a scattering of sawmill hamlets—Port Townsend, Port Gamble, Port Madison, Seattle, Bellingham Bay—began to appear. In 1853 the Territory of Washington was created, with its capital at Olympia, the customs station at the head of Puget Sound and terminus of the Cowlitz corridor road from the Columbia River. The original petition from local settlers had called for a Territory of Columbia, embracing all the area north and west of that river. Congress, playing its own geopolitical games, decided to extend the lower Columbia line eastward along the Forty-sixth parallel to provide an approximate halving of Oregon and, to avoid confusion with the District of Columbia, decided to call it Washington instead. The territorial census of 1853 recorded just under 4,000 residents.

North of the new international boundary, the British government decided that a colony of British subjects should be established on Vancouver Island to help deter "the encroaching spirit of the U.S.," but the political climate of the day warned that it must be done without cost to the taxpayer, and so the Hudson's Bay Company was again pressured to undertake the task. Accordingly, the colony of Vancouver Island was formalized with a governor seated at Fort Victoria, but after the first year the governor and the chief factor were the same man; and because the company wished to forestall any really substantial colonization, the results were meager. A considerable portion of the people shipped in, and especially the miners sent to work the Nanaimo coalfield, deserted to California. By 1855 a semblance of a settlement in a small block of surveyed lands, with roads, mills, schools, and a church, was apparent, but there were only a few hundred settlers. As a colony the formal undertaking anchored on Fort Victoria was as yet less substantial than the informal developments it had been designed to replace in and around Fort Vancouver.

ASSINIBOIA

Tensions among the Hudson's Bay Company, the British government, and settlers arising from uneasiness over American pressures along the international boundary were not confined to the Northwest Coast. In the Red River Basin, American traders became much more aggressive in luring trade from Assiniboia to markets south of the border. By the early 1840s rival American and Hudson's Bay Company posts were spaced along the boundary from Grand Portage to Turtle Mountain. Pembina, the old métis cluster on Red River just south of the line, was the main focus of tensions (fig. 14). The Hudson's Bay Company attempted to enforce its monopoly over all fur trade within its territories, but American traders paid two to four times the price for furs and robes and the métis had no strong allegiance to the company. As hunters, traders, and settlers, they were indifferent to invisible boundaries drawn across the uniformities of nature, and they were very difficult to police. In 1843 the first in what soon became a rapidly expanding line of Red River carts carried a load of furs and robes from Pembina to Mendota, a hamlet in the shadow of Fort Snelling, the American military post on the upper Mississippi. A loose cluster of settlements had grown up here around the mouth of the Minnesota River and the Falls of St. Anthony in the Big Woods (mixed hardwood forest) just beyond the edge of the prairies. The first settlers here were in fact Selkirk Colony refugees: métis, and Swiss and other soldier-colonists who had left during various

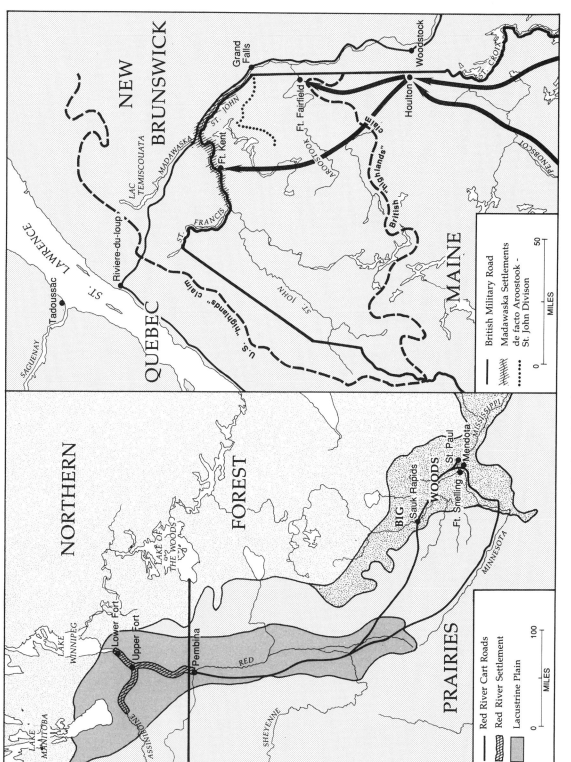

14. Borderlands: Red River and Madawaska.

difficulties in the colony. Together with the American Fur Company personnel (many of whom were Scots or French of Canadian origins) such people made this connection a natural social and commercial link without strongly conscious political implications. In 1844 the Hudson's Bay Company attempted to stamp out this illegal diversion, and as tensions with the United States over Oregon and other issues flared, three companies of British soldiers were sent to Assiniboia by way of York Factory and gave tacit military support to the company's house searches, seizures, and other efforts to suppress smuggling (the company even tried to insist on inspecting all mail). When the international situation eased, these soldiers were withdrawn, and a year later a body of armed métis so directly intimidated the local court in the trial of a convicted smuggler that no punishment was exacted. From this point on the company gave up its enforcement campaign, and this de facto end of its trading monopoly in Assiniboia was recognized and celebrated on both sides of the border.

At midcentury the geopolitical future of Assiniboia was quite uncertain and attracting a variety of interests. It was a considerably more substantial colony with an obviously greater potential than had been apparent in its Selkirk days. More than 5,000 settlers were aligned in their narrow lots along the Red River all the way to the border and along the Assiniboine to Portage la Prairie (edging there into higher, drier soils that were proving good for grain). It was still very remote and facilities were limited, but there were mills (including several windmills) and an agricultural improvement society, a public library, and more schools and churches (the Roman Catholics and the Anglicans each had a cathedral here serving an extensive diocese), and there was a nucleus of educated leaders among the Scots, English, French Canadians, and métis who were beginning to look beyond the fading paternalism of the Hudson's Bay Company toward some other political arrangement. One possibility was the creation of a British Crown Colony, as had just been done for Vancouver Island, maintaining the Red River–Hudson Bay–London link as a direct governmental, rather than a company, tie. However, despite the continuance of that old commercial orientation, by the 1850s much the most flourishing link was south to St. Paul. Every year now several hundred Red River carts screeched across the plains to that booming town below the falls (declared by a British visitor to be "the best specimen to be found in the States of a town still in its infancy with a great future before it"), where the steamboats came upriver from Prairie du Chien, Dubuque, or Galena serving the settlers surging up the Mississippi in the wake of the withdrawal of the Sioux from the Big Woods and adjacent prairies of the new Territory of Minnesota (1849). Mail, machinery, and all manner of goods could be brought to Pembina and Assiniboia far more efficiently than by the laborious old waterways of the northern woods, and the facilities were being extended and improved every year. Railroads were reaching west from Chicago, steamboats began coming all the way up from St. Louis, and a stage line connected St. Paul to Sauk Rapids. In 1855 George Simpson reluctantly reported to the governor and committee that the New York–St. Paul route would now prove far superior to York Factory for the Venerable Company itself even though it risked the interception of the fur business by the American metropolis. And the booming sales at the Sauk Rapids land office were portentous for a vast region. The Territory of Wisconsin, created in 1836 and admitted as a state twelve years later, now had more than 300,000 citizens, and the geopolitical implications of that wave spreading into Minnesota became a matter of intense speculation on both sides of the international line.

Farther east a number of other nagging boundary disputes, all arising from the inaccurate maps and inexact language of the 1783 treaty were finally settled in the Webster-Ashburton Treaty of 1842. The easiest to resolve was the line between Lake Superior and Rainy Lake. Boundary commissioners sent by the two powers to establish this line in the 1820s could not agree on where to begin and responded by making extravagant territorial claims, but these were so obviously askew from the treaty makers' intent that once the diplomatic climate was right for an amicable resolution there was little difficulty in finding one. The boundary river and por-tages on either side were declared open to users from either country.

In the far northeast, matters were much more complicated and controversial. The territorial issues involved Fort Montgomery, an American fortress at Rouses Point, which, because of an early surveying error, was found to be on British soil; a minor dispute over the uppermost sources of the Connecticut River; and a major conflict over the northern boundaries of Maine.

MADAWASKA

The treaty of 1783 clearly intended to divide the Republic and British North America along the border between New England and Nova Scotia, but no exact separation had ever been unequivocally established during a century and a half of European presence in the area. In the late 1820s, having failed between themselves to find a solution, the contending parties submitted the case to William I of the Netherlands for arbitration. The king decided that the documents relating to the original treaty were so inconclusive that a compromise partition was the only feasible solution, but the United States (under pressure from Maine) claimed that the king had thereby exceeded his assignment and refused to accept his award. The geographic features most pertinent to the dispute were the Aroostook and the upper St. John river basins, containing excellent timber and some potential farm-land; the St. John–Témiscouata–St. Lawrence route connecting the British At-lantic colonies with Quebec City and the Canadas; and the Madawaska settle-ments, a strip of French settlers extending along the St. John for sixty miles above

Grand Falls (see fig. 14), a colony originating in the great expulsion of 1755, when some Acadian families found refuge here among the Malecite Indians (they were later joined by some from Canada, but the leaders would always assert their Acadian ancestry). There were no British or American settlers in these areas before the 1820s, but then a few squatters and timber cutters drifted in, and the dispute was suddenly intensified in 1831 when the State of Maine sent agents to organize Madawaska as a town, causing a clash with New Brunswick authorities, who had heretofore provided some minimal oversight. A few years later Maine pushed a road northward into the Aroostook Valley, and Americans began to compete for resources and jurisdiction with the British. Maine militia built a blockhouse on the lower Aroostook in 1839, and British troops were stationed at several points along the St. John River and Lake Témiscouata; no overt clash occurred, and for the next several years there was a de facto partition of the disputed area: the Americans holding the Aroostook Valley, the British the upper St. John. One modification of the latter was important, however, for Maine agents also built a blockhouse at the mouth of the Fish River in the upper reaches of the Madawaska settlement and reasserted the town government and United States claim. The British made no formal effort to expel this American foothold in the midst of what had been an exclusively British colonial area.

When Daniel Webster and Lord Ashburton undertook their determined diplomatic effort to settle these boundary problems, military matters were prominent in their minds. Reverberations from the Canada rebellions still echoed, and a number of other problems extraneous to this boundary had exacerbated relations between the two countries. For the United States a major need was to rectify, by minor boundary adjustment, the embarrassing situation of Fort Montgomery, the million-dollar bastion guarding the Champlain corridor. For the British it was imperative to have a winter road between the St. Lawrence Valley and the Atlantic, as the instructions to Ashburton (written under the guidance of the duke of Wellington) emphasized: "The most indispensable condition for the security of our North American Possessions is to be found in a direct and constant communication between Quebec and the Sea at the Port of Halifax." Reciprocal accommodation of these military needs posed no difficulty for the principal negotiators, and they were prepared to find an acceptable partition without getting hung up on the ambiguities of the 1783 treaty. But Webster's actions were severely complicated by the participation of representatives from the states of Maine (especially) and Massachusetts (which had reserved a half interest in Maine's public lands when it released the area for statehood), who, as might be expected, resisted giving up any territory. The territorial dispute was soon narrowed to the Madawaska settlement. It appeared that the United States would agree to the St. John River as a boundary (and would indemnify Maine and Massachusetts for loss of timberlands); but the

Madawaskans had petitioned Queen Victoria not to hand them over to the Republic, and Ashburton argued against sundering a community (although the king of the Netherlands had done so) and proposed a geometric line just to the south. But ultimately the British desire for an end to the problem and a general diplomatic accord with the United States overwhelmed any concern for the people most directly and severely affected, and the Madawaska colony was cut in two, leaving about 4,000 Acadians on the New Brunswick side and perhaps 1,000 or so in the state of Maine. We may note that the St. John River became a boundary *only* where it cut through this settlement; on the west the disputed territory was partitioned along an arbitrary geometric line drawn through uninhabited country between Maine and Quebec (that this line was drawn east of the actual watershed, and therefore farther from the St. Lawrence, was considered to be a concession by the United States and a strategic gain for Great Britain). There was of course nothing unusual in the relative unimportance of existing communities to the geopolitical decisions of diplomats in distant capitals, but a special factor may have been involved in this case. American spokesmen repeatedly argued that these Acadians were not relevant to any British legal claim because they were "fugitives," "neutrals," "a distinct race, a people by themselves," and did not constitute a truly British presence. Aside from its legal connotations, such characterizations were not incongruous with the attitude of a good many British officials in New Brunswick and Nova Scotia toward the intractable, unassimilable French in their charge.

CANADA

For Canada the issue was not the specific location of the boundary but its larger meaning for life in North America. Any serious dispute between Great Britain and the United States must reverberate upon the Canadas, the great hostage. Maine and Oregon came in succession after the rebellions of 1837, and each generated loud talk south of the border about driving monarchical Britain from the continent and creating the greater North American republic that nature had intended it to have. The usual journalistic and congressional bombast need not be a cause for alarm, but occasionally things got rather more specific and ominous, as in a series of articles in the *National Intelligencer* in 1845 by Matthew Fontaine Maury, a U.S. naval officer and frequent writer on strategic affairs. He decried the Ontario peninsula of Upper Canada as a "dangerous . . . thrusting of foreign territory beyond the safe and natural limits of national boundaries," and declared its annexation to be far more important militarily than that of Texas. The British press and government, misjudging Maury's significance, protested this "lust of the United States Government and people to appropriate the territory of their neighbors"—Texas had been annexed and U.S. armies were ready to march into Mexico—and gave renewed attention to the defense of Canada (undertaking, among other things, a set of martello towers to guard the naval approaches to Kingston).

But these military tensions quickly eased after the Oregon treaty and the chronic problem of economic competition with the United States returned to the fore. Heavy government investment in canals and channel improvements during 1845–48 made the St. Lawrence a superior waterway (nine-foot minimum depth, steam-powered propeller vessels) to the Erie Canal, yet the power of New York and the diversity of American facilities continued to draw much trade from the most productive districts of Canada West. In the late 1840s the Laurentian commercial system suffered a severe depression, and the coincidence of this stress with a set of major political changes ignited an explosion in the capital of that system, Montreal. The British repeal of the Corn Laws, ending Canadian preference in the British market, seemed a body blow to the colonial economy; and the installation of responsible government (essentially "home rule") appeared to fix the French majority in power in Canada East (Quebec). When Parliament and the governor-general approved into law the Rebellion Losses Bill (referring to the events of 1837 in both Canadas), an issue of deep emotional symbolism (those opposed saw it as a payment to traitors), there was an angry, ugly outburst in Montreal. A mob stormed the Parliament building, harried the members out, and burned it and the homes of several leading politicians to the ground (the capital, never fixed in place, was moved to Toronto). A few months later, in October 1849, an impressive body of Montreal citizens issued "An Address to the People of Canada," calling for "A FRIENDLY AND PEACEFUL SEPARATION FROM BRITISH CONNECTION, AND A UNION UPON EQUITABLE TERMS WITH THE GREAT NORTH AMERICAN CONFEDERACY OF SOVEREIGN STATES." The document rehearsed a lengthy set of grievances and alternative remedies before concluding that union with the United States was the only feasible solution. But it was a rocket that faded as suddenly as it had flared. It ran into an almost solid wall of "ingrained resistance to the United States," continued pride in the British connection, and in Canada East majority satisfaction with the newly won French dominance of local affairs. Furthermore, there was little evidence that the United States would welcome such a move. The New York and Vermont legislatures passed resolutions endorsing the idea (noting, correctly, that the original Articles of Confederation had provided for the admission of Canada to the Union), but the federal government maintained a strict neutrality, and Canadian annexation did not become a lively issue in a United States so deeply preoccupied in 1850 with the problems of holding the existing federation together.

The Montreal manifesto was a very narrowly based economic protest, a cry of despair from the small but hitherto powerful body of English merchants who felt themselves abandoned by London and suddenly imprisoned in an antithetical French state (a few radical French anticlerics also signed the manifesto). Within a year an economic recovery was underway and many signators regretted their rash act; within four years a reciprocity treaty with the United States appeared to provide the integration of continental economies that had been the essential goal of the annexationists, allowing Canadian access to the huge American market, American access to Canadian fisheries, and opening the St. Lawrence, Canadian canals, and Lake Michigan to vessels of both nations. Nevertheless, this brief localized event was symptomatic of deeper unresolved matters. The emergence of responsible government had put Canada United into a new context but done nothing directly to resolve the deadlock of government. The French-English issue remained paramount. There was no sign whatever that the French were being assimilated as Lord Durham had designed; indeed, the only workable government was, in effect, a double premiership and cabinet (and agreement that the capital would alternate every four years between English Toronto and French Quebec, bypassing bicultural but disgraced Montreal). But the political philosophies of the two peoples were at odds on many basic issues (especially religion and education); Canada West, having surpassed its French partner in population, was increasingly unhappy with equal representation of the two parts, and the pressure to find some alternative to this awkward geopolitical union was mounting.

By midcentury, therefore, the official boundary between the United States and British North America had been defined with new precision all the way across the continent. And so it stands today (there would be a few minor squabbles over local demarcations)—and so the boundary as a basic topic disappears from our histories after the events of 1846. But at that time there could be little that was conclusive about that line. Any study of the map and reflection on the past must give rise to important questions. How *permanent* would it be?—on a continent as yet not half occupied by aggressively expanding and competitive peoples. How *permeable* might it continue to be?—along half its span, local peoples (métis, Chippewa, Sioux, Blackfeet, Kootenay, Okanogan, Coastal Salish) were unaware of or simply paid no attention to it. And what, in any longer view, would it *separate?*—at the moment the political patchworks on either side, the shaky federation of states on the south and the awkwardly combined Canadas on the north, were nearing geopolitical crisis. And would it continue to be a boundary between *two sovereignties?*—if a fully transcontinental United States was beginning to be generally regarded as feasible (railroads were the decisive factor), few persons were even thinking about creating a single geopolitical entity in place of the distant and disparate pieces of British America. And what would a political boundary between *two vast English-speaking societies* mean?—spokesmen on both sides of the line foretold an inevitable convergence and eventual unification of an Anglo-Saxon North America—and this despite the fact that the one solid *nation* of North America was French Quebec.

However subsequent history might answer these questions, our perspective is grounded on a simple geographical principle: a boundary line creates a border zone that becomes an important fact of life, day by day, for all who live within it. Even though the line remains unchanged, we shall need to pay attention to changes within that zone, to see how all these many peoples and polities respond to that line and, in the larger view, to get some sense of what it means for them to share a continent.

7. Annexation and Conquest: Texas and the Hispanic Borderlands

Just five years after the Adams-Onís Treaty had defined a boundary all the way from the Gulf of Mexico to the Pacific Ocean, the United States of America found itself facing a new geopolitical entity along the entire length of that line, a state modeled to some degree in name and concept on itself: the United States of Mexico. There ensued a new era in American international relations and in the contact and confrontation of Anglo-Americans and Hispanic-Americans in several regions. When the first phase of that era ended thirty years later, the boundary line and the political relations between them had undergone drastic changes.

At the outset these two republics were very nearly identical in size: the United States of America c. 1.8 million square miles (not including any territorial claims on the Pacific Slope), Mexico 1.7 million square miles; and they were not grossly unequal in population: the United States 9.6 million (1820 census), Mexico c. 6.2–6.5 million (various estimates). Such comparisons underscore how immense were the changes of the next thirty years. By annexation, conquest, and purchase the United States of America took over one million square miles of Mexican territory (and made serious attempts to obtain considerably more). Such an enormous addition to the one state (larger than the Louisiana Purchase) and subtraction from the other (more than half of its national area) must have profound effects upon their relative positions and potentials on the continent. And even though the area transferred contained but a very small proportion of Mexico's population, the marked differences in demographic growth over those thirty years had given the United States three times the population (more than 23 million in 1850) of Mexico (estimated 7.5–8 million). Clearly there had been an enormous shift in the balance of forces in North America.

Contrary to common American assumptions, these vast Mexican cessions were not simply the logical, inevitable result of American vitality and "manifest destiny" (the term first appeared during this time). However unequal the expansive power of the two states might be, historian specialists working their way through the labyrinth of domestic and international politics of the several states involved (including Britain, France, and Spain) have revealed how uncertain and contingent it all was at every stage. We must avoid getting lost in that maze, but in order to understand such immense geopolitical changes we do need to know something of the geographical character of the two states in collision, of the specific areas and types of areas in contention, and of the wide variety of territorial issues under consideration at various times. Having already sketched the American reach westward and something of the character of its frontiers, we now give special attention to the geopolitical character of the United States of Mexico, a topic all the more important because of its general neglect in American accounts of the tempestuous events relating to these momentous changes. (To avoid confusion, when used alone, "United States" will always refer to the United States of America.)

MEXICO

The United States of Mexico was successor to the main body of the great imperial realm of New Spain (which had also included the captaincies-general of Guatemala and Havana). In simplest geographical terms it consisted of a densely populated core region amidst the rugged volcanic plateau of central Mexico and extensive but much more thinly populated areas to the south and east and far to the north and northwest. The new state remained anchored on the famous old capital city in the Valley of Mexico (or Anáhuac, land of the Nahuatl—older Indian names for localities and territories found favor in the self-conscious new state). This area was one in the set of richly productive high-lying basins that extended laterally across the narrowing body of the continent from the steep escarpment on the east, where the snow-capped cones of Orizaba and Cofre de Perote towered over the narrow (and seasonally pestilential) lowland at Veracruz, westward through the old Aztec and Tarascan countries into Jalisco, where the strong regional capital, Guadalajara, stood poised at the junction of roads leading across the mountain edge to the rugged Pacific shore. Well over half the population was concentrated in this ancient heartland where the distinctive Mexican civilization had been forged in all its rich human diversity over the three centuries since Cortes. On the south and east the state extended through the heavily Indian country of Oaxaca and Tabasco on either side of the Sierra Madre and on beyond the narrow waist of Tehuantepec into the ancient Mayan lands along the Guatemala border, a boundary that was for a time uncertain and disputed and for a much longer time quite unmarked over most of its extent across the rugged mountains of Chiapas and the jungly scrub of the wide, water-scarce limestone platform of Yucatán.

Northward from the core the pattern was like a great fan, with thin lines of sporadic settlement stretching a thousand miles or more through the dry basins or along arid coastlands between the diverging mountain ribs of the broadening continent. The oldest of these extensions was along the Pacific Coast, where the

Spaniards had followed the Indian route through a sequence of small lateral tropical lowlands to the Culiacán (northwestern limit of native high culture) and Rio Yaqui (region of a major "barbarian" tribe), thence turning inland away from the severe desert coast of Sonora along a line of frontier missions, ranches, and presidios to Tubac and Tucson on the upper waters of the Gila. The old Jesuit missionary system strung along the arid peninsula of Baja California was an early branching across the narrow Sea of Cortes (Gulf of California) of this northwestern movement, from which the more famous Franciscan chain along the coast of Alta California to San Francisco Bay was a late eighteenth-century extension.

Much more important to New Spain, and in time to the newly independent Mexico, was the thrust directly north from Jalisco wherein the Spanish, in "one of the greatest break-throughs of New World history," had founded a series of big mining camps within the Gran Chichimeca (the lands of the "barbarian" nomadic tribes), such as Zacatecas, San Luis Potosí, Durango, and Santa Barbara, and in 1598 had reached far beyond these to impose their rule upon the Pueblo Indians in the hopefully named (but lamentably poor) *Nuevo* Mexico on the upper Rio Grande del Norte. A third line of outreach diverged to the north and east from San Luis Potosí to Saltillo and Monterrey, from where a short branch led to the lower Rio Grande and a long, tenuous line to San Antonio de Bexar and on to the frontier outpost of Nacogdoches deep in the piney woods of east Texas (fig. 15).

An important feature of this geographical pattern was the almost complete lack of lateral connections between these diverging northerly extensions. The initial land route across the severe desert—the real American Sahara—between Sonora and Alta California was soon severed by the belligerence of the Yuma Indians along the lower Colorado River and never restored. The Californias were in effect overseas provinces served by occasional ships from San Blas (as, on the southeast, was Yucatán, connected only across the sea to Veracruz); *californios* often referred to Mexico as "la otra banda"—the other shore. Missionaries had penetrated the barrancas to make contact with all the peoples of the Sierra Madre Occidental, and an occasional trader might make his tortuous way between the Pacific Slope and Parral or Chihuahua but there was no regular trafficway across that formidable barrier anywhere north of Durango. Similarly on the high northern plateaus, there were only a few trails across the broad bolsons between Durango and Parral on the west and Saltillo and Monterrey in the Sierra Madre Oriental. There were no direct links whatever between Texas, New Mexico, Sonora, and Alta California. Each of these was a remote isolated terminus of Hispanic society lodged in the midst of Indian country. The outer edge of that widely spread fan of Mexican sovereignty displayed on the maps of North America was thus an abstract tracing across 2,000 miles of wilderness mostly devoid of Mexican settlements.

As with the United States of America, the sheer extent of the state was a

15. Mexico.

This portion of J. Calvin Smith's "Map of North America" (which was itself an inset on his large "Map of the United States of America, Canada and Texas"), published in 1843, offers one of the most accurate depictions of Mexico of its time, and we can readily add Texas (then independent) to obtain a good idea of the original Mexican federation. Note how "Indian Territory" and the "Great American Desert" seemed to provide a broad buffer zone within the borderlands. (Courtesy of the Library of Congress)

challenge to cohesion. The airline distance from Yucatán to northernmost California was equal to the transcontinental breadth between New England and Oregon. More pertinent was the fact that the distances from the capital at Mexico City to San Antonio, Santa Fe, and Monterey in Alta California approximated, respectively, the distances from St. Louis to Santa Fe, the upper Missouri, and the Willamette Valley. Long treks across broken, barren, and dangerous lands were features common to both countries, although in the 1820s such pathways in Mexico had been longer in use and were better served by regional centers and permanent outposts than analogous routes in the United States. An important contrast with the northern republic as a whole was the almost complete absence of navigable rivers and thus the insulation of Mexico from the impact of the steamboat, which at this very time was revolutionizing transportation on the Ohio, Mississippi, and Missouri systems. Reasonably good roads, though often steep and tortuous along many stretches, connected towns within the central region and these with the one major port of Veracruz, but even here, and everywhere else, the great medium of commerce was the pack train. Couriers and travelers moved on horseback (usually in parties, often with armed escort) and ox-carts hauled the heaviest of goods, but the basic circulation of the nation, the binding of its regions, depended on an enormous system of men and mules and burros plodding the trails marked out by Indians and Spaniards over the centuries. The one important alteration in these old patterns was Mexico's relaxation of restrictions on coastal commerce. Within a few years the new town of Tampico became an important competitor for the trade of San Luis Potosí, Zacatecas, and Durango; Matamoros began to serve Coahuila; and a number of small ports, such as Matagorda and Brazoria, emerged in the wake of the Texas colonizations. On the Pacific coast Mazatlán and Guaymas became official ports, and Mazatlán soon surpassed Acapulco in the diversifying Pacific traffic.

There was also an important shift in external articulations. The fact that Spain did not recognize the independence of Mexico until 1836 complicated and undercut the role of Havana as the great transatlantic way station, and New Orleans emerged as an important focus of Mexican activity. It was a burgeoning commercial center, and its Spanish and French heritage and populations made this cosmopolitan city attractive to Mexicans seeking refuge from the political turmoil in their homeland. Through much of the nineteenth century New Orleans was an important base of leadership, propaganda, and marshaling of resources in the continuing crisis of Mexican politics, the number and variety of exiles fluctuating with the varying fate of contending factions.

The problem of holding so extensive an area together was of course not new; Spain had faced that issue, successfully if not always easily, over a long period of time. But once the imperial hold was broken and the vice-royalty became an independent republic (after the brief Iturbide interlude), the philosophy and strategy of the matter became an open—and fundamental—question. The issue quickly took shape as a contention between "federalists" and "centralists," between those who wanted the member states of this new union to have a relatively high degree of autonomy and those who insisted that a strong authority seated in the national capital was essential to the survival of a united Mexico. Broadly, it was a contention between the more liberal and democratic on the one side and the more conservative and authoritarian on the other, but such simple polarities were blurred and often shattered by intense factionalism generated by personalities, specific policies, and opportunities. The constitution of 1824 was a relatively liberal instrument that endorsed the ideals of regional autonomy and recognized nineteen founding states of the republic, but whereas regionalism was an old if uneven fact of life rooted in the human geography of so large and diverse a land, republican federalism was a new and foreign concept. The imperial experience had provided no effective preparation; Spain itself was only now in the earliest stages of its intermittent trials with liberalism. Thus while the geopolitical structure was composed (more or less) of the old territorial parts, it was not vitalized by politics grounded in the creative experience of colonial assemblies. As José Mora, a leading liberal of the time, summed it up: in the United States of America "everything was done before separation from the mother country" whereas in Mexico "everything remained to be done." Furthermore, the disintegration of empire, the process of obtaining independence, was critically different in the two cases. The Spanish Empire came apart at the seams more from a loss of power at the center than from an upwelling of revolts in the periphery. The subordination of Spain to French rule and blockade of the continent by British forces had made it impossible for Spain to assert force upon its overseas domains. After 1821 the Spanish army held only a small fortress at Veracruz and gave up that toehold four years later. Although independence did not come to Mexico simply by default, it required nothing like the desperate concerted effort by rebel forces from nearly every part of the colonial area, as in the British North American case (the Hildago revolt of 1810 and other tremors that threatened to engulf the whole country in racial and class war had been ruthlessly suppressed by essentially Mexican forces). Having not really forged a nation in the crucible of revolutionary struggle, leaders of the new Republic of Mexico found it difficult to bolt the many parts together by political engineering. In the deadly contests for power, personal loyalties to strong local leaders tended to outweigh devotion to new abstract principles.

Fundamentally, Mexico was more a nation than a federation, but in this, too, there were difficulties. The Spanish impress had been comprehensive in extent but varied greatly in depth and character. The great diversity of peoples was routinely generalized into four main groups: Indians (those who were still firmly of Indian tongue and Indian ways), mestizos (*castas*), creoles (*criollos*—American-born *blancos*), and Spaniards (*gachupín*—European-born *blancos*). National leaders might urge and national documents declare the abolition of these as categories of people and determinants of status, but they perforce continued to have powerful

meaning in daily life. Large areas, some densely occupied, displayed the old imperial pattern of a small White minority dominating a large Indian majority (as in
Yucatán), but insofar as these broad groupings of peoples were concerned the main
political struggles of the early republic arose more from long-festering antagonisms
between the two categories of Whites. The *gachupín* constituted a tiny portion of
the population but had a powerful role in the Mexican economy and society. The
refusal of Spain to recognize the fact of Mexican independence intensified resentments against this group. Widely presumed to be royalists, they came under much
harassment and two formal decrees of expulsion. By 1830 probably most had
departed—and thereby had removed a good deal of leadership and wealth from
many institutions (especially the church, judiciary, and army) and important
portions of the national economy (especially commerce and manufacturing)—but
the purging of such "loyalists" was no cure for more basic problems of nation-
building.

Yet it must be emphasized that Mexico had the basic essentials for nationhood.
Its many factions might disagree bitterly, bloodily, over the control and direction of
the body politic yet never falter in their pride in and allegiance to Mexico as a great
state grounded in a rich and distinctive heritage. Such feelings may indicate no
more than an elemental, skeletal nationalism, but the process of self-examination
and deeper formulation leading toward broader social mobilization was underway.
It would be a long, diffuse, and uncertain process, as it is in most nations—
including the United States of America. (It is interesting to note that the Mexican
author of the first comprehensive description of the United States to appear after
Mexican independence emphasized that the North American republic had "no
absolutely national character" because it was deeply divided into three disparate
regions [characterized by New England, Pennsylvania, and Virginia] and in those
divisions lay "the germ of the future dissolution of the United States.") One
fundamental step in national self-consciousness had already been taken through
the help of Alexander von Humboldt. For nationalism requires a geopolitical as
well as historical and cultural vision, and the great geographer's renowned work on
New Spain proved richly appropriate to the need. As Henry C. Schmidt states,
"Humboldt's book changed the concept of Mexico. . . . Insofar as he posited
Mexico as an autonomous historical entity at the same time removing it from its
Spanish context and opening it to the wider western world, Humboldt laid the
conceptual basis for national identity that would be elaborated by intellectuals well
into the twentieth century." This fact of a deeply grounded even if as yet vaguely
formulated Mexican nationalism must be kept clearly in mind as we consider this
new state's relations with the older republic to the north. It is all the more important that we do so because it was a fact not at all clearly understood by most
American statesmen and spokesmen of those times, who apparently had no sense

of the affront they gave by assuming that this new republic would be willing to sell large parts of its territorial heritage for cash. While the brand new state was trying to shape an internal political design, the first American envoy arrived with instructions to try to renegotiate the Sabine boundary—in effect to buy Texas (there were as yet no Anglo-American colonies in that area). David Weber notes that in 1825, Secretary of State Henry Clay "carried Yankee ingenuity to its extreme by suggesting that United States acquisition of Mexico's entire northern frontier would benefit Mexico by placing her capital in a more central location" (one wonders if the Mexicans in response asked for the return of Louisiana as an analogous benefit they might confer on the United States). With that kind of geopolitical impudence from its expansive neighbor no Mexican administration could be unconcerned about its northern regions.

FRONTIER PROVINCES

That concern was, all the while, a double one: how to bind those several distant and different parts to the main body of the nation, and how to secure that whole vast perimeter against external dangers. The history of Texas, the only direct border zone between the two republics at the outset, well illustrates the general issues and responses to them. As noted, the problem of Texas had been recognized by the Spanish years before: the need to increase its population, assimilate its people, administer it efficiently, and guard it securely. The new Mexican state was well aware of this inheritance, and the first report of its Commission on Foreign Relations minced no words about the dangers: "If we do not take the present opportunity to people Texas, day by day the strength of the United States will grow until it will annex Texas, Coahuila, Saltillo, and Nuevo León like the Goths, Visigoths, and the other tribes that assailed the Roman Empire." A major program of colonization was undertaken, and in 1828 a scientific expedition was sent to assess the geographical qualities of the area (fig. 16). Until a sizable body of reliable citizens could be formed it was decided to keep this frontier territory bound to Coahuila. To promote public order and national security new garrisons were established at key points along the coast and main road. From time to time such policies were reviewed and revised to fit changing circumstances.

But as we also know, after little more than ten years the results contradicted the intent. The general rationale was plausible but the performance inadequate. Much the most important body of colonists was Anglo-American (and not Hispanic- or Franco-Louisianan, as some officials had hoped); the program for a strong counterimmigration of Mexicans (every state was to supply 5,000 colonists for Texas) was never implemented; various plans to recruit Irish and German Catholics yielded little; the transformation of these immigrants into good Mexican citizens, inherently difficult at best, was defeated by the feebleness of the potential inte-

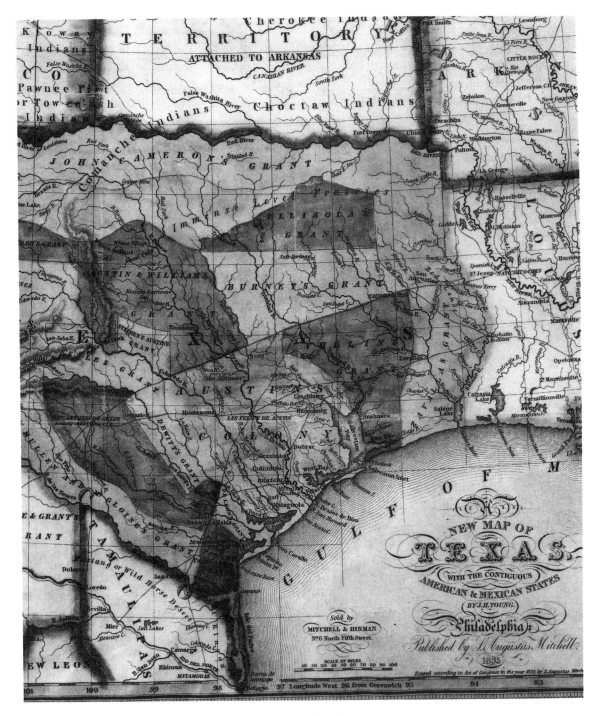

16. Texas, 1835.

J. H. Young's map is an improvement over Stephen F. Austin's version of 1830, on which it is partly based, but both were aimed at American emigrants. The coastal zone and its water entrances are exaggerated; the focus is on Austin's Colony, with the suggestion of San Felipe, Austin's capital town, as a thriving interior crossroads, when in fact it was never more than a ramshackle hamlet. Americans as yet knew little about other parts of this borderland. Note that the boundary of Texas is set firmly on the Nueces, with TAMAULIPAS written boldly across the Rio Grande (Rio del Norte). (Courtesy of the State Historical Society of Wisconsin) grating instruments of state, church, and commerce; the army became so en-meshed in civil wars in the central region as to leave frontier garrisons under-manned and ill-equipped, and these eventually found themselves to be tiny outposts in the midst of hostile territory. Nevertheless, Mexico was not powerless, and the Texan secession was achieved at considerable cost, as the Alamo and Goliad attest. That the Anglo-American triumph came at San Jacinto, deep in the woodlands and coastal prairies of east Texas, attested to the decisive changes those people had already wrought in the human geography of the Mexican borderlands.

California was an interesting variant of the frontier problem. Secularization of the Indian missions, the most substantial settlement system in the province, was ostensibly a move toward national integration. Mexico had declared the civic equality of all peoples, and the avowed objective of the missionary program, here as elsewhere, had always been to create communities of good Catholic citizens. But secularization was an inherently difficult process to manage, and it dominated California politics for years. It was of course resisted by the Franciscans, and the response from Indians was generally not in accord with the stated objectives. Only a few stayed on their small allotments of land, more drifted off to catch on as servants and laborers, many simply disappeared from any Mexican surveillance (some had revolted against the missions earlier); in the late 1830s large numbers died from smallpox. By that time the whole system was a shambles and the church proved unable to minister effectively anywhere in the province (there was no resident bishop in any of these frontier territories, or in many other states, because the Vatican withheld appointments pending Spanish reconquest or at least firm conservative Mexican rule).

Secularization was also designed to loosen the church's hold on lands and make room for colonists. But again, where to find settlers for such a remote frontier? Unlike Texas, there was no adjacent source; California was so detached that small groups of families could not simply make their way there. Because of that it became, to a small extent, Mexico's Australia: a place to send convicts to scratch out a living in punitive isolation. The most substantial colonization effort, the Hijar-Padrés attempt, foundered on opposition from californios, who saw it as a political scheme to compete with them for control of mission lands. Mexican leaders were acutely aware of the dangers of thinly populated frontier territories, but the example of Texas warned against fostering foreign colonies, and unable to effect any substantial domestic program, Mexico left California to grow by natural increase and casual infiltration.

The famous rancho era that blossomed in Mexican California was sustained by the export of hides and tallow, an exchange initiated when English and Yankee traders began to tap the cattle resources of the missions in the early 1820s. This burgeoning commerce, along with whaling, maritime furs, the China trade, and other Pacific ventures, began to give California more effective links with other parts of the world than with Mexico itself. Through such connections and from a straggle of American explorers and mountain men probing the westernmost expanses of the continent, a variety of foreigners came to these remote shores, and some of them stayed, settling in, perhaps marrying into one of the californio families. Even though Mexican development programs had accomplished little, the scale of such infiltrations was not alarming. Until the 1840s no Visigoths seemed to be threatening this far corner.

In all the lands between Texas and California it became increasingly apparent that the major issue was not the building up of colonies to stave off foreign encroachment but the securing of old settled districts against Indian depredations. By the 1830s the nomadic tribes, always a danger, had become "better armed, better mounted, and more successful than ever at defending their lands and striking offensive blows deep into Mexico." The Comanche on the eastern plains and the many bands of Apache in the mountains were raiding deep into Coahuila and Chihuahua, even reaching as far as Zacatecas. This increase in Indian power was closely related to the impact of the Santa Fe Trail upon what had been one of the most isolated regions of the Mexican world. The nomadic Indians had responded as avidly as the Hispanos and Missourians to new commercial opportunities. There were new markets for horses, mules, wool, furs, and hides, and traders were not overly concerned about where and how such goods might have been obtained. Firearms became much more plentiful, and old alliances and interdependencies between Indian tribes and New Mexican officials were undermined. Any affront to an Apache or Comanche leader threatened to open old grievances and unleash new waves of killing and plundering. By the late 1830s the settlement frontier in Sonora had receded as ranches along the San Pedro and Santa Cruz were abandoned and a remnant of mestizos and Christian Indians huddled in the vicinity of Tucson and Tubac. In New Mexico the governor used lavish grants to try to expand colonizations along the northern and eastern margins of the old settlement core as a bulwark against Indian dangers. Such officials were also aware that the American policy of shoving Indians westward would eventually impinge upon them, for as one observed, the Indian nations on the plains were "like balls in a row," wherein an impulse on the first "is passed along until it reaches the last" and "in time we will probably have them on top of us."

The impact of this St. Louis connection had also radiated widely across northern Mexico in more positive economic ways. By the 1830s some Missourians were routinely carrying their goods to Chihuahua and a few ventured much farther south. Droving trails were opened across the Sierra Madre Occidental to Sonora, and westward by way of the San Juan, the canyonlands, and across the Mojave to Los Angeles, to bring mules and horses east to the American market.

And so while Mexico City administrations were arguing the need and searching for ways to bind frontier territories more firmly to the body of the nation, Texas, New Mexico, Chihuahua, Sonora, and Alta California were being enlivened and altered by external connections. Nacogdoches and San Antonio, Santa Fe and Taos, El Paso and Chihuahua, Guaymas and Hermosillo (Pitic), Monterey and the landings around San Francisco Bay were all in some degree cosmopolitan localities whose bilingual merchants and shippers were in many cases more closely bound up with New Orleans or St. Louis, New York, Philadelphia or Boston, London, and the Pacific world of Hawaii and China than with Mexico City. And such commercial connections influenced much else: newspapers, books, and views of the world; fashions, travel, social contacts, and where to send the children off to school. Except in east Texas, it was not a case of foreigners taking over, for they were a small minority and often closely allied through partnerships and marriage with leading Mexican merchants and families. Such ambivalent orientations were therefore not necessarily ominous, but they did represent a divergence and differentiation that pressured toward some real measure of regional autonomy. All of the frontier territories actively sought full statehood within the federal system, and aside from the separation of Sonora from Sinaloa (in 1824 these had been bound together in a new state of Occidente), none of the proposals (separation of Texas from Coahuila; creation of the states of Hidalgo [New Mexico] and Montezuma [Alta California]) were enacted. As it turned out, frustration of such efforts heightened rather than lowered centrifugal pressures.

Mexican federalism reached a crisis in 1834 when Antonio Lopez de Santa Anna's new dictatorship abolished the constitution and declared all states and territories to be mere administrative districts under a rigidly centralist government. This radical act provoked a radical response: an upwelling of revolt against the center in many parts of the country. And such actions in turn provoked civil strife within these regions and severe counterattack from the center. In the later 1830s the Mexican state was foundering on the classic dilemma of federalism.

As their leaders always proclaimed, these revolts were not (with one prominent exception) against Mexico, but only against the subversion of Mexico to arbitrary centralist rule. But the central authority, ever-conscious of the dangers of disintegration, felt that it must respond ruthlessly to any challenge; it must assert the ultimate superiority of power at the center. To the obvious example of the collapse of the Spanish Empire there was added, during these very years, the disintegration of the Central American confederation next door. The United Provinces of Central America (essentially the former Captaincy General of Guatemala) had been one of the successor states, along with Mexico, on the breakup of the Spanish Empire. Did its collapse and the emergence of an independent Guatemala, Honduras, El Salvador, Nicaragua, and Costa Rica represent a next, inevitable, stage in this geopolitical devolution? From our perspectives today the potentials for nationhood must appear very different in the two cases, but Mexican leaders viewing the defection of Zacatecas, Texas, New Mexico, Sonora, California, and Yucatán could have no such confidence. Certainly the kinds of particularisms and philosophical factionalisms that tore the Central American union apart were amply evident in Mexico. And so, as is highly likely in such geopolitical situations, there was a desperate attempt to hold the structure together by force.

Texas was clearly a special case. Only here did "ethnicity" (to use a modern term) gravely compound the issues between center and periphery, between the national core and the outlying provinces (the Mayan revolt in Yucatán was a later example). Only here was permanent secession and annexation to another state an avowed alternative (and here, as elsewhere, the *initial* rebellion was ostensibly directed at restoration of the federal constitution). One logical response to such a situation would have been to recognize that geopolitical fact and seize the advantage of it: to grant independence to the Anglo-American Texans and thereby excise an alien people, an unattractive region, and a dangerous kind of borderland from the body of Mexico. A boundary drawn along the Guadalupe, San Antonio, or Nueces (perhaps preserving San Antonio de Bexar as a frontier station) and extended in any way to the northwest would have separated the two nations by a broad, desolate border zone that could be of little foreseeable interest to colonists or entrepreneurs of the aggressive *norteamericanos*. British diplomats apparently advised Mexican officials to do just that, and President Lamar of the precarious Republic of Texas was willing to pay $5 million in return for a fixed boundary (he would of course have opened negotiations by insisting on the Rio Grande) and formal recognition from Mexico. But nations do not live by logic. Mexican leaders were, understandably, too proud, precarious in office, and fearful of further disintegration to admit defeat and accept such a loss. Texan support for secessionist Yucatán, complicity in other such schemes, and claims to and attempted invasions of New Mexico reinforced Mexican fears and determination to reconquer.

Formal recognition of an independent Republic of Texas by the United States, Great Britain, and France did not entail recognition of its specific territorial claims. These far exceeded its grasp. Texas claimed the Rio Grande as its southern and western boundary and selected a location for its new capital town of Austin as being strategic and symbolic within that frame: at the intersection of the great imperial highways of the future between the gulf ports and Santa Fe and between the Red River and the lower Rio Grande, and on the inland edge of current settlements pointing to the vast frontier beyond the Balcones escarpment. In fact, Texas remained anchored on the bottomlands and coastal prairies of the old Austin Colony and adjacent districts, its traffic focused on Galveston Bay (to which there were repeated efforts to remove the capital). Three attempts to assert Texas power over Santa Fe were ignominious failures; only once was a force dispatched south of the Nueces, and that in retaliation for a Mexican strike at San Antonio and Goliad. Throughout the years of the republic, the country between the Nueces and the Rio Grande remained unsettled and unsecured from either side; maps of the time referred to the "Mustang or Wild Horse Desert," and it was known as a dangerous haunt of Indians, "mustangers," and "prairie pirates."

But even though this huge periphery remained beyond control for the time being, the core of Texas was being strengthened day by day. Land was offered on generous and simple terms, slavery was legalized, and settlers came in from the whole breadth of the American South. Good cottonlands lured planters with their slaves, and the proportion of Blacks to the total population (perhaps one in ten in Mexican Texas) rapidly increased. Northern lawyers and merchants founded and flocked to aspiring ports and towns. The republic's programs to expand and strengthen the settlement frontier gradually took shape in Henri Casto's Alsatian colonies west of San Antonio, the sizable German immigration moving into the hill country from its new base at New Braunfels, and the scattering of Anglo-Americans lured into the large frame of the Peters Colony in the Black Prairies and Cross Timbers in the north. As "expansionism" became a rallying cry in American politics in the 1840s this influx became a surge, with "Texas fever" rivaling "Oregon fever." By 1845 the population was 125,000, an increase of 75,000 in ten years.

All this firming of the Anglo-American hold should have made it clear to any Mexican leader that Texas was irretrievable. But its separate existence was a nagging complication. The refusal of the United States to welcome Texas into the Union in 1837 not only shocked the Texans, it greatly surprised the Mexicans. The United States had been so blatant about its desire for Texas, and so persistent in trying to purchase or pressure Mexico out of it, that complicity of the American government in fostering the Texas secession was assumed. In fact, although the American press and many of the American people were exuberant over the Texan triumph, the government was very circumspect, and historians have concluded that the United States was not directly involved. And the reason for that was obvious enough: Texas was an ominous problem for the United States as well as for Mexico, intensifying as it did the internal struggle over a formidable complex of moral, constitutional, and geopolitical issues that was shaking the federation to its foundations.

Failure to enter the Union put Texas in chronic crisis. Whatever its potential, it had no money, and its uncertain political status and the probability of further warfare made investors wary. Desperate for financial and diplomatic support, Texas turned to Great Britain and found considerable interest in its case. The idea of a buffer state that might deflect American expansion found favor with influential statesmen, and the possibility that a British guarantee of Texas independence might induce Mexican recognition and settlement of boundary issues was earnestly discussed. But any such British intervention was inflammatory to American suspicions of "perfidious Albion" and further fueled by contentions with England over Oregon and California.

Pressures toward a resolution mounted. It appeared that either Texas would be formally and firmly established as an independent state, as some Texan leaders had come to prefer, or it would be annexed to the United States, as most Anglo-American Texans seemed to have assumed. In either case, the political risks, domestic and international, seemed to be high for all involved. In the United States powerful interests lined up on opposite sides. In 1843 John Quincy Adams threatened a Northern secession if Texas were annexed; in the following year John C. Calhoun threatened a Southern secession if it were not. In June 1844 a treaty of annexation, reluctantly endorsed by Sam Houston, was, after long and bitter debate, soundly defeated in the U.S. Senate. Attempts soon thereafter by the United States to open negotiations with Mexico, evidently with the hope of purchasing Texas and part of California, failed. Meanwhile, British support for Texas proved to be less firm than its proponents had hoped. British abolitionists were strongly opposed, British bondholders were impatient with impecunious Mexico, and, as the negotiations over the Maine and Oregon boundaries were demonstrating, these North American disputes were relatively minor matters to a global power and none of them worth the risk of war with the United States. In 1844 James K. Polk campaigned on a platform that called for "re-annexation of Texas" (claiming that the treaty of 1819 was a giveaway) and the "re-occupation of Oregon" (the treaty of 1818 was a backing down), and his victory offered outgoing President Tyler the public endorsement needed to get a simple annexation resolution (interpreted as the admission of a state rather than a treaty with a foreign power) narrowly approved by Congress in March 1845.

It was then Texas's turn, and its new president, Anson Jones, delayed a national decision until he had received a treaty of recognition from Mexico (hastily procured under British pressure). Jones, who favored independence, then submitted both documents to the Texas Congress, which, on July 4, 1845, unanimously approved annexation. On December 29, President Polk signed the act admitting Texas to the United States. The new boundary thereby created between the United States and Mexico was left unspecified to be "adjusted" between the two countries.

An American national interest in California developed more slowly, under quite different circumstances, but eventually became closely linked with the Texas issue. As early as 1818 an American diplomatic agent stopping over en route to Oregon had warned of the feebleness of the Spanish hold on California and of Russian designs on San Francisco Bay, "the most convenient, capacious and safe [harbor] in the world." The Russians soon receded from the scene to be replaced by the British as a worrisome presence. Apparently the first official American move was Andrew Jackson's attempt in 1835 to sound out the possibilities of purchasing the strip of land lying north of 37°N (so as to include San Francisco Bay), or even 36°N (to include Monterey). Nothing came of this overture but the idea remained in the air, and over the next few years Americans were served more and more accounts of California's attractions and importance, its political turmoil and uncertain future. In 1841 Lieutenant Wilkes, as part of his strategic explorations of the Pacific, confirmed the qualities of San Francisco Bay ("one of the most spacious, and at the same time safest ports in the world") and stressed how vulnerable the whole area was: "Although I was prepared for anarchy and confusion, I was surprised when I found a total absence of all government in California, and even its forms and ceremonies thrown aside." Wilkes assumed that the whole thinly populated region would soon be formally detached from Mexico and thought it likely that California would be joined to Oregon to form an independent state that might eventually "control the destinies of the Pacific." Other visitors remarked on the feebleness of the Mexican hold and impending change. George Simpson concluded that "the only doubt is whether California is to fall to the British or the Americans."

This perceived power vacuum (there was in fact *some* government, and between 1836 and 1840 a capable californio governor had instituted various reforms) was the result of conflicts within California as well as within Mexico. Although there were common complaints against Mexican neglect and the poor quality of officials sent to this remote corner of the troubled nation, the secession against Santa Anna's dictatorship had come from Monterey and exacerbated chronic contention between the northern districts and the southern, anchored on Los Angeles. This sectional fight recurrently verged on civil war and sapped what little strength the californios might have mustered against foreign encroachment.

In the 1840s there were worrisome intrusions by land as well as by sea. Unruly gangs of American mountain men began to find the mild valleys beyond the Sierras a seductive winter refuge. In 1841, in response to alluring descriptions by resident Americans, the first overland farmer-emigrant party branched off from the Oregon Trail and headed for the Sacramento instead of the Willamette; more came year by year, getting their wagons across the Sierra Nevada for the first time in 1844; a few came south from Oregon or with caravans from Santa Fe. Many of these immigrants began to form loose clusters of settlement near New Helvetia, the fort-farm-workshop site developed by the defiantly independent Swiss colonist (and Mexican citizen) John Sutter in the midst of his large land grant in the Sacramento Valley. Sutter was happy to profit from the sale of land, supplies, and services to such people, and the river leading from the Sierras to his place became known as Rio de los Americanos (today's American Fork). The traditional hospitality of the californios was sometimes strained but never generally withdrawn from these newcomers. There were mutual advantages, and land and privileges were readily dispensed in return for fees and favors. But a rising influx of American colonists spreading their hold upon large districts apart from Mexican settlements and beyond the control of Mexican officials was enough like Texas to cause the Mexican government to protest to Washington that such foreign settlers were no longer wanted in California.

Of course, the United States government neither could nor wished to control such movements. Its intentions were made clear in 1842, when the American commodore in charge of the Pacific patrol, mistakenly inferring that the United States and Mexico had gone to war over Texas, hurried his two warships from Peru to Monterey, landed unopposed, ran up the American flag, and claimed California for the United States. His apologies and embarrassed withdrawal the next day could hardly cover the fact that he was acting on contingent orders. More complicated and contentious (and still controversial today) were the actions of Captain John C. Frémont, an American officer with influential political connections who conducted three forays into California at the head of various parties of soldiers and irregulars. Just whose orders, if any, he was acting upon remain uncertain, but an intent to foment revolt and ensure the American seizure of California seemed obvious enough, then and now. Frémont's widely read account of California and its attractions based on his first two expeditions helped raise the public consciousness of this Eden. His brazen defiance of Mexican officials and his return (from Oregon) and assumption of leadership over a nervous American group that had proclaimed the independence of California (the ephemeral "Bear Flag Republic") in the summer of 1846 made him a leading participant in the quick American capture of the province at the outset of the American-Mexican War.

Much of the political rationale for such aggressive American actions argued the need to rescue this "waif" from a lurking Britain. As Waddy Thompson, American minister to Mexico in the 1840s, put it, while there might be many uncertainties about the future of California and appropriate American policies, one thing *was* certain: "It will be worth a war of twenty years to prevent England acquiring it." There was no denying a British presence and interest—it had been there longer than that of the Americans—and as the American intentions became more obvious, some californios made overtures for a British protectorate. After an American army had crossed the Rio Grande, the Mexican government, grasping at straws, offered to mortgage California to the British in return for a war loan and protection of the province; they also negotiated with a Jesuit colonizer to bring in 10,000 settlers from famine-stricken Ireland. But the British refused to be drawn into such a provocative position, and Father McNamara gave up when he arrived to confirm his land grant and found the Stars and Stripes flying over Monterey.

James Polk came to the presidency determined to obtain not only Texas and Oregon but a large swath of Mexican territory. In 1845 he sent John Slidell to try to negotiate a comprehensive conclusive settlement with Mexico. The most pressing concern was to establish the boundary between newly annexed Texas and Mexico, but the most important issue, in Polk's mind, was the bay and harbor of San Francisco, for "if these should be turned against our country by the cession of California to Great Britain our principal commercial rival, the consequences would be most disastrous." Slidell was empowered to offer up to $20 million for any boundary directly west from New Mexico that included San Francisco, $5 million more for a more southerly line that would include Monterey, and a further $5 million for New Mexico as well. Mexico refused to receive Slidell and discuss such a drastic dismemberment, and news of this overture set off angry protest demonstrations.

Having failed to obtain his objectives by diplomatic pressure and purchase, Polk set about to obtain them by force. He ordered American troops to advance beyond the Nueces and take up positions on the Rio Grande. When this entry into disputed ground provoked a Mexican countermove and skirmish, it was quickly blown into a full-scale war. Polk declared to Congress and the nation that by sending an army north of the Rio Grande, "Mexico has passed the boundary of the United States, has invaded our territory and shed American blood on American soil. She has proclaimed that hostilities have commenced, and that the two nations are now at war." Although it seemed to a good many Americans, in Congress and elsewhere, that the United States had provoked the battle on ground to which Mexico had some plausible claim, there was no halting the public fervor despite deep misgivings about where all this might lead.

Polk seems to have been quite sure of where he wanted it all to lead: to the acquisition of all those lands he had sought to purchase. David Pletcher, a keen analyst of these events, states that "there was never any question that Polk regarded permanent possession of California as the first goal of the Mexican War." Accordingly, American naval forces and Frémont's irregulars (acting under secret instructions) took over northern California, then moved to occupy the southern districts. Here they ran into resistance and had to be helped by General Stephen Kearny's force coming overland across northern Sonora from New Mexico. Kearny had earlier marched from Fort Leavenworth to the outskirts of New Mexico, where he halted until he had negotiated a surrender of that province. Subsequently, a small force was detached to capture Chihuahua city, and the army on the lower Rio Grande took Monterrey and (after a major battle) Saltillo. Within ten months American armies had seized control of northern Mexico from Matamoros to San Diego and San Francisco. Polk assumed that Mexico would now give way and negotiate an end to the war by ceding its frontier territories in return for a "generous" cash payment. When Mexico refused to make so great a sacrifice of its honor and substance, Polk, fearing an erosion of his political support during any protracted stalemate, determined to strike a decisive blow—"for peace," as he put it—and ordered American forces to invade the heartland and seize Mexico City itself if that proved necessary to force a capitulation.

As this campaign got under way, the president and his cabinet drew up a set of demands and sent a minor diplomat, Nicholas P. Trist, to accompany the army and initiate negotiations as soon as the Mexicans proved ready to talk. When the invaders under General Winfield Scott had fought their way to the outskirts of the capital, discussions began. A draft treaty was prepared but quickly rejected by the Mexican cabinet (it almost certainly would have been rejected by Polk's cabinet as well, for Trist had given way on the touchy matter of the Nueces–Rio Grande issue). Therefore the war was renewed and Scott's capture of the citadel of Chapultepec and occupation of Mexico City brought the negotiators back to the table. After many weeks a new treaty was presented to both governments and, with minor modifications, signed by the two in the suburb of Guadalupe Hidalgo (the Mexicans insisted on a site away from the presence of armed Americans) on February 2, 1848. The U.S. Senate approved the treaty (thirty-four to fourteen) a month later; three months after that an anguished Mexican Congress, recognizing that "the territorial cessions were like an amputation performed to save the patient's life," did the same.

The Treaty of Guadalupe Hidalgo involved a variety of issues between the two parties (land claims, indemnifications, and so on), but geography was the crux of the matter. This war began over disputed territories, the main objectives—of both sides—had always been defined in terms of specific territories, and at each stage of the war as their armies ranged across much of the Mexican nation and their warships blockaded its harbors, American leaders pored over maps to consider how big a bite to take out of their victim. It is difficult to appreciate the immense geographical scope and portent of those discussions. We have lived so long with the results and, as with the Oregon dispute, the outcome has been so commonly represented as the logical, more or less inevitable—even equitable (on the grounds that corrupt, chaotic Mexico did not deserve to rule those lands)—result of American development that it is useful to consider the geography of this great alteration with care.

These territorial decisions of the 1840s were on a scale with those enormous transactions of previous centuries when European diplomats played geopolitical games with continents across the seas. But this was a different era and a different context. No *national* government had ever faced such a range of apparent possibilities for extending its territory and reshaping itself on such a scale (the nearest precedent, Louisiana, was huge in size but presented in one piece for a simple decision: take it or leave it). In a democratic republic it was perforce a prospect that lay before not only the president and his cabinet, but before Congress, an array of special interests, and the American public. We shall confine our examination to those alternatives that received cabinet-level consideration, noting, however, an extreme position, which is simple to state if mind-boggling to ponder: gobbling up the whole of Mexico. As David Pletcher notes, while Trist was negotiating the cession of the northernmost provinces, "a large part of the American public was blundering toward the conviction that the United States must annex all of Mexico." Such an upwelling was so alarming to those Americans opposed that they tried to put the Congress on record (to quote one of many resolutions) "that the present war with Mexico should not be waged or prosecuted 'with a view to conquest,' either by the subjugation or dismemberment of that Republic." Such resolutions were part of the tangle of politics attempting to put a halt to a war that had spread far beyond initial objectives, to prohibit any annexations, to embarrass Polk, to gain party advantage; none were passed. Despite some vociferous supporters in Congress, there was little likelihood that such a vast engorgement could have been approved, and the movement deflated with the arrival of a specific treaty for debate, but such overweening talk was a blatant exhibit of some of the more virulent forces at work in this realignment of geopolitical positions on the continent. Furthermore, a more limited version of such American control in the form of a military protectorate over the whole of Mexico was discussed at the highest levels—and supported by one faction of Mexicans. Such an occupation was necessary, it was argued, to restore political order and commercial relations, to enforce payment of debts and prevent European interventions; it was—we can now see—a rehearsal for an argument that would impel American forces to invade the West Indies and Central America time and again in later decades.

For President Polk and his cabinet the territorial issues were narrowed to a few specifics (fig. 17). One was insistence on United States control of the strip between the Nueces and the Rio Grande. Everyone agreed that the land itself was worthless, but having proclaimed it as American soil, moved troops into it and thereby sparked the war, no victorious government could consider backing down on the matter (hence the anger when Trist, defying instructions, gave it away in that first, stillborn, treaty). Mexico, of course, felt honor-bound in the same way, and had to be battered into submission. As is so often the case, here political emotions were heavily invested in a local territorial issue of little intrinsic geopolitical significance. Beyond such self-justification was the really important territorial matter: San Francisco Bay and a broad Pacific frontage. There was really no argument about the bay. Even anti-expansionists who deplored the "insane thirst" for territory as "the great American disease" might agree that San Francisco would be a

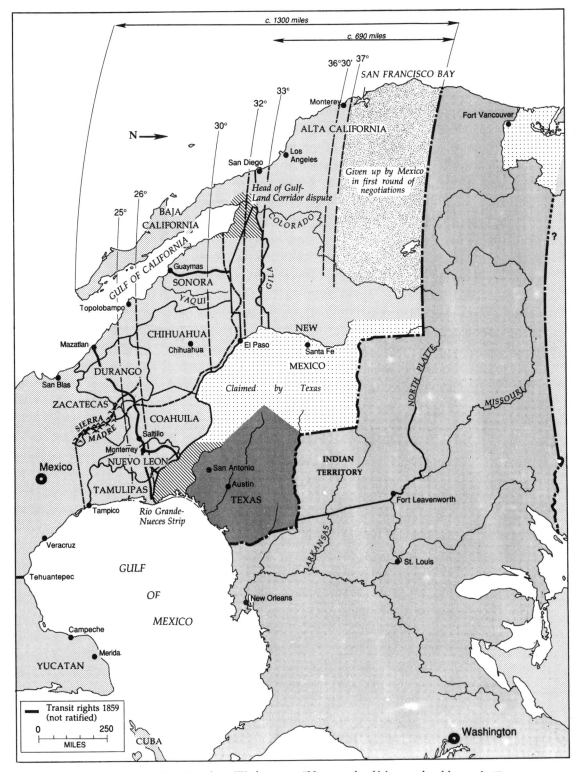

17. The View from Washington: "How much of Mexico should we take?"

valuable addition, and the well-publicized threat of British intervention helped offset any scruples. And the Mexicans saw this—and saw the Americans streaming into the Sacramento Valley—clearly enough to yield it in the first round of negotiations, proposing 37°N as the new boundary. That was far from enough to satisfy most Americans, but how broad a frontage was necessary or desirable and how broad the connecting band of territory across the barely charted desert and mountain wastelands should be generated serious differences among American decision makers.

Geographically these differences were of such magnitude as to make the casual manner in which they were assumed to be feasible alternatives stagger the modern student who reflects on their implications. The Americans were of course acting with that luxury of choice given to a powerful aggressor that has beaten a weak neighbor into submission. Polk and several cabinet members wanted to annex both Californias and all of Mexico north of 26°N—a belt of territory more than a thousand miles wide north to south and embracing four Mexican territories, three states, and parts of four others. Latitude 26°N was chosen as a simple geometric boundary west from the mouth of the Rio Grande (they seem to have ignored the fact that the lower course of the river swings slightly south of that line). There were also strong supporters for even more; such persons argued that for "defensive" purposes the line ought to begin farther south on the Gulf of Mexico (some would include Tampico) and be drawn along the "Sierra Madre" for some distance, thence along 25°N or 26°N to the Pacific. (The common maps of the time, by Disturnell, showed the Sierra Madre *Occidental* as the great spine of Mexico.) Such a boundary would bring into the United States all of Tamaulipas and Nuevo León and parts of San Luis Potosí, Zacatecas, Durango, and Sinaloa (Sam Houston and Jefferson Davis proposed different amendments of this sort in the congressional debates on the final treaty). On the other hand, other members of the cabinet had their minds set firmly on California harbors and argued for a separation along the Rio Grande to the southern boundary of New Mexico and thence westward to the Pacific, thereby annexing only New Mexico and Alta California. For convenience, to avoid disputes over antecedent Mexican boundaries, and to ensure obtaining the Gila Valley and San Diego, this latter line was soon shifted to 32°N. The maps they relied on showed such a line intersecting the head of the Gulf of California, giving the United States access to that sea whether or not the whole peninsula was taken. In the end Polk gave way to this 32°N line as the minimum acceptable, with Baja California as desirable but not essential.

Mexico was not without leverage in these negotiations. It had not surrendered, only joined in a truce; a renewal of fighting was always possible, even likely, as had been proven before. The American expedition to Mexico City had been a risky (and costly) venture; the American presence there was vulnerable; the possibilities for guerrilla activity were almost limitless. Furthermore, the bewildering instability of Mexican governments was a constant threat of delay or repudiation of any agreement, and the American government, acutely aware of the dangerous pressures within its own fragile federation, was eager for an end to this controversial affair.

Although Mexico gave up San Francisco Bay early on, it tried hard to exclude New Mexico. After all, New Mexico had been part of New Spain and Mexico for more than 200 years. Whatever their grievances with Mexico City, argued the foreign minister, these people wished to remain members of "the Mexican family." "Could the government go to sell Mexicans like these as they would a herd of sheep? No!" Mexico offered a boundary of 36°30'N on the Pacific, giving up Monterey, in return for holding New Mexico. But the Americans were adamant, pointing out that Mexico would be relieved of much trouble and expense in having to defend a "remote and detached province . . . which can never be advantageous to her," and assuring that these people would in fact enjoy an unprecedented freedom and prosperity within the bosom of the vigorous northern republic. American officials tried not to mention the uncomfortable fact of these tens of thousands of residents they would be "purchasing," dismissing them as "an inconsiderable portion of the Mexican people." They were insistent on obtaining that territory for two reasons: the unresolved legal claims of Texas on all lands east of the Rio Grande (thereby including Santa Fe and half of New Mexico), which threatened to become a festering sore for all three parties; and the desire for good overland routes to California ports. In the American Senate an anti-expansionist amendment to exclude "the State of New Mexico with a population of about one hundred and fifty thousand [a considerable exaggeration] hostile people unwilling to be united to us, and unfit to be trusted with a participation in our free form of government, the principle of which they are utter strangers" was defeated eighteen to thirty.

Ultimately, the only real compromise involved more local features along the boundary between the Rio Grande and the Pacific. Forced into such a division, Mexico tried for a boundary along the Gila River and westward to a point just north of San Diego (in early negotiations Trist had accepted 33°N but had been rebuked by his American superiors). The Mexicans pleaded that the central government had no authority to give away pieces of sovereign member states (Chihuahua and Sonora). They were also adamant on the need for a land connection to Baja California. The United States insisted on San Diego, pointing out (correctly) that the traditional boundary between Alta and Baja California lay south of that harbor, but gave way on the 32°N line. The Americans did specify navigation rights on the Colorado River across that land corridor even though Trist warned the Mexicans that this arrangement "would inevitably give rise, in a very short time, to the old Mississippi question over again."

One additional topic generated a good deal of interest but was not included in the treaty. The old dream of a canal across the narrow waist of the Americas was an integral part of continental visions and Pacific destinies in the 1840s. Panama, Nicaragua, and Tehuantepec were the most obvious possibilities, and many Americans thought that transit rights on the Tehuantepec route should be an absolute requirement in any treaty settlement. Trist was instructed to try for it, but found that Mexico had granted a concession for a canal some years earlier that was now held by a group of British capitalists, and the topic was dropped from the negotiations. By the time of the final debates on the treaty, an American naval engineering report on serious problems with this proposed route had undercut some of the enthusiasm.

The Treaty of Guadalupe Hidalgo imposed a new boundary across North America from sea to sea. Whatever the feelings on either side about such a transfer of territory and people, this new separation line at least had the merit of cutting through only two small settlement districts along its nearly 2,000-mile extent. One was the lower Rio Grande, colonized by the Spanish almost 100 years earlier. Most of the several thousand settlers and all of the small towns were on the south side (partly because the river provided, at times, some impediment to Indian raiders). Americans were not unfamiliar with the area. American steamboats had occasionally provided service along a short stretch of the river. Fort Brown, established in support of the American troops Polk had ordered in to train its artillery on Matamoros, sheltered the first nucleus of Anglo-American settlement (soon formalized as Brownsville). Farther upriver where the main road crossed the river, the Americans established another fort, and the old pueblo of Laredo began its new border role, while the embryo of a Nuevo Laredo appeared with the Mexican custom station and guard on the western bank. The other settlement district was in two parts north and south of the ridge where the Rio Grande cuts through to form El Paso del Norte on the road to New Mexico. The two parts were of quite different age and origin: the downriver oasis was a string of mestizo and Christian Indian refugee villages dating from the great seventeenth-century revolt of the Pueblo Indians in New Mexico; the upriver section in the Mesilla Valley had been initiated by a Mexican empresario only in 1843. The treaty allowed residents of the transferred territories up to a year to remove themselves and their possessions back onto Mexican soil if they wished to do so. All the villages on the west side of the river in this area (excepting Paso del Norte—later Ciudad Juarez) were founded by Hispanic refugees from the new American jurisdiction.

For the rest of its length the new boundary cut through "empty" country: that is to say, it cut across the hunting and gathering areas and the networks of trails binding together the homelands of Apache, Papago, Maricopa, Yuma, and Diegueño Indians. The treaty made reference to these people only in collective terms as "savage tribes" who must be forcibly restrained by the United States from incursions across this newly imposed invisible line.

The Treaty of Guadalupe Hidalgo undertook a comprehensive redefinition of the geopolitical relations between the United States of America and the Republic of Mexico, but it did not mark an end to the pressures for further change. The border became a turbulent zone, especially along the lower Rio Grande, where the intermittent activities of bandits, filibusters, and secessionists produced a motley array of raiders and refugees on both sides of the river. On the Pacific Slope, Sonora and Baja California became familiar to many fortune seekers en route to the California goldfields, and the feeble Mexican hold and rumored riches of these territories prompted a number of schemes. A French entrepreneur negotiated with Santa Anna to bring in thousands of footloose Frenchmen who had flocked to San Francisco and the Sierras and to form a colony in Sonora that would serve as a buffer against the Indians and Americans, a protracted affair that disintegrated into fruitless filibustering. Meanwhile, William Walker, the restless Tennessee adventurer, sailed from San Francisco with a small force, seized La Paz, the capital of Baja California, and tried to detach that territory and Sonora from Mexican rule; six months later the bedraggled remnants of this filibuster were driven across the border by Mexican militia and surrendered to American authorities in San Diego (two years later the irrepressible Walker set sail again and seized control of Nicaragua).

Walker's illegal meddling was an embarrassment to the United States because it impinged upon Franklin Pierce's program to purchase another swath of Mexican territory. Pierce had come to the presidency in 1853 with such an intent, and serious difficulties in establishing the actual boundary west from the Rio Grande (difficulties arising from the defective maps used for the treaty of 1848) provided the excuse for attempting a comprehensive renegotiation; Santa Anna's chronic need for money impelled him to respond. The principal quest was for a band of country west from El Paso to provide a southern route for a Pacific railroad. In 1847 Trist had been instructed to try to get the entire Valley of the Gila for that purpose after General Kearny's expedition had reported favorably on it. The negotiations of 1853 were entrusted to James Gadsden, a South Carolina expansionist who was an active promoter of a railroad between the gulf states and the Pacific. Gadsden was given a list of six alternatives to try for. The maximum would have taken most of Nuevo León and Coahuila, including Monterrey and Saltillo (following the line proposed in 1848 by Jefferson Davis, who was now secretary of War), a strip all along the Rio Grande to give the United States control of both banks, a swath west from El Paso, and all of Baja California. In the end, Gadsden had to settle for a line approximating his minimum alternative, just enough for the railroad route. He got that only because Santa Anna was desperate for the $15 million the United States was willing to pay for this 30,000-square-mile cession. Much of this addition was uninhabited desert, but it included the homeland of the Papago, a few Hispanic settlements along the Santa Cruz, and all those hapless Mexicans in the Mesilla

Valley who in the wake of 1848 had moved across the Rio Grande to stay on Mexican soil. A few of these families would move yet again to find refuge around Casas Grandes.

This addition of the Gila Valley failed to satisfy the appetite of American leaders. In 1857 President James Buchanan, who had been a member of the fervently expansionist Polk cabinet, instructed his minister to Mexico to offer $12 million for a boundary west along 30°N from the Rio Grande to the Rio Yaqui and thence to the sea, a chunk that included half of Chihuahua, most of Sonora, and all of Baja California. In the next year he sought congressional support for imposing a military protectorate upon northern Chihuahua and Sonora and pressuring Mexico for further territorial indemnities. His minister actually obtained a draft treaty granting transit routes and various commercial and military concessions across Tehuantepec, north-central Mexico (to Mazatlán), and Sonora (to Guaymas) in return for loans, but it was rejected by the U.S. Senate. Mexican negotiators were careful to refer to these proposed relations as an alliance rather than a protectorate. There was strong sentiment among all parties against any further territorial cessions, but the liberal group that took power after the deposition and exile of Santa Anna was quite ready to seek economic help from the United States. Despite the humiliation of the war and Mexico's dismemberment there was, in some important circles, open admiration for American growth and power. Over the course of these tumultuous years many Mexican leaders had gained familiarity with the United States as officials, travelers, or exiles, and they continued to be avidly interested in, even though understandably wary of, their giant neighbor. Meanwhile, Americans became almost entirely absorbed in their own problems and Mexico faded from the national view. We know, of course, that with the Gadsden Treaty the boundary between the United States and Mexico was fixed in place. Except for brief mention of minor incursions the topic therefore disappears from American histories—and then rather suddenly and with some alarm it reappears in the current events of the late twentieth century as a place of massive immigration and challenging problems. But here, as elsewhere, we are concerned with a zone as well as a line, and the borderland we live with today began to take shape as soon as Brownsville appeared across the river from Matamoros and has been a regional and national fact of life ever since.

Two other areas became involved in the renegotiations of the Anglo-Hispanic border during these years. Even before the Treaty of Guadalupe Hidalgo was ratified the American president and Congress were confronted with a new territorial issue—one not of their making but very much to the liking of some. It came in the form of a plea from the creole leaders of Yucatán for military help in suppressing the fierce revolt of the Mayans that seemed to threaten the White minority with extinction. In return, the envoy suggested that the United States assume the

"dominion and sovereignty of the peninsula." Yucatán was an area of strong regional pride and unsteady allegiance to the Mexican state. Its leaders had long
sought a special autonomy, and in January 1846, the Yucatecan assembly, citing
chronic neglect by Mexico, had declared independence. Later that year Yucatán
proclaimed its neutrality in the American-Mexican War. In early 1847 the Yucatecan envoy had sounded out the Polk administration about annexation, but the
president, judging the prospects for approval by Congress as unlikely, merely sent
arms to help the Yucatecans defend themselves against the Mexicans. A year later
Polk was much more favorable to occupation and possible annexation, citing the
need to save the Whites (they now held only the few towns) and, as usual, warning
that because of Yucatán's "vicinity to Cuba, to the capes of Florida, to New
Orleans, and indeed to our whole southwestern coast, it would be dangerous to our
peace and security if it should become a colony of any European power." Expansionists now whipped up a fervor, but the mood of Congress had shifted against
further acquisitions, the British threat was denounced as illusory, and news of a
truce between the creoles and Mayans quickly deflated the agitation. When the
Mayan unrest resumed in 1851, Yucatecan leaders were ready to submit to Mexico
in return for help in ending the so-called caste war. In 1855 the peninsula, soon
divided into two states to appease the rival cities of Mérida and Campeche, was
reintegrated into the Mexican union.

CUBA

Cuba also reemerged as an important territorial issue at midcentury. The flaring
of expansionism inevitably directed attention to that nearby island and invoca-
tion of those "laws of political gravitation" that John Quincy Adams had enunci-
ated forty years earlier. Cuba continued to be a special kind of place. It was still a
Spanish colony in the midst of a liberated volatile Hispanic America; it was a
prospering planter society, now the leading supplier of sugar to the world; and it
was still a slave-based society and economy, replenished by the continuing import of African captives, within a contracting and increasingly constricted realm
of American slavery. The British had abolished slavery in their West Indies in
the 1830s, the French did so in 1848, and the United States was in crisis over
further westward extension of slavery within its own bounds. Cuba thereby took
on new significance within the unstable geopolitical patterns of the time, and a
variety of interests became involved in the seething affairs of this strategic island.
There were those Cubans and Americans who worked for a free Cuba and
freedom for all Cubans; there were those Cubans and Americans who worked for
an independent Cuba firmly in the hold of its planter oligarchy; there were those
Cubans and Americans who schemed to transfer, by whatever means, this remnant of European empire into the North American union. And all of these

agitations involved Cubans and Americans in both Cuba and America: there were several thousand Cubans, exiles, agents, and others residing in the United States, chiefly in New Orleans and New York; and there were a thousand or more Americans, agents, merchants, speculators, sojourners, even a number of American planters (Northern as well as Southern) lured by the profits in sugar, residing in Cuba, chiefly in Havana and along the north coast: Cárdenas was known as an "American city"; American engineers and machinists came in seasonally to run the sugar mills and railroads. Inevitably there was a good deal of coming and going between island and mainland (fig. 18).

In 1845 a senator from Florida introduced a resolution in Congress asking the president to undertake negotiations with Spain for the cession of Cuba. After brief debate that resolution was withdrawn, and interest in the topic was soon deflected by the war with Mexico. As that war drew to a close and it became clear that the United States would extract large territorial cessions from its Hispanic mainland neighbor, a shrill chorus of propagandists began to argue the advantages, the need, indeed the inevitability, of an American takeover of Cuba. The Polk administration was a sympathetic listener. On May 10, 1848, during the Yucatán debates (which tirelessly emphasized the importance of Cuba and Yucatán together as the "lock and key" to the Gulf of Mexico) and immediate aftermath of Guadalupe Hidalgo, President Polk recorded in his diary: "I am decidedly in favour of purchasing Cuba & making it one of the States of [the] Union." With only partial support from his cabinet he dispatched an envoy to Madrid with power to offer up to $100 million. The inept overtures of that agent produced a famous reply that sooner than transfer the island to any power Spain "would prefer seeing it sunk in the Ocean." That rebuff did little to alter the pressures for change, however. Secretary of State Buchanan was soon stating (in a private letter): "We must have Cuba. We can't do without Cuba, & above all we must not suffer its transfer to Great Britain." Over the next few years several filibustering schemes were given indirect support, and two set out from New Orleans, but none achieved a secure foothold on the island.

The official statements of the United States at this time always focused on the strategic imperatives of geographic position. In 1852 Secretary of State Edward Everett defined this delicate matter to an understandably suspicious Spain:

> The island of Cuba lies at our doors. It commands the approach to the Gulf of Mexico, which washes the shores of five of our states. It bars the entrance of that great river which drains half the North American continent, and with its tributaries forms the largest system of internal water-communication in the world. It keeps watch at the doorway of our intercourse with California by the Isthmus route. . . . Under certain circumstances it might be almost essential to our safety.

But of course there was always much more involved than simple strategic location

18. The American Gibraltar, Havana, 1853.

A modern lighthouse towers over the ancient (1589) Morro Castle to guide ships to the narrow channel leading past the much larger and later fortress of La Cabaña into the capacious harbor, which by this date is alive with steamships as well as sail. "Havana is crowded with Americans," noted a visitor of that time, and they came via scheduled services on these big side-wheel vessels from New Orleans, Baltimore, Philadelphia, and New York to enjoy the vitality of this compact, densely built Spanish colonial city. The twin towers of the cathedral and the large bulk of the governor's palace overlooking the Plaza de Armas provide the expected cultural landmarks in such a towns-cape, but beyond the old fortified wall and its enfiladable open space has arisen the new town, here rimmed by a tree-lined ornamental paseo and focused on the new barrel-roofed railroad station. (Courtesy of Leví Marrero) in any movement to change Cuba's geopolitical status, and some of these interests became blatant. Franklin Pierce committed his administration to "detach" Cuba from Spain, by purchase if possible, by other means if necessary. In marked contrast with the expansionism that coveted much of Mexico, the main driving force in this Cuban policy came from the planter oligarchy of the American South working in league with some of their counterparts in Cuba, and it was powered more by fear than by any confident sense of "destiny." The great specter was "Africanization"—that out of spite against local revolutionaries and American aggressors (and under pressure from European powers) Spain would emancipate all slaves. The American concern therefore became a more compelling version of an old theme in this corner of the Republic: just as the free Blacks of Spanish Florida had made that border territory seem an intolerable threat, so the Florida Straits would be an insufficient moat to protect North America from the inflammatory example of a free Cuba—which might turn into another Black Haiti.

American proponents of annexation usually gave assurances that Cuba would come into the Union with the consent of the Cubans, by which they meant the dominant planter minority. They were confident that this group was so fearful about its slaves (there had been many local uprisings), and so uncertain of its support from Spain, that it would welcome the sheltering power of the United States. The main body of these American expansionists certainly sought the extension of slavery within an expanding federal union ("the safety of the South is to be found only in the extension of its peculiar institutions . . . —towards the equator"), but the need to ensure the hold of Cuban planters upon their slaves in Cuba in order to ensure a like hold in the American South was also fundamental. That became all too clear in the notorious "Ostend Manifesto," a private position paper prepared by senior American diplomats in Europe. Spelling out a rationale for American policy toward Cuba, it recommended purchase if possible but seizure if necessary to prevent "Africanization," and this "on the very same principle that would justify an individual in tearing down the burning house of his neighbor if there were no other means of preventing the flames from destroying his own home." Soon leaked to the press, this extraordinary document was a serious embarrassment to the American government at home and abroad. Caught in a tangle of Cuba revolutionary movements and whipsawed by American sectional politics, President Pierce repudiated the Ostend statement and withdrew support from General John Quitman, a Mississippi filibuster who was readying an invasion force of several thousand men. The push to detach and annex Cuba slacked off for the time being. James Buchanan, who succeeded Pierce, reaffirmed his support of the annexation of Cuba along with obtaining more territory from Mexico, but such ideas became overwhelmed by the impending threat to the

Union itself. Disillusioned about American support, the various factions in Cuba had to find other ways to work for the basic changes they sought.

Cuba and Puerto Rico lay in the eastern sector of that long Anglo-Hispanic border zone that now extended from the Atlantic to the Pacific. Such a zone had first appeared more than a century ago as the English had fixed their hold upon Carolina and Georgia on the northern margins of Spanish Florida. It was a frontier of repeated conflict and major alteration, and there was little reason in the 1850s to think that it had become firmly set in place. That Cuba was important to the United States had been apparent for fifty years—ever since the purchase of Louisiana. Havana was the obvious Gibraltar of the American Mediterranean, and American politicians of every stripe agreed that it must not fall into the hands of a rival power. But there were other geographic realities no less basic but rather less obvious than these simple conformations of land and sea. There was the human geography of the main peoples of the American subtropics. Only when those broad patterns are brought into view does the full strategic significance of Cuba come into focus. Only then does the position of Cuba at the intersection of three great worlds—Hispano-America, Anglo-America, Afro-America—become clear. The human interests and emotions bound up with those confronting, overlapping, interconnected worlds were a guarantee of continued stress and strain in this part of America. Furthermore, each of these broad areas was an unstable divided world: the Hispano-American between the many independent states and the remnants of the Spanish Empire; the Anglo-American between Slave States and Free States; the Afro-American with the broader realms of slavery, emancipation, and the independent state of Haiti. Such internal divisions magnified the potentials for explosive change.

The bitter regional-sectional strains that endangered the United States were deeply entangled in these extensive and complicated revisions of the Anglo-Hispanic frontiers. The famous federation of the North, from which had emanated so much derisive comment about the innate inability of its Hispanic neighbors to create and sustain viable modern nations, was plunging headlong toward its own disintegration. Mexicans, especially, might find some ironic satisfaction in that spectacle, but if such a convulsion might bring some relief it would not likely put an end to pressures from the north. American expansionism had not been powered by any one interest or section, and it was by now so heavily imbued with a set of cultural attitudes and continental presumptions that whatever the outcome of that intramural struggle it would surely continue to reverberate with powerful effects upon the whole length of this cultural border zone.

8. Spanning a Continent—and Ocean

On July 6, 1848, James K. Polk, presenting copies of the ratified Treaty of Guadalupe Hidalgo to Congress and the nation, noted with obvious satisfaction that "New Mexico and Upper California . . . constitute of themselves a country large enough for a great empire, and their acquisition is second only in importance to that of Louisiana in 1803." Including Texas, the cessions from Mexico were equal in size to Louisiana, and their 918,000 square miles added to the 287,000 of Oregon meant that the United States had been enlarged by more than 1.2 million square miles; the country had grown by 64 percent in two years. It would have been quite "un-American" not to have taken pride in such a dramatic change. Surveying the list of these additions, James DeBow, superintendent of the United States Census, offered a gratifying set of comparisons:

> The territorial extent of the Republic is, therefore, nearly ten times as large as that of Great Britain and France combined; three times as large as the whole of France, Britain, Austria, Prussia, Spain, Portugal, Belgium, Holland, and Denmark, together; one-and-a half-times as large as the Russian empire in Europe; one-sixth less only than the area covered by the fifty-nine or sixty empires, states, and Republics of Europe; of equal extent with the Roman Empire or that of Alexander, neither of which is said to have exceeded 3,000,000 square miles.

In his message to Congress, President Polk went on to point out that

> Rich in mineral and agricultural resources, with a climate of great salubrity, they embrace the most important ports on the whole Pacific coast of the continent of North America.
>
> By the acquisition of these possessions, we are brought into the immediate proximity with the west coast of America, from Cape Horn to the Russian possessions north of Oregon; with the islands of the Pacific Ocean, and, by a direct voyage in steamers, we will be in less than thirty days of Canton and other parts of China.

Thus did he emphasize that the United States had not only spanned the continent, it was now positioned within a vast new oceanic world.

Polk, of course, had been made well aware throughout his tumultuous term that not everyone shared his geopolitical vision. Still, with the war over and the treaty signed, he was startled to hear his successor, Zachary Taylor, remark, as they rode together in the carriage up Pennsylvania Avenue to the inaugural ceremony on March 5, 1849, that "California and Oregon were too distant to become members of the Union, and that it would be better for them to be an Independent Gov[ern]ment." Polk noted in his diary that the general was no doubt "a well meaning old man" but was "uneducated, exceedingly ignorant of public affairs, and . . . of very ordinary capacity." Taylor's view of the future pattern of North America, however, had a respectable history. It was widely understood that the United States was a continuing experiment in how extensive a modern republic could be. That it could span the Appalachians and bind the Atlantic Seaboard and the Mississippi was by now substantiated. Canals and a thousand steamboats provided convincing demonstration. The steamboat itself had been hailed as a revolutionary invention "enlarging the sphere of republican government," but except for the tediously winding Missouri arching through the northern plains, steamboats were useless on the shallow rivers west of the woodlands, where broad, braided channels showed more sand than water through much of the year. Whether an effective government of the people, by the people could be further stretched across 2,000 miles of plains, mountains, and deserts to Pacific shores remained debatable.

The very idea of extending republican government across the continent from a capital on the Potomac had provoked derision during the earliest debates on proposals to effect an American occupation of Oregon: "Can any legislator seriously think of extending [this country's] limits four thousand miles west of the mouth of the Missouri? Does any one believe that such an extension can be made, without parting the chain of our Union?" The speaker got a lengthy response from colleagues who did so think and believe, but his point was an obvious factor in defeat of the measures. Such doubts persisted even as geographical knowledge expanded. As we have noted, Lieutenant Charles Wilkes, leader of the great American Exploring Expedition, who certainly had an expansive geographical view of his country and its place in the world, thought it most likely that Oregon and Upper California would become united to form a new Pacific republic. And such was the opinion of America's most respected elder statesman, John Quincy Adams. From the time he had served as James Monroe's secretary of State, Adams had spoken confidently of the inevitable march of the Anglo-Americans across North America and had taken pride in having negotiated a firm United States reach to Pacific shores. When he was speaking for the ears of Europeans he might imply that Oregon would be part of the Union, but he really saw his "transcontinental treaty" (Adams-Onís) as a means toward a plurality of Anglo-American republics, as he reaffirmed to his congressional colleagues during the Oregon treaty debates in 1846: "I want the country for our western pioneers . . . for them to go out to make a nation that is to arise there, and which must come from us as a fountain comes from its source, of free, independent, sovereign republics." That American pioneers could, and would, cross the continent was being demonstrated year after year, but emigrant wagons were a one-way traffic; nothing was being hauled back; there was no effective interaction (the famous caravans to and from Santa Fe covered less than half the distance to the Willamette Valley).

But Taylor and Adams were among the last spokesmen for this geopolitical view (and both were soon dead). It faded quickly in the late 1840s and may be said to have essentially disappeared on September 9, 1850, with the admission of California as the thirty-first state in the Union. (Though it might still be called forth as a threat, as it was by California's first representative, who warned his congressional colleagues in 1852 that California's position in the Union "is a delicate one"; separated "by thousands of miles of plains, deserts, and almost impossible mountains" from the other states, "anything like neglect falls with stunning force" and, "however repulsive the idea may be," gives rise to thoughts "of a separation, and the establishment of an independent Republic on the Pacific.") In his inaugural address, Franklin Pierce, successor to the Taylor-Fillmore administration, declared the end of that era of American geopolitical thinking:

> The apprehension of dangers from extended territory, multiplied States, accumulated wealth, and augmented population has proved to be unfounded. The stars upon your banner have become nearly threefold their original number; your densely populated possessions skirt the shores of the two great oceans; and yet this vast increase of people and territory has not only shown itself compatible with the harmonious action of the States and Federal Government in their respective constitutional spheres, but has afforded an additional guaranty of the strength and integrity of both.

That was whistling in the dark to drown out the voices threatening that integrity, but the reality of a transcontinental republic was now generally accepted. The decisive factors of course were not presidential pronouncements but the presence of large numbers of American settlers on the Pacific Coast and the many plans afoot to connect them far more effectively with the main body of the nation. The United States had hardly gotten California and placed it under military authority than tens of thousands of Americans had gotten to it by foot, horseback, wagon, sail, or steamship. That great surge to the goldfields transformed the visionary idea of a railroad all the way across North America into an assured eventuality.

The first formal plan for such a railroad had been put forth in December 1844 by Asa Whitney, a New York merchant involved in the China trade. The general idea was soon taken up by various civic and commercial interests, and began to be discussed in Congress and state legislatures. An issue of such immense geographical portent inevitably generated fervent competition among all the cities and states aspiring to become the eastern terminus of the first transcontinental axis of the nation (it was generally assumed that such an enormously expensive project could not be duplicated along a second route for a generation or more). In Congress this intense commercial geographical issue was quickly entangled in bitter party rivalries relating to the federal role in internal improvements, land policies, and "the accursed question of slavery." The first Pacific Railroad Bill in Congress (1853) tried to defuse sectional opposition by proposing two routes, a northern (following Whitney's Prairie du Chien to Puget Sound plan) and a southern (from some point between Memphis and New Orleans to California), but it generated furious complicated contentions and ended by authorizing only that the Army Topographical Engineers undertake engineering surveys and general assessments of five possible routes (fig. 19).

These "Explorations and Surveys to Ascertain the most Practical and Economi-

19. The United States West of the Mississippi, 1859.
D. McGowan and George H. Hildt's map was based on Lieutenant Gouverneur K. Warren's official map of 1857 accompanying the Pacific Railroad Surveys. Published in St. Louis, this commercial offering emphasizes routes emanating from that center, including those to the newly discovered gold regions in what is now Colorado. A minor feature of interest is the appearance of a territory of "Arrizonia," then being proposed in Congress. (Courtesy of the Library of Congress)

cal Route for a Railroad from the Mississippi River to the Pacific Ocean" were designated by reference to parallels of North latitude:

47° and 49° from St. Paul (and Duluth)
41° west from Council Bluffs (and Chicago)
38° west from St. Louis

35° west from Memphis

32° west from Vicksburg (and New Orleans)

The surveys got under way in 1854 and were soon providing American leaders and public with an immense enrichment of knowledge and understanding about their vast new western territories. The number of routes defined in the task by Congress was evidence of the enormous difficulty of national decision about this fundamental geographical question, but the scale and the intense national interest in this investigation was evidence that the United States had determined that neither the Continental Divide nor any other massive physical feature would interfere with the reality of a transcontinental state.

Fears of over-extension of the national domain had certainly faded. The very appearance of such an instrument for conquering distance at just this time seemed but another step in some larger plan, as Mr. Washburn assured his congressional colleagues:

> Annexation, thus far, seems to have proceeded *pari passu* with our preparation and ability to receive and govern what we have acquired. Adaptation has kept company with extension. When Louisiana was purchased, Fulton came with the steamboat, and made New Orleans nearer to Washington than Savannah had been before. When Texas was annexed, the railroad had been introduced; and now, practically, her capital is nearer that of the Union than St. Louis was . . . And when California added another star to our banner the telegraph was ready to announce the fact from the Bay of Fundy to the Gulf of Mexico in less time than Puck agreed to put a girdle around the earth. And the Sandwich Islands, when the Pacific railroad is built, will, measured by time and expense, be nearer this city than Bangor was when Maine was admitted into the Union.

Washburn was explaining why a Whig from Maine was not opposed to all annexations. New Englanders had their own expansive visions and had brought the Pacific into view from quite a different perspective.

While Pacific railroads were causing great excitement in the Mississippi Valley, commercial interests on the Atlantic seaboard were also giving keen attention to far less costly and more fully Atlantic-to-Pacific routes via Panama, Nicaragua, or Tehuantepec. In 1850 the United States and Great Britain agreed that the two powers would enjoy full equality of access to any such transit facility that might be developed. That did not end national rivalries among various government and private interests to gain advantage over these strategic positions. Led by Cornelius Vanderbilt, New York investors in 1849 obtained a concession for a Nicaragua ship canal and soon had their Atlantic and Pacific steamship services connected by way of roads and lake steamers to serve California-bound traffic. But their canal project collapsed when they were unable to attract British financing, and in a few years the overland route was disrupted by local political turmoil. By that time the Panama

Railroad had been completed by another American firm and was soon flourishing on the basis of U.S. mail contracts, passenger traffic, and Latin American freight. Meanwhile, the promising Tehuantepec route (practicable and providing a shorter way to California) remained mired in American and Mexican politics. A railroad finally begun in 1859 lay uncompleted for many years.

All of these routes, internal and isthmian, were designed to connect the main body of the nation with San Diego, San Francisco, the Columbia River, and Puget Sound. It is important to remember that those ports were already connected to a vast new maritime world. By the 1850s, this new Pacific frontage of the United States was linked, in some cases quite routinely, with Mazatlán, Callao, and Valparaiso, with New Baranof (Sitka) and Kamchatka, Canton, Tahiti, Australia and New Zealand, and, pivotal to all these, the Hawaiian Islands. Yankee seafarers and merchants had become leaders in all kinds of Pacific activities: maritime furs, hide and tallow, lumber and sandalwood, whaling, and the China trade. Yankee missionaries had stations in Oregon, Hawaii, Micronesia, China, Siam, and Borneo. A U.S. naval squadron (usually two or three ships) had patrolled the Pacific since 1822; a government-sponsored expedition had carried out scientific explorations from Antarctica to the Strait of Juan de Fuca; after the first treaty with China in 1844, American clipper ships moved in on the coveted tea and silk trade; in 1853 Commodore Matthew Perry used polite force to crack open the door to Japan.

The grand patterns of winds and currents and a position at the northeastern corner of the island-studded southern and western Pacific made the Hawaiian Islands the principal way station in all this new traffic (fig. 20). Ships rounding Cape Horn bound for the Pacific coast of North America swung west and north with the equatorial currents and trade winds to Hawaii and thence north and east to pick up the westerlies and the clockwise circulation in the North Pacific to carry them across the 2,500 miles of empty seas to Oregon and California. From the 1820s on Hawaii was the main base for Pacific whaling. The California Gold Rush was an immense stimulus to traffic, drawing ships from China, Australia, and South America as well as from Atlantic America and Europe. Thus, at midcentury the most isolated cluster of Polynesia had become the thriving crossroads of a new Pacific world. The volume was impressive: on November 20, 1852, there were 131 whalers and 18 merchant vessels in port at Honolulu; that was the peak recorded in the shipping records of the time, but not far above average, and there may have been nearly as many at Lahaina on Maui, the other important anchorage in these islands. The provisioning of vessels for the long voyages across the vast reaches of the Pacific had thus become a major business. Cattle, white potatoes, sugar, coffee, and citrus had been added to the native production of hogs, chickens, taro, breadfruit, bananas, sweet potatoes, and seafoods. Mercantile houses serving the

20. The Americas and the Pacific.

This fine opening plate in *Maps of the Society for the Diffusion of Useful Knowledge,* volume 1, published by Charles Knight and Company, London, in 1844, well displays the emptiness of the North Pacific and the strategic position of the Sandwich (Hawaiian) Islands. Note that this English atlas, published just as the Oregon dispute was heating up, shows a division along the lower Columbia River. (Courtesy of the George Arents Research Library, Syracuse University) variety of markets imported wheat and flour from Chile and lumber from Oregon, as well as a great array of manufactures from Europe and eastern America (fig. 21).

These diversifying contacts had a heavy impact on island populations. Although the Polynesians were less vulnerable than the American Indians, European diseases took a heavy toll. The 1853 census count of 73,134 inhabitants was a reduction from perhaps 300,000 at the time of Captain James Cook's first contacts seventy-five years earlier. There were more than 2,000 foreigners, from many parts of the world, but chiefly from the United States. There was obviously much contact between the Hawaiians and the *haoles* (the 983 "part-Hawaiians" listed in the census must surely be an undercount). Hundreds of Hawaiians served on foreign ships; Hawaiian laborers show up in Hudson's Bay Company brigades early on (and leave their name—"Owyhee"—imprinted on southwestern Idaho). The small size of the islands, the ease of contact, and the rapid rise in the volume and intensity of interactions generated strong pressures for culture change.

One critical change took place very early: the creation of a single Hawaiian Kingdom under Kamehameha I, who with the use of European arms subdued all rival chiefs. After his death in 1819, his successors were faced with the need for adroit adaptation to a rapidly changing world. In this they were assisted by a number of foreign advisers, some of whom held office in the Hawaiian government. The most prominent of them, Robert Wyllie, was a Scot (he was foreign minister during a critical time), but most of the influential foreigners were American. The first formal constitution, adopted in 1840, drew heavily on the American example, though in this case designed to support a monarchy. That document in effect defined the Hawaiian Islands as a Christian nation, and the first government-

Honolulu, Oahu, Nov. 1840. J. D. Dana from shipboard.
Wilkes Exploring Expedition.

sponsored school system was operated by Protestant and Catholic (French) missionaries. That system was designed to train a national leadership, and instruction was at first entirely in Hawaiian, but yielding to pressure from parents, some instruction in English was begun in 1853. In the late 1840s the Great Mahele, a comprehensive transformation of the indigenous land system, was undertaken. Allocations were made to the monarchy, the government, and individual freeholds; when completed, in 1850, foreigners could purchase and hold land on equal terms with Native Hawaiians, opening the way to plantations, ranches, and industries and a quite unequal influence upon the whole economy and polity.

The competing foreign interests were jealously monitored by British, French, and American residents, consuls, diplomats, and visitors (the Russians were also early participants but were expelled in 1817). In the early phase the British had

21. Honolulu, Oahu, November 1840.
This fine panorama of a bicultural capital town was sketched by James Dwight Dana, professor of geology at Yale and one of the naturalists on the Wilkes Exploring Expedition. It clearly shows a Polynesian settlement now studded with Western buildings. On the left, the tallest flag flies over the old fort and residence of the local Hawaiian governor. The shorter flag and tower just behind marks the Seaman's Chapel; farther to the right is the small flag of the American consulate, near the large, uncompleted Roman Catholic church. The tall palms mark the royal grounds, lying in front of the old volcanic crater already known as the Punchbowl. The very large structure on the right is Kawaihao Church (with tower uncompleted), the principal seat of the New England mission. Not included here is a third panel of Dana's sketch that extends the view along the taro beds and fish ponds of Waikiki to Diamond Head. (Courtesy of the Hawaiian Mission Children's Society Library)

regarded the Sandwich Islands (Captain Cook had named them after the earl of
Sandwich, first lord of the Admiralty) as an informal protectorate. As foreign
interests intensified, the king of Hawaii requested that Britain, France, and the
United States join in a formal declaration recognizing the kingdom as "an Independent State" that they would never subordinate as a possession or protectorate. In
1843 Britain and France did so; the United States, citing the special constitutional
process required, declined to join in such a treaty, but declared its support of that
position separately. Such proclamations masked a tense, unsteady balance of
forces. Hawaii was a rich prize for any imperial maritime power, and warships of the
three contenders were a common presence in these island waters. After a comprehensive review of the British strategic position in 1846, a new first lord of the
Admiralty declared his preference for a single great base at this "Malta in the centre
of the Pacific." Acknowledging that French opposition would make that impossible
for the moment, he urged his government to move quickly to obtain San Francisco,
"the Key of the N. W. Coast of America," but British diplomats, eager to settle the
Oregon dispute, were more concerned with problems elsewhere. At the moment
the French were ominously pressuring the Hawaiian Kingdom over various indem-
nity and equality of treatment issues, but much the most important developments
were those taking place on the Pacific Coast of North America. As Oregon and
California came under American control the annexation of Hawaii became a topic
of discussion; after the Gold Rush it was a matter of lively agitation by a variety of
interests. Even before the sudden emergence of a volatile American California, the
British consul in Honolulu had warned his superiors: "I do think the tide of
Emigration, now setting so strongly Westwards from the United States, will extend
to these Islands & in the course of time thereby endanger their free action,
especially as the Western Settlers cannot, at all times, be controlled either by the
Local Authorities, or their own Government."

   In Hawaii there were sharp differences among the Americans themselves on the
question of annexation. The missionaries were divided or ambivalent on the topic
and on what they saw themselves as having wrought. Some might find satisfaction
in "the fact that the Hawaiian Islands are already a virtual colony of the United
States, a missionary offshoot from the stock of New England" and that the "Heart
of the Pacific" would soon display the same society and "Anglo-Saxon Blood" as the
mainland. But others, probably most, could only read disaster in that prospect:
"The native Hawaiian race would be trampled in the dust. Thus it has been with
every tribe of Indians who have come in close contact with the Whites. For the
sake therefore of the aboriginal race, if we can be independent and enjoy peace, I
wish not to be *annexed* and pray it may never be consummated." That the king of
Hawaii and his subjects preferred independence and peace there can be little
doubt, but when it appeared that they might have neither, the king and his council
looked to the United States for shelter; in 1851, fearing a French take-over and

failing to get reassurance of British protection, they formally asked to become an American protectorate. The Fillmore administration was wary, the local situation soon eased, and no action was taken, but the annexation movement gained strength in the islands as well as on the mainland, especially in California and New England. The local American commissioner got the Hawaiian leadership to accept the idea of annexation as an alternative should independence prove impossible to sustain. The Pierce administration was open to the idea but did not wish to initiate such a move. When fears arose in the islands that an irregular group of Americans might simply seize control and declare an independent republic, the Hawaiian government began negotiations with the American commissioner for incorporation into the Union. A treaty was drawn up providing for immediate admission as a state, the royal family to be pensioned off with annuities. But it generated strong opposition in Hawaii and ominous noises from France and Britain, and when the old king soon died, his successor put an end to the proposal. The treaty never reached the U.S. Senate, and if it had would almost certainly have been defeated, for statehood had become an inflammatory issue (some interpretations of the event suggest that the treaty received nominal support from influential persons in Hawaii because they assumed that the statehood provision insured its defeat).

For the time being, interest in annexation faded in the islands and on the mainland, but the American predominance in Hawaii continued to increase and the strategic position of the islands guaranteed that the geopolitical relation between the United States and this corner of Polynesia would remain a topic of keen concern to American statesmen. The United States was firmly implanted in the Pacific world.

This far-ranging oceanic outreach of Americans during the first half of the nineteenth century is a forceful reminder that American expansionism must not be viewed as simply a great *westward* movement by a government and people across the continent to fix claim to a thousand-mile territorial frontage on Pacific shores. Rather, it should be seen as a powerful *outward* movement, putting pressure on the borderlands to the north and south as well as thrusting westward, and ranging out to sea to place islands and coastlands near and far under American commercial, cultural, demographic, and political influence. The great gateways and "jumping-off places" for Oregon and California were not just St. Louis and the Missouri river towns but New York, Philadelphia, and Baltimore, Boston and Salem, New Bedford and Nantucket, Charleston and Savannah; the seats of incipient empire southward were New Orleans and New York; and we might even detect the faint reverberation of America's internal dynamism across the Atlantic to West Africa, where in 1847 the independent Republic of Liberia emerged from the several Afro-American settlements established just south of Sierra Leone by American colonization societies in the 1820s.

At midcentury, the United States was three times larger than the original

Union. To American eyes half of this great transcontinental expanse was essentially empty, and thus Henry Wansey's characterization of the new United States—"a vast outline with much to fill up"—was as apt in the 1850s as it had been in the 1790s. But of course it was not really empty of people nor unused in its resources. By these vast extensions of its bounds, the Republic had brought under its jurisdiction a great array of new peoples: more than a hundred Indian tribes, of half a dozen broad cultural types; French Louisianians; the varied Hispanic Americans of Texas, New Mexico, northern Sonora, and California; the métis of the northern plains; the Mormons in their refugee commonwealth in the Great Salt Lake Basin; the heterogeneous swirl of people pouring into northern California. Such additions reinforced the general truth and compounded the continuing reality of the United States of America as, at once, a set of regional societies, a federation, a nation, and an empire.

9. Empire: The Geopolitical Management of Captive Peoples

By the 1850s the evidence of empire was widely apparent in many forms. Although the United States had asserted its sovereignty broadly across the continent, half of its territory was as yet unorganized and most of those lands were as yet unceded by indigenous peoples. Much of that half of the country had been recently acquired, but the imperial character was also still discernible in lands held for half a century, as in French Louisiana and the northern Great Plains. Indeed, much of the plains as well as large areas of the newer territories remained unsecured dangerous country wherein Anglo-Americans entered at risk, usually in armed parties.

As in most young empires, this dependent area was not a tranquil realm. Whole regions, such as California, were in flux, and movement, pressure, tension, and conflict in some degree were found almost everywhere. An unmistakable mark of imperialism was to be seen in the 100 military posts, serving as bases for the nearly 200 companies of troops assigned to police frontiers, patrol trafficways, oversee captive populations, and open military roads for the efficient application of imperial power (fig. 22). The generals commanding the several military departments had plenty to keep an eye on. The first Anglo governor of New Mexico had been assassinated by a small rebellious group of Taoseños, and resentments over Anglo domination were widespread; bandits and Indian raiders roamed almost at will along the Mexican border and in many parts of California; the army was in the field in pursuit of Indians in Texas, the Navaho country, the Great Plain of the Columbia—and still hunting remnants of the Seminoles in Florida; prospectors and drifters ranging out of the Sierras in search of gold were trespassing and pillaging the Indians and creating waves of disorder across the Pacific Slope; the several overland trails across the Far West were swaths of tension and trouble;

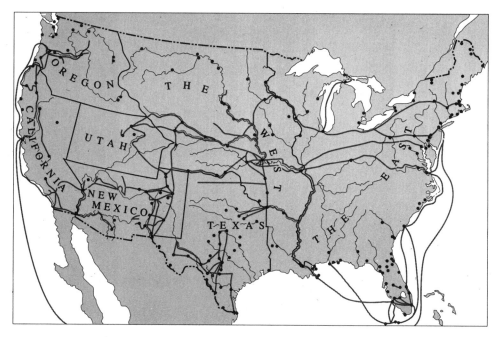

22. Troop Movements, 1857–58.

This combines information from two original maps in the National Archives: "Map Exhibiting the Lines of March Passed over by the Troops of the United States During the year ending June 30th 1858" (War Dept., Office Expl. & Survey, Nov. 1858) and "Map of the United States Exhibiting the Military Depts. & Posts 1860."

settlers and speculators moving in upon newly opened tracts in Iowa, Nebraska, and Kansas were generating pressures for the next stage of forced concessions. In 1857 the national government ordered 3,000 troops across the plains to Utah to quell a reported rebellion of the Mormons.

Although there was plenty of political discussion and controversy over virtually every episode and policy in these matters, rarely did anyone speak of the United States as an empire in the old generic sense of a geopolitical structure exhibiting the coercive dominance of one people over other, captive, peoples. Only rarely, at moments of decision over huge annexations of conquered territories, might some voice cry out against converting "the Republic which our fathers created for us into an Empire, and our unpretending National Government into a great Power bearing imperial sway over distant provinces and dependencies." By the 1850s, certainly, the great majority of American leaders and people accepted such dominance matter-of-factly as an inevitable part of national life during this phase of national development, while denying that they wished the United States to be an empire or even in fact that it was one. In view of this contradiction—still part of the national mythology—it is important to define somewhat more systematically the imperial character of the American geopolitical structure at this time.

A basic, first problem of empire is how to accommodate—how to structurally encompass—a bloc of people who have separate cultural identity and claim to a specific territory and who clearly cannot be quickly assimilated into the body of the ruling imperial nation. As one of the great processes of world history, imperialism has taken many forms and strewn the earth with many examples of how such subordinate areas can be organized and articulated within an overall political structure. We shall limit our concern to those geopolitical strategies most pertinent to the American case.

1. Protectorate. In the simplest forms of such relationships, the subordination of a people and their territory is formally recognized by treaty but they are left largely undisturbed. Such treaties typically declare the mutual respect and friendship of the two parties and the promise of protection from external dangers in return for acknowledgment of the exclusive political supremacy of the imperial state. Initial American treaties with Indian groups usually took some such form. However, such relationships in the American case were inherently unstable and temporary for two reasons: the United States never regarded them as anything but a prelude to negotiations for drastic concessions by the Indians of all or most of their lands, and the United States was unable, or unwilling, to commit the military resources necessary to provide such protection, although time and again it made some gesture of doing so. Basically, these protectorates were not sustained because the United States did not wish to perpetuate such territorial arrangements.

An important exception to this stance was the case of the Pueblo Indians in New Mexico, and that of course stemmed from the exceptional character of these Indians, who lived in compact permanent villages on their small tracts of intensively cultivated lands in a region far removed from the main pressures of American settler expansion. With too little land to covet, the relatively peaceful Pueblo towns were regarded as islands of stability amid the resentful Hispanos and dangerous "wild" Indians. Thus they were quickly confirmed in their lands, which in effect merely reaffirmed a Mexican practice evolving out of several centuries of often tumultuous Spanish-Pueblo relations. Here the United States was simply the latest in a succession of external rulers and accepted the established imperial pattern.

2. Indigenous State. A more formalized and coherent form of indirect rule is that which recognizes a local ruler and assigns him to administer his people and territory as a surrogate of the imperial ruler, all the while under the eye of a resident agent who sees that he rules in such a way as not to interfere with any important interests of the empire. Such "native states" are more likely to be the product of an alliance rather than of direct conquest, as was the case with many of the most famous examples in modern history, the "princely states" of British India. Had the United States accepted the protectorate as offered, Yucatán might well have become such a state. Various proposals for American Indian states, such as those of the Cherokee, were versions of this concept, distinguished by their provisions of direct representation in the United States Congress but insisting on internal autonomy as Indian polities. The United States refused to accept such territorial insulation and political autonomy.

3. Minorated Society. A favored technique of American empire was to flood the annexed area so heavily with Americans as to change the position of the indigenous society from a majority to a minority without actual displacement or diminution in number of the captured population. Obviously this can be done only if there is sufficient land and lure, valued resources of some kind, to accommodate the influx.

The calculated move to set the boundary of the potential State of Louisiana so far north as to enclose enough land to ensure an American majority within a few years was the first application of this technique. Just to the east, the small Creole populations around Biloxi and Mobile were swallowed up in the capacious territories of Mississippi and Alabama. In the case of Texas, the Anglo influx came well before annexation so that the residual Mexican population of Bexar and the Rio Grande was a small minority from the beginning of American rule. In Alta California, the influx came suddenly, undesignedly, and uncontrollably immediately after annexation, overwhelming everything in its path. Repeated efforts were made all through the 1850s to divide the state and set aside southern California as a separate territory. That movement was led by the Californios, who were still the majority population south of Monterey and the Tehachapi; the compelling issue then voiced (by local Anglos as well as Hispanos) was the uneven burden of taxation imposed on ranching properties, but the ethnic factor underlay the secessionist agitation. In the context of the American empire, what these Californios tried to obtain was what the New Mexican Hispanos had—reluctantly—been granted.

4. Direct Rule. One of the most common types of imperial territories is the province under direct rule, wherein the imperial state assigns a governor and selects high officers to rule the territory. These imperial officials seek the cooperation of the local elite of the subordinated territory and may try to disturb local customs as little as possible, but the basic laws, courts, and language of the empire are imposed.

Such was the case of New Mexico, first under military government and then under territorial officials (some of whom were cooperating Hispanos). Despite American intentions, New Mexico did not become another Louisiana for a long time because, as the territorial legislature admitted ten years after annexation, there was still "no prospect of a numerous and speedy immigration." Its boundaries were extensive (even after various reductions), but most of the land was pastoral or Indian country, and so the Hispanos remained the majority population forcibly bound to the United States but generally considered unfit for statehood (despite more than sufficient numbers) for sixty years. (It should be noted that there was also strong local opposition to statehood as endangering Hispano cultural integrity.)

Hispanic New Mexico was in some ways analogous to Lower Canada (Quebec) within the British Empire: a conquered province, a people of foreign tongue and culture, resisting the pressures for acculturation but splintered into factions partly by those pressures; governing themselves in important ways but heavily penetrated by an influential minority from the imperial society whose political influence and resources put them into ever-greater command of the provincial economy. However, there was nothing akin to the broader dualism of the Laurentian geopolitical situation in the newly annexed American Southwest.

The Territory of Utah, which under Governor Brigham Young functioned in many ways more as the de facto Mormon State of Deseret than a routine territory of the central government, was another variation of this kind of imperial holding. The tensions and conflict arising from Mormon pressures toward an "indigenous state" and federal insistence on a normal "direct rule territory" underlay the dispatch of the American army to this part of the empire.

5. *Drastic Reduction and Dependency.* A common imperial strategy applied to weaker "tribal" peoples, especially when they occupy lands coveted by the stronger, expanding people, is to reduce them to a small reserve of the least desirable lands and make them dependent upon allocations of essential supplies and support from the imperial power. Because they can no longer sustain themselves in their age-old ways of life, such captive peoples are placed under enormous pressures to change themselves into a people more closely conforming to the dominant patterns of the conquering power. Ostensibly, such culture change may be intended to release such people from dependency and enable them to become full participants in national life; realistically, for the first generations so treated, "reduction" almost inevitably refers to a drastic diminution not only of territory but of numbers and cultural vitality as well.

This technique was just beginning to be applied in these newly acquired lands of the Far West, as in the case of the initial treaties with the Yakima and related Indians in the Columbia Plain, and would in time be brought to bear on almost all the Indians of this vast realm. The famous Spanish mission system in the Californias was a relatively mild version of this kind of program—mild in that it was designed to fix nomadic Indians in place by means of agriculture and local industry, a concentration on what the imperial agents (the missionaries) regarded as the best lands rather than removal and reduction to the poorest areas, and its primary objective was to create Christian Indian communities that could survive amid the usual pressures of imperial life. To describe and classify it as such of course is not to deny the coercion, suffering, and rebellion attendant upon that specific case. It does, however, help us see more clearly that the typical American Indian reservation created before the 1850s was the product of a much more severe policy.

6. *Complete Removal to a New Reserve, with Programmed Acculturation.* When the balance of power between conqueror and conquered is enormously in favor of the former, the imperial state may decide to exercise that power in a truly radical way: to uproot an entire people, remove them to a specified reserve in an entirely different part of the empire, and resettle them there under a program designed to remold them into a people more appropriately conformed to imperial desires.

The American program to remove all of the Indians from east of the Mississippi River to a set of newly demarked tribal areas in a new Indian Territory was one of the great examples in modern world history of the application of this imperial technique. It is clear that the concept of drastic removal as an appropriate tool was widely supported in the United States. In the 1850s, even as the main program established in the eastern prairies was already being deformed by relentless White expansion, there were calls from various parts of newly acquired territories for further mass removals. One of the earliest acts of the California legislature was to petition the federal government to reject all pending treaties and instead remove all Indians from the state. By that time, such an interest and request may be regarded as entirely routine. More startling—and telling—was the suggestion by Secretary of War Charles Conrad in 1853 that the entire population of New Mexico ("61,000 souls" exclusive of "wild Indians") be uprooted and resettled elsewhere. The local resources were so meager and the military costs so great, he said, that "to protect this small population we are compelled to maintain a large military force at an annual expense nearly equal to half the value of the whole real estate of the Territory. Would it not be better to induce the inhabitants to abandon a country which seems hardly [fit] for the inhabit[ation] of civilized man, by remunerating them for their property, in money or in lands situated in more favorable regions?" Even though the proposal seems not impelled by a desire to gain control of a captured people's lands, it is no less drastic in its removal of people from their homeland to suit the convenience of the imperial power. After all, "re-munerating" for property and promising lands "in more favorable regions" were familiar phrases in many an Indian treaty. In view of the notorious imperial history of the United States, the protesting cry of Missouri and Santa Fe traders and others "that such a proposition could have been conceived in this enlightened age, will test the credulity of the historian" seems rather wide of the mark (they were concerned of course that it would remove themselves—"American citizens"—and their businesses as well as the New Mexicans). Massive removal would continue to be a basic American policy for another thirty years "in this enlightened age."

The widespread use of such a technique of imperial management was of course favored by the sequential acquisition of new territories that appeared to be sparsely inhabited. The Louisiana Purchase made possible the grand removal program of the 1830s; the Mexican cession seemed to provide ample space elsewhere for California's Indian survivors; Secretary Conrad may well have had southern California itself in mind as an appropriate region for the resettlement of New Mexicans. Obviously, without such recurrent additions of new territory, an empire will eventually run out of available areas sufficiently empty and marginal to serve the purpose and must thereby shift to other techniques (what would have been done with the more than 60,000 Indians in the gulf states if there had been no Louisiana Purchase?).

We should also note that an important region within this western empire had been created by the decision of Mormon leaders to uproot and remove their whole people to a refuge in distant marginal lands rather than endure the persecutions and pressures for conformity within the main body of the nation. In so doing, such people saw themselves not as enacting a story in any way comparable to that of the beleaguered Indians but as an exodus, lamentations, and building of a new Zion comparable to that of the ancient Israelites. Spacious empires loosely held may provide insulated ground for utopian experiment as well as imperial management, as the larger history of Europeans in the Americas also attests.

GEOGRAPHIC PATTERNS WITHIN IMPERIAL TERRITORIES

If we are to understand the geography of empires we must also focus on the most important features in the daily life of empire: the basic patterning of contacts and relations between the imperial people and the captive people. For convenience these may be viewed in terms of some commonly recognized categories.

Imperialism is, first of all, a *political* phenomenon, an unequal power relation-ship between two discrete peoples organized in territorial terms. The dominance of the one over the other is visibly expressed by the presence of imperial agents supported by coercive power (governor or commandant and lesser officials backed by police and military forces). Such persons and forces are stationed at carefully selected points within a network of routes linking them together and the territory as a whole to the capital and core of the imperial state. The establishment of a logistic system for the efficient application of military power upon the subordinate province is always a high priority in imperial policy.

Governing requires contact between agents of the two peoples, and the inequality of political relationships imposes an inequality of *social* relationships so as to create an obvious stratification. The conquerors become, ipso facto, an ethnic elite—"aristocracy and empire [are] naturally linked." In any relation beyond the most minimal of protectorates, imperial officials will likely be accompanied by many other representatives of the empire (traders, merchants, lawyers, missionaries, teachers, opportunists of many kinds). Such people will tend to cluster in a few advantageous localities and will likely live in juxtaposition with, but in some degree segregated from, the subordinate population, the more so wherever there is a marked cultural or racial difference between the two peoples. Any considerable influx will create a set of bicultural localities containing separate residential and commercial areas. Those areas will of course be visibly distinct, set apart by barriers of some kind (walls, gates, open spaces), and display the characteristic architecture of the two cultures. Much of that contrast may emerge routinely from the ordinary buildings and spatial forms of the two, but these will likely be accompanied by more calculated emblems of empire. To ensure domination at minimum cost and trouble, imperial states seek to invoke respect for their power and may do so by visible display not just of armed might but of an architecture of authority: the adornment of significant places (capital, gateways, crossroads, shrines, historic sites) with offices, governor's residence, armories, post offices, schools, churches, and other major facilities built on a scale and in a style that physically emphasize the presence and power of the imperial state. The landscape of empire is manipulated to create symbols of authority so as to induce a shift in the *psychological* focus of the captive population. The intent is to subordinate indigenous symbols and gain allegiance not simply from fear but from a respect and even admiration for the cultural attainments and superiority of the ruling power.

Imperial expansion is always predatory and will seek to extract wealth from newly acquired territories. The means of doing so are innumerable: through direct political action, as in confiscations and taxation; through entrepreneurial initiatives, as in the establishment of new businesses and the penetration of indigenous ones; through more subtle, insidious means, arising from alterations of laws and the operations of courts relating to property, tenure, and inheritance. Wealth also flows into the captive province through indemnities, wages, and investments, and from purchases of supplies and services. All of these new *economic* relations are visible in various resources, facilities, and movements of goods and people.

Thus new imperial provinces are penetrated by new people, organized within a new system, bound by new ties, and integrated in many ways into the larger structure. In short, they display a new human geography; in the longer term such articulations and sustained contact will produce *cultural* change, most markedly in the minority people.

The character and degree of such geographic changes can vary greatly with specific circumstances. In some cases, the newly imposed pattern may be very nearly concordant with the old, with the imperial agents simply replacing indigenous personnel, as when General Kearny hoisted the American flag over the Palace of Governors in Santa Fe and moved in to preside over an American New Mexico. Local administration was disturbed as little as possible; the use of English and the line of authority reaching to Washington instead of Mexico City were the only obvious alterations. But of course a more visible imperial geography and landscape was soon discernible: in the stone, brick, and milled lumber of distinctive Anglo-American structures (imperial officials never accepted adobe as a suitable material); in the ethnic clustering and emergence of bicultural "old town–new town" pairs (such as Las Vegas and Albuquerque) with their English newspapers, Protestant churches, and schools; in new economic activities, traffic patterns, and in much else. So, too, as we have seen, the Americans at first simply took the place of French officials in Louisiana, but New Orleans, booming from the sudden congruence in the bounds of its political and economic hinterlands, soon took on a visibly bicultural form and polity (analogous to the development of Montreal under British rule), even as the French Creoles were confirmed in their civil laws and society.

Such continuities in human geography—concordant or duplicative patterns—are most likely where there already exist in the imperial province obvious centers and trafficways and economic activities readily linked with those of the imperial state. Santa Fe and New Orleans were well-established trade centers with influential Anglo-American residents and close mercantile ties with the United States for some years before annexation. But where imperialism imposes rule upon a people greatly different in culture and economy with no infrastructure that the conqueror can readily put to its own use, it will create a pattern much more of its own design and likely quite discordant with that of the indigenous people. Such was the case with most of the army forts, agencies, and trafficways established by the United States with reference to its many Indian territories. Although army troops and Indian traders made use of many well-worn trails, in general imperial facilities and logistics were projections of an alien system designed to serve the bordering, penetrating, and traversing members of the conquering power. And of course wherever the policy of uprooting, removal, and resettlement into thinly occupied lands was applied, the result was the creation of a human geography new to conqueror and conquered alike.

Because American imperialism took this drastic form so extensively up to this time, it is useful to review that policy in light of some of these generic features of empire.

INDIAN REMOVAL AS AN IMPERIAL POLICY

The first decades of the nineteenth century marked a decisive shift in the balance of power between Indians and Whites in the United States. After the Jacksonian era there could be little doubt about the eventual complete subjugation of all Indians to American jurisdiction on American terms. Indian policy was a major national issue, the accompanying debates and discussions provided a rehearsal and refinement of the racial and cultural attitudes of the dominant power, and the historical geography of the changing relations between the two peoples offers a stark display of some fundamentals of American polity and society, and of the Indian predicament and response.

At the opening of the century American policy was grounded in official recognition of the Indians as "resident foreign nations," of a desire for geographic separation of the Whites and Indians, and of the duty of the central government to negotiate for the orderly relinquishment by the Indians of their "excess lands." The concept of "resident foreign nations" was a means of distinguishing them from the member states of the Union and a recognition of the group identity of each Indian tribe. The very fact that the United States entered into treaty relations with Indian tribes gave these tribes a unique position within the American system. Such treaties, however, were primarily instruments of land transfer, the legal device by which the United States sought to achieve its primary policy objective of "expansion with honor." These documents were regarded as decisive exhibits confirming repeated assurances to the Indians that lands would never be taken from them without their consent—hence the need to obtain Indian signatures by whatever means from however small a faction to legitimate the transfer in American interpretations of the law. As a French historian has put it, such treaties "were essential to the making of history," by which is meant "falsifying reality and making this falsification history."

In the early stages of this national process the main pattern of land cessions was accompanied by the withdrawal of the Indians toward the margins, away from the advancing front of White settlers, with the U.S. government assuming little responsibility for the consequences within the remaining unceded Indian country. After the Creek wars and American seizure of the Floridas, however, the southeastern Indians were surrounded and reduced to a hard core of tribal lands, beleaguered islands amid the swirl of settler expansion. It was this geopolitical situation, so unsatisfactory to the Southern states and citizens, combined with the accession of Louisiana and its vast reaches of apparently empty or nearly empty lands, that was primarily responsible for the translation of "withdrawal" and "reduction" into "removal" to a distant sanctuary, reinstituting geographic separation on a continental scale.

Obviously to many, probably most, Americans, removal was simply an expedient for getting rid of the Indians, pushing them farther into the wilderness to fend for themselves. But practicalities of the matter brought forth specifications of American protection and assistance. Nor was removal in itself generally regarded as a final solution to this difficult national problem. Even Jefferson, with his grand vision of allocating all west of the Mississippi to the Indians, did not regard such a geographic design as permanent. "When we shall be full on this side," he wrote in 1803, "we may lay off a range of States on the Western bank from the head to the mouth, & so, range after range, advancing compactly as we multiply." The primary concern was American "advance," not geographic separation of the two peoples. Removal was merely a postponement, at best a buying of time for other processes to work changes in the very nature of Indian society. All formal territories within the federal structure were regarded as temporary, with the critical difference that Indian territories, unlike White, required more than an increase in population to qualify for statehood: they required a comprehensive transformation of Indian life.

By the 1830s the status of the Indians had been redefined as "domestic dependent nations" whose "relation to the United States resembles that of a ward to his guardian." As guardian the United States decreed that the good of its wards required that they be made into typical Americans as rapidly as possible—that they be changed from nations into citizens, from communal life into individual life, so that in their new Western Territory, as Isaac McCoy envisioned, there would be "no greater partiality for the metes and bounds" of tribal areas "than is felt in one of our States or Territories for the lines of counties." As with so much of American Indian policy, hope for such change sprang from a set of attitudes and theories about the nature of Indian societies that had, as subsequent history would demonstrate, little relation to reality.

American Whites commonly assumed that any two or more Indian tribes could and should, whenever appropriate to larger purposes, easily cooperate, amalgamate, fuse into some larger body, or dissolve into individual family units. This assumption rested on a widespread belief that all Indian tribes were basically alike, that they had no real history, that they were not really "nations" in any European sense. That was of course a unity and stereotype entirely of European making, beginning with Columbus's initial act of naming and declaring a general category that could have no meaning whatever to the indigenous American peoples of the time. A corollary was the view of Indians as static societies; their primitive habits were attuned to nature's endless rounds yet with no close attachment to the soil, for they were basically nomads, roaming, hunting, gathering; their agriculture was no more than a kind of random gardening. Indeed, so loosely bound were they to any locality that they could be shifted to another without serious disruption; pleas about the pain of leaving their homelands and the bones of their forefathers could be dismissed as a ploy to impede negotiations (and could have little persuasive power upon a people who had been leaving homelands and ancestors behind— even an ocean away—for generations).

Policies based on such assumptions were constantly bedeviled by contradictions: the deep-rooted, tenacious distinctions of tribes one from another; the long, complicated history of relations among tribes, with keenly remembered patterns of enmity or amity; the fact that the Indians involved in the relocations of these times were in no case rootless wanderers. The role of agriculture in Indian economies did vary, but especially among the Cherokee, Creek, Choctaw, and other southeastern nations agriculture was a well-developed ecological system (borrowings from which had been critical to European survival and success in subtropical America). Where hunting and gathering were a more important basis of subsistence the bond with familiar localities was no less, for one must know nature intimately to gather its fruits. White assumptions about Indian economies generally ignored the whole intricate web of relations—seasonal, ceremonial, religious, psychological—that bound Indian societies to nature in general and to localities in particular. Americans did not understand much about Indian cultures, nations, societies, nor, with a few conspicuous exceptions, did they try very hard to do so. Indians were a policy problem, and the solutions, if any, seemed clear enough.

Insofar as cross-cultural understanding is generally possible, there was certainly no lack of opportunity for Indians to become acquainted with American society, for it was all around, and not only the rougher outer fringes, because many Indian leaders traveled widely and knew something of American towns and cities as well as of frontier outposts and farms (and it was official government practice with reference to remote tribes who might be "in total ignorance of our power" to bring "a deputation of their chiefs through the more populous parts of our country, and letting them see for themselves how comparatively feeble they are"). But for all their variety and tribalism, Indians were united on at least one important thing: their rejection of American society as a model, a higher level of community life. That fact must be emphasized because Americans find it so surprising, puzzling, difficult to accept that all during these years and long after few Indians freely chose to become ordinary American citizens (whereas thousands of Whites elected to leave their own society—civilization itself—to become Indians). Indians were quite willing to marry Whites, but not to become "White"; they were willing to adopt various tools and techniques, ideas and systems, but never to remake themselves into full participants in the "American way of life," despite all the opportunities, assistance, exhortations, and pressures to do so and the obvious, endless pain and penalties of not doing so. That such a change might carry its own disabilities, that neither as individuals, families, or small groups would Indians be welcomed in most American communities, and certainly not as equals (there were strong pressures to categorize them as a "non-White" or "colored" population), seems beside the fact, for there is little evidence that they ever sought such a resolution of their predicament.

The most basic feature of the Indian side of this relationship, therefore, was the *continuity* of Indian societies, of tribal identities wherever possible, of "Indianness" whatever the case. The encounter with Europeans was a new phase of Indian experience, unprecedented in character, difficulty, and danger—but not the beginning of history itself (which is not to say that the Indian conception of "history" was at all similar to the Euro-American). Such intercultural contact was a fact of life that had to be faced, and it might be accompanied by strong attractions as well as painful disruptions. As the United States became a powerful, expansive force, every Indian society caught within its bounds was eventually plunged into crisis over how best to respond, and every tribe was factionalized by such pressures, but the internal quarrel was always over the form of resistance, not over the possibility of dissolution and surrender to White civilization. Even where these contentions tended to be "full bloods" versus "mixed bloods," as was often the case, survival was defined in terms of *group* survival, preserving as large a measure as possible of communal life, kinship bonds, consensual authority, seasonal and generational rhythms and rituals, languages, traditions, and mythology within radically altered and constricted geographies.

That the human geography of Indian America must be radically altered—eventually effaced as a discrete pattern—was never extensively questioned by American leaders and public. They were agreed that Indians were a primitive people who must, by the laws of nature and history, give way to more advanced peoples. As Robert E. Berkhofer, Jr., has emphasized, Indians were regarded as deficient in comparison with Whites: uncivilized, un-Christian, unenlightened, living in communal groups with little sense of formal organization or private property; unindustrious, undisciplined, given to sporadic outbursts of savagery. History proved their inferiority: their failure to withstand the shock of encounter with Europeans, their vulnerability to disease, their inability to compete with White societies. In spite of any good qualities they might have (and many Whites acknowledged a certain nobility in the best of Indian leaders) and however valiantly they might resist (and they had earned more than a little respect for their fighting abilities and bravery), they were doomed to fail; they were a vanishing race.

It was a special complication of American history that they were not vanishing fast enough. The amazing dynamics of American expansion, the sheer success of the Republic, brought about repeated collisions between the two peoples. Therefore the United States had to deal with Indians in some comprehensive way, and as most spokesmen acknowledged that it would be immoral willfully to promote their extinction as persons, some means of salvation must be undertaken. Because it was apparently going to take some time to change them into productive citizens, they must meanwhile be removed and protected and aided by the American government.

The really relentless pressure in all of this, of course, came not from any widespread sense of obligation to save the Indians but from the desire to get hold of their lands. Although fueled by greed, such desire was also grounded in the routine assumption that family farms ought to take precedence over tribal uses, and such a change was further magnified and ennobled in this case as being fundamental to the essence of America, wherein land ownership was regarded as being the foundation of democracy, the stabilizer of society, the insurance of liberty. Continued access to cheap lands and the westward advance of settlers was therefore the surest sign of American social health and progress, and thus "under the ideology of Americanism," as Berkhofer noted, "geography took a moral as well as an economic dimension"—with most Americans shrugging off the corollary that any full sense of morality would have to account for the changing geography of the beleaguered Indians as well as the advancing Americans.

By virtue of its revolutionary triumph the United States asserted sovereignty over all the land within its geopolitical bounds. Indians had merely a "right of occupancy" on the sufferance of the United States, and when it pleased the American government to modify the scale and locale of that occupancy, it found legal means of doing so. Tocqueville's well-known ironic comment on American practice that "it is impossible to destroy men with more respect for the laws of humanity" glosses over the cynicism with which such laws were used. By signing treaties Indians became locked into an alien juridical system over which they had no direct influence. In such an unequal relationship treaties turn out to mean whatever the dominant party wants them to mean. Even the most sophisticated adaptations to the ensnaring system do not ensure its protections. The Cherokee were considered to have seriously undermined their strong legal case for retention of the last remnant of their homelands when they formalized their own state government, for the State of Georgia immediately pointed to the American Constitution, which states that "no new State shall be formed or erected within the Jurisdiction of any other State" (Article IV, Section 3). More obviously, the Cherokee lost because they (and by inference any other tribe or all Indians together) were less important to the Union than was the State of Georgia. The federation was fragile and the central government unwilling to risk the alienation of another Southern member (the Cherokee case coincided with South Carolina's assertion of "nullification" over the tariff). When the irresistible force (Georgia) met the immovable object (the Cherokee), the federal government put its weight behind the force, and the object was violently moved a thousand miles westward.

During this tumultuous time a common metaphor recurs time and again in treaties, orations, discussions, and debates to describe the relationship of Americans with the Indians. It had been set forth explicitly at the Treaty of Greenville (1795). At the signing ceremony, following the conclusion of this first violent chapter of American dominance, the Indians publicly declared "we do now, and will henceforth, acknowledge the fifteen United States of America to be our father"; to which the victorious General Anthony Wayne replied: "I now adopt you all, in the name of the President of the Fifteen Great Fires of America, as their children." This paternal image was a mutually acceptable metaphor; it humanized abstract concepts of political authority, just as "Great Fires" conveyed a sense of the state as a community. Not surprisingly, it became a favorite image for White Americans; *The Great Father* serves as the appropriate title for Francis Paul Prucha's magisterial survey of relations between the United States government and the American Indian right down to our own time.

It is an obvious and appealing metaphor: it is a father's duty to care for his children, to protect them, to help provide for their basic needs, to point the way, to lead them through inexorable change, and to help them find a suitable place in the larger society; the good father knows what is good for his children; he may listen to them, but he is not bound by their wishes, and he may admonish and chastise them when needed. His is the superior experience, knowledge, and wisdom; he is in charge because that is the way God, or Nature, has ordered life to be. It is easy to understand how natural and compelling such an image was to a people who regarded Indians as primitives who must be nurtured and disciplined into civilized beings. And it is important to recognize the sincerity with which many officials, agents, and friends of the Indians sought to apply it, to make it an appropriate expression of the protection, education, and change to be achieved. As Bernard W. Sheehan, after a thorough study of these times and this topic, has remarked: "surely the breadth and intensity of the discussion belies the charge of hypocrisy" in any comprehensive sense.

It is of course notorious that the image was tarnished by reality—but, after all, parenting often is. If the father was unable to do, or at least did not do, all that he had promised and hoped to do, if the children did not respond as the father hoped, if they turned out to be surprisingly, exasperatingly different and difficult (they are, after all, adopted and of unknown origin)—need we be surprised? Should we abandon the image because it seems to correspond more closely to common experience than to some exalted ideal of fatherhood? Certainly Americans generally have not thought so, for its use has endured.

But let us apply this paternal metaphor just a little more closely to the actual case. Let us think of the United States as a household with two sets of children, one natural, the other adopted. The natural children are much the more numerous and stronger, and they wreak havoc on the adopted children, stealing their goods, beating them, at times depriving them of shelter and subsistence. It is only natural that the weaker children resist as best they can and in various ways (but are so disparate among themselves as never to band together very effectively); they retaliate in kind, and from time to time it is open warfare, with killings and maimings on both sides. The father makes a feeble attempt to keep order in his house; he loudly denounces such mayhem and repeatedly professes his concern for his adopted children and promises protection (as Lincoln, deflecting the complaints of a delegation of Plains Indian chiefs, said: "You know it is not always possible for any father to have his [natural] children do precisely as he wishes them to do"); but he is in fact under the control of his natural children and is goaded by them into punishing the despised and weaker set, eventually exiling them into a far corner of his property, and when they resist, beating them, and if they really fight back, killing them.

In the real world no society tolerates such fathers or such children; such horrifying families are forcibly, legally dismantled, and society assumes responsibility for punishing such behavior and finding some means of caring for its victims. In this American case, the paternal metaphor leads us ineluctably into the pathology of the family.

What are we to do with such a metaphor? We cannot simply ignore it, for it is a historic terminology used formally at the highest levels, and it has permeated and shaped American thought and practice over a long period of time. But no sensitive person can continue to use it in such a way, for surely the reality of the case is too apparent and painful. And so we must find another way to describe the actual relationship between the United States government and Indian peoples, a way that defines the relative positions of the two peoples, makes plausible the various policies and actions pursued, and places this aspect of national history in broader perspective.

We will be better served by a concept and set of terms long available, familiar at the time, and fully appropriate to the American case: the language of empire. American conquest, subordination, and management of the Indians as a distinct people within the national polity is but one example in a long array of harsh interracial encounters and stark cultural collisions. The American case, like every other, has its specific context and special features, but it is no more than a variation within one of the most common geopolitical patterns in world history. Nor would one have to search far into that history for examples, for they were apparent in several parts of the world at that time. In the very years that the United States was declaring and erecting a "permanent Indian frontier" drawn longitudinally through the woodland-prairie margins of central North America, the Russian Empire was building an arc of forts from west to east along the northern edge of the Kazakh Steppe in Central Asia in an attempt (equally futile) to stabilize the borderlands between its Siberian settlers and Turkic nomads. In general terms, the two situations, responses, and results were strikingly similar. The Russian-Kazakh encounter featured a long prelude of trading posts, sporadic clashes, and ominous changes in native economies and culture. It involved frontier squatters, harassments, and mutual retaliations, with Russian expansions aided by opportunistic and corrupt local officials in defiance of central authorities who made some attempt to uphold treaty protections. The Russian Empire also assumed sovereignty over all lands, with allocation of tracts to native groups and subdivision of "surplus" lands to Russian settlers; it superimposed a new geopolitical order, with boundaries designed to confine and divide native clans from one another and undermine traditional patterns of authority; and it imposed the Russian language, laws, taxation, and schools, thereby giving critical influence to interpreters and various agents and intermediaries. It pressured the rather marginally Muslim Kazakh nomads to settle down and become good Christian farmers. In the face of mounting disruptions, havoc, and murder, the pleas of Kazakh leaders to the imperial government to impose some restraint on its Russian citizenry and uphold elemental principles of humane relations have a hauntingly familiar ring to any student of American Indian history.

There were, however, critical differences in the two cases: in the balance of power and in the character of empire. The Kazakhs were far more numerous than the Indians and therefore not so easily pushed aside; they had never been so decimated by disease or debilitated by contact as to suggest that they were a "vanishing race," even though Russian spokesmen might assert as confidently as Americans that by the "laws of history" nomadic peoples (in this case herders) must give way to settled farmers. The Kazakhs might be shoved around and diminished in territory but they could not be readily removed en masse, and, therefore, if the empire insisted on expanding in that sector it had little choice but to incorporate them as an ethnic and geopolitical component. That of course was something the Russian Empire had done with a long list of peoples over several centuries. It was a sprawling structure encompassing a great patchwork of territories, many of which were primarily ethnic ("racial" in nineteenth-century terms) in definition and content.

The United States was also a huge and expansive structure that captured and encompassed many different peoples, but it refused to allow them that kind of geopolitical presence. That issue was central to the debates over Indian policy and fundamental to the subsequent character of the United States as a society and polity. As we have seen, several different imperial designs were actually formulated and extensively discussed:

1. A large protectorate in distant and less desirable margins of the country, incorporating many different peoples, with no more than a limited program for cultural change—as in the proposed northwest Indian territory of the 1820s;
2. A formal indigenous state, modeled extensively on the pattern of American states but wholly under internal Indian control—as in the Cherokee design; and
3. A large Indian territory formally subdivided among the various tribes and under close supervision and cultural programming by the imperial government, with a capital town, general council of tribal representatives, and nonvoting delegates to Congress—as in committee proposals of the 1830s.

What the United States did create was a semblance of this third type: the geographical framework without the political substance, a special territory of something over 100,000 square miles (about the size of Missouri and Arkansas together) for something over 100,000 people, but it was (despite all treaty assurances to the Indians) obviously regarded as a temporary geopolitical accommodation, a kind of holding pen awaiting the further diminution, dispersal, and assimilation of its inhabitants.

The generic marks of imperialism were readily discernible in this 1840s Western Territory, even if not wholly classic in form nor complete in substance:

1. The presence of an imperial governor (though some distance removed, in the Superintendency in St. Louis—the original proposal had a governor seated at Fort Leavenworth) and his district agents (though not housed in a calculated symbolic architecture of power);
2. The presence of military garrisons and depots at strategic sites, from where periodic shows of force and ceremonial escorts were sent out to perform in the theater of empire (formal meetings where warriors paraded and orators offered solemn assurances of their mutual respect and perpetual friendship), as well as to punish offenders and suppress resistance;
3. The mixed-blood population and the variety of translators and other intermediaries present in the localities of sustained contact (but as yet without stabilized social segregations and stratifications); and
4. The assigned cultural agents and their instruments of change: schoolteachers, missionaries, farmers, and other artisans; along with the whiskey dealers, unlicensed traders, land swindlers, and other unauthorized persons preying upon a captive people.

The principal variation from common imperial patterns was the absence of formal systems of tribute, taxation, and other means of economic exploitation. The obvious explanation was the absence of ready wealth from newly resettled Indians and the confident expectation of eventually taking from them the most coveted resource: their "excess" lands.

So, too, the modern reader of Indian treaties is saved from choking on the clotted hypocrisy of those solemn assurances—"perpetual peace and friendship"; "protect against all disturbance"; *"a permanent home, . . .* which shall, under the most solemn guarantee of the United States, be and remain theirs forever"—if it is understood to be the language of empire, drawing upon the standard vocabulary of diplomacy, the formal etiquette of adversaries, the rhetorical disguise of actual power relations and feelings between the two parties.

Of course, Americans have never been very comfortable with such language, being inclined to regard it as the product of a cynical Old World inappropriate to the politics of the New. And despite all this stark exhibit of imperial features, American statesmen and the American public in general steadfastly refused to think of the United States as an empire with reference to its captive Indian populations. Americans who argued against Indian removal tried to insist "that a degree of independence [as an enclave] within the context of the surrounding white society was legally and politically possible as well as morally desirable," but any such design was firmly rejected. American leaders, backed by strong majorities, time and again made a conscious decision not to tolerate that pattern of human diversity within their country.

RACISM AND EMPIRE

That the United States wanted the territories it obtained but not the people who lived in them does not make it exceptional in the history of imperialism, as many a ruthless conquest attests. It does place the American case in a particular broad category of imperialism and attendant cultural collisions.

One of the most common geopolitical events in world history is the conquest of densely settled productive regions by disciplined forces coming out of some distant, lean periphery. Conquest may yield plunder at the cost of much destruction but longer-term imperial interest requires the continuance of the indigenous population and economy so as to continue production of the wealth that first attracted and now sustains the conquerors in their ruling position. In such cases, the conquerors are often less technically advanced, less economically sophisticated, and would disdain to do the basic labor required to produce such wealth.

The United States case is clearly the opposite kind of conquest and encounter. Here the indigenous economies were producing almost nothing that was of interest (aside from the quickly distorted and destructive fur and deerskin trades) and little to sustain an imperial superstructure, whereas the conquerors had the tools to create far more of their own kind of wealth and sustenance by colonizing it with their own people. In such situations, if the conquered people can be put to work within newly imposed or dominated systems they may be accepted as a useful presence (such as Hispanic sheep herders on American ranches in the semi-arid Southwest), but if not, there will be great pressures to shove them aside as entrepreneurs move in to organize exploitation of newly acquired territories. In the American case, almost all of these annexed peoples were regarded as an encumbrance, a complication, a costly problem; further, not only were they regarded as weaker societies, they were considered to be inherently inferior peoples who must by the inexorable processes of history be replaced by superior, successful people. That attitude was of profound importance in shaping the character of this continental empire.

The broad social ranking of these "other peoples" was quite clear (in simplest form): French Louisianians–Mexicans–Indians–Blacks. There were numerous gradations and nuances within and among such categories. The French Creoles included persons of European ancestry as well as many of mixed racial origins, but even those at the top of the local hierarchy were not accepted as equals, for as Lord Durham, taking into account the situation of both French Louisianians and French Canadians, had observed: "It is not any where a virtue of the English race to look with complacency on any manners, customs or laws which appear strange to them; accustomed to form a high estimate of their own superiority, they take no pains to conceal from others their contempt and intolerance of their usages." It was generally understood by the dominating power, however, that such people were assimilable and indeed must eventually disappear into a triumphant North American "Anglo-Saxonism." As young William Gilpin (who would become an avid geopolitical spokesman for a Greater America) reported to his father from New Orleans in 1837, while the town was still Gallic in flavor, "the Anglo-Saxon is pushing aside the Frenchman and eating him up."

In Anglo-American eyes, the French were tainted by their tendency to mix and socialize too freely with other races. Obsessed with White-Black relationships, Anglo-Americans were inclined to lump all people who had any apparent trace of Indian or Black ancestry into the general category of "colored," with varying recognition of subgroups. Officials struggled to fit human variety into a few simple categories. The Census Schedule of 1850 defined "White, Black, Mulatto, or Domesticated Indian. Free or Slave" as the appropriate classifications; "Mestizo" was mentioned in a footnote as another mixture (improperly defined as "the issue of the Indian and the Negro"). The Census of 1860 added "Half-breeds" to the list for some states and territories (in a most erratic and unreliable manner: 55 in New Mexico, for example); that had long been the common English term for the residue of French métis in the northwestern territories (404 listed for Wisconsin).

This deeply ingrained sense of color and social prejudice was of course magnified by the clash of Anglo-Americans and Hispano-Americans. The Texas Republic came out of what was widely perceived as a "racial" war and set a pattern of attitudes further broadened and intensified by subsequent encounters. Even though early relations between Anglos and Hispanos in New Mexico and California were mutually advantageous and often cordial, these, too, served to build a picture of Mexicans in general as an ignorant and indolent people demonstrably incapable of self-government. Americans readily concluded that such was a natural result of their being a people degraded by promiscuous mixing—"half breeds and mongrels," to use a common derision in American lingo. Such a population was hardly a good prospect for American citizenship. Horsman's remark that the recurrent argument about annexation of Mexican territory "was primarily an argument not about territory but about Mexicans" does not really apply to Texas and California, or even New Mexico, but was surely true with reference to the further annexations so avidly sought by influential leaders. The expansionist argument that the Mexicans would inevitably recede before the Anglo-American tide was more difficult to sustain the deeper they pushed their boundaries into Mexico. It was also made more difficult after thousands of American soldiers had tramped a thousand parched miles through the scrub-covered countrysides of semi-arid Mexico. It was apparent that there were tens of thousands of inhabitants in those difficult lands and no great fertile expanses awaiting the industrious colonist. Contemporary statistics readily available to interested Americans showed that the coveted band of additional territory between Tamaulipas and Baja California contained about a million people—good reason indeed to question the incorporation of such an acquisition into the body of the Republic (modern assessments put the figure closer to 600,000). Still, the combination of sheer arrogance, ignorance, and vainglory with reference to such additions must not be underestimated: Buchanan, eager to obtain Cuba, remarked that of course it must be speedily "Americanized—as Louisiana has been"—at a time when that Hispanic island was home to more than a million people, including 600,000 Blacks.

One way out of the dilemma posed by such populations was to cast aside this need to "Americanize" and assimilate them and simply proceed to conquer and rule these territories as an obvious empire. There were people quite willing to undertake such a task, most notoriously the Knights of the Golden Circle, a small extremist Southern group that envisioned a tropical slave-plantation empire under American military rule expanding around the Caribbean, but that was too blatant—and far too Southern—to be supported by a deeply divided federal republic. These Hispanic and Afro-American borderlands did impede American expansion. Even that leading architect and general of the cause, James K. Polk, occasionally expressed doubts about annexing large numbers of Mexicans. Frederick Merk concluded that the main reason why "continentalism" stalled and began to fade after midcentury was "a national reluctance to add peoples of mixed blood to a blood that was pure, and an unwillingness in some parts of the population to have unfree blood as well. Only those people should be admitted to the temple who would qualify someday for equal statehood in the Union, and this requirement the colored and mixed races to the south could not meet."

As Merk's choice of words suggests, American racism had begun to take on a new emphasis and stridency. Reginald Horsman has traced the mutation of *Anglo-Saxon* in American usage from its early connotation of a distinct politico-cultural heritage—the great principles underlying the law and liberties and constitutional government—to an overt emphasis upon the natural, historically demonstrated, superiority of the English-British-Germanic-Teutonic "race" (definition of *Anglo-Saxon* in this sense was flexible, and readily adaptable to the context and prejudice of the user). At the same time an "American school of ethnology" emerged that produced scientific tomes defining the types of humankind and expounding on their fatefully divergent destinies in the modern world—anthropological corollaries to the geographical interpretations of Arnold Guyot.

Americans were ripe to receive such teachings not primarily because they felt any need to excuse their treatment of Mexico and Mexicans but because they had long been struggling to rationalize the continuing enslavement of Africans and the progressive extermination of Indians. These populations were relegated to the bottom layers of the American classification of peoples, but the two remained sharply differentiated. Theoretically the possibility of assimilation was always open and indeed urged upon the Indians: they could become full citizens if they would shed their Indianness. Practically it was widely assumed that the Indians were doomed to extinction from their curious inability or dogged refusal to cope with modern civilization; in either case they would not endure as a distinct body of people to complicate the geopolitical structure of the federation. Black Americans were a captive people in a critically different sense, imported as alien chattels with never a claim to a territorial identity or status. Their presence constituted the deepest human problem and exposed the worst contradictions in American life: eagerly purchased for their labor but generally despised as a people, unwanted as a social presence, feared as a potentially rebellious force. American agonizing over how to effect an eventual abolition of slavery was compounded by the White dilemma over what to do with free Blacks—that is, how to keep such a potentially large body of people from participating fully in American society and polity, and how to contain the explosive pressures inevitably generated by such denial. This painful plight of American Blacks will be more fully examined in our consideration of the United States as a nation.

In the broader view of history, Americans were not alone in having a model for humankind and a rationale for expansion. Other versions of such national missions were already evident or being formulated elsewhere in the world. Because the American case involves such self-conscious talk about purity and inferior races with reference to peoples and territories, the modern student may find the most telling parallel in the way German intellectuals (even more imbued with ideas of nationalism and the new sciences than the Americans) were proclaiming the expansive mission of the German people. As A. P. Thornton noted:

> Their belief in racial superiority did not incline the Germans to practice reciprocity in their dealings with other nations. No true reciprocity, in such a situation, was possible; and it would be hypocritical to pretend that it was. The idea of Pan-Germanism could never adapt itself to the presence of other races. . . . The Germans conquered, or planned to conquer, *territories* and *areas*, not nations. Germans needed above all, if their ideas were to grow and develop fully, space. If the space was not physically there, it had to be created. It had to be cleared. They spoke of *Lebensraum*, as if the provision of room for German elbows was the only function such cleared areas would have. They saw themselves as constantly faced with a Task. When not actively at work on this Task, they were betraying the cause for which they stood.

The point of this assessment is not to imply that the United States should not have expanded across North America but only to help us see more clearly than the lens of nationalism commonly allows on what terms it did expand and with what consequences for the peoples—all the peoples—of the United States. In running roughshod over other peoples caught in their path, Americans behaved as strong societies have most commonly behaved through all human history. "It is clear," said Philip Mason in his thoughtful survey of such matters, "that dominance by one group of people over another is something of which no race or period has a monopoly; it is as old as the Pharaohs and springs from passions that are common to all men." A notable feature of the American case has been the extraordinary resistance to any forthright admission that the United States was an empire, imposing its rule upon captive peoples and their homelands. As the young philosopher Josiah Royce, writing in the 1880s about his native state, observed: "The American as conqueror is unwilling to appear in public as a pure aggressor; he dare not seize a California as Russia has seized so much land in Asia or as Napoleon, with full French approval, seized whatever he wanted. The American wants to persuade not only the world but himself that he is doing God service in a peaceable spirit, even when he violently takes what he has determined to get."

More important than this characteristic "squeamishness" and "hypocrisy" with which Americans regarded and represented their methods of expansion was the refusal to recognize the geopolitical character of what they had created. The United States was, from its beginnings, an empire in very basic ways. It was, further, a special kind of empire, and that fact was directly connected to some of those same characteristics that Americans took so much pride in presenting to the world as the marks of a new kind of society and polity. The United States was a *democratic imperialism,* a mass-driven force of special character and power. That fact was especially apparent in its dealing with the Indians. With reference to most Indian territories the central government was not the primary agent directing White expansion. It did not commonly send out its armies ahead of its citizens to conquer these peoples and drive them off their lands; rather, it sent them out, time and again, to impose order upon the chaos arising from the unbridled aggression of its frontier citizens trespassing into Indian territories. But always, ultimately, it put its power in support of such populist aggression because in this federal system the central government was the hostage of its member states, and in those constituent democratic republics the leadership was accountable to the citizenry, as an Indian agent (himself involved in crass speculations) explained bluntly to the restive Potawatomi in 1858: "Let me impress upon your minds, my Red Children, that the white people who make the laws and elect the president and all other officeholders are the government themselves, and when they determine by a large majority to effect anything against the poor Indian, the President himself, though he might want to do right toward you, has not got the power to do it." The theoretical protections of the three branches of government and separation of powers were of little account, as the Cherokee case demonstrated. The fundamental fact in the workings of this American process of expansion was the general agreement at all levels as to the eventual outcome desired, whatever differences there might have been as to the handling of any specific case.

As a result, the United States was an unusually severe imperial power. It demanded more than simple submission to political authority: it decreed the drastic displacement of native peoples from their homelands, and it undertook a program to pressure them into abandoning the most basic features of their way of life, of their identity as a people. Such contempt for the culture of subordinated groups, intolerance of their existence as separate and vital societies, and indifference to their survival as people were not, to be sure, unprecedented. But the United States was the most massive and systematic case of its time and notable as well for enveloping the whole drastic process with assurances to the people involved and to the rest of the world of its special virtues and noble intentions.

In an impassioned plea to his fellow Californian legislators not to petition the federal government to remove all the Indians from the state, J. J. Warner asked: "Will it be said that the land is not broad enough for them and us? or that while our doors are open to the stranger from the uttermost parts of the earth, we have not spare room for the residence of the once sole inhabitants of our magnificent empire?" The paradox of welcoming immigrants while trying to get rid of the indigenous population was obvious enough, but it must not be extended to suggest a tolerance of diversity in the one while refusing to accept it in the other. Those variegated immigrants were expected to conform, to make themselves into Americans on American terms; they were to become *individual*, English-speaking, law-abiding citizens with no intervening allegiance to their native culture or society. That was the kind of freedom conferred by American membership and protected by the Constitution. It was not unusual, nor presumably would most people think it inappropriate, for the receiving nation—the *charter society*—to lay down the terms of membership for those who sought to immigrate and join it. A nation whose origins and dynamics were so obviously bound up with transatlantic migration and so conscious of itself as a new and continuing creation must have some vital concern about the compatibility and coherence of its citizenry.

It is quite a different matter to require such assimilation from people who have been conquered or annexed against their will and who have no escape. When the balance of power is so heavily weighted in favor of the dominating power and the pressures to conform are driven by a powerful sense of national mission and a deep sense of racial and cultural superiority, the outlook for the captured people is ominous indeed; for such hapless victims *e pluribus unum* means social annihilation in one form or another.

Imperialism is usually a bloody business, empire-building a rough affair, imperial management a coercive trade—so much so that the very word and concept have, by the late twentieth century, become commonly regarded as denoting a political evil that must be abjured and expunged wherever it might remain. But such a view would seem to be naive and selective in what it likely recognizes as imperial; it glosses over the fact that the political "self-determination" of every aspiring self-defined "people" or "nation" is hardly a feasible goal in any prospect that involves a close look at the number of such peoples on the face of the earth. Therefore the problem of how to create political frameworks that can accommodate human variety in territorial units will long be with us. In humane terms that has ever been the positive challenge of empires: how to create an encompassing geopolitical system that can accommodate cultural diversity in the form of discrete, territorially delimited societies on a sustained and not destructively subordinate level. Sustained contact between unlike peoples will surely lead to culture change, but even if initiated and maintained under forceful auspices, not all of it need be deleterious for the subordinate people. As innumerable examples in the history of nations attest, it may lead to a broadening of views and opportunities, to stimulating interaction and creativity with manifestly beneficial results (perhaps more apparent to those generations who inherit such results than to those who live through the early creative phases of them).

The United States refused to accept that geopolitical challenge. Its leaders held fast to a vision of the nation that had no place for diversity in such terms. They insisted on seeing America as a new, unique creation unsullied by older, European models. They had established a new kind of state for a new kind of person, and their *novus ordo seclorum* had no place for rival cosmologies; their vaunted liberty and equality were available only in terms of a fundamental conformity. The Constitution, drawn up when more than half of the national territory was unceded Indian lands, made no provision for the geopolitical accommodation of such people, and subsequent addition of a great many more Indian and other societies brought no constitutional amendments in support of their cultural integrity; it is a document for a nation, not an empire, a set of rules and protections for a people that is uniform rather than diverse in its basic cultural character.

It has generally been agreed that it could hardly have been otherwise. As Reginald Horsman, an incisive critic, put it: "Enlightenment did not mean cultural pluralism and to ask the early nineteenth century leaders to believe in this concept is to ask them to transcend their century." It is of course true that every "century" tends to be shaped by a particular view of the world, by some set of ideas about human nature and society, and tends to force observable evidence into the pattern of that view. The idea of the Indians as a vanishing race, their tribal extinction as a lamentable necessity of "progress," might in itself account for their exclusion from the great initial design for the Republic. But their continued, complicating, exasperating presence forced American leaders to think about the problem, and it is not quite so obvious that they would have had to "transcend their century" in order to think in terms of imperial alternatives. The problem of incorporating disparate cultures within the bounds of orderly political states—"pluralism" by whatever name—was age-old, always on exhibit in the world and certainly in that century. Statesmen steeped in the classics could have drawn as readily upon the Roman Empire as upon the Greek republics for their concepts and models, but they rarely did, for the image was not compatible with their ideals (Sam Houston, in his usual forthright manner, had no hesitation in pointing out that the Anglo-American "love of domination and the extension of their territorial limits, . . . is equal to that of Rome in the last stages of the Commonwealth and the first of the Caesars").

The great majority of American leaders and public alike were so obsessed by nationalism, by their sense of superiority and destiny, by their aspirations for themselves and their country that they were either blind or indifferent to the realities of American imperialism. And the power of their position and potential was such as even to becloud the view of the most discerning critic of the century. Writing in the 1830s, Alexis de Tocqueville concluded the first volume of his monumental analysis of *Democracy in America* by noting that, suddenly, in his own day, two great nations had appeared on the world scene—the Russians and the Americans—each advancing "with ease and celerity along a path to which no limit can be perceived." Having examined the plight of the American Indians, been thoroughly tuned in on the swirl of debates, and actually seen bands of the Choctaw in the midst of removal ("I was witness of sufferings that I have not the power to portray"), he assumed their ultimate extinction and went on to draw this comparison of the two great forces moving across the continents (he was writing before the major confrontation of Americans and Mexicans):

> The American struggles against the obstacles that nature opposes to him; the adversaries of the Russian are men. The former combats the wilderness and savage life; the latter, civilization with all its arms. The conquests of the American are therefore gained by the plowshare; those of the Russian by the sword. The Anglo-American relies upon the personal interest to accomplish his ends and gives free scope to the unguided strength and common sense of the people; the Russian centers all the authority of society in a single arm. The principal instrument of the former is freedom; of the latter servitude. Their starting-point is different and their courses are not the same; yet each of them seems marked out by the will of Heaven to sway the destinies of half the globe.

We should not be surprised if Americans eagerly embrace so flattering a comparison. But such a statement removes the Indian from our view rather too hastily and completely. We must not dismiss the 300,000 people that lay to the west of those advancing American plowshares quite so readily; we might indeed make use of his comparison but observe that for all the weaker tribal peoples that lay in the paths of these two Juggernauts, the one that gave "free scope to the unguided strength and common sense of the people" was much the more to be feared. Insofar as Kazakhs and Choctaws were concerned, there was reason to believe that the despotic empire of Nicholas I offered better prospects for cultural survival than did the democratic American "empire for liberty" under Andrew Jackson and his successors.

We cannot "undo" history, but we can undo common understandings of history and put in their place interpretations that offer a better view of what actually happened and how we might best comprehend it. To recast the history of Anglo-American expansionism into imperial terms is merely one basic shift in perspective that can help Euro-Americans gain a clearer view of our national past. At the same time, we must seek the help of members of these many indigenous captive peoples to discern far more clearly that we as yet do the variety and richness that lie underneath the imposed unity of the concept "Indian"; to help us appreciate the tenacious hold on ancestral cosmologies and cultures and the responses and adaptations that have allowed survival in the face of powerful and comprehensive pressures—that have together forced upon a resisting, begrudging American nationality the fundamental fact and power of *in uno plures*.

10. Continentalism: Objectives, Modes, Visions

The expansion of the United States across the North American continent—prodigious in scale though it was—was not really surprising. After all, the nation was an outgrowth of a vigorously expanding Europe, and it had been fitted out at its birth with even more effective tools for rapid advance. By 1800 the spread of the American people westward into their half of the Mississippi Valley was obviously a powerful movement that the Indians could not stem and the central government could not manage. So, too, the extension of the sovereign limits of the United States beyond their original bounds had ample precedent. The political map of North America had been redrawn time and again as a result of diplomacy and war among the European imperial powers, and once the United States became an independent actor its national leadership could be expected to attempt further alterations to enhance its security and prospects.

Yet, however much politicians and the public talked about "manifest destiny" and "natural boundaries" there was nothing foreordained about the United States becoming a transcontinental state and adding the particular areas it did eventually obtain. As we have seen, these bounds were the result of a complex series of events that involved surprises and compromises as well as specified geographical objectives. It will be useful to summarize some of the geographical thinking and modes of expansion employed in the creation of this momentous territorial frame.

GEOGRAPHICAL OBJECTIVES

As a national policy, American territorial expansion began with a specific, focused, and limited objective: to obtain control of the lower Mississippi so as to gain unhindered access to the Gulf of Mexico. Such an addition was defined in exact geographic terms—the Island of New Orleans—and justified as being the most critical part of a *natural geographic system* upon which the United States was dependent for its prosperity and security. The occupation and annexation of westernmost Florida might have been rationalized on the same geographic grounds (rather than as part of the Louisiana Purchase), for it completed American control of both banks of the entire Mississippi waterway.

An interesting extension of this concept applied to this "same" natural system began to appear in the 1820s in support of the annexation of Cuba. President Monroe, replying to Jefferson's encouragement about adding Cuba to the Union, stated, "I have always concurr'd with you in [that] sentiment. . . . I consider Cape Florida, & Cuba, as forming the mouth of the Mississippi." American expansionists readily took to the idea that the Gulf of Mexico and the Gulf Stream were logically and essentially American waters, a concept broached by Jefferson as early as 1806 during the maritime troubles with Britain and France. Despite some talk of Florida as an obvious *natural appendage* to the Republic, that was not the main consideration of those who worked most assiduously for its annexation. But once Florida was obtained, the strategic significance of that peninsula and Cuba together to the coasts and commerce of the United States became a standard theme.

The other great natural geographic system was not a cause of similar concern. The northern boundary between the secessionist republic and the continuing British Empire bisected the Great Lakes but left all but seventy miles of the St. Lawrence, their sole natural outlet, under British control. Removing that hold and bringing the whole system under the American flag became a logical and attractive objective of the War of 1812 but had nothing to do with the initiation of that conflict. Indeed, the American areas most directly bound into that hydrography were strongly against the war. Before the surge of American settlement into the broader Great Lakes region was well under way, the completion of the Erie, Champlain, and Oswego canals had made the new American waterway system manifestly superior and thereby defused any potential American pressure for redefinition of boundaries or controls relating to this great natural—but naturally limited—trafficway. That ill-conceived war had forced Americans to accept the fact that the British Empire was not weakening and receding, as the Spanish obviously was, but remained a mighty presence in Atlantic America. It is worth noting that the United States made no attempt to negotiate a recession of British positions overlooking vital American sea-lanes, as in the Bahamas, Bermuda, Nova Scotia (a natural appendage?), or Newfoundland. After 1815 a growing mutual interest in the flow of Atlantic commerce must have softened any American sense of vulnerability, despite occasional diplomatic crises.

The idea of an American extension to the Pacific Ocean developed slowly and uncertainly. The prospect of transcontinental commercial traffic was envisioned by Jefferson, assessed by Lewis and Clark, and attempted by the Astorians, but with no convincing success and no determined effort on the part of the U.S. government to ensure a formal territorial reach across the continent (fig. 23). The Adams-Onís Treaty, which did formalize such a claim, was considered at the time to be a personal diplomatic adjunct of more important territorial issues. On the other hand, the American claim to rights on the Columbia River, initiated by Gray's exploration, was never challenged, and when the United States did turn its attention to the Pacific Coast access to the best harbors—Puget Sound on the north, San Francisco Bay on the south—became specific objectives. As we have seen, however, the initial interest was not so much in securing a broad oceanic frontage for a transcontinental state as in ensuring use of these prized anchorages for Pacific commerce. The United States tried repeatedly but failed to gain direct territorial access to the Gulf of California, with the port of Guaymas as the main

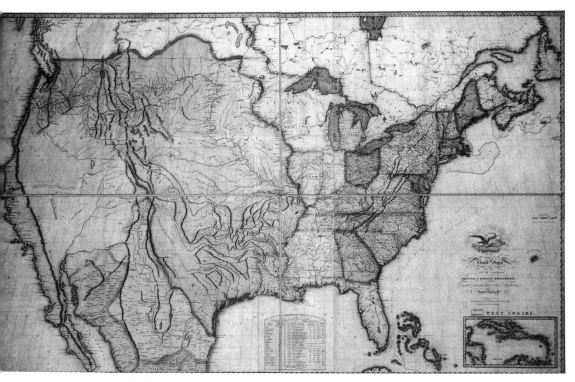

23. "Map of the United States with the Contiguous British
and Spanish Possessions," 1816.

John Melish was a Scot who traveled extensively in the United States in 1806–7 and returned to settle in Philadelphia in 1809. Advertising himself as "Geographer and Map Publisher," Melish formed the first company devoted solely to such works, and this 1816 map was the first to show the United States as a transcontinental state. In an accompanying booklet he noted that at first he had intended to carry the map only to the continental water divide, but finding that "there was no map in existence presenting an *entire view* of the United States territory," he decided to carry it to the Pacific Ocean, for "part of this territory unquestionably belongs to the United States" and "in tracing the probable expansion of the human race from east to west, the mind finds an agreeable resting place on its western limits." He admitted that western boundaries remained uncertain. His map became well known, was used in treaty negotiations—and who can tell what influence his delineations and his stress upon "the beauty and symmetry of the map" may have had upon American perceptions of the appropriate frame for their country? (Courtesy of the Library of Congress)

point of interest. Navigation rights on the lower Colorado River across Mexican territory would prove to be of little value because of the limitations of the river itself.

Discussions of territorial change were accompanied by a great deal of talk about *natural boundaries*. The concept had been current in European intellectual and political circles for some time and was intrinsically attractive to Americans involved in thinking about enlarging and reshaping their country on a continental scale. The idea that the gross lineaments of nature provided a logical framework for the political partitioning of the earth had great appeal to the rationalism of the time. It was also an idea readily put to the service of nationalism, and not only by expansionists who discerned "the finger of nature" pointing out appropriate additions but by those who saw "natural barriers" that must cause "a permanent separation of interests" between peoples on either side and thus fix a limit to national expansion.

The Louisiana Purchase shifted the western boundary of the United States to the Continental Divide. It seemed obvious to many people that here, surely, "nature has fixed limits for our nation; she has kindly interposed as our Western barrier, mountains almost inaccessible, whose base she has skirted with irreclaimable deserts of sand." But such a conviction, common through the 1820s, was undermined by the rapidly enlarging experience of Americans in crossing those mountains and deserts and extending systems of operation spanning the continent. Once the idea began to take hold that a transcontinental republic was actually feasible, the Pacific Ocean became the obvious "natural" boundary, with no concern about the formidable array of mountains and deserts that intervened between the Rockies and the coast (fig. 24).

Rivers were the most obvious linear feature on the coastal plain of Texas, and a sequence of them was proposed at various times as appropriate boundaries. The Rio Grande was the largest lying well westward of the frontier of Anglo-American colonization and became the great issue in boundary-making in this sector. Such a natural feature was clearly discernible but also clearly not much of a barrier—hence (in part) the strong interest of some American leaders in pointing to the Sierra Madre as the natural boundary and a more "defensible" line. Selection of the Rio Grande and the Gila as the principal basis for the boundary in the first treaty with Mexico was more a matter of politics and convenience than a strong belief that these were "natural boundaries" in any compelling sense.

The list of specific territories that American administrations generally decreed to be *essential* additions to the national domain is not long, but that of course is partly because of the huge extent of some of the additions obtained. In 1803 Jefferson's sights were focused on the Island of New Orleans, but had he not gotten the whole of Louisiana in one amazing transaction, we may well assume that he or his successors would soon have declared it essential to have the upper Mississippi and Missouri valleys as well—and would have applied relentless pressures to get them. Once the United States decided that it must have San Francisco Bay and, having defeated Mexico, was able to insist on having all of Alta California, then in turn all the land lying east of that long Pacific frontage became "natural" additions.

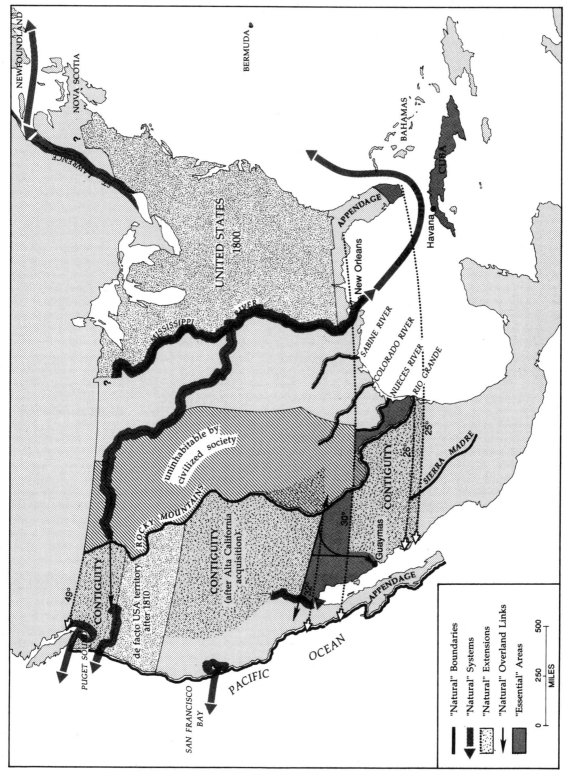

24. Continentalism and Some "Natural" Geographic Concepts.

Legend:

"Natural" Boundaries
"Natural" Systems
"Natural" Extensions
"Natural" Overland Links
"Essential" Areas

MILES
0   250   500

Labels on map:

NEWFOUNDLAND
NOVA SCOTIA
ST. LAWRENCE
BERMUDA
BAHAMAS
CUBA
Havana
UNITED STATES 1800
MISSISSIPPI RIVER
APPENDAGE
New Orleans
SABINE RIVER
COLORADO RIVER
NUECES RIVER
RIO GRANDE
uninhabitable by civilized society
ROCKY MOUNTAINS
CONTIGUITY (after Alta California acquisition)
de facto USA territory after 1810
CONTIGUITY
49°
PUGET SOUND
SAN FRANCISCO BAY
PACIFIC OCEAN
Guaymas
CONTIGUITY
SIERRA MADRE
APPENDAGE
25°
26°
30°
32°

The United States had no claim whatsoever to New Mexico (except through the extravagant pretensions of Texas) and did not covet its meager resources. New Mexico was taken as a spoil of war in order to gain southern routes to California (and to encompass those complicating Texan claims). The road from Missouri to Santa Fe was a well-established commercial route, but extensions westward to California were not, and the sudden patterns of traffic to the California goldfields seemed to demonstrate that an additional piece of northern Sonora must be obtained in order to control the best route. Such annexation in turn generated further expansionist agitations, especially renewed efforts to obtain Sonora and Baja California and thereby ports on the Gulf of California.

An even simpler kind of geographic "logic" can be discerned, by which the limits of the United States should provide an appropriate symmetry or compactness on a transcontinental scale, to create that "magnificent parallelogram of our domain," hailed by Senator Benton in 1849. Such was explicit in the emphasis on "continuity" and "contiguity" with reference to extension of the Forty-ninth parallel boundary from the Rockies to the sea, and it was implicit in the attempts to establish a southwestern border along 30°N (approximating the line of the Gulf Coast), 26° (west from the southern tip of Texas), or 25° (west from the southern tip of Florida).

The shape of the United States is the result of historical chance as well as geographic calculation, and none of it is "natural" in any forceful sense of that term. Statesmen and propagandists read geography in their own terms. Through the lens of nationalism and expansionism, "natural" appendages and systems, barriers and boundaries appeared wherever needed, and with proper adjustments in angle and perspective a compelling contiguity and propinquity of almost any desired territory could be brought into clear view. By midcentury natural limits seemed much less prominent and obvious than they had only a few years earlier. It was becoming widely agreed that the highest mountains and the broadest oceans imposed nothing insuperable to a vigorous and hopeful people, as was attested by the reality of a transcontinental state and the agitations to annex the Hawaiian Islands. However one might read the configurations of the continent, the application of steam and electricity to the conquest of distance had made it hard to discern any "natural" limits to national expansion.

We should remember, however, that this overweening confidence in an expansive American destiny was but one side of the coin; on the other was the image of a United States as a contender among dangerous rivals. Early in the century France was generally regarded as the world's most powerful state, and the negotiation for Louisiana was initiated out of alarm over French control of the mouth of the Mississippi and fear of new French designs for developing an American empire. Despite the well-remembered history of French friendship and assistance during the American Revolution, the removal of such a power from the North American scene was regarded as an event of enormous geopolitical significance. The British persisted as a formidable presence throughout this time. Elimination of the British from North America would have been welcomed but was never really a prospect, except momentarily in 1812. Annexation of Canada was a logical adjunct of that war, and the idea would flare up amid public agitations from time to time, but it was never accepted as a specific policy objective by any administration thereafter. The Americans saw Britain as an aggressive jealous power that was ready to exploit any opportunity to curb, annoy, or belittle the United States. The British ability to dispatch armies to any shore and back them up with the world's most powerful navy was something to be reckoned with. Andrew Jackson's marvelous triumph at New Orleans could not efface the memory of the British burning of Washington. American intervention or involvement in the Floridas, Cuba, Texas, Mexico, Yucatán, California, and Hawaii was in some degree motivated by fear of the British. American bluster and relative intransigence in the Maine and Oregon negotiations was in part an effort to gain respect, to show the British that the United States could not be pushed around. In this larger international context, American expansionism could be rationalized as a means of self-preservation.

MODES OF EXPANSION

All historical accounts recognize the agency of both pioneers and politicians in the creation of a transcontinental nation. Pioneers have long been a celebrated feature in American mythology. As Ray Allen Billington put it: "The true hero of the tale [of his *Westward Expansion*] was the hard-working farmer who, ax in hand, marched ever westward until the boundaries of the nation touched the Pacific." As for politicians, Thomas Jefferson and a variable set of others have long been recognized as visionary statesmen who helped ensure the greatness of the nation. The actual history of the case was of course much more complex and controversial than such generalizations may suggest. As Thomas Hietala stated, "The United States used many tactics to expand its domain, and like other empires it created legitimizing myths to sanction that expansion."

We may well begin our review with a caution against any simple categorization of *private* and *government* modes of expansion implied in the common mythology. Governments may make use of private individuals or groups in informal or secret ways (as was notorious in some filibuster cases); citizens may act in the belief (true or false) that they are not only serving their own interests but in some larger sense tacitly doing the government's will as well; and of course the two may find their separate initiatives converging into a mutually reinforcing effort. In the earliest days of the Republic, Secretary of State Thomas Jefferson had laid out a tantalizing prospect of just such an ambiguous relationship as a means of expansion. "Governor Quesada . . . is inviting foreigners to go and settle in Florida," he reported to President Washington. "This [invitation] is meant for our own people. . . . Our citizens have a right to go where they please . . . . I wish a hundred thousand of our inhabitants would accept the invitation. It would be the means of delivering to us peacefully, what may otherwise cost us a war. In the meantime we may complain of this seduction of our inhabitants just enough to make them [the Spanish] believe . . . it very wise policy for them, & confirm them in it. This is my idea of it." The Florida case did not develop in quite this way, but it did become a notorious example of complicated government (both national and state) and private actions and interactions. On the other hand, Jefferson's greatest accomplishment as president was the direct result of his own personal initiative and we may well begin our list with that simple and remarkable case.

1. Purchase. Deeply ingrained Euro-American concepts of property and sovereignty made American statesmen regard cash purchase as much the simplest and best means of acquiring new territory. Ideally, such a transaction was freely undertaken as beneficial to both parties, effectuated by an exchange of goods, and sealed by joint signature of a definitive document. For a society that regarded land as a commodity such a mode of transfer was highly attractive, so much so that the process was insisted on even if one of the parties had to be heavily pressured into participation: whatever the imbalance of forces, the resulting document would legitimate the acquisition, as notoriously the case in treaty after treaty with the Indians. Thus, in a message to Congress in January 1803, Jefferson referred to the increasing unease of the Indians "at the constant diminution" of their territory, *"although effected by their own voluntary sales"* (emphasis added); such fictions endlessly repeated served to ease Americans' conscience about their relentless expansions: "We paid for it, its ours."

In such an environment the Louisiana Purchase was an especially satisfying transaction. Begun as an offer to buy a small strategic region and enormously enlarged in scope at the suggestion of the seller, it was quickly accomplished as a simple exchange by mutual consent—a clean deal. Such a triumph must have greatly reinforced the idea of purchase as a wonderfully effective means of expansion. If one great piece of the continent could be bought, why not buy more whenever it was needed? After bidding for the Isle of New Orleans, West Florida, and East Florida, which resulted in Louisiana, the United States attempted to buy Cuba, Texas, New Mexico, various portions of Alta California, Baja California, and all or portions of Sonora and Chihuahua. Of these, the only piece obtained by simple purchase was northernmost Sonora, from a Mexican dictator desperate for funds. After Louisiana the only large territory obtained in an equally simple, untainted transaction was Alaska (which most Americans at the time thought not worth the price).

Of course, large payments were a part of treaties with Spain and Mexico to cover assumptions of American claims against those states and to ease the pain and induce acceptance of territorial cessions obtained by force or threat of arms. As in the case of treaties with the Indians, such transactions eased the American conscience about the nation's methods of expansion. Thus James Buchanan, in his annual message to Congress in 1858, referring to recent attempts at "honorable negotiation" with Spain for Cuba, stated: "We would not, if we could, acquire Cuba in any other manner. This is due to our national character. All the territory which we have acquired since the origin of the Government has been by fair purchase from France, Spain, and Mexico or by the free and voluntary act of the independent State of Texas in blending her destinies with our own." This kind of calculated hypocrisy could exasperate those on the other side of the negotiating table. As the Mexican commissioners who initially rejected the proposal that New Mexico and Alta California be ceded as a purchase put it: "It was a new experience inconsistent with any ideal of justice to wage war on a people on the only ground that that people refuse to sell territory which a neighbor would buy from them."

There was a further imbalance in such matters in that Americans might have a special respect for cash payment as a mode of transfer of territory, but we may well presume that they would be only buyers, never sellers. As Gene M. Brack noted: "President Polk knew that Mexico could offer but feeble resistance militarily, and he knew that Mexico needed money. No proper American would exchange territory and the national honor for cash, but President Polk believed that the application of military pressure would convince Mexicans to do so. They did not respond logically, but patriotically." Aside from the obvious hypocrisy, it seems likely that American statesmen never quite appreciated the difference in dealing with a Mexican *nation* rather than a European *emperor*.

2. Assertion of Claims and Diplomatic Compromise. When the United States of America assumed its place as a major presence in North America, the continent was as yet incompletely parceled out among imperial powers. Vast claims had been asserted, but much of these were unoccupied (and large areas never yet seen) by Europeans and undefined by adjudicated boundaries. Robert Gray's discovery and exploration of the lower Columbia River put the new republic into the competition. Jefferson was eager to put a more official imprint upon this entrepreneurial outreach. It took him more than a decade to do so, but he was determined to create an American swath across the continent. As Bernard DeVoto put it, "The dispatch of the Lewis and Clark expedition was an act of imperial policy. Even while he moved to buy New Orleans the President of the United States was moving to possess Louisiana"—and, we should add, Oregon. Although Jefferson was open to the idea of a separate Pacific republic, he wanted to ensure the spread of the

American people across the continent whatever the eventual geopolitical arrangement.

This dual private and government interest in strengthening American claims to disputed ground continued spasmodically for another forty years. The Astorian entrepreneurial venture resulted in several outposts in the Columbia Basin; all were ephemeral, but the main one, Astoria overlooking the great oceanic entryway, remained an important symbol of the American claim. Repeated though unsuccessful attempts followed in Congress to reassert that presence with a military post. Later the entrepreneurial efforts of Wyeth and others and the cultural outreach of American Protestant missionaries were followed by extensive official reconnaissances led by Wilkes and Frémont. Such activities were all grist for the diplomatic mills, although the ultimate division was not closely bound to the actual territorial impress of the contending parties. The Willamette Valley settlers greatly reinforced an American hold on Oregon but did not directly affect the boundary settlement.

Dispute over the northeastern corner of the United States arose from inadequate treaty maps but eventually also became a compromise division of territory in which both private individuals and public officials played a part. In this case the private players were land speculators and timber cutters and the public officials were agents of the State of Maine who set up blockhouses, built a road, organized towns, and thereby constricted the options of the federal government and pressured toward a particular line of compromise.

3. Military Conquest and Annexation. Most American presidents during these decades indicated in one way or another a willingness to use armed force if necessary to support territorial acquisition. Of course, as Frederick Merk noted, "Propaganda designed to prepare for the seizure of territory has a characteristic language," and such proposals or actions were usually couched in terms of national defense and honor, or in response to grave dangers and provocations. The results varied from complete failure in the case of the invasion of Upper Canada to very extensive success in the case of Mexico. Territories added as a direct result of military invasion and conquest were the Nueces–Rio Grande strip, New Mexico, (Alta) California, and, in effect, East Florida. It should be noted that the two Mexican provinces were not simply occupied by American forces pending an armistice and the outcome of treaty negotiations; they were formally annexed immediately, by military proclamation.

Military occupation of the Mexican capital and other strategic places gave American leaders the privilege of considering whether to take much more territory and there were strong pressures to annex Tamaulipas, Nuevo León, Coahuila, Chihuahua, Sonora, and Baja California. Of course, there was no assurance that such areas could have been obtained. Mexico might have resisted such vast cessions and reopened hostilities, and the American administration might not have found support at home for a prolonged war.

4. *Military Protectorate and Eventual Annexation.* The American military presence in Mexico also allowed the United States to consider imperial alternatives, such as imposition of a military protectorate upon all or large parts of Mexico. Support for such an action was commonly argued in terms of the need to establish order and enforce payment of debts, but the possibility of further cessions of territory was usually apparent. Buchanan's repeated requests to Congress to support him in establishing American military authority over portions of Chihuahua and Sonora in order to halt Apache incursions came in the wake of Mexico's refusal to sell those provinces. His agent negotiating for land grants, transit rights, and military protection for the construction of railroads across Mexico to Guaymas and Mazatlán assured his superiors that such corridors "would have fenced off and consecrated to American use, ultimately to American ownership, the very territory" Buchanan sought. The concept of American military intervention into borderland states was generally regarded as a policy option. Henry Clay had stated the general principle clearly in 1810: "I have no hesitation in saying, that if a parent country will not or cannot maintain its authority in a colony adjacent to us, and there exists in it a state of misrule and disorder, menacing our peace, and if moreover such colony, by passing into the hands of any other power, would be dangerous to the integrity of the Union, and manifestly tend to the subversion of our laws; we have a right, upon eternal principles of self-preservation, to lay hold of it." Clay was referring to West Florida, but the argument would reappear time and again in messages and debates and was as readily applied to Mexico as to a colonial power, and to distant Hawaii as to adjacent Cuba. The case of West Florida could be cited as an example of such a protectorate and annexation, but it and several other cases of official military intervention are probably best considered as part of another, more complicated category.

5. *Filibuster.* The term *filibuster* is of Dutch Caribbean origin, referring to piracy (freebooter, free booty) and came to be applied to any leader or band of warriors and their actions in trying to seize control of a particular territory and subvert it from its sovereign affiliation. Such armed independent groups are not uncommon in thinly occupied, loosely governed, ill-policed borderlands. They had been an important feature amid the imperial competitions in Tropical America in previous centuries, and they were much in evidence during this time of imperial disintegration. In the expansion of the United States filibuster actions were important in the acquisitions of West and East Florida; they were of some minor significance in Alta

California (Frémont and the "Bear Flag" irregulars); they were failures in Texas, Cuba, and Baja California. The threat of such interventions in these and other areas, such as Sonora, Chihuahua, the Rio Grande Valley, and Hawaii, however, was a factor of some importance in diplomatic and strategic issues of the day. An important if often elusive feature of these adventures is the extent to which they were fostered by the American government as a means of acquiring territory. Some of these actions were clearly viewed by national leaders as very much in the interest of the United States, as in the cases of the Floridas; some were encouraged for a time and then dampened, as in the case of Quitman's Cuban expedition; others, such as William Walker's foray into Baja California, were purely private geopolitical schemes but if successful would surely have gained the keen attention of the United States. There is much variety in the very nature of these volatile and often quixotic and ephemeral affairs. Filibuster forces might include citizens of the country being attacked as well as Americans and other opportunists, and their encouragement might come more from sympathetic interests within, say, Mexico or Cuba than from the United States.

6. *Annexation by Request from a Foreign State or Population.* The Hawaiian Kingdom was an interesting variant among these cases. Here the presence and influence of a small number of American commercial and cultural agents, in conjunction with fears of filibusters and of military interventions by rival imperial powers, led to an official petition for protection, and later for annexation. Even those Americans who were uncomfortable with most other methods of acquiring territory might find little objection in such a voluntary act. As the United States commissioner in the islands stated: "We must not take the islands in virtue of the 'manifest destiny' principle, but can we not accept their voluntary offer? Who has a right to forbid the bans?" There were in fact a variety of interests willing to halt—or delay—such a marriage. Other foreign requests (actual or incipient) to join the United States came from the beleaguered Creole leadership of Yucatán and the despondent Montreal merchants; both actions were quickly deflated by improving local circumstances.

7. *Settlers and Secession.* As noted, the idea that American settlers would move relentlessly into bordering regions of adjacent countries (with or without invitation from governing authorities), become the dominant population, and eventually seek to secede and annex themselves to the United States was regarded as an effective mode of territorial expansion from the earliest days of the Republic. Jefferson from early on saw it as the likely means of taking over Louisiana as well as Florida. West Florida was the first place where something of this sort did happen, although complicated by other features. The great example, of course, was Texas,

which was colonized in part by Anglo-Americans responding directly to Mexican invitation and in part by Anglo-Americans spreading westward as the outer edge of a broad folk movement more or less indifferent to international boundaries.

There were really no other obvious cases of settler conquest in this sense. The scattered incoherent groups of American emigrants in the Sacramento Valley were not decisive to the annexation of Alta California, which must be credited to American military occupation and the long-building determination to acquire San Francisco Bay. And the substantial presence of settlers in the Willamette Valley was in a part of Oregon never at serious risk in any diplomatic negotiation with Great Britain. Americans took the lead in organizing a government in that region, but there was no authority from which they had to secede. It has been said that New Mexico was "a conquest of merchants," but such a statement must not be misinterpreted. American traders in New Mexico might have welcomed annexation and been a factor in the negotiations for a peaceful takeover, but their presence had no direct bearing on the American decision to annex that province—it seems clear that it would have been taken even if there had been no Americans there at all. Similarly, David Weber's conclusion that "the American frontier had literally spilled over onto the Mexican frontier and forged new economic, demographic, and cultural links to the United States. America's political incorporation of the Mexican frontier between 1845 and 1854 represented the culmination of a process as much as it did the inauguration of a new era" is pertinent but must not lure us into thinking that such a process was either inexorable or decisive to the change in sovereignty.

It is also appropriate to note that "settler sovereignty," like purchase, was for Americans only. The numerical dominance of other peoples, no matter how deeply rooted as settlers, was no deterrence to American annexation, as the cases of Louisiana, New Mexico, the Rio Grande Valley, and the Madawaska emphatically demonstrated (fig. 25).

History is too complex to be fitted neatly into a set of categories, but such an exercise does illuminate the primacy of two main means of expansion of the territory of the United States: by purchase and by some form of violence (military invasion, filibuster, revolt). The "hard-working farmer who . . . marched ever westward" was fundamental to the creation of a transcontinental *nation,* but such pioneer heroes were working very largely within national boundaries won by American statesmen and warriors. Nor were those territories obtained primarily to serve those farmers. The Jeffersonian ideal of a democratic republic grounded on a citizenry of yeomen farmers was a powerful image, and it had become widely accepted that a thriving American nation required a spacious frame, but once Louisiana had been purchased, the Republic was spacious beyond all but the most

Legend: ○ attempted or threatened ● accomplished

	Purchase	Assertion of claims and compromise	Military invasion and annexation	Military protectorate and annexation	Filibuster	Annexation by request	Settlers and secession
ISLAND OF NEW ORLEANS	○						
WEST FLORIDA	○		●	●			●
EAST FLORIDA	○		●	●			
LOUISIANA	●						
CUBA	○				○		
UPPER CANADA			○				
MONTREAL						○	
MAINE		●					
OREGON		●					
TEXAS	○				○		●
NEUCES-RIO GRANDE STRIP			●				
TAMAULIPAS			○		○		
NUEVO LEON			○		○		
COAHUILA			○		○		
CHIHUAHUA	○		○	○			
SONORA	◐			○	○		
NEW MEXICO			●				
ALTA CALIFORNIA	○		●				
BAJA CALIFORNIA	○				○		
YUCATAN				○		○	
HAWAIIAN ISLANDS						○	

25. Territories and Modes of Expansion, 1800–1859.

expansive dreams of the time. The need for room for the millions to come was a common theme of nationalist and expansionist rhetoric, but the great additions of the Far West could not be very persuasively rationalized in such terms. Despite rose-colored evocations, it was generally believed that those distant lands were mostly barren plains, mountains, deserts, or impenetrable forests on the rainy, rugged Pacific Coast. Orators might speak of the pioneers in Oregon, but in the main they talked of commerce, security, or some larger strategy or general "law of progress" in support of these acquisitions. If some (but not all) Southern spokes-men insisted that the lands of Texas were essential for continued progress, that was part of a quite different and more complicated geographic concept developed by Southern interests.

THE UNITED STATES AND NORTH AMERICA

The world must become "familiarized," said John Quincy Adams to his cabinet in 1819, "with the idea of considering our proper dominion to be the continent of North America. From the time when we became an independent people it was as much a law of nature that this should become our pretension as that the Mississippi should flow to the sea. Spain had possessions upon our southern and Great Britain upon our northern border. It was impossible that centuries should lapse without finding them annexed to the United States." It was not the first—and far from the last—time that he would expound on the simple equation "that the United States and North America are identical." In this view continental dominance was more than an appropriate national objective—"pretension"—and more than a conse-quence of an inevitable recession of European empires, it was something funda-mental and inexorable: "a law of nature."

The vision of a fully continental United States and the conviction that it was foreordained, part of Nature's Plan, became ever stronger through the first half of the century, such that when John L. O'Sullivan wrote in 1845 that our claim to Oregon "is by right of our manifest destiny to overspread and to possess the whole of the continent which Providence has given us for the development of the great experiment of Liberty and federated self-government entrusted to us," his phrase instantly entered the national vocabulary and mythology. Such rhetoric and con-victions helped shape official policy. American expansion must not be understood as old-fashioned aggrandizement, Secretary of State Edward Everett explained at length to a no doubt weary and skeptical Spanish minister in 1852, for it was impelled by "the law of progress, which is as organic and vital in the youth of States as of individual men." European immigrants were pouring across the Atlantic and the United States was "filling with intense rapidity, and adjusting [its territorial relations] on natural principles"; and therefore even though the American presi-dent did not wish to take Cuba, it must eventually happen because nothing can "resist this mighty current in the fortunes of the world."

That "mighty current" was nothing less than "the geographical march of his-tory" fulfilling the God-given role of the several continents as the grand earthly "theatre of human societies"—so Americans had been assured by one of Europe's brightest younger geographers in 1849. Arnold Guyot, a Swiss scholar who had studied with the great Humboldt and with Karl Ritter and had followed his countryman Louis Agassiz to the United States, delivered a series of twelve lectures at the Lowell Institute. It is hardly surprising that his eloquent presentations (in French) of Asia, Europe, and North America as the successive settings for "the three grand stages of humanity in its march through the ages"—the first continent serving as the cradle, the second stimulating the flowering of culture, the third providing "the simplicity and unity of plan" on an extensive scale for the great culmination and diffusion to all the world of the blessings of (Northern European Protestant) civilization—were warmly received by his Boston audiences. And they engendered an appropriate New England missionary response: translated and serialized in a local newspaper, they were soon published as a book, *The Earth and Man*, which, endorsed by eminent figures, enjoyed great attention through several editions.

By midcentury it was obvious to everyone that the United States was the dominant presence in North America. The very terms *America* and *American* had become appropriated through common usage to refer, unless otherwise qualified, to the Great Republic, its citizens, and its characteristic features, a pretension of no little annoyance to many others in North America and the Western Hemisphere. It was a republic on an enormous new scale, and its internal vigor and expansiveness were utterly unmatched. Its population of thirty million was more than ten times that of British North America and threefold greater than that of its Hispanic neighbors immediately to the south. But just what form and extent this overpowering American continentalism might take was not entirely clear. Within the diffuse body of sober reflections and oratorical effusions of the time one might detect several versions of the North American future.

There was the vigorous spread of the American people, imbued with their unique sense of freedom, carrying with them a distinctive vision and form of society and polity. Such an expansion was regarded as inevitable and beneficial, as in this typical congressional flourish: "Our people, with a spirit of enterprise unparalleled in the history of men, are pushing onward, scattering in their train the blessings of enlightened liberty." By its innate attractive power this new version of society would perforce assimilate all lesser European peoples, such as the French of Louisiana. And it seemed logical to many Americans that their British neighbors, who already shared so much in North American experience and English heritage, would surely join themselves to this powerful current, casting off their archaic monarchical ties (and Lord Durham had spelled out how all those French Canadians would—out of self-interest—assimilate to this encompassing Anglo-American presence).

In the early years, especially, the emphasis in this Jeffersonian version of Crevecoeur's "American, this new man" was on the emergence of a new kind of *society*; whether these new persons organized themselves into a single or eventually into several republics was less important. If there was a divergence, said Jefferson in

1803, "It is the elder and the younger son differing. God bless them both, & keep them in union, if it be for their good, but separate them if it be better." But few were as easy and tolerant of such a prospect; others had a darker sense of human nature and history. John Quincy Adams from early on insisted that political unity was essential to the integrity of the general concept: "The whole continent of North America appears to be destined by Divine Providence to be peopled by one *nation*, speaking one language, professing one general system of religions and political principles, and accustomed to one general tenor of social usages and customs. For the common happiness of them all, for their peace and prosperity, I believe it indispensible that they should be associated in one federal Union." His concern for that Union had been given much stronger expression in a letter two months earlier. If the separatist tendencies of New England Federalists were not squashed, he had warned in 1811, "instead of a nation, coextensive with the North American continent, destined by God and nature to be the most populous and most powerful people ever combined under one social compact, we shall have an endless multitude of little insignificant clans and tribes at eternal war with one another for a rock or a fish pond, the sport and fable of European masters and oppressors." Warfare over boundaries and petty territories was one of the curses of Europe, and fear of (what might later be called) the "balkanization" of America became a recurrent theme in continentalist rhetoric.

Mexico, of course, must recede in the face of this American expansion. Texas had proved the irresistible power of the Anglo-Americans and exposed the chaos within Mexico. The collapse of the Spanish Empire had left a vacuum, an array of fragments rather than a nation. Unable to govern itself, Mexico came to be regarded as a legitimate spoil of war, its frontier provinces "waifs" awaiting the blessings of American protection and nurture. It was a new phase in the centuries-old competition between the English and the Spanish in the New World, and the Americans were eager to redraw the map to their advantage. Just where Nature intended the separation between Anglo-America and Hispanic-America to be was not entirely clear. In the aftermath of American victories over Mexican forces a good many read the conformation of the continents as indicating an obvious division at Panama. The more extreme voices proclaimed all of Mexico, Central America, and the Greater Antilles as necessary parts of the American empire ("our India is south of us"), to be conquered, annexed, and somehow incorporated into a greater United States. Others would place all those areas under American military occupation to ensure economic penetration and the beneficent spread of American influence. By the 1850s there were certainly widespread assumptions that this entire area was of geopolitical significance to the United States, that these waters must become an American Mediterranean, that nothing should be allowed therein that might conceivably threaten the security of the transcontinental republic.

There was also near unanimity in believing that, while it might be part of America's mission to bring the blessings of liberty and enlightenment to these peoples, they would never be equal, for they were a lesser, darker breed. That, too, was assumed to be part of God's Plan and proven by history.

Given these general convictions about American destinies and the specific expansionist commitments of several American presidents and many influential leaders, it is perhaps surprising that the United States was not even larger than it was by this time. When one has reviewed all the geopolitical contentions it is not difficult to imagine a considerably more extensive framework: a Greater United States. Obviously, such imagination must force a whole series of "might-have-beens" through the intense struggles of American domestic politics (to say nothing of the international assumptions necessary), but there were such powerful interests in favor that it is not wildly implausible to imagine a United States that, leaving British North America intact, did annex Cuba and a much larger chunk of Mexico and made Yucatán into a formal protectorate (fig. 26). Such a speculation underscores the point that the actual southern limits of the United States are no more "natural" or "logical" or "appropriate" than other boundaries might have been. Of course, the social and geopolitical implications of the extension of Anglo-American sovereignty so much more deeply into the Hispanic-American and Afro-American worlds are enormous—and quite incalculable. There may be no great merit in pursuing such a supposition; it is simply worth remembering that there were loud voices and important interests calling for exactly that kind of enlargement of the United States in the 1850s.

It is also important to remember that there was all the while a contrary, reverse side to such matters. Not all Americans were carried along by this strong tide of expansionism. There was in fact deep resistance to it in almost all of its phases. It is useful to reflect that there were always those who had a different vision of an advantageous shape and size and content for their country, a different opinion as to its appropriate position on the continent. Even though we cannot sort out all of their feelings and self-interests in the matter, we have no reason to assume that those who were cautious, who opposed these large annexations, who condemned the "insane thirst" for territory as "the great American disease," were any less interested in a strong, secure, and prosperous United States than were those who urged these additions. Apparently such persons did not believe that a successful American republic required anything like its present extent and shape; they read geography in a different way and had a different understanding of the "law of progress."

Reflecting on the arguments, complexities, and contingencies of these great geopolitical issues it is at least as easy to imagine a Lesser United States as it is a Greater one. For example, if we start with a consummated Louisiana Purchase (which came so fortuitously and simply), we may assume that a transcontinental

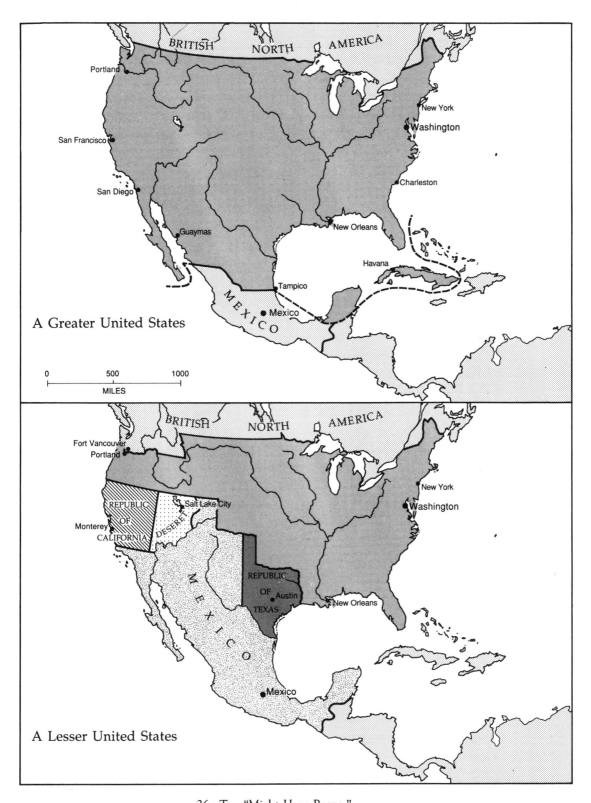

A Greater United States

0   500   1000
MILES

A Lesser United States

26. Two "Might-Have-Beens."

United States would be created because the American claims to the lower Columbia were superior. But, as already noted, the Oregon boundary settlement might
well have resulted in a narrower American corridor. And suppose that the Mexican
government, however bitterly and reluctantly, had decided to recognize what their
British advisers and some of their own strategists had argued: that Texas was
irretrievable; that the most astute thing to do was to recognize Texan independence
and seize the advantage of it—work out a boundary settlement (accepting President Lamar's $5 million offer) and help create a buffer state, guaranteed by the
European powers, between Mexico and the aggressive United States. A radically
different set of geopolitical circumstances might plausibly have followed from such
a resolution: a continuing independent Republic of Texas; an infiltrated but continuing Mexican state of New Mexico; a de facto independent Commonwealth of
Deseret beyond the canyonlands of the Colorado where neither the Spaniards nor
the Mexicans had ever exercised any authority (the Mormons willing to make a
handsome payment to be left alone and Mexican officials accepting this disciplined
body of colonists who had such ample reason to oppose the United States); and,
out of the swirl of the Gold Rush, a new Republic of California, as had been
predicted by persons of the most extensive knowledge and vision. Was there ever a
region better designed by Nature for separate geopolitical existence than Alta
California—a land so distinctive and attractive, set apart by the great unbroken
wall of the Sierra Nevada backed by desert wastelands, fronting on the world's
greatest ocean, focused on one of the world's most magnificent harbors? Mexico
was fortunate to retain hold of the much less desirable lands south of the
Tehachapi.

And thus we can set forth a transcontinental United States displaying the
plausible results of a sequence of complicated international geopolitical issues of
the first half of the nineteenth century (see fig. 26). In retrospect it seems reasonable, "natural," almost "inevitable," doesn't it? If it is hardly conceivable that the
United States could have been closed out from the Pacific, it is only a little easier to
imagine that it might have gotten more. There were always those who dreamed of
more, agitated for more, insisted that California, at the very least San Francisco
Bay, was essential to the health and future of America. But to such people, and
specifically to those in Congress who doubted the viability of our more limited
transcontinental nation, we may retort in stentorian tones (turning Senator
Breckenridge's theme [p. 13] on its head):

I would ask, sir, what is the honorable gentleman's standard extent for a republic?
Does it require a continent? Is not a country reaching 3,000 miles from sea to shining
sea broad enough for a republic? Does the Goddess of Liberty require a vast expanse of
impenetrable mountains and inhospitable deserts for her sustenance? Are not the
wonderfully fertile lands where rolls the mighty Oregon a foothold for a glorious

future? Was Athens an extensive republic? Mark you, sir, liberty depends upon the qualities of men, not upon expanses of geography. . . . [etc., etc., for seven more columns in the *Annals of Congress*]

Well, we need not pursue this fantasy further either; such "what ifs" of history may be seductive, but they can prove nothing. Yet again, they can jar us out of habits of mind, loosen images so familiar, so constantly put before us, so deeply imprinted on our national consciousness that they are assumed to be fixed and inevitable. It is a fresh and forceful way of reminding ourselves that there was no destiny manifest, certainly no "physiographic destiny," nothing natural or inevitable about those annexations and the eventual shape of the continental United States. Even if "expansionism" was a powerful force it need not have resulted in the pattern that did in fact emerge. The point has been forcefully put in a more radical version of such a "counterfactual geography" by Eric Wolf:

> The republic was neither indivisible nor endowed with God-given boundaries.
> It is conceivable that things might have been different. There could have arisen a polyglot Florida Republic, a Francophone Mississippian America, a Hispanic New Biscay, a Republic of the Great Lakes, a Columbia—comprising the present Oregon, Washington, and British Columbia. Only if we assume a God-given drive toward geopolitical unity on the North American continent would this retrojection be meaningless. Instead, it invites us to account in material terms for what happened at each juncture, to account for how some relationships gained ascendencies over others. Thus . . . the United States was . . . [never] a thing propelled toward its unfolding goal by some immanent driving spring, but rather a temporally and spatially changing and changeable set of relationships, or relationships among sets of relationships.

That the United States was "a temporally and spatially changing and changeable set of relationships" was in fact very widely understood in the 1850s. That is clear enough from the fears and fervors surrounding all these issues of annexation. Expansion was always a contentious matter. It could hardly have been otherwise in such a complex, precariously balanced, dynamic political structure. Every addition of territory altered the shape, content, and prospects of the whole, but always differentially with respect to the existing parts, and never with any certainty as to just what the impact might be. As Daniel Boorstin emphasized, "not the 'manifestness' but the uncertainty of the national destiny was the first great motive and emotive power of the national life." To a great extent, as Hietala has shown, the expansionists themselves were running scared; driven by "anxiety, not optimism," they hoped that "territorial expansion would encourage nationalism and foster internal harmony"; they discovered instead that it "exacerbated partisan and geographical divisions and ultimately precipitated disunion and civil war." Such a result was one of the more important of the many ironies of American history.

Thus, as the century moved on past its midpoint these various concepts of continentalism and visions of a single great North American society and polity became more difficult to see across the chasm opening within. The United States had always been at once a federation, a nation, a set of regional societies, and an empire. Now nation and federation seemed to be threatened by regionalism and imperialism in new forms. As Boorstin concluded: "The continental extent of the nation and the means of associating or disassociating its parts . . . were not settled until the Civil War resolved them in a sea of blood."

PART TWO
EXPANSION:
THE GROWTH OF A CONTINENTAL NATION

North and south, east and west, city and country, from the 1780s to the 1850s the most powerful influence in the shaping of American society was space. The ideas about space, the uses of space, the projects across space, and the accommodations to space, above all else, charted the basic changes that occurred between these years.

Robert H. Wiebe

Prologue

We turn our attention inward: to the formation of a genuinely continental America lodged as firmly and fully in the Mississippi Valley as on the Atlantic Seaboard—and ignore, for the time being, the distant and barely attached Far West beyond the Great Prairies. Our concern is with regional and national formations.

It is not easy to prepare a coherent picture and general assessment of one of the most rapid, prodigious, and portentous set of geographic developments in modern world history. Given the complexities of the topic, we can offer no more than a relatively simple sketch, but drawing from our special perspective we can hope to present a fresh view of some important features. We begin by roughing out a general outline and then sharpen our focus upon several different bodies of people so as to fill in some characterizing regional details. We make no attempt to limn a fuller picture because the whole process of regional formation was still so much in flux and incomplete.

The unprecedented challenge of holding together such an ever-enlarging and differentiating expanse and, indeed, of making it an ever-more efficient interacting whole, directs our attention to the extension and elaboration of a national infrastructure. Our concern is not so much to measure these developments as to mark them upon the map so as to give some sense of the emerging geographic structure. Americans were unusually self-conscious about nation-building, and they had much to say about this continuous geographical shaping of their country. We shall give considerable attention to their visions and programs for the whole—and reserve for later consideration the tensions that arose among the parts and the failure of these ties and cement to hold the nation together.

1. Filling in the Framework: Migration Westward

While warriors and statesmen were creating a spacious frame for the American republic and empire the dominant body of the American people was rapidly expanding in numbers and in space to create a broadening, relatively contiguous, continental nation, pressing to and even beyond political borders on the north and south and extending from the Atlantic seaboard onto the margins of the great western prairies. The growth of population through all this period was astonishing: running about 33 percent each decade, the total rising from 5,306,000 in 1800 to 23,192,000 in 1850, a rate far exceeding that of any other large area in the world. Historical demographers credit about 21 percent of this growth to immigration, virtually all the remainder to natural increase (annexed populations accounting for less than 1 percent). Such fecundity was a source of great satisfaction to expansionist politicians, who regarded it as their most powerful weapon and excuse. As an Indiana congressman put it, in 1846: "I invite you to go to the West, and visit one of our log cabins, and number its inmates. There you will find a strong, stout youth of eighteen, with his better half, just commencing the first struggles of independent life. Thirty years from that time, visit them again; and instead of two, you will find in that same family twenty-two. This is what I call the American multiplication table." Some such multiplication, even if not this exact table, was widely apparent, and he went on to imply that you would not likely find the twenty-two all in one place because "the greater portion of this multiplying mass of humanity have their faces turned toward the setting sun." (We might presume that the twenty-two includes several young grandchildren; not necessarily, but a dozen pregnancies and a dead wife would be more likely than twenty births from the same mate.)

At the beginning of the century the inland margins of White settlement could be traced in the general form of a great wedge extending from the Genesee Country of western New York to the upper Ohio and closely along that river to the mouth of the Wabash, thence back southeastwardly to central Tennessee and bending around the Cherokee lands on south to coastal Georgia. Fifty years later settlers had spread across the plains of southern Michigan and the hills of southern Wisconsin and were pushing rapidly up the shallow river valleys of eastern Iowa, and the general frontier line was a broad arc extending from Green Bay to the Permanent Indian Frontier along the western boundary of Missouri and Arkansas, with a broad southwestern embayment curving deeply into Texas; the Coastal Plain from Corpus Christi on the west to the Suwanee River on the east was under vigorous development (the Florida peninsula was virtually empty). The area newly opened to colonization in this half-century exceeded half a million square miles, an expanse far larger than any European state west of Russia, and was home to about 10 million Americans in 1850, 44 percent of the nation's total.

The initial spread of this population across this vast area constitutes the most famous era of the "westward movement" of the young American nation, and the concomitant experience of penetrating the wilderness, breaking the land, creating farms, founding towns, and forming civil societies in this great "frontier" has long provided the basis for the most famous—and endlessly controversial—generalizations about the emergence of a distinctly *American* civilization. We shall have occasion to comment further on such matters, but our first task is to bring into focus some of the larger patterns within this great swirl of activity.

These fifty years of expansion were far from being one vast uninterrupted development. Historians, such as Malcolm Rohrbough, who have provided us with a richly annotated general view of the topic have emphasized its many *pulsations* (reflecting primarily the booms and busts of a volatile national economy) and broader *phases* (reflecting more basic changes in human geography and technology). The first of these phases began in the 1790s as an array of land tracts was put on the market in western New York, Pennsylvania, and the Ohio Valley, and the first of the federal lands in Ohio were surveyed and made available. Meanwhile, settlement in Kentucky and Tennessee was spreading outward from prospering nuclei in the Bluegress and Nashville basins, and farther south a still experimental emphasis on cotton was generating strong pressures from several older districts. In all of these areas this was a time of difficult pioneering, suffering from meager facilities, chronic commercial instabilities, geopolitical uncertainties, and mounting fears about Indian retaliations. The war initiated in 1812 marked a tumultuous transition into a new phase.

The shattering of Indian confederations in both the Northwest and Southwest was followed by a much stronger surge of expansion, indeed, "one of the great immigrations in the history of the western world." These were the famous "flush times" in Alabama and all the gulf states, while north of the Ohio the frontier was pushed beyond the narrow tributary valleys into the higher, richer plains broadening out from central Ohio across Indiana and Illinois. Within five years after 1816 five states were carved out of these western territories, and dozens of new steamboats were revolutionizing commerce on these western waters.

A third phase, emerging in the 1830s, was in many ways an elaboration and extension of the second but marked by the complete removal of the Indians, the full impact of the canal age, and the emergence of the railroad from an experimental supplement to a primary medium of transport. An even greater expanse of lands was made available and six more states were created by 1848. We may take the gold rush to California, which for the first time began to lure emigrants in large numbers away from this Mississippian West (the emigration to Oregon had been a minor prelude) and to alter the whole national perception of the West and its possibilities, as marking the onset of still another phase in the 1850s, and one that carries us beyond our present concern.

It has become common to refer to this vast movement as taking place in the *Transappalachian West*. It is of course true that for most Americans of the time this new country lay beyond a broad wall of mountains, but not for all of them, and such a designation tends to ignore or marginalize major expansions on the Coastal Plain beyond the southern end of the Appalachians (it also generalizes those mountains with a name that though extant was not the most common usage of the time: *Allegheny* and *Cumberland* for the northern and southern sectors, respectively, of that chain). Similarly, although most of this expanse was part of the *Mississippi Valley*, drained by the waters of that vast system, that, too, excludes most of the gulf states with their sequence of streams leading directly into coastal embayments, as well as the entire Great Lakes system on the north. Another common term of the day, the *Western Waters*, was more inclusive and gave an appropriate emphasis to the importance of waterways as routes of emigration and commerce. In the early phases of this colonization the great waterway central to so much of this movement made it convenient—and, for a brief time, official—to divide the whole area into two parts, *Northwest* and *Southwest* of the River Ohio, but such directional terms faded or shifted in location as the extent and shape of the nation changed. We need not select from nor adhere to these contemporary terms, but it is well to be attuned to their geographic connotations. As for simply *the West*, we can hardly avoid making extensive use of the term, but we must always remember that it is heavily charged with many mythic as well as locational meanings.

This momentous geographic development was not a broad sweep westward but an uneven advance along several pathways, the direction and volume responding to Indian cessions, land qualities and accessibilities, speculative promotions and popular fervors, resulting in a continuous reshaping of the outer edge of the frontier and of the relative position of every city and subregion within this burgeoning half of the nation. It was, of course, basically an expansion from the several regional societies of Atlantic America, and we must look more closely at the major streams of migration and map the general pattern of their deposits that laid the foundation layers of what Daniel J. Elazar has called "the 'geology' of settlement" in these western lands.

In the north the strong westward expansion of New Englanders had begun to spread over New York State and northernmost Pennsylvania in the 1790s (see *Atlantic America*, 348ff.). The Mohawk Valley, the one great natural breach westward through the mountains, funneled the main flow to the new town of Utica, from where it fanned out into an array of attractive districts (fig. 27). The Genesee was much the most famous of these, a name broadly applied to the lakes country as well as to a specific river and valley. The Genesee Road leading west from Utica along the northern margins of the uplands to Geneva and Canandaigua provided the main avenue of entry. A number of other roads, more difficult in profile but more direct from Connecticut and the lower Hudson Valley, led across the Catskills into the many valleys of the upper Susquehanna and converged on the Genesee. By 1800 there were 100,000 settlers in these lands, and the last big tract, held by the Holland Land Company and covering the entire western end of New York State, was readied for the market. Joseph Ellicott, the agent in charge, set up his headquarters at Batavia, near the eastern entrance, and gave high priority to extending the road on to Lake Erie, where he laid out an elaborate plan for New Amsterdam, at the mouth of Buffalo Creek—a site, he assured his Amsterdam backers, "designed by nature for the grand emporium of the Western world" (he also intended to develop therein a network of canals but nothing could save the name: residents and visitors alike persistently called it Buffalo).

Some of this emigrant traffic moved on, following the ancient elevated beach-line, past Presque Isle, where Pennsylvanians had laid out their own western emporium in the town of Erie, to the famous Western Reserve of Connecticut. Much of this northeastern corner of Ohio had been purchased by the Connecticut Land Company, which surveyed the town of Cleveland (originally Cleaveland) at the mouth of the Cuyahoga River. Some of these large tracts, like a number of others in New York and Pennsylvania (and Upper Canada as well), were exhibits of the "developer's frontier": speculations wherein the investors expended a good deal of money and effort not only to survey and sell lands but to provide a basic infrastructure of roads, towns, mills, inns, and in some cases model farms as a means of luring settlers (and increasing the price). At a quite different scale and intent was the old Yankee practice of a group of intending emigrant families forming a company to purchase a small block of lands to establish an entire community in a particular district, as was done in several areas of the Western Reserve and also in newly opened federal lands just to the south, as at Granville, Delaware, and Worthington.

As already described with reference to the northern borderlands, before 1812 minor branches of this Yankee exodus flowed northward into adjacent Quebec and westward across the Niagara River into Upper Canada. It should also be noted that while this general colonization movement was strongly dominated by New England emigrants, it was augmented by varying inflows from the Hudson Valley, New Jersey, Pennsylvania, and even Maryland. Some of the major land jobbers were based in New York or Philadelphia, and roads were also pushed into western

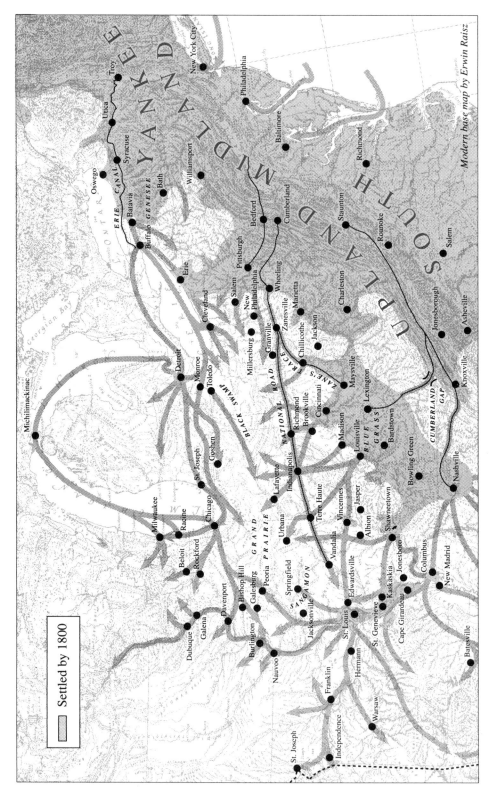

27. Westward Migrations: Northern Paths.

New York from the Susquehanna Valley and northwest from Pittsburgh into the Western Reserve.

In detail this northern belt of expansion was very uneven and selective, reflecting in part the varied character of the land. It was everywhere a terrain remolded by the continental glacier and characteristically patchy, with areas of swamp and high-lying bog, of sand and gravel, of steepened slopes and drumlins, but also of rich valley bottoms, terraces, and, especially, gentler uplands mantled with well-drained and fertile glacial drift. The dense forests of mixed hardwoods were broken in numerous places by old fields and village sites of the largely vanquished Iroquois, and the whole country was laced with streams and spotted with lakes and attractive mill sites. The early settlers tended to avoid the often swampy Ontario lake plain as unhealthy, but most of this new region was at least equal in quality to New England, and much of it was superior to the mountainous western and northern districts from where the greatest number of emigrants were drawn.

After a strong surge into central New York this movement slackened; the Holland Company lands and the Western Reserve developed much more slowly than their promoters expected; the war and depression of 1812–19 were a major interruption. Yet all this while Upstate New York was being formed and furnished as a major economic and social region with a powerful new instrument for geographic change. The building of the Erie Canal had a strong local economic effect, and its completion in 1825 impelled a great boom that ramified far afield. The canal realigned the western trunk route, giving birth to a set of new towns—and allowing Buffalo to begin to fulfill its envisioned role. This greatly enhanced avenue of commerce was extended by sail and steam to Cleveland and Detroit and other ports sprouting along the shores of Lake Erie. At the same time the natural barrier that had insulated Michigan from ready land connection with Ohio was breached by a long-awaited federal road across the Black Swamp, a dreaded thirty-mile-wide morass paralleling the Maumee River, the legacy of a once-larger Lake Erie. More accurate reports on the nature of the land between Lakes Erie and Michigan now challenged earlier assertions that it was all a swampy wilderness, and by the 1830s settlers were pouring in, fanning out from Monroe or Detroit across a broad belt of very attractive country with its many oak openings toward Flint and Grand River, and especially westward along the territorial roads toward St. Joseph. Some followed the curving moraine around the end of Lake Michigan to the boomtown of Chicago, and by the late 1830s this west-flowing stream was spreading across northern Illinois and edging into Wisconsin. Beloit, Rockford, Moline, and Galesburg were quintessential Yankee communities, and a New England influence was implanted in many others beyond the area of domination, such as Peoria, Decatur, and Urbana.

The distinctive character of this western colonization was unmistakable, but it was a second-generation emigration coming far more heavily out of New York than from New England itself, as is attested by the enduring imprint of those peculiar New York names on the map of these western states: the several Genesees, Geneseos, and Batavias; Oneida, Onondaga, and Oswego; Chemung, Canandaigua, and Unadilla; Manlius and Marcellus; Utica, Syracuse, and Ithaca, as well as New Buffalo, New Troy, and the like. The appearance also of a Watervliet, a Kinderhook, and a Rensselaer, referring to a deeper layer of Hudson Valley settlement, remind us again of the variety of peoples in this great northern stream. By 1840 the population of this "Third New England" beyond Lake Erie was about 350,000; ten years later it exceeded 1 million quite apart from its heterogeneous cities.

This long latitudinal reach was paralleled and impinged upon by other major migration streams. These laid down a more complicated pattern stemming from two different bodies of people competing for some of the same ground, overlapping and becoming intertwined as they extended westward. The basic differentiation was between emigrants coming out of the great Midland source region of Greater Pennsylvania (a movement reinforced in its later phases by transatlantic immigrations through New York City, Philadelphia, and Baltimore) and migrations out of the old Greater Virginia region, which included Tidewater Maryland and areas reaching into North Carolina, together with its new western outliers in the Bluegrass and Nashville basins.

Both of these movements established footholds north of the Ohio River before 1800. Virginia retained rights to a large block of military bounty lands lying west of the Scioto River. These were reached via Maysville (Limestone), Kentucky, with Chillicothe, the territorial capital located on Zane's Trace where the Scioto Valley broadens out northward toward the Pickaway (Piqua) Plains, as the main forward seat of aspiring Virginian gentlemen farmers and speculators. The great Midland foothold lay just to the west in a tract between the Miami rivers where Cincinnati soon emerged as the premier center of the Ohio Valley. It was in a peculiarly advantageous position: at a northerly bend of the Ohio where the great river leaves its typical course through the rugged hills and cuts into the softer rolling glaciated country, providing easy access to the fertile plains of western Ohio and central Indiana.

In 1804 the federal government made its vast fund of lands available on better terms to the ordinary settler, reducing the minimum purchase to a quarter-section (160 acres) with provision for four years' credit. Even before surveys could begin and land offices opened, speculators and squatters were swarming into the broad swath of government lands lying between Cincinnati and St. Louis. Tracts around the old French settlements at Vincennes and Kaskaskia were the first opened; Jeffersonville (opposite Louisville) and Shawneetown became the river port gateways. Land offices were next set up in a line of inland towns: Brookville–Terre Haute–Palestine–Vandalia–Edwardsville, and these were soon succeeded by another set farther inland. By the early 1830s all the lands south of Lake Michigan had been put on the market. Meanwhile, the first large tract in Missouri was opened (1811), a wedge of settlement quickly extended up the Missouri Valley, and the opening of the Santa Fe Trail gave rise to a sequence of upriver towns competing to serve this new overland commerce. At the end of the 1820s the rush to the lead mines inland from Galena soon created another major outlier of St. Louis–based expansion on the upper Mississippi, a decade ahead of the main farmer's frontier.

The great majority of the people moving north across the Ohio and up the Missouri and Mississippi were part of the Greater Virginian migration stream, a part drawing ever more heavily upon Kentucky, Tennessee, and western North Carolina. Such pioneers found the rough unglaciated hill country of the Ohio Valley and Missouri entirely familiar in kind, and they readily worked their way back into the coves and recesses of the Ozarks. By these colonizations they were extending the northern and western margins of the Upland South, a major American region that had begun to take shape after the Revolution. As they spread northward up the streams of Illinois they came onto a much more gentle and open land where the hardwood forests gave way to prairies in their many variations: small prairies and big prairies, flat prairies and rolling prairies, dry prairies and wet prairies, open areas studded with widely spaced groves and "barrens" with no trees at all. Such country was not necessarily strange to these people—there were openings and barrens in Kentucky—and they had no aversion to making what use they could of such lands, but for practical purposes they hung along the margins where there was wood for building, fuel, and fencing, soils easily tilled once cleared, free range for hogs, and a variety of game. They let their cattle graze on the prairie and pushed their fields into it where they could, but sodbreaking was an arduous task requiring heavy plows and many oxen and was beyond the means of many of these pioneers. As the valleys filled, land pressures mounted, and evidence of success with prairie farms accumulated, it became increasingly routine to select land "well-proportioned with prairie and timber," while still skirting the Grand Prairie and other broader expanses. Only in the late 1830s and early 1840s, with the development of self-scouring steel plows, did prairie farming become really attractive, and by then many of the new settlers arrived with enough capital to hire sodbreakers and fence builders and to purchase and ship in timber from a distance. Most of these later migrants were not Upland Southerners but representatives of one of the more northerly migrations.

The Midland stream spread westward rather more slowly than those to the north and the south. Zane's Trace and the National Road provided a main entryway into

Ohio; others took the Ohio River to Cincinnati for the roads leading into Indiana and Illinois, while St. Louis became a dispersal center for lands to the north and west. A characterizing feature of this extension from Greater Pennsylvania, setting it rather sharply apart from bordering streams, was its marked diversity of peoples, especially the many subgroups of British and German colonial stock. That variety was to be found in all the main settlements from Zanesville to Indianapolis, Peoria, and Burlington. Equally characteristic and more readily visible were the many towns and districts imprinted with the mark of a single sect or denomination. Thus the Quakers, emblematic of the originating society, established settlements at Mt. Pleasant and Salem, just inside Ohio, followed by a thin sprinkling farther west (as at Westerville, Leesburg, and Wilmington), and a more extensive pattern fanning out from Richmond, Indiana, into easternmost Illinois (as at Georgetown). Many of the Quakers in Indiana came from North Carolina, electing, as sectional tensions increased, to leave the South and to make a new start on free soil. Various Pennsylvania German sects were also deposited in many localities along this corridor: the Moravians at New Philadelphia, near the site of their early missions among the Delaware Indians; the Amish filling districts just to the west (Strasburg, Millersburg) and later founding new settlements farther on (Englewood, Ohio; Goshen, Indiana; Forrest, Illinois); Dunkards at New Lebanon; Rappites in their commune at Harmony, Indiana (but later selling out to the Welsh utopian Robert Owen and returning to Pennsylvania). A more general concern for maintaining the German language and culture led to the formation of the German Settlement Society of Philadelphia and to the founding of Hermann, Missouri, as the western nucleus of a riverine district that grew by both domestic and foreign immigration into the "Missouri Rhineland." Such ethnoreligious patterning was augmented by the immigration of German Roman Catholics, who imprinted numerous localities (such as Somerset, Ohio; Oldenburg and Jasper, Indiana; Highland, Illinois; and Westphalia, Missouri) with a landscape all the more distinctive for being obvious cultural islands within the scattered country neighborhoods of Upland Southerners. However, there were also Roman Catholic communities indigenous to the Upland South: created by Maryland Catholics who had moved westward alongside their Greater Virginia kin to establish Bardstown and a number of hamlets in central Kentucky.

By the 1840s the immigration of Germans, representing all the varied regions and religions of the homeland, and Irish Catholics was rapidly increasing. They swelled the population and vitality of Cincinnati and St. Louis and such booming river and lake ports as Burlington, Davenport, Dubuque, Milwaukee, and Chicago. The Irish provided much of the labor to build the many canals connecting the Great Lakes with the Ohio and Mississippi, and they created "little Dublins" and eventually Catholic parishes in the towns along those waterways. The Germans were prominent as artisans and industrialists as well as farmer-settlers on the Iowa frontier. Other immigrant streams, much smaller in volume and visibility, added further variety to this socially complicated intermediate region, such as the much-publicized (but not markedly successful) English farm colonies in southern Illinois (Albion); the Welsh settlers who began to pick open the coal and iron measures in the southern Ohio hills (as at Jackson); the Cornish miners lured to the lead diggings of Wisconsin; and the first of the Scandinavian colonists (at Norway, on the Fox River, and the Swedish religious commune at Bishop Hill, Illinois).

There were also even more conspicuous domestic migrations, most notably those of the Mormons. The beginnings of the Church of Jesus Christ of Latter-day Saints in Upstate New York and the building of their first temple at Kirtland in the Western Reserve were congruent with the New England origins and Puritan affinities of the founder and shapers of this new movement, but its distinctly North American dimensions (as asserted in the Book of Mormon) were brought to the fore when Joseph Smith proclaimed Independence, Missouri, as the seat for the building of the New Zion. The removal to and founding of several settlements in western Missouri engendered so much strife that the Mormons soon moved to yet another designated gathering place at Nauvoo, on the Illinois bank of the Mississippi River, which they soon built into a thriving center, momentarily the largest city in Illinois. After further conflicts and the murder and martyrdom of their leader in 1844, the main body of Mormons under the leadership of Brigham Young removed to their final isolated refuge in the Valley of the Great Salt Lake. We shall trace the development of a distinct Mormon culture region in the Far West in due course; for the moment we may simply identify them as one of the many groups contributing to the diversity, dynamics, and, especially in their case, the turbulence of these early streams of migration. This variety of peoples was sufficiently common throughout this Midland migration belt to make the countryside of every subregion and even most of its counties a mosaic, every large town and many a county seat a meeting point of contrasting (and often contending) socioreligious groups.

As for expansions in the Old Southwest, there was a steady extension and thickening of settlement in Kentucky and Tennessee, states that grew by 342,000 in the first decade of the new century. There were no federal lands in these two states (and western Tennessee was not open to colonists until 1818), and the first new thrust of the advancing frontier in this general area was southward out of Middle Tennessee into what was to become Alabama Territory, where the federal government had opened a land office in Huntsville to peddle the tract lying north of the great southerly swing of the Tennessee River. The vanguard of settlers and speculators overlooking the long stretch of Muscle Shoals on the Tennessee was one of several posed on the perimeter of the huge block of unceded Indian lands in the Southwest. On the east Georgians were filling in the long cession between the Oconee and Ocmulgee rivers that had been extracted from the Creeks in 1804. At the southwest corner an American city was rapidly growing within and around the Spanish grid of Natchez, perched on the bluff overlooking a Mississippi landing. By 1812 this bustling city of 9,000 was the commercial and cultural focus of a booming cotton district and connected to New Orleans by the first regular steamboat service on the river. Crude military roads led eastward to Washington and on to St. Stephens in the more insulated Alabama district. Federal land offices had been opened in both of these inland towns in 1803; eight years later most of northern Louisiana was opened to American settlement (fig. 28).

A rather chaotic swirl of geopolitical changes altered the context for American expansion along the Gulf Coast. The shattering of the Indian hold, reducing the once-formidable nations and confederations to residual homelands, and the successive annexations of the Floridas opened up a whole new scope for speculation and settlement. A broad belt of land reaching from the Tennessee River on the north to Mobile Bay was wrested from the Indians. In March 1817, the Territory of Alabama was created; in August the first lands of the Creek Cession were put up for sale at Milledgeville; by November a North Carolina planter reported that "the Alabama Feaver rages here with great violence and has *carried off* vast numbers of our citizens." The lands first marketed and of greatest interest to speculators and emigrants were the river bottoms along the Alabama, Cahaba, and Tombigbee, lying amid parallel belts of black prairie soils and sandy loams curving across the center of the territory. The Federal Road, the old military track across the Creek Country west from Augusta and Milledgeville, funneled thousands of families from the Georgia-Carolina Piedmont into this new frontier. Thousands of others came out of Tennessee and Carolina by way of Huntsville and Florence, following roads that led southward to the new river towns of Tuscaloosa and Columbus (Mississippi). The older Alabama and Tensaw districts extending along the river bottoms north from Mobile were a third source region and entryway. In the southwest the New Purchase from the Choctaw in 1820 was followed by a similar surge of expansion from the Natchez district. Vicksburg and Yazoo City were laid out at advantageous river sites, and the state capital was shifted from Washington to a more central location at Jackson on a low bluff overlooking the extensive prairies beyond the Pearl River.

The great power behind these migrations was the coincidence of soaring prices for cotton and the sudden opening of lands especially suited to its cultivation. All the while, however, many kinds of country less attractive to commercial speculation—the sandy and gravelly soils of the flatwoods and piney hills, the heaviest canebrakes and swamplands, the rougher hills and districts remote from

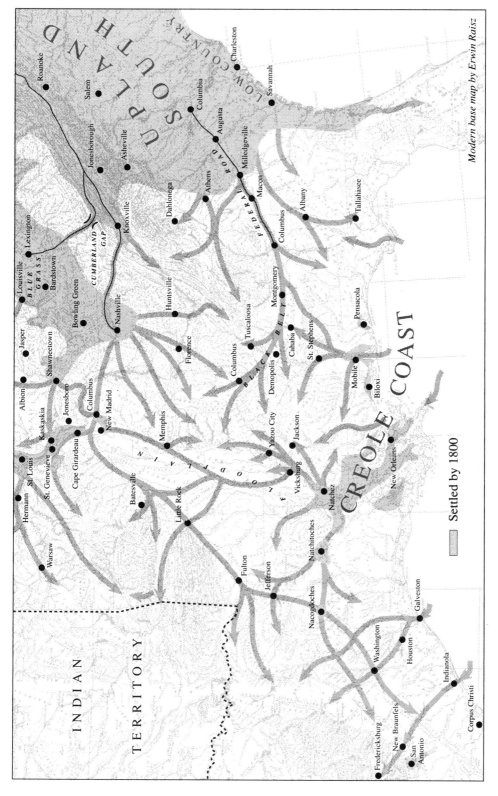

Modern base map by Erwin Raisz

INDIAN TERRITORY

UPLAND SOUTH

LOW COUNTRY

FEDERAL ROAD

BLUE GRASS

CUMBERLAND GAP

BLACK BELT

FLOOD PLAIN

CREOLE COAST

Roanoke
Salem
Jonesborough
Asheville
Knoxville
Dahlonega
Athens
Columbia
Augusta
Milledgeville
Macon
Charleston
Savannah
Lexington
Louisville
Bardstown
Bowling Green
Nashville
Huntsville
Florence
Columbus
Tuscaloosa
Montgomery
Columbus
Albany
Tallahasee
Jasper
Albion
Shawneetown
Jonesboro
Columbus
New Madrid
Memphis
Demopolis
Cahaba
St. Stephens
Mobile
Pensacola
Biloxi
Kaskaskia
St. Louis
St. Genevieve
Cape Girardeau
Hermann
Batesville
Yazoo City
Jackson
Vicksburg
Natchez
New Orleans
Warsaw
Little Rock
Fulton
Jefferson
Natchitoches
Nacogdoches
Washington
Houston
Galveston
Indianola
Corpus Christi
Fredericksburg
New Braunfels
San Antonio

Settled by 1800

28. Westward Migrations: Southern Paths.

the main roads and waterways—were being occupied in common Southern back-woods fashion by stockmen-hunters. Drifting out of all the older settlement re-gions, such people infiltrated every district and spread restlessly and relentlessly across the entire Gulf South from the Carolinas deep into Texas. Creating loose clusters of kith and kin, such pioneers supported themselves on their cattle and hogs, patch farming and kitchen gardens, hunting, fishing, and trading, with only occasional connection with the rapidly extending commercial world.

In the 1830s the removal of the Indians and the successful secession of Texas from Mexican rule opened the last great expanses of these humid subtropical lands. The final reserves of the Choctaw and Chickasaw on the west and of the Creek and Cherokee on the east had been beleaguered islands reconnoitered and infiltrated well before any legal cession, and they were now quickly overrun from every side. West of the Mississippi, land seekers spread up the White and Arkansas rivers. In 1839 Henry Shreve completed six years of arduous work in clearing the Great Raft, a 160-mile blockage of debris on the Red River, and thereby added a waterway to the several land routes funneling streams of settlers into East Texas. In the 1840s the "Texas fever" was raging, depleting the older states as the Alabama fever had done a generation earlier.

By the 1850s these waves of Southern migration had reached halfway across Texas, seeping into the Cross Timbers, lapping up against the long escarpment of the hill country—a thousand miles west of its Atlantic Seaboard source regions. It was the longest and much the broadest of these several westward expansions, and for the most part it was remarkably homogeneous in population, as Milton New-ton, Jr., looking eastward from his native Texas, emphasized:

> When in 1811, Hidalgoist Bernardo Gutierrez went overland from the Sabine to Washington, D.C. [he was seeking support for a reassertion of the Mexican revolu-tion] he passed through a single, relatively uniform cultural medium, that of the Upland South, virtual sole possessor of the Old West. He would have found a vast, fertile land about the size of New Spain, occupied by armed and agile republican-Protestants, Freemasons all (as he was), milling constantly west and southwestward. After having encountered the first log-built farmstead in Sabine Parish in Louisiana, he would have learned the cultural landscape of the entire million square miles he was next to traverse, allowing of course for those whose prosperity had permitted them to make more polite versions of the same plan.

Almond Parkins pointed more directly to the vital threads of this great fabric: for three hundred years Southern expansion was "for the most part the dispersal and reassembling of the same families. . . . One will find the family names of Colonial Virginia all over the South even to the western border of Texas"; Barnes Lathrop, a specialist on this movement, concluded that "the typical East Texan derived from the back-country folk of the Carolinas, and the pivot of his westward progression had been either Tennessee or Alabama." As this specification indicates, much of this expansion involved long-distance migration, and in fact the latest phase involved some of the longest relocations, for as the success of cotton production became manifest, the newest western regions drew planters and small farmers alike directly from the oldest South—the worn-out tobacco lands of Tidewater Virginia and North Carolina. Coastal South Carolina and Georgia, based on a more stable form of production in the rice lands, did not contribute proportionately in volume, but they nevertheless contributed important kinds of people who would play a critical role in shaping the sociopolitical direction of this newer South.

In spite of the great preponderance of this basically homogeneous "Southern" population, there were localities and districts, old and new, of exceptional variety. Central Texas was the only region of the Gulf South where this massive sweep of Southern land seekers was joined by others coming in directly from Europe. The Republic of Texas had actively sought such immigrants to populate its vast spaces and shore up the defenses against retaliatory Indians and Mexicans. Germans were much the largest group, dominating a number of districts in a broad belt of varied country extending from coastal Carlshafen (Indianola) to Fredericksburg deep in the hill country two hundred miles to the west. New Braunfels on the rich prairies near the base of the uplands became the most important nucleus. In the 1850s a trickle of Bohemians, Moravians, Sorbians (Wends), and Poles, drawn from German-ruled homelands, added to the ethnic variety of the area.

As elsewhere in North America the rapidly swelling influx of Irish also left its mark, but rather less broadly. Following the shipping lanes to the big coastal and river ports, the Irish remained more confined to such entry points because there was less demand for their labor in industrial projects inland. In time their most conspicuous mark would be their religion and its institutions, and the erection of new dioceses provides a useful clue to their spreading presence: Charleston (from Baltimore) 1820, Mobile 1829, Natchez 1837, Little Rock 1843, Galveston 1847. At the start each of these was an almost empty frame, with no more than a scattering of the faithful and few if any churches, but in each case the intensive efforts of a few priests and nuns eventually created an important presence. The Creole Coast, already harboring a rich diversity of peoples and traditions, provided a rather more substantial base upon which to build, and after twenty years of labor the first bishop of Mobile (a French-born priest sent out from New Orleans) was able to turn over an impressive number of parishes, missions, and facilities, including Spring Hill College, to his Irish-born successor. As the old primary focus of this West and a link with the wider world, New Orleans in some degree imitated New York City in receiving a great variety of immigrants from Europe, the Caribbean, Hispanic America, and from many states north and south.

As a result of these broadly latitudinal migrations the same sequence of peoples might be expected to be found north to south along the Mississippi in 1850 as that found along the Atlantic Seaboard in 1800. And in general such was the case, although by that date the migrants on that western margin were most commonly from an inland region one generation removed from the seaboard societies. Thus Upstate New York was the leading source of settlers for Wisconsin and northern Illinois, Ohio for Illinois and Iowa, Kentucky for Missouri, Tennessee for Arkansas, Alabama for Mississippi, Mississippi and Alabama for northern Louisiana. Convergence and interpenetration along the margins of these movements were considerable, especially in the Ohio Valley and Missouri and in the significant contributions of Tennessee and Kentucky to Texas, but such complications in pattern were not new in kind because the old seaboard source regions were not always sharply distinct either, as exhibited in the Yankee penetration and spanning of the Yorker Hudson Valley and Pennsylvanian migrations far southwestward in the Great Valley and onto the Carolina Piedmont.

Such migrations were not simply inland extensions of the several regional societies of the Atlantic Seaboard, however. These fifty years were a time of momentous change and development in all areas, old and new, and we should not expect regional characteristics and contrasts to remain unmodified over such a span of time. The emergence of cities ever-more closely connected through networks of radically improved transportation added an important complication to these broad patterns. Everything seemed to be in flux; the internal content and structure of the United States was being continually, markedly, often quite unpredictably, reshaped. Nor could it all be readily charted and measured, even by the most astute students, for this changing geography was bound up with changing and often sharply contrasting perceptions, attitudes, and emotions about just what the shape of this great republic was—and ought to be.

2. Occupying New Ground: Colonization, American Style

The transformation of the United States into a truly continental America, with nearly half of its population residing in the new states of the West, was a development of prodigious proportions in time and space. Even though the fecundity ("the American multiplication table"), restlessness ("Though they have generally good houses, they might almost as well, like the Tartars, dwell in tents. Everything shifts under your eye"), and deep-rooted aggressiveness ("from the first discovery of America to the present time, one master passion, common to all mankind—that of acquiring land—has driven, in ceaseless succession, the white man on the Indian") of the Americans were well recognized at the time, other features must also be taken into account. Some attention must be paid to the character of the stage and the institutional and social context of this drama, and the acts in its unfolding more clearly defined.

As noted with reference to imperial expansion, the federal government assumed responsibility for negotiations with the Indians and under relentless public pressures concentrated on their orderly removal so as to make their homelands available to American land seekers; further, it became generally understood that wherever such removal was not effected rapidly enough Americans were tacitly free to trespass with impunity, defend themselves with guns, and drive the Indians from such lands by whatever means they wished to employ. All along this western front, therefore, the presence of armed men and fortified outposts, whether of the U.S. Army, territorial militia, irregular bands of Whites, or family stockades, was an integral part of American settler expansion.

Early land seekers might regard expulsion of the Indians as a dangerous and tardy process, but relatively few actually had to fight, and however this removal was accomplished the land was then perceived as empty and untrammeled. Even though it was not a virgin wilderness, it was easily viewed as such because the Indians had left behind no cities (these had disappeared centuries before, leaving a scattering of great mounds to whet the curiosity of this new wave of settlers), and their semi-permanent towns and villages could be effaced in a season. The location of such sites, with their old fields and connecting trails, might influence the choice of land in some localities, but such faint tracings could not shape the overall patterns of the much denser subsequent settlement. Aside from a few French and Spanish settlements Americans did not have to share this vast realm with other peoples.

ENVIRONMENTAL CONDITIONS

Not only was this huge area essentially empty, it was a familiar kind of country. That it could be described as such not just in guidebooks and promotion tracts but in letters sent home from the vanguard of pioneers was fundamental. As Archer Butler Hulbert, one of the great students of this mass movement, has written, it was the reports of these agriculturalists

> naming the soils and shrubs and trees and grasses that were already known to them; describing conditions which they had already been wont to overcome; presenting the exact terms of a battle they knew they could win. Always and everywhere that, and that alone, was the unquestionable magnet—the evidence that success with soil could be won on terms of farm or plantation life as the prospective emigrants knew it; that known reactions of soil to weather would be experienced; that wood with which they were used to working lay ready at hand; that all the old tricks of the trade would work in the new land.

This is not to say that North America presented a simple set of uniform latitudinal belts through which the pioneers could move without any adjustment; only that for a thousand miles there were no really critical environmental differences that might bar the routine westward extension of established systems of pioneering. The broad mass of the Appalachians was far from being the great "barrier" that many later interpreters of this American expansion assumed it to have been. It had been successfully penetrated all along its eastern margins from the Catskills to the Great Smokies before the Revolution, and in the reassertion of such movements after the war this rugged upland was not only crossed by way of several major routes, it was routinely penetrated and in time permeated by American settlers. As we have seen, Yankees streaming westward through the Mohawk Valley encountered familiar glaciated country all the way to southeastern Wisconsin. If the moraines and till plains and swamplands were much more extensive than the New England version of such things, that posed no problem. Similarly, Carolinians skirting the southern end of the mountains might encounter—perhaps in different order, depending upon their route—the same belted sequence of flatwoods, sandy plains, red hills, black prairies, and piedmont uplands as would be apparent in any traverse of their home state. In between, in the lands beyond the Cumberland Plateau, the rich and rolling limestone soils of the Bluegrass and Nashville basins were western versions of the Great Valley of Pennsylvania, western Maryland, and the Shenandoah, while much farther west, beyond the Mississippi, the Ozarks and Ouachitas were another Appalachia. Of course, there was always much to be learned in detail about local conditions in every district. Only direct trial could reveal the response of particular lands to various crops and tillage—how soon the big flats would dry out in the spring, how soon the north slopes would warm up, how far inland the leeward lakeshores would prove advantageous for fruit—but the results of such experience were routinely added to the folk knowledge of every pioneering community.

It was commonly remarked that nature seemed to be designed on a grander scale beyond the mountains: the mighty rivers, the vast floodplain of the Mississippi, the seemingly endless forests—and then the broadening plains and eastern embayments of the great prairies. These last would pose special problems, but they gave notable pause to the swarms of promoters and land seekers alike only in their higher, drier versions farther west; by sticking close to the woods lining the many streams, the prairies of Illinois and Iowa were readily penetrable.

It was soon powerfully apparent to any newcomer that western weather was also on a grander scale. There were greater seasonal extremes of heat and cold, and far more violent changes, sometimes in a matter of hours, accompanied by spectacular thunderstorms, cloudbursts, hail, blizzards, or, most awesome of all, tornadoes. These weather phenomena were in part unexceptional and in part peculiar to North America in their intensity. The great seasonal range of temperatures was primarily a simple matter of continentality—of moving away from an oceanic seaboard inland toward the continental source regions of the air masses that usually controlled such things in this global belt of the westerlies. But the violence, the power of the great storms that swept across the region was generated by the peculiar conformation of North America in which the broad uninterrupted lowland extending from the Arctic Ocean to the Gulf of Mexico became a collision course for the bitterly cold dry air of the Yukon and Athabasca and the thick warm air surcharged with moisture spreading northward from the tropical seas. The zone of encounter was controlled by the shifting sinuosities of the stratospheric jet stream and experienced at the surface in the passage from west to east of front after front along the cyclonic storm tracks across the great lowlands. In time, it would become more clearly understood how so much of the weather experienced by generations on the eastern seaboard was a reverberation or residue of these vast continental systems.

These extremes of weather, punctuating the seasons with memorable episodes, might well strike those who experienced them as marking an important difference between East and West, but it was the more general patterns of the seasons, weather over the longer term, the averages—climate—that were critical to the success of an agricultural people, and here experiences in the West were strongly reassuring. In general, all the crops and methods of home, all the old tricks of the trade, worked and often worked wonderfully well in these new lands. In spite of the greater continentality, the average seasonal isotherms ran more or less latitudinally, and the precipitation was about the same on either side of the mountains. These were the critical features. Essentially it didn't matter how cold it got in a particular winter; what was important was how soon it warmed up in the spring and how long before the first killing frost in the fall. Indian agriculture had demonstrated its adaptation to the whole broad region; now an ever-expanding American folk knowledge, accumulations of weather data from various places, and a slowly developing science enlarged general understanding of such vital matters. These consistent patterns across the eastern half of the continent were confirmed in the first general scientific work on the climate of the United States, by Samuel Forry in 1842, and again, in much richer detail and concept, in Lorin Blodget's landmark book on climatology published in 1857. Blodget drew on several years of systematic data collection initiated by the Smithsonian Institution and new understandings of a world system of analogous climates.

Research on weather and climate had been initiated by the Surgeon General's Office of the U.S. Army out of concern for the health of troops in their widely scattered posts. Such a focus called attention to a rather more ambiguous aspect of western weather and environment. On the one hand, many a guidebook and traveler reported on the vastness of the skies, the clear, bracing air, the exhilarating freshness of it all, and increasingly a journey to the West for a "change of air" and its presumed curative effects became a common prescription for those suffering from consumption (tuberculosis), dyspepsia, and various other diseases and complaints. It was generally understood that the higher and drier areas within the West were to be preferred; in the 1840s Josiah Gregg, the popular reporter of experiences along the Santa Fe Trail, wrote persuasively about the "travel cure in the Prairies." Yet the extensive incidence of fevers—"the ague"—and similar afflictions could hardly be glossed over. Such fevers were known in the East as well and had been a hazard since very early attempts at European planting on American shores. That newcomers to a region might suffer a bout of sickness was taken for granted—"country seasoning," it was called—after which those who survived might be more or less free of severe recurrences. But in this, too, the West appeared to be on a bigger scale. One seemed never far from "miasmic waters": swamps, bogs, stagnant pools, shallow lakes, sluggish rivers, floodplains, bayous, all clogged with vegetation. It was a luxuriant environment for mosquitoes, as every traveler painfully discovered, and "malarious diseases" were endemic. Blodget boldly asserted that "India itself has not been more certain to break the health of the emigrant than the Mississippi valley," though he softened the embarrassing comparison by stating that "the American forms of disease were always attended by a much smaller ratio of mortality." Just how much the still-considerable American mortality and disability affected population growth is difficult to estimate, but if these slowed migration to the West it was hard to notice. For this great interior region was at once a magnet and a magnifier; it exerted a powerful draw upon the people of older areas and it enlarged their visions of the possible: "One acquires as he proceeds westward, largeness and expansion of his ideas. . . . thought swells away into the vast dimensions of the majestic rivers and boundless tracts over which the eye expatiates."

OBTAINING LAND

In the western portions of the original thirteen states (including the whole of Kentucky and Tennessee) lands were made available by the state, mostly through grants to war veterans or the sale of large tracts to proprietors who acted as wholesalers to individual settlers or lesser speculators. Some proprietors attempted to manage the settlement process to maximize profits, surveying and classifying lands as to quality and withholding some from the market to await a rise in price. Considerable investment was often made in facilities and services—roads, mills, inns—and especially in the development of one or more towns to ensure their prominence and maximize profits from the sale of town lots. Thus Marietta was designed to serve the large Ohio Company tract, Cleveland to be the "capital" of the Western Reserve, and Buffalo, Batavia, and Maysville intended by the Holland Land Company to shape the urban pattern of westernmost New York. Even extensive investment could not ensure the success of a particular place, however, as Charles Williamson's extravagant expenditures on Bath, New York, would demonstrate. The patterns of mature settlement, lines of communication, and especially networks of interregional connection were quite beyond any single developer's control. So, too, those older states that controlled their public domain might decree the laying out of a townsite at a few strategic locales, as did, for example, New York at the mouth of the Oswego River (Oswego) and Pennsylvania at Presque Isle (Erie). Georgia ordered the creation of a series of "trading towns" at or near the head of navigation on major streams as large land tracts were opened by successive Indian cessions, and these fall-line towns (Milledgeville, Macon, and Columbus) became important centers in the regional system. But west of these jurisdictions most of the land was first marketed by the federal government according to a set of standard procedures initiated in the Land Ordinance of 1785.

This federal system was at once simple and comprehensive (fig. 29). Under the direction of the geographer of the United States, each large block of lands designated for sale had first to be surveyed and mapped according to the township and range system. A distillation and compromise from a variety of colonial precedents and new proposals (notably Jefferson's radically rational system of geographical hundreds), this famous American template required the laying out of an east-west baseline and a principal meridian as the controlling framework for a set of rectangular townships, each six miles square, with each township subdivided into thirty-six rectangular sections of one square mile each, and every square labeled according to a simple numbering system. No provision was made for the formal designation of locations or reserves for roads, towns, or millsites; the original act did make clear, however, that the surveyors were to be good field geographers and not merely geodetic workmen, for each was instructed to note carefully in his field books "at their proper distances, all mines, salt-springs, salt-licks, and mill seats, that shall come to his knowledge; and all water-courses, mountains and other remarkable and permanent things, over and near which such lines shall pass, and also the quality of the lands." Under the pressures to get the land on the market as soon as possible, such notations tended to become rather perfunctory (and the title of the national officer was soon changed from geographer to surveyor general). That the government ought to classify land into a set of graded qualities was debated time and again. That such a scheme would allow more equitable pricing and stimulate sales was countered by fears that it would favor speculation and reduce total proceeds. Before the Graduation [in price] Act of 1854 no such differentiations were made; all land was offered at the same fixed minimum price, surveyors' notations remained incidental, and it was left entirely up to buyers to make their own judgments about quality.

Once the points of this grid were marked on the land and officially recorded, a

Detail of a Township

Detail of a Section

Area of Townships

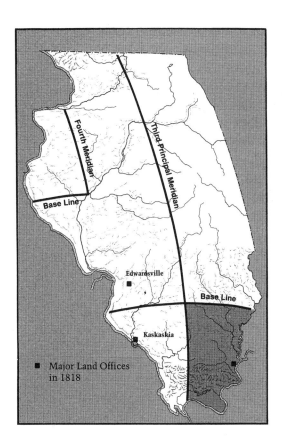

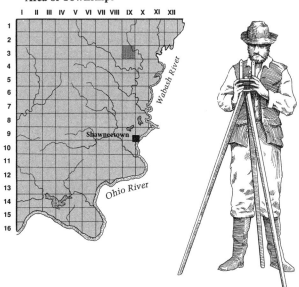

Surveyor at Work

29. The Federal Township-and-Range System.
(By Tom Willcockson, courtesy of David Buisseret; © by the University of Chicago.
All rights reserved)

federal land office could be opened in some convenient place near the threshold of
the tract and the public sale of lands begin. The size of the units offered and the
level and mode of payment were, expectedly, matters of intense and chronic
controversy. Pressures for the right to purchase smaller units led to recurrent
reductions in the minimum size parcel available: from one section (640 acres) to a
half section (320 acres) in 1800; to a quarter section (160 acres) in 1804; half of a
quarter (80 acres) in 1820; and a quarter of a quarter section (40 acres) in 1832.
Each reduction not only put land within reach of a larger number of purchasers, it

increased the flexibility of design for those who could purchase more than one minimum unit. For example, the first purchaser of 160 acres made up of four 40-acre units in some newly opened neighborhood had nineteen ways to shape and orient the four squares, a flexibility of immense advantage in the search for an optimum mix of good land, water, woodland, and access to road or river. But it would take time before actual land seekers and local residents would routinely think in terms of a rectangular landscape. As John Mack Faragher noted about the settlement of the Sugar Creek district in central Illinois: "The lines that surveyor Angus Langham drew across the land helped families to locate their claims precisely, but otherwise they had little impact on the shape of settlement during the first quarter-century of the American period. The look of the landscape was determined not by an abstract grid, but by cultural traditions of kinship and resource use in association with natural patterns of woodland and prairie." Only as the woods were cleared, fields were laid out, and, especially, the local road system neared completion was this repetitive rectilinear pattern manifest (and only much later, when it could be viewed from above—first from balloons, then from airplanes—did it become famous as a distinctive human imprint on the earth).

In 1800 federal land was made available at $2 per acre, with one-fourth down and four years to pay the remainder. Over the next twenty years Congress tinkered time and again with various adjustments, discounts, extensions, and other forms of debt relief before ending credit sales. The act of 1820 reduced the minimum cash price to $1.25 per acre, where it remained for many decades. On the assumption that buyers would pay more for the best lands, sale was by auction.

Reference to these formal procedures may mislead as to the common process of obtaining land. Such laws represent the desire of the national government to manage the orderly advance of settlement, whereas in fact such expansion ran largely out of control. From the first years of the Republic, Congress had attempted to prohibit Americans from encroaching on the public domain until it was formally opened to settlers. The act of 1807 authorized forced removal, fines, and possible imprisonment for any such trespass. But the matter was highly contentious. Whereas the one side argued that to allow people to "locate themselves upon the public lands without much regard to lines or boundaries, and with very little respect for the rights either of the Government or their Indian neighbors" was to risk chaos and fuel speculation, the other insisted that this vanguard of settlers was creating homes for their families and by their improvements bringing great benefit to the whole country and increasing the value of adjacent lands; they had transformed the derisive term *squatter* into an honorable one, they represented the strength and future of the Republic; and blame should rest on the government for not putting sufficient land on the market to meet an obvious demand. Such sturdy pioneers, it was fervently argued, had earned the right to "preemption"—that is, to purchase the lands they actually occupied, at the minimum price, once such tracts were officially surveyed and readied for sale. After a few futile attempts to remove squatters from lands in Ohio, the federal government abandoned any consistent effort at control, the act of 1807 became essentially a dead letter, and settlement before survey became a common practice. Indeed, it reached such proportions that in 1838, when Congress was again debating the topic and was preparing for the first sale of land in Iowa, at least fifteen thousand people were already resident there, the town of "Burlington and all the land for miles around had already been claimed. Hundreds of houses had been erected . . . ; the town already had a mayor and alderman. . . . Most of the first claimants had sold out to advantage and other men had bought and sold lots for years, and had even given deeds, but not a single lot in town or an acre of farmland was legally owned by an individual." General acceptance of squatting as part of the formal process of obtaining land came only with the Preemption Act of 1841, but Congress had legitimated particular cases many times in the years before, and that law was "merely declaratory of the custom or common law of the settlers."

Although nearly all the recurrent reforms in legislation purported to aim at getting government lands directly into the hands of "bona-fide settlers" rather than absentee owners, there were countless ways of evading the intent of the law. Large land jobbers were much reviled on the frontier as greedy parasites who corrupted officials, retarded settlement, created tenancy, and in general reaped where they had not sown. Yet their apologists at the time (and some historians since) argued that they provided badly needed capital and credit and other useful services in helping the prospective settler locate land and get started. In some degree the government directly fostered speculation by setting a minimum price below market value, yet large speculators seem neither to have made huge profits nor to have significantly retarded settlement. Because of the complexities of the transactions involved it has proved impossible to measure and assess the role of speculators with any precision for any considerable district. And that points to the most basic feature of the settlement process: that it tended to be suffused in speculation. Large absentee landlords were convenient scapegoats, but there were speculators at every scale, local as well as distant, those who dealt in hundreds as well as in thousands or tens of thousands of acres, including large numbers of settlers who sought to profit from the sale of surplus land (or the whole farm) whose value had been increased by their presence and improvements. Claims clubs were organized not only to protect the family farm until title could be secured but to fend off competing speculators. In spite of the auction system, competitive bidding for government land was often suppressed by buyers banding together to ensure acquisition at the minimum price.

Of course, the intensity of speculation in western lands rose and fell (and was an intricate factor in) the more general business cycle. An Iowa country editor summed up the situation that had prevailed just before the Panic of 1857:

It is amazing how completely our citizens were filled with the desire of sudden riches. Credit was easily had—eastern currency flooded the country—imaginary towns sprung up everywhere—lands were fictitiously high—usury was unscrupulously asked and willingly promised—farms were neglected—debts were left to run on unasked about, goods and groceries bought on credit, land alone selling for ready money at exorbitant rates. In short, every one was a professed speculator. . . . Then followed the wrecks of fortunes and the crash of business. It was natural—it could not have been otherwise.

It was "natural," certainly, in an America wherein real estate speculation as a way to wealth was as old as Jamestown. Although a conscientious application of the laws and other feasible reforms might have resulted in a more equitable distribution of lands directly into the hands of those who would turn them into productive farms, it clearly would have required a powerful central government with a large bureaucracy and strong armed forces to have disposed so great an expanse of lands to millions of people in a truly orderly manner.

OCCUPYING LAND

As for the modes of occupying and domesticating the land, these had been worked out in the Atlantic Seaboard source regions during the long prelude to national expansion. The famous symbol of American pioneering, the log cabin in the forest clearing, was derived from a scene most common in the early and broadening advance of Upland Southerners across the Interior. It pointed to an American system of expansion, a complex of Native American and European crops and animals, tools and techniques, involving a close dependence on local resources of pasture, woodland, and stream for a diversity of foods, fibers, medicinals, fuel, and building materials, and it implanted a distinct pattern of settlement upon frontier districts. The rifle, ax, and hoe were the essential tools. Patches of ground were cleared by girdling and burning, with plantings in the ashes among the stumps. Indian corn and hogs provided a subsistence base that was supplemented by a variety of produce from the garden (pumpkins, squash, beans, peas, cabbage, cucumbers, turnips, and perhaps potatoes) and the hunt (especially deer, bear, turkey, pigeon, and fish); cattle (for milk as well as beef), poultry, and quick-maturing peach trees provided important dietary additions. Log cabins and out-buildings were readily constructed according to a few basic folk designs—and as readily expanded by simple additions. A typical frontier "settlement" was a loose string or cluster of such family homesteads along a creek or line of springs, con-nected with one another by paths and with the whole district by pack trails and droving roads with some commercial outpost. Adapted to living off the land with minimal dependence on outside supplies, such a mode of colonization was highly efficient in spreading a population thinly over a large area.

Based on their research in both Europe and North America, the geographers Terry Jordan and Matti Kaups concluded that this highly successful American pioneering system first arose in the lower Delaware Valley as the invention of Savo-Karelian Finnish immigrants working in close association with the local Delaware Indians; that it was the Scotch-Irish who "subsequently supplied the largest single genetic input to the backwoods population, setting the colonization machine in rapid westward motion"; and that this vanguard complex was rapidly displaced in the area of its origin by "an evolving, expanding Germanic core" (such ethnic identities are general characterizations of what was, in most times and places, a more diverse participation; "Germanic" here refers to the English and various continental Germanic peoples).

Reference to this displacement brings attention to the important fact that an efficient pioneering system is not necessarily well adapted to progressive intensification in place. Geared more toward family subsistence and freedom than commercial production and formal sociopolitical development, many of these people had neither the tools nor the motivation for "progress" defined in prevailing American terms. They sat lightly on the land, ready to sell out, pack up, and move on to flee the onset of new people and closer settlement. They were a deliberately marginal people; as one Southerner "drifter" put it: "I had been reared to the belief and faith in the pleasure of frequent changes of country." Such folk tended to dominate the stage in contemporary accounts of the frontier, and they became celebrated thereafter as symbols of American intrepidity and independence. Yet anything like complete displacement over any considerable territory was probably rare. Some families would elect to stay on to "improve" their properties and join with subsequent newcomers in developing the locality. A sprinkling of specialists with their mills and smithies would soon appear, the search for commercial products and improved links with the wider world would be intensified, and local trade centers would emerge (fig. 30).

As the volume and pace of western expansion increased, the simplicity of the stereotypical succession blurred and the role of the famous pioneering wave changed and diminished. By the 1830s, certainly, in many areas the typical frontier squatter was no longer the backwoods family purposely living on the outskirts of national society but a petty speculator, or the agent of a greater speculator, alert and eager for the next wave of land seekers and development. Men with capital were buying virgin land, hiring laborers to clear the forest or break the sod, fence the fields, and build homes with milled lumber. In the South, where the full cotton system had been experimentally developing during the early phases of western expansion, plantation owners in Virginia and the Carolinas were selling off their worn-down lands and moving their entire estates, livestock and slaves, tools and household goods to large tracts in the Southwest, where the slaves were set to work

30. The Pioneer Settler and His Progress.

The first two panels of a four-stage sequence as presented by Orasmus Turner in his *Pioneer History of the Holland Purchase of Western New York,* Buffalo, 1849. A few important features, extracted from Turner's extensive captions: No. 1. Winter: the pioneer and his young wife, with their livestock; rude log house hastily built in the fall with roof of peeled elm bark, window of oiled paper, floor of halves of split logs, door of hewed planks; a little hay piled on small hovel; ox sled for hauling. No. 2. Summer: baby, calf, and pigs have arrived; chimney added to house; flowers, vines, kitchen garden, rail and brush fences; neighbors helping to clear more land; corn, potatoes, beans, and pumpkins growing among stumps and felled timber; crude bridge across stream. (See fig. 34 for panels 3 and 4) at clearing the great forest and architects soon hired to supervise the erection of appropriate mansions (mostly in the towns). Industry and commerce, towns and cities, full-fledged governments and social institutions were now part of the frontier scene rather than gradually emerging in later phases. Technology played a major role in this acceleration of development: first the steamboat, then the railroad, and a great increase in the volume and variety of industrial goods made available nationwide.

The more traditional American system of pioneering thus was quickly overtaken by and in some areas essentially excluded by a far more elaborate *American system of regional development.* And this system, too, had its famous symbol: the instant town mushrooming on the frontier even before much of the forest had been felled or fields cleared in the countryside. Less romantic to a later age than the log cabin, the town was far more potent in the shaping of the nation. It represented an intense investment of energy and capital from the East to transform new outlying districts into fully integrated parts of the whole.

Although especially apparent from the 1830s onward, urban centers had long been an essential part of the frontiering process in a way obscured by agrarian, Turnerian interpretations. "The towns were the spearheads of the frontier," asserted Richard Wade thirty years ago in his iconoclastic book *The Urban Frontier:* "planted far in advance of the line of settlement, they held the West for the approaching population." He was referring especially to Lexington, Louisville, Cincinnati, and St. Louis. As James Vance subsequently displayed in *The Merchant's World,* a thin scattering of such collection points and wholesaling centers, each with its own hinterland and connection to major entrepôts, was the characteristic pattern of the Atlantic system as it penetrated ever deeper into North America. Such early centers served the archetypal backwoods frontier as well as more specialized systems devoted to the Indian trade, furs and skins, minerals, forest products, and the support of military outposts. But this primary pattern became caught up in the new dynamic of the nineteenth century. As settlement thickened and new avenues of commerce multiplied the number of such mercantile centers, their external connections and relative positions could be quickly altered and their future threatened. The ensuing regional patterns, contingent on countless decisions, could not be confidently predicted, and even premier centers at naturally strategic sites had to join in the self-promotion and competition.

Urban speculation, like so much else, was encouraged by the minimal regulation of such things. A landowner needed no special legislative approval, license, or franchise to subdivide property into town lots and offer these for sale. One needed only to file a plat, displaying any design one wished, with a local county office. As John Reps has shown in his great series of books on American urban plans, some quite remarkable designs were proposed and some actually marked out upon the ground, but the vast majority were simple grids of linear streets framing rectangular lots, with perhaps a square or two set aside for public purposes. Such regularity, simplicity, and uniformity defined an American pattern dominant in every new region, impressed upon every kind of natural site, and offered at every scale from village to metropolis. It confirmed that the primary purpose was not to found communities but to sell lots. Wherever there was a surge of settlement into some attractive district land prices soared and fueled "the mania for . . . buying and selling house lots." Rohrbough, writing about Michigan in the 1830s, caught the flavor of this frantic geographical competition:

> Newspapers displayed the endless opportunities of the day. . . . Every inlet on either of the two lakes, every promontory on the two roads running east and west, the falls of every river leading inland, every prospective county seat, or indeed any vacant field, all were prospective town sites. The proprietors needed a smooth tongue, a suitable location, and the help of a number of urban fixtures—a mill and a hotel, a few stores, plus artisans and mechanics to serve the farmers from the countryside—to begin the village's career.

During the full fervor of such boom times towns might be planted almost as thickly as farms—or so it seemed to a facetious western newspaperman in 1837 (just before the bust): "If the plethora of town making did not cease, it would be necessary to petition Congress to reserve one or two sections in each township for agricultural purposes."

Local trade centers did of course emerge before or amid this plethora of paper towns and not necessarily as formally platted and promoted places. They might begin as no more than a general store, tavern, and post office (perhaps all in one building, operated by one family) at some crossroad, junction, or stopping place along a main road, adding a few more facilities—perhaps a gristmill or blacksmith shop—as the surrounding country was domesticated. Such small service centers, each with its limited radial trade area, emerged as the base level of a nascent hierarchy of central places. It was at the next tier of that pattern that the competition became intense: among those centers providing a larger array of services and even competitive stores on the same street. In boom times some of these larger places seemed to appear almost overnight with several mercantile houses, inns, banks, newspapers, lawyers, doctors, schoolteachers, and a variety of other shops and mills and services. Such places obviously represented the importation of capital and special skills from the East, and each saw itself as engaged in an intense competition with other places to secure dominance over its particular district.

GEOPOLITICAL FRAMEWORKS

Although a town could be initiated by any promoter, if it grew in substance it eventually had to organize a city government under state charter. But the powers granted tended to be very limited: authority to tax to provide police, health inspections, simple market regulation, streets and bridges were common, whereas water supply, fire protection, libraries, and poor relief were very often at first provided, if at all, by private or voluntary associations. One indispensable facility for any aspiring town was a local newspaper (and more than one, if possible) to focus citizen attention on worthy local causes and be an effective voice in vital competitions with other places. Almost all papers also served as the voice of a national political party, and many were initiated and subsidized for such purpose. The footloose opportunistic newspaper editor-publisher was also common among this frontier throng.

American governments did not usually design and initiate towns directly (a brief federal experiment in founding ten towns in Alabama was an unimportant exception), but they could be an active force in shaping the patterns of urban settlement. To govern required that there be a central place for governmental services. State legislatures usually selected locations for a capital and various state institutions and of course could influence the fortunes of particular places by support for specific projects, such a roads and bridges, canals, and railroads. Throughout the new territories and states the primary framework for local government was the county (although varied regionally in its specific powers and modes of operation). This geopolitical framework tended to be a coarser grid fitted upon the basic survey pattern, modified by major natural features, and readily extended or subdivided as settlement expanded and thickened (fig. 31). The location of a county seat (an American term, first recorded in 1803) was regarded as a major geopolitical decision. This decreed focus, with its cluster of buildings and officers, was considered as certain to attract a host of other facilities and services and give that place a marked advantage over other aspiring towns, though in fact such limited political functions alone were not enough to sustain much of a town. At all these levels of government, officials were of course subjected to intense pressures from local boosters and land speculators. Nor were such decisions necessarily final. County seats could be moved by popular vote, or counties could be subdivided to create the need for another seat and undercut the centrality of the older one; thus "county seat wars," sometimes involving intimidation and violence, became legendary in American folklore.

Counties were created by state or territorial governments, and these latter were created by Congress. Obviously the formation of these higher jurisdictions involved geographical decisions of fundamental importance. The shaping of states, especially, fixed American political life into a permanent framework—though one of ever-changing internal character and relative power—and we will need to look more specifically at some basic and specific features of the topic when we shift our focus to the federation. Suffice it here to note that even the most thinly settled outer margins of the nation were placed under the jurisdiction of courts and a set of

31. United States Counties, June 1, 1860.
Marked variations in size reflect differences in the significance of county government, as well as
in terrain and population density. The influence of the federal rectangular survey system becomes increasingly apparent in post-1800 settlement areas. (Courtesy of the Library of Congress)

administrative officials. However far the vanguard of pioneers might outrun effective order, it was rarely even momentarily technically beyond legal authority.

INFRASTRUCTURE

Transportation facilities were an especially powerful instrument in shaping new
patterns of settlement and development; steamboats enlivened riverbanks with
aspiring ports at every feasible landing, and the railroad was soon acknowledged as

the great determinant of local fortunes, founding strings of new centers and blighting all it bypassed as the depot became a new focus of American social and political life. And here, too, American governments played a remarkably limited role. A program for a national network of roads, canals, and waterways was presented by the secretary of the Treasury in 1808. The international crisis postponed debate, but the ensuing war only magnified the need, and various versions of such a program were considered until President Jackson's veto of a road bill, ostensibly on constitutional grounds, in 1830 put an end to any such comprehensive scheme. Thus one National Road, authorized in 1802 as a means of binding the incipient state of Ohio into the Republic, and a few crude military roads to far frontiers were about all the central government undertook directly. Meanwhile, the State of New York's sensational success with the Erie Canal stimulated a flurry of state projects, especially in Pennsylvania and Ohio (as well as an expanding system in New York). But virtually all such sponsorship, including several state railroad projects, ended with the Panic of 1837.

All this while, of course, turnpikes, bridges, canals, and, later, tramways and railroads were being built by private enterprise. Such projects had to be licensed by state authority, and their promoters lobbied relentlessly for subsidy and favor from governments at all levels, but such facilities as well as the actual systems of carriage—stagecoaches, wagon freighting, canal boats, steamboats, and railroad trains—were operated by private companies under minimal official regulation. Mail service and other essential government transport, such as shipments of ordnance and supplies to military posts, were normally undertaken by contract with private operators. This entire national infrastructure was shaped far more by private corporations in pursuit of profit than by government assessment of the basic needs of the nation, its regions, and its local districts. As a result the geographic patterns and pace of these basic developments were also strongly, and increasingly, influenced by speculation and competition. Western regions became as thickly papered over with proposed railroads as with towns, and much of the capital raised never resulted in the laying of any track. Lines actually completed were often opportunistic as to local routes and built and operated at minimum standards rather than providing substantial facilities as part of an optimum network. On the other hand, intense competition meant that few possibilities for traffic were long ignored, routes and services could be quickly adjusted to ongoing changes, and pressures toward the creation of larger and more efficient systems to dominate particular intercity and interregional connections were growing. By the 1850s such larger regional strategies were driving railroads across Iowa with little regard for the current margins of settlement or immediate traffic.

The social infrastructure was also left almost entirely in private hands. That, too, had been debated since the formation of the Republic. Jefferson, among others, had envisioned a nationwide system of public schools, graded to serve appropriate levels and specialties, but such ideas were far too expansive and radical to attract general support. It was initially proposed that some portion of the income from public lands be dedicated to the support of education and religion. Only the former was approved, in the form of declaring that the income from the sale or lease of Section 16 of every federal township be set aside, under the authority of the territorial or state legislature, "for the use of schools" (in 1848 a second square mile in each township [Section 36] was added to this reserve). But such provision did not in itself result in the creation of statewide—or even local—public school systems. There remained keen controversy over the desirability or degree of tax-supported education at any level of government. New England towns took the lead in establishing public schools, and in 1837 Yankee-dominated Michigan became the first state to make a constitutional commitment to establish a comprehensive system, but it would take many years for such ideas to be effected and diffused—and always with marked regional differences.

Repeated attempts to establish a national university in Washington failed, and before 1862 special congressional land grants for the support of particular institutions of higher learning were rare. State governments were much more active, chartering a considerable number of universities and colleges as public institutions, but many of these were long delayed in funding and long stunted in development.

Education, therefore, was very largely left to private initiative: to parents to hire tutors, to local groups to support a private school, to religious denominations to found an academy, seminary, or college. Teachers and schoolmasters searching for a niche were not uncommon among the fluid populations of new districts. Because community leaders regarded schools, and especially colleges, as emblems of culture and civilization, they were prized acquisitions in competitions for city status. Hence, as Boorstin noted, whereas "in Europe a college or university would be found in an ancient center, in the United States it was more likely than not to appear in a town whose population and prosperity lay all in the future"; indeed, "much the larger number of new colleges was founded in the western outposts and on the fringes of settlement." Generated by "denominational initiative, upstart enterprise, [and] booster optimism," the whole process was swept along by speculation, and the West was soon littered with "ghost colleges" as well as ghost towns.

The situation of religion in America was much less ambiguous but no less competitive. The first amendment to the Constitution declared that "Congress shall make no law respecting an establishment of religion, or prohibiting the free exercise thereof." Given the variety of religions already rooted in America, the result tended toward an increasing competition among a growing number of denominations to expand their position and numbers. Although families tend to be conservative in such matters, to adhere to the same faith generation after generation and to carry it with them from place to place, migration and resettling far from home—perhaps more than once—tends to loosen such allegiance, especially when the new settlements are accumulations of people from different regions. Furthermore, there were more general influences within this new democratic republic tending to make religion increasingly a matter of adult choice, an individual decision made in a kind of marketplace of religions where several brands were on display and being actively promoted. Such a characterization risks trivializing matters of deep personal meaning, but it is nonetheless especially pertinent to areas of new settlement where community patterns were as yet relatively open and unstable, where, in many places, most of the people had no church affiliation at all.

Certainly leaders of the various churches saw great opportunity, indeed a great Christian challenge and duty, in these new regions—"it is . . . plain that the religious and political destiny of our nation is to be decided in the West"—and they set about to reach out and bring these extending and growing populations into their fold. The most famous method was that of the traveling evangelists and the great camp meetings, an American phenomenon initiated at Cane Ridge, near Lexington, Kentucky, in 1801; a "revival of revivalism, at a strategic time and place," it did much to shape "the future of the country's denominational expansion." The emergent denominational pattern was ultimately shaped by the founding of churches in specific places rather than by sporadic camp meetings and revival sessions of this Second Great Awakening, although new religious movements would also upwell from such fervors.

Each of the major churches developed a distinct strategy for expansion that was shaped by its doctrines of faith and order. In areas of open competition, simplicity and adaptability were great assets, and the Baptists and the Methodists proved most effective. The former were entirely local in initiative, authority, and support and were often served by self-appointed and self-supporting lay ministers. Such congregations were only loosely associated as a broader religious body, without hierarchical supervision, and they readily split off into new groupings. The famous Methodist circuit riders were under regional and national authority, but the whole system was so flexible in its operational geography and personnel assignment and in its peculiar combinations of local lay leadership and periodic ministerial visitations that it proved highly effective in bringing a sustaining churchly presence to whole regions well before there were sufficient people and resources to build actual church structures. Other denominations also undertook missionary activity in the West, but the more formal and traditional they were in doctrine, worship, and authority, the more they tended to expand only as a nucleus of followers in some established community committed themselves to build a self-sustaining church under a trained ordained leader. There were many pressures and changes in these matters; Presbyterianism, especially, despite its strong formal and traditional roots, mutated into several new organizations in the West.

Religion was therefore present in the early stages of regional development. Itinerant ministers roamed through even very thinly settled districts; "in new areas denominational leaders read maps with an intensity that challenged land speculators and prospective settlers"; townsite promoters set aside lots, and civic boosters often donated land and money for the building of churches so as to acquire such symbols of morality and order. The diversity of settlers and the variety of denominations meant that the larger towns might have half a dozen churches aligned along Main Street, or Church Street, or clustered about the square, or in some other pattern—but always indicative, by their kind, size, and position, of important characteristics of the local society, for "as they gauged a region's shape and development," the denominations "subtly imposed identities upon areas waiting for guidance."

GENERALIZATIONS

This brief sketch of the American case records an extraordinary combination of conditions:

1. the huge expanse of good-quality lands made available at very modest price;
2. the essential emptiness of the area, its familiarity in kind and ready domestication by established systems of pioneering;
3. the prevailing principle that beyond establishing the most elementary frameworks for public order, the government was not to control or manage the processes of settlement and development but leave all to private initiative; and
4. the concurrent revolution in transportation facilities that ensured ever-more efficient connections between new places in the continental interior and the great entrepôts of world commerce.

No other settlement frontier opened on the several continents during this century came close to offering so much to so many under such little restraint.

Such a grand and attractive prospect generated a movement that was further propelled by its own momentum. As the success of early western colonizations became manifest and the physical practicalities of a great continental republic seemed assured, the haste to participate and share in the expected rewards was intensified. A key feature of this American dynamic was not the actual conditions at any particular moment but the confident belief that a mighty surge of growth and prosperity would eventually take place. Such confidence was grounded on obvious geographic realities: unroll the map, look out from any vista, take a passage down any of the great rivers or a traverse anywhere across those broadening plains, and it was obvious that this land would become the home of millions of citizens with thousands of towns and dozens of thriving cities serving them.

Just where those towns and cities would be and how those citizens would arrange themselves across the region, however, was less obvious. Surely it must depend in considerable part on the people themselves, acting freely, in concert or in competition with one another. The rampant boosterism of the time was in general simply part of the endemic speculation, rooted in economic self-interest and employing a similar hyperbole, but it also had a geographic specificity and a community dimension that warrant a closer look. In his study of five Kansas towns, Robert Dykstra emphasized the special, momentary character and importance of this early stage of development. It was a time of "marked fluidity when the opportunities for *recruiting* the acknowledged attributes of city status—population, major transportation facilities, capital investment—were perhaps better than they would ever be again. Even geographical advantage, that most important of fortuitous variables, required human agency for translation into urban prosperity. To the dedicated town-builder this appeared self-evident." Don Harrison Doyle expanded upon this prevailing "booster ethos" in his study of Jacksonville, Illinois:

> An underlying assumption of this ethos was that urban prominence was not decided by geographic location and natural resources alone; rather it was decided by the collective will of the community or "public spirit"—a favorite expression in the booster's lexicon. The virtues of communal energy, enthusiasm, and enterprise would somehow find their just reward in what the boosters repeatedly referred to as the "open race" of competing towns striving toward growth and progress. The prices to be grabbed in this frenzied race—the county seats, colleges, railroads, mail routes, and state asylums—were the makings of great cities. They would be won by aggressive lobbying and pork-barrelling in the halls of government, by vigorous fund-raising, and by local donations of land, all aimed at luring the unclaimed asset to the ambitious town. The race was quick-paced because so many of these prizes were awarded only once. If a community was rapidly established as a prominent city, it was sure to reap the bounty that fell upon the early leader.

Doyle further pointed out that this "booster ethos flowed naturally from the nineteenth-century ideology of individual social mobility, which promised that industrious young men of good character, if unobstructed by artificial barriers of class or monopoly, would inevitably be rewarded in the 'race of life.'" Compared to the cult of individual success, however, "the ideology of boosterism was pragmatic: it recognized that one town's success took place at the expense of its rivals."

These observations cut through the banalities of American boosterism to focus on the fundamental reality: this was a decisive, dynamic, formative period in the human geography of these western regions. The strident tone of booster rhetoric betrayed a well-founded urgency and anxiety during a phase of unusual geographic malleability and uncertainty. Boosters were generally correct in believing that the reshaping of the human geography was rapidly, relentlessly under way and that the relative position of their town with reference to all other places in the region would become more or less fixed; however (like industrious young men with faith in individual social mobility), they tended to exaggerate greatly the power of local leaders and "the collective will" to determine their place within the emerging settlement hierarchy. Although enterprise could make a difference, there were usually rather severe limits on what local entrepreneurs themselves could do. If they had chosen a good site in the first place, they might ensure that their town survived in the competition with nearby places for the trade of the local area, but most of the decisions critical to a rise to real city status were likely made elsewhere. Major investments in industrial and commercial facilities, in railroads and shipping concerns that bound these new regions firmly into national networks, were made in the established centers of economic power. At best local boosters could hope to convince Eastern capitalists that their town might be of interest to some larger corporate strategy. As the region became more completely colonized the settlement system itself became increasingly inexorable in fixing villages, towns, small cities, and regional centers into a relatively stable pattern. That is to say, the size and the spacing of each level in this central place hierarchy was determined by distance and technology and the number of services that any given population would support—by how far and how often people would normally travel to purchase different classes of goods and services. The symmetries of such a pattern of market centers would be disrupted here and there by the incidence of important industries, and proportionate relations among the several levels of such places would in time be affected by improvements in transportation and rising standards of living, but the basic patterns of this formative period would provide the settlement matrix for all subsequent local history.

This massive experience in occupying new ground was not only a great American drama, it came to be seen as one of the great episodes in the creation of the modern world. Inevitably, it has generated a vast literature, yet much of what has been written has been anchored upon a single seminal—and very geographic—thesis, and it will be useful to measure our generalizations against that famous formulation.

From the time of their resounding revolution and the formation of the Republic, Americans had a tendency to regard themselves as pointing the way for all humankind. And as the United States grew so greatly in extent and substance some philosophic observers came to see that not only was their society and polity a model for the future, but the ongoing drama of their westward expansion was, in effect, a reenactment of the human past. In 1824 a reflective eighty-one-year-old Thomas

Jefferson observed that a cross-sectional traverse of America would reveal a giant diorama "of the progress of man from the infancy of creation to the present day":

> Let a philosophic observer commence a journey from the savages of the Rocky Mountains, eastwardly towards our sea-coast. These he would observe in the earliest stage of association living under no law but that of nature, subscribing and covering themselves with the flesh and skins of wild beasts. He would next find those on our frontiers in the pastoral state, raising domestic animals to supply the defects of hunting. Then succeed our own semi-barbarous citizens, the pioneers of the advance of civilization, and so in his progress he would meet the gradual shades of improving man until he would reach his, as yet, most improved state in our seaport towns.

Such a view of the "march of civilization" was a perfect geographic expression of Enlightenment philosophy. It would become further empowered by social Darwinism allied with American continentalism and receive its classic statement near the end of the century in Frederick Jackson Turner's address on "The Significance of the Frontier in American History." Taking a cue from the Italian economist Achille Loria that "colonial settlement is for economic science what the mountain is for geology, bringing to light primitive stratifications," Turner asserted that

> the United States lies like a huge page in the history of society. Line by line as we read this continental page from West to East we find the record of social evolution. It begins with the Indian and the hunter; it goes on to tell of the disintegration of savagery by the entrance of the trader, the pathfinder of civilization; we read the annals of the pastoral stage in ranch life; the exploitation of the soil by the raising of unrotated crops of corn and wheat in sparsely settled farming communities; the intensive culture of the denser farm settlement; and finally the manufacturing organization with city and factory system.

Upon this areal pattern and historical sequence Turner constructed his famous thesis that "the existence of an area of free land, its continuous recession, and the advance of American settlement westward, explain American development."

Some of the larger implications of Turner's interpretation will be explored in later sections. For the moment let us focus on this "continental page" of history and magnify it so as to see more clearly some of the details in each sector and stage. Figure 32 displays Turner's six-stage model as a set of geographic diagrams, with annotations derived directly—or readily inferred—from Turner's various versions of the topic. Even such an elementary formalization imposes a rigidity foreign to Turner's own free-flowing metaphors and characterizations, but it seems essential to any effective geographic assessment of his notoriously elusive concept. (In some of his evocations Turner included a "miner's frontier"; Dahlonega, Galena, and California attest to its pertinence, but the exploitation of such sporadic resources was anomalous to the more general concept of social progression in the same geographic space, and it has been omitted in this presentation.)

As Richard Hofstadter, a severe critic, noted: "The initial plausibility of the Turner thesis lies in the patent fact that no nation could spend more than a century developing an immense continental empire without being deeply affected by it." When examined at the scale of these diagrams, moreover, Turner's depictions of this succession of actors and their roles in the transformation of the West accorded well with common understandings. Three generations of observers had described the American drama in something akin to these categories, and it seemed to fit especially well the earliest and best-known sector of the frontier: the spread into Kentucky and the Ohio Valley. By the 1890s the landscape of Indiana or central Illinois—or, more telling, Turner's home country in southern Wisconsin—was indeed a "palimpsest" inscribed with many clues to these several layers of development.

The Turner thesis was of course a product of its time, and with the hindsight of another century we now see things rather differently. His emphasis upon geographic and economic dimensions of history was an important broadening of perspectives, but his simplistic, optimistic view of society as an organism evolving inexorably from simple to complex is now regarded as a serious misreading of the nature of society and history and his characterizations of each stage are viewed as inadequate representations of profound transformations. Drawing upon the evidence already offered in our survey of nineteenth-century developments, and adhering (rather arbitrarily) to a six-stage model, we can readily construct an alternative formulation (fig. 33). The principal differences arise from a sharper focus on selected imperial, capitalist, and cultural features of the American case. In such a view the triumph of Euro-American society involved a high degree of cultural change and violence arising from a long, complex interaction between disparate societies; subsequent patterns were shaped by national and capitalistic systems operating out of frontier urban centers and subject to volatile shifts in the levels and character of activities; stages of exploitation become blurred in the scramble of varied and competing interests to gain control of resources, with profit-taking rather than home-making the primary motivation. In this view "development" refers to changes wrought by specific peoples with their instruments and power rather than to an evolutionary sequence led by modern Europeans; it is cultural, contextual, and contingent rather than unilinear and deterministic; it refers to marked transformations in societies and regions but always obtained at a cost; it reduces "progress" from an expanding beneficence to a cultural appraisal, subject to critique.

Such an alternative formulation offers a better sense of the swirl and complexity of the American scene and would seem to fit especially well the later American Midlands frontier such as that developing around, say, Peoria, Davenport, or Chicago. But even though it may have a considerably wider application in general and provide a useful introduction to a complex topic, we must not reify it as "the

WILDERNESS	TRADER'S FRONTIER	RANCHER'S FRONTIER	
High Plains / Camp / Village / Prairie / Forest	Fort / Agency / Post / Mission		
palisaded villages temporary camps	trading post army fort Indian agency	temporary camps cowpens	
tribal society	pathfinders of civilization disintegration of savagery	stockmen prospectors drifters	
primitive dependence on natural resources	exploitation of wild beasts	exploitation of free grass	
routine seasonal movements to gardening, gathering, hunting grounds intertribal trade in rare resources (copper, obsidian, etc.)	white and métis hunters, trappers, and traders furs and skins exchanged for blankets, trinkets, tools, guns and alcohol	cattle herding on open range of public lands seasonal drives to distant markets	
buffalo trails footpaths porters canoes	pack trails canoes bateaux	droving trails packhorses supply wagons	
tribal rule over traditional territory	national instruments as wedge to open Indian country	federal territory unorganized vigilantes	
pagan religion	Christian missionaries	no public institutions	

32. The Classic Turnerian Pattern.

FARMER'S FRONTIER	INTENSIVE AGRICULTURE	CITY AND FACTORY
isolated family clusters	farmsteads small towns	commercial city industrial centers rich rural countryside
first wave of settlers pre-emption	second wave of settlers purchasers	merchants industrialists immigrant workers
exploitation of virgin soil	diversification and conservation	science and technology
squatter settlement on attractive lands patch farming, corn, hogs, cattle hunting, fishing livestock, tobacco, whiskey to markets	denser settlement all land claimed crop rotations staple exports of wheat, meat, cheese, etc. via local trade centers	full range of commerce industry scientific agriculture wholesaling large mills factories shipping services banking
pioneer wagon roads ferries arks flatboats	turnpikes stagecoaches bridges steamboats, canals	railroads steamboats frequent intercity service
federal territory first counties	statehood county framework completed	state counties municipalities
itinerant preachers camp meetings family tutors	rival evangelical churches town schools	all churches schools } { private colleges } { public rural schools

NORTH AMERICAN TRADITIONAL SYSTEM

MODERN

INDIAN SOCIETY	IMPERIAL FRONTIER	MERCANTILE FRONTIER	
palisaded villages seasonal camps	army post sutler Indian agency trading post	collection, supply and service center winter quarters	
tribal society refugee Indians traders white transients	reduced and relocated tribes federal agents metís intermediaries licensed and illicit traders	wholesale merchants frontier contractors peddlers, craftsmen cattlemen, farmer-traders, métis	
subsistence on seasonal resources ecological balance furs and skins for exchange	national agents for conquest, clearance and acculturation zone of interaction	forward base of international commercial system	
gardening gathering specialized crafts hunting expeditions intertribal trade fairs integration of foreign complexes: horses guns tools	altered Indian economy plows oxen cattle hogs stockmen squatters trespass and conflict gardening peddling	staple collection from wide hinterland ravaging of selected resources: furs, skins, hides pioneer ranching farming local gardens mills	
footpaths porters canoes travois	pack trails patrol routes wagon roads bateaux	wagon freighting bateaux keelboats flatboats	
longhouses bark huts wigwams seasonal shelters	stone forts frame official housing log cabins	wood brick stone log houses regional types	
tribal authority client subordinates	military enforcement of sovereign claims federal Indian reserves	federal territory first counties remnant reserve	
indigenous religion shamans prophets	assigned Christian missionaries	itinerant preachers church services in local halls	

33. An Alternative Pattern: American System of Regional Development.

W O R L D   S Y S T E M

SPECULATIVE FRONTIER	SHAKEOUT AND SELECTIVE GROWTH	TOWARD CONSOLIDATION
Proposed r.r.		
rival townplats initial land clearing millsite development	selective survival regional and local centers ghost towns	railroad-founded towns central place infilling complete occupance
swarms of speculators land agents land seekers town promoters investors merchants laborers	exodus of promoters, people, capital stranded settlers successful investors	rural to urban migration immigrant workers ethnic districts civic leadership
competitive profiteering conflicting claims to most properties rapid turnover	concentration of property control heavy indebtedness distant owners—local tenants	integration with national system economic and social differentation
influx of capital speculation in land, industries, services rapid emergence of commercial agriculture assault on woodlands	development of best properties staple productions wheat meat livestock tobacco hemp abandoned industries	diversified mechanized farming domesticated landscape industrial corporations complex import-export regional economy comprehensive services
steamboats roads turnpikes proposed canals proposed railroads	steamboats abandoned canals undercapitalized railroads	steamboat systems canal by-passes rival railroads rural road network
milled lumber brick stone national styles	redundant buildings replacement building	architecture of wealth and status mass produced housing cast iron storefronts
early statehood rapid county formation county seat rivalries	state empty counties shifts of county seats	state counties towns cities
rival churches missionary societies	impoverished churches survival of leading denominations	all denominations dioceses synods conferences

American frontier process." The absence of any mention of slaves and cotton plantations is only the most obvious regional variation missing in these patterns and notations. And so we may well conclude these attempts at generalization with Carl Sauer's acerbic comment that Turner's "plot of a westward-moving pageant in six scenes was good drama but was not our history," and his early insistence that "the eternal pluralism of history asserts itself on the American frontier: there was no single type of frontier, nor was there a uniform series of stages." We must now sharpen our focus to look more closely at the specific pluralism of the American case.

3. Planting New Societies: New England Extended

"Amongst all the columns of emigration" within "the great flood of civilization which has poured over the vast regions of the West," the "two great masses . . . [of] the New England and the Virginia columns" deserve special attention, concluded Michael Chevalier, one of the more reflective and well-informed of the many Frenchmen reporting on the United States in the 1830s. (Sent by the Ministry of the Interior, he spent two years examining American canals, railroads, banks, and other facilities and institutions.) "The Virginian and the Yankee have planted themselves in the wilderness, each in a manner conformable to his nature and condition." They "are very unlike each other; they have no great love for each other, and are often at variance."

There was nothing really new in his characterizations or in his nomination of these two peoples for special attention. It was generally understood that New England and Virginia were distinct societies. So different were they in institutions, motivations, and temperament—in their whole "way of life"—that each was often referred to as a "nation," or, as we might more likely put it today, an "ethnic group." The stereotypes of these two—the energetic, entrepreneurial, practical, moralistic, duty-bound New Englander and the easy, pleasure-loving, hospitable, paternalistic Virginia country gentleman—were widely employed, with countless emendations, flattering and unflattering, in American conversation and literature. The vividness of these caricatures of Yankee and Cavalier had taken on new intensity and meaning in Chevalier's time because the two peoples were now more clearly seen as direct competitors in the next great stage of American development: shaping the design of the American West and thereby the character of a newly, truly continental America.

New Englanders were well prepared for such a contest. For two hundred years they had been exhorted on their moral responsibility as a "chosen people" in this new world. The admonition to build model communities, to be "as a City upon a Hill," was considered as appropriate for the great western prairies as it had been amid the drumlins of Massachusetts Bay. One of the most respected of these voices was that of Timothy Dwight, influential teacher, president of Yale for more than twenty years, a man of impeccable Puritan lineage. In the 1820s, near the end of his life, he set forth his vision of America as a "vast empire" studded with "innumerable villages" of "beauty and cheerfulness," "flourishing towns and splendid cities," and "seats of various useful manufactures." In all of these places there would of course be churches "diffusing, like so many stars, light and splendor over the whole horizon," but of equal, fundamental, importance would be

> neat schoolhouses stationed at little distances, diffusing each over its proper circle the education necessary to every human being, and contributing to create a new national character. . . . To these . . . add, at distances somewhat greater, the vast collection of superior schools communicating more extensive information to a multitude. . . . Within every twenty thousand square miles . . . a college, where literature and science will shed their light. . . . Here and there seats of professional science, in which is taught whatever is known by man concerning medicine, law, policy, and religion; . . . [and finally] those national institutions designed not so much to teach as to advance the knowledge of man.

Here was a model settlement geography, comprehensive, symmetrical, hierarchical, covering all the levels from village to nation. It was of course understood as New England writ large, grounded in that deep-rooted sense of community represented by the New England town.

Timothy Dwight never traveled farther west than Niagara Falls, but what he saw, he liked. New Hartford, just beyond Utica, "is the first New England settlement which we found in this region," he reported on his first journey in 1799:

> Accordingly it presented us with a very neat church, ornamented with a pretty steeple. The houses also are built in the New England manner, and are generally neat, and for so recent a settlement are unusually good. The lands are good and well cultivated, and everything wore the cheerful air of rapid improvement. . . . No settlement merely rural since we left New Lebanon [a Shaker community just beyond the Massachusetts border] can be compared with New Hartford for sprightliness, thrift, and beauty.

Some years later, after several similar journeys, he could record, with obvious satisfaction, that "great numbers are continually crowding into this state for commercial as well as agricultural purposes" and that "New York is, therefore, to be ultimately regarded as a colony from New England." By that time, the vicinity of New Hartford had several textile mills and a thriving academy as further testimony of Yankee enterprise.

There were soon dozens of such villages sprinkled thickly across New York and, in time, on farther west, and they represented a notable cultural imprint. "Built in the New England manner" referred to materials, proportions, styles, arrangement, and finish: everything of wood, capacious but unpretentious, trim and restrained in design; white houses set upon spacious lots facing a village green or elm-lined streets, all neat and tidy in comfortable irregularity. The whole scene was a conscious expression of landscape as at once a mirror and a mold of society—or so Timothy Dwight would have his readers believe. In his emphasis on what was implicitly the traditional village Dwight was idealizing a feature that was actually undergoing significant change. Although the concept of the town as the frame for the community was deeply embedded in this regional culture, it was only in this early federal era that town centers, which in rural districts had often consisted of no more than a meetinghouse and a tavern, were rather quickly transformed into substantial villages of merchants, millers, and professionals amid a diversifying countryside. As Joseph Wood has shown, those white steeples rising above the spacious green of the embowered villages were now the marks of a much-intensified nucleation within a regional system of central places bound together by new turnpikes, stage services, and greatly extended lines of commerce. The ornamentation of those steeples, moreover, was an indication not merely of greater prosperity but of a more active concern for outward order and appearance (and a new enthusiasm for white paint), a new self-consciousness of the links between landscape and society. The westward spread of New Englanders routinely imprinting their mark upon a succession of frontier regions thus coincided with the efforts of a growing body of New England writers to place the image of the New England village before the American public as the ideal model for domesticity and community. This burgeoning literature would be brought to fruition by Emerson and a bevy of popular novelists in a romanticization that was impelled not only by the contest for the West but even more by ominous new problems closer at hand: urbanization, industrialization, immigration, and the politics of mass democracy (fig. 34).

This model design was also changing in the spacious new lands of the West. Colonial and federalist architecture mutated into new forms, most notably into a Greek Revival vernacular in exuberant variety, lining village streets and country roads with wooden temples (a truly remarkable sight to Europeans: "houses with porches of Ionic pillars begin to be scattered by the roadside," reported Harriet Martineau, approaching Buffalo). A few years later fashion-conscious clients might choose from a set of Italianate designs of cube-shaped structures with elaborate cupolas and cornices, or even the radical new octagon developed by an Upstate New Yorker to maximize efficiency and health. Such houses were as common on prosperous farms as in the villages, and there the usually modest New England barn had become enlarged and uplifted onto a stone basement to become the bilevel bank barn adapted to the needs of dairying and diversified farming in New York and the Western Reserve. These Yankees had emerged as the keenest students of improvements in the field and the garden as well as in the workshop and

34. The Yankee Settler and His Progress.

No. 3 in Orasmus Turner's quartet (see fig. 30). Summer, ten years later: a comfortable house added to the relic log cabin, surrounded by flourishing garden, orchard, and paneled fence; small barn, thirty or forty acres in crop and enclosed by rail fences; framed plank bridge; farmer busy at haying, wife at the well, half a dozen of their children at the log schoolhouse (upper left corner); the whole premises beginning to have a look of thrift, comfort, and even plenty. No. 4. Winter, forty-five years since the start in the wilderness: the independent farmer and his wife in their well-earned comfort and prosperity amid a fully domesticated landscape, served by a well-made road and stone bridge; railroad and village with church, school, tavern, a few stores, and mechanic's shops in background; the farmer has secured lands for his sons in the western states; the wife has fitted her daughters for "the vicissitudes, trials, and duties of life." Although easily taken as the typical American sequence, the vernacular architecture in Turner's final panel anchors it specifically in New England Extended.

the home, and with missionary zeal they published farm journals and invented the county fair to instruct the multitudes.

Wheat was the preferred pioneer crop in these northern frontiers and was the commercial staple for a generation or so through a succession of districts from the famed Genesee Country to northern Illinois. In the wake of declining yields of wheat these same areas soon became leading producers of rye, oats, and barley, of orchard fruit, nursery stock, and market garden produce, of potatoes, poultry, and, most conspicuously, dairy products. From a minor specialty in colonial New England, dairying spread into the Berkshires, the Mohawk Valley, and thence rapidly westward with the canal era. In 1851 the first successful cheese factory in the United States was built in Rome, New York, and such facilities, producing on a scale and with a consistent quality much favored by buyers, began to transform an industry that had already become another distinguishing mark of these Yankee-lands and of the Yankee farmers settled among others: "Some Milk 30 or 40 cows," reported Gershon Flagg from Urbana in west-central Ohio, "these are New england people. The country people [mainly from Kentucky and North Carolina] never make any cheese." Such juxtapositions were always vivid displays of cultural contrasts. Solon Robinson, reporting in 1845 on Bunker Hill, a small New England settlement a few miles northeast of Alton, Illinois, reported that "there is more grass [for dairy cows], more fruit trees, more barns, more good houses, more scholars at school, and more readers of agricultural papers in this eight year old settlement, than there is in some of the oldest settlements in the State, where the population is double." That Robinson was a Connecticut-born journalist no doubt colored his view, but observable differences in culture permeated the scene—in the way each most commonly worked horses (New Englanders by double reins, Southerners by a single line) and raced them (New Englanders in harness on an oval, Southerners astride on a quarter-mile straight track); in diet, dialect, and decorum.

It must not be supposed that this spread of Yankees was essentially a rural colonization accompanied by preachers and teachers; it everywhere "included a proportional number of mechanics, manufacturers, merchants, physicians, and lawyers," said Timothy Dwight, who happily accepted the idea that a New England influence could be spread by canal contractors, road builders, and innkeepers as well as by clergymen. Indeed, the rapid, intensive development of local industries and long-distance commerce was a marked feature of this enterprising people, many of whom were "intelligent, acute, versatile, ready when disappointed in one kind of business to slide into another." The Yankee propensity "to form villages" and "naturally unite themselves into corporate unions, and concentre their strength for public works and purposes" was as likely to show forth in support of the practical arts and material progress as it was in more social and philanthropic causes.

It was the latter, however, that became the most noted, and notorious, instruments in the contest for the West. The creation of schools and churches was not simply a local routine of Yankee colonists; it was a calculated strategy of New England leaders deeply concerned with the larger issues at stake. Missionary societies in Massachusetts and Connecticut devoted themselves to the support of such work; cadres of specialists were sent to the front and strategic positions taken up for the conquest of whole regions (military phraseology was common among such Christian soldiery). The Calvinist Plan of Union brought cooperation with the Presbyterians and made major training centers of Princeton as well as Yale, Auburn Seminary in Upstate New York as well as Andover; Marietta, Western Reserve (at Hudson), Oberlin, Wabash (Crawfordsville), Illinois (Jacksonville), Knox (Galesburg), Olivet, Beloit, and Grinnell colleges became notable outposts in the field of battle. Other instruments of social causes such as the American Education Society, American Tract Society, American Sunday School Union, and American Temperance Society, as well as more radical movements calling for abolition of slavery or women's suffrage, and experimental utopian communities such as Oneida and the early Mormons were all rooted in Yankee ground—that is to say, in Yankee political culture. New England was the primary seat of what Daniel Elazar has termed "moralistic" politics, one of the three basic regional formations that have shaped American political society. Here the purpose of politics was understood to be the creation of a better society; government was a positive instrument dedicated to the well-being of the commonwealth; politics was a noble calling and a proper concern of every citizen. Such, at least, were the ideals, and they fostered an energetic interventionist mode of political action devoted to solving social problems that would have an impact nationally all out of proportion to the numbers of Yankee citizens.

This great column of emigration and subsequent strategic and logistic activity created what became recognized at the time as a vast "New England zone." In fifty years the Greater New England of Atlantic America had become a New England Extended reaching to the upper Mississippi Valley. But such labels and commentaries need closer assessment. As Frederick Jackson Turner, one of the keenest interpreters of these changing geographies, warned long ago: "It must not be supposed that New England in [New York] was the same as New England in the homeland." Turner went on to assert that the "New York Yankee" was "less conservative, less Puritan, more adaptable, and more tolerant of other types than the Yankee who remained in the land of his birth." Such a distinction would be contradicted by other historians who demonstrated that at least some of these Yankee emigrants were more conservative and less tolerant, having undertaken a new errand in the wilderness to reestablish what had been lost in lax, secularizing, strife-ridden Massachusetts. Such matters are not easily assessed nor really central to our concerns. What we can say, from our geographical perspective, is that although these Yankees flooded thickly across this northern belt, they had to share most localities with settlers from elsewhere to a degree unlike anything in their New England experience. Adaptation and toleration arose from such uncontrollable variety; the old Puritan prescriptions for congregation and town, the old ideal of community had to be modified in some degree to meet the new social geography. And of course, in broader political and social terms, the State of New York, with its strong legacy of an Anglo-Dutch landed and mercantile oligarchy and its powerful role in the initial land market and all subsequent developments, could never be simply transformed into a Yankee commonwealth, nor could the Yankees hope to dominate Ohio, Indiana, or Illinois, whose longitudinal reach crossed three broad belts of western migration.

Furthermore, after the first generation or so of colonization, these western regions were not being reinforced so much from New England as from new immigrations following the main avenues of commerce. The Irish poured into Boston and dispersed into all the southern New England mill towns, but the Irish—and later the Germans—of Upstate New York came by way of New York City and spread westward along the canals and railroads. Syracuse offered a good display of the diverging character of places along these enlivening facilities (fig. 35). The countryside was almost entirely Yankee, the uplands to the south were dotted with little villages, and Pompey, one of the nearest, was the seat of a notable academy; but Syracuse itself was entirely the product of the Erie Canal, laid out astride that waterway in 1820 to form a new crossroads of commerce a short distance from several earlier hamlets that served the primitive salt industry around the swampy shores of Onondaga Lake. The largest of these simple industrial villages was Salina, which by the time Syracuse was platted a mile away had already accumulated a considerable Irish population and was soon the site of the first Roman Catholic church in the area. But Syracuse boomed so vigorously that it absorbed Salina and several other salt villages and was incorporated as a city in 1848. The open land between the Salina and Syracuse plats was subdivided into streets and lots and quickly filled by a heavy influx of Germans, who established their own Roman Catholic, Lutheran, and Evangelical churches and an array of institutions and industries. Meanwhile, the central sections of Syracuse were filling up with other deposits from the ever-enlarging stream of migrants, including enough German Jewish peddlers to found a synagogue in 1839 and a trickle of free Blacks settling along Canal Street and forming an African Methodist Zion Church in 1841. By 1856 Syracuse, with a population of 25,000, had twenty-six houses of worship representing thirteen denominations, including eight distinctly ethnic congregations. Other upstate canal towns were similar in general, each with its own specific proportions, as were those in northern Ohio. The rural Western Reserve might be obviously "New England in miniature" over most of its extent, but the canal

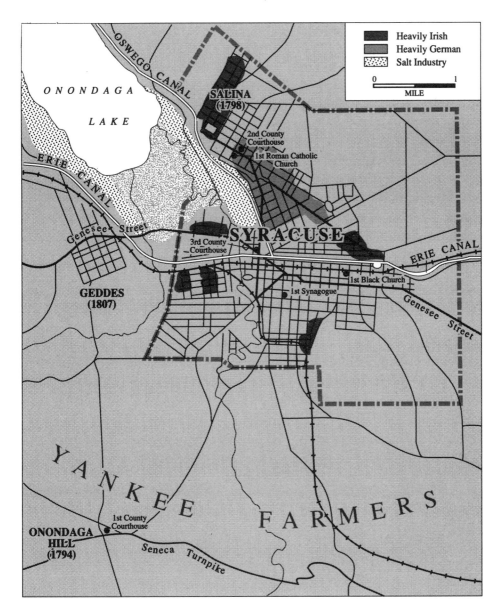

35. Syracuse, New York, c. 1860.
(Principal sources: Clarke map, "City of Syracuse, 1860"; Bigelow [1978])

branching southward was known locally as the "Irish Ditch," Akron and Ravenna each had their "little Dublin," and by 1850 Cleveland also had several German and Jewish congregations and several hundred Blacks.

The importance of these western divergences was not so much in the variety and numbers of such peoples as in the local context and attitudes. "The New England States . . . pride themselves on their populations being homogeneous," noted Harriet Martineau, "while that of the other States is mongrel." Such homogeneity was being relentlessly altered in fact but stoutly resisted in mind, and that made the Yankee-Irish encounter a simple, stark confrontation between "Americans" and "foreigners" in every New England city. In these western lands there was a marked divergence in character between urban and rural populations, but nearly everyone in these booming canal towns was a newcomer; variety, mixture, and instability were normal, influxes of new people were welcomed as a measure and means of development (however resisted in social intercourse). Thus, although the marks of New England were readily apparent, they did not quite add up to a replica of New England, and it is important to define more clearly just what kind of geographical shaping was taking place. We may quite properly think of a *New England Extended;* indeed, it is essential to recognize such a pattern as important and indelible. Such a term refers to the firm impress of initial migration streams resulting in a distinctive regional landscape of material forms, basic political and social frameworks for community life, and a set of firmly held—and asserted—religious and political beliefs. This extended regional reach was reinforced by continuing links between homeland and colonies, the routine social ties between those who moved and those who stayed—mail and marriage and family visits—as well as more calculated institutional and commercial links with Boston, Harvard, Yale, and other seats of Yankee culture and enterprise—the recruitment of leaders, preachers, teachers, the dispatch of business agents of every kind. Yet everywhere beyond the Berkshires these Yankee lands were being penetrated by other peoples and interests and bound into other vital connections. New York City was not only the main portal for new immigrants, it was the main focus of commercial life and, inevitably, a swelling source of cultural influences. Try as it might, Boston could never extend its tentacles westward and effectively divert traffic from the Hudson and therefore was left somewhat marginalized from these burgeoning Great Lakes and western systems. In all but one of these western states Yankees were a minority, in many cases a vociferous and influential minority, but nonetheless forced by the capacious boundaries of these new geopolitical units to compete for political power with large bodies of people who had very different outlooks and agendas.

New England Extended was thus a zone of strong influence, but it was not the western salient of a discrete culture region in the sense that New England itself surely was. Nor were these western districts a discrete region by themselves, for there was too much difference and too few essential ties between, say, Upstate New York and northern Illinois to qualify as such. Each of these areas was part of something larger, but for some time it was not really obvious what that encompassing structure might be. If they were obviously part of "the West" to those who viewed them from New England, that famous term had no clear regional meaning in any cultural sense. What would become clearer, year by year, was the fact that all these Yankee lands were being knit together ever more efficiently and intricately into a larger complex that was increasingly discerned and defined as the North. Shaped by new networks of intercity commerce and coalitions of business and political interests, such a pattern was the most profound and powerful geographic change to emerge in American national life, and these Yankees spread across the northern reaches of the United States would have a major role in giving it meaning.

4. Planting New Societies: Virginia Extended

In marked contrast with that of New England, the Virginian column had marched massively forward without such a panoply of propaganda, without special cadres dispatched by seaboard strategists to implant institutions critical to the contest. There was little awareness of any such regional competition because it did not really exist at the time. The Virginians were far in the lead, having reconnoitered and staked out Kentucky before the American Revolution. In the scramble for Ohio Valley lands after the Revolution, the New England–based company that founded Marietta was simply one among many speculations and had no obvious "ethnic" connotation. Any sense of conquest referred to the "wilderness" and "savagery"; any idealized image focused on the explorers, the Indian fighters, the log cabin in the clearing of intrepid pioneers as the "advance-guard of civilization"; any sense of moral cause was bound up with a general view of such expansion as integral to and expressive of the "Progress of Mankind."

Virginian expansion was in large part a folk movement, a routine process of families searching out new lands to their liking where they could create local societies of their own kith and kin with the least possible interference or constraint. The result was a system of pioneering and a pattern of landscape and society no less distinct, even if far less self-conscious, than that of their belated Yankee competitors, and one we have already described as the stereotypical "American" mode of colonization.

Those in the Virginian column were preeminently the creators of a frontier of preemption, ranging usually well ahead of formal government surveys and sales. Such people were long practiced in marking out claims by metes and bounds to enclose only the more desirable lands, creating complicated, discontinuous patterns of occupance. But here, as elsewhere, land speculation was an old profession, and in Kentucky and Tennessee, especially, the first wave of settlers was sometimes dispossessed by a wealthier class who could afford the litigation and lobbying to obtain favorable rulings out of a maze of conflicting claims. And, contrary to the stereotype of pioneering, men of means were sometimes first on the ground in this earliest of western expansions as well as in later speculative surges. That was especially true for the best ground, as in the famed Bluegrass of Kentucky and Middle Tennessee.

This system of settlement spread a scattering of population over a wide area and variety of country: over bottomlands and mountain coves, thin-soiled hills, knobs, and ridges, as well as over the rolling richness of the limestone basins. In the newer states the rigid orthogonal framework of the federal survey system was eventually superimposed, requiring many local adaptations and often leaving dispersed squares of unclaimed land that continued to be used as woodlots, livestock range, and hunting grounds. This colonization had a commercial dimension, even if that was not as central to its purpose as elsewhere. On the better lands substantial farmers were soon marketing livestock, tobacco, wheat, hemp, or (in parts of Tennessee) cotton, and adorning their properties with a comfortable house with detached kitchen, springhouse, smokehouse, stillhouse, corncrib, double-crib barn, stables, and a few slave cabins. The most common house across the whole region was the "double-pen dogtrot": two basic rooms (pens), each of four log walls, separated by an open walkway (dogtrot) under a single roof, with a chimney at one or both gable ends (or a chimney in the middle, making it a "saddlebag" rather than a dogtrot). There was great versatility in this simple plan. Such structures could be well built with hewn logs and plastered over, and they could be readily enlarged by adding a second story, porches, shed attachments at the rear, and enclosure of the walkway to create a center hall entryway (fig. 36). There were many ways of asserting social status from a common form: a good many plantation homes were basically "log mansions," with plaster or board sheathing and a bit of ornamentation, a classical portico, or some New Orleans ironwork. The double-crib barn was essentially the same structure and as readily adaptable to special needs. Another common dwelling type was what has become known as the "I-house," a one-room-deep, two-story, center-entry structure. Built of milled lumber or brick, it was a favorite second-generation house, replacing necessarily cruder dwellings, and it, too, was easily enlarged and trimmed with stylish detail.

This characteristic architecture confirms that this expanding frontier was not in fact a simple projection from classic Tidewater Virginia but was, rather, an extension of what came to be known as the Upland South, a distinct regional complex formed in the Great Valley and Piedmont during the late eighteenth century, drawing strongly upon the Delaware Valley and Greater Pennsylvanian sources as well as those of Greater Virginia. The towns reflected the same antecedents, in various combinations and adaptations. The county was the primary frame of local government and the county seat the primary focus and often the only hint of urban life. A marked tendency toward greater formality and regularity in town planning

36. "View of a Farm on the Illinois Prairie," 1833.

Karl Bodmer was a Swiss-born artist who accompanied the German naturalist-geographer Prince Maximilian of Wied-Neuwied in his journey to America and travels far up the Missouri River to investigate the Plains Indians. Bodmer became famous for the superb portraits and landscapes he painted in that remote interior, but he sketched and painted avidly from the time he first glimpsed American shores and also provided us with some of the most accurate and penetrating pictures of the vernacular landscape. His patron elected to spend the winter at New Harmony, Indiana, and trips in that vicinity brought Bodmer into contact with something really new: "He had begun to see the raw, real frontier" of America (Goetzmann). Here, in some small prairie west of the lower Wabash, he gives us a rare view of a pure Upland South farmstead: the double-crib log barn, the log (dogtrot?) house with wide roof overhang and end chimney, the well-sweep and rail fences. There is also a suggestion here of a rectangularity in fields, but we cannot be sure if that displays an individualistic Southerner being disciplined by a national system or merely the tidiness of a German artist (who finished this painting from his sketches after his return home). (Courtesy of the Joslyn Art Museum, Omaha, Nebraska)

that laid out a grid with a designated public square owed more to Pennsylvanian than Virginian models, but a large courthouse in the middle of that central square symbolized a polity that was assertively Virginian (fig. 37). It was—to continue with Elazar's terminology—a "traditionalistic" political culture wherein the main purpose was the maintenance of public order and the social system. An obvious

37. Courthouse at Mount Vernon, Indiana, 1833.
Karl Bodmer decided to interrupt his winter sojourn at New Harmony with a trip to New Orleans. This took him overland to the Ohio River at Mount Vernon, where he waited a few days for a steamboat. In this careful watercolor of the Posey County courthouse in this southwestern corner of Indiana he has again offered us a pure Upland South scene: an elaborate formal symbol of public authority planted in a spacious square with a town as yet barely forming around it. (Courtesy of the Joslyn Art Museum, Omaha, Nebraska)

social hierarchy and paternalistic leadership were accepted as normal and natural; real power was concentrated in "an established elite who often inherit their 'right' to govern through family ties or social position," and ordinary citizens were not expected to play an active part in local political life. It was in fact a litigious and rather raucous society, as attested by the size and prominence of lawyers' row, jail, and perhaps even stocks and gallows, which together with the essential hotels and taverns might occupy much of the frontage facing the square. The protection of property and position was fundamental.

Although churches—Baptist, Methodist, Campbellite, Presbyterian, and the new (1810) evangelical Cumberland Presbyterian—were eventually fairly thick on the ground, ranging from isolated chapels and halls serving country neighborhoods to more substantial buildings in the larger county seats and few cities, they were never the symbol and focus of community life as in New England. In Nashville, for example, a masonic hall faced the courthouse square years before any permanent church building existed in the town, and Methodist Bishop Asbury, on his third visit in 1812, recorded his bitterness about "a community that put the courthouse in the central location, where the church 'ought to be.'" Anglican churches were few and an almost certain sign of direct Virginian planter influence. Schools were not at all common, and there was protracted political resistance to any public funding of education. The Presbyterians were the most active in founding denominational academies and colleges, but with few exceptions—notably Transylvania and Centre in Kentucky—these, too, played a limited role in regional society.

This Upland South was a rural society through and through. It had its necessary trade centers and in time a few small cities, but all were in an important sense indigenous growths, their industries confined to elementary processing of rural products, their populations drawn from or closely identified with the surrounding countryside. Lexington and Nashville had developed from stockaded outposts to the preeminent mercantile centers, dominated by a small elite of bankers, lawyers, and politicians, but they were closely connected by marriage and interest with the leading planters, and members of the two groups might well have both town houses and country estates. The primary model for such a society was the true Kentucky colonel, the country squire with a distinguished record of militia service, whose "plantation" was not one of vast fields of staple crops worked by gangs of slaves but one of rich pastures neatly fenced and full of high-grade livestock, together with an array of Black stable hands, drivers, and house servants. Such farms might actually be more dependent on commercial crops of tobacco, wheat, and hemp, but their fame rested on their blooded stock and their pleasures were manifested in livestock shows, racing meets, and hunts. To themselves and many observers such planters were an American version of the English country gentlemen; in actual derivation they were perhaps more directly American "Celtic cowlords." In such a countrified world, the rapid rise of Louisville in the steamboat age represented something much less indigenous: anchored in the region, as attested by its distilleries, tobacco warehouses, and ropewalks, but filling up with outsiders who were busy binding it into quite different strands of the American system.

As in any folk culture, people were keenly aware of family connections and kept the several generations and collateral relatives in touch with one another even across the mountains and the expanse of several states. They were also well aware of themselves as a people, even if they had no clear general name for the whole. They tended to identify with states, as Kentuckians or Tennesseans, or referred to themselves as from a major district such as East or Middle Tennessee. Genuine Virginians would of course proudly assert their origins, and their prominence and self-confidence gave a strong flavor to western society: their young men "seem to feel that they have an hereditary claim to command, place, and observance," noted Timothy Flint, who saw an urgent need to discipline and purify them with appropriate institutions. Kentucky, the famous offspring of Virginia, was itself "proudly exalted, as a common mother of the western states" and, as Flint observed, aspired "to stamp the impress of her character upon the country that is growing up in the Valley of the Mississippi." It was this kind of lineage, leadership, and character that allowed commentators to identify this column as "Virginian."

It is not wholly inappropriate to think of the broad pattern of this migration as Virginia Extended, but, as already indicated, it is more accurately denominated as the Upland South, emanating from a culture hearth that partook of and blended elements from colonial Pennsylvania as well as Virginia. Its diversity of European-derived peoples—chiefly English, Scotch-Irish, and German—were already well integrated within a common regional culture before transappalachian migration, retaining their particular identity chiefly through their religious affiliations; its Africans were as routinely locked in place but much less numerous and widely distributed than in most of Virginia (a minor variant were the several small clusters of kinship groups of "mixed blood," locally known by some collective name—such as Issues and Goins—and surviving by endogamy in marginal areas bypassed by major movements). There were no significant additions to this formative amalgam of peoples.

But even though this Upland South presented a remarkably uniform cultural surface, it was even less of a functional region than New England and its extensions. There were few effective commercial ties and little two-way traffic between the eastern hearth and Atlantic ports and these western settlements. East Tennessee, lodged in the southwest extremity of the Great Valley, could maintain contacts with Baltimore and Philadelphia and also developed droving trails across the mountains to the Asheville Basin and Carolina Piedmont, but all beyond the Cumberland Plateau was bound to the great rivers of the West and focused on New Orleans. "Western" issues were therefore of primary importance, yet there was nothing like those Yankee-style exhortations and strategic programs for the seizure and shaping of the West. In time, after finding themselves engaged in such a contest, a greater self-consciousness and more explicit programs and symbols would emerge, or at least be urged upon the inhabitants by regional leaders, but for the great bulk of these people the main interest remained, as always, in land and liberty, in the continued open possibility of easy access to new lands free from governmental restraint or interference. William Blount, though himself a notorious speculator and powerful politician, the elite of the elite in early Tennessee, must have been near the truth when he asserted that every man who arrives in this western country "appears to feel and I believe does in reality feel an Independence & Consequence to which he was a stranger in the Atlantic States." And as for government and formal responsibilities, the common attitude of these Southerners was never more succinctly suggested than in the lure set out by a Mexican Texas land commissioner to his fellow Anglo-Americans in 1834: "I am convinced that Texas must prosper. We pay no taxes, work no public roads, get our land at cost, and perform no public duties of any kind."

We should note, parenthetically, that Virginia had the greatest practical visionary of all during these vital formative years. But in spite of his love for his native state, Thomas Jefferson's designs for the West were far from being a Virginia Extended. To be sure, that fundamental of Jeffersonian democracy, the yeoman farmer, could be extrapolated from the Virginian scene, but his ideal community and polity for that citizenry could not; for Jefferson not only wanted all public lands surveyed according to a rigid geometric plan, he argued for many small states, subdivided into counties, and each county formally divided into hundreds as the appropriate scale for genuine community life ("of such size that all the children of each will be within reach of a central school in it"). These "little republics" together would provide "the main strength" of the great Republic. He acknowledged the New England town as his model, in contrast to the "large and lubberly division into counties" of Virginia and most of the rest of the country. But even had they known of such ideas and despite their respect for such an eminent countryman, Virginians and other Upland Southerners, like the people of any strong regional culture, would have routinely shaped their West according to that with which they were fully familiar rather than experimented with some novel abstract design for "ordered liberty."

5. Planting New Societies: Midlands Extended

One finds no reference to a "Pennsylvania column" advancing in contention for the Great West nor, later, of a "Pennsylvania Extended" in quite the same sense as the term has been applied to New England and Virginia. Yet even though Michael Chevalier dismissed it as only a nameless "auxiliary," there certainly was a Midland migration stream, and it not only left its mark, but it was to be of decisive importance in the shaping of that broader West.

The imprint of this migration was as strongly reminiscent of its source region as was any other. Such people could fit their common modes of settlement to the rigid geometry of the federal survey system with only minor adjustments and, especially in the undulating prairies, the resulting orderly landscape of large, contiguous, diversified farms with their characteristic architecture—capacious four-over-four houses and forebay barns if a German district, I-houses and English barns elsewhere—was clearly a western version of southeastern Pennsylvania, needing only a long forested ridge in the near background to replicate the home scene. Similarly with the towns. It was not uncommon for observers to refer to them as "little Philadelphias," but most towns in Pennsylvania were not four-square, and the more significant feature was the focus on a market square; courthouse and churches might face on the square, but commerce occupied the symbolic center.

This primacy of commerce was undergirded by the prosperous countryside and local industries. The Midland migration carried in a long tradition of diversified commercial agriculture based upon corn, small grains, and livestock, together with tobacco, broomcorn, buckwheat, and other specialties, and by the 1840s the distinctive features of the later famous American Corn Belt began to appear in favored areas. The Scioto Valley and the Bluegrass were early western cattle-fattening areas, but it was the emergence of a band of districts extending from the Miami and Whitewater valleys across central Indiana and through the Sangamon Valley of Illinois specializing in hogs that formed the main nucleus of that larger pattern. Superior breeds of hogs (such as Poland China, developed in the Miami Valley) were fattened on corn and then driven or shipped a short distance to the big packinghouses in the river towns. Cincinnati became famous as "Porkopolis," with its large factories rationalized for efficient use of labor and by-products (from lard, bone, bristles, and skins), and there were important smaller works in such towns as Madison, Terre Haute, and Peoria. And as in colonial Pennsylvania, these western towns were soon full of industrialists, artisans, and mechanics, and flour mills, distilleries, breweries, sawmills, woodworking plants, and farm implement factories were dotted through the region. These Midlanders along with their Yankee neighbors were in the forefront of development and adoption of new plows, rakes, seed drills, corn planters, reapers, and threshers in the 1840s and 1850s. It was especially in this Midland zone that town promotion and city growth were an integral part of the frontier process, and the "American system of regional development," with its rapid emergence of relatively dense rural and central place patterns, was most fully displayed.

The other telling feature of this migration was its marked diversity of peoples. It was just that sort of variety in the source regions of Pennsylvania, New Jersey, and New York City that had produced still another American political culture. Daniel Elazar has labeled this regional type "individualistic" and described it as one in which government is viewed as a kind of marketplace, with politicians as brokers mediating among contending interests—and taking their fee. In such an environment politics is a business, a profession (and, necessarily, a rather "dirty" one) that holds out rewards to those who earn them in serving their supporters; political parties are viewed not as instruments of ideology but more as business corporations working to ensure the "profits" of the principal investors. It was a practical politics, designed to deal with diversity and contention by means of compromise and trade-offs, temporary agreements and shifting alliances. A party embracing such a concept was likely to be a rather loose coalition, with an easy tolerance of sociocultural variety.

Such a form of politics could not be simply imported intact and applied; it had to be adapted to the special conditions of counties, cities, and states in the West, and its larger relevance is to be found not within the narrow confines of the main Midland migration stream but within those Western communities that had to accommodate not only characteristic Midland diversities but significant numbers of Yankees and Upland Southerners as well. That broadens our view to include the Ohio Valley and Old Northwest, with special attention to the states of Ohio, Indiana, and Illinois, and to cities, large and small.

Contentions arising from cultural diversity were apparent from the beginning: in the rivalries for territorial leadership among gentry opportunists in Ohio; in the first rural area of convergence where "Pennamites" moving up the Mahoning Valley encountered Yankees in the easternmost county of their New Connecticut; in the U.S. Congressional Lands where the settlers, "almost exclusively from Pennsylvania, Virginia, and Maryland . . . formed such a motley society that few or no persons from New England would settle among them"—but in fact a good many did; in the compromise (rather like New York) between county and township powers in local government (Illinois later allowed each county to choose); in the growing cities such as Cincinnati, from the first a Middle States enclave in an Upland South environment, where there was not only a widening social gap between the rich on the hills and the poor below but the early emergence of social districts identified in regional, racial, and immigrant ethnic terms. Germans and Irish created their own communities and forced American society to adapt to their presence as well as themselves adapt to their adopted nation. As a broader West took shape, the most obvious contention was that between the two most contrasting political cultures, the moralistic and the traditionalistic. It was, of course, that contrast in types and self-conscious rivalry that had drawn so much attention to the Yankees and Virginians. Commentators on these two great columns of western migration usually predicted some sort of convergence and blending of the two in this arena and speculated on what kind of distinctly "western" product would ensue. Chevalier, for example, while extolling the assiduous enterprise of the Yankees, thought that the Virginians' natural talents for leadership would eventually make them the dominant strain within the new "third type of the west, which is now forming and already aspires to rule over others." He foresaw, however, not a quick and easy blending but a long stimulating period of "wholesome rivalry" and "interchange of ideas and sensations." "History shows," he asserted, "that the progress of humanity has been constantly promoted by the reciprocal action and reaction of two natures, or two races, sometimes friends, oftener enemies or rivals," and, after a long peroration on historical examples, he offered the reassurance that "there is no country in which dualism is more admirably developed than in the United States; each of the two natures has an open field, each a distinct career of industry; each possesses in the highest degree the qualities necessary for its peculiar position . . . [and] the young giant that is growing up in the West seems destined to . . . bind together the North and the South in his vigorous gripe [sic]." His countryman, Tocqueville, writing at the same time, spoke more broadly of the American tendency to intermingle and assimilate: "the differences resulting from their climate, their origin, and their institutions diminish; and they all draw nearer and nearer to a common type."

These unusually perceptive men may well be excused for such oversimplification on this particular topic. They could cite evidence in support of their predictions, and they were writing before the full imprint of the Midland migration was apparent in the West. But their main error—as that of a multitude of observers since— was to overestimate the ease and rapidity of blending and assimilation in America. It seemed such a natural process, such an obvious component of "progress," whereas in fact these regional, ethnic, and religious identities were fundamental and enduring. They shaped the local patterns of society and politics all through these formative years, and they continue to do so in some real degree today (as demonstrated in Elazar's *Cities of the Prairie*); which is not to deny that integration and assimilation have taken place, but such leveling processes have not yet effaced the uneven surface of the deposits laid down by these streams of migration.

A first stage in the necessary adaptation and accommodation of deeply rooted differences was completed by the 1820s when it became clear that Ohioans would insist on popular (local) sovereignty as an American (Jeffersonian) birthright but also would empower state governments, courts, and schools to channel individualism into (federalist) social order. Over the next twenty years, as James De Bow later observed, the values of the commercial town "quietly and almost imperceptively" spread over the whole country so that "by the 1840s the norms of the town prevailed among respectable Americans everywhere." It was during this time and in this process that Midland political culture exerted a critical influence. As John Murrin put it: "While the Republic's self-announced progenitors, New England and Virginia, fought out their differences into the Civil War, the middle states quietly eloped with the nation, giving her their most distinctive features: acceptance of pluralism, frank pursuit of self-interest, and legitimation of competing factions." Whereas Yankees and Upland Southerners tended to line up on opposite sides of issues, whether it be taxation, education, public improvements, powers of government, or whatever, Midlanders brought a focus on private economic interests that helped to bridge that chasm and build a broader consensus. Yankees, after all, were ever keenly concerned with economic development (and a good many of those Midland investors and entrepreneurs had New England forebears), and paternalistic leaders of the South were ever concerned with their own economic well-being, so grounds for a common program at local, state, and national levels existed. The most obvious manifestation of such a coalition was the Whig party, with its broad base of middle-class supporters and strong commitment to national programs of economic development. In the West as in the East it represented a New England and Midland coalition with important support from Southern banking and commercial interests (as represented by Henry Clay of Kentucky and his program for an "American system"). At the local level such coalitions might be broadened further in support of community projects, although boosterism tended to blur party lines only temporarily. More fundamental was the fact that so many counties in this zone contained people from diverse streams of migration, and such patterns of diversity were further extended by the railroads. Thus one newspaper noted in 1858 how the Illinois Central had opened southern Illinois "to middle state and New England ideas" and changed the "political physiognomy" of the country along its route: "Jonesboro is a mile and a half from the railroad. The station is called 'Anna' and is as large as the town itself. The station is Republican; the town is democratic." Jonesboro was able to hang on to the county seat, but Anna quickly surpassed it in population and services.

The Democratic party stood in stalwart opposition to the larger Whig (and, later, Republican) agenda throughout the Ohio Valley states. Yet it, too, owed something to the Midland political culture, for the party was a loose coalition of highly diverse groups: Southern farmers, Northern laborers, Irish Catholics, and others finding common cause in what they perceived as intolerant, homogenizing, centralizing Whig pressures. Patterns of migration had thus made this set of multicultural western states contested ground between these evolving, unstable political composites.

Each migration stream also had its characteristic religious denominations, but here, too, Pennsylvania contributed something new and important. American Methodism took on shape and substance in the Lower Delaware Valley during the early years of the Republic. Breaking from its Anglican roots and simplifying its doctrines, essentially untainted by old political and ecclesiastical disputes, it developed a remarkably effective strategy of proclaiming its optimistic message and sustaining local congregations through its centrally directed circuit-rider system. Although the great success of early Methodist expansion into Kentucky and Tennessee is famous, its penetration of Upstate New York is perhaps an even better clue to its astonishing growth. Working up the Susquehanna, Lycoming, and Tioga valleys the Methodists soon organized several districts into a Genesee Conference and by 1812 had surpassed the traditional Calvinists as the largest and most vigorous church all across the great westward extension from New England. When the next generation of Yankees moved farther west they were as likely to be Methodists as Congregational-Presbyterians. It was apparent that the kind of personal Christian perfectionism they proclaimed had found a ready reception among a striving citizenry committed to progress in every sphere of life. Methodism thereby became a very "American" religion; penetrating every region of the country, by 1840 it was the largest denomination in the United States, but its strongest support remained in a belt of country stretching from Philadelphia across central and southwestern Ohio through central Indiana: more than any other, the Methodists represented Midland Protestant America.

More than either of its companion columns, this Midland reach into the West maintained strong and effective commercial ties with its source region. Pittsburgh and Wheeling were its portals to the West, Cincinnati its earliest forward base, and improving connections across the mountains with New York City, Philadelphia, and Baltimore became a matter of national as well as regional concern. For a time it was difficult to compete with nature's great artery flowing down to New Orleans, but first with the help of steamboats and soon with the railroads ever-more powerful east-west sinews of communication and commerce were developed so that the entire set of western cities from Louisville and St. Louis through Burlington, Milwaukee, Chicago, and Toledo were bound into an interregional system that disclosed an emerging North in everyday functional terms. That geographic reality was in fact fundamental to the rather sudden intensification of sectional stress and instability in the 1850s and the convulsion that followed. As Cayton and Onuf have put it:

> To a great extent, the economic issues that had divided Jacksonians [Democrats] and Whigs had been resolved by the early 1850s. The question was no longer whether the transportation revolution would transform the region. It had. Banks were there to stay. And the ambivalence many midwesterners had once felt about commercial capitalism was no longer a crucial factor in the region's political life. . . . [T]he meteroric success of . . . new parties shifted the debate away from economic concerns to those of culture. The questions that divided them were no longer related to the ways in which the market revolution would take place but centered on who would define the values and create the institutions of the new world to which it had given birth.

In such a redefinition of the contest, these three basic political cultures would play an even more crucial role than heretofore—as would a fourth, whose emergence we must now examine.

6. Planting New Societies: The Cotton Belt and South Carolina Extended

When we turn our attention farther south we do not see a distinct "column" marching parallel to those expanding out of New England, Pennsylvania, and Virginia, yet by 1850 what may well be called South Carolina Extended was becoming one of the bolder patterns in the fabric of America. It is important to get a proper geographic sense of just what had taken place.

As we have seen, the basic settlement system and cultural imprint of the Upland South was spread broadly across the nation. The culture hearth of that highly efficient pioneering complex extended into the South Carolina Piedmont, and it was as readily adapted to the Gulf states as to the Ohio Valley. Thus, after half a century of expansion one could find common elements in local landscapes and society all the way from central Texas to the Potomac and from northern Florida to central Illinois. In that view the really distinctive parts of this more southerly South were the older subtropical plantation areas of the Carolina-Georgia Low Country and the Creole footholds at Mobile, Biloxi, and French Louisiana. The geographic pattern we seek to understand can best be traced as an interpenetration and binding together of these two culture types.

This linkage emerged from the diffusion of two quite distinct systems. The lesser of these was the Anglo-American cattle-herding complex that spread from its origins in the cow pens of the pine barrens back of Charleston across all the lean sandy piney woods, savannas, and canebrakes of the Coastal Plain deep into Texas, encountering and in some degree blending in people and practices along the way with various creole herding systems: that of the Spanish-Seminole cattlemen of West Florida, the French and Cajun herders of Louisiana, and influences stemming from Mexican Texas. This "creolization" of a South Carolina complex would be fundamental to the later rapid transformation of an emptied Great Plains into the great Cattle Kingdom, the momentary world of the famous American cowboy. But our present concern is with the creation of another famous—and far more important—world, one in which it would be proudly proclaimed: "Cotton is King."

Cotton had long been cultivated by Europeans in the West Indies and tropical fringes of North America as a garden plant and ornamental. In the aftermath of the American Revolution a superior kind of cotton (probably from Barbados) was introduced into the Low Country of South Carolina by way of the Bahamas. The long, silky fibers of this Sea Island cotton commanded a good price in the burgeoning English textile industry, and Eli Whitney's famous improved device to separate the fiber from the seed radically altered production potentials. Local planters were quick to respond but soon discovered severe environmental limits to expansion. But if repeated efforts to raise this cotton farther inland failed, hardier, coarser varieties (especially "green seed") yielded well on the upriver alluvials and better piedmont soils, and spurred by the rapidly expanding demands, Upcountry farmers began to clear the woods, break ground, and plant all they could of a crop that could double their usual income in a year's time. There was a sudden demand for labor, and farmers who had been scarcely involved if at all in slavery began eagerly buying as many slaves as they could, while planters from the rice lands of the Low Country began to enlarge and consolidate their scattered inland investment properties and to shift a portion of their energies and facilities, including gangs of slaves, to the production of this new staple. Thus in the early 1800s a belt of country combining the inland hinterlands of Columbia and Augusta emerged as a new thriving cotton district connected down the rivers to Charleston and Savannah, where an array of commission agents (factors), bankers, merchants, and shipping services provided the vital connections to markets and suppliers in Liverpool, London, New York, Philadelphia, Baltimore, Boston, and elsewhere (fig. 38). After a decade or so of trial, during which breeds of cotton, systems of cultivation, and networks of marketing (long hindered by blockade and warfare in Europe) were worked out, cotton underwent an enormous boom after 1815: the price doubled, steamboats drastically reduced shipping costs on the rivers, and, as Roger G. Kennedy has helped us see, in "an extraordinary burst of wealth" Savannah planters and merchants, with the help of a bold and talented young English architect, created an ensemble of buildings that transformed that small Georgia port out of the shadow of older and elegant—but rather staid—Charleston.

During this same time a generally analogous development was taking place in the southwest corner of the nation. Before 1803 the Natchez District occupied exactly that position and was a fertile foothold of a remarkable set of Northern "scientist-planter-entrepreneurs" who readily added cotton to their experiments with tobacco and indigo. As in South Carolina, cotton had long been present in a small way on the downriver plantations, chiefly in a variety known as "creole black seed," which the French had brought in years before from Siam. The Natchez planters worked energetically to find hardier and higher-yielding breeds. Native cottons from central Mexico were tried with some success, and during the 1810s a natural hybrid of Mexican and local cottons was discovered in the field; assiduously isolated and propagated, it proved to be a markedly superior plant, immune to common diseases, high yielding, and much easier to pick, and it became the basis for American upland cotton, the standard of the industry. Some Natchez planters specialized in providing this superior seed (first marketed as "petit gulf") and continued in that role through the development of further improved varieties for several decades. These Mississippi planters were in an even better position to make the most of the early cotton boom. As Kennedy states, "after they had oligopolized their base on the loess hillocks around Natchez," they "shifted capital (millions of dollars in capital in some cases) northward into the lowlands along the east side of the Mississippi, which were denied smaller farmers by the high cost of ditching and draining." These "river planters" (as they were soon called) developed their own systems of plowing and tillage suited to these deeper soils, continually tinkered with improved designs of gins and presses, employed the largest gangs of slaves to produce the highest yields and quality of cottons in the country, and with their profits adorned Natchez, Washington, Vicksburg, and a few lesser places with an elegant architecture of enduring interest. Their vital connections were first with nearby New Orleans, where Anglo-American planters and merchants were using the profits from sugar, cotton, and the booming Ohio Valley trade to create their own elegant Garden District alongside the old French grid, and more critically with Philadelphia, New York, and London, the real sources of capital and culture.

These two new geographic formations, responding to the same set of forces, alike in general structure and character, differing in agronomic and cultural details, were the primary culture hearths of the great American Cotton Belt that took shape so rapidly and portentously over the next four decades. The spread of cotton cultivation across the South was largely—though not entirely—an extension from these nuclear areas: from South Carolina eastward into North Carolina and westward from Georgia across the Black Belt of central Alabama, which emerged in the 1830s as a kind of a belated geographic replica of these hearths wherein Montgomery, Selma, Demopolis, and Tuscaloosa emerged as prosperous seats in the geographic heart of the broadening Cotton Belt, while Mobile, providing the pivotal external linkages, was quickly transformed (with the help of a Yankee architect) "from a Caribbean village into a Classical Revival city"; meanwhile, the river planters of Mississippi were extending their reach or their influence across the floodplains of Louisiana and Arkansas, enveloping the old creole center of Natchitoches. Farther west, the prospect of good cotton lands along the Brazos had lured the first Anglo-Americans out of the Gulf states into the Austin Colony, and expansion from that early implantation combined with a later influx into the "redlands" of East Texas made Texas a rising producer and Galveston, its white villas glittering along the strand of its narrow island, a prospering and cosmopolitan cotton port.

The edge of the earliest Texas cotton district lay closer to the sea than elsewhere because of marginally better soils and lower autumn rainfall than in the flatwoods of the Coastal Plain everywhere to the east. The northern margins of the Cotton Belt came to be defined as along the line marking at least 210 frost-free days and was anchored by districts in northeastern North Carolina (a southward contraction from early trials in southern Virginia), southern Tennessee (a contraction from the Nashville basin), and the loessal bluffs and Mississippi floodplain lying in the northerly hinterlands of Memphis (a city that developed into a major cotton

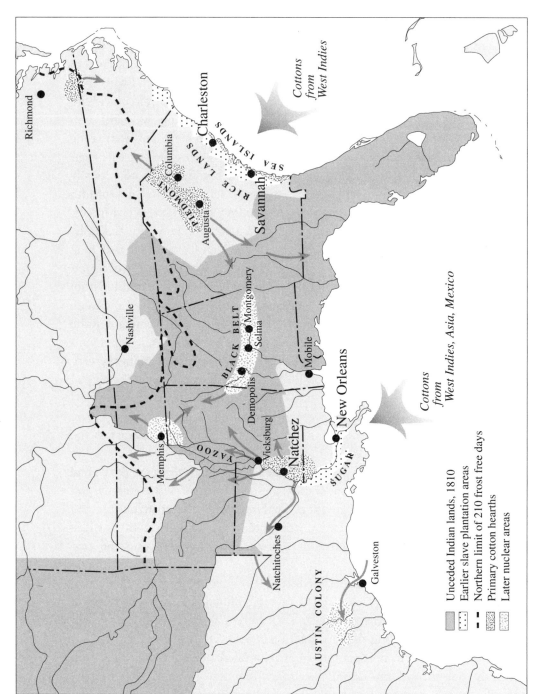

Richmond

Charleston

Columbia

PIEDMONT

Augusta

RICE LANDS

SEA ISLANDS

Savannah

Cottons
from
West Indies

Nashville

Montgomery

BLACK BELT

Selma

Demopolis

Mobile

New Orleans

Cottons
from
West Indies, Asia, Mexico

Memphis

YAZOO

Vicksburg

Natchez

SUGAR

Natchitoches

AUSTIN COLONY

Galveston

Unceded Indian lands, 1810

Earlier slave plantation areas

Northern limit of 210 frost free days

Primary cotton hearths

Later nuclear areas

38. Early Formations of the Cotton Belt.

market and service center). Although there remained much potential good land in the jungly swamps of the Mississippi floodplain and in the black waxy prairies of Texas, there were reasons for some concern in the 1850s about impending limits to cotton expansion. The endless arid plains beyond the central Texas hills must surely define the eventual western limit, and, perhaps more important, a generation or so of relentless cropping on the rolling red hills had already brought ruin to some of the older districts in the Piedmont. Erosion was especially severe in these friable soils under row-crop cultivation in a climate characterized by heavy summer downpours. By the 1850s extensive tracts in the Piedmont were "a perfect waste . . . washed into Gullies from 3 to 4 feet deep—now growing up in briars and pine saplings." Better farming practices, such as contour plowing, cover crops, and manuring were much discussed but slow to be applied. It was far from a new problem, as the worn-out tobacco lands of Virginia testified, but it was not one to which Americans had as yet demonstrated much creative response. The common attitude toward soils was the same as that toward the great forests and the vast flocks and herds of wildlife: they were nature's riches to be plundered by those lucky enough to get there first. When they were exhausted, the most common American response—North or South—was to pack up and move on to fresh ground in the West. An Alabama senator complained in 1855 that the small planters of his state "after taking the cream off their land . . . are going farther west and south, in search of other virgin lands, which they may and will despoil and impoverish in like manner." Such rapacious agriculture combined with the characteristic restlessness and speculative attractions to expand the limits of this Cotton South so rapidly.

It was quite apparent at the time that there were two rather different sets of cotton farmers in this vast new agricultural region. In the simplest sense they were the rich and the poor, the big planters and the small farmers, but they also tended to be regionally and locally sorted according to good land and poor land, deep soils and shallow, quickly exhausted soils. The contrast between the river planters and the upland farmers in Mississippi was a major exhibit. Rothstein suggested that the two were sufficiently different as to constitute a "dual economy" within the South not unlike that commonly characterized as "modern" and "traditional" co-existing in our present world. He offers the Natchez planters as striking an exhibit of the former:

A large proportion came from distant non-slaveholding areas—from Northern states or from abroad. These "aliens" quickly established close ties of kinship and friendship with the core of leading "native" planter families . . . and with them formed a fairly cohesive self-conscious group. Their links to the market place were often far more direct than those of their smaller neighbors; their holdings were not only larger, but ostensibly more profitable, than the generality. In addition, their common interests were broader, encompassing all phases of market-place activity, while their social and

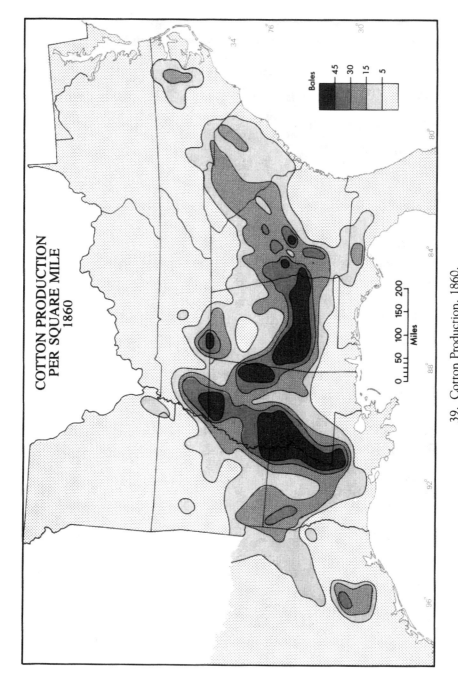

39. Cotton Production, 1860.
(Reproduced from Hilliard, *Atlas of Antebellum Southern Agriculture*.
Copyright © Louisiana State University Press)

political ties to the larger world outside the South were as strong as their attachment
to the region which gave them wealth.

The reality of those wider connections sometimes came in for criticism, as in a
local newspaper in 1842: "The large planters—the one-thousand-bale planters—
do not contribute most to the prosperity of Natchez. They, for the most part, sell
their cotton in Liverpool; buy their wines in London or Le Havre; their negro
clothing in Boston; their plantation implements and fancy clothing in New Orleans." And, in fact, the gulf between these cosmopolitan planters and the more
ordinary Mississippi farmers would be rather starkly exhibited in the staunch
Unionist stance of the Natchez Whigs (it is said "that the Confederate flag never
flew officially" over the city). However, the War demonstrated that the more
fundamental feature of this Cotton South was just the opposite: the binding of rich
and poor, big and small cotton farmers in a common geopolitical cause.

As we have seen, the very structure of the emerging cotton hearth in South
Carolina involved both Low Country and Upcountry interests, and the quick
profits from cotton paved the way for ever-closer relations: in the common commitments of both areas to cotton and slavery; in advantageous marriages between new
wealth and old; in mutual investments in Piedmont plantations and Charleston
properties; in the founding of institutions designed to serve both regions, such as
the College of South Carolina in Columbia; in political reapportionment that
finally broke the stranglehold of the minority Low Country elite. All of this was
taking place rapidly during the first fifteen years or so of the cotton era, and
although it did not put an end to internal tensions, it did so reconstitute the
sociopolitical character of the state that South Carolina was in an excellent position to exert a very marked influence upon the newer Gulf states. In some cases this
was the work of big planters, as noted by Kennedy, who put it in architectural
terms: "In 1814 and 1815 Wade Hampton I became the first eastern entrepreneur
to invest heavily in Louisiana plantations. After him came many others; the
constant travels of these investors between their East Coast and their Mississippi
Valley holdings were a necessary preliminary to the crossbreeding of the Caribbean
cottage (our convenience term for a complex phenomenon) and the now somewhat tired tradition of columnar architecture [of the Upland South]." But there
were important links at all levels. South Carolina contributed large numbers of
migrants to every state lying to the west; in the case of Mississippi more than from
any other source and most heavily to the upland cotton area in the northeastern
counties. And more crucial than numbers were the contributions to sociopolitical
leadership. In every courthouse town—"the center of civic life, of legal order, and
of the literati"—among the lawyers, judges, newspapermen, doctors, and teachers
there were likely several natives of South Carolina or those who had been trained

in its colleges or law offices in Charleston or Columbia, and they gave a marked coloration to political life.

This South Carolinian style of politics emerges so blatantly and becomes such a powerful force in the affairs of the Republic that we must acknowledge it as a distinct political culture, even though it does not appear in Elazar's comprehensive scheme but remains submerged in the broader "traditionalistic." Traditionalistic it was, and it was clearly akin to that broader Southern type in many ways, but what comes to the fore, under the special pressures of the time, is the more specific tradition of a South Carolina whose lineage leads directly back to Barbados and the West Indies during the heyday of imperial planter domination. Those tropical societies were dangerous, unstable affairs, dedicated to the rapid amassing of wealth and status through the ruthless exploitation of land and labor by a militant master class. The main working units in such societies were not the paternalistic plantations of Virginia country gentlemen but scatterings of holdings worked by gangs of slaves under local overseers, while the owners indulged in their "brittle, gay, showy style of life" in the safer confines of the towns. Such a system fostered a "proud and mettlesome school of politics" that may be termed "hegemonic," wherein the purpose of politics was power to preserve the rule of a master class. Often accorded a fierce loyalty by an underclass, yet ever-conscious of being a vulnerable minority amid deadly dangers, it was a leadership that was authoritarian in all its tendencies, ready to ride roughshod over opposition; contentious, irascible, exhibiting "a fierce and quixotic pride," such an elite was quite ready to resort to violence to maintain its sway or, if sensing an opportunity, to expand its conquests.

These and related features were readily discernible in the Low Country politics that so long dominated the least democratic state in the Union, they flared forth for all the nation to see in the Nullification Crisis of 1833, and under mounting pressures from "moralistic" voices in the North, the shrill defiance of the "fire-eaters" began to be heard much more widely across the Lower South. Whereas in the 1830s observers of America had focused on Yankees and Virginians contending for the West, twenty years later the main event was a far greater drama on a larger stage. If in common depictions it was now the North and the South contending over the future of the Republic, those who looked more intently often summarily defined it—and some tried to dismiss it—as Massachusetts versus South Carolina.

At midcentury James De Bow, superintendent of the 1850 census, struggled to find a new classification of states and territories that would reflect both "the great geographical divisions of the country" and "political or social" elements. He offered an arrangement that first divided the country into three great sections: East (Atlantic), West (Pacific), and Interior (Mississippi Valley); then divided each of these into North and South, using slavery as a basis (except for California—

"which is sufficiently Southern"). It was already apparent, however, that the more critical divisions within the North and the South were not between Atlantic and Interior but latitudinal, following the great migrations and their subsequent differentiations. By that time "the Cotton States" was a common reference, and it gave rise to eventual recognition of an "Upper South" and a "Lower South" as convenient terms for the two great halves within this greater half of the nation.

The great distinguishing mark of the Lower South was its heavy involvement in staple production through the use of Black slaves (fig. 40). This more inclusive regional term encompassed the rice and sugar plantation areas as well as the new cotton belt. And these older areas compounded the involvement with slavery and the West Indian model. De Bow calculated that these three crops accounted for more than 80 percent of all the slaves employed in field labor in the United States. In the Carolina Low Country and Louisiana sugar districts slaves made up as much as 80 percent of local populations; by 1850 several cotton counties or parishes in the lower Mississippi floodplain and the Alabama Black Belt were approaching such proportions. Blacks made up more than 40 percent of the population in every state from South Carolina through Louisiana and were a majority in three. Elsewhere only the old tobacco districts of eastern Virginia and North Carolina or the newer areas of concentrated wealth in the Bluegrass and Middle Tennessee were at all comparable. The development of such patterns had of course involved the movement of hundreds of thousands of Blacks as well as Whites into newly opened western lands and, in later stages, of special traders moving thousands of redundant slaves to the booming markets in the West.

This greater emphasis upon staple production and slavery left its imprint on the landscape in the greater number of working complexes of slave cabins, overseers' houses, commissaries, gins and presses, and a wide array of attendant facilities. In this more subtropical latitude, utilitarian buildings tended to be more simple and open; creole influences, such as raised floors to allow air circulation, wide verandahs, and "shotgun" cottages, seeped inland; mules were preferred over horses for field work. Farms were less diversified, although many plantations produced some corn, meat, and vegetables, and in some cases slaves were allowed to cultivate small plots. There was also a sharper division between town and countryside because so many planters preferred the social life and safety of the one over the other. As elsewhere in the broader South, the greater number of actual farmers and cotton growers lived on their small properties and may have even worked alongside their few slaves; with little capital, they had to use the impending crop as collateral and were chronically in debt. And most of the hamlets and towns strewn thinly over the countryside certainly seemed to travelers as meager ramshackle places. Coming alive only during the marketing season, few were little more than a scattering of simple wooden houses, a store, tavern, cotton gin, and blacksmith;

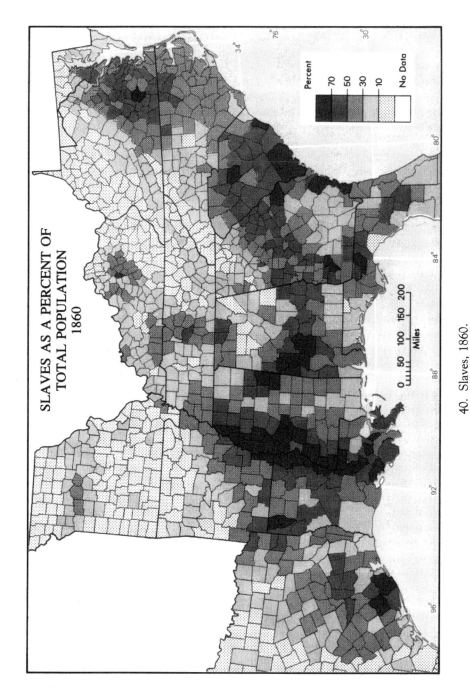

SLAVES AS A PERCENT OF
TOTAL POPULATION
1860

Percent

70
50
30
10
No Data

0 50 100 150 200
Miles

40. Slaves, 1860.
(Reproduced from Hilliard, *Atlas of Antebellum Southern Agriculture*.
Copyright © Louisiana State University Press)

they were stunted by there being so little to do because so much of the trade was handled directly by cotton factors in the entrepôts. Any sense of community was narrow and shallow, civic promotion hardly known.

The social model for the region was on display in Charleston and Natchez in those elegant creole townhouses sustained by a dispersed set of productive properties (and the mortgages held on others) in the industrial-agricultural hinterland. These places were quite unlike urban centers in other regions. The social structure was more sharply differentiated between rich and poor, cultural and civic institutions were fewer, and the relegation of commerce and industry to a lower status was more obvious (as in Natchez-under-the-hill). In fact, a good deal of both the cultural and the commercial life of the region was in the hands of "foreigners." As Fletcher Green noted: "There was hardly a college in the South prior to the Civil War that did not have a Yankee president, and some of them ten or more professors. . . . In like manner nearly all the tutors and governesses in the homes of the wealthy planters were New England Yankees." As bankers, merchants, shippers, industrialists, railroad men, publishers, doctors, and speculators of many kinds, Northerners were a conspicuous presence in all the larger centers and some of the smaller ones as well. Commonly recognized as external opportunists, their foreignness was not necessarily a permanent mark of significance because many a Yankee married into a local family and assimilated to Southern ways; some even became important voices in support of the Southern cause. But most did not assimilate so completely, and these enduring cultural distinctions would be vividly displayed with the onset of secession in the exodus of thousands of these Northerners and the return south of hundreds of Southern students from Northern colleges and seminaries.

We began this topic by standing with Michael Chevalier as he watched the "great flood of civilization" pouring over "the vast regions of the West." We have now looked at it closely enough to see that the West meant quite different things to the several different peoples dominating those columns and that, broadly speaking, these constitute nothing less than different versions of America, different designs at the levels of locality and region with profound implications for the nation and federation as a whole. For New Englanders the West was a missionary field wherein communities were to be shaped in accordance with strict moral directives to create a better society. For most Midlanders the West was a land of illimitable resources and opportunities for individual speculation and corporate development. For Virginians the West offered land and liberty, the chance to combine family property and personal freedom to an extent only dreamed of in older regions. For South Carolinian planters and their Creole associates the West became a region in which personal and class power and privileges had to be asserted in defense of a distinctive way of life.

Just how these four versions of American life might co-exist within a single framework would become the great geopolitical test of the American federation and nation. De Bow's use of slavery to establish the largest regional groupings of the several states was a commonplace by midcentury, but along every sector of its length that notorious geopolitical division failed to coincide with the patterns resulting from these great columns of migration. Furthermore, the new North and South so defined by that separation were far from being coherent regions in other respects. Such incongruities reinforce the need for our geographical perspective on the engrossing issues of the era.

7. Color in the Plantings: The Afro-American Presence

Had those commentators who pointed to the Yankee and Virginian columns as the most important to the destiny of the nation been more prescient, they might well have given special attention to the coffles of Black slaves being led along the old tracks into the cotton lands of the Southwest, for it would soon become notorious that the geographical expansion and economic invigoration of the slavery system was the central feature of an ominous federal crisis. This larger geopolitical issue will be examined in due course; it is sufficient here to emphasize that Blacks were participants in all of these westward migrations, northern as well as southern. Closer examination will also quickly reveal that however few their numbers, and whether slave or free, the very presence of Blacks was always a topic of concern at local and statewide levels. Thus, much as one might like to describe the changing geography of Afro-Americans as simply one important component of the American people—present from the earliest colonial period in nearly all regions of European North America—we are confronted with the stark reality that Blacks have never been regarded by the dominant population as just another ethnic group but rather as a distinct caste, a separate, subordinated category of people whose presence in any number is regarded as a "problem." Then—as now—"the significance of race in the American past can scarcely be exaggerated."

Underneath such a national generalization lay important regional variations in the context of Black-White relations—differences grounded in local history, legal status, numbers, employment, and other factors bearing upon the character and vitality of Afro-American life. When this westward expansion got under way the four distinct kinds of colonial Black society were still apparent: the strongly African Carolina Low Country type; the more complex interracial creole society of Louisiana; the patriarchal rural society of Greater Virginia; and Blacks in the North, a largely urban minority population mostly free, living in more varied and somewhat less restrictive relationship with Whites. These Black populations were routinely extended westward as integral parts of their encompassing regional societies, yet all such migrations by Blacks, whether free or captive, were challenged in some degree, and attempts to curb, contain, and in some way control the residence and status of these people became an insistent American activity.

The greatest efforts were directed at the containment of slavery as a legal institution within the United States. Too explosive an issue to be faced directly at the Constitutional Convention, the most the opponents of slavery had been able to obtain was a prohibition against any further imports of slaves after a twenty-year interim. At the time it was often stated—by voices in the South as well as in the North—that slavery was a burden, an unfortunate, even evil, system that somehow must eventually be ended. Limiting its growth, some argued, would help confine it until it withered away through its inherent inefficiencies and internal difficulties. Such a prohibition (taking effect in 1808) must indeed have reduced the growth of the Black population from what it might have been, considering the volume of slaves that continued to be shipped across the Atlantic to the American tropics for two decades thereafter, and even later to Cuba and Puerto Rico (there seems to be little evidence of any significant amount of smuggling of slaves from the islands into the United States). Hardly mentioned at the time but now logically apparent was the genetic and cultural significance of the end of these annual infusions of Africans and their innate "Africanness" into North America. However brutal and constrained and unidirectional that link had been, the severance of this centuries-old transatlantic connection must have affected the shaping and vitality of Afro-American life.

Internally a geographical containment of slavery to the area south of the Mason-Dixon Line and the Ohio River was established early on by the separate actions of the northern states, in some cases through a gradual extinction, such as declaring all newborn persons free (thus there were more than 2,000 elderly slaves in New Jersey as late as 1830) and by federal prohibition of the importation of slaves into the new Northwest Territory. That proved to be a stable, though not unchallenged, line. Attempts to make the Mississippi a similar western barrier were not successful. The purchase of an entire Afro-American society in 1803 prompted various unsuccessful efforts to impose gradual emancipation on, or at least to prohibit any further transfer of slaves into, Louisiana. The first attempt to extend the crucial latitudinal divide beyond the Mississippi shook the federation to its foundations. Northern pressures to make Missouri a free state (with gradual emancipation of the slaves already there) failed, but the Compromise of 1821 did fix the boundary farther westward at 36°30′N. A few years later the abolition of slavery in newly independent Mexico nominally circumscribed its continental bounds, limiting it to the southern United States, but the tacit admission of Anglo-American planters with their slaves into the Austin Colony penetrated that western boundary, and the subsequent formal recognition of slavery by the Texas Republic shifted it, ostensibly, to the Rio Grande. Debates on the admission of Texas to the Union reopened the topic and produced various proposals for specific western limits to slavery (such as 100°W) whatever the ultimate boundaries of that new state might be. The protracted debates over slavery in the territories failed to establish a firm limit, and even the admission of California as a free state was not regarded as an unalterable barrier.

The selective focus of the antislavery forces in Congress was very apparent: "instead of being challenged where it prevailed, slavery was challenged where it did not exist." Such a strategy rested not only on a moral insistence that one must stop the spread of an evil but on a belief that if slavery were contained in the South it would die a natural death, for it was an archaic socioeconomic system unsuited to an industrializing, individualistic, capitalist world. A specific geography of this gradual demise was often sketched, wherein slavery would recede southward from the expanding forces of modernization to its final stand in the tropics. Such a view was even brought in support of the annexation of Texas, as in this version by Mr. Stone, a Democrat of Ohio: "With such a climate and soil as Maryland, Virginia, Kentucky, and Missouri possess, slave labor never can be profitable. Admit Texas into the Union, and what will be the result? The slaveholders in these several states will emigrate to Texas. The strongest motive which operates upon the human heart (self-interest) will lead them there. A quarter of a century will not pass before [these border states] will become free states." He presumably did not please his Southern Democrat allies by going on to say that these emigrating slaveholders would be succeeded by frugal enterprising Yankees who would vitalize the economies of these states. In fact, slavery was markedly declining and industry expanding in Delaware and Maryland, and the relative strength of slavery was lessening all across this northerly zone. The number of slaves in Virginia was barely increasing, Kentucky passed a law against further importation (but repealed it in 1849), and there were seasonal sales of surplus slaves to more southerly markets; there was also a marked increase in the number of free Blacks in these states.

The idea that adding more slave states would somehow hasten the demise of slavery found its most fervent exponent in Robert J. Walker of Mississippi, serving as Polk's secretary of the Treasury, who argued in a published and widely circulated letter that Texas would "act as a safety valve for the whole Union" by drawing planters and slaves, as well as free Blacks from the North, into its vast spaces and that these Blacks would eventually diffuse on southward into Mexico and Central and South America where (as a supporting senator from Illinois phrased it) "the whole black race will . . . find a refuge among a kindred population." Such a contrived argument invited the kind of derision expressed in this rejoinder by Senator Miller of New Jersey:

If I correctly understand [this] plan for the abolition of slavery, it is by means of what may be called the draining system. Texas is to be the last great reservoir into which each state will pour its stream of surplus slavery. The negro, through a thousand years of servile pilgrimage from generation to generation, is to drag his weary way from the Delaware to the Del Norte, exhausting, in his painful march, every field of labor by the sweat of his brow, until the whole race shall be congregated in one dark mass of worn out, profitless slaves, beneath the sunny skies of Texas. Then and there is to terminate the long and wearied march of slavery. . . . I cannot conceive how we are to get rid of slavery through the process of annexing foreign slave States to the Union, by opening new and more profitable fields for its employment.

The idea that spreading slavery into new areas would somehow weaken it had received its most succinct answer years before from the Baltimore political theorist Daniel Raymond: "Diffusion is about as effectual a remedy for slavery as it would be for smallpox."

The most common Northern stance in these recurrent contentions, however, was likewise an easy target for scorn. That most Northern leaders focused on limiting the spread of slavery while promising not to interfere with it where it was established invited Southern ridicule and exposure: "What kind of ethics is that which is bounded by latitude and longitude, which is inoperative on the left, but is omnipotent on the right bank of a river?" asked Senator James Barbour of Virginia during the Missouri debates; and he scoffed at Northerners' solicitude for the slave: "Let us hear no more of humanity—it is profaning the term. Their object is power." Forty years later, near the end of the weary congressional struggle, Senator Jefferson Davis sternly intoned the same refrain:

What do you propose, gentlemen of the Free-Soil party? Do you propose to better the condition of the slave? Not at all. What then do you propose? You say you are opposed to the expansion of slavery. . . . Is the slave to be benefited by it? Not at all. It is not humanity that influences you . . . it is that you may have an opportunity of cheating us that you want to limit slave territory. . . . It is that you may have a majority in the Congress of the United States and convert the Government into an engine of Northern aggrandizement.

The North was exposed to such ridicule and accusation because it was abundantly clear that its great interest was not in abolition but in containment—of free Blacks, as well as of slavery.

Attempts to exclude Blacks from all the new Western territories and states date from discussions at the Ohio statehood convention. No restriction was built into that constitution, but concern over "the menace of Negro immigration" resulted in a succession of measures (usually known as the "Black Laws") designed to discourage entry and domicile (such as a requirement that each Black immigrant post a $500 bond as a guarantee of good behavior). Negotiations for the Missouri Compromise were prolonged by a clause in the proposed state constitution advocating such laws as may be necessary "to prevent free negroes and mulattoes from coming to and settling in this state, under any pretext whatsoever." This provision was accepted by Congress, with the addition of an ambiguous qualifier, after a debate that called attention to the fact that every Northern state had laws specifically designed to constrict the civil rights of free Blacks in many ways. Legal prohibitions on Black settlement in the West markedly increased thereafter. In time, Indiana, Illinois, Michigan, and Iowa enacted exclusion laws. Although such laws were not rigidly enforced, they were a latent threat to the security of Black residents and may be presumed to have discouraged Black immigration. One thing is clear: they represented the feelings of most Whites, as evidenced by wide margins of approval in various public referendums.

The numbers of Blacks in these Northern states could in themselves be little cause for alarm. A concern commonly voiced was that these states would become a dumping ground for emancipated slaves. Over the years a number of masters had crossed over to Ohio or Indiana and freed their slaves, antislavery agitation within Kentucky continued to be vigorous, and more stringent laws in several slave states declared that newly manumitted slaves must be expelled from that state—such things gave rise to the specter of hoards of indigent Blacks pouring across the Ohio to swamp the poorhouses and jails of every Western county. Such people were considered to be indolent and ignorant, a wretched underclass that would ever be a burden and a problem, and many a community in the Ohio Valley used force or threats or held mass meetings to devise some means to rid themselves of such a population. And just as pressures within Kentucky reverberated into the Old Northwest, so each successive Western state could claim the same need for exclusion acts; as a delegate to the Iowa convention put it, if free Negroes were not prevented from settling there, the neighboring states would drive "the whole black population of the Union" into it.

Visions of great waves of free Blacks moving to the North and West were an effective polemic—"Shall the Territories be Africanized?"—because of the widespread and deep-rooted antipathy of American Whites to *any* Blacks in their communities. The overriding interest was to reserve the West for Whites only. Because it was generally assumed that Blacks were inherently inferior, they could never be full citizens and therefore were not an appropriate people for a democratic republic. David Wilmot, whose famous proviso against slavery in all the territories ignited the crisis of the late 1840s, was candid about his motives: "I plead the cause and the rights of the white freemen [and] I would preserve to free white labor a fair country, a rich inheritance, where the sons of toil, of my own race and own color, can live without the disgrace which association with negro slavery brings upon free labor." As abolitionism gained in notoriety (if not so much in strength) and as people thought more about what it might mean, there was a more general determination to exclude Blacks from the national patrimony of Western lands. From the 1840s onward there were numerous attempts to enact specific exclusions, and once the Dred Scott decision (1857) declared unequivocally that Blacks were a "separate and degraded people" and not citizens, administrative rulings quickly confirmed the already-common denial of rights under the various federal land acts. Such moves were not made without protest, but it is clear that a great majority of Whites endorsed them. An Ohio representative well phrased a common view: "I sympathize with them deeply, but I have no sympathy for them in a common residence with the white race. God has ordained, and no human law can contravene the ordinance, that the two races shall be separate and distinct. . . . I will vote against any measure that has a tendency to prolong their common residence in this Confederacy, or any portion of it."

If the two races should not live together, then they must live apart: *apartheid*, to use the Boer word that firmly entered our vocabulary a century later. But where? Given the vast territory of the United States, surely some place might be found? At least some people thought so and, from time to time, tried to initiate the creation of such a refuge. In 1816 the Kentucky Abolition Society, noting that "great numbers of slaves have been emancipated" only to be denied local citizenship and debarred from entry into most of the states and territories, petitioned Congress to look to the "vast tracts of unappropriated lands" and "cause a suitable territory of lands to be laid off as an asylum for all those negroes and mulattoes who have been, and those who may hereafter be, emancipated within the United States." The Committee on Public Lands gave it a terse and cynical rejection. As sectional tensions mounted, any hint of the idea of all-Black settlements, colonies, enclaves, territories in the American West produced vehement warnings and denunciations. Fear of such a thing lurked in the debates over establishing the new Indian Territory on the edge of the Great Plains in the 1830s. Opponents warned that to allow the Indians to have a formal area and to send a delegate to sit in the House of Representatives would be "the entering wedge of something more," a precedent that would inexorably lead to similar territorial representation by the "deeper colored races." In 1848 Congressman William Duer of New York offered a resolution to effect exactly that, asking that "the Committee on Public Lands be instructed to inquire into the expediency of setting apart a portion of the public lands for the exclusive use and possession of free black persons"; no sale of land "to white persons" would be permitted, and when the area reached an appropriate population, it would be organized as an ordinary formal territory of the United States. When an opponent accused him of proposing to establish "a State of negroes within the confines of these United States," Duer insisted that he intended only a territory, not a state.

As we might expect, Thomas Jefferson had given much thought to this matter, as to so many other topics relating to the geographical shaping of America. As a young man in the Virginia legislature he had chaired a committee to consider plans for gradual emancipation and deportation. In his first year as president, prompted by a Virginian inquiry on the need to establish a penal colony for "insurgent negroes," Jefferson reviewed a wide range of geographical possibilities for the removal and resettlement of American Blacks in general. He declared the idea of establishing a Black colony in Ohio or farther to the west to be incompatible with his vision of the American future: "It is impossible not to look forward to distant times, when our rapid multiplication will expand itself beyond [our present] limits, & cover the whole northern, if not the southern continent, with a people speaking the same language, governed in similar forms, & by similar laws; nor can we contemplate with satisfaction either blot or mixture on that surface." No "blot or mixture on that surface"—there, in the first year of the new century, on the eve of the first huge accession of territory, from the pen of its greatest geopolitician, the theme for the subsequent shaping of the American empire—and nation—was set forth. However expansive and optimistic that theme might have been to the American people in general, it was unmistakably ominous for any people who stood in their way—or any "colored" people caught in their midst. Any Black colony in the West would presumably conform in language, government, and laws, yet would be inescapably regarded as a blot.

If not the West, where else? Africa—"obviously," their "natural home." The idea of shipping freed Blacks back across the Atlantic—"repatriation"—was an old one and by 1800 had become a reality in the colony of Sierra Leone, founded by British philanthropists on the west coast of Africa. Initiated at Freetown with a shipment of Black Loyalists from Nova Scotia, the project was of interest to Blacks as well as to Whites. In 1816 the American Colonization Society was formed to expand upon this concept and initiative. Through a combination of gifts and threats a foothold was eventually obtained from local Africans at Cape Mesurado, 250 miles down the coast from Freetown. Here in 1822 the town of Monrovia was laid out and about 150 American Blacks began the physical creation of "Liberia." Annual shipments over the next forty years brought in more than 10,000 to the area. In the 1830s individual state colonization societies became active and sponsored a number of settlements; "Maryland in Liberia" at Cape Palmas, the most substantial (and separate) of these, received direct legislative support and added another 1,100 colonists to this American effort (fig. 41). The more expansionist leaders of this general enterprise envisioned a thriving "Americo-African" colony as the initial base of a civilizing—and profitable—empire. The results were disappointing and burdensome. Little was actually produced for export; disease and strife with local Africans took a heavy toll. In 1839 most of the settlements were united in a Commonwealth of Liberia and efforts made to get the United States to

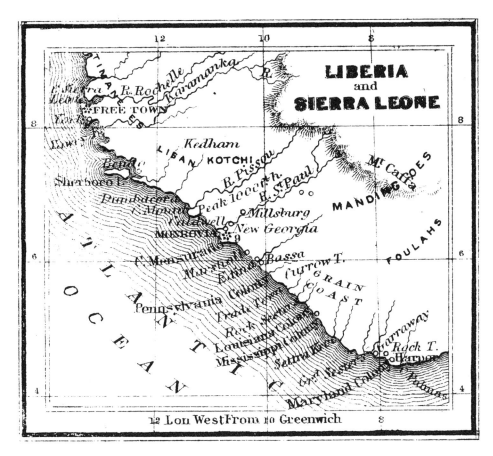

41. Liberia, 1853.

"Egypt" and "Liberia and Sierra Leone" rate insets as areas of special interest on the full-page "Map of Africa" in *Smith's Quarto Geography*, an elementary schoolbook published in New York in 1853. The map shows the location of four of the state-sponsored colonies along the Grain Coast adjacent to the original Liberia at Cape Mesurado ("Mensurado" on this map).

assume sovereignty over this anomalous geopolitical creation. Failing in that, in 1847 the distressed directors ordered the colonists to proclaim independence. Thus the American version of Sierra Leone, a peculiar Afro-American Christian colony, was cut loose as the Republic of Liberia in which a few thousand Black immigrants from North America claimed sovereignty over a substantial piece of Africa and several hundred thousand (no one had much idea of just how many) Africans. The new state was soon officially recognized by the leading European states but, very pointedly, not by the United States until 1862.

African colonization was promoted as a great *national* project beneficial to all

Americans, Black and White alike. It early received some indirect federal support (from funds appropriated for the Atlantic antislave trade patrols), it was endorsed by Congress in 1832 (but vetoed by Andrew Jackson), and it was sustained by both state and voluntary contributions from all sections of the country (only South Carolina proved intractable). But the colonization movement was an unstable coalition of different, often divergent, and even contradictory interests. It "drew its strength from humanitarianism and fear alike": it was a philanthropic movement to improve the life of Blacks and to Christianize and civilize Africa; and it was promoted as an urgent and practical means of removing a population subversive to slavery. Harshly attacked from one side as an instrument of abolitionists and from the other as a cover for securing slavery, the central concept that had brought such a muddle of White interests together became more and more explicit: it was a *deportation* project; its real objective was to get rid of free Blacks, whose very presence was regarded as a threat to order and stability and the "purity" of America.

"Back to Africa" was inevitably a troublesome and divisive concept for American Blacks. There were those who supported the idea even before the American Colonization Society got under way: Paul Cuffe, a Black shipmaster from Massachusetts, sponsored and conveyed a small group of American Blacks to Sierra Leone in 1815. Such programs held out hope of a degree of freedom and dignity and future prosperity beyond anything that seemed likely in America. The proclamation of a Black-ruled Republic of Liberia stimulated further and larger designs, most notably those of Henry Highland Garnet and the African Civilization Society and of Martin Robison Delany, an energetic Black nationalist who set forth expansive ideas for African development, touted a trans-African railroad, and undertook explorations and negotiations for an American Black colony in the Niger Delta. In marked contrast were the larger number who bitterly rejected the whole concept as a White scheme to "expel the colored man entirely from the country" (and it prompted some groups to drop "African" and substitute "colored" in their name and in common parlance). "We do not mean to go to Liberia," declared Frederick Douglass; "Shame upon the guilty wretches that dare propose, and all that countenance such a proposition. We live here—have lived here—have a right to live here, and mean to live here."

Historians Mary Frances Berry and John W. Blassingame, after reviewing various African schemes, concluded that "judging by the letters received by the society and those reprinted in a number of newspapers, about 20 percent of the free blacks supported emigration between 1817 and 1861." Even so, with a free Black population numbering half a million in the 1850s and with shipments carrying at most a few hundred annually to Africa, it was obvious that this highly controversial movement had as yet generated no ameliorative momentum.

If not Africa, where? Haiti—of course. The American tropics had always seemed to many persons to be the logical outlet for North American Blacks, as Jefferson had noted in 1801: "The West Indies offer a . . . practicable retreat for them. Inhabited already by a people of their own race & color; climates congenial with their natural constitution; insulated from the other descriptions of men; nature seems to have formed these islands to become the receptacle of the blacks transplanted into this hemisphere." It was generally assumed that some sort of negotiation and program of transfer would be required (rather than rely on some fanciful "natural drainage"), and the emergence of the independent Black state of Haiti opened a specific place to begin. The very existence of such a nation, created by the only successful slave revolt, in the heart of the planters' world, made a deep impression on North American Blacks. And as it gained some greater degree of security the Haitian government sought ties with and became a focus of interest for American Blacks. In the 1820s branches of the Haytian Emigration Society were formed in the major cities. Although a few White sponsors were also involved, the migration of several thousand Americans to Haiti was very largely by Black initiative. But the failure of the Haitians to provide land and aid as expected and the generally difficult conditions and cultural distinctiveness worked against any large continuing influx, and it was soon apparent that the free Black state in America was no more effective as an outlet than was the one in Africa. A great variety of other places in and around the Caribbean were nominated as attractive prospects. There was much vague talk of Central America and Mexico. Benjamin Lundy, a Quaker well versed in such things (he was involved for a time in Haiti), actually obtained an empresario grant in Tamaulipas to resettle manumitted families, but the Texas revolt intervened before anything could be accomplished. In the late 1850s Frank P. Blair, Jr., a prominent Missourian, energetically promoted in Congress and in public a scheme for federal and state cooperation in gradual emancipation involving the U.S. purchase of large blocks of land in several Central American countries for the subsidized resettlement of freed Blacks under continued American assistance and political protection. He was confident that the border states would respond and that the exodus of Blacks "would be succeeded by the most useful of all the tillers of the earth, small freeholders and an independent tenantry. The influx of immigrants from Europe and the North, with moderate capital, already running into Maryland and Virginia, would, as these States sloughed the black skin, fill up the rich region round the Chesapeake bay." But, however much White communities might long to "slough the black skin," Blair found no significant support for his programmed "drainage system" because it was too late for such gradual measures. Following the abolition of slavery in the British and French colonies a trickle of North American Blacks did voluntarily go to Jamaica, Trinidad, British Guiana, and elsewhere. Some of these had been recruited by labor contractors who were finding it difficult to lure local freed Blacks off their small plots and home islands to new plantations and industrial projects. But again the number actually involved in all these movements was infinitesimal when measured against proclaimed needs or desires. Furthermore, free Blacks were complexly bound into Southern society, and the idea of forceful expulsion of American-born persons—even if "colored"—was simply too gross a contradiction of American ideas to find overt support from many Southern leaders.

If not Africa or the tropics, where? In the aftermath of a race riot in Cincinnati in 1829 (precipitated by an attempt to enforce the Ohio Black Laws), a national conference of Black leaders urged that endangered Blacks consider moving to Canada. There were obvious practical advantages. Blacks were already there (as part of the founding Loyalist colonies), gradual emancipation had ended slavery, and American Blacks could walk to freedom (with the additional need, on the main routes, of a boat ride across the Niagara or Detroit river). With some Quaker assistance, the Cincinnati refugees established Wilberforce, deep in the woods north of Peterborough, but such an isolated colony could not thrive, and thereafter American exiles tended to congregate around established centers near the portals of entry, such as St. Catharines on the Niagara Peninsula and various towns east of Detroit.

These Canadian places, in other words, became the northernmost terminals of the "underground railroad," the name given to a system operating to extract slaves from the South and conduct them secretly to safety. Emerging into prominence in the 1840s, its extensions into Canada became more important as attempts to enforce the fugitive slave laws increased. Famed for its individual exploits and moral purpose yet clandestine in its operations, it was readily defined in American mythology as an efficient system operated by a hierarchy of managers, conductors, and agents along an intricate set of routes by which as many as 100,000 were helped to freedom. Modern reassessments suggest a smaller volume, much less system, and a limited White role. It was much more an informal folk operation by Blacks, and its success gives further significance to the many small Black communities created in the course of westward migrations across the free states and territories. Such places now became way stations on a set of pathways that cut right across the grain of the main patterns of American movement. There remains much uncertainty about the whole operation, but southeastern Pennsylvania, southwestern Ohio, and southern Indiana were the main passageways out of slave territory, with dispersal routes in the West threading through Quaker and Yankee districts and, for some, on into Canada West.

In fuller perspective, of course, all of these efforts at deportation or refuge are distinctly minor compared with the great expansion in space and growth in numbers of the Black population, free and slave, within the United States. They are important, however, in what they reveal about the peculiarities of the American situation: that in spite of the presence of several million Blacks, the idea of getting rid of all of them could receive so much serious attention and effort. As Friedman concluded about the Liberian program: "Like other apparent panaceas . . . , black repatriation was an unworkable abstraction that drew Americans away from confronting and resolving the many and varied problems of a multiracial society."

The census at midcentury enumerated 3,639,000 Blacks, making them 15.7 percent of the population of the United States. Chiefly because of the impact of European immigration they were a declining proportion, even though a vigorously growing body of people. Of these, 434,000, or about 12 percent, were free, 3,204,000 slave (and thus slaves constituted 13.8 percent of the American population). Such accounting showed that Blacks were not just a Southern population but were present in all regions, and indeed in almost every county in the country, North as well as South (confirming that exclusion laws were never fully effective) (fig. 42). The overall population surface was of course highly uneven, with much the heaviest concentrations in the main plantation areas. There had obviously been a great shift of Blacks from the older areas to the new, but the numbers and modes of movement have proved difficult to define. Demographic calculations suggest that about 800,000 slaves were moved from the Atlantic states to the new western regions between 1800 and 1860. The great majority of these persons were taken west by their masters as a routine part of colonization. Professional slave traders were always part of the system and became especially active after the annexation of Texas and continuing expansions in the Mississippi floodplain. In the rising tensions of the time, the visibility of public auctions in the cities (and especially in Baltimore, Washington [outlawed in 1850], Alexandria, and Richmond) and of the long lines of fettered Blacks clanking along the main roads to the Southwest became a focus of comment by foreign travelers and abolitionist wrath. Coastal shipments were a relatively minor part of the pattern, chiefly of service to many smaller Gulf ports. New Orleans was much the most important destination and distribution center, and notorious as a market for "fancy girls"—young mulattos gathered from across the South for the brothel and mistress trade.

New Orleans continued to be the great center of the most complex Afro-American society, with its basic segmentations by language and religion as well as slave and free, its intricate gradations of color and status, its close interlockings with Whites of every class, its relative defiance of rigid codes and constraints, its celebratory festivals and general richness of sociocultural life. The creole countryside mirrored much of this same variety and was especially notable for its patterns of extended families of free coloreds dominating whole districts as planters and slaveholders. Slavery on a sugar estate might involve the worst of laboring conditions, and as a formal system Louisiana slavery was little better than any other, yet the local context was so different that the range of potentials for Afro-American life was greater here than elsewhere in the South.

The Carolina Low Country, centered on Charleston and extending as a type

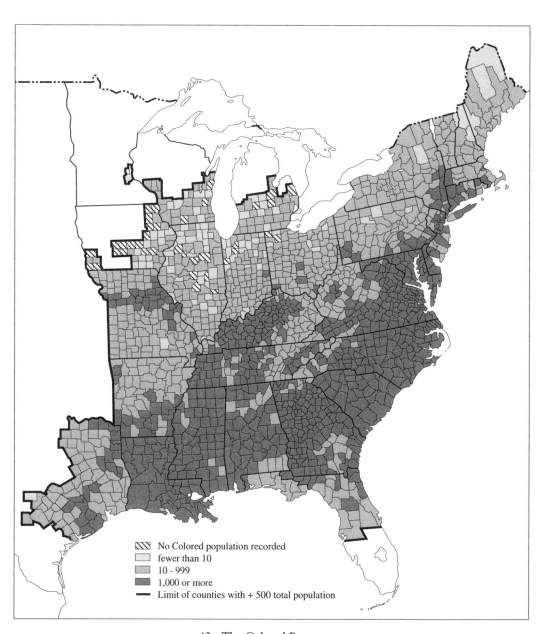

Legend:
No Colored population recorded
fewer than 10
10 - 999
1,000 or more
Limit of counties with + 500 total population

42. The Colored Presence.
As recorded by county in the census of 1850; the map is designed to emphasize the extent and comprehensiveness of this presence rather than proportions or densities.

from Cape Fear into northern Florida, continued as another distinct Afro-American society. Although some broad analogies with Louisiana might be drawn, it was a simpler social scene, with sharper racial lines and clearer separations, and Charleston was far less vibrant and cosmopolitan than New Orleans. Such things reflected both differences in origin and more recent history. It was not an expanding or prospering region; staple productions were confined to a narrow coastal environment, the Upcountry cotton boom was past, and populations were barely growing. It remained by far the most African of North American areas. Blacks made up 70 percent of the population in the Charleston District (city and countryside) and 85 to 90 percent in adjoining coastal areas. Living so largely apart from Whites, concentrated in such large numbers, working under a task system that allowed considerable free time, cultivating their own gardens—it is not surprising that here African influences in language and religion, music and dance, foods and folk medicine, family and social life should remain the strongest. Charleston was an exceptional island within this African scene, with its thousands of light-skinned servants and artisans, workers and hangers-on (and a small free mulatto elite) living in intimate structured contact with Whites who passed the harshest codes and vented the shrillest talk about White supremacy to cover their fearful insecurity as a small ruling minority in the midst of such an African American region.

While these two old planter regions played an important role in the emergence of the Cotton Belt, they did not impress their forms of Afro-American society widely upon it. The complex creole heritage of Louisiana could not of course be imitated, and only the richest areas—where the numbers of slaves were great, the Whites were few, and the masters preferred their mansions in towns—tended toward the South Carolina type. Most of the Cotton Belt was more Virginian in social character: a rural countryside compexly patterned with a wide variety of holdings, some with large numbers of slaves, most with a few, many with none at all, with, everywhere, Whites and Blacks living and working in close association. Afro-Americans were therefore much less separate and socially autonomous, fewer in relative number, having to form thin networks of contact among neighboring farms and plantations, always more vulnerable to interference and to the shaping influences of White society. In general, compared with the Low Country or Creole Louisiana, slavery in the cotton lands was much less rooted and stable, a looser, rougher sort of system focused on driving a labor force to wrench the profits out of farm and forest as quickly as possible, ready to shift to some new frontier whenever opportunity beckoned. As such it also diverged from its Virginian prototype, which, especially in its diffusion across the Upper South, involved fewer numbers of slaves, a greater diversity of tasks and skills, and—in its model form—presumed a more patriarchal authority and care of the extended family, Black and White alike. In the Upper South also slaves were employed in urban and industrial work (often negotiating their own terms of employment and "boarding out," free from direct supervision), the number of free Blacks was increasing (in Maryland approaching equality with the number of slaves), and the older, simpler patterns of White-Black relationships were being modified.

The city of Baltimore represented a transition into a different Afro-American context. It was in fact a peculiar hybrid society. There were 3,000 slaves, and slave traders, auctions, and patrols were a routine part of the urban scene; far more (more than 25,000) of the Blacks were free, by birth or by manumission, yet the general conditions of their life displayed how limited such freedom was in America: free from the shackles of slavery, but hedged in on every side by the harshest social discrimination; free to labor for their own support, but denied all but the most menial and insecure jobs; free to live without supervision, but "crammed into lofts, garrets and cellars, in blind alleys and narrow courts" in the most squalid and segregated of conditions. Such things actually got worse farther north in the "free" states, as studies of antebellum conditions in the "Little Africas" and "Niggertowns" of Philadelphia, New York City, Boston, and other cities confirm. Yet there was another dimension to it. Denied any real integration into American life as full citizens, Blacks resolutely adapted segregation to their own purposes. They set up shops and services for their people, organized mutual benefit associations, burial societies, and fraternal orders, established churches and schools, published newspapers, and sponsored meetings on community problems. In the larger cities the sheer numbers of Blacks could support a small but growing body of business and professional people, and such leaders formed intercity networks and national (or, more usually, northern) organizations concerned with abolition, civil rights, and the welfare of Blacks, activities expressed most fully and directly in the Negro Convention Movement that met, irregularly, from 1830 onward. Such things were of course best developed in the larger urban concentrations, but conditions were analogous elsewhere. Even in the smallest of settlements Blacks were forced and drawn together; though few in number, wherever they could link a set of families, form a church and a mutual aid society, or serve as a receiving station for migrants and a way station for transients, they created a vital nucleus of Afro-American life.

All the while, there were exceptional cases of Blacks who forged a successful career in a largely White world, such as Frank Johnson, the leading musician, concertmaster, and composer of Philadelphia, Samuel Ringgold Ward, minister of all-White churches in New York City, or Free Frank, enterprising pioneer and town-founder in western Illinois. But such lives only displayed a kind of capricious flexibility in the dominating society, a perversely tantalizing potential so remote from the realities facing most Blacks as to offer no useful guide to the possibilities of Afro-American life.

The chronic internal struggle over the goals of Afro-American life has been between the integrationists and the separatists: the one insisting on full equality, access, social mobility, and routine individual dignity within an assimilating national society; the other, despairing of any hope of that, asserting with pride Black differences and insisting on separate space and economy and full social and political autonomy with facilities equal in quality to those of the encompassing society. The bitterness of the Black situation in America is grounded on the hard fact that neither goal has proved possible.

Americans are obsessed with color as if it were a fundamental human distinction. Throughout the nineteenth century, White Americans were in such basic agreement about Black inferiority that no model of an American society accommodating the two peoples on anything like equal terms was seriously considered. As Frederick Merk summarized: "The concept of a society consisting of two races, each free, each possessed of equal rights under the law, and entitled to equal opportunity and dignity, was, in the North, deemed contrary to sober reality; in the South it was deemed unthinkable." Just as the severity of the United States as an imperial society is attested by the common plight of the American Indians, so the severe selectivity of the United States as a national society is attested by the chronic plight of American Blacks.

8. Making New Pathways: Waterways, Roads, and Rails

Only "by opening speedy and easy communication through all its parts" can "the inconveniences, complaints, and perhaps dangers" arising from "a vast extent of territory . . . be radically removed, or prevented," said Albert Gallatin in his landmark report to Congress in 1808. "Good roads and canals will shorten distances, facilitate commercial and personal intercourse, and unite by a still more intimate community of interests, the most remote quarters of the United States."

Whether or not anyone had as yet used the phrase, it must have become more obvious year by year that America was an unprecedented "experiment in transportation." The sheer size and character of the Republic made it so: its "vast extent," its natural separation by a rugged mountainous expanse into divergent drainages, the relentless spread of its population ever more distant from established centers, its special need to nurture an informed citizenry and community of interest.

The ground for this grand experiment was favorable. Given its size, the young United States was relatively well situated for commerce: a long, well-indented coastline; the vast dendritic drainage of the Mississippi-Ohio-Missouri system, with few interruptions on the major streams; and on the north the Great Lakes, offering broad surfaces for sail (but a spectacular break at Niagara and severe constrictions on the St. Lawrence). And of course the spread of population had been shaped by this basic geography, fitting human patterns to natural systems. The great westward wedge of settlement was aligned with the Ohio, and the relative value of lands and sites in all districts was closely attuned to the prospects for getting produce to market and intercepting lines of traffic. The harvesting, processing, and shipping of the products of farm and forest were geared to the seasonal variations: the high water of spring and early summer, the low water of fall and early winter, the ice of midwinter and the ice flows and jams that followed; the high winds and rough seas of the equinoctial seasons, the mist and fog of northern coasts. Many modest local improvements had been made—short bypasses and channel deepenings, lighthouses and breakwaters—but it was commonly agreed that much more was needed. The United States was a vigorously expanding frontier of a vigorously expanding world system. American pioneers were participants in a capitalist society wherein it was not enough simply to be in touch, to have some sort of seasonal access to market and a source of special supplies; there was the need for continuing development for expanding productions and profits. And for American towns and cities it was not enough to secure an initial niche in a network; there was the need to be alert and responsive to every possible competitive advantage in a system undergoing almost continuous geographic change. "Speedy and easy communication" was therefore a compelling and comprehensive concern in America.

That Americans knew how to build truly "good roads and canals" had just been demonstrated in the Philadelphia-Lancaster Turnpike and the Merrimack Canal. This turnpike was America's first superhighway, an "artificial road," that is, a roadbed carefully grounded, shaped, and surfaced and carried across streams on substantial stone bridges; an immediate success, it was soon extended to Columbia on the Susquehanna. The canal, an artificial channel with masonry locks connecting Boston with the lower Merrimack River, was hailed by Gallatin as "the greatest work of its kind completed in the United States" and, because of successful experiments in its construction and operation, declared by a modern historical authority as "important to the transportation geography of the United States all out of proportion to its length and facilities." These examples of new standards in transportation spurred many imitators. "Turnpiking" became a virtual mania in Pennsylvania and the Northeast. Most pairs of cities along the seaboard were soon connected, and as New Englanders spread into western New York, the Seneca Turnpike, Great Western Road, Catskill Road, and others began to extend improved trafficways west from the Hudson. And there was a great deal of interest in canals, not just as local improvements of river navigation but as a means of extending the competitive reach of mercantile centers, as Boston had done.

How to pay for such capital improvements was an insistent question. Canals, especially, were very expensive, with no return whatever until completed; and although many turnpikes were little better than "natural roads," a proper one was not cheap to build or maintain. Where the distance was not great, the terrain favorable, and traffic assured, private corporations readily responded to the potentials envisioned. More formidable projects looked to state legislatures for help, as in the case of roads across the Allegheny Front to Pittsburgh. But many people saw that such efforts were opportunistic and piecemeal and could never result in a proper national system of communications. Only a comprehensive national plan, supported where necessary by the national treasury, could overcome the limitations and jealousies of states and cities and private interests.

When Ohio, the first state carved out of federal territory west of the mountains, was admitted to the Union, the central government agreed to help bind it more effectively with the seaboard. A portion of the proceeds from the sale of federal lands therein would be allocated to the building of roads to, as well as within, the state. The congressional committee reviewing the matter found that the states of Pennsylvania and Maryland were already extending roads into their western districts and recommended that the federal government undertake to connect Cumberland, Maryland, on the upper Potomac, with the "river Ohio . . . opposite to Steubenville . . . a little below Wheeling." After brief debate this first formal "national road" across the boundaries of three states was authorized.

This action generated a great deal of interest and controversy (including strong dissent from Pennsylvania and Maryland), and since such a road could be no more than one small piece of the system desired, the Senate requested that Secretary of the Treasury Albert Gallatin make an assessment of national needs.

THE GALLATIN PLAN

Gallatin reviewed the public roads and canals already built or under way and incorporated these into his overall scheme (fig. 43). His recommended program consisted of four geographical parts:

1. **Parallel land and water trafficways along the Atlantic seaboard,** consisting of:
   a. a Great Turnpike from Maine to Georgia, passing through all the principal seaports;
   b. a protected coastal waterway from Boston to Savannah, making use of canals across the four great necks: Boston to Providence (better than a shorter cut across the base of Cape Cod); New Brunswick to Trenton; Delaware-Chesapeake; and the Dismal Swamp Canal connecting Norfolk to Albemarle Sound.
2. **A series of east-west connections between Atlantic streams and western waters,** consisting of numerous river improvements, and where rivers and ca-

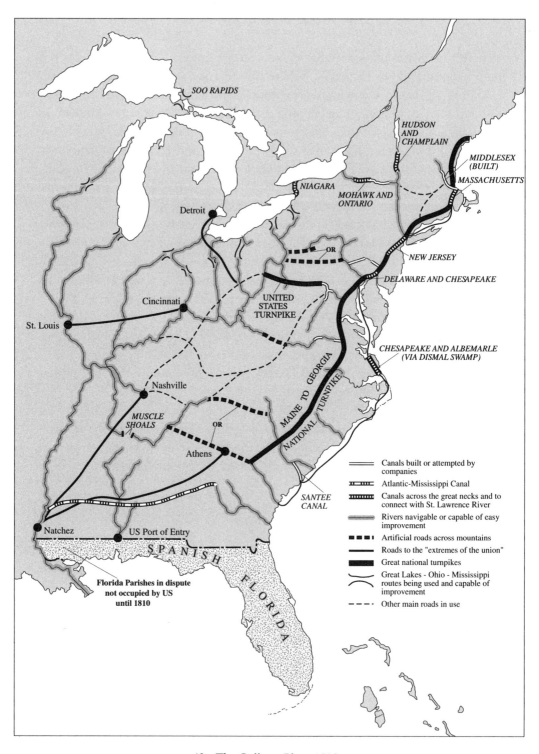

SOO RAPIDS

HUDSON
AND
CHAMPLAIN

MIDDLESEX
(BUILT)

MASSACHUSETTS

NIAGARA

MOHAWK AND
ONTARIO

Detroit

OR

NEW JERSEY

DELAWARE AND CHESAPEAKE

Cincinnati

UNITED
STATES
TURNPIKE

St. Louis

CHESAPEAKE AND ALBEMARLE
(VIA DISMAL SWAMP)

Nashville

MAINE TO GEORGIA

MUSCLE
SHOALS

OR

NATIONAL TURNPIKE

Athens

SANTEE
CANAL

Natchez

US Port of Entry

S P A N I S H

FLORIDA

Florida Parishes in dispute
not occupied by US
until 1810

Canals built or attempted by
companies

Atlantic-Mississippi Canal

Canals across the great necks and to
connect with St. Lawrence River

Rivers navigable or capable of easy
improvement

Artificial roads across mountains

Roads to the "extremes of the union"

Great national turnpikes

Great Lakes - Ohio - Mississippi
routes being used and capable of
improvement

Other main roads in use

43. The Gallatin Plan, 1808.

nals were not practicable, a set of artificial roads across the mountains. These several links were:

   a. Susquehanna or Juniata to the Allegheny

   b. Potomac to the Monongahela and Ohio (by the U.S. Turnpike already authorized)

   c. James to the Kanawha

   d. Santee or Savannah to the Tennessee

   e. eventually a long canal across the Gulf Plains connecting tidewater Georgia with the lower Mississippi (all of Florida was still under Spanish control).

3. Connections between the Great Lakes–St. Lawrence system and Atlantic and Mississippi Valley streams, including the following canals:

   a. Lake Champlain–Hudson River

   b. Lake Ontario–Mohawk River

   c. Lake Erie–Chautauqua Lake

   d. Lake Erie–Allegheny River

   e. Lake Erie via Cuyahoga-Muskingum rivers

   f. Lake Erie via Sandusky-Scioto rivers

   g. Lake Erie via Maumee-Miami rivers

   h. Lake Erie via Maumee-Wabash rivers

   i. Lake Michigan via Chicago Creek–Illinois River

   j. Green Bay via Fox-Wisconsin rivers.

4. Improvements ("on a much less extensive scale") **of roads leading to points on the extremes of the interior of the Union:**

   a. Muskingum to Detroit (with sloop connections to the upper lakes)

   b. Cincinnati to St. Louis

   c. Nashville, Tennessee, or Athens, Georgia, to Natchez.

As this last category suggests, Gallatin's plan comprehended the political as well as commercial interests of the United States. To facilitate the mail, "the prompt transmission of information of a public nature," and "the means of a rapid concentration" of the federal army and state militias "on any given point" were part of the basic purpose. Gallatin also acknowledged the special problems of federalism in moving ahead with any such program: "As the expense must be defrayed from the general funds of the union, justice, and perhaps policy not less than justice, seem to require that a number of local improvements, sufficient to equalize the advantages, should also be undertaken in those states, parts of states, or districts, which are less immediately interested in those inland communications."

As an official proposal the Gallatin plan was lost in the turmoil leading to war in 1812, but because it was both a comprehensive inventory and a thoughtful assessment of geographic possibilities, it set the basic framework for discussion after 1815, debated in some degree in virtually every session of Congress for a generation until overtaken by new technologies and geographic contexts. Many of the facilities Gallatin proposed were actually built even if not as a concerted program under national direction and subsidy. Our concern for the moment is with this changing geography, with the evolving networks of transportation improvements whatever their sponsorship or financial success.

WATERWAYS

At this early stage transportation developments were focused in the densely settled districts, especially in the concern of major ports to improve access to hinterlands and of various states to improve vital intrastate connections. Many actions related to a peculiar historical geographical feature of the Atlantic seaboard, which Vance has called the "misplaced entrepôt." The North American colonies were initiated by seafaring peoples who sought the most attractive points of attachment to continental shores. A spacious, well-protected harbor with room enough for local settlements was sufficient lure for the implanting of a nucleus that might in time develop into an important provincial capital and commercial center in an Atlantic world. In only a few cases did such early footholds also enjoy good waterway access deep into a productive hinterland, most notably at New York (and belatedly in the case of the later emergence of Norfolk), much less so in the cases of Savannah and Philadelphia, hardly or not at all in the cases of Charleston, Baltimore, New Haven, and Boston. As populations and productions developed ever farther inland such places found themselves ill-positioned to capitalize on this newer phase of American development (they were in that sense "misplaced," though it seems anachronistic to call them "English mistakes"). The need to overcome such geographical problems became a paramount concern of local commercial interests. The many geometric boundaries cutting across river basins and therefore complicating the intra- and interstate implications of various projects were a further colonial legacy. As Vance notes: "The misfit of entrepôt to hinterland, of harbor to source of its cargoes, and of potamic transportation to the colony or state charged with developing a first effort at internal improvements accounts for most of the early canal-building efforts in the United States." Such concerns underlay Boston's interest in the Merrimack Canal, Charleston's in the Santee Canal, and Philadelphia's in early schemes to create a waterway via improvements on the lower Schuylkill and a canal to Middletown on the Susquehanna. This Pennsylvanian program was designed to provide a complement to the Philadelphia-Columbia turnpike, the two facilities to serve as the eastern segments of connections by land and water across the state; both were also intended to intercept downstream Susquehanna traffic from reaching the Chesapeake and Baltimore.

Interest in providing thoroughfares across the divide to western waters was quickened by the Gallatin report. The State of New York began to look beyond meager improvements in the Mohawk River and commissioned a reconnaissance for a canal westward to the Great Lakes. Before any such project could be undertaken, however, a new phenomenon rather suddenly came into view, altering perceptions and horizons and heightening the stakes in intercity, interstate, and interregional rivalries.

A number of Americans had begun to experiment with the adaptation of the steam engine to propulsion in water in the earliest years of the Republic. In 1790 James Fitch had a small boat in regular passenger runs on the Delaware above Philadelphia but was unable to compete with long-established services by sail and stagecoach. The great breakthrough did not come for another seventeen years, when Robert Fulton's *Clermont* steamed 130 miles up the Hudson to Albany and back. Fulton and his partner, Robert Livingston, thereby obtained the monopoly on steam navigation that the New York legislature had offered as an incentive, forcing a rival inventor (and former associate), John Stevens of Hoboken, to take his boat to the Delaware, where he reestablished the long-defunct service between Philadelphia and Bordentown. From these inaugurals steamboat service spread fairly rapidly to adjacent coasts and rivers. Steam ferries were soon operating in New York Harbor and up the Raritan to New Brunswick to connect with the new "Flying Machines"—stagecoaches designed for a rapid ride across New Jersey to Bordentown. Similarly, steamboats were soon plying downriver from Philadelphia to New Castle to connect with stages across the narrow neck to the Chesapeake and boats to Baltimore. In 1815 steamboats began operating between Baltimore, Norfolk, and Richmond, and expansions within the Chesapeake soon followed. Extensions eastward from New York were a bit slower, in part because of assumed difficulties in navigating Hell Gate and the oceanic waters of Long Island Sound, and in part because of the inhibitions of the Fulton-Livingston monopoly. Direct service to New Haven was begun in 1815, soon followed by extensions up the Connecticut to Middletown and Hartford as well as east to New London and, in 1822, Providence. Meanwhile Boston and Salem, famous seats of the American sailing marine, showed less interest. Not until the middle 1820s was there anything like regular service to Portland, Bath, and other Maine ports, as well as to Saint John, New Brunswick.

The expansion of steamboating was actually more rapid on inland waters. A year after the *Clermont*'s demonstration run, a boat was put in service on Lake Champlain to provide a Whitehall–St. Johns waterway link between Albany and Montreal. Developments on the Great Lakes were slower for lack of established traffic, the greater hazards these often stormy waters presented, and the irruption of war. Canadian shippers at Kingston launched the first steamboat on Lake Ontario in 1816, Americans followed in the next year, and by 1822 there were good boats connecting the main Lake Ontario ports and down the St. Lawrence as far as

Prescott. Lake Erie service began with the famous *Walk-in-the-Water* in 1818, but this not very efficient vessel was wrecked in 1821, and for some years afterward there were only two steamboats in regular service between Buffalo and Detroit.

Fulton and Livingston had regarded the Ohio-Mississippi system as their greatest potential and moved quickly to establish domination. Their first boat, launched at Pittsburgh, reached New Orleans in January 1812 and began regular runs between New Orleans and Natchez. The development of sufficient power—and navigation experience—to move briskly upriver was of course the really radical innovation and key to success. In 1816 the first ascent from New Orleans to Louisville was made, and soon boatyards along the Ohio were busy building and improving on these newfangled vessels, U.S. mail contracts were obtained, and pioneer captains were probing up the Tennessee, Missouri, upper Mississippi, and a dozen lesser tributaries. By the early 1820s more than seventy steamboats were offering a variety of services including more or less regular links between New Orleans, St. Louis, Louisville, Cincinnati, Pittsburgh, and Nashville (fig. 44). The biggest and fanciest of these vessels were primarily passenger carriers, but others became the main workhorses of the river replacing most of the keelboats, although flatboats and arks continued to carry a good deal of seasonal farm and forest produce to market and emigrant families with their livestock and belongings westward to river landings leading to frontier land offices. Meanwhile, steamboats were also introduced on major rivers of the Coastal Plain, first on the Savannah, later on the Alabama, Tombigbee, and the Red River below the Great Raft.

By 1825 it was clear that the steamboat would transform the nation's transportation. The potentials for river and lake navigation could be readily calculated, and although experiments had not as yet provided similar assurance about oceanworthy vessels, the prospect of comprehensive coastwise connections could be as readily imagined (fig. 45). And in the autumn of that year every citizen of America was soon made aware that a new dimension had been added to this transport revolution. In October a grand flotilla left Buffalo and proceeded eastward across New York State to the accompaniment of cannons booming every mile and festivities in every town, culminating in an elaborate ceremony in New York Harbor, where Governor De Witt Clinton tipped an elegant keg of Lake Erie water into the tidal waters of the Atlantic to mark the completion of the Erie Canal. The engineering triumph and immediate commercial and financial success of the world's longest modern artificial waterway ignited the "canal mania" that swept across America for the next twenty years. Now began in earnest, under state and private auspices, the effort to provide the great system outlined in Gallatin's proposals.

The Erie Canal, making use of the sole natural break through the Appalachian barrier (the summit west of Rome was less than 500 feet above sea level), was the most obvious and easiest of these grand links. The full line of that canal, however,

44. Cotton Boat, 1833.

While on his winter trip to New Orleans, Karl Bodmer sketched the *Lioness*, a 160-ton side-wheeler laden with 1,500 bales of cotton, near Baton Rouge. Built in the year previous at New Albany, Indiana, and based in New Orleans, the *Lioness* was typical of workhorse craft on the river and, not untypically, was lost within the year. (Courtesy of the Joslyn Art Museum, Omaha, Nebraska)

was not determined by nature. The simplest and shortest connection between the Hudson and the Great Lakes was by way of the Oswego River to Lake Ontario. That link was built but the main line was carried westward along the ancient beachline to Lake Erie (necessitating another 150-foot rise over the Niagara escarpment). The compelling navigational advantage of that longer route, of course, was to bypass Niagara Falls and provide direct access to all the western lakes; a persuasive political and commercial advantage was to serve the famed Genesee Country and other western districts with a trans-state waterway.

Three major effects of the Erie Canal were immediately apparent:

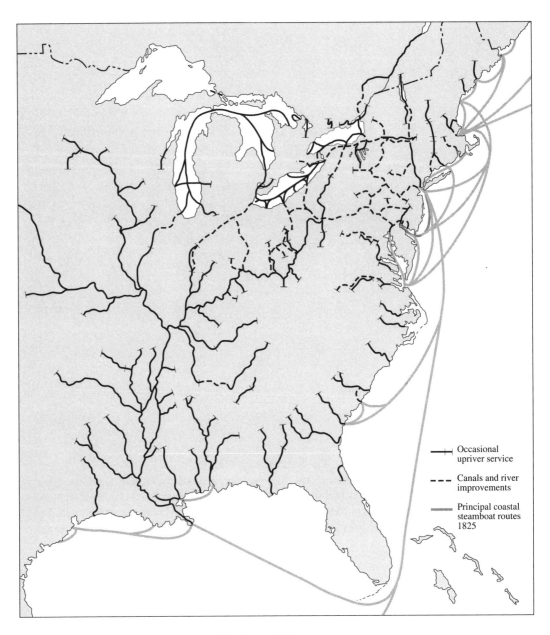

45. Potamic America.

1. It so drastically reduced the cost of shipment as to give immediate commercial stimulus to all it touched, further enhancing New York City's preeminence, creating a series of boomtowns at strategic sites (especially Syracuse and Rochester), and ensuring the construction of several lateral feeders to spread the economic benefits throughout Upstate New York.

2. It impelled rival states and Atlantic ports into frantic actions to create their own competing connections across the Appalachians.

3. It was the catalyst for the building of canals between Lake Erie and the Ohio River to form the long-envisioned linkage of the three great natural waterways.

Thus in 1825 Ohio passed a bill to undertake the Ohio & Erie Canal between Portsmouth and Cleveland; in the following year Pennsylvania broke ground for the Main Line Canal between the Susquehanna and Pittsburgh; a combination of state and federal interests gave renewed impetus to a Chesapeake and Ohio canal by way of the Potomac; and (some years later) the James River and Kanawha Company was reincorporated to reinvigorate George Washington's plan for a Virginian waterway to the Great West.

But if "it was the Erie Canal that assured that there would be an American Canal Era," there was no way to assure that any other state or region could come close to duplicating the rewards that accrued to New York. Indeed, as Vance notes, New York was "the only part of America where a comprehensive system typical of France and the Low Countries was constructed," and that was surely because of its natural advantages as well as its political initiative. Several branch canals were authorized even before the Erie was completed and others soon added, so that within a few years there were connections to Lake Champlain, Lake Ontario, the larger Finger Lakes, and via both the Chenango and the Chemung rivers to the Susquehanna on the southern border. Such branches were primarily feeders to the trunk line, rather than transits to other outlets, and traffic on the Erie was so heavy that within ten years surveys for its enlargement were under way. Eventually Pennsylvania would have an even greater mileage of waterways than New York but to far lesser advantage. Many of its short canals and river improvements facilitated the shipment of coal, but nothing could compare with the Erie Canal. When Pennsylvania's trunk line was hurriedly completed ten years later, it turned out to be a costly, inefficient patchwork of two railroads, two canals, and several sets of cable cars on incline planes to cross the Allegheny Front. "In its peak year, 1845, the Pennsylvania Mainline carried a total of 83,972 tons in both directions. That same year the Erie rose above a million tons of freight for the first time." Pennsylvania had earlier taken the lead in the building of major roads, and it was these, soon supplemented and then replaced by railroads, rather than canals that would bind it securely into the rapidly developing national network. Farther south, the canal along the Potomac did not reach Cumberland until 1850, and faced there with a thriving railroad running parallel for many miles and on past toward the Ohio, the company abandoned its transappalachian goal and settled in to carry coal to the industrial seaboard. Virginians had pushed the James-Kanawha canal only just beyond the Blue Ridge before they, too, halted at that point.

West of the mountains the much easier task of extending canals across the low divide south of Cleveland and Toledo and following along the various tributaries of the Ohio was carried forward so that by the early 1840s those ports had connections with Pittsburgh, Marietta, Portsmouth, Cincinnati, and Terre Haute (but not with Evansville until 1856). The long-sought but repeatedly delayed short link from Chicago to the Illinois River was not finished until 1848. Other pieces of Gallatin's plan completed during this time were the Welland Canal, bypassing Niagara Falls (on Canadian soil with the aid of American investment), the Morris Canal and the Delaware & Raritan across New Jersey, the Delaware & Chesapeake, and the Dismal Swamp Canal. Following the annexation of Florida there were numerous proposals and surveys for some sort of cutting west from the St. Johns River to the Gulf of Mexico, the now obvious alternative to Gallatin's proposal for a long link across the Coastal Plain.

Thus, a generation after Gallatin's report a combination of artificial roads, canals, and the unanticipated presence of the steamboat provided "speedy and easy communication" through large portions if not quite all the parts of the nation as he had proposed. The nation's waterways had become linked on an extensive scale, but it must not be thought of as a single network, for it was divided into several distinct functioning parts. There was the Atlantic coast and its tidal rivers. Here the impact of the steamboat was not really revolutionary, and these waters continued to be alive with all manner of sailing vessels. Regular steam packet service connected the major ports between Boston and Norfolk; it did not extend the whole length of the seaboard because the traffic did not demand such service. Smaller steamboats on a number of southern rivers were important local improvements for a scattering of southern ports. In the Northeast a much denser network of canals, rivers, turnpikes, tramways, and short railroads gave the larger ports ready access to diversifying hinterlands.

The New York canals represented another distinct segment of the national system. That the ever-mounting traffic was mainly from local agricultural and industrial districts is suggested by the fact that Rochester (20,000), the booming flour-mill city at the falls of the Genesee, was larger than Buffalo (18,000). Great Lakes sloops and steamers and the tributary canals of northern Ohio made up a third segment, feeding into Buffalo (or, on Lake Ontario, into Oswego). The movement of merchandise and migrants via the Erie Canal and on west to Michigan was still gathering momentum as attested by the small populations (1840) of Cleveland (6,000), Detroit (9,000), and Chicago (5,000). Although the canals across Ohio allowed multiple connections between Lake Erie and the Ohio River, these, too, were primarily local facilities with much of the traffic divided along a Youngstown–Coshocton–St. Mary's line.

It was on the great rivers of the West that the new innovations had their greatest impact. As a memorial from citizens of Cincinnati (seeking congressional aid for river improvements) put it: "Of all the elements of the prosperity of the West—of all the causes of its rapid increase in population, its growth in wealth, resources, and improvements, its immense commerce, and gigantic energies—the most efficient has been navigation by steam." By 1840 steam powered an immense commerce: more than 500 boats serving over 5,000 miles of the Ohio-Mississippi system. Most of these boats were built along the upper Ohio and Monongahela near the iron foundries and metal-working shops. Pittsburgh, Cincinnati, Louisville, St. Louis, and New Orleans were the great operational centers on this vast river network, each with more than a thousand arrivals annually. The inherent flexibility of the medium made patterns of service unstable, but by 1840 several types were apparent: trunk line service, some of it operating on regular schedule, between major pairs of cities (that between Cincinnati and Louisville being the heaviest); local service from major cities to minor landings and up the smaller streams; transient service ready to respond to shipping needs anywhere on the system.

In 1840 New Orleans was one of the great commercial centers of the nation, with a population (100,000) equal to that of Boston or Baltimore. But although steamboats carried passengers upriver in style and great numbers at astonishing speeds, its overall traffic was still heavily unbalanced, its commercial facilities geared to downriver shipments and exports from a constantly expanding hinterland. The steamboat had not altered traffic patterns nearly as much as many people had anticipated. In 1815 a Pittsburgh newspaper had hailed the new invention as the weapon with which to win "western independence" from the hold of "the Pennsylvania and Maryland waggoners . . . [and] the mercantile states of the Atlantic . . . [which] have for many years succeeded in diverting the trade of the West from its *natural channel*." But in fact those waggoners continued to provide a vital trunk line service in defiance of nature, with haulage made easier by improvement of roads and shorter by westward extensions of canals and railroads. And it was not just a matter of the relatively short distance of this overland connection; it was also the long-established relations with and superior services available in those mercantile states, because the commercial, financial, and industrial facilities of Baltimore, Philadelphia, New York, and Boston exceeded anything offered by the great entrepôt of the Mississippi system, New Orleans.

RAILROADS

By 1840 the performance and potential of an even more radical application of steam transport was coming to the fore as the decisive instrument in interregional relations. As with the first turnpikes and canals, most early railroads were portage roads—local improvements within existing waterway facilities, as in the case of the Mohawk & Hudson (1832), bypassing the tedious lockage around Cohoes Falls;

the Champlain & St. Lawrence (1832), from the Richelieu to the steamboat landing for Montreal; the New Castle & Frenchtown (1832) across the Delaware-Chesapeake neck; the Tuscumbia & Decatur (1832) around Muscle Shoals. The considerably longer Philadelphia & Columbia (1834) also functioned as part of the larger Pennsylvania system, offering more efficient service than the longer and limited Union Canal, but it was much more than a portage line, for it provided an alternative to turnpike wagons and stages for the highly productive agricultural counties and inland towns along its eighty-two-mile route.

To capture and enlarge upon the existing traffic between pairs of cities was another obvious incentive to railroad promoters, well represented by such early lines as the Camden & Amboy (1834), serving Philadelphia and New York; the Philadelphia, Wilmington & Baltimore (1838); and the lines radiating from Boston to Lowell, Worcester, and Providence (all completed in 1835), making it the first "hub city" of American railroading.

The South Carolina Railroad, whose 136-mile track made it, for a moment in 1833, the longest in the world, represented a more urgent geographic strategy: "It was a Charleston enterprise to save Charleston" by a line to the Savannah River in the hope of diverting much of the burgeoning Piedmont traffic to its "proper" South Carolina outlet. The line was not a great success. The city of Augusta prohibited any connection across the river, and Savannah began to push its own railroad inland to ensure dominance of its Georgia hinterland. A number of other southern ports, especially Petersburg, Portsmouth, and Wilmington, did the same, and by 1840 these three tap lines had converged to form the first long interstate link on the southern seaboard. Any map showing such connections could be deceptive, however, for these were very lightly built lines designed more to ease the seasonal produce of farm to port rather than to provide rapid long-distance links (for which there was little demand among these small cities). Of much greater significance was another pioneer railroad undertaken as the curative strategy of another endangered port. In 1827 a group of merchants gathered to "take under consideration the best means of restoring to the city of Baltimore that portion of the western trade which [had] recently been diverted from it by the introduction of steam navigation and other causes." From that meeting came the formation of the Baltimore & Ohio with the "audacious" proposal to build a 200-mile railroad across the Appalachians to reorient the Ohio Country to Chesapeake Bay. This was to be Baltimore's instrument in the race with Philadelphia to answer the challenge of the Erie Canal.

The Baltimore & Ohio was noteworthy for its strategy, scale, and construction. It has been called "the university of railroad engineering" because here more than anywhere else the essential characteristics of American railroading were first developed. Begun with intentions to follow well-studied English practices, by the time it had reached Harper's Ferry (1834) its engineers had worked out new designs of roadbed, alignment, locomotives, and passenger cars to suit the very different economic and geographic conditions of North America. Construction through the mountains was slow, and Wheeling was not reached until December 1852. The B&O was the first railroad company to receive engineering aid from the national government. Army engineers surveyed the route and were in charge of the first track laying. During the next nine years they were detailed to assist dozens of private companies as "the railroad craze was superimposed on the canal mania." As the B&O and various short lines began to demonstrate the success of this latest innovation there was a scramble to join in the competition of transappalachian lines. The depression of 1837 imposed a long interruption, but eventually seven such lines were completed in the years 1850–53. From north to south these links were:

Montreal with Portland
Ogdensburg and Montreal with Boston
Buffalo with Albany, with further rail service to Boston and New York City
Dunkirk with New York City
Pittsburgh with Philadelphia
Wheeling with Baltimore
Chattanooga with Charleston and Savannah

This remarkable flourish of completions marked an important new stage in the rapidly changing geography of North American transportation. All of these lines were projections of vital importance to major commercial and civic interests. The competition was of course not all directed at capturing a single prize but at obtaining some significant share of the range of rewards perceived, and these varied with regional circumstances. Portland was seeking to take advantage of its position as the nearest ice-free port to the winter-bound St. Lawrence. Boston was seeking to overcome the well-established power of the Hudson River to intercept eastbound commerce. A railway to the Hudson had provided a welcome improvement for passengers and mail but could divert little tonnage from the riverboats, and an attempt to bypass the grand junction at Albany with a railroad cutting across a corner of the Catskills was abandoned before completion. However, Boston's search for a "new Northwest Passage" via Ogdensburg and Lake Ontario steamboats would prove but a feeble challenge to the superior position and facilities of New York City.

The State of New York gave a selective response to railroad promoters: for some years it deterred Albany-Buffalo lines from carrying freight in competition with the Erie Canal; yet it encouraged the building of the New York & Erie across the "southern tier" to provide some sort of equivalent service to those more landlocked counties and to divert traffic from following Susquehanna routes into Pennsylvania. By 1852 two trans-state systems (of different gauge) existed: the New York Central, a new corporation formed from the seven companies that had built segments of the Albany-Buffalo route; and the NY&E from Piermont on the lower Hudson to its first objective, Dunkirk (it soon built a branch to Buffalo, much the more important port). By the late 1840s it was realized that railroads could even compete with long-established Hudson River services, and two lines, one along the river, the other inland, were completed by 1852.

Pennsylvania hurried its line forward to avoid losing out to Baltimore in the railroad age as many felt the state had lost out to New York in the canal age. In 1857 the entire Main Line system of canals and railroads was sold to the private Pennsylvania Railroad Company (which soon abandoned the awkward portage railroad facility). Efforts (rather analogous to the NY&E) to connect the Susquehanna with Pennsylvania's port on Lake Erie (Sunbury & Erie Railroad) fell far short of completion.

The singularity of the southern link formed by the convergence of lines from Charleston and Savannah at newly named Atlanta and by extension on to the new town of Chattanooga on the Tennessee River was not for any lack of vision and schemes for many other connections. In the early 1830s army engineers had been assigned to survey lines running from Memphis to Savannah, to Charleston, and to Kingston, near Knoxville. This last was in anticipation of an eventual extension by way of the Great Valley to connect with Baltimore, a link strongly favored by influential Tennessee interests. Such surveys immediately brought loud calls from an impressive array of South Carolina leaders for the building of a railroad between Cincinnati and Charleston.

As Vance notes, each of these transappalachian railroads was at once a *developmental line* stimulating new traffic from a belt of territory paralleling its route (the New York Central and Hudson River lines having the least immediate impact because of the efficiency of waterway services), and an *interregional trunk line* across the divide linking Atlantic and interior commercial centers. With regard to the second function, companies soon realized that merely reaching these western waters was not in itself a decisive strategy: there was the relentless need to extend further so as to capture western produce before it ever reached a river landing or before it was diverted by a competitive rail line to a rival port.

By the time these trunk lines had reached the Great Lakes or the Ohio River more than 1,500 miles of railroad had already been built in the transappalachian West. But it took more than simple articulation between eastern and western lines to form coherent interregional systems. The overall pattern of early railroad building in the West was rather a muddle, in part because of narrow intrastate programs and in part because so much of the region was still in such a malleable formative stage that there were few obvious major points upon which to anchor larger strategies. Here, as in the East, many of the first railroads were tap lines inland from some river or lake port; but here as well each state responded to the first flush of the railroad era with elaborate intrastate plans designed to serve local constituencies and with little concern for larger regional linkages. All of these programs fell victim to the Panic of 1837, but various segments were eventually built with or without public subsidy. For some years larger visions continued to focus on links between the great waterways: east-west across southern Michigan, north-south across Ohio, Indiana, and Illinois, complementing or competing with existing or authorized canals. It is instructive to note that none of the three states bordering southern Lake Michigan originally shaped their main system to focus on Chicago, which would so soon become the obvious great nexus. Although a Chicago-Galena line was early undertaken, the main axis of the Illinois program was to extend from a point on the Illinois & Michigan Canal (Peru-LaSalle) due south to the grand confluence of the Ohio and Mississippi rivers (the new town of Cairo); the limited focus envisioned for the overall system was granted to Illinois's rival to St. Louis, the vigorously promoted city of Alton.

Although B&O interests had projected a line directly west from the upper Potomac through Parkersburg and Cincinnati to St. Louis as early as 1843, the concept of such extensive east-west linkages did not appear with much force until the trunk lines building west from Atlantic ports actually reached the thresholds of the West. Once that happened, however, the opportunity to purchase control of various segments and franchises and push such connections forward was quickly seized and the rapidly changing geography of settlement offered new goals. Thus, within a few years the New York Central had reached Chicago by two routes, on either side of Lake Erie, the one by way of the Great Western across Canada and through Detroit, the other via the Lake Shore Route through Cleveland and Toledo; the Pennsylvania had obtained connections to Cincinnati and Chicago; and the B&O had accomplished its aim of "the American Central Line" direct to the Mississippi opposite St. Louis.

Several thousand miles of railroad were built south of the Ohio River during these same years, but the network formed was significantly different. Charleston, especially, and half a dozen other Atlantic ports had lines reaching into, and in some cases fanning out across, their Piedmont hinterlands. By the late 1850s one could travel by rail from Virginia all the way through the Carolinas and Georgia into Alabama—but only slowly and with many deviations and changes, including several changes in gauge. There was no trunk line along the seaboard because there was still little demand for such service. The completion of the long-sought line between Memphis and Charleston in 1854 was also celebrated in great "marriage of the waters" ceremonies at each terminus, but this symbolic uniting of the Mississippi with the Atlantic was so far south and through such a homogeneous economic region that it could do little to overcome the natural union of those waters by way of New Orleans. The extension of the Virginia & Tennessee through Bristol and Knoxville to a junction with this Memphis line at Chattanooga was hailed as the long-awaited Great Southern & Southwestern Mail Route, but here, too, there was little more than mail and a few passengers in need of such a full traverse, although such lines did provide welcome and important alternatives for shipments to and from eastern Tennessee. By 1850 long-complacent New Orleans mercantile interests had become alarmed over traffic diversions and began to agitate for a series of long tap lines to Nashville, St. Louis, and Texas. Before the decade was over lines northward from New Orleans and Mobile had intercepted the Memphis-Chattanooga traverse and provided indirect connections with Nashville and Louisville. Overall, the railroad pattern across the southern states was much less dense, more dispersed in orientation, fragmented in operation, and generally less substantial in construction than that in the North.

The rate of railroad building in the United States during the 1850s was astonishing. By the end of that decade more than 30,000 miles of track had been laid and many thousands more were clearly in the offing. The map of these lines reveals a pattern spread across all east of the Mississippi and half a dozen tentacles reaching into Iowa and Missouri (fig. 46). But as already suggested, there were marked variations in density and many complications in the actual patterns of service. The many companies, patchwork of construction, different gauges, and lack of bridges across major rivers and even of connections within major cities greatly affected the movement of passengers and freight. Yet, the transformation of this general pattern into a truly national network was clearly under way in the North. Each of the major northern trunk lines was anchored on a single Atlantic port and had contrived to establish direct links with all or most of the Western commercial centers, and each was making rapid progress in developing efficient interchange, through-car services, and coordinated schedules. The heaviest traffic of all was on the shorter lines tapping the immediate hinterlands of these ports. Fanning into burgeoning industrial districts, those lines were increasingly becoming interlaced, and in so doing began to offer alternative connections. Thus by 1860 the "Allentown Gateway" route was being promoted as a shortcut leading from Reading and all points west directly across northern New Jersey to New York Harbor. Railroad traffic along the seaboard between these rival ports moved over the lines of a series of separate companies and was still broken by transfers within each city and ferries across the great rivers and estuaries, for there were no bridges across the lower reaches of the Susquehanna, Delaware, Hudson, Connecticut, or Thames. (But the prospect of such crossings seemed clearly confirmed with the completion of John Roebling's spectacular Suspension Bridge across the Niagara Gorge in 1855.)

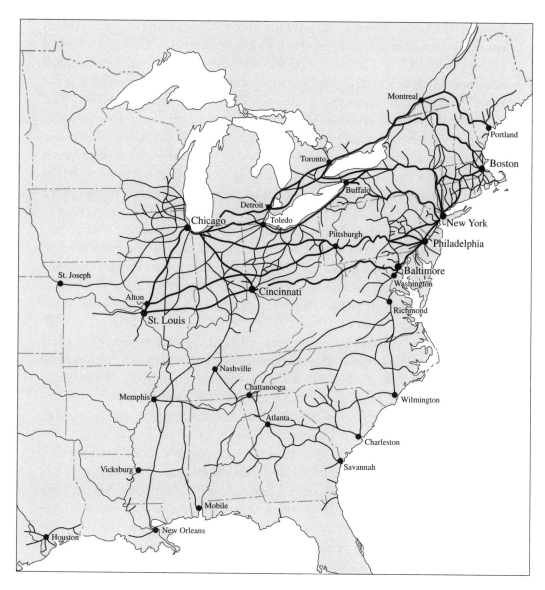

46. Railroads, 1860.

Incipient trunk lines are marked with a heavier line. (Principal sources: *Mitchell's Traveller's Guide*, 1860 [in Garrett]; *Colton's Series of Railroad Maps, No. 3*, 1860 [in Modelski]; Baer, *Canals and Railroads of Mid-Atlantic States*)

It should be noted also that Canadian railroads were an integral part of this evolving network, developed in direct response to the potentials for capturing an important share of traffic from the American West. The prospectuses of both the Great Western and the Grand Trunk specified that they were international in

concept: the Great Western "designed not only to facilitate the internal traffic of
the Province of Canada . . . but also to form a connecting link in the great chain of
Railway from the city of Boston . . . to the Mississippi"; the Grand Trunk designed
to gather the traffic accumulating "at the *débouchure* of the three largest lakes in the
world" [at Sarnia] and convey it "in one unbroken line through the entire length of
Canada into the St. Lawrence at Montreal and Quebec" and, in winter, via the St.
Lawrence & Atlantic (which the Grand Trunk absorbed) to Portland. Critical to
such visions and competition were the removal of U.S. duties on Canadian goods
in transit and of British restrictions on American ships in the St. Lawrence. By the
early 1850s more than half of the imports to Upper Canada came by way of the
United States.

The most significant geographic feature of the North American railroad pattern, therefore, was not its overall extent, impressive as that was, but the emergence of a series of latitudinal trunk lines operated as single- or joint-company
systems connecting the big Atlantic ports with the primary commercial centers of
the West. Buffalo, Pittsburgh, Cincinnati, St. Louis, and Chicago were clearly
major nodes in this interior network, along with Cleveland, Detroit, and Milwaukee as lesser articulation points, and all of these were major junctions of
railroad and water transport. This northern network was physically unconnected
with the southern, for the Potomac and the Ohio were unbridged at Washington,
Cincinnati, Louisville, and Cairo, nor did any single company operate lines connecting across these waterways. A major structural divide had already emerged in
the national network.

Another important feature of the northern pattern was the many lines that
reached westward from St. Louis, Chicago, and Milwaukee. The Mississippi had
been reached at eight points above St. Louis, bridged at two (Rock Island in 1855
and Clinton in 1858), and several lines were being extended across Missouri and
Iowa. This westward momentum was intensified by a new goal: not just to tap the
rich lands of these newly opened prairies but to gain a strategic position with
reference to the eventual Pacific Railroad, the future transcontinental axis of the
nation. In 1859 the Hannibal & St. Joseph was the first line to reach the banks of
the middle Missouri, the assumed central threshold of that grand national project.

That first railroad bridge across the Mississippi was barely completed before it
was struck and badly damaged by a steamboat—probably on purpose. The ensuing
court case eventually made clear that both forms of transportation must be allowed
passage, but the geographic impact of the latest phase of the transport revolution
was already clear. As Israel Andrews put it, in the introduction of his massive
report to Congress in 1852:

> Modern commerce has sought, and is constantly creating, at great expense, artificial
> channels; and this is so true of the United States, that such channels have, in a great

degree, superseded the natural routes; for the reason that the direction of American internal commerce is between the *agricultural,* and the *commercial and manufacturing* districts, which are *not* connected by the two great outlets, the Mississippi and the St. Lawrence rivers. Produce leaving Burlington, Iowa, following its natural outlet, is landed at New Orleans; or, leaving Detroit, and following its natural course, at Quebec. By the changing influence of artificial channels, it is now easily borne to New York, Philadelphia, Boston, or Baltimore.

"Artificial channels" included canals as well as railroads, of course, and the Erie Canal and some of the shorter canals continued to carry a very considerable traffic. But all interior waterways were yielding in some degree to the railroads, and the least efficient were being put out of business. There were many potential complementarities between railway and waterway services, but the speed, frequency, and regularity of the newer mode allowed a rapid capture of much of the passenger and lighter merchandise traffic. The whole relationship was unstable, responding year by year to the rapid ramifications of railroad service. When the B&O first reached Wheeling, for example, a new line of large and fancy steamboats was formed to provide coordinated service to Cincinnati and Louisville, with free transfer of passengers and baggage from the one mode to the other; but this arrangement lasted only a season because even indirect railway links between these cities began to cut into the long-thriving steamboat trade. Shipping on the Great Lakes expanded all the while to serve rapidly developing forestry and agricultural frontiers, but much of the passenger business was lost and several railroad cut-offs, such as Toronto to Collingwood, Fort Erie (opposite Buffalo) to Goderich, and Detroit to Grand Haven, sought to capture some of the freight through faster service. Along the Atlantic coast the situation was similar, with steam and sail still providing important waterway links but the railroads, even with many interruptions in movement, taking over the lighter traffic.

TELEGRAPH

Still another mode of connection must be added to this rapidly elaborating network, an innovation as revolutionary in impact within its special field as any of these others. The development of the telegraph system got under way a decade or so after the beginnings of the railroad, and because it made opportunistic use of railroad right-of-ways and its profits depended on intercity connections, the pattern of its spread conformed rather closely to its revolutionary predecessor in overland communication. There were, however, a few important variations, arising from the special character and value of the telegraph.

After years of trying, Samuel F. B. Morse finally received an appropriation from Congress in 1843 to build an experimental electromagnetic line between Washington and Baltimore. The success of his famous first transmission—"what hath

God wrought!"—on May 24, 1844, soon spurred extensions, though no further government support. Within three years lines connecting Washington and Boston (with a break at New York, where the problem of spanning the Hudson defied solution for several years), and New York City to Albany, Buffalo, and Toronto were in place. The most obvious advantage of the telegraph was the instantaneous transmission of commercial intelligence. High priority was hence given to lines reaching eastward to intercept, at the farthest point of land, westbound steamships from Europe. A Boston to Halifax line was completed in 1849 and extended via undersea cable to St. John's, Newfoundland, in 1856. Similarly, within the United States there was keen interest in connections between the Northeast and New Orleans, and by the time a link from Washington was made in 1848, rival companies were stringing wires to that port by way of the Ohio Valley.

The telegraph was an instant sensation but not an immediate commercial success. Unregulated competition and litigations, undercapitalization, and technical problems hindered reliability of service and public confidence. In the 1850s, however, with consolidation of companies, interregional compacts, and improved equipment, the telegraph quickly became an indispensable tool of commerce, government, and many kinds of social communication. The Associated Press was formed to coordinate the dissemination of news nationwide. Railroads belatedly realized that the flimsy lines of wires alongside their tracks could become a wondrously efficient tool for traffic management, and a growing interdependence between the two modes strengthened both. By 1860 there were about as many miles of telegraph as railroad binding cities, regions, and all eastern North America together. There were also confident expectations of an extension of both facilities across the continent to bind California to the nation and repeated attempts in 1857 and 1858 to lay a cable under the Atlantic between Newfoundland and Ireland. The failure of those efforts was no cause for despair; a rival company was soon proposing to establish, by means of an alternative island-to-island route (Greenland-Iceland-Faeroes), what was by then regarded as an inevitable and essential connection in this new phase of modern communication.

THE SYSTEM IN THE 1850S

The United States (and the Canadas) had an overall transportation complex of enviable versatility and density by the 1850s. Much of Gallatin's design had been built in one form or another and was reasonably discernible within the far denser pattern. Steamboats had transformed the circulatory potentials for waterway traffic, though nature's basic framework of Atlantic, Great Lakes, Ohio-Mississippi remained (with the Gulf Coast added through the acquisitions of the Floridas and Texas). Nearly all of the canals Gallatin had recommended were in use, as were the turnpike connections across the Appalachians, but in many cases the railroad had superseded these facilities. The roads across the Appalachians were still used as droving trails and by emigrant families and various itinerants, but the loss of mainline freight and passenger traffic meant a loss of state and metropolitan interest and a rapid decline in quality. Roads and turnpikes had been largely reduced to feeder lines aimed at the nearest railroad depot or river or canal port. The brief flurry of speculation in plank roads (Syracuse to Central Square in Upstate New York being the first, in 1846) quickly subsided in the face of excessive maintenance costs and railroad competition. Canals and river service had been more selectively and less drastically affected. Wherever there was bulk freight with low time demand, such as lumber, stone, cotton, and some grain, steamboats and canal boats continued to carry large tonnages. And in fact the growth of population and agricultural and industrial production in all regions meant an ever-larger traffic to be moved and could, in the main shipping seasons, tax the facilities of the entire complex.

The general purpose of the Gallatin plan had been to bring the most modern service to every region (by central government aid, direct or indirect, where necessary). Because it was conceived as a single framework for optimal development there was no place in it for any close duplication of routes or interception of traffic by one center from another; confined to waterways and roads, there was little to be gained from competition. In pattern it was a rough, though incomplete, grid. It was assumed that state and local interests would do much to fill in with turnpikes, canals, and river improvements so as to provide the facilities needed for every district. The envisioned result was perhaps best summarized by William Blodget, a Pennsylvanian writing a few years before Gallatin, extolling the value of such internal improvements. It was quite possible, he said, to bring every part of the country within twenty to twenty-five miles of efficient transportation, thereby opening every inland town, every village in America, to the cheapest markets of the world, promoting industry and trade, distributing a universal plenty of food at a common price, multiplying information, and "thus converting the entire country into *one great city* without any of the disadvantages that attend the residence of mankind, in great numbers together, on the same spot."

Such an idyllic geography combined some of the strongest aspirations of American culture: the primacy of the market, the virtues of rural life, and the quickening touch of the modern world. If the pattern at midcentury was not quite as simple and meliorative as Blodget had envisioned in 1805, it had, beyond all expectations, transformed the American situation. On the basis of the rapid succession and cumulative complex of turnpikes, steamboats, canals, railroads, and telegraph lines one could certainly declare that America as an experiment in transportation was a success. The challenge of binding Pacific shores into the main body of the nation could be confidently undertaken because the United States was now, in the

1850s, the best exhibit that a new phase in the historical geography of the world had begun: the great continents, no matter how broad or remote, could be opened up, brought into touch with, and bound ever more tightly into the world system.

9. Tying the Parts Together: National Programs

"The people of these United States are spread over an extensive territory, and . . . [because] politically speaking, there is in the United States but one order or grade known—*that of the people*, . . . [there] arises the imperious necessity in a Government thus constituted of tying together the whole community by the strongest ligatures. This your committee believe can best be effected by the construction of roads and canals." So stated Senator Abner Lacock of Pennsylvania in 1817 in what had begun, essentially, as a resubmission of the Gallatin plan. His report was in response to President Madison's urging of Congress to devise a constitutional means of undertaking just such a comprehensive system. Later that year Madison surprised his congressional associates by vetoing the bill they had prepared and passed. His highly controversial action did little to quell the issue, however; committees on roads and canals continued to examine the situation, offer lengthy reports, and insist on the national urgency of the matter until thirteen years later, when President Jackson's veto of the Maysville Road Bill essentially ended efforts to implement a national transportation program. Both vetoes were ostensibly on constitutional grounds. Historians have examined the contending philosophies and politics of this complicated issue in a large literature. Our concern is with a few geographical issues that seem to warrant further commentary.

The Gallatin plan was a design fitted to nature. The basic framework was one of circumferential waterways, with the Ohio River as a central axis, augmented by a series of artificial connections between the several great hydrographic basins to form a vast interconnected network that touched every state and territory east of the Mississippi. It was a design drawn up in the last years—almost the last moment—of what Lewis Mumford (following Patrick Geddes) called the *eotechnic* age. One of Mumford's many contributions to our perspectives on "technics and civilization" is his emphasis on the character of this long preparatory period, the essential prelude to what has been commonly termed the Industrial Revolution. In terms of transportation and industry it was the wood-wind-water era, characterized by sailing ships, canals, waterwheels, and windmills. It was an oceanic and potamic age, brought to a peak in America in two famous creations: the clipper ships, those sleek wooden vessels gliding across the high seas under towering sails at record speeds; and the Erie Canal, that long utilitarian artificial waterway that stimulated the economic development of a major part of the country. The canal builders were bringing the inland waterway system of the United States to its eotechnic culmination during the same years the clipper ship was being brought to perfection, but the country cousins of those oceanic queens, the sloops and keel-boats and other older river and coastal craft were little changed, and the canal boat, proceeding at the pace of a horse, while far more efficient than a wagon, was little faster and could not by itself increase the pulse of the national circulation.

It was that remarkable hybrid of old and new technologies, the steamboat—a wooden vessel propelled along the liquid paths of nature by wood fed into an iron firebox to heat the metal-sheathed boilers of a steam engine—that, coincident with the canal era, revolutionized the inland waterway system. (It should be noted that steamboats were not well suited for use on most canals because the waves generated by paddlewheels quickly damaged the earthen banks.) All rivers and coastal waters were generally open to any entrepreneur (exclusive franchises, such as Fulton obtained from New York and Louisiana, were exceptional and eventually invalidated). Services expanded quickly into all feasible natural channels wherever any possibility of traffic was discernible. The geographic pattern was thus in large degree already latent in nature and quickly established. Many detailed improvements, of course, could be made, such as the removal of snags, channel markings and minor deepenings, slack-water weirs and lockage. Such efforts could extend the mileage a bit farther upriver or make the season a little longer, and had the railroad not arrived for another generation no doubt a good many more such extensions would have been made (perhaps along the line of Charles Ellet's vast scheme for western rivers, published in 1853), but the basic spatial and seasonal patterns of nature remained fixed and formative.

The improvements came quickest in the designs of the boats themselves. There was a rapid evolution in a relatively simple technology, and also a marked divergence in character—in hulls, paddle assemblies, and engines—between a "Hudsonian" type, developed for tidal river, coastal, and Great Lakes conditions, and a "Western" or "Mississippian" type adapted to the special conditions of western river navigation and the abundance of cheap fuel. The Mississippian type, especially, represented an American folk experimentation at its best (and in its carelessness about safety devices, at its worst). The great floating passenger palaces racing between the river cities were the wonder of their time, but the smaller sidewheel or sternwheel, shallow-draft, "run-on-a-heavy-dew" steamers chugging up the twisting channels of dozens of western rivers, cheap to build and cheap to operate, were more basic to the transport revolution. The remarkable reductions in marketing costs of western farmers rather than the speed of passenger travel was the more fundamental change. By 1840 the western steamboat had reached its essential form, and it would soon begin to reach its essential geographic limits within the Mississippi system. In the high-water season boats could make their way far up the Missouri, greatest of the western tributaries, but the broad, braided, shallow, shifting channels of other prairie streams were hardly penetrable, if at all. No feasible expenditure could make the Platte a waterway into the farther West.

The steamboat had an ambivalent impact upon the interregional connections of the United States. On the one hand, the conversion of the Mississippi system into an effective two-way commercial thoroughfare seemed to enhance greatly the potential of New Orleans as a national entrepôt; on the other, that same conversion also made the Pittsburgh–St. Louis segment into a far more effective east-west trafficway, bound by improving facilities across the divide ever more closely with the great Atlantic seaports. At the same time, Great Lakes traffic was oriented much more strongly to the Erie and Hudson than via the several canals across the low divide connecting with the Mississippi-Ohio. Thus while steamboats were revolutionizing river travel and fitting traffic flows to the potamic template, steamboats and canals together also did much to reinforce the latitudinal ties of the nation.

The railroad—the iron wheel on the iron rail on a roadbed laid right across the lesser corrugations of nature—was the more fully revolutionary instrument and the very symbol of the new "coal-iron-steam" age (though in North America wood remained the principal fuel for many years). And even though Great Britain was the great seat and source of the *paleotechnic* for all the world, and the earliest American experiments began with British concepts and equipment, "almost from the first morning two distinct rail systems were emerging" on opposite sides of the Atlantic. Problems of distance between settlements, terrain, capital, industrial costs, and uncertain traffic, together with a more speculative environment, pressured Americans toward cheaper construction, which in turn required special adaptations in engineering and rolling stock. In contrast with the British system (displayed in its highest form in Brunel's Great Western line with its splendid double-track roadbed carried directly across the country via great cuttings, tunnels, and stone viaducts), American practice was to build cheaply, conforming more closely to the natural lay of the land, with the intent of using the earnings to reconstruct and upgrade the physical quality and capacity of the line. After a few formative years Americans became confident they could build railroads anywhere (and would eventually prove it by stringing narrow-gauge lines to dozens of mining camps in the most rugged recesses of the highest Rockies); it was in the United States under conditions of diverse experimentation, intense competition, and minimal regulation that the railroad first exhibited its nearly limitless expansibility.

Most of the earliest railways were integral parts of existing waterway systems, their tracks in some cases terminating on incline planes to the water's edge. Even the first lines across the mountains were mainly conceived as long portages, terminating at the nearest river or lake port (Wheeling, Pittsburgh, Dunkirk). The first prospectus for a railroad as a long-distance overland axis, that of the Great Western Railway in 1829 (a forerunner of the New York & Erie), suggests how uncertain the competitive prospects of the new mode seemed. The main line was to run from the lower Hudson across southern New York, northern Ohio, Indiana, and Illinois to Rock Island on the Mississippi, *avoiding* contact with the Great Lakes on the north and "at the most advantageous distance" from the parallel National Road on the south. Momentarily there seemed to be a vision of canal and lake vessels, railroad, turnpike, and Ohio riverboats as providing four complementary, noncompetitive east-west trunk lines (fig. 47). The 1830s was a period of vigorous steamboat and canal extension as well as of railroad experimentation, but by 1845 the superiority of this radical overland instrument in directness, speed, frequency, flexibility, regularity, and reliability was becoming obvious. Early railroading was plagued with delays and accidents, but less severely than steamboating (thousands of lives were lost in steamboat boiler explosions before an 1852 act improved standards and inspections). Only in the face of the railroad threat did steamboat companies really move to provide scheduled frequent service on the main rivers. The shift of passengers and light merchandise from river to rail in the 1850s was accelerated by the coincidence of a sequence of unusually dry years that severely impeded western river service just as the railroads were rapidly extending their tentacles across the interior states.

The railroad was far less closely fitted to nature than the steamboat, but it could be constrained in other ways. In its early stages most states attempted in some way

47. Four Complementary Trunk Lines, c. 1830.

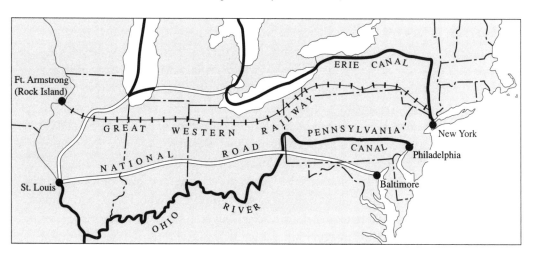

to shape a network to serve their own interests. The usual aim was to ensure rail service to every major constituency, and they might also try to shield the intrastate system from external encroachment. Thus the North Carolina legislature authorized a long railroad axis (by joint state and private funds) from a new port at Morehead City to the Great Smokies at Asheville, specified that it be of a different gauge from that of bordering states, and explicitly prohibited the Richmond & Danville, building southward in Virginia, from approaching within twenty miles of the North Carolina Railroad tracks. Similarly, Pennsylvania long thwarted a Baltimore & Ohio branch to Pittsburgh and tried to block the New York & Erie from building across Pennsylvania's corridor to Lake Erie. New York prohibited the NY&E from building into New Jersey or Pennsylvania and impeded Massachusetts lines from effective connections at Albany and Troy, just as Augusta and Georgia had fended off the South Carolina Railroad. Although state participation faded rather quickly, a good deal of the disjointed, patchwork character of the evolving national railroad network could be traced to it. Such impediments were overcome not by federal intervention in the interests of a more rational national system but rather by private corporations trying to maximize their control and profits. The American railroad network was shaped primarily by relatively "conservative metropolitan capitalists" who had access to the best information, credit sources, mercantile and manufacturing connections, and engineers—as well as political influence. Geographically, such persons tended to work in the interests of a city rather than of a state; of a center, a focus, or a terminus rather than of a large bounded territory. Railroad corporation leaders were often a team representing the mutual interests of several commercial centers along a particular route, and they would not hesitate to consider building across state boundaries or intercepting traffic that flowed to a rival center (such as the Northern Central, running straight north from Baltimore deep into Pennsylvania—the railroad equivalent of the Susquehanna River) or, indeed, of shifting allegiance from one center or route to another if the commercial prospects seemed to warrant. Nevertheless, in these early decades the opportunities were still so wide open that the main incentive was to dominate a swath of territory between a pair or set of centers rather than to multiply connections and invade the territory of another company. There were as yet few interpenetrating branch lines among the trunk line companies. The principal railroad competition, therefore, was between distant major centers, wherein the shipper had a choice of through routes between Chicago or St. Louis and Atlantic seaports.

The harnessing of electricity in the telegraph was the first hint of Mumford's *neotechnic*. Instantaneous communication was certainly a radical step, with wide ramifications in commercial and political life, but so long as this new power was confined to transmitting information rather than extending to the movement of goods and people, it functioned within a paleotechnic world dominated by the railroad. The close relation between the patterns of telegraph service and the pattern of railroads has been noted, but there was a marked difference in the internal geographic character of the two systems. Because telegraph lines and stations were so simple and cheap to build, there was soon intense competition and even extensive duplication of telegraph lines (there were three competing lines between Philadelphia and Boston and between New York City and Buffalo by 1850). Various compacts and consolidations sought a way out of debilitating rivalries. The Six Nations' Alliance (1857) and the North American Telegraph Association (1859) were fragile, incomplete attempts to establish the concept of regional territorial monopolies. Both may be seen as initiatives of corporations working privately and without government restraint to create something like a rational national system out of an almost chaotic competitive situation.

The idea of a comprehensive governmental program for transportation development was not rejected without a struggle. The Gallatin plan of 1808 was set aside because of more pressing concerns, and when it reappeared there was a noticeable shift in emphasis, reflecting an embarrassing national experience arising from those concerns. Gallatin had mentioned, almost as an afterthought, "that the facility of communications, constitutes, particularly in the United States, an important branch of national defence." It remained for the appalling difficulties attendant on the movement of goods, ordnance, and men during 1812–15 to bring that issue to the fore. Thereafter the imperative need for military roads to critical frontiers became an important feature in every national plan. As Secretary of War John C. Calhoun put it, the facts of "the late war" were "too recent to require details, and the impression too deep to be forgotten."

There was of course a prominent precedent for such undertakings in the National Road, authorized in 1802, to link the Potomac with the Ohio, and in fact federal funds had been used to hack out several minimal military tracks through the wilderness (such as Nashville to Natchez) and more of these would be authorized (such as Plattsburgh to Sacket's Harbor), but only after 1815 was the concept of a set of major highways radiating from the national capital to the national frontiers put forth as a national necessity. In addition to progressive extensions of the National Road westward, the geography of the issue became focused on two new connections: Washington to New Orleans and Washington to Buffalo, designed to connect the "seat of the General Government to . . . two frontiers which will be imminently exposed in the event of a war." Each segment was the subject of special reports, surveys of alternative routes, and separate proposals; in 1830 they were combined in one bill to construct "from North to South," from Buffalo to New Orleans, "a great interior artery" by way of Washington, "the heart" of the "body politic" (fig. 48). As earlier, the issue generated a torrent of debate. Arguments over constitutional matters and funding were compounded by geographical issues.

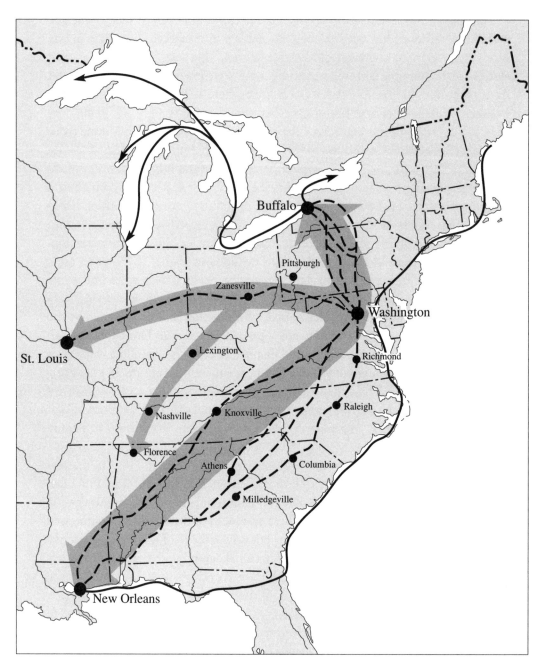

48. National Roads.
Principal connections and alternative routes surveyed.

Three alternatives were extensively assessed for the New Orleans road: a western route, by way of the Great Valley through eastern Tennessee; a middle route, traversing the Piedmont and crossing the main rivers "at the head of boat navigation"; and an eastern route along the fall line touching "the head of sloop navigation." A succession of committees attempted to weigh the advantages of each route in terms of national defense, the mail, commerce, "accommodation of population," and "political considerations" (linking the seats of government, tying East and West), but could reach no firm conclusion. What was politically intimidating for committees proved even more difficult for Congress. In the intense debates over specific routes the whole plan threatened to unravel from amendments altering the original design, such as a proposed extension from Buffalo to Lake Champlain and Boston, and a deflection of the western route to Memphis. During these years there was also a vigorous campaign in support of another major addition (or, in some views, alternative): a national road connecting Zanesville, Ohio (on the National Road), with Florence, Alabama (just below Muscle Shoals on the Tennessee), where it would connect with an earlier military track to Lake Pontchartrain and New Orleans. The main argument in support of this "great interior artery" was its utility for the movement of troops from the interior to southern frontiers. As Calhoun had explained: "Opposed in principle to a large standing army, our main reliance for defence must be on the militia, to be called out frequently from a great distance, and under the pressure of an actual invasion." Because Kentucky and Tennessee "have no frontiers of their own," their militias became the main "disposable force" to be thrown into the balance on any front. It was a bill to finance a piece of this road within Kentucky (the Maysville Road) that Andrew Jackson vetoed in 1830, ending fifteen years of attempts to create a system of national roads.

The one piece of the program that survived in this chronic controversy was the first National Road, but even it was so controversial that funding and construction of its several extensions were long delayed. Surveys from Wheeling to the Mississippi were authorized in 1820, and to the capital of Missouri in 1825; but the road did not reach Columbus until 1833, and a year later Congress turned the project over to the states. Illinois graded as far as Vandalia and projected it to Alton, but the Panic of 1837 put an end to this and all other such state enterprises. For a while there was also an attempt to marshal federal support for the Chesapeake & Ohio Canal as a parallel trunk line "peculiarly national in its character." "Passing through the centre of the Republic," linking the "seat of the National Government" with the inland navigation network, touching thereby "eleven states of the Union," it would be "at once a powerful bond of Union . . . in a time of peace— and, in war, the most efficient means of national defence." Such a role dictated a larger-than-ordinary size, and the C&O was designed for a considerably larger capacity than the Erie Canal (just nearing completion).

The concept of national roads and canals of course was more than military in its intent; it always included the transport of mail and persons to "facilitate the administration of Government: and more especially, in a country like ours, to make known, by a rapid circulation, the political disquisitions relative to public measures." In a "political system of confederate Governments," especially, "any thing calculated to facilitate the intercourse between the several States, may be considered as a complement of the system." Hence it was common to emphasize the need "to connect the seat of the Federal Government, by the shortest lines of communications, with the capitals and great cities of the several states" as well as with "the most exposed and remote frontiers." The route of the National Road beyond the Ohio River was thus directed through four state capitals; the long-advocated Atlantic Seaboard turnpike was to pass "through the capitals of the States south of Washington toward the seat of government in Florida"; the Zanesville-Florence Road would pass through Nashville (but in Kentucky through Lexington rather than Frankfort). Under the Board of Engineers for Internal Improvements, army surveyors reconnoitered and submitted maps, plans, and estimates on dozens of routes in addition to these main axes, but in the end no comprehensive system was federally funded.

Such a national program was not only thwarted by constitutional scruples and political squabbles, it was overtaken by technology. As early as 1819 Calhoun pointed to the sudden new importance of steamboats, "now introduced on almost all of our great rivers." By means of the Mississippi "aided by the force of steam", an "irresistible force" could be concentrated "at once" to any point along the southern frontier. Just such a possibility was soon brought to bear against the very concept of national military roads; Mr. Carson of North Carolina ridiculed the whole idea of federal roads to New Orleans and the gulf: "What! bring men from the State of Ohio across the states of Kentucky and Tennessee? Aye, and across the Ohio river, too, with its current teeming with steamboats ready to waft the soldiers and provisions to the point of destination." Such, also, was the point of the Tennessee congressman's amendment to divert that road to Memphis, "where the steamboats are passing every hour in the day and night." Furthermore, "the powerful agency of steam" was soon offering another alternative. Carson chided the Virginia chairman of the House committee for his support of military roads and his obsession with the C&O Canal when it was apparent that the railroad was "a system of road intercommunication" superior to anything yet "devised by human ingenuity." His was apparently the only congressional voice on record that spring of 1830 to declare the turnpike and canal age over ("exploded") and the railroad revolution at hand, but within a few years the railroad mania would sweep over the land and with it the need to rethink national transportation strategies.

The central government, as already noted, provided important assistance to railroad development as it had to roads and canals, but no new comprehensive program on the order of the Gallatin plan was drawn up and debated in Congress. The nearest thing to such a scheme was the "System of Railroads" tirelessly promoted by General Edmund Pendleton Gaines. Gaines was a Tennessee resident much involved in local commercial promotions. He was a widely experienced career officer who had served in wars and on every frontier except the Atlantic coast and had supervised army work on rivers and roads, but he was also an assertive and controversial figure who became notorious as a man ready to prescribe radical changes on a vast scale for the security of the nation. As early as 1826 he was arguing for the replacement of most permanent fortifications with a system of steam-propelled floating batteries supported by a system of canals and turnpike roads radiating from the central inland states. In 1830 he turned to railroads, the "greatest improvement or discovery known to military history" which "is destined soon to produce an entire change in the mode and manner of military operations." He was active in various railroad promotions, instrumental in getting army engineers to survey several routes from Memphis to the Atlantic, and was an honored guest on the inaugural run of the Tuscumbia Railroad around Muscle Shoals in 1835. By that time he was drawing up a program for a system of railroads radiating to army posts along the entire western frontier. Three years later he had expanded this scheme into "A System of Rail Roads, leading from Kentucky and Tennessee—the two great Military States of the Union, embracing the principal disposible force of the Republic—to the six grand Divisions of the National Frontier" (fig. 49).

Although his detractors could point to a self-serving emphasis upon Memphis and the "central states," Gaines's rationale was grounded in the familiar geographical logic that the Kentucky and Tennessee militias constituted the chief "disposable force" that might be shuttled rapidly by railroad or steamboat to any frontier. These states embodied the secure heart of a nation surrounded by enemies, and Memphis was the key place: the highest point upriver "at which navigation has never been interrupted by ice," and

> the position at which the *greatest number of efficient volunteers*, with the greatest quantity of *Iron-Lead-Coal-Hemp-Leather-Horses-Cattle-Timber & Lumber* of all kinds necessary for *Floating Batteries, Steam ships of war, Gun carriages & all other purposes for an Armory, arsenal or Naval Depot*, together with an everlasting supply of every description of *Subsistence needed for one million men*, and the same number of draught or dragoon horses annually—all which supplies can be obtained in the valleys of the Mississippi & its principal tributaries, and transported to Memphis *in a shorter period of time and at less expense than at any other spot in America.*

Gaines's proposals received a cool reception in the War Department; undeterred, he lobbied aggressively for them with public officials, sent a memorial to

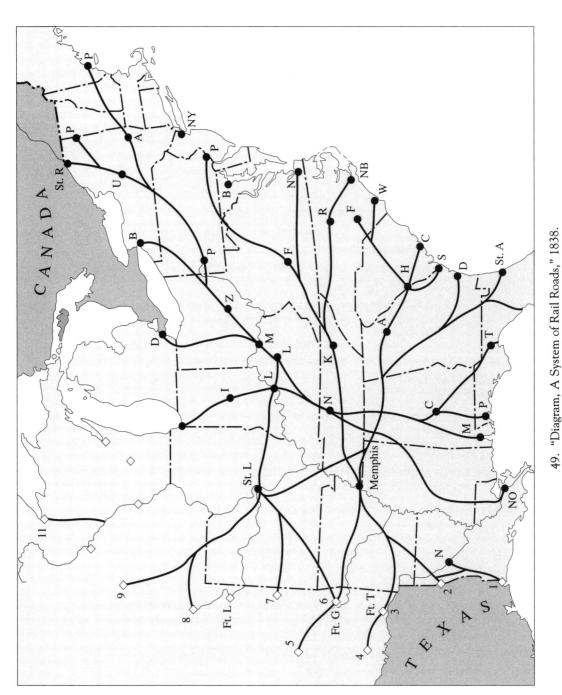

49. "Diagram, A System of Rail Roads," 1838.

Adapted to a modern base map from the original by Edmund Pendleton Gaines in the National Archives. The numbers refer to the line of existing or recommended army forts on the western frontier.

Congress, and appealed personally to the secretary of War. He could hardly have endeared himself to his fellow officers and superiors by claiming that his plan "will be a *thousand times more certain*—and infinitely less costly in *money, human life,* and *national honor than any former means of national defence*" and asserting that anyone with an ounce of sense would recognize that the arrival of "steam power" spelled an end to "the *quackery* of old European systems . . . with which we have been encumbered, as if with a millstone about our necks." Gaines was a rancorous person who flouted the system within which he served (Winfield Scott came to believe him insane). Insisting that all who opposed him were animated by party and personal interests, it is not surprising that he made little headway with his grand system. Furthermore, our knowledge of history and human institutions tells us that military establishments and politicians tend to respond to new realities reluctantly and most likely only under emergency pressures and after bloody experience. More important, from our perspective, is the fundamental flaw in Gaines's geopolitical thinking. His system of railroads had a geographical logic, but it was more that of an abstract "spatial geography" than of the actual human (and political) geography of the nation. The Gaines plan was a center-periphery design, wherein the center was the invulnerable core area in the territorial heart of the nation, the periphery all the exposed frontiers. Militarily, one could give way on the periphery while awaiting reinforcements and counterattack from the center; his arguments for the strategic significance of Memphis specifically accepted the possibility of losing Boston and the arsenals and navy yards at nearby Watertown, Charleston, and Springfield. But no national government could embrace a strategy that allowed the loss, even temporarily, of these and other seaboard centers. Such a plan put the most populous portions of the country at peril. In terms of manpower and ordnance the real core of the nation was anchored on the Northeast, not in the Mississippi Valley. Furthermore, inspection of Gaines's railroad map reveals some curious features. While his southern routes seem to reflect those already surveyed or under serious discussion, his lines drawn to the northern and eastern frontiers are flourishes with little relation to the realities of terrain, canals, railroads, or even major cities. His system shows no railroad connection to Cincinnati, New York, or Baltimore (and ignores the B&O, under construction to Wheeling), nor to Boston or Washington, which two, astonishingly, are not even on the map. Even though in some textual versions he makes some vague reference to tying in with local systems, and even allowing for greater familiarity with recent developments in some regions than others (but he had served in war on the St. Lawrence frontier), it is hard to account for—or excuse—such aberrations. On such evidence the Gaines plan appears to be a geographical design so warped by regional and hometown obsessions and fanatic personal promotion as not to have merited serious national debate. The man *was* prescient with reference to some of the realities of the new technological age, but as actual facilities appeared and their power was demonstrated in daily commerce, even conservative military minds could recognize important new potentials. By 1856 the quartermaster general stated: "I can safely say that the rivers, canals, and railroads, with their present means of transportation, taken together, have more than quadrupled the military power of the western States for defensive purposes, by the facilities they afford for the rapid and certain movement of troops and military supplies."

Steam power did not immediately take over the transport of mail. A House report of 1840 investigating "irregularities" in the New York–New Orleans mail found problems with all forms of transport, in various segments, and especially with river service. Schedules even between major cities on trunk lines were unreliable and anything like regular service to lesser centers was impracticable. It is "unreasonable to expect heavy steamboats to stop at every small office on the banks of the rivers to exchange mails when there is no other business"—indeed, some post offices had been "procured at mere woodyards for the evident and only purpose of compelling the boats to stop." The report concluded that for letter correspondence horseback was "a mode of conveyance not surpassed in certainty by any hitherto invented." It was apparently in that year that the first railway post office car (for the sorting of mail en route) was put in service (between Norwich and Worcester). Congress had already decreed all railways to be post routes; within a few years routes had been classified and rates standardized, and postal contracts became a routine form of government aid to railroads. Thereafter steamboat mail service receded rapidly as rails were extended. Meanwhile express companies specializing in the rapid delivery of small packages had mushroomed along the main routes, and although technically prohibited from carrying letters, they so encroached upon the official postal service and so exposed its high rates that in 1851 the postal service shifted from pricing by distance to the simple three-cent stamp for any destination within the United States (an idea borrowed from Britain, but radical in its application to so vast an area).

By the late 1850s the entire national population—excepting only the Far West and Texas—was within six days' travel of New York City or Philadelphia, a remarkable compression of the operational distance-scale of the nation. Americans had always been on the move ("if God were suddenly to call the world to judgment," said a visiting Spaniard in 1847, "He would surprise two-thirds of the population of the United States on the road like ants"), but large numbers of them were now moving with unprecedented ease and efficiency. It had not been a simple progression; each new facility had brought its own special benefits: the smoothness of the slow canal boat a welcome relief from the bruising jolts of the stagecoach; the best of the steamboats, with their lounges, saloons, staterooms, dining rooms, and ever-attendant servants, setting an entirely new standard of luxury travel. The railroads had not equaled that; most were still somewhat jerky, soot-begrimed affairs, but the best were rapidly improving (George M. Pullman tried out his first sleeping car on the Chicago & Alton in 1859). It was of course their speed and regularity of service that had transformed travel. The very focus and intensity of the experience had changed, the detail of the roadside or waterside landscape dissolving in a blur to be reformulated at a new scale and with a kinetic quality, giving a real sense of annihilating space. Such acceleration altered the sense of place; towns "were no longer spatially individual or autonomous: they were points in the circulation of traffic that made them accessible . . . , places visited by the traveler became increasingly similar to the commodities that were part of the same circulation system." Although midcentury America was still in the earliest stages of this transformation, it was discernible: both the exhilaration and the stress were part of public discussion. Furthermore, the railroad forced into being new modes and a whole new scale of management. The train was an unprecedented "machine ensemble" in which roadway and vehicle were technically conjoined; and the railroad company was a new geographic phenomenon, a highly complicated, carefully coordinated linear system extending over hundreds of miles. Learning to handle such things under the pressures of investors and competitors was intensive practice for a truly national—continental—scale of life in the modern world.

Steam had certainly quickened the pulse of the nation, but it had not yet linked quite all of the seats of government. Washington was connected by railroad to the capitals of every state east of the Mississippi except Michigan and Florida. Baton Rouge, Little Rock, and St. Paul were still served only by steamboat. No rail line as yet tied Texas into the national system, and of course with the general assumption that California and Oregon must be bound into the Union with iron rails, the idea of a national transportation plan suddenly reappeared in the 1850s—and with it came all those intransigent political, financial, and geographical issues that had bedeviled leaders and legislators during the first thirty years of the century.

All arguments in support of a national transportation program rested, ultimately, on the general proposition that ease of communication and frequency of intercourse among the different parts of the federation were the best insurance of the Union. Jefferson had said so, Gallatin had stressed the point in the introduction to his great report—"no other single operation, within the power of government, came more effectively tend to strengthen and perpetuate [the] union"—and it was a theme tirelessly repeated, adjusted to changes in the scale of the need and new modes of communications. At the outset, this relationship rested on the assumption that economic interdependence was the most powerful cement of union. Gallatin's plan was part of a larger strategy to ensure that the United States became one vast national market in which the specialized productions of each region were exchanged for those of others. It was thereby tied to, and in important circles tainted by, concurrent promotion of a national bank and related facilities. With the defeat or deflection of such national systems the rationale became rather more diffuse, simply stressing the assumed virtues of interregional contacts.

That this common reference to strengthening the union was more than a cliché seems apparent from the many references to *disunion* that appear from an early date. Thus Calhoun, arguing in support of his program in 1819, said "We are great, and rapidly—I was about to say fearfully—growing. This is our pride and our danger; our weakness and our strength." Although he recognized that the American people had proved that a republic could thrive in so large a frame, "we are under the most imperious obligation to counteract every tendency to disunion. . . . Let us, then, bind the republic together with a perfect system of roads and canals. Let us conquer space." Eight years later the Mercer Committee on roads and canals, while noting "that the possible separation of the United States into distinct political communities should never be adverted to," hailed the steamboat as removing "the ancient doubt . . . among the most sceptical as to the practicality of enlarging the sphere of Republican Government, to almost any territorial extent, without endangering its freedom or durability." By the 1840s it became commonplace to aver that such remarkable improvements in communication would "give to the republic one national heart and one national mind." Within a few more years the railroad was hailed as the decisive instrument for union on an unprecedented scale: "The vision of an ocean-bound Republic is now a reality," exclaimed Mr. Yates of Illinois in 1852, and "the iron bands of commerce" ensure "impregnable bonds of union" because "wherever the iron horse travels, he will carry, not only the rich production of our soil, but our laws, our liberty, and our religion." Thus

> the fears of disunion growing out of the increased extension of territory no longer alarm the patriot. It will be no matter how far Charleston is from New York when, sir, they can have constant communication with each other in a few days. Rome, by her military prowess, spread her empire over the world; and her eagles winged their triumphant flight over conquered provinces; but these provinces were beyond the reach of the Roman lawgiver. The eloquence of Cicero thundered in the forum, but reached no further than the ears of the conscript fathers and the Roman populace. But not so with us, when the message of the President can be read in the most distant State on the day of its delivery. Not so with us when we travel by steam, print by electricity, and talk by lightning.

An eloquent oration, but Mr. Yates never confronts the fact—so apparent in the great forum in which *he* was thundering—that people in the different sections of the American empire might not like what was being communicated in presidential messages and congressional debates with such remarkable efficiency. Early in the century "cementing the union" usually referred to the need to bind East and West together across the mountains. By Mr. Yates's time "increased extension of territory" was not so much the cause for alarm as were the strains that had appeared along another divide—as his reference to Charleston confirms. Many years earlier an opponent of the "roads and canals" bill of his day ridiculed the whole idea of roads as a "remedy" for disunion. If indeed they were, he said, the priorities were all wrong: before building to New Orleans, Buffalo, or wherever, you had better "encircle South Carolina."

The failure of the United States to establish some sort of transportation plan for the common good, in spite of the imperative need voiced by so many prominent spokesmen over so long a time, was the result of many factors. The constitutional issue arose from conflicting interpretations of the power of the central government to undertake such works within the body of the states, a federal question that became entangled in issues of governmental powers over property—and eventually, by implication, over slavery.

Lurking within the arguments unleashed by this long succession of proposals was the issue of "centralization" and all the varied fears that that political concept generated in the young republic. Years before he was president, Madison had warned that "enlarging federal power to promote 'general welfare' necessarily led to greater *executive* prerogative, patronage, corruption, and tyranny." Much of the successive committee efforts to define a workable bill focused on methods and agencies for the actual allocation of funds for specific projects. Whatever the formula, politicians tended to receive such proposals "not so much as a design for a [transportation] system, but as an invitation to the public trough." The cynic will assume that such a response is inherent in the nature of politicians, but there was also something more involved, inherent in the nature of the general issue itself: route decisions are place decisions; every specific project was an exercise in geographical discrimination, favoring some places over other places. Moreover, such choices were considered to be powerful and indelible, for every major road and canal shaped the geography of its region and thereby the pattern for the future. As Larson has emphasized, local representatives believed that "it mattered absolutely . . . who designed and constructed the roads and canals, because that first conquest of space would fix forever the opportunities for growth enjoyed by distant places within the nation." In no other issue, therefore, were geography and politics so intricately and locally exposed and debated—and repeatedly stalemated. The pork barrel appeared so prominently because Congress found it so difficult and often impossible to make such fundamental geographic decisions. It was not a current version of the Gallatin plan that Madison vetoed but a bill that allocated federal funds to the states for internal improvements in proportion to their population, a formula that completely subverted any possibility of a national design.

The word *centralization* had both political and geographic connotations. To cry out against turning the United States into "one grand, magnificent, consolidated empire" was not only to oppose the concentration of political power in Washington but to oppose the corollary tendency of making that particular place the main geographic nexus of national development. Looking to European examples it seemed almost a geopolitical law that the capital city be the primate city in every important regard. To a European observer, such as William Newnham Blane, it was a surprise to find that "the worst feature in the conduct of the [federal] government is, that the members, arriving from different parts of the Union, have very often shown a decided hostility to the place." He was appalled at the indifference or opposition to works of "general benefit" (such as the National Road) and at the jealous struggle among the various states to obtain the national mint, the bank, and the military college. "Now had all these establishments been fixed at Washington," he said, "they would have been under the immediate eye of Government, and would have added to the importance and ornament of the metropolis." But Mr. Blane, like most Europeans, was thinking in the familiar terms of London and Paris, of kingdoms and empires rather than of a federal republic; most Americans did not want an ornamented metropolis at the center of their world. In France all roads radiated from Paris; in the United States there was a determined and successful effort not to have them radiate from Washington. In the Gallatin plan Washington was the junction of the two great inland arteries: the north-south Atlantic seaboard turnpike and the axis to be formed by the C&O Canal, National Road, and Ohio River, but these were only built in fragments and did not become the thoroughfares envisioned. The 1820s plans for national military roads would have greatly magnified the centrality of Washington, but these, too, came to naught. It seems reasonable to infer that the latter schemes would have gotten much more support had the country actually been in danger, but Americans felt increasingly secure in the main body of their country during these decades. And while Washington might be the command center, it was not really central to the main sources of military strength, to manpower, ordnance, supplies, and subsistence. Much of that lay to the north.

This imbalance in the basic geographical morphology of the nation underlay much of the difficulty and division over such national programs. The core of the country was anchored, as it always had been, on the New York City–Philadelphia nuclear area, with increasingly substantial extensions westward to Buffalo and Pittsburgh. When Mr. Hemphill of Pennsylvania pointed out how the Chesapeake & Ohio Canal would, in conjunction with the Erie Canal, New Jersey canals, and the Chesapeake & Delaware, create "an island in the heart of the Union," he surely won few supporters outside that favored area since most of his fellow legislators would not acknowledge that to be the true "heart of the Union" and would certainly resist enhancing it in any way. The fact that the United States had no single "natural" center and several alternative routes to its most obvious central axis, the Ohio River, meant that there would be keen sensitivity to any perceived discrimination in favor of any particular place or route. Calhoun counted on just such jealous self-interest to help realize his program: "The interest of commerce and the spirit of rivalry between the great Atlantic cities will do much to perfect the means of intercourse with the west. The most important lines of communication appear to be from Albany to the lakes; from Philadelphia, Baltimore, Washington, and Richmond to the Ohio river; and from Charleston and Augusta to the Tennessee." In the heady flush of the new railroad age the sphere of such competition seemed to be enlarged in scale and possibilities. A ruler on a map would show that Charleston was the same distance from Cincinnati as was Philadelphia, and at a South Carolina rally in 1836 it was pointed out that a railroad would allow "the South . . . to compete with eastern cities for the trade of Ohio, and, with a branch to Louisville, for the trade of Indiana. The connection with Cincinnati, from a political point of view, meant detaching a powerful confederate from the East, as far as commercial and social relations would do it, and might keep Ohio a friend to the South on the slavery question." The hope was utterly unrealistic, because Charleston could never compete with the great Atlantic ports of the North for the Ohio Valley trade, but the proclaimed purpose was at least an open recognition that the interests of different centers, states, and regions were not only competitive but could be antithetical in fundamental ways. That truth challenged all those clichés about good roads and canals being "to the body politic what the veins and arteries are to the body natural" and "whatever benefits one of the parts is a benefit to the whole." Such a view, said Mr. Barbour of Virginia forthrightly, was "too lofty a magnanimity, too expansive a patriotism, for me to pretend to," when the real truth was that "the different States have different and opposing interests" and "the moment this [central] Government attempts to control and regulate the whole, then the conflict begins." Larson's conclusion that "a national system . . . promised to consolidate the union . . . and that is precisely why no program was ever passed," would seem to be confirmed by a geographical as well as a more specifically political perspective. Whatever the number of projects and mileage of facilities distributed among the various constituencies, there was no prospect of remolding the human geography of the United States so as to equalize the proportionate advantage of its many cities, states, and regions. On the contrary, every national design purporting to benefit the whole seemed likely, whatever its intent, to consolidate further the ties between the northeastern seaboard and the West.

Furthermore, historical changes affected geographical as well as constitutional matters. Those who would design a transportation framework for the United States during these years were working within an unstable context. Large additions to the national territory and the continually expanding margins of settlement kept generating new needs and proposals. At best, Congress might select a few "grand and leading" projects, for the human geography was being altered day by day and it was "impossible to foresee all the channels through which our inland commerce may take its direction." So, too, each new technology altered the possibilities and forced reassessment of previous plans. The rapid emergence of first the steamboat and then the railroad seemed to undermine old assumptions, imperil established centers and trafficways, and open up such a range of new possibilities as to make politicians leery of committing themselves to vast expenditures to fix in place any specific facility "for the good of the whole."

Finally, and most important, transportation facilities were being extended year by year, often at an astonishing rate, through the initiatives of the several states and, especially, of private corporations (often aided in various ways by governmental favors). In spite of the absence of a formal national program—or perhaps *because* of such absence—Americans had indeed "conquered space" to an extent far beyond what Calhoun or any other leader of 1819 could have imagined. The 1860 census listed more than 5,000 miles of canals and slack-water navigation and nearly 31,000 miles of railroad in operation. If the overall pattern was not the closely integrated, balanced, nonredundant national system some may have wished, it surely represented a vigorous response to national needs, for no sizable settled district of the main body of the nation lay beyond the enlivening touch of those modern services. If it was not a truly national network designed specifically to bind "the whole community together with the strongest ligatures," its lines were laced through most of the Republic and, by all expectations, would soon reach the remainder. Although created by many agencies and reflecting many special and limited interests, the overall pattern had a good deal of bold long-range strategic planning embedded in it. By assiduously preventing consolidation and centralization under the power of a government seated in the national capital, political leaders had left the design of the American transportation system very largely in the hands of "conservative metropolitan capitalists" seated in a few great Atlantic seaports. In time, after further consolidation among themselves, it would become much more apparent how centralized and national their designs could be.

10. Creating New Centers: Cities and Systems of Cities

One of the most notable features of this great era of expansion, widely remarked by citizens and visitors alike, was how new cities seemed to "spring up amidst the forests with inconceivable rapidity." Captain Basil Hall from England, passing through Rochester in 1827 shortly after the opening of the Erie Canal, sketched a representative scene: "Everything in this bustling place appeared to be in motion. The very streets seemed to be starting up of their own accord, ready-made, and looking as fresh as new, as if they had been turned out of the workmen's hands but an hour before—or that a great boxful of new houses had been sent by steam from New York, and tumbled out on the half-cleared land." There were "great warehouses, without window sashes, but half-filled with goods"; mills full of people "at work below stairs while at top the carpenters were busy nailing on the planks of the roof"; everywhere the streets were "crowded with people, carts, stages, cattle, pigs, far beyond the reach of numbers;—and as all these were lifting up their voices together in keeping with the clatter of hammers, the ringing of axes, and the creating of machinery, there was a fine concert, I assure you!"

Rochester had actually been founded some years earlier, but it became a real boomtown only when this obvious fine mill site at the Falls of the Genesee was crossed by the new east-west trunk line. In general the Erie Canal was simply a major improvement in a sequence of trafficways following this natural lowland cutting across New York State, but it immediately displayed how even a realignment of only a few miles in the avenue of commerce could greatly affect settlement systems and urban futures. Bisected by this vital waterway, upstart Syracuse, Rochester, and Lockport quickly surpassed Cazenovia, Geneva, and Canandaigua, towns which had been impressing a generation of travelers as elegant places assured of prosperity.

Town-founding and speculation were exercises in geographical prediction: which locations would become the main centers within the developing commercial networks of the region and nation? It was commonly accepted that "the forces of geography fundamentally determined the success or failure" of the attempts to create cities in the wilderness. Such language was ambiguous. On the one hand, "geography" most obviously referred to the "lay of the land" and its particular physical features. If at times it seemed as if every nuance of nature was seized upon as a propitious site for a town, bolder features that seemed certain to channel traffic were the most coveted, such as river junctions, falls, great bends, and bridgepoints; lake harbors, promontories, and isthmuses; valley corridors and central points within basins and embayments. On the other hand, it was also understood that nature was not a simple template and that when fully settled the human geography of any region would not be just a reflection of its natural surface but would have been shaped by human choices of exact sites, routes, and activities. And because the results did depend, very basically, on human choice and initiatives, getting there first and getting something under way, the power of a *headstart* in shaping the context of subsequent initiations was also important: as one traveler (visiting Louisville and vicinity) put the common understanding, once "capital and population" have fixed a location "they will keep it. Experience proves that a city once became populous and wealthy, will in the ordinary course of events triumph over natural disadvantages; and by means of capital and industry, maintain its superiority over neighboring towns more favorably situated." Success in town-founding and city-building was an inexact science but a generalized process. It required a keen eye for and careful study of advantageous *sites* (exact location) and *situations* (broader contexts), early and vigorous *promotion,* and tireless attention to whatever *influence* could be brought to bear to enhance that place at the expense of all competing places.

The vast arena of the American experiment makes it necessary to recognize that this kind of geographic prediction and competition was conducted at several scales. Viewed within the confines of a region, a close reading of the map might reveal many attractive locales for modest speculation. For example, in 1804 Judge William Cooper (James Fenimore's father), seated comfortably in his own attractive village in the midst of his lands just north of the Catskills, nominated a dozen undeveloped sites in frontier New York as places "which cannot possibly fail to become important, unless crippled by their proprietors." A sample of these potential "emporia" suggests the kinds of locations that gleamed in the eye of the speculator:

> the mouth of Buffalo Creek [Buffalo, 74,214]
> the straits of Niagara below the falls [Lewiston, 1,014]
> the first falls of the Genesee [Rochester, 43,877]
> the greater Sodus (bay) [Sodus Point, 200]
> the Oswego falls [Fulton, 3,192]
> the head of navigation of the Black River [Dexter, 429]

The appended names of the towns that did emerge at these sites, together with their populations in the state census of 1855, suggest how immensely varied the results could actually be—differences surely beyond the power of proprietors.

When speculators turned their attention to the whole transappalachian West, they saw an essentially empty wilderness. The scattering of trading posts and small towns on various waterway sites, such as Detroit, Vincennes, Kaskaskia, St. Louis, and Prairie du Chien, seemed to offer no sure guide to the shape of the western urban pattern. New Orleans was the only substantial center firmly fixed in place, and developmental strategists focused on the great natural features of the grand trunk steam: the Forks of the Ohio, the Falls of the Ohio, and the Confluence of the Ohio and Mississippi. The Gallatin report brought a number of other locales into the strategic picture: the terminals of the several transappalachian turnpikes, canal ports on the Lower Lakes, and the junctions of each of the connecting canal-river routes between the Great Lakes and the Ohio or Mississippi. And almost decade by decade the steamboat and the railroad would each further alter the strategic value of these and other places within the rapidly developing networks and contentions.

On closer view, even the boldest of these apparently "natural sites" did not dictate an exact location or ensure a singularity of development. The Forks of the Ohio was a location as strategic in its commercial potential as it had been in military operations (fig. 50). A small town emerged on the point of land in the shadow of Fort Pitt before the Revolution, and a formal plan for a larger one was laid out immediately after. But the simple geography of any major river junction suggests the possibilities of rival centers on the opposite banks of the joining streams as well; and these soon appeared at the Forks, one of which, the town of Allegheny, initiated by the Commonwealth of Pennsylvania, was soon thriving (its annexation by Pittsburgh in 1907 added 107,000 to the corporate metropolis).

Similarly, because the Falls of the Ohio was in fact a two-mile stretch of usually unnavigable rapids, it offered four obvious sites: at the portage terminals above and below the obstruction on either side of the river. In fact, six distinct towns (and several more plats) eventually took on some substance in this strategic locale (fig. 51). These emerged as a sequence of pairs, reflecting changing circumstances in river traffic. The first two, Louisville (1779) and Clarksville (1783), were laid out above the falls on the south bank and below the falls on the north bank, respectively, by George Rogers Clark, who had encamped there with his frontier militia during forays against the British at Vincennes and Kaskaskia. As river traffic increased, Jeffersonville (1802) and Shippingport (1803) emerged on the banks opposite the first two towns. In 1814 proposals for a canal bypassing the river obstructions prompted the laying out of Portland and New Albany opposite each other just downriver from any presumed canal terminus, and these two were soon thriving on the new steamboat services even before the canal was finished. The differential growth of these half-dozen places was a reflection not only of their unequal command of river commerce (related in part to the nature of the river channel and dockage safety) but of their success in tapping the trade of extensive hinterlands: Louisville commanding that of the long-productive Bluegrass Basin; New Albany reaching westward into the rapidly developing Wabash Valley.

That the largest city in the American West was not at one of these boldest of natural features of the River Ohio attested to the importance of hinterland control. Even if not so obvious as the Forks, the Falls, or the Confluence, the great northerly bend of the Ohio was readily seen as an attractive locale. But here, too, there were several specific sites and no certainty as to which would prove the best. Indeed, John Cleve Symmes, proprietor of the Miami Purchase, platted his towns at the mouths of the two largest streams flowing in from the north (North Bend on the Miami and Columbia on the Little Miami) and sold off the site of Cincinnati in between. Cincinnati's promoters regarded its position opposite the mouth of the Licking River as their greatest advantage, but radial access into Ohio and Indiana would soon prove to be far more important than any route into Kentucky.

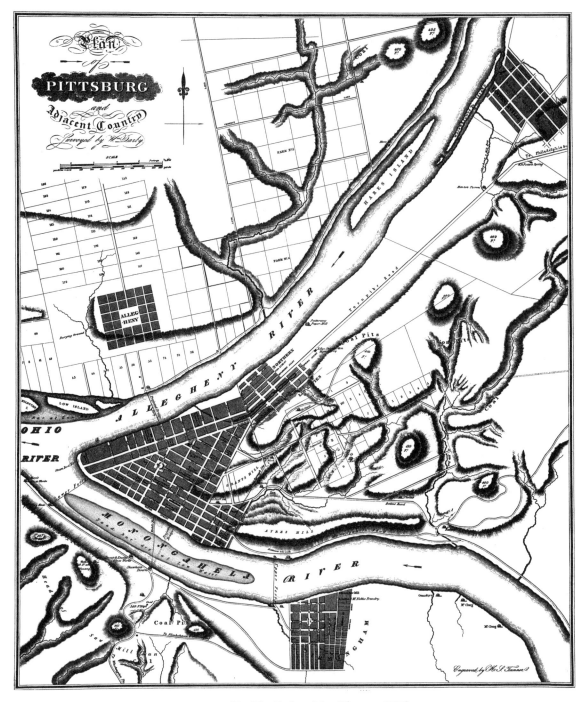

50. The Forks of the Ohio, c. 1815.

Initiated in 1784 by the heirs of William Penn and named for the British statesman who a generation earlier had secured the place from the French, Pittsburgh was soon a thriving industrial as well as transportation center. William Darby's nicely detailed map of the awkward plat, designed to serve two riverfronts on this compelling but constricted site, identifies coal pits, foundries, glassworks, sawmills, cotton mills, a paper mill, gristmill, nail manufactory, and steamboat yard; and the appearance of *Birmingham,* laid out on the Monongahela by an Englishman in 1811, and *Manchester,* just down the Ohio (off the map), proclaimed the industrial expectations of a location as strategic to new resources as it had been to military operations. (Courtesy of John W. Reps, from the Geography and Map Division, Library of Congress)

And, indeed, the city potential of what seemed to many persons to be the greatest strategic location of all would prove, time and again, to be chimerical. Prominent in the objectives of one of the earliest speculative companies in Transappalachia was a town to be laid out "as near the Junction of the Ohio and Mississippi as the nature of the ground will admit." The Revolution canceled that effort, but the same idea reappeared in the "Town of America," touted in 1809 as certain to be the premier commercial center of inland America; in the town of Cairo, laid out in 1818 on the "Nile of America" and named for what was claimed to be its obvious analogue; in a new Cairo, replatted in 1835, extravagantly promoted in England (and scathingly derided by visitor Charles Dickens), shored up by lavish private and state investment, but attaining only 1,756 people by 1857 and these attracted more by the new prospect of railroad than by river commerce. For some puzzling reason, nature's grandest junction seemed to defy the geographical laws of city growth.

The other major confluence locale of western waters became, for a short while, the scene of a vigorous, if always uneven, rivalry. The city of St. Louis had a long head start, an excellent site on a low bluff alongside the main Mississippi channel, and an advantageous situation just below the junctions with the Missouri and the Illinois. From among a number of speculative ventures the town of Alton, on the Illinois side where the long wall of bluffs to the north gives way to the rich bottomlands flaring inland along the east side of the Mississippi, began to emerge as a leader. Just as enterprising Yankees a generation earlier had founded Troy on the eastern bank of the Hudson just upriver from Albany and set out to challenge the Anglo-Dutch merchant dominance over the trade of that great pivotal location, so eastern entrepreneurs (backed in part by Cincinnati merchants) challenged the Anglo-French establishment of St. Louis. They worked tirelessly to make Alton the primary focus of turnpikes and railroads, and their position (analogous to that of Troy) with reference to the Lake Michigan–Illinois River waterway (which they assured would be the western equivalent of the famed Erie Canal), and the possibility of intercepting traffic from the upper Mississippi caused many people to agree that Alton might well become preeminent in this grand central locale of inland America.

To the north, strategic sites on the lower Great Lakes would in time prompt similar speculations. With the completion of the Erie Canal, Buffalo became the grand western emporium its founder had assured his Dutch banker bosses it would in time become. The rapidly extending tentacles of commerce directed attention to the other end of Lake Erie, where there were at least three plausible contenders for principal entrepôt. Detroit had a long head start, but it was twenty miles upriver from the end of the lake and part of its old hinterland was now foreign ground. Maumee (Toledo) and Sandusky harbors, each with the assurance of canal connections south to the Ohio, appeared to many persons to be better prospects.

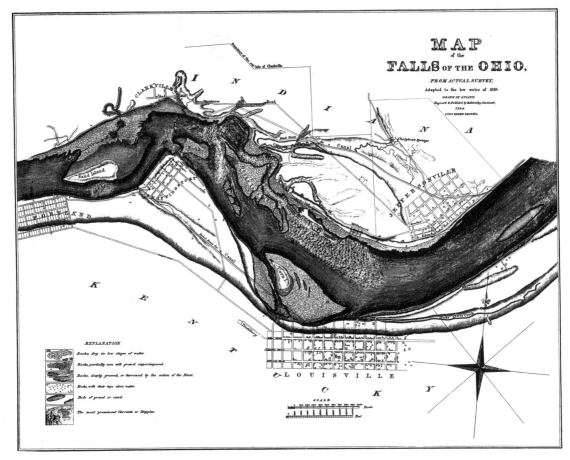

51. The Falls of the Ohio, 1824.

Five of the six townsites are shown, with New Albany just downriver off the map opposite Portland. Louisville's leadership would not be harmed by completion of the canal along the south bank route shown. These stereotypical town plats give no hint of a vanished variant. As John Reps has detailed, William Henry Harrison, governor of Indiana Territory, influenced the proprietor of Jeffersonville to follow the ideas of its namesake and leave every other square open for "turf and trees" as a specific against the generation and spread of yellow fever. These Jeffersonian ideals, however, soon succumbed to speculative fever, and in 1817 the town was replatted into ordinary lots. (Courtesy of John W. Reps, from the Geography and Map Division, Library of Congress)

That the city near the southern end of Lake Michigan became the greatest boomtown of all—the wonder child of urban America, for several decades the fastest growing city on earth—was a surprise to contemporary students of such matters. The location was not an obvious site in early American visions of the West. The town was initiated not by private speculators but by the State of Illinois, which directed its canal commissioners to lay out a town on the Chicago River for speculative sale in the hope of raising money to help finance a Michigan-Illinois canal. The original plat of 1830 did not actually include the harbor or any lake frontage. Work on the canal did not begin for another six years, but after a modest start, speculators did begin to pour in and fueled a frantic boom, which was only momentarily deflated by the Panic of 1837 (fig. 52). Such activity represented the vanguard of the northern migration stream, and many other towns were founded at this time, among which Michigan City and Milwaukee were for a while regarded as Chicago's contenders for preeminence. Railroads, not canals, would make Chicago the great "Key of the West," and that is why its location was not so obvious in early speculative assessments that had focused on advantageous points on nature's passageways.

In that pioneer perspective on western waters, one of the earliest towns of Transappalachia was an anomaly. Lexington was inland, eighty miles from the Ohio, twenty-five miles from Frankfort, the head of the very limited navigation on the Kentucky River. But Lexington was not founded by people ranging inland from the big rivers, and it was not a speculation of continental strategists; rather, it was established by Virginian migrants in the midst of the wonderfully attractive Bluegrass Basin that opened out after the long wagon haul through the mountains. Lexington emerged as the seat of influential families, a place of culture and prestige, "capital" of this New Virginia, the "Athens of the West." The wealth generated from its productive hinterland sustained its preeminence for several decades; Lexington was not surpassed by Louisville until well into the steamboat age. But when one form of steam power was soon followed by another, Lexington began to vie desperately for railroad connections to shore up its commercial position. These were eventually obtained, but they could do little to offset Lexington's marginal position within the larger regional context.

Most early railroads were built as adjuncts of waterways, as portages or tap lines binding ports and hinterlands. This quickly made them primary instruments in local urban competitions, and in providing iron pathways more directly through the country, railroads also fostered the founding of many new towns, because speculators readily adapted the old axiom and proclaimed that wherever a railroad line crossed a turnpike, river, canal, or another railroad, there, too, "is a place of business." But it took much more than that to assure growth, as many an ephemeral town and crossroads hamlet would attest. Inevitably, railroad building and real estate speculation became intimately entwined. In the West, where they were a pioneering instrument, railroads became active founders of towns. The Illinois Central became an influential innovator in such activity (even though technically prohibited by its charter), laying out thirty-three standardized town plats, spaced approximately every ten miles along its line, with Centralia as a larger center to

52. Chicago, c. 1853.

A portion of a lithograph by D. W. Moody, after a drawing by Geo. J. Robertson. As David Buisseret notes, this is Chicago "at the height of its development as a port and canal town, before the railroads had made any serious impact." The Chicago River is lined with factories and warehouses served by a variety of vessels, while the railroad lines, from the west and along the lakeshore from the south, are almost bare of such facilities. But the large level space just south of the river mouth and in front of the Illinois Central depot has just been created for large railroad yards and the erection of huge grain elevators, and the booming city will fill in all but the lands toward the far horizon in a matter of a few years. (Courtesy of the Chicago Historical Society) serve as a division point, with machine shops and other services. The standard plat was bisected by the railroad, with the north-south streets numbered, the east-west named after trees (in rigid order: Mulberry, Hickory, Walnut, Chestnut, Oak, Locust, Poplar, and Ash). Some such patterning would become routine in the later western states.

In the larger field of competition it was the trunk-line railroad, providing new or much more direct and efficient interregional connections, that became a major influence on the emerging urban hierarchy. While established river and lake cities sought to consolidate and enhance their positions by adding railroad connections, inland centers might, for the first time, aspire to become a major focus in the national system. One such place was Indianapolis. It was of course sustained by its capital functions and central position within Indiana. The National Road passed through, other roads radiated to the corners of the state, and the city leaders had put high priority on railroad connections to the Ohio and the Wabash. But as western railroad developments began to provide direct service between all the major cities, local visions and aspirations expanded to discern central Indiana as "an isthmus of dry and level land" through which east-west routes would be naturally channeled between the hilly country along the Ohio and the swamps and sandy wastes of the glaciated plains to the north. Furthermore, as these lines would necessarily be crossed by those connecting Chicago and Lake Erie ports with Cincinnati, Louisville, and Alton-St. Louis, Indianapolis leaders began to sense a new pivotal position that would make their city the "Great Railroad Center" and "wholesale emporium" for the entire West. By 1860 there were seven spokes in this railroad hub, but these were of very unequal significance and the city had been bypassed by several trunk lines. Indianapolis was no longer a mere minor outpost of Cincinnati, but neither was it a wholesale rival. Its 19,000 residents put it comfortably ahead of such Indiana competitors as Richmond, Terre Haute, and Lafayette, but it was only one of several similar cities in the West. Railroads were essential for survival but gave no assurance of triumph in urban competitions.

It was widely assumed that one great city would dominate the American interior. Cincinnati emerged as the early leader, the Queen City of the West, nearly twice as large as its nearest competitor by 1820. It increased that margin well into the 1840s, until a great spurt of growth brought St. Louis even with it (at 160,000) by 1860 (fig. 53). Cincinnati's leaders did not accept the growth of such a rival as the inevitable result of continual westward expansion. They cultivated links with merchants in Alton, Quincy, Peoria, Davenport, Galena, and other towns and sought to improve service connections so as to bypass St. Louis. Yet many people saw a compelling logic in St. Louis as the "great commercial emporium of the continent." It was central in so many respects: within the body of all the country east of the Rocky Mountains; within the narrower span of the productive West

53. Cincinnati, 1848.

This view is but one panel of a set of daguerreotypes showing the full sweep of the riverfront by W. J. Porter that are said to be "the finest examples of city panorama of their time." This is the Queen City at the peak of river activity (more than 4,000 steamboat arrivals in 1847). The broad slope suggests the normal variations in the height of the river, and great floods have already occasionally swept over this lowest river terrace solidly lined with four-story utilitarian buildings housing all sorts of shipping services. (Courtesy of the Public Library of Cincinnati and Hamilton County)

between the Appalachians and the High Plains; and midway along the course of the Mississippi and pivotal to all the great junctions of the western river system. William Gilpin's pseudo-scientific geographical rationale for the eventual shift of this service point farther westward to the junction of the Missouri and Kansas rivers (Independence and Kansas City) and his vision of a great "Centropolis" there within the Great Basin of the Mississippi—the "Amphitheatre of the World"— owed more to his grandiose boosterism than to his much proclaimed borrowings from Alexander von Humboldt.

Joseph W. Best's vision for Toledo was equally self-serving, but rather more plausible at the time. Very aware of the rapid development of a northern latitudinal axis of commerce in the 1840s, he saw Toledo as the logical focus for a fan of canals and railroads drawing the produce of the West to this head of "our great central lake" for water shipment on to the Atlantic, making use of major enlargements under way of the critical canal connections to the Hudson and on the St. Lawrence. Best acknowledged Chicago as the leading contender of his Maumee city for such a role, but when he first proclaimed his idea railroads were no more than feeder lines and Chicago was little larger than Toledo. Chicago's phenomenal growth from 5,000 inhabitants in 1840 to 109,000 twenty years later ended any such pretensions for Toledo but did not yet resolve the issue of primacy. How much of the trade of yet-to-be-developed Wisconsin and Minnesota might become tied to Milwaukee or Green Bay? Would a major entrepôt emerge on the upper Mississippi and establish direct rail connections with the East (as indeed momentarily seemed to be the case with Davenport in the boom times following completion of the railroad bridge across the Mississippi)? What service centers would arise on the middle Missouri (Kansas City, St. Joseph, Council Bluffs?) and how would these be connected into the national system? The human geography of the expanding West was still far too fluid and unpredictable to be certain as to which city—if any one— would dominate this vast region.

Of course, much more than primacy in the West was at stake in the dynamics of American city development. Although the topic received little systematic analysis, embedded in much of this booster rhetoric, intense sense of competition, and strategies pursued by individuals and civic groups were some intuitive understandings of normative patterns of settlement geography likely in a society with so few institutional constraints. There was a commonsense recognition of *urban hierarchy*: of great cities, middle-sized cities, smaller cities, towns, villages, and crossroads hamlets. Whatever the informal or arbitrary definitions of these terms as to population size and function, there was obviously some kind of order in this ranking; that is, there were fewer towns than villages, fewer small cities than towns, etc.—or so it seemed. Such differences were most obviously related to differences in the size of trade areas served and the number of services provided at each level. Later urban theorists would work out a systematic spatial patterning, a nested hierarchy of such trade centers, as a major insight into settlement geography (central place theory), but they were studying static patterns—a cross-section of an assumed completed stable system. Such logical relationships were not readily apparent a century earlier, when instability and irregularities among such categories of places were so widespread. Given the environment of the expanding nation it is not surprising that the talk and actions of urban promoters were largely concerned with the role of cities at the upper levels of any such urban ranking, with cities as *entrepôts* rather than centers serving the immediate needs of a surrounding countryside.

Entrepôts are places of collection, deposit, and shipment of one or more staple commodities in exchange for provisions, supplies, equipment, and other services provided to the entire collection area. In such relationships the exchange does not take place at each level of the hierarchy but is a direct transaction between specialized dealers in the entrepôt and producers and consumers throughout the hinterland—wholesaling, in the full sense of the term. Such trades may begin with unspecialized merchants, but as volume and regularity increase and new staples emerge, specialists appear, including bankers, brokers, and insurance agents, as well as those providing warehousing, processing, and transportation services. Such persons and their special facilities, including merchant magazines and credit agencies, constitute an *intelligence complex*, a concentration of the best knowledge of mercantile conditions in their broad tributary region. Newcomers seeking to share in an expanding trade will be strongly attracted to such a center, and so competition in wholesaling tends to cluster in established cities. If developments in some distant part of the hinterland tempt some agents to shift to a new forward location, others will likely remain in the older center and concentrate on improving efficiencies of service so as to thwart such interceptions—or narrow either their specialization or their reach. The two vital functions of such entrepôts, therefore, are control of exchange and the physical handling of commodities. So far these were largely dependent on the same facilities, or at least followed the same routes, but the telegraph had opened the possibility of an important divergence between lines of information flow and the routes of commodity shipment.

Toward midcentury, interest was also increasing in cities as *industrial centers*. This was a direct reflection of the emerging paleotechnic era, moving beyond the simple gristmill, sawmill, slaughterhouse, and forge to the processing of raw materials on a mass scale and the manufacture of specialized goods for marketing far beyond immediate trade areas. Factories need no longer hug the tumbling streams. As a prescient writer exclaimed in 1836, "what a revolution must follow" should steam power actually become the cheapest form of power: "in which case our great cities and their suburbs will become the theatres of manufacturing." Cincinnati's leadership in meat processing was a reflection of a superior location with reference to hog production and waterway transportation as well as of its entrepreneurial vigor. But the dynamics of American expansion brought major shifts in the patterns of industry as well as of commerce. By the late 1850s the great westward expansion of agriculture and emerging railroad networks had brought St. Louis and Chicago into this industrial picture, together with numerous smaller centers in Illinois and Iowa. Meat-packing was of course especially responsive to such westward expansions of agriculture, but so was the burgeoning iron and engineering industry in the West, with its emphasis on agricultural implements and railroad equipment. Civic boosters tirelessly pointed out the great opportunities awaiting the industrial investor, but in fact the risks were high and the geography of major industries difficult to predict in so dynamic an environment. What was becoming apparent was the strong tendency toward industrial concentration, for particular kinds of industry as with specialized wholesaling to cluster, and for the same reasons: to take advantage of established intelligence centers and infrastructure and be in a position to learn of and respond quickly to production or marketing opportunities. In some cases the need for skilled labor was an added incentive. By the 1850s this trend toward concentration of both industrial and wholesaling activities, together with the radical efficiency of the railroad, had driven many small factories, forges, and mills out of business. Clothing, hardware, machinery, processed foods, and even lumber and bricks for houses might be shipped surprisingly long distances from major production centers, undercutting smaller, inefficient, undercapitalized firms in other cities as well as those in small towns and villages. There was thus no simple urban hierarchy in the patterns of industry.

Finally, there was surely some general understanding, even if little clear exposition, that all of these competitions in the West were, in larger view, a jockeying for position within a comprehensive national system of cities. The main base, the central control point, of that system became ever-more firmly fixed and prominent during these years. Although early in the potamic stage of western expansion the prospect of New Orleans rising to rival New York as a national focus may have seemed plausible to some persons, New York's primacy was never in fact in danger. The volume of traffic at New Orleans increased prodigiously, but the great Mississippi Valley entrepôt remained subordinate to and dependent upon New York City for financial and commercial services. New York City was the great metropolis of the western Atlantic World, the control point for American commerce, the financial center of the American system. By the 1840s many states had laws requiring local banks to keep funds in New York City banks as a means of ensuring smooth, nationwide transactions; in the 1850s six of every seven banks in the country participated in that system. With its more than one million inhabitants (including the 266,000 in Brooklyn), in 1860 New York City was clearly the real "Centropolis" and in many ways the effective "capital" of the United States.

Looking outward from that center and pinnacle, it was easy to see several distinct alignments in the American system of cities. The most obvious was the seaboard axis of the national core area, pivoting on New York and extending to Baltimore on the south and Boston on the north. Philadelphia, so long the cultural capital and leading center of colonial America, was now little more than half the size of New York; Boston and Baltimore were less than half the size of Philadelphia. Such rankings did not represent a simple hierarchy but a differential combination of basic supports. All were important ports and industrial centers, and all had vigorously developing local hinterlands and trunk-line connections into the West. Washington was a specialized outpost dangling off the southern end of this axis, connected by rail and telegraph but entirely different in support and significance (Georgetown being a distinctly minor port).

Looking inland, as a writer of 1860 pointed out, "you can easily trace [upon the map] two great lines of cities dotting, like great jewels, the chain of trade and intercourse between East and West." The northern line extended from the Albany-Troy pivot through a close succession of smaller cities along the Erie Canal axis to Buffalo and thence to Cleveland, Detroit, and on to Chicago and Milwaukee. A parallel axis, much less urbanized, connected Philadelphia to Pittsburgh, beyond which the old river alignment of Cincinnati, Louisville, and St. Louis was clearly apparent. In between these obvious lines was a fainter string of small cities along the more direct overland routes between these major centers. Thus Buffalo and Pittsburgh were the great gateways to the transappalachian West (while Wheeling, Baltimore's initial gateway, was left far behind); Cincinnati was the dominant center of the older West anchored on the Ohio (with double the population of all the cities at the Falls); St. Louis and Chicago were analogous and competitive for the main focus of the New West of the upper Mississippi Valley (fig. 54).

South of these alignments there was nothing of similar pattern. New Orleans stood alone as a metropolis, equal in size to Cincinnati or St. Louis, four times larger than any other city in the South. There was no obvious urban axis. Along the Mississippi, Memphis (23,000) was much the largest of the river towns. Nothing developed at Cairo because the local area was unproductive and the site plagued with fevers and floods, there was no break-in-bulk service to perform, no compelling reason for steamboats to stop, and it was quite impossible for an upstart to dislodge Louisville or St. Louis as a regional center. Montgomery (36,000) was the fastest growing city in the South, three times the size of any other fall line town— and these towns did not constitute an urban alignment in any functioning sense because there was little overland connection between them; each was tied to the nearest port. Throughout this southern half of the nation the principal ports as well as the inland trade centers remained remarkably small in comparison with those of the North. Charleston (41,000) actually declined in population between 1850 and 1860, a markedly aberrant American pattern. Within such an overview the Virginian cluster of Richmond-Petersburg, rival cities twenty-two miles apart with a combined population of 56,000 (72,000 if extended to include Norfolk) looms large, but its civic leaders had good reason to be deeply disappointed with their relative status. Richmond, especially, had striven to become a Virginian Baltimore: a major Atlantic port (perhaps in association with Norfolk as the deepwater harbor) with direct canal and railroad links to the Ohio Valley and the expanding West (fig. 55). Richmond had some thriving local industries, but strenuous promotion and various state subsidies had failed to establish any of these connections. At stake, as its leaders tirelessly proclaimed, was not simply greater popula-

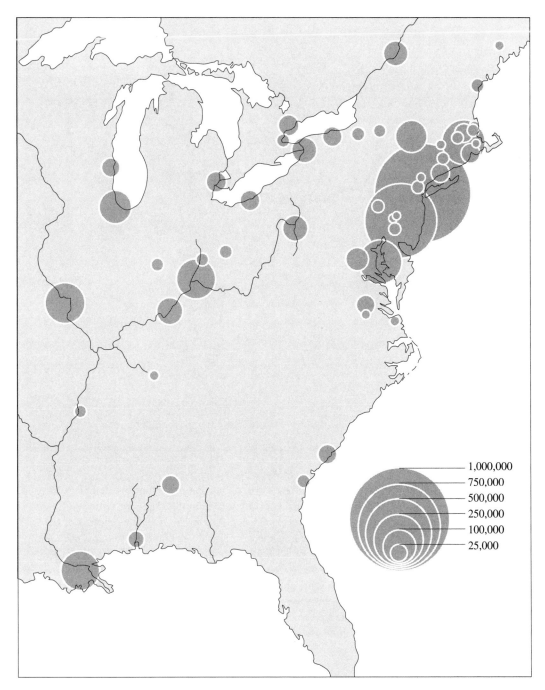

1,000,000
750,000
500,000
250,000
100,000
25,000

54. The Pattern of Cities, 1860.

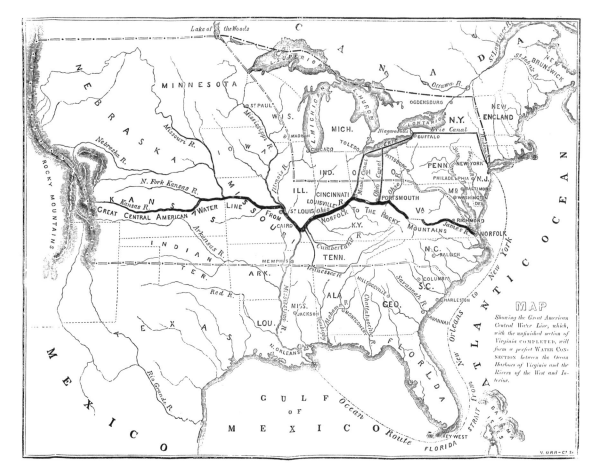

55. Geographical Hyperbole, Virginia.

As late as 1857, Norfolk and Virginian interests were pointing to the need to complete the James-Kanawha canal as the key to a magnificent commercial future. In this fantastic effusion, connecting Norfolk—"the great central sea-port of the Atlantic"—with the junction of the Ohio and Mississippi—"the grand converging and diverging point of full *ten thousand miles* of inland steamboat navigation—a vastly *greater amount* than any other gathering point *in the world!*"—would make "Virginia an EMPIRE OF EMPIRES; Norfolk the QUEEN CITY OF THE ATLANTIC; and realize here, at a Southern port, and on Southern soil, the most sanguine hopes of SOUTHERN COMMERCIAL AND FINANCIAL INDEPENDENCE." The anticipated traffic divides between New York, Norfolk, and New Orleans are shown on the map; the continued dominance of waterways over railways is rationalized in the accompanying pamphlet. (Courtesy of the Virginia Historical Society)

tion growth but "freedom from commercial vassalage." These Virginian cities aspired to become the southern anchor of the national seaboard axis (as Jefferson had envisioned long ago); after all their efforts, they found themselves increasingly bound and subordinate to the established centers of that axis. They were not alone in that quandary. As a Charleston paper put it in 1860: "At present, Norfolk, Charleston, Savannah, and Mobile are but suburbs of New York, Philadelphia, and Boston" (it might well have added Baltimore). Recognizing such links brings into view a coastal alignment reaching from New York through these southern ports to New Orleans (and minor extension to Galveston), but it differed from the others in being a maritime pattern that allowed direct links between any of these ports and New York without intermediate stops (though ships often called at several ports).

These alignments are worth noting because urban development must be understood within a national context. Such lines were of course major avenues of commerce—but they did not include all such avenues, as was apparent in the case of the Mississippi River, a major commodity export route. More significantly, they were the major arteries for the pulsations of the body commercial, for the movement of agents and messages between major control points of the system. As such they shaped the main lines of diffusion of entrepreneurs, ideas, capital, and business affiliations, and these in turn shaped the character and scale of urban development, and to some degree the pattern of worker migration.

The results of these several decades of intensive city promotion confirm no simple formula for success. At the outset physical geography appeared to be the critical factor in determining the most advantageous localities for growth. Entrepreneurial energy and capital invested in the early stages might make the difference among nearby competing centers. Local triumph simply broadened the scale of rivalry into a phase of intense regional competition when cities "like imperial states, . . . carved out extensive dependencies, extended their influence over the economic and political life of the hinterland, and fought with contending places over strategic trade routes." As the winners in these contests emerged and their tributary areas were more clearly defined, it became almost impossible for others to challenge their positions because urban growth became increasingly circular and cumulative; that is, the tendency of like activities to cluster continually enhanced the possibilities for further growth of established centers. Once this stage was reached, civic promoters, no matter how capable they might be, could not force towns upward in the urban hierarchy. As Lukermann has put it: "In a very real sense the system or over-all economy has the decision-making power. It creates its own environment. It pulls in towns that fit. It adopts from a population of potential aspirants those that have a situational advantage, given the system." His "very real sense" is of course a broad generalization in which a vast complex set of decision makers is subsumed under an abstract "system," but the emphasis is pertinent. "Situational advantage" refers to a commanding strategic position within the human geography of a particular area. The system creates its own environment, its own centropolis, pivots, gateways, and nodes within a particular network of places. The American pattern was a rich representation of that process. Yet the American system was also so remarkably dynamic in many important ways, still expanding in space and in commerce and industry, that the position of any particular city, whatever its size, rank, and role, remained in some degree uncertain, and thus a prospect for continuing speculation.

These cities had taken on an increasingly American look. It was not that more of them were more distant or separated from Europe—quite the contrary, they were in ever-closer touch with and avid receptors of European ideas and fashions; all these places were, after all, creations of and fervent participants in an expanding Atlantic cultural and commercial world. But the context of civic life and the conditions for city building were so different as to make these New World centers increasingly divergent in character. American cities displayed an exaggerated emphasis on a narrow spectrum of urban life. If, as Sherry Olson has phrased it, "a city is a projection of society on the ground," the nineteenth-century American city mirrored in its form and fabric, in its volatility and mutability, a society narrowly obsessed with commercial speculation and material progress; it was "a municipal environment dedicated to any and all growth as good." In America the city came to be "treated not as a public institution"—not as the geographic context of an urban society—"but as a private commercial venture to be carved up in any fashion that might increase the turnover and further the rise in land values."

The grid pattern, so ideal for the commodification of land, became the almost universal spatial form of such ventures, not only in the new Western cities but in the design of extensions to the older ones—as most notably in the Commissioners' Plan of 1811, which imprinted an unrelenting grid upon almost all the remainder of Manhattan Island. A concomitant feature was the minuscule proportion of land commonly reserved for public facilities and amenities, such as parks, playgrounds, promenades, schools, libraries, and cemeteries; most of the space for such purposes had to be obtained later—usually with difficulty—by philanthropy or a citizens' campaign focused on some pressing need; even the municipal government itself might have to bid for land to obtain space for the city hall, courts, and jail. In such a speculative atmosphere land sales and construction were usually independent of each other, undertaken by different persons, and actual building might be piecemeal and scattered over the usually capacious original plat (the "urban shell," to use Conzen's term). As needs or opportunities arose, that plat could be readily modified both internally by the insertion of new streets and subdivision of lots (urban repletion) and externally by adding new plats at the edges (urban accretion), usually opportunistically by new land promoters working independently of any civic design or authority. American cities thus expanded erratically in form and fabric at the edges, blurring the distinctions between town and country.

"Around 1850 . . . the sky above the city grew darker, and a smell of coal smoke could be detected in the air." Much of that was associated with the railroad, which, as Lewis Mumford stated, "carried into the heart of the city not merely noise and soot but the industrial plants and the debased housing that alone could thrive in the environment it produced. Only the hypnotism of a new invention, in an age uncritically enamored of new inventions, could have prompted this wanton immolation under the wheels of the puffing Juggernaut." Mumford was a severe critic of American cities—which were so far from his vision of how rich urban life might be for all—but his polemic was grounded in common evidence. Nevertheless, it must be recognized that the railroad, by its very nature and import, brought a crisis in land allocation to every city, old or new, in Europe as well as in America. Although some greater care in the granting of space might have been made in many cases, no civic authority in America could or wanted to resist the intrusion of this radical space-conqueror; in the open competitive environment of that critical formative geographic era, growth and prosperity did in fact depend upon superior railway connections. And so every city avidly enticed railroads and readily ceded to them streets, public squares, waterfront, and large acreages, all with deeply disturbing and long-lasting effects upon the patterns of urban life (Syracuse became a notorious example: for nearly a hundred years dozens of trains every day ran at grade level through the heart of downtown, directly in front of City Hall, repeatedly halting all street traffic, showering pedestrians with soot, and begriming several blocks of the principal business buildings).

Railroads had impelled the second great cycle of urban building in the nineteenth century. The first, and shorter, canal phase had peaked in 1837 and abruptly collapsed; recovery appeared in the early 1840s and continued until 1857 before easing off rather erratically into the onset of war. City buildings (the urban fabric) were increasingly expressive of the new industrialism. Balloon-frame wooden buildings, initiated in Chicago in the 1830s (and made feasible by the mass production of nails), had become the dominant mode of residential and much commercial construction in the newer cities of the West, while machine-made pressed brick and cast-iron facades, developed in the East in the 1840s, were soon being applied throughout the nation. These last were often elaborate in ornamentation, yet perfect representatives of the new age: industrial products stamped out in standardized form, available in a multitude of designs, marketed by catalog nationwide, easily shipped, mechanically assembled, and readily tacked onto simple frames. With such cheap and quick products, whole districts could be built or expanded rapidly and individual buildings altered or replaced with relative ease (urban repletion), and this dynamic character of the American city was one of its most striking features.

There were of course noticeable differences between the older cities on the eastern seaboard and the newest ones in the West, especially in residential areas.

Row houses of three to four stories, varying in type and quality from handsome bow-fronted brownstones, through many different styles (often peculiar to a particular city or region, such as southern New England three-deckers), to barren tenements designed to cram the maximum number of persons into a narrow space, were characteristic of the larger eastern cities, whereas individual houses (mostly of wood in the newer northerly cities, many of brick in the older riverports) on open lots prevailed throughout the West. But the commercial cores of these cities tended toward an increasingly similar face. Along the broad, paved, gaslit streets back from the compact lines of waterfront warehouses were long vistas of three-to-four-story business blocks, the buildings mostly rather simple cubes of brick or stone, but more and more now dressed ornately in cast-iron facades, the whole scene punctuated by the symbolic architecture of special functions: the templed bank, steepled churches, domed or cupolaed city hall or courthouse; the elaborate cornice of a great hotel might loom over the scene, but it was rarely as yet balanced by a great railway station nearby, for most urban depots were little more than rude trainsheds (fig. 56). The density of these central business districts bespoke the laws of concentration and the intensity of competition as well as the absence of public green spaces and the natural limits on feasible heights of urban activities. A breakthrough in building height came in 1857 when Elisha Graves Otis installed his patented safety passenger elevator in the handsome five-story Haughwout Store on Broadway. In the next great building boom the combination of such elevators and new steel-frame construction techniques would provide the way for American cities to create their most famous distinctive feature.

During these years a few people began to talk about how to design and build better cities, especially in response to the worrisome challenges of the new industrialism. But so much of what was proposed took the form of a utopian or romantic escapism, or in other ways failed to confront the massive realities of American privatism and capitalism, that little was effected. American cities came to look and to perform—or fail to perform—as they did because they were indeed "projections of society on the ground." They were developed and continued to be redeveloped piecemeal under conditions of intense competition (within and among cities), few political constraints, and no overall planning or design. They were shaped by thousands of individual entrepreneurs, large and small, in accordance with prevailing ideas about businesses and buildings, and with minimal specialized advice. There were no urban planners because no city government wanted one, would have known what to do with one, nor had the authority to make effective use of one. There were architects, but very few in proportion to the volume of construction undertaken, and such people were usually employed only for the more monumental or signature buildings. (The American Institute of Architects was founded in 1857 and headed for twenty years thereafter by Richard Upjohn, British-born

56. Utica, New York, 1848.

Lewis Bradley's detailed depiction of his hometown offers a good midcentury example of a small (c. 16,000) thriving commercial and industrial city. Uticans might well have entitled the scene "the Gateway to the West," for the view is from a position over the Mohawk River (as if tethered in a balloon) looking from the railroad station and hotels bordering Baggs Square westward up Genesee Street (the right of the diverging pair), the foremost turnpike across the state. The Erie Canal, barely visible in the upper left corner, curves through the middle of the city (bridges are visible in the middle distance), and the building in the center at the corner of Genesee and Baggs Square housed the headquarters of the first commercial telegraph company in the world, with lines recently completed to Buffalo and Albany. Steeples (*l. to r.*, Episcopal, Dutch Reformed, Presbyterian) and smokestacks (mostly steam-powered textile mills) punctuate this federal and classical townscape, while in the upper right distance is the enormous New York Asylum for the Insane, a pioneering humane institution and one of the greatest Greek Revival buildings in America. (Courtesy of the I. N. Stokes Collection, Miriam & Ira D. Wallach Division of Art, Prints and Photographs, the New York Public Library, Astor, Lenox and Tilden Foundations)

and trained ecclesiastical specialist, whose greatest creation, Trinity Church, was at the time the most famous landmark in the New York City skyline; Upjohn's simplified Gothic renditions of smaller stone or wood Episcopal churches established a new distinctive style that was already imprinted across the land from Providence to Galena.) In the older cities, especially, there were persons with ideas and talents eager to have a hand in reshaping the American urban scene, but they would have to join with wealthy and influential citizens and try to insert some of the amenities of life and landscape that were so apparent to American visitors in Europe's great cities and so utterly absent in their homeland. In the 1850s the first great example of such action got under way. The grim prospect that the rigid frame of streets and blocks and solid infilling of brick and stone would continue its relentless spread over the whole of Manhattan ignited a campaign to rescue a generous portion of the rocky, irregular remainder of the island before it was too late. Led by a small but politically influential social elite who were convinced of the imperative need to apply the best of current social and scientific philosophy to the shaping of modern urban life, this movement generated sufficient support to cause the city government to begin purchase of a 500-acre tract (it was a telling example of American limitations on government that the city had to obtain special legislative approval for such acquisitions). In 1858 Frederick Law Olmsted and Calvert Vaux, having won the design competition, began their remarkable work of transformation. Central Park, the first large public park in America, was a stunning success and Olmsted became the foremost practitioner of an environmental design movement that left its mark on many an American city. He was one of a small but growing group who saw these mushrooming cities as the most telling exhibits of the course of modern civilization, the most vital centers of American life, and who worked assiduously to create more humane civic environments. Such dedicated people would effect some important ameliorations, but they could scarcely touch the controlling dynamics of American urban development.

11. Harnessing New Forces: Industries and Industrial Regions

Almost any route of travel in the early years of the Republic would confirm that Americans were an industrious people. Gristmills and sawmills, forges and smithies were part of the common scene; tanneries, distilleries, and paper mills, carriage works and furniture factories were to be found in most of the older districts; shipyards, ropewalks, and chandleries in many a seaport; in the larger coastal cities there were clusters of workshops, with artisans busy at dozens of special trades; and in town and countryside alike important volumes of foodstuffs, cloth, boots and shoes, and other items were being manufactured in ordinary households for the commercial market. All of this activity represented the American eotechnic: dispersed and small in scale, artisans working with local materials but flourishing on the lavish availability of wood and waterpower, enjoying the widespread accessibility provided by river and coastal shipping, and serving rapidly expanding regional markets.

Nevertheless, many leaders of the new nation did not look upon this bustling scene with content. "Until we manufacture more," the *Boston Gazette* declared in 1788, "it is absurd to celebrate the Fourth of July as the birthday of our independence," and two years later Congress requested the secretary of the Treasury to give his attention "to the subject of Manufactures, and particularly to the means of promoting such as will tend to render the United States independent on foreign nations, for military and other essential supplies." Hamilton's "Report on Manufactures" became an early landmark in official efforts to create a national economic policy and his recommendations of various forms of protection and subsidy a recurrent feature of American politics. An upsurge of commercial prosperity, stimulated by wars in Europe, postponed the pressures for a time, but the tariff, especially, soon reappeared as a basic, and divisive, national issue. Our concern is not with such legislation, for, however these policies may have influenced the pace of development in targeted industries, we may agree with Thomas Cochran that "industrialization seemed bound to advance in the United States on the basis of culture, geography, and resources regardless of [international] competition."

With reference to culture, in the early decades of the nineteenth century a multitude of initiatives by both government and private agencies relating to such matters as banking, credit, and insurance, property rights and corporations, taxation and tariffs went a long way in shaping a distinctive American "business culture." One of the most important components of that culture had long been apparent, for it was a major legacy of the British colonial societies created on this North American seaboard. As Albert Gallatin summed it up in 1810:

> No cause, indeed, has, perhaps, more promoted in every respect, the general prosperity of the United States, than the absence of those systems of internal restrictions and monopoly which continue to disfigure the state of society in other countries. No law exists here, directly or indirectly, confining man to a particular occupation or place, or excluding any citizen from any branch, he may, at any time, think proper to pursue. Industry is, in every respect, perfectly free and unfettered; every species of trade, commerce, art, profession and manufacture, being equally open to all, without requiring any previous regular apprenticeship, admission, or license.

The great virtues of such ostensible domestic social mobility were magnified by the continuing ease of movement between the mother country and its assertively independent offspring, despite English attempts to monitor such emigration. Although Hamilton's statement that "it is the interest of the United States to open every possible avenue to emigration from abroad" was based on the assumed need to expand the manufacturing labor force without detracting from agriculture, later assessments would stress the often critical importance of the emigration of artisans (Jefferson was wary of large immigrations from monarchical Europe, but as for "useful artificers"—"spare no expence in obtaining them"). The contributions of a few of these skilled persons are famous, those of many others well documented, and the general movements of and contacts among what Anthony Wallace has called the "international fraternity of mechanicians" were fundamental to this formative stage of American industrial development. As our focus is more on places than on persons we shall look at only a few of these emigrations and innovations that were critical to the emergence of important industrial districts.

The story of Samuel Slater, the English apprentice who memorized the design of Sir Richard Arkwright's automatic spinning machine, emigrated from Derbyshire to New York, and with capital support from Moses Brown was lured to Rhode Island to build an American version of Arkwright's mill at a falls just north of Providence, is famous in the annals of American industry. Slater and Brown did not thereby initiate the American textile industry, for tens of thousands of yards of cotton and woolen goods were being produced by family manufacture (nor did they introduce Arkwright's ideas, for various versions of his machine were already being tried), but they did build the first waterpowered mill equipped with effective machinery, they clearly represented the critical alliance between the new technicians and mercantile capitalists, and to an important degree they directed the rapid transformation of textile-making along particular lines in a particular region and thereby made Providence and the Blackstone Valley "the nation's nursery of manufacturing."

The spread of the "Slater system" of spinning mills serving home weavers was rapid. The Blackstone and a dozen other streams running rapidly through the nobby, glaciated hill country of southern New England provided a great many mill sites; the small mills themselves could be readily constructed by local millwrights, carpenters, blacksmiths, and masons, and once success was demonstrated ample merchant capital was available.

The spread of early woolen mills was not dissimilar. Introduction of the key machinery and system is usually credited to the Scholfield families from Yorkshire, who began near Boston and within a few years had built machines in half a dozen other localities. Other English emigrants were soon involved, and the machinery was quickly elaborated and diffused. Such factory success brought demands for better wool, and the importation of merino sheep from Iberia to upgrade American flocks soon transformed the industry.

A third component of the New England textile revolution was that begun by Francis Cabot Lowell and his Boston merchant associates at Waltham in 1813, based on newer machinery and integrated operations (spinning, weaving, bleaching, dyeing) on a considerably larger scale than any heretofore. The success of the Waltham mill led to many imitations in the 1820s, and in 1831 Lowell and his Boston Associates took the next step of creating an entirely new textile mill city at a great falls on the Merrimack River. Lowell, Massachusetts, was so impressive in scale, famous in concept, and successful as an investment that it spurred the development of an array of new mill cities on the major rivers of New England, such as Chicopee and Holyoke on the Connecticut; Lawrence, Nashua, and Manchester on the Merrimack; Brunswick and Lewiston on the Androscoggin; and Waterville on the Kennebec.

Nearly all this while, textile mills were being established elsewhere in the country as well, in part by direct diffusion from New England, as in the Upper Hudson Valley and area around Utica, and in part by separate initiatives, of which some of the more important were at Paterson (first with cotton, later silk), Philadelphia and vicinity, and Baltimore. There was a sprinkling of mills in the land of cotton, mostly in the Piedmont, from Rocky Mount and Salem through the Spartanburg district into northern Georgia. Some were initiated by artisan colonists from New England, others by avid Southern industrial promoters, such as William Gregg at his new mill town of Graniteville, South Carolina. But there was a great difference between these Southern mills and those in New England: the difference between a few factories turning out a limited range of goods (in most cases of cheap quality for local markets) and an industrial *region* of great density and complexity, employing tens of thousands of workers of every necessary skill to turn out a great diversity of products; with dozens of machine shops building every piece of equipment; inventors and tinkerers working continuously to enlarge and improve on machine designs; buyers, brokers, and agents of various kinds monitoring every aspect of production and marketing; and competing corporations and adventurous capitalists alert to every possible advantage. This New England regional complex had an interdependence and an inner dynamic that shaped the role of the textile industry in the national economy.

Geographically, the industry spread inward along the rivers of New England, eventually studding the great waterpower sites with clusters of large mills and housing for workers. Mill towns were connected by river, canal, turnpike, and eventually railroad to major mercantile centers, which imported the raw cotton, shipped the finished goods, and served as general supply centers and managerial and financial headquarters. Providence and Boston had the most extensive hinterland systems. By the 1840s a new development, the use of steam power, brought a near cessation of the spread upriver and saw the establishment of large mills at tidewater, not only in these two major centers but in such old fishing and whaling ports as Portsmouth, Salem, Fall River, and New Bedford.

The textile industry was only one component (or set of components) within this regional industrial complex. In southern New England, especially, the rivers became lined with other kinds of manufacturing that were also undergoing intensive transformation and expansion. The old Yankee traditional crafting of a great array of tools and trinkets, housewares and notions was rapidly translated into leadership in a variety of new factory-produced goods requiring close tolerances and fine finish: clocks, locks, brass, silverware and tinware, cutlery, tools and hardware, firearms, engines, and much else. Because of the role of particular inventors and entrepreneurs, production was often clustered in a particular locality, such as locks at Stamford, clocks at Waterbury, other brass items in the Naugatuck Valley, and builders' hardware in New Britain. Of special importance was the production of firearms in a number of places, of which New Haven (Whitney) and Hartford (Colt) became the best known but Springfield was the most significant.

The War Department established its first national armory at Springfield, Massachusetts, in 1794. Although at first muskets were produced by gunsmiths using traditional methods, a persistent interest in improving efficiency and quality, close working relationships with private firms, and a sequence of creative inventors and machinists eventually made this armory "a world leader in the manufacture of firearms and a showcase of production techniques," representing a crucial step forward in the Industrial Revolution. The key concept of interchangeability of parts was French in origin, brought to the United Sates by Jefferson and others, nurtured by American officers familiar with French military doctrines, and cannily publicized by Eli Whitney (and later Samuel Colt). But interchangeability of parts was in fact very difficult to achieve on any major scale because it required unprecedented care with new forging and milling techniques—in short, success awaited the invention of "machine tools." The first real success was evidently achieved in the 1820s by John Hall, who began in Portland, Maine, but was induced by the government to set up a small rifle factory at another national armory at Harpers Ferry, Virginia. David Hounshell has noted that "it is fitting that John Hall's Rifle Works was situated at Harpers Ferry, a point where two rivers ran together. At the Rifle Works, two important streams of development of Manufacturing technology flowed together into a major stream that runs through American history. There, the idea of uniformity or interchangeability of parts was combined with the notion that machines could make things as good and as fast as man's hands, or even better." From our more specific geographic perspective, however, it is not the simile of confluence that attracts attention but the fact that the major stream that runs through American technological history was fed by swelling sources in New England, for Hall's achievements were soon carried from his small factory on the Potomac to be emulated and greatly extended at Springfield on the Connecticut, and it was there that a distinct American "armory system" spread into a proliferating variety of productions—pins, brass clocks, sewing machines—in the factories of New England.

Thus emerged a southern New England industrial region (fig. 57), varied district by district in product emphasis and factory type, but these overlapping in area (as at Springfield and Chicopee) and interlocking in function (as in the production of textile machinery). It was a region of industrial diversity and intensity, with easy internal movements of labor and capital, anchored on metropolitan centers

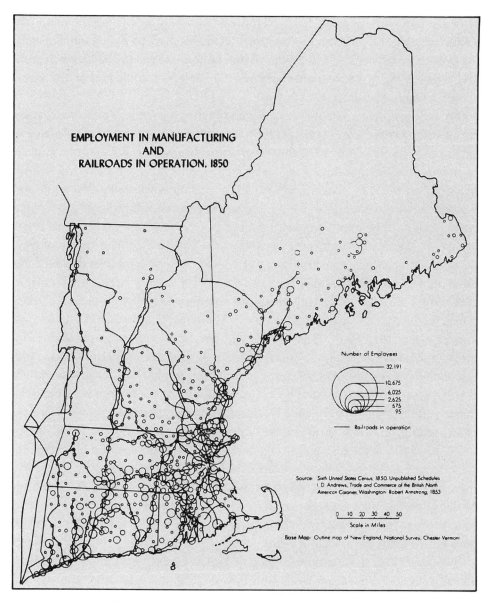

57. New England Manufacturing Employment, 1850.
(Reproduced from Leblanc, *Location of Manufacturing in New England in the Nineteenth Century;*
courtesy of the Department of Geography, Dartmouth College)

(Boston, Providence, and to some extent New York City), with output increasingly concentrated in large specialized industrial satellites (Lowell, Lynn, Manchester), but with a number of intermediate diversified manufacturing and service centers (Worcester, Fitchburg, Springfield, New Haven), and some industrial production in virtually every town. New England heavily dominated the nation in textile capacity and productions (two-thirds to three-quarters of the total, depending upon how measured), and produced one-fifth to one-quarter of all machinery and engines, but a much higher proportion of machine tools and of the more complex and high-valued equipment.

An associated but ultimately very different pattern emerged from the concurrent development of another major component of the new industrial age: the steam engine. As inventors perfected these increasingly versatile machines, machinists in dozens of workshops turned out the boilers, pipes, valves, frames, and wheels required. As the use of steam spread, larger and more specialized factories appeared; yet the technology remained simple enough and sufficiently tied to older crafts, such as those of millwrights, boat builders, and carriage makers, that large numbers of local firms continued to participate. The geographic dispersal of production was apparent from the first. Machinists in Philadelphia and New York fitted out the first trial steamboats, but by 1820 Pittsburgh had become a major center for both steamboat and stationary engines, and western demands soon spread production downriver to Cincinnati, Louisville, St. Louis, and a number of smaller places. Although Oliver Evans had developed high-pressure engines in Philadelphia to run his new "continuous process" flour mills as early as 1802, and his son set up an engine manufacturing plant in Pittsburgh in 1812, the application of steam power to the many simple but heavy tasks so long done by water or muscle power—grinding, sawing, turning, blowing, pressing, pounding, pumping, shearing, dredging, hoisting, spinning, weaving—did not really expand rapidly until the 1830s. Such demands thereby coincided with the enormous stimulus given to steam power and the whole engineering industry by the railroads. By the 1850s there were large locomotive works in Philadelphia, Paterson, Lowell, Taunton, Manchester (fig. 58), and Schenectady; yet, typical of the industrial patterns of the time, more than fifty manufacturers of railroad engines and cars in eighteen states have been identified for that decade.

By midcentury large factories employing hundreds, even thousands, of workers and turning out a great variety of machinery, engines, and other capital and consumer goods were to be found in all of the major cities and in many smaller places, the latter being especially numerous in southern New England and parts of Pennsylvania, which were emerging as the premier industrial regions of the United States. New England manufacturing, as we have seen, was associated with the great density of waterpower sites, early leadership in factory production of textiles, and a tradition of skills and inventiveness that avidly responded to new machinery and engineering demands, the whole sustained by ample merchant capital and entrepreneurial leadership. Pennsylvania had some of the same ingredients but with important differences in emphasis, direction, and resource base. Philadelphia had

58. New England Manufactures.

In 1856, when this print was published, "Amoskeag" was famous primarily as the largest cotton textile mill complex in America. In the following year, the Amoskeag Manufacturing Company became the Manchester Locomotive Works and expanded into one of the leaders of the industry until merging with the newly formed giant, the American Locomotive Works, in 1901. The engine shown is a classic 4-4-0 "American" type, which dominated the American scene for forty years, and the fine touch of Yankee artisans is well displayed in its decor and finish. (Courtesy of the Division of Transportation, National Museum of History and Technology, Smithsonian Institution, Washington, D.C.)

been a beehive of industries since its foundation. Early German colonists, especially, had included an unusually rich array of artisans who were soon busy producing metal goods, glass, paper, and textiles, and the agricultural hinterland provided an incentive for large and improved processing plants, such as Evans's new mills. And here, as in New England, commercial leadership, capital, and connections throughout the Atlantic World played an essential role. The critical difference was in the sources of power. Pennsylvania had waterpower, but nothing like the density of mill sites in glaciated New England; its great bounty was coal, especially anthracite, but translating that gift of nature into a real resource was difficult. The incentive to do so came from the iron industry and from the relentless expansion of cities.

American growth was putting heavy pressures on fuel supplies. The iron industry was consuming whole forests for charcoal, driving up costs and putting some districts out of production, and "urban America in 1830 was almost wholly dependent upon wood for fuel; and it was in trouble." The great cities of the seaboard were reaching farther and farther afield. New York City consumed several million cords a year, shipped in from Maine and the New Jersey Pine Barrens as well as downriver from the Catskills and Adirondacks. One important new response was the development of fuel-efficient cast-iron stoves, which became popular and plentiful by the 1840s, but these in turn added to the demands for iron.

Early in the century the basic iron industry in America consisted of hundreds of small furnaces and forges, loosely clustered in a number of districts, most of which were aligned with the trend of the mineral-bearing uplands from eastern Massachusetts through the Taconics, the Highlands of New Jersey, across southeastern Pennsylvania, and along the Blue Ridge in western Virginia into eastern Tennessee; there were also important outliers in the eastern Adirondacks and western Pennsylvania and soon-expanding developments in the Ohio Valley. It was a pattern reflective not only of the widespread occurrence of surficial iron deposits but the even wider availability of wood for charcoal (as well as waterpower for bellows and hammers).

The English, having ravaged their forests long ago, had been experimenting with the use of coal for smelting for several generations, achieving success with high-grade bituminous for coking in the eighteenth century and with the carbon-rich anthracite of South Wales early in the nineteenth. Such British experience was as crucial to the American coal and iron industries as it was in textiles. It was an Englishman who first made use of anthracite for steam power in Pennsylvania, a Welshman who, by specific invitation, came from Swansea to set up the first anthracite-fueled blast furnace at Catasauqua near Allentown, and all the while English, Cornish, Welsh, and Scottish miners and ironmasters were pouring into Pennsylvania. Special machinery and firebrick were imported from Britain also, but local machine shops, iron mills, ovens, and kilns, all a direct heritage of the earlier American iron industries, were soon supplying most of the exponentially expanding needs. By 1840 railroads were consuming one-third of the demand for iron; rails were still being imported, since it proved difficult to adapt American ores to the mass production of high-grade iron, but such problems were soon overcome and several rail mills built.

Canals and tramways had tapped the Schuylkill and Lehigh coalfields by the 1830s and initiated a rapid, competitive expansion in those districts; further extension into the Shamokin and Wyoming fields by several railroads brought a multiplication of shipping lines to the seaboard, as well as to Upstate New York and Canada (fig. 59). By 1860, production of Pennsylvania anthracite had increased more than fortyfold in thirty years, and it was being marketed throughout the Northeast.

Meanwhile the enormous bituminous coal measures of the Appalachians were being developed. Soft and sooty compared with the almost carbon-pure anthracite, the many grades of bituminous were more easily adapted to use in steam engines and stoves but were not really successful for iron smelting until the discovery of the excellent Connellsville coking coals in the late 1850s. The bituminous fields nearest to tidewater lay just upriver from Richmond, and a modest amount of this Virginian gas and steam coal was shipped to coastal urban markets, where it competed with that from Nova Scotia. Only when the C&O Canal and the B&O

59. Anthracite Coalfield.

Shown is a portion of S. Harries Daddow's "Map of the Anthracite Coalfields of Pennsylvania," published by Benjamin Bannan, Pottsville, Pennsylvania, and attached as an appendix to Daddow and Bannan's *Coal, Iron, and Oil; or the Practical American Miner*, 1866. The numbers refer to specific collieries, which are listed in the legend (not shown). (Courtesy of the Rare Books and Special Collections, the University Libraries, the Pennsylvania State University)

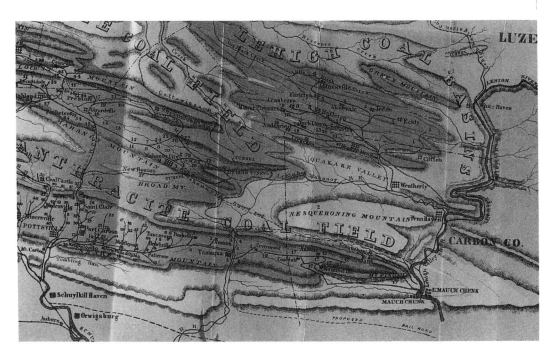

Railroad finally reached Cumberland could the seaboard cities tap into the main reserves. By that time these enormous Appalachian riches had already made such places as Brownsville, Pittsburgh, Steubenville, and Wheeling memorable sights. Even before 1820 the "eternal veil of smoke" hanging upon these western towns was a source of disgust to many a visitor ("a cloud which almost amounts to night"; every object *within* the house "stained, soiled, and tarnished" by the enveloping soot), and pride to many a promoter ("this smoke it is that must enrich America"). By the 1850s demands of homes and shops and, especially, steam engines had brought the production of these western bituminous fields to a level only a little short of eastern anthracite.

America's first heavy industrial region, therefore, developed in continuity with the furnaces, forges, and machine shops of early Pennsylvania, but on the basis of a vital new resource and a set of new technologies. The key resources were the coal measures of the Schuylkill and Lehigh valleys and the iron ores of the anthracite district, nearby Lebanon, and northern New Jersey (fig. 60). The coal-shipping centers of Mauch Chunk and Pottsville, and the big new blast furnaces and iron mills at Pottsville, Allentown, and Phillipsburg were central to these basic re- sources, but such industrial towns were simply specialized centers within a greater manufacturing complex. Philadelphia was the obvious anchor of this industrial region. Here lived the men who owned the railroads and the bulk of the coal mines and iron mills, here worked most of the big commission agents who marketed iron and iron products nationwide, and here, in the city and its environs along the Delaware and up the Schuylkill from Manayunk to Norristown, was the most diversified array of iron mills and engineering works, as well as major productions of glassware, bricks, paints, dyes, drugs, and the most variegated output of finished textiles—everything from lace to oilcloth—in the nation. Clearly, Philadelphia and its hinterland loomed very large in the new industrial America. It was not quite so obvious that another great center served this emerging industrial region. For Philadelphia and the anthracite valleys were linked by several canals and railroads right across New Jersey to New York Harbor. Important industrial towns lay along those routes, notably Trenton, Boonton, and Paterson, and they came into focus on what was the largest (by value of output and, barely, by employment) manufac- turing center in the United States.

New York City's role as the premier financial and commercial center of America tends to obscure its significance in manufacturing. Its immense array of workshops produced the greatest variety of consumer goods, but it was also a major seat of heavy engineering works, machine shops, and ironwork. It was the largest builder of steam engines, largest maker of cast-iron stoves and storefronts, principal seat of marine engineering, and much else. In 1860 the number of employees in manufac- turing in New York (102,969) and in Philadelphia (99,003) far exceeded that of

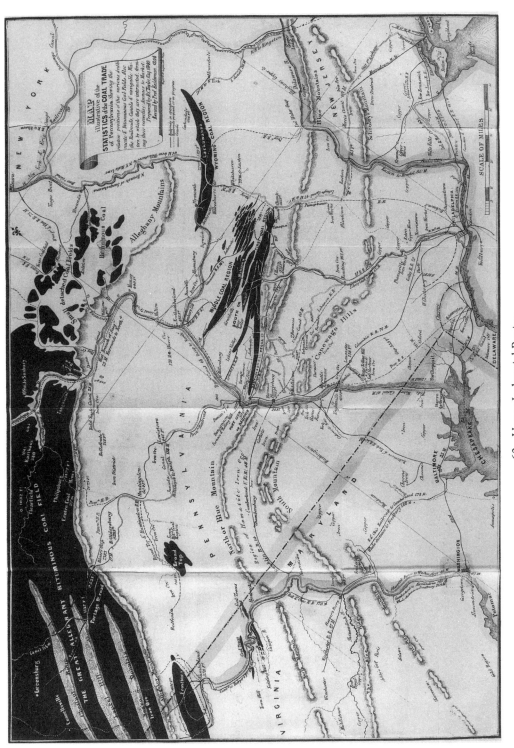

60. Heavy Industrial Region.

This fine map, originally prepared by R. C. Taylor in 1849 and revised to 1854 by S. I. Haldeman, clearly shows the concentrated anthracite districts and their connections by water and rail to Philadelphia and New York City (extreme lower right corner). Published in R. C. Taylor's *Statistics of Coal*, 2d ed., 1855. (Courtesy of the Rare Books and Special collections, the University Libraries, the Pennsylvania State University) any other city; furthermore, as Cochran emphasized, "the coal, iron, and clothing business" of the two cities "were so intertwined . . . that it is more realistic to think of one great manufacturing complex from Wilmington to New York. From 1843 to 1860 this megalopolis was probably the most rapidly growing large industrial area in the world."

Once we begin to trace the regional outlines of these new manufacturing areas, the position of New York City becomes even more impressive, for it had ready access to southern New England and thereby served as an important industrial as well as commercial link between these two premier regions. Much of the metal goods of New England was marketed through New York jobbers. Furthermore, as we look beyond this nuclear area to identify outlying manufacturing districts of the 1850s, it is apparent that New York had a richly productive hinterland extending throughout the state, dotted with new industrial plants, many of which were in some degree bound up with those in the city. Foundries and factories in the Hudson Valley could be fueled with anthracite via the Delaware & Hudson Canal. Adiron-

61. Troy, New York.

A view across the Hudson from the Watervliet Arsenal of a thriving industrial center. At least four foundries and stove factories are shown, along with great piles of Pennsylvania coal, and there were larger ironworks just downstream (to the right). Rivercraft include two schooners, two sloops, and a steamboat. The remarkable multi-spired building on the hill is not an artistic exaggeration; it was the new home of Troy University, a short-lived Methodist institution. This engraving appeared in J. H. French, *Gazetteer of the State of New York,* 1860.

dack ores and Pennsylvania coal supported major ironworks at Troy (fig. 61) (especially stoves and the nation's largest bell foundry) and Watervliet (federal arsenal), which, with the locomotive works at Schenectady, cotton mills at Troy and Cohoes, and lumber mills at Glens Falls and vicinity, made the Upper Hudson an important industrial district. Albany-Troy also constituted the greatest lumber marketing center in the United States. Westward along the Erie Canal there was a sprinkling of factories typical of New England, such as a number of textile mills and the Remington Arms plant at German Flats, but most industries were involved in processing the harvests of farm and forest, the volume and variety magnified by the prosperous diversified output of the region and by rapidly mounting shipments of grain from the West. The flour mills of Buffalo, Lockport, Rochester, Oswego, and Fulton were now an industry of national importance. The most prominent of the newer factories were the agricultural implement works, whose forges and mills could now be fueled by Pennsylvania coal. Troy and Auburn were important, and in 1846 Cyrus McCormick selected a Brockport firm to be one of the principal manufacturers of his reapers.

A more specialized outlier of this new industrial America was that focused on Pittsburgh and ramifying into half a dozen valleys above and below where the many charcoal furnaces and forges were being replaced by large coal-fired facilities. There were seventeen rolling mills within five miles of the Forks in 1858, and several more downriver, especially at Wheeling. Steam engines and railroad equipment were the most notable products of the many engineering works; there were copper mills, pressed glass works (an American invention), and the nation's largest potteries, established by English emigrants on the basis of the fine clays around East Liverpool. The iron supply came largely from central and western Pennsylvania, but a few trial shipments of rich ore from Marquette in Upper Michigan together with experimental use of the Connellsville coking coals provided a hint of the future, though the magnitude and significance thirty years hence of the marriage of Lake Superior ores and Appalachian coal for the industrial power of the United States could hardly have been imagined.

Each of the large cities of the West was an industrial center of regional importance, with outputs varied in part by particular local resources. Cincinnati, together with nearby towns in the Miami Valley, was the most diversified. By 1860 St. Louis had railway access to the iron ores at Pilot Knob in the St. François Mountains and could anticipate larger productions from its several rolling mills. Chicago had only one iron mill (re-rolling rails for the insatiable railroad expansions), but it was the greatest lumber marketing center in the West, with a wide array of furniture, sash and door, and other woodworking shops; it was serving farmers with more than 5,000 reapers annually from McCormick's famous factory; and new industrial plants were being extended along the Chicago River. Chicago's strategic position within the expanding agricultural West was becoming clearer every year, but because most of the developed farmland lay to the east and because the new implements were requiring much more iron (and often high-grade steel), plants poised near the edge of the main iron-producing region, such as those in Canton and Massillon, Ohio, appeared to be in an advantageous position.

We may complete this reconnaissance by noting the special position of Baltimore. It was connected by river, canal, and railroad to the Pennsylvania anthracite and iron districts and drew upon them to some extent, but it lay at some distance and rather detached from these, and its principal focus was westward, to its own coalfields just beyond Cumberland, to the Ohio Valley, and, as always, its own immediate agricultural hinterland. Baltimore had added ironworks, large railroad shops, and a variety of other manufactures to its older milling industry, but, rather like the cities across the mountains, it remained heavily geared to commerce (with coal as a new export item).

The general geographic pattern of this industrial America was therefore fairly clear: a set of major and distinctive regions in the Northeast, with New York City and Philadelphia as great foci and manufacturing centers themselves; the Hudson-Erie Canal belt and Pittsburgh and the valleys as important extensions or outliers of these; and the several large cities spaced through the West. The really striking feature is the absence of any major industrial center south of Baltimore–Louisville–St. Louis (south of the B&O Railroad). There was of course a scattering of factories across the South, some of considerable size and efficiency, and there were even a few small clusters of furnaces, forges, mills, and workshops of various kinds, but the great majority of these manufactories were engaged in elementary processing of local materials, and the total investment, employment, and output was far below that of the major districts in the North. There were a few notable mill towns, such as Graniteville and Prattville (a major producer of cotton gins), but no Lowell or Paterson, nothing like a Blackstone Valley or Lehigh Valley, and nothing remotely like a Philadelphia or New York City—or even a Cincinnati. New Orleans, the one large city of the South, was a minor manufacturing center.

Some of the reasons for this great contrast may become clearer through a look at the most impressive single industrial complex in the South: The Tredegar Iron Works on the banks of the James River in Richmond. The original plant was designed by an engineer from the famed Tredegar Works in South Wales. Initiated in the 1830s to serve local railroads, the firm soon obtained state and national orders for ordnance (such as an iron ship, cannon, chains), and Boston builders later helped set up an engine factory. By 1859 it was the fourth largest ironworks in the United States, employing about 800 workers in its furnaces, foundries, rolling mill, machine shops, and locomotive works. The Tredegar was also near bankruptcy, not simply because of the sudden severe economic crisis in a South teetering on the brink of secession, but because it was inherently uncompetitive. Most of its raw iron was now purchased from Pennsylvania furnaces because its older Virginia sources were neither sufficient in quantity nor competitive in price. It burned mostly Virginia coal, easily transported by canal, and imported only a small amount of Lehigh anthracite; but virtually all copper and bronze, many parts, and much of its machinery had to be purchased in the North. Furthermore, the works had to pay a premium to lure skilled workers to a slave state. Northern and British ironmasters and machinists objected to working alongside Blacks, in part because they considered it demeaning, more importantly because they feared (with reason) that the owners hoped to replace them once their Black slaves had acquired the requisite skills. As a result there was a high turnover, chronic labor shortage, and little concerted attention to improvements and innovations. The Tredegar survived on the basis of the Southern market, but only by offering more liberal—and risky—credit to Southern railroads, and by the occasional preference given a regional company by a Southern state. Within the South the Tredegar Iron Works loomed large—as would soon be dramatically apparent; within the nation it was distinctly marginal both economically and geographically. Viewed at that scale, Richmond was no more successful in industrial than it was in commercial competition.

The danger in the South's dependence upon the North or Europe for all kinds of capital goods and all but the most basic consumer goods was an urgent theme in many an oration and editorial in the region. The penalty was soon imposed, the disability long endured, and the reason why the South did not participate more fully in this great structural transformation of the national economy has long been debated among economic historians. Such analyses lie outside our focus, but our geographic perspective does suggest that the topic must take into account not only the more obvious economic factors of production but an understanding of this new industrialism as a *cultural system* that emerged in certain localities, was nurtured in a few special districts, and then spread as an increasingly integrated system to advantageous areas farther afield. We are dealing therefore with a specialized version of a *culture hearth*, and the simple formulation earlier specified for that concept (see *Atlantic America*, 52–53) may be usefully applied.

In a development wherein so much depended upon sequences of very specific inventions, improvements, and adoptions, we may take the "stimulus of contact" to refer to the easy movement and intense interaction among numerous creative and skilled persons. Such persons tend to cluster in areas of greatest opportunity and stimulus. As a writer of 1859 noted: "superior mechanics and dexterous workmen manifest a . . . preference for cities and an abhorrence of isolation; hence, if for no other reason, extensive mechanical or manufacturing operations must be conducted at a great disadvantage in isolated localities." That he was touting the attractions of Philadelphia does not taint his assertion, for that city was indeed a great exhibit of such truth. As Cochran noted: "In Philadelphia by 1810 there were half a dozen ironworking shops within four blocks of each other that collectively constituted a machine tool industry, a basic requirement of industrial progress. It is this convergence of machine work in a few urban areas, rather than an occasional invention, that assured the continuation of technological progress." The founding of the Franklin Institute in 1824 by master mechanicians and manufacturers further exemplifies the kind of formalization and intensification of industrial culture that only major centers could sustain (the initiation of Rensselaer Polytechnic Institute in Troy that same year is an equally pertinent illustration).

The "stimulus of pressures" was most intense at the corporate level wherein competition among firms for sheer survival put a high premium upon entrepreneurial and managerial leadership. The willingness to take risks, a genius for promotion of a product, and the ability to impose order upon complex operations and discipline upon a large body of workers were talents that this new culture learned to respect and reward. The "instrument of expansion" of this cultural system consisted of interlocking complexes of capitalist enterprise: merchant capital, credit facilities, and variable sets of interdependent companies armed with the latest technology and organization. The application of such an instrument to the exploitation of a large body of resources to produce goods for a rapidly expanding market provided ample "stimulus of resource rewards." Such an industrial complex generates an internal dynamic, powered by the incentive and the instruments for growth and its very success generating continuing infusions of capital, skills, and labor for further expansion.

The development of an industrial region will surely be shaped in part by such geographic particularities as the waterpower potentials of New England and the anthracite resources of Pennsylvania. Such features must be taken into account, but whereas they may guide the patterns of expansion they cannot of themselves provide the impetus. For that we must look to the cultural character of the antecedent societies of these regions and the long nurture of entrepreneurial and artisanal talents that would be poised to respond ("pre-adapted," as some would phrase it) to new technological and economic opportunities.

Such a general cultural formulation may be comfortably fitted upon a more specifically economic one, such as David Meyer's concept of "regional industrial systems," with its close attention to such fundamentals and growth factors as efficiencies in power applications and factory productions, radical reductions in transport costs, the role of hinterland demands and interregional trade, the large and varied infrastructure demands generated by phenomenal urban growth, the close forward and backward linkages within particular industries, and the creation of a strong capital goods sector. Once such an industrial system becomes firmly consolidated within a particular area with the capability of serving much of a nation's needs it becomes a dominating force. Subsequent major industrial complexes are not likely to be independent of it but, rather, extensions from it, bound to it for many essentials even if operated by local corporations. In this sense we may say, as with the national system of cities, that the system creates its own environment and shapes the highly uneven geography of development. With reference to the most notable case of such variation in the United States we must conclude that in the period we are examining there was no possibility of the South nurturing an industrial region at all comparable to that of the Northeast. That the South might have had more factories than it did in fact develop seems obvious enough because there was room for choice in countless particulars, but no set of decisions by any group, class, or other combination of Southerners could have created a diverse internally dynamic autonomous industrial system. Richmond could have become an important national center of manufacturing only by becoming an extension of the national nuclear area—only by tying into that complex so as to serve as the southern end of a closely interdependent region with easy and intensive circulations of capital, entrepreneurs, inventors, artisans, and all the specialized goods and services sustaining and steadily enriching a genuine cultural system. The Tredegar case suggests that there would have been grave difficulties in doing so even if such links had been vigorously sought by the civic and manufacturing leadership.

Industrialization therefore compounded the regional imbalance in economic power apparent at the beginning of the century. There had been concern about that from the start. Hamilton had tried to reassure the nation that there was no need to fear such a regional differentiation. He argued that such differences in production would in fact strengthen reciprocities, that "mutual wants constitute one of the strongest links of political connection" and therefore it was "unfounded" and "mischievous" to think of "the Northern and Southern regions . . . as having adverse interests" in the national promotion of manufactures.

Hamilton was not alone in misreading the future impact of industrialism—nor should we expect anyone to have foreseen with much clarity the radical transformations of the paleotechnic. Hamilton, Gallatin, and others were living in an eotechnic world, when manufacturing was still literally that: the handcrafting of goods, perhaps with the help of waterpower and the new possibility of making use of some clever little machines. Agriculture was obviously fundamental to any national economy, commerce a natural exchange arising from regional differences in the kinds of things produced. Any enlargement of manufacturing must be complementary to these two. It was especially important that increases in industrial development not divert labor from agriculture nor "retard or prevent the population of the Western Wilderness," for it was generally understood that "the conversion of this extensive wilderness into cultivated farms" contributed immensely "to the population, strength, and real riches of the country." Occasionally there was some challenge to such thinking, as in an 1804 memorial of the "Artists and Manufacturers of Philadelphia," which denounced any idea that "the prosperity of the citizens, in old established situations, were to be sacrificed to new projects and land speculators [in the West]." But political realities at the national level suggested caution, and Hamilton was careful to specify that manufacturing was most suitable for those "large districts which may be considered pretty well peopled"; having "fewer attractions to agriculture . . . , they exhibit a proportionably stronger tendency towards other kinds of industry. In these districts may be discerned no inconsiderable maturity for manufacturing establishments." Furthermore, the newest factories, using machinery and division of labor, made possible the "additional employment of classes of the community not originally engaged in the particular business," most especially women and children (others would specify residents of almshouses, orphanages, and prisons). Hamilton also pointed to "the composition of our towns" and the "large proportion of ingenious and valuable workmen, in different arts and trades, who, by expatriating from Europe, have improved their own condition, and added to the industry and wealth of the United States." Therefore, he said, "in respect to hands for carrying on manufactures, . . . we shall in great measure, trade upon a foreign stock, reserving our own for the cultivation of our lands and manning of our ships."

Such arguments reflected a general theory of regional development in which manufacturing becomes appropriate at a certain stage and serves as a complement to agriculture and commerce. There was also the need to find specific kinds of places suitable for these new activities. Hamilton and a group of associates attempted to show the way. They formed a corporation to create a "National Manufactory" with a diverse array of mills and factories at the Great Falls of the Passaic ("one of the finest situations in the world"). It was only fifteen miles from Jersey City on the Hudson, and New Jersey itself had the right qualities: "It is thickly populated—provisions are there abundant and cheap. The state having scarcely any external commerce and no waste lands to be peopled can feel the impulse of no supposed interest hostile to the advancement of manufactures." It also "appeared prudent to take a position in that state for the purpose of interesting New York and Philadelphia." Although they got underway, digging canals and laying out their company town of Paterson (named after the New Jersey governor) within their generous concession, the program soon foundered on inadequate capital and labor unrest. The real assets of the place were so solid, however, that a thriving industrial city did soon emerge.

Meanwhile, Tench Coxe, a Pennsylvanian associate of Hamilton, set forth plans for a large manufacturing town on the Susquehanna, which included a great many mills, 800 brick and stone houses (graduated into several sizes and prices), schools, churches, library, and taverns. He conceived it as a prototype for more such places and thought that these would be best situated on the west bank of the great river in central Pennsylvania on the borderland between the well-settled country to the east and the highland frontier on the west, "an auxillary to Philadelphia, as Manchester, Leeds, Birmingham, and Sheffield, & c. are to the seaports of Great Britain." Coxe also argued for the location of factories at various state capitals, and in a letter to Jefferson stated that the same concept "may apply happily in the federal district." These capitals mostly lay near the head of river navigation, with waterpower available, but it seems clear that Coxe and others of the time were also looking for a strong governmental hand in the location, design, subsidy, and promotion of a new kind of manufacturing city. The concept of a special state land reserve (and exemption from militia service and taxes) was apparent, for example, at Paterson.

Such, however, would not be the case in the United States. New industrial settlements emerged directly from the efforts of private manufacturers, without government design or sponsorship. David Humphreys has been cited as the creator of "the first true mill town." It was he, following a brilliant career as a statesman, who brought from Spain the first flock of merino sheep and undertook to transform the production of wool and woolens in America. He purchased a site at Rimmons Falls on the Naugatuck River in southwestern Connecticut and created a new community. His textile machines were tended mainly by orphans brought from New York City, for whom boardinghouses were constructed. At an early stage of his project Humphreys toured factories in Europe and returned determined to preclude the evils thereof. Neat white-painted buildings, gardens, schools, and a variety of programs and awards characterized this paternalistic community and made it famous as a model village as well as producer of America's best woolen cloth ("others may prefer the cloths of Leeds and London," said Henry Clay in 1810, "but give me those of Humphreysville"). Meanwhile Samuel Slater gradually developed a village model as his operations expanded to a succession of sites upriver from his first factory at Pawtucket (fig. 62). Slater built tenements to house entire families and offered work to all of employable age. He also provided a store, school, church, and "extended his power over as many phases of his workers' lives as they would tolerate." Such mill villages were duplicated, with varying degrees of paternalism, throughout the "Slater system" area of southeastern New England.

The most famous of these early American industrial centers was on a very different scale but not radically different in concept. The Merrimack Manufacturing Company purchased entire control of the waterpower and land at the site and set about building a large complex. As Dunwell stated:

> Although the investors foresaw eventual growth of the community to over twenty thousand inhabitants, they had no comprehensive city plan in mind. . . . At most,

they anticipated a series of adjoining industrial units, each comprising a group of mills and its associated housing, all arranged for maximum hydraulic efficiency.

Yet this aggregation of manufacturing units would soon become the most astonishing industrial city in American history and take the name *Lowell* in memory of the Waltham promoter who proved the feasibility of a large-scale integrated system. . . . In reality, the new city was neither visionary nor novel, being a limited dream of limited men desiring maximum corporate profit on a long-term investment.

Lowell became internationally known not just because of its size and success but because of its landscape and social environment—and its easy accessibility from Boston and astute promotion by its prominent corporation. Its most famous feature was the "Lowell girls," a labor force recruited from New England farm families and housed in large brick boardinghouses under comprehensive supervision, with churches, libraries, and lecture halls devoted to their edification. For a decade or so such laborers flocked to the mills and proved to be highly dependable and industrious workers; most stayed only a few years and then returned home or went on to

62. Globe Village, Massachusetts, c. 1822.
A new four-story cotton mill alongside the Quinebaug River provides the focus of this view of a typical Slater village just west of the Blackstone Valley. In the left foreground are two tenement houses and the store, and upstream is an earlier (1814) cotton mill. This deceptively idyllic rural scene is attributed to young Francis Alexander. Alan Burroughs called Alexander, son of a Connecticut farmer, "a dependable craftsman" who painted with "simplicity and clarity" before he went off to Europe and became suffused with sentimental and aristocratic influences. (Photograph courtesy of Old Sturbridge Village)

something else, and they generally regarded their Lowell experience as both valuable and respectable. This local recruitment, ample supply, and regular turnover—
this "circulating current from the healthy and virtuous population of the
country"—was basic to the Lowell concept: it ensured that factory work, labor
relations, and living conditions would escape the well-publicized horrors of English
industrial life.

The New England mill villages generally, and the Lowell scheme especially,
were widely idealized at the time because they seemed to represent exactly what the
philosophers of national development had sought: manufacturing as a comfortable
complement to rural life; "the machine in the garden"—unobtrusively. "Widely
distributed . . . at salubrious spots," making use of special categories of surplus
labor, drawing upon the deep regional cultural traditions of industry, discipline,
thrift, and obedience to paternal authority, "many of these early factory towns
appeared to be peaceful, ordered, traditional communities to those who lived and
worked in them."

But of course they were not really traditional, for they were based on a radically
new technology which was ultimately beyond the local community's power to
control and manage. The regularity and uniformity of machine labor and production might, in its early stages, seem to fit in well with traditional concepts of
harmony and efficiency and the social virtues undergirding a tranquil republic, but
a more fearful dimension became ever-more apparent: a massive, relentless regi-
mentation that threatened to turn human beings into machines. Furthermore, any
particular mill, no matter how large, became an ever-smaller part in an ever-
enlarging system and subject to forces and decisions quite beyond the control of
any single corporation.

The challenge of accommodating this new industrialism (the word begins to
take on such meaning during this time) to larger and valued qualities of American
society would preoccupy social philosophers for the next hundred years—from,
say, Nathaniel Hawthorne to Lewis Mumford. Such critical voices would always be
hard to hear above the paeans to progress, but some of the problems were already
obvious. By the 1850s the utopian image of New England factory towns was
becoming tarnished. Intense market competition and business depressions undermined stability. Many of the small mill villages were owned by a single proprietor
and could be closed down or sold entire. In the larger mills labor problems soon
emerged. Even the "Lowell girls" became restive over wages, hours, and stultifying
supervision. Furthermore, the continued expansion and competitiveness of the
larger complexes made them ever-more discordant with and less and less sustained
by the surrounding rural society. Managers seeking more labor turned increasingly
to immigrants, whole families of them, and provided them with less care and
supervision, and thus the very thing that the founders had spoken against—factory

workers as a separate caste—began to emerge. As is so often the case, some such people had actually been there from the first, but were generally unacknowledged. The careful stratification of living quarters at Lowell (and elsewhere) featuring a mansion (for the manager), modest single houses (for overseers and skilled workers), and boardinghouses (for the ordinary machine tenders) left the Irish day laborers, who had dug the canals, built the dams and mill structures, and continued at menial jobs, to fend for themselves. Their shantytown "paddy camps" on nearby vacant land were not part of the famous landscape, but in the 1850s more than half the labor force in the mills was Irish.

The advent of steam power further undermined the desired agrarian-industrial symbiosis. As Anthony Wallace noted, once "the reliable steam-driven factory could be . . . placed alongside a railroad beside a harbor, within a great city . . . the wilderness lost its plausibility as a site for industry." He was describing the change that overtook the lesser number of "Christian capitalist" communities lining the millstreams of southeastern Pennsylvania, and his exposition of Rockdale is a useful reminder that while the great attention given to these early industrial communities in America has been almost entirely focused—then and now—on New England, similar kinds of places were to be found in other regions.

It is even more important to make clear that there were other kinds of industrial communities, equally representative of this new era, but utterly obscure in comparison with these famous New England showplaces. Travelers of the time might well remark upon particular iron mills or engineering works or even make a point of visiting unusual mining facilities, such as the remarkable gravity coal tram system at Mauch Chunk in the Lehigh Valley, but neither they nor more general social commentators were likely to extol Pennsylvania towns as models for the American industrial future (fig. 63). There were company towns in that region also, and corporations developing mines and mills in the mountains often had to provide some workers' housing and a mercantile store, but the result was likely to seem a shantytown in comparison with the brick blocks and avenues of New England and with none of the vaunted moral supervision by proprietors. And of course there were no "Lowell girls" with their literary societies; the heavy labor required was supplied by the muscles of male immigrants, mostly Irish, Welsh, Scottish, or English. These Pennsylvania valleys could be picturesque in the romantic sense of the time, but the actual scenes were quickly transformed into hills ravaged of their forest cover, valley floors crammed with canals, railroads, and the shambling structures and rubble of industry, the waters running red and green with wastes, the whole atmosphere thickened by a gray pall of smoke and dust and grime. It challenged the skill of any artist to portray such a scene as a harmony of man and nature—as in the now-famous rendition of *The Lackawanna Valley* by George Inness in 1855. As Leo Marx has shown, the very attempt to do so, and the fact

63. Mauch Chunk, Pennsylvania, 1845.

Mauch Chunk ("Indian" for Bear Mountain) was set up as a company town by the Lehigh Coal and Navigation Company. Located where the Lehigh River cut through the eastern end of the southernmost anthracite field, it quickly became a major shipping point. At first a primitive tramway brought the coal from the mountain to the coal barges (mules hauled the empty cars back); in 1844 a new system, powered by stationary steam engines, was installed and became a major tourist stop. The company began selling lots to the public in 1832, and by the time of this sketch, this seat of newly formed Carbon County has begun to spread from its riverfront up the steep narrow valley. In 1953 the town was amalgamated with its residential satellite, East Mauch Chunk, and renamed Jim Thorpe. (Courtesy of the MG-219 Philadelphia Commercial Museum Collection, Pennsylvania State Archives, Harrisburg)

that the painting was commissioned by the railroad company, were important clues to American attitudes about these new forces. But we must also cut through that sentimentality and recognize clearly what was already discernible at midcentury: that the dominant patterns of industrializing paleotechnic America would come to resemble the ravaged valleys of Pennsylvania much more than the model mill towns of New England.

In an essay included in the first extensive national *Report on Manufactures,* in 1833, Samuel Slater, by then a highly successful and esteemed industrialist, declared:

If the people of this country desire to be a civilized and powerful people, they must cultivate and promote those arts of life which form the elements of civilization and power. An exclusively pastoral or agricultural nation can never be formed into a polished or a powerful community.

Twenty years later whatever one might think of its civilization and polish, there was no disputing the power of this American community. The United States was surging forth in industrial production, American machinery was being exported to other industrial nations, and "the American system of manufactures" was becoming a topic of keen interest among rival producers in other countries. The pivotal event in a general recognition of this status was the Crystal Palace Exhibition of 1851 in London. If it was not generally appreciated that the extraordinary building itself (essentially a vast greenhouse), erected in an incredibly short time, was a perfect illustration of American methods, the production and performance of American machines such as McCormick's reaper, Hobbs' locks, and Colt's repeating pistols, made it apparent that not only had America "clearly developed a native technical tradition equal in vitality to that of the industrial nations of Europe," it was actually well ahead in the application of machine-production techniques (Hobbs and Colt soon thereafter set up factories in England). Two years later the New York Industrial Exhibition offered an American version of the same kind of show and even though this imitation (America's first world's fair) could hardly equal the sensational impact of the original, it did help to confirm the impressive advances of American manufacturing, a fact certified by several British experts who had been sent by parliamentary order to assess that situation. The Committee on Machinery of this expedition was especially concerned with firearms and, upon their recommendation, the main British armory was soon equipped with American machine tools to revolutionize the production of Enfield rifles.

Such transatlantic interactions underscore those "intensely dynamic reciprocities of America and Europe" that were thematic in Victor Clark's early landmark *History of Manufactures in the United States,* and Thomas Cochran's more recent and specific emphasis on the "geocultural" importance for technical progress of this close interaction between "two rapidly advancing cultures with a common language." Industrializing America must be understood in the context of an Atlantic World as well as of a continental expanse full of resources, challenges, and opportunities for an especially enterprising people. Whatever the sources might be, by midcentury both the tools and the attitudes essential to a continued acceleration of industrial expansion seemed to be in place. The real "American system of manufactures" was something more than the efficient use of machines to produce machines, it involved a new scale of production and an inventiveness, an openness, an avid national commitment to create an environment in every way congenial to capitalistic enterprise. As Cochran concluded, whereas "Europe modified industrialism to fit its various cultures, . . . American culture more readily changed to suit new conditions."

That industrialism, like so much else, had taken on special characteristics in America was celebrated at the time and has been acknowledged ever since. But we must also keep in mind what our reconnaissance has given us a start on: that, as always, there were marked differences from region to region in such things, a geography of attitudes as well as artifacts relating to the harnessing of these forces.

12. Cementing the Parts Together: An American Nation

"The United States form, for many, and for most important purposes, a single nation. . . . In war, we are one people. In making peace, we are one people. In all commercial regulations we are one and the same people . . . America has chosen to be, in many respects, and to many purposes, a nation." So declared Chief Justice John Marshall in 1821. That forty-five years after the Declaration of Independence he felt the need so to declare and to spell it out was a reflection not only of a common mode of judicial pronouncement but of a good deal of uncertainty and some outright opposition to the idea. A few years later, in a debate over the funding of "national" roads, Senator Smith of South Carolina warned against this "insidious word": "the term National was a new word that had crept into our political vocabulary," he said, but "it was a term unknown to the origin and theory of our Government"; indeed, it had been specifically expunged from the draft of the Constitution.

Yet if the Constitution did not explicitly declare a nation, it implicitly defined the framework for one. It clearly created a political unity, empowered it, and required that it be given allegiance. That the nation so defined was a callow creature and limited in its powers was obvious enough, but it could legitimately claim the name. Washington, Jefferson, and many other statesmen used the term, often with emphasis upon its basic connotation (as when in his Farewell Address Washington warned of regional divisions as a threat to the "community of Interest in *one Nation*"). Nevertheless, there *were* special features to the American case. The United States was clearly not the product of a deep-rooted nationalism, a cumulative, insistent force asserting the claims of a self-conscious ethnic group to a homeland. Revolution and independence had been unexpected events, arising from the grievances of many separate colonies, and in a very real sense, "the American nation was a by-product that [at the outset] nobody wanted." "Thus," as John M. Murrin goes on to say, "in the architecture of nationhood, the United States had achieved something quite remarkable. . . . Americans had erected their constitutional roof before they put up the national walls," and "the Constitution became a substitute for any deeper kind of national identity." American nationalism therefore was unorthodox in being connected first of all to a set of principles rather than to an ancestral place.

Yet, if the foundations are firm, erecting the roof before the walls may be entirely appropriate. The American edifice was solidly grounded: its people shared a common language, laws, and institutions, and the rich colonial experience of expanding upon and domesticating a new world; and although the Revolution had been unforeseen, the experience of mobilization, warfare, triumph, and consolidation was a powerful nationalizing process—indeed, it would come to be regarded as a classic, generic case. For a generation after the Revolution there was, expectedly, much emphasis on differentiating America from Europe, asserting the special virtues of American polity and society for all humankind; there was also, inescapably, a preoccupation with basic security, with protecting the newborn state from the imperial machinations of the great powers (foreign reports were dominant in American newspapers). Nevertheless, both the worst (the burning of Washington, D.C.) and the best (Jackson's triumph at New Orleans) of that experience served to reinforce nationalism. In 1816 Albert Gallatin sensed a new level of pride and sensibility among the people: "They are more American; they feel and act more like a nation."

Just what it meant to feel and act like a nation was not entirely clear, however, and it became a topic of avid discussion over the next several decades. That America was something quite different from Europe no longer needed such strident assertion, for every European observer confirmed it (though not all agreed that it was something better). Americans could therefore turn from the Atlantic and their colonial past and focus intently upon their national future, on what they as a people had in common, what held them together, and how they might best strengthen themselves for the building of a continental republic (domestic news soon submerged foreign in American papers).

There was a paradox in the accelerating growth of nationalism in the United States concurrent with a persistently minimal central government establishment. The Jeffersonian political triumph of 1800 initiated "a movement that was national in scope and universal in its ideological appeal," yet one in which the central concept of freedom was grounded not only in "natural law" ("all men are created equal") but also in an instrumental, utilitarian concept ("appetitive, rationalistic, propulsively self-improving economic man") that called forth the greatest possible freedom of enterprise. The central government was thus restricted to the most rudimentary internal national tasks: to deliver the mail; to coin money and collect revenues (including the sale of federal lands); to guard the perimeter against foreign foes. Nevertheless, even such limited responsibilities contributed something to nation-building.

The Post Office was at once the simplest and most comprehensive of these systems. Administered from the General Post Office in Washington, D.C., it distributed the mail by railroad, steamboat, sail, stagecoach, sulky, horseback, and foot to all the people. As a spatial pattern directly reflective of the population surface, it was recurrently adjusted to the expanding margins of settlement and differential growth. This routine delivery service was not simply a matter-of-fact obligation of government. The need to distribute newspapers (conveying business intelligence and political discourse) as cheaply as possible was accepted from the beginning as a necessary cost "to help the fragile republic cohere as a nation." Such a principle was fraught with definitional and regional implications, however, and "the development of postal policy and administration also presents one of the clearest examples of federal involvement in the nineteenth-century economy and in day-to-day business affairs." A major issue was the fact that cheap rates favored the circulation of metropolitan over local papers. A North Carolina representative warned against allowing "the poisoned sentiments of the cities" to destroy the local country papers, which were the organs of "our country opinions, our provincial politics, . . . our conservative doctrines." When in response to such pressures Congress in 1851 allowed free postal circulation within the county of publication and imposed stiff distance-gradation zones on all other destinations, opponents decried it as an internal "tariff" on information that would have an insidious tendency, in the words of Senator William H. Seward of New York, "to denationalize this Union." The policy was abandoned the following year and replaced with a single nationwide rate of one cent for all regular newspapers.

This primary concern for the diffusion of business and political information was always evident. Personal letters incurred heavy distance charges until 1851, when a three-cent nationwide rate was initiated. However, most newspapers always carried varied fare, mostly reprinted from exchanges, and magazines and special interest publications multiplied rapidly during this era. Bound books were first accepted as mail in 1851. The federal postal system therefore became an immense network of channels for communication of great importance to this expanding society: "it provided for redundancy in the circulation of news, supplied a varied diet of information, accommodated complex messages, and permitted any point in the network to send information to any other point." By its role in routinely facilitating supralocal communication through a wide variety of literature the postal system was perforce a nationalizing instrument—even if not necessarily a decisive one (fig. 64).

The ring of military posts along the edges of the national domain, sporadically adjusted to territorial annexations and advances of the imperial front against as yet unsubdued Indians, might seem a sharp contrast to the comprehensive coverage of the postal service, but such an inference would be seriously misleading. For these peripheral fortifications were but the terminals of one of the earliest complex national systems. As Cynthia A. Miller has shown, once we trace the networks by which the forces on these frontiers were supplied with food, clothing, shelter, fuel,

64. A Quasi-Official Map of the United States, 1841.
This is the eastern half of a large map produced by David H. Burr, a well-established surveyor and map maker who served as topographer to the U.S. Post Office Department, 1832–38, and geographer to the House of Representatives, 1838–47. Burr compiled information from post-masters throughout the country and also published a set of large state and regional maps showing post offices and routes. This national map is a distillation from those postal sheets, and the density of place-names offers a general sense of the density of settlement. (Courtesy of the Library of Congress)

arms, equipment, and men, we can discern several sets of systems anchored diversely in the core of the nation (fig. 65). Political patronage had some influence on the pattern of regional armories and arsenals, but the major facilities reflected rather closely the structure of the national economy. Thus for many decades virtually all army uniforms were made in Philadelphia, most of the small arms and swords came from New England, heavy ordnance was apportioned among four manufacturers (West Point, Georgetown, D.C., Richmond, Pittsburgh), and most of the wagons and camp equipage were produced in various factories in the Northeastern industrial regions. Subsistence was obtained through contract bids from suppliers in the agricultural regions most accessible to the frontier posts, and firewood, hay, and horses were procured from more local sources. All except these local items were distributed through regional arsenals and depots by the most efficient means of transportation. Always working with niggardly budgets, the quartermaster was quick to make use of canals, steamboats, and railroads almost as soon as these were put in service. As we have seen, the army helped to create this infrastructure, and we must recognize the national importance of the engineering training offered by the United States Military Academy at West Point (founded in 1802). Adding the naval dockyards, Naval Observatory, Hydrographic Office, and Naval Academy at Annapolis (1845)—all operating as a militantly separate system—completes the main framework of this official establishment that was ultimately under central command from Washington, D.C.

Keeping this system supplied with manpower was a chronic problem, for military service was not commonly regarded as one of the attractive options in this land of opportunity. There was an attempt to recruit within the regions of army regiments and naval bases, and (except for the brief emergency of 1813–15) at first only citizens were technically eligible to serve. Such policies proved so insufficient, however, that the citizenship restriction was removed in 1828, the recruiting services turned to the great ports, and within a few years immigrants made up 40–50 percent of the annual intake of about 1,000–3,000 men to be sent to the many army garrisons. Even though the numbers involved at any one time were small, the cumulative effect of rotating thousands of men year after year through what was perforce an assimilating and nationalizing process cannot have been negligible.

A geographical perspective on the military establishment thus reveals a "proto-military-industrial complex" seated in the national core and a system of systems under central command in the capital designed specifically to display an American presence and power around the borders of the nation, offering, in short, an assertive definition of the national space.

There was really nothing else of comparable importance. Whereas in most independent states, kingdoms, and empires central bureaus and departments played major roles in shaping systems of education, public health, police, banking,

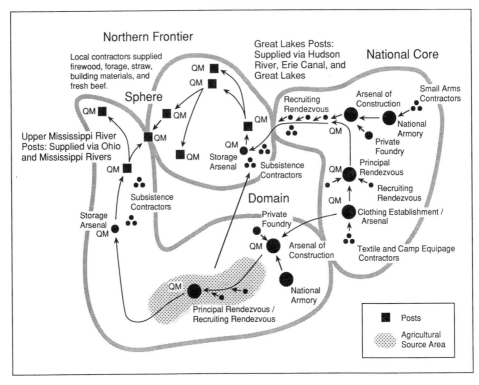

65. The U.S. Army Logistics Complex.
This diagram offers a simplified version of the several quartermaster (QM) systems supplying the outposts on the northern frontier in the 1830s and 1840s. The "Principal Rendezvous" within the National Core is New York City, that in the Domain is Newport Barracks, across the river from Cincinnati. (Courtesy of Cynthia A. Miller)

commerce, and much else, there was strong resistance to any hint of such a thing in the United States. Repeated efforts to create some sort of "Home Department" with some of these responsibilities reached an early peak in the 1820s in efforts to establish a Bureau of Public Economy and receded with the veto of "national roads" and the collapse of the Whiggish "American System." When a Department of the Interior was finally created, in 1849, a reluctant President Polk registered his "serious objections to . . . its consolidating tendency," though in fact it long remained no more than a conglomerate of miscellaneous bureaus.

One of those new subdivisions of Interior presumably did exert a subtle nationalizing influence. The General Land Office, in charge of the survey and sale of public lands, continually expanded the impress of the national order upon western America. As noted, the full imprint of that rigid rectangular design only gradually emerged as the countryside became ever-more domesticated, but it worked its way into common consciousness. In the early years of the Republic travelers might remark, as did Timothy Flint, upon "the beautiful simplicity of the limits of farms, introduced by our government, in causing the land to be all surveyed in exact squares"; by the late 1850s half the nation had been laid out in such manner, and it was generally understood that "the grid objectified national, not regional, order, and no one wondered at rural space marked by urban [Philadelphian] rectilinearity." In its simple, rational, repetitive pattern with uniform spacings and the complete absence of common lands, it was the perfect landscape display of some fundamental national concepts.

A more overt, readily visible (if more sporadic) mark of the national presence was the slowly increasing number of governmental buildings designed specifically to make a statement about America. The Capitol itself was of course the central symbol, but its influence was not immediate or direct. Domes were much in fashion and the focal building in Washington underwent three versions over a span of more than fifty years before it became the monumental symbol of world fame. In 1800 "there was no universally acceptable image of what an American capitol should be," and for years thereafter attention was focused on the state level because nearly every state, old or new, undertook some sort of capitol project. It was generally understood in that early period that states were the basic sovereign entities and primary representations of republican values, whereas the central government was a more abstract, minimal superstructure. And so the states took their inspiration from examples in their midst: first Bulfinch's elegantly domed statehouse in Boston, and in the 1820s Stephen Hills's "marriage of dome, rotunda, portico, and balanced houses" in Harrisburg that "united for the first time the architectural symbols of American democracy" (fig. 66). In the Jacksonian era a simpler classical temple was selected by several states, reasserting those civic virtues first declared by Thomas Jefferson in Richmond.

The first Greek Revival buildings in the national capital complex (the Treasury and the Patent Office) were also begun in the 1830s, but that distinctive style had already been established as a national symbol by the central banking system (which Jackson had forthrightly dismantled). The main building of the Second Bank of the United States was begun in Philadelphia in 1816 under the powerful influence of Nicholas Biddle, who soon became its president. Biddle was passionately devoted to the Grecian model and by the time of its demise in 1833, "the bank had scattered twenty-six money temples around the country. These structures, makeshift or magnificent, established a federal presence and a collectively approved architectural symbolism of stability and order, which could impart the aura of real stability to even the most speculative banking enterprise" (fig. 67). Of course, the Greek Revival became a fervent fad in America during this time, gracing town and country alike (in some regions) in endless variations of expression and purpose, and this was not simply an emulation of governmental examples. It has been

Southern view of Harrisburg, Penn.

66. The Capitol at Harrisburg, c. 1856–60.
John Warner Barber's pen-and-ink sketch shows how Stephen Hills's domed statehouse dominated the townscape of a small city (c. 12,000) that was also thriving as an industrial and
commercial center. The large building on the left with central tower and tall smokestack
alongside was a new cotton mill. The covered bridge was completed in 1817, the first across the
Susquehanna; the railroad bridge dates from 1839; log rafts and arks were still a feature of traffic
on this broad, shallow river. (Courtesy of the I. N. Stokes Collection, Miriam & Ira D. Wallach
Division of Art, Prints and Photographs, the New York Public Library, Astor, Lenox and Tilden
Foundations)

suggested that it was peculiarly suited to American predilections not only because
of assumptions about its republican symbolism but because "columns could be
added at will—often with little expert knowledge—to provide a temple for everyone, whether banker or legislator or tradesman," or, indeed, farmer, not unlike the
simple, measured, uniform squares of land. However, it long continued to have
special power as a symbol of government and to spread under national (as well as
state, county, and city) auspices. Especially from the 1840s onward, "towns everywhere clamored for federally funded buildings as an indication of stature. And
Congressmen obligingly served them up" and post offices (heretofore commonly in
rented quarters), courthouses, customshouses, armories, arsenals, hospitals, and
asylums added an unmistakable national imprint to many a local scene. In 1850 the
newly created Office of Construction (Treasury Department), failing to stem the

wanton spread of federal favor, gave a new emphasis to central planning and standardization of design. (The Smithsonian Institution's new medieval castle rising midway on the Mall might seem a contradiction of such policies and indeed was meant to be an "antidote to the ordered mentality of the grid and the bare geometry" of Grecian architecture—but a cultural institution could be indulged in its pursuit of fashion without compromising the conviction that classical temples were the proper housing for authority.)

Turning from these more tangible evidences of national systems and symbols, we must note the formal bonds of citizenship. Here again the Constitution offered no

67. A National Imprint.

This small structure of 1834 in Louisville was one of the more elegant of the "money temples" that Nicholas Biddle's Bank of the United States placed in the main commercial centers. It also testifies that the calculated symbolism of stability was not locked into a rigid repetitive style, for here the two Greek columns have been tucked under a massive Egyptian Revival portico. The architect was James Dakin, a New Yorker, who, along with his brother, Charles, left a major imprint on several Southern cities. It now houses the Actors Theatre. (Photo by Richard Tripp, Courtesy of the Actors Theatre of Louisville)

explicit definition of such status nor how it might be acquired. There was the uncertainty inherent in this federal structure about the relation between state and national citizenship. Territorial or "birthright citizenship" was widely implied (for example, in reference to the requirement that the president be a "natural born Citizen"), yet everyone knew that it did not apply to all the people. Whole categories were excluded, subordinated, or marginalized. Indians were a separate, dependent population, themselves members of specific tribes or nations and as such generally ineligible for citizenship. Individuals who abandoned tribal society and elected to become members of White communities—as Indians were repeatedly urged to do—might become citizens, but the ways of doing so remained informal and uncertain. Other exclusions were defined in social practice and in the laws of the individual states. Slaves were obviously not citizens, but the status of "free colored," and especially free-born Blacks, was not so simple. Because color prejudice was so deep and widespread, designers and caretakers of the Union concentrated simply on how best to deny citizenship to this growing body of residents. Definition was left to individual state practices, reinforced from time to time by judicial decision. Over the years state courts came up with an array of contrived categories—"subjects," "denizens," "quasi-citizens," "wards of the state"—until 1857, when the Supreme Court declared, in the Dred Scott case, that no African-American could become a citizen of the United States by birth. Such a convoluted conclusion was based on an interpretation of citizenship as being consensual as well as natural, that it depended in part on the formal consent of the people, and, further, that such consent had been obtained for Whites by the popular ratification of the Constitution. (That all women as well as all Blacks had been excluded from such voting was routinely ignored at the time.)

Immigrants were yet another category, and the Constitution assigned Congress the task of establishing "a uniform rule of Naturalization." Initially defined as a process requiring two years of continuous residence in the United States, the sudden influx of French refugees soon after the French Revolution brought a change to five years in 1795, which the panicky Alien and Sedition Acts soon increased to fourteen years; in 1802, however, it was returned to five years, where it has since remained, despite occasional calls for a much longer probationary period (reacting to the unprecedented influx of Roman Catholic "aliens" in the 1840s, the Know-Nothing party wanted to require twenty-one years of residence). Naturalization itself remained a simple process: essentially one could become a member of the American household by swearing allegiance to the political abstractions inscribed on the constitutional "roof"—or, one might better say, inscribed on the frieze or pediment of the national temple.

Naturalization provided legal incorporation into the national family but was no guarantee of warm social acceptance. So long as the inflow remained small there was little debate (although a degree of uneasiness was often expressed) about the general principle of welcoming European immigration; humanitarian ideals were well buttressed by the need to increase the labor supply and push up land prices. But as the volume and character of this influx changed and as new ideas about race and destiny and progress took hold, a new consciousness and concern about just what constituted "the American people" emerged. In his *Compendium* of the 1850 census, James De Bow devoted separate sections to the White, Free Colored, and Slave populations, and relegated the 407,064 "unrepresented and untaxed" Indians to a footnote (observing that "the number of Indians (taxed) domesticated and absorbed in the population cannot be ascertained"). Most of these differentiations were of course pertinent to one of the basic reasons for conducting a census: the requirement of decennial reapportionment of congressional representation. But De Bow also offered a new set of categories: "The present population of the Union may be said to consist of, *first* the number who were in the country on the formation of the government in 1789, and their descendants; *second,* of those who have come into the country since that period by immigration, and their descendants, . . . ; *third,* of those who have been brought in by annexation, as in Louisiana, Florida, New Mexico, etc., and their descendants." In its context such a scheme might seem to be no more than another item among De Bow's compulsive demographic calculations, but it was a clue to something more subtle and important. For in pointing to a distinction between the old stock and the newcomer, between colonial and immigrant, it coincided with the emergence of genealogical societies, the definition and veneration of the "founding families" of the nation, a sharpened sense of "Americans" and "foreigners." Furthermore, such distinctions were fundamental to Chief Justice Roger Taney's grounding of United States citizenship in a charter group; as Kettner summarized, "Those citizens who created the Union in 1789 formed a closed community in which membership was restricted to descendants of the founders and to aliens co-opted by the process of naturalization." Taney's opinion, resting more "on the social fact of prejudice and discrimination" than on legal precedence and logic, was specifically directed at Blacks, but those who arrogated to themselves the status of founders of the nation naturally saw assimilation of the unprecedented volume of immigrants to the standards and values of their "synthetic Anglo-Saxonism" as a crucial challenge.

The processes of assimilation certainly proceeded, but not always with the speed or in the direction so desired. The national government assumed no role, directly or indirectly. There was no naturalization program, no national school system, not even an official language (though there was at times a good deal of debate about such things). Left to the routines of social intercourse, cultural change was shaped by the patterns of encounter, by the local social geography of living spaces, occupations, recreations, numbers, ages, and sex ratios and by attitudes about behavior, religion, and ethnicity on the part of the peoples in contact. Some groups (such as many Germans) worked hard to resist assimilation and to maintain a strong cultural identity as a distinct ethnic segment of the already-diverse American people; with others (especially Irish Roman Catholics), the strong local barriers to assimilation only magnified and invigorated their ethno-religious consciousness. And there were many other variations in the patterns of integration; cultural pluralism had been a characteristic of American society since the early European implantations on North American shores, but the great annual waves of immigration in the 1840s and 1850s altered the proportions and magnified the power of such infusions, permanently affecting the content, style, and vitality of American life.

Such infusions, as we have seen, were highly uneven in regional impact (fig. 68). The contrast between North and South was extreme: 90 percent of the nearly 2.2 million foreign-born residents recorded in the 1850 census lived north of the Potomac–Ohio River boundary (extended to include St. Louis and the "Missouri

68. Foreign-Born and State Populations, 1850.
This cartogram was created by Jane and Richard Wilkie, for Wilkie and Tager, *Historical Atlas of Massachusetts*; it has been redrawn for this book. (Courtesy of R. Wilkie and the University of Massachusetts Press)

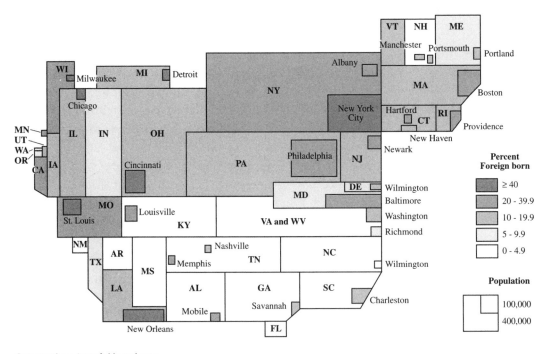

Cartogram base: Area of cities and states
determined by population size

Rhineland"), and about half of the small remainder were localized in and around New Orleans and Louisville; large districts in the South were virtually untouched (there were fewer than 20,000 in all of Georgia, Alabama, and Mississippi combined). Proportions were highest in the newest areas of the northwest (more than a third of the settlers in Wisconsin were foreign-born), but actual numbers were largest in the Northeast (more than a million in New York–New Jersey–Pennsylvania). Here, therefore, was a sharp, deep, and widening cleavage within the expanding body of the American people. To speak of the United States as a *pluralistic* society was a generalization that glossed over stark regional differences. In general, the North was pluralistic, but not wholly nor equally so. Southern New England, with its Irish-Yankee confrontations, was more clearly a *segmented* society, while northern rural New England was a minor residue of the self-consciously *homogeneous* society of Puritan-Yankee origins. Except for the *racially stratified* Creole Coast, and the lesser variations of central Texas, the entire South remained the same simple *biracial* society most of it had always been. The United States is better viewed overall as a *complex* nation encompassing several kinds of regional societies markedly altered in proportions and positions from those of colonial America (compare *Atlantic America*, table 2, "A Classification of Colonial Societies"). The mass immigrations of midcentury therefore not only intensified the social pressures within many American communities, they further strained the very idea of an "American ethnicity" as undergirding a national unity.

Most educational leaders seemed to regard this social geographic complexity of America as a primary challenge: "education for assimilation" was but a subset of the broader need to promulgate an "ideology centered on Republicanism, Protestantism, capitalism" to ensure the coherence of the whole. Yet however widespread may have been public approval of such an objective, there was everywhere stout resistance to any national formulation of such a program. General fears of centralization (in light of European developments often referred to as "Prussianization") combined with various convictions about the waste and futility of advanced education for a practical, democratic people long sustained an unusual degree of local control, yielding only grudgingly to statewide standardizations. Thus, "America had schools, but . . . America did not have school systems," and in place of such systems there emerged an unstable mixture of local public, quasi-public, philanthropic, private, parochial, and other church-related schools, varied in curriculum and quality and in presence and proportion from place to place. By midcentury most Northern states had some semblance of statewide standards for elementary public education, while the South relied heavily on private tuition-based academies. In his fresh perspective on nationalism, Wilbur Zelinsky called attention to the peculiarity of this American pattern. "The criticality of educational strategy" for fostering a common sense of a national past and character has been almost universally accepted, he noted, "but what sets the United States apart from virtually every other country is its lack of a fully centralized educational bureaucracy, one responsible for formulating and administering the curriculum throughout the entire public school system."

It would be little exaggeration to say that instead of an official centralized educational bureaucracy the United States had a self-appointed educational establishment. As Elson put it: "New England can justly be termed the schoolmaster of the nation." To the leadership and prevalence of Yankees as teachers and as founders of schools and colleges—giving substance to Timothy Dwight's vision for the nation—must be added their role in designing statewide standards, creating normal schools to train teachers and develop curricula, and writing and publishing textbooks. Although the most famous schoolbook of the time, *McGuffey's Eclectic Readers,* was the product of a Midlander (who spent his last thirty years as a professor at the University of Virginia), the Yankee dominance was unmistakable. These textbook authors "emphatically believed that there was such a thing as national character and that they had a duty to help form and preserve it." They set out to create a usable past, a national myth, and a definition of American virtue as the basis for the civic education essential to a coherent continental republic. Their books accepted as axioms "that the law of history is one of steady and inevitable progress toward greater material wealth and comfort as well as toward greater virtue and freedom," that the United States was in the vanguard of that progression, and that New England set the standard—was "the measuring rod"—for the nation.

At the adult level, the appearance from 1834 onward of volume after volume of George Bancroft's "gravely rhetorical" *The History of the United States of America from the Discovery of the Continent* confirmed that America was providentially leading the advance of liberty and justice. Although he was too learned and well trained (a doctorate from Göttingen) to depict all American history as simply an emanation from Plymouth Rock, Bancroft submerged the regional varieties of American development under "generalities about the wholeness and unity of the nation" grounded upon implicit Yankee virtues. Reviewers immediately praised "his patriotic zeal" and "the *Americanness* of his approach," and this towering evolving work was soon joined by other strongly romantic treatments of national themes.

By the 1850s, however, the tendency of school texts "to treat all of American history as a gloss on New England's came under spirited attack." Southerners were especially sensitive to Yankee "claims of patriotic eminence," and as the issues of slavery and union came to the fore textbook writers, who had heretofore tended to ignore the existence of sectionalism, became increasingly polemical and divisive, leading to denunciations and calls for *Southern* books in their place—but with little substantive response. Less blatant was the instinctive resentment and resistance of a larger proportion of newer Americans to the overweening Protestantism of the prevailing "education for assimilation." In 1852 the Roman Catholic leadership issued a call for sacrificial efforts to establish parochial schools, and many Lutherans, Mennonites, and others expressed similar concerns. Thus, although the rapid expansion of schooling and literacy offered a common grounding in the essentials of American character, the discordance between this unilinear, mono-cultural myth and the complex, pluralistic reality of the United States—the failure to develop a past equally usable to all sections of the Republic—represented a serious weakness in this fundamental tool of nationalism.

These pedantic expositions of nationalism were of course merely substantiating and formalizing the populist patriotism long expressed in exuberant and exhausting celebrations of February 22 and July 4. The "invention" of George Washington as "a full-blown national hero" was "the most remarkable symbolic feat of the Revolution"; the cult burgeoned during the event and was fully in bloom after his death in 1799. The Fourth of July came to called "the National Sabbath" and was readily enlarged to include reverence for the Constitution, "the sacred document of the national religion." This "holy nationalism," this sense of America as blessed by Providence, an instrument of the Almighty in the creation of a great moral society, was endemic in patriotic and political orations, an expression of American na-tionalism as a "civil religion." It was also indivisible from some central themes of the churches themselves, for "despite the competition among them, all the [lead-ing] denominations identified with the nation and worked to unify American culture under evangelical Protestantism." A parallel development in religious literature "evolved a myth of the American Christian past, one of the most power-ful myths to inform the history of both American religion and American society," insisting "that America had always been a Christian nation, from the settlement of Virginia and Massachusetts Bay to the writing of the Constitution." In fact, al-though religion had always been present, it was there in many different (and often conflicting) forms and had been relatively feeble in most of the colonies, important more as a badge of ethnic identity than as an influence on the direction of develop-ment. But a great upwelling had since taken place, and as Jon Butler has put it, by the 1850s America was "awash in a sea of faith": "Religious syncretism and creativity extended across antebellum society and easily rivaled the American ingenuity and adaptability evident in exploration, politics, and technology. White and black, rich and poor, literate and illiterate—Americans of all kinds, if not yet all Americans—brought forth religious movements astonishing in their variety, numbers, and vitality." However, "Americans who shared a common religiosity did not yet share a common religion," for "region, class, and especially race all con-strained the flow and dispersion of America's rising religious currents." Thus the formal expression remained within the great and growing number of denominations, as was made clear in the concurrent "landscape sacralization"—the common midcentury American cityscape prominently studded with the towers and steeples of competing churches.

As Bernard Bailyn has noted, "no other society in the world ever conceived of religion" as such an individual, voluntary affair, leaving people free to join, depart, change, and create religious institutions as they pleased. The major denominations emerged as nationwide networks of great importance: "They not only furnished millions of people with a primary relationship of belonging; they also afforded opportunities unmatched elsewhere for gaining experience in voluntary organization, developing lay leadership, and regulating human behavior. Their network of representative units gave ample occasion for communicating local concerns to their national leaders and for transmitting the authority of the leadership to the local units." Each denomination was perforce an extensive geographical system. Some of the most prominent churches remained distinctly regional in extent: the Congregationalists—and their deist offspring, the Unitarians and Universalists—essentially confined to New England Extended; the Quakers largely to the Midlands and New England outliers; the several Lutheran groups mostly to the Midlands; the Campbellites to the Upland South. But the Baptists, Methodists, Presbyterians, and Episcopalians were fully national in their operations, as was the Roman Catholic church, even though its presence in the South was locally concentrated. However much these ecclesiastical systems differed in concepts of authority, they all operated at district or regional levels within some sort of territorial organization—varying from the very loose and changing associations of the Baptists to the formal rigidities of Roman Catholic dioceses—and however equal in technical status such units might be, there was always at least some sort of informal hierarchy because, inevitably, some parts or places were more influential than others: sees, and headquarters, and the gathering places for some sort of periodic nationwide assembly—be it called a general association, conference, synod, convention, or plenary council; seminaries and institutes and religious orders of special influence; publishing houses and auxiliaries of extensive outreach. On the other hand, there were always powerful leveling influences and resistances to centralization in these as in other American systems. Thus among the Methodists—that most American of denominations—the idea of establishing a central university, supported by the entire church and offering the best of training for leadership, was repeatedly raised, and just as often defeated. Competition with local interests, jealousy over the selection of such a place, and the chronic shortage of funds, as well as the very nature of the concept, militated against such proposals; yet in fact Wesleyan University in Connecticut (established 1831) trained most of the professors in the many Methodist colleges in the North, as Randolph-Macon College in Virginia (1830) did for the South.

Such a regional differentiation was of more than incidental and internal significance. The fact that three of the largest nationwide systems broke apart into wholly separate Northern and Southern networks before midcentury was widely recognized as an ominous warning about the depth and comprehensiveness and strength of American nationalism.

Still, the United States did function as a national unit in many mundane ways, and more effectively and efficiently with each passing year. Such practical affairs were bound up with those innovations in transportation and communication that radically enhanced the movements of people, goods, and messages and thereby strengthened and quickened the pulsations of national life. If not quite every town and district was yet touched by the magic of these new iron and electric arteries, few were far beyond their reach and all could assume they would eventually be so enlivened.

The United States was one vast national market in which all goods (except slaves) could move from one state to another without restriction (except at times for minor complications relating to temperance laws). Although most consumer goods were marketed only locally or regionally, the larger potential was discerned early on, as by this Cincinnati writer: "A steamboat, coming from New Orleans, brings to the remotest villages of our streams, and the very doors of our cabins, a little Paris, a section of Broadway, or a slice of Philadelphia, to ferment in the minds of our young people, the innate propensity for fashions and finery." And the news of fashions and finery was also being broadcast across the land with increasing effectiveness in magazines and newspapers. *Godey's Lady's Book,* founded in Philadelphia in 1830, "became a household standard," featuring the latest in Parisian modes, while *Frank Leslie's Illustrated Newspaper* (1855) and *Harper's Illustrated Weekly* (1857), offering more diverse fare for a broader readership, became the leaders among a growing number of mass-marketed national magazines. Steam had worked a revolution in this realm, and with new presses and binding machines, "the publishing industry by the 1830s could turn out books as rapidly as nails or matches." Americans were by far the most voracious newspaper readers in the world; almost every town of moderate size had a daily paper, some had several (more than 250 in the nation by 1850), and even small and remote centers had a weekly: "no nation at any time was so thoroughly covered by the press."

There was no really successful national newspaper—although there were usually several aspirants, such as *Niles' Weekly Register* and the *National Intelligencer;* instead, there developed an extensive system of newspaper exchange that promoted a wide diffusion of information. To facilitate this system, post offices allowed newspapers to be sent free to the editors of other papers. The volumes of such exchanges recorded during a particular week in 1850 well reflect the principal nodes in the national circulatory system:

New York City	c. 35,000
Philadelphia	9,800
New Orleans	3,000
Boston	2,600
Cincinnati	2,000

The telegraph soon led to a newsbrokerage system. The first such association was created in 1846 when several newspapers in Upstate New York contracted to be supplied with state news generated in Albany. Three years later a New York City Associated Press was formed, with correspondents in ten other cities in North America, and by the late 1850s, having fought off rivals, this organization (backed by the city's seven leading newspapers) clearly emerged as the "nation's news-broker." Following an intense competition during the regularization and expansion of steamship service on the "Atlantic ferry," coinciding with the consolidation of the nation's telegraph system that had unlocked "a national marketplace of goods and services" for every business, and concurrent with "the nation's new-found ability" through telegraphy and journalism "to communicate more rapidly, more widely, and more voluminously with itself," New York City emerged as the control center for American as well as foreign news: "Everything of interest occurring in any part of this country is telegraphed at once to the general office in New York, copies being dropped at all intermediate points on the route, and the other parts of the country being supplied from the central office." In this as in so many other ways New York assumed a position of great national power that in every European country was firmly, designedly anchored upon the imperial or state capital. Kielbowicz reports that detailed surveys of total subscriptions to newspapers and periodicals in several small communities during this era revealed that "surprisingly, few individuals in either the North or the South took Washington, D.C. news-papers."

In an early issue of *Niles' Weekly* an essayist assured readers that, adding to the "cementing quality" of commerce, the press would become a vehicle for "uniformity of opinion and conduct." That clearly did not prove to be the case in the most pressing of national matters, but the rise of mass journalism and accelerated communications did create a national forum, broadened the base of political parties, and coincided with a remarkable increase in political participation: whereas only 9 percent of eligible voters cast ballots in 1820, more than 50 percent did so from 1832 onward. And despite the rising intensity of political dispute among various constituencies and broad sections of the country there was, over much of the same period, a deepening sense of nationhood, a common pride in their "American-ness." As Wilbur Zelinsky, who ranged far beyond the usual materials to examine an array of ceremonies and symbols in the landscape as well as in print, noted:

Nowadays it takes much flexing of the imagination to reconstruct the situation as it existed during the early nineteenth century when not just statesmen, bureaucrats, and professional warriors, but virtually all poets, dramatists, musicians, artists, and novelists threw themselves, heart and soul, into the nationalist cause, eventually to be joined by the rank and file of the population. At a certain point, which I would place in the 1820s or 1830s in the United States, nationalism saturated the community.

But his geographical perspective allowed him to proceed beyond this simple reinforcement of common suppositions:

> Because the evidence remains so fragmentary, we must be more reserved in speculating about the historical geography of nationalism in the United States than about its history. Nevertheless, such data as we do possess all point toward a single hypothesis: that nationalism seems to have developed earliest and most vigorously in the New England and Middle Atlantic states, then subsequently grew lustily in those sections of the Middle West settled from this northern segment of the Atlantic Seaboard, while it lagged far behind in the South.

It is important to be clear about what is being stated in these two quotations because they are grounded in what was a fundamental ambiguity of American nationalism. Insofar as it expressed simple pride and patriotism, participation in a glorious history, and the promise of a greater future, nationalism surely did "saturate" the whole country. All regions could draw equally upon the Revolution and life under the Constitution; all had participated fully in the expansion and development of the United States. But when it came to the formulation, articulation, and dissemination of the specific doctrines of this civil religion, to defining the moral qualities of the national character and the commitments to the national purpose, nationalism was primarily the product of a specific part of the country, a design promulgated in and diffused from a particular region. Thus the surface of nationalism, like most everything else, was uneven, with peaks and highlands and lower levels, in places marked by sharp changes in gradient; the formula prescribed to smooth and cement the parts together would not bond equally well on all these surfaces. Insofar as the South increasingly perceived "national" to be a code word for "uniformity" in terms threatening its interests, it would increasingly resist the spread of that "insidious" word and concept, and insist, in its place, on the basic primacy of federalism and regionalism in the shaping of America. In 1866, in the bitter aftermath of "the lost cause," the Southern apologist Edward A. Pollard gave vent to this Zelinskyan distinction: "It was Yankee orators who established the Fourth-of-July school of rhetoric, exalted the American eagle, and spoke of the Union as the last, best gift to man. This *afflatus* had but little place among the people of the South. . . . In the South the Union was differently regarded. States Rights was the most marked peculiarity of the politics of the Southern people; and it was this doctrine that gave the Union its moral dignity."

13. Morphology: The Shape of the United States, 1850s

In spite of enormous expansions in territory, population, and geographic development, the United States remained firmly anchored on the same nuclear area.
Nothing had effectively loosened it from the basic New York City–Philadelphia
axis, with its extensions to Boston and to Baltimore on either side, a pattern that
had been clearly evident by 1800.

These great Atlantic ports, together with their immediate hinterlands, still
constituted the main part of the *core* of the nation but were now augmented by two
long salients of diversified development: the Hudson–Erie Canal belt across Upstate New York, and the more tenuous extension across central Pennsylvania to
Pittsburgh and its radial industrial valleys. During the 1850s expansions in the
anthracite districts and the building of several rail lines from them northward along
the glacial valleys of New York to connect with the Erie Canal cities and Lake
Ontario ports were serving to bind these salients together and thereby consolidate
an enlarged core area.

By all measures of concentration and intensity this area (in general, six states
plus Wilmington-Baltimore) was the functioning heart of the nation. About a
third of the U.S. population lived here. The diversity and value of its productions
towered over every other region and notably dominated the new capital goods
industries. William N. Parker emphasized the developments "around and within
this industrial net" of cities during this time: "Like some complex sea organism, the
society of the Northeast had grown older and even more structured, piling up layer
upon layer of occupations and social groups, adding function to function through
complex interdependent internal markets and contractual arrangements." All of
the great networks were anchored here. Canals, steamboats, and especially railroads had bound the West to these northeastern seaports, and much of the traffic of
the lower Mississippi and Gulf ports was focused here as well. News, books and
magazines, fashions and finery, hardware and home furnishings, immigrants and
ideas—and contagious diseases—were all diffused across the nation primarily from
this corner of the seaboard (though New Orleans was another important entry for
the last of these).

When Alexis de Tocqueville remarked in the early 1830s that "the United
States has no metropolis," "no great capital city, whose direct or indirect influence
is felt over the whole extent of the country," he was complimenting the Republic
on its good fortune. He was also measuring the American situation against that of
his own country. Twenty years later America still had no Paris, but New York City
(fig. 69) certainly had some of the attributes of that famous metropolis. Now twice
the size of Philadelphia, it was clearly the main anchor of all those extensive
networks, and the real capital of the nation in so many respects: the great nexus

CITY OF NEW YORK.

69. New York City, 1856.

This dramatic scene by C. Parsons, published by N. Currier, brings the commercial node of the
nation and western anchor of the Atlantic World into clear focus. Miles of busy docks line the
North (Hudson) River and East River (right) and ferries are making routine crossings to a dozen
harbors around the margins of this complicated estuary, connecting with railroads fanning out
across the country. The towering spire of Trinity Church on Broadway at the head of Wall Street
provides a quick reference to the financial and commercial heart of the nation in the near
foreground: just to the east is the Grecian temple roof of the Customs House, and further on the
dome of the Merchants Exchange, and all through this lower end of Manhattan are the banks,
brokers, stock and commodity exchanges, shipping agents, taverns, and inns expressive of the
life of the premier port. The large round structure at the southwest tip of the island is Castle
Garden, built as a fortress, converted in the 1820s into a theater and resort, and now the great
immigrant receiving center (until superseded by Ellis Island in 1892). This angle of depiction
gives emphasis to the density and uniformity of the built environment in the years just before the
invention of the safety passenger elevator. (Courtesy of John W. Reps, from the Division of
Prints and Photographs, Library of Congress)

between the Old World and the New, the primary portal of immigration and imports, the control point of finance, commerce, and information, the managerial headquarters of the national market. In such ways New York City filled the role expected in modern complex societies, that of a single great center, seated within the core and dominating the whole; the foremost exhibit of authority, focality, intensity, and general influence on national life.

As noted in our initial assessment of such abstract patternings (*Atlantic America*, 400–406), however, the United States was not a model case. The most obvious departure was the placing of the highest political authority in a compromise site deliberately separate from the large commercial cities. In symbol and substance Washington was an undisputed *federal* capital but a very weak *national* capital. Poised on the critical cultural borderland, it was the scene of periodic negotiated adjustments in the balances of power among the member states and contending regions of this complex geopolitical association (adjustments made necessary primarily by the continuously changing human geography of the country). It was the undisputed command center of the military, but that was a feature more of imperial than national significance—it commanded no police force keeping an eye on ordinary citizens. It exercised astonishingly little direct control over the forces that shaped the nation. As we have seen, even in the sale and settlement of public lands the central government was usually scrambling to catch up with and legitimate decisions and actions already defiantly carried out by thousands of its citizens. To an important degree this lack of power was attributable to the continuing strength of Southern influence, because that section was most opposed to centralization, fearing that it would lead to interference with its vital sectional interests. It seems likely that had the core area possessed greater formal political power it would have adopted some sort of "American system" of Federalist-Whiggish lineage so as to make centralization serve its own sectional interests. How much a greater Northern influence might have enhanced the physical and symbolic ornamentation of Washington cannot be known, but it would surely have made that federal city more of a national capital as well. In fact, the negation of central power and planning was well exhibited in the diminution of the size of the nation's capital reserve: in 1846 Alexandria merchants obtained the retrocession of the Virginia corner of the District of Columbia rectangle to enable them freely to undertake a railroad to the west to counter the B&O invasion of the Shenandoah Valley.

In the simple model of the nation-state the core area offers the best display of important characterizing features of the culture. To put it thusly is, to a degree, a tautology, for it is the core area that sets the standard, that selects and defines what is "best," "proper," or deemed most appropriately "representative" in such things as dress, design, dialect, and social behavior. To say that "the core area sets the standard" is of course an abstraction referring to a kind of authority that may be less easily specified and traced as to actual power and place but has nevertheless an important influence on the character and direction of the whole. Leaving aside for the moment the difference between what the leaders of a particular society may wish to see displayed as characterizing features and what a reasonably acute and detached observer might offer as descriptive of the same, we may note some geographic particulars of the American case.

Peter Dobkin Hall has elaborated on the long-standing claim of Boston as "the nation's center of culture and capital" throughout this period. In addition to the obvious leadership in education and social reform, Hall has focused attention on the New England concern for the development of "character," on its response to the emerging world of private corporations, and on the vitalizing links between these two. The result was the socialization of a disciplined, dependable, predictable citizenry essential "for the creation of modern, large-scale organizations," and "a cadre of men in all sectors of activity, widely dispersed and strategically placed" who were adept at governance, participation, and protection of purpose of these new powerful instruments. Hall stresses not only the outward penetration of the nation by such men but the invigoration of local New England institutions under the auspices of state laws encouraging endowment trusts. In marked contrast, New York law was so hostile to such trusts as to cripple private support of philanthropic institutions, and therefore, "however wealthy New York might be, it had no universities or other cultural institutions comparable to Harvard or Yale, the Massachusetts General and Philadelphia Hospitals, or the Boston Atheneum." As this suggests, the Quaker establishment had led Pennsylvania closer to the New England position, but most states, like New York, adhered to the so-called Virginia Doctrine designed to curb such management and protection of private wealth. Boston could not rival the power of New York City as a financial center, especially in its influence on the operation of the national system, but it was a major source of capital and the seat of networks of Yankee capitalists who dominated many major corporations, especially in railroads, insurance, and investment banking.

As Hall has noted, "New England did not influence nationality by making the nation the subject of New England powercenters or even by making it adhere to political causes favored by New Englanders." Rather, it "established a cultural basis for nationality" that shaped a broader leadership and citizenry for corporate life on a continental scale in a new technological world.

In this geographic perspective, therefore, the United States had three capitals: Washington as the federal political center; New York City as the primary financial, commercial, intelligence, and in some ways (especially in consumer goods) cultural center (fig. 70); and Boston as the seat or source of individuals and associations seeking actively to shape the moral character of American life. Philadelphia remained a prestigious and important city, but overshadowed by the assertive

70. "Wall Street, Half Past 2 O'Clock, Oct. 13, 1857."

This painting by James H. Cafferty, a well-known artist of the day, and his associate, Charles G. Rosenberg, a specialist on architecture, depicts a dramatic scene at the onset of the Panic of 1857, referred to at the time as the "Western blizzard" whose "destructive power and chilling effects had surpassed all other financial gales." Grace M. Meyer, in her commentary on the painting, also offers a quotation from the *New Orleans Crescent* that well expressed the fear and hatred such events produced in other parts of the country: "New York, with fifty-seven suspended banks; New York, with her hundreds and thousands of bankrupt merchants, importers, traders and stock jobbers; New York, with her scores of thousands of starving workmen; New York, with her rotten bankruptcies permeating and injuring almost every solvent community in the nation; New York, the centre of reckless speculation, unblenching fraud and downright robbery; New York, the prime cause of four-fifths of the insolvencies of the country; New York, carrying on an enormous trade with capital mostly furnished by other communities." (Courtesy of the Museum of the City of New York, Gift of the Hon. Irwin Untermeyer) power of New York City and Boston. At midcentury there could be no doubt about the increasing dominance of this multicentered core area in the life of the nation.

All the rest of the contiguously settled area of the United States constituted the American *domain*. By definition it was dominantly American in allegiance and general character, but less densely settled, less intensively developed, less tightly bound to the national center than was the core. Domains are realms in which distinct regional variants arising from different physical environments, resources, local economies, and mixes of peoples are likely to show through the veneer of national culture. Viewed from the center such areas tend to be regarded as remote, "provincial," lagging "behind the times"—by implication, inferior. The response in the regions to such presumptions is likely to be mixed. Although there will almost certainly be some resentment of the dominating power of the center and core and some resistance to pressures to conform to national roles and standards defined therein, there may also be avid interest in developing more effective links so as to even out these disparities and share more fully in the fruits of modern life. The need to do so is commonly apparent in the continual drain of talented people from the domain to the richer and more diversified cosmopolitan centers of the core. (Dr. Johnson, seated with Boswell in the Mitre Tavern, gave classic expression to the generic principle at work: "Sir, the happiness of London is not to be conceived but by those who have been in it. I will venture to say there is more learning and science within the circumference of ten miles from where we sit than in all the rest of the kingdom.") The American case has its own special complexities in such geographic relations.

Northern New England and New York, mountainous western Pennsylvania, and the Pine Barrens of New Jersey were districts of the domain upon the margins of the core (fig. 71). Generally regarded as local "backwoods" locked into a subordinate role, gravitation of young adults from these areas to nearby cities and industries was an established pattern (Vermont and New Hampshire were nearly stationary in population). But the great provinces, of course, were those of the West and the South, each subdivided according to migration streams and further parceled into areas tributary to major ports. Ethnic enclaves of captive populations, most notably in the Creole Coast, added further complexity and a vivid diversity—as attested by Timothy Flint in Natchitoches, experiencing "indescribable emotions" in trying to read the "mouldering monuments" in the graveyard of that "very ancient town" where "Spanish, French, Americans, Indians, Catholics and Protestants lie in mingled confusion."

The South, even in broadest definition, was a perfect exhibit of classic domain characteristics: a large province differing in so many respects from the core; a regional culture (or cultures) rooted in distinctive physical conditions and historical origins, with emblematic economies, societies, and landscapes; a huge area

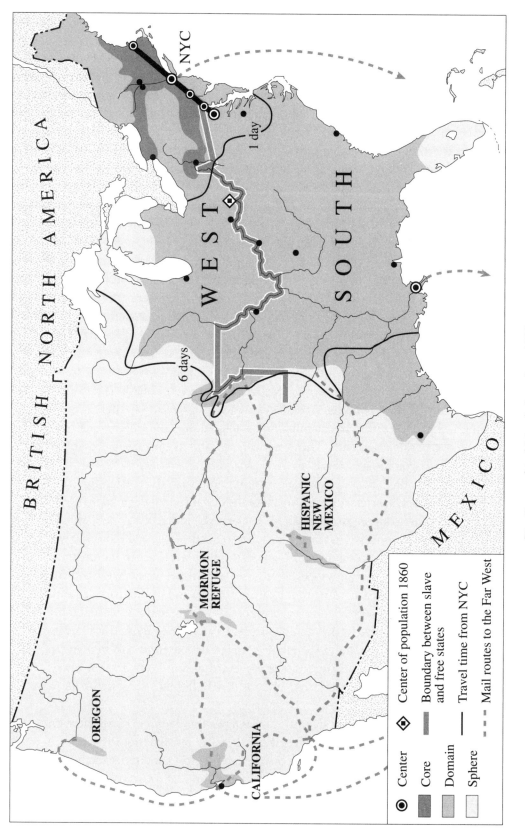

71. Geographical Morphology, Late 1850s.

Center

◎ Center of population 1860

◈ Boundary between slave and free states

Core

Domain

Sphere

◈ Center

Boundary between slave and free states

Travel time from NYC

Mail routes to the Far West

NYC

1 day

6 days

BRITISH NORTH AMERICA

WEST

SOUTH

MEXICO

OREGON

CALIFORNIA

MORMON REFUGE

HISPANIC NEW MEXICO

only loosely articulated into national networks. From 1820 onward slavery became the primary focus of regional self-consciousness, accepted as a defining characteristic by North and South alike. By the 1850s the power of the core was expressed in the end of comity among the states over the issue of fugitive slaves; this lack of mutual respect for laws reflecting provincial mores imposed a serious restriction on Southern security, mobility, and participation in national life, undercutting the benefits of association in a federal structure. (The crucial issue, of course, was not simply a lack of respect but the utter incompatibility of state laws relating to individual rights and freedom on either side of a long provincial boundary.)

The West, in marked contrast, was so much an emanation from and continuing extension of the core that differentiation was largely a matter of lower densities and complexity and of distance and interior location. Its agriculture featured old Eastern staples on a larger scale; its industries were similar in type and diversifying along Eastern lines; its population continued to draw on Atlantic sources and thereby fully reflect the newer immigrations. Buffalo and Pittsburgh, the great gateways between the core and the West, were not, therefore, poised on any obvious cultural divide. They were, for the moment, operational divides between eastern and western railroad companies, but these were being ever-more closely articulated and would soon become absorbed into single Atlantic-to-Mississippi systems. That kind of integration would be a basic step in the further westward extension of the core area of the nation later in the century.

Yet, not all Westerners sought closer integration with and emulation of the East. Some rejoiced in their distance and distinction from it, for they saw themselves positioned in the true heartland and destined to shape the future of the nation. In certain terms there *was* something peculiarly "American" about it, for the Old Northwest was the first great experimental ground for the new Republic with reference to Indian removal, federal land surveys and sales, and the evolutionary development of states out of territories; it was also the scene of a significant degree of convergence and intermingling of several streams of migration in the extensions of American society. Having been created by the United States to accommodate its own expansion on its own terms, with none of the lingering encumbrances of a European colonial past, these Western states were easily regarded by local citizens as more purely "American." And it was seductively easy to enlarge upon such features, combine them with the special position and prospects of the region— removed from the corrupting influences of aristocratic Europe, central and secure from all foreign dangers, and possessed of the richest land ever provided by a beneficent Providence on a scale such that "here every farmer in the world may become a freeholder in rural bliss"—and proclaim this West, this Garden of the World, to be the purest America, the real "body of the American eagle." Here, therefore, was the seat of a rival claim about the shaping of America, a challenge to the actual dominance of the Northeast core, an assertion of representativeness, of a standard by which America could best be measured. Here, in short, was the flowering of an agrarianism, isolationism, and exceptionalism that would long endure as an important geographic tension in American national life.

The West was indeed becoming a great exhibit of the burgeoning American business civilization and its thickening layer of middle-class culture. It was a society of aspirants: its Main Streets vitalized by the "deep American optimism about the effects of American expansion"; its freestanding homes of the latest tasteful design, each on its own ample plot of ground, "an index of progress, both personal and national"; its productive farms neatly ordered by fences and hedges and the latest machinery. But in fact such things were not peculiar to the region, and the very grounding of some of its asserted superiority was being compromised, for the West was rapidly urbanizing and industrializing, being flooded with European immigrants and brought in closer touch with—and dependent upon—the East and Europe. It was, in other words, emerging as the western half of an American North.

Such a North, however, was not yet a clear subdivision of the United States. Although "North" and "South" had become common geopolitical terms in discussions relating to the intensifying federal crisis, they carried no exact regional reference. The existence of slavery was not a simple key (as Delaware demonstrated), and indeed (as we shall see) even actual secession could not provide a clear delineation. Whereas South and West were common regional labels (albeit with many variations in application), there was no similar designation for a complementary North/East, that area usually being apportioned (as in the census summations) between New England and the Middle States (which sometimes included Ohio and Maryland, because of common industrial interests). There was, in fact, a growing resistance—and fear—in both the South and the West to the very idea of an emergent North.

Of course, a considerable degree of vagueness, variety, and even incongruity in regional perceptions and delineations was to be expected in such a rapidly changing geographic structure. The annexations and boundary settlements of the late 1840s had dramatically altered the shape of the country. By such acts the *sphere* of the United States had been formally extended to a long Pacific frontage. The term is derived from the classic concept of a "sphere of influence," referring to a peripheral area open to penetration and a measure of control by an imperial power. In decisive contrast with the domain, local indigenous people remain the majority population. In general, at midcentury the sphere included the western half of the national territory, all beyond the "western frontier"—which referred at the time to a defensive line of outposts, a limit rather than an advancing edge of settlement as in later Turnerian usage. The common assumption, basic to all policy then and thereafter, was that this entire area should become in due course fully integrated with and its people assimilated into the main body of the nation—or, in our morphological terms, that this vast sphere be transformed into a set of American domains. There were various ways of accomplishing this, and some of the processes and results were already evident, most obviously in the sudden influx into northern California, the continuing colonization of Oregon, and the development of connections to these distant regions, including surveys for a Pacific railroad. The Mormon colonization of the Valley of the Great Salt Lake was a peculiar variant of uncertain outcome: a body of people indisputably "American" in origin but dissenting and diverging from some basic norms of American society and withdrawing into western isolation to put up determined cohesive resistance to assimilation. The New Mexican Hispanos represented a more common imperial case, and territorial officials worked to get the processes of change under way. In a plea to Congress for aid in setting up schools, they stated that the people were eager to educate their children in English as well as in Spanish so that they might "take rank with the great body of enlightened freemen of the Union, to which they now belong" (in fact, such petitioners represented a small minority—and they got no response from an indifferent Congress). As for the rest, we have already described the various imperial policies employed by the United States to manage its captive peoples. Much of this huge area was not yet under effective control (and it had no accepted name as a major part of the country—census reports simply referred to it as "California and the territories"), but the army was in the field in several sectors and American power and proclivities made it certain that the human geography of this Far West would be drastically altered.

To this categorical area of influence must be added the Hawaiian Islands, where the United States was clearly the favored, though not unchallenged, imperial presence. Furthermore, the sudden expansion and consolidation of the American position in the Pacific had created new strategic interests, most especially in the trans-isthmian passageways across Nicaragua and Panama, marking these alien areas as potential additions to the American sphere (as Cuba had been targeted for thirty years).

These qualitative concepts—center, core, domain, sphere—bring into clearer focus critical geographic features of this dynamic nation. Applying the same model to the United States at different times in its history reveals not only some rather obvious changes but important lines of continuity. The most patent features of this half-century of massive reshaping were the vast increase in the extent of the sovereign borders (successive large geographic additions to the American sphere) and the vigorous westward march of American colonization (continuous expansion of the American domain). The broad extent and geographic balance of that advance is attested by the continuing westward shift of the center of population (as later calculated by the Census Bureau) approximately along the Thirty-ninth parallel. In 1800 that balancing point was just west of Baltimore (affirming the formal centrality of the new national capital), and by 1860 it lay in the Scioto

Valley of southern Ohio (almost exactly on the latitude of Washington). The implications of that alteration of the population surface were of course manifold and only in part manifest at the time. One of the more obvious to any reflective person at midcentury was that Virginia, the largest in area and most populous and powerful single unit in the sixteen-state federation of 1800, was now only sixth in area, fourth in population, and had had its congressional voice reduced from 22 (in a total of 106) to 13 (in a total of 233) in a federation of thirty-one states. Moreover, it remained as marginal to the nucleus of the national system—to the American core—as it had been in 1800, and the implications of that position were now far greater. Not only had the center of population moved into Ohio (rather than "continually advance[d] in a south-western direction," as James Madison had predicted), that large western state was becoming bound ever-more firmly into the primary networks of the nation; Ohio was an incipient part of an enlarged core while Virginia remained eccentric to such forces and essentially defeated in its larger competitive strategies.

Such underlying patterns and trends in regional power and influence, so much less obvious than expansions in territory, population, and settlement, had always caught the attention of the more astute observers of the shaping of this remarkable new nation. Tocqueville had concluded that "the civilization of the North appears to be the common standard, to which the whole nation will one day be assimilated." A generation later an experienced British student, Thomas Colby Grattan, spelled out in the introduction of his two-volume work *Civilized America* just how an American national character had come to be:

> Although the genuine Yankee is only he who belongs to the part of the country called New England, the term "Yankee," as the cognomen of the entire national family, is now as appropriate to the Union at large as are the distinctive appellations given to the people of other countries.
>
> Yankeeism is the general character of the Union. Yankee manners and feelings are as migratory as Yankee men. The latter are found everywhere, and the former prevail wherever the latter are found. Yankee connections and interests are spread throughout the land, and are gradually neutralizing all opposing influences. The Yankee mind, in short, is stronger than that of the other races, and is subduing them all. It is consequently important, towards the knowledge of the American character, to study that of the section which gives the prevailing tone to the rest. New England is therefore of surpassing interest.

And indeed New England was of great interest and importance in the 1850s—as it had always been—but Grattan had been British consul in Boston and was less well acquainted with the rest of the nation. Had he spent an equal time in Charleston or Mobile, or indeed in Cincinnati or St. Louis, he might have recognized that as yet "Yankee" and "American" were not quite the synonyms he assumed.

PART THREE
TENSION:
THE SUNDERING OF A FEDERATION

*A federation is the most geographically expressive of all
political systems.*

K. W. Robinson

Prologue

W hen we shift our focus to the internal geopolitical structure of the United States we are again confronted with a remarkable case. No federation before or since has enlarged itself by the almost routine sequential addition of so many new territorial units. We shall be concerned with the design of these parts and with how they were fitted to and altered the overall structure.

Because federations, by their very reason for being, must cope with important regional differences, it is not surprising that the addition of so many new units might generate serious stresses within the enlarging structure. Such strain did not arise from the simple number or size of these additions but from the rapidly changing human geography within them, and eventually this national building became so rickety that all the struts and bolts and cement that had been assiduously applied failed to hold it together.

The breaking of this large edifice, its partial collapse, and its forceable reconstruction are the most famous—and fascinating—events in American history. Our concerns with this mighty drama are, characteristically, confined to a few geopolitical matters. We shall pay little attention to personalities and parties, battles and generals, or the larger human dimensions of this conflict—and refrain from any general assessments of rights and wrongs. Nevertheless, we may hope that this very conciseness, this severe selectivity in the service of our special geographical perspective, may help us to see certain basic features rather more clearly than when these things are enmeshed in richer panoramic narratives.

We shall carry our study only to the point where a minimal program for putting the whole structure back together again was initiated, and leave the actual rebuilding to later examination.

1. The Shaping of New States

The expansion of the United States across the continent in less than half a century posed unprecedented geographical problems and opportunities. Among the most important, fundamental to the ensuing character and operation of the federation, was the recurrent need to subdivide huge areas of land into new constituent geopolitical units. As Congressman Samuel Vinton of Ohio, in one of the many debates over the topic, put it: "The question of the formation of new States and their admission into the Union, has always been regarded, and ever must be, as often as it arises, one of grave importance. Few questions upon which Congress is called to act can exert a more vital and abiding influence upon the confederacy. . . . It is a proceeding that gives a new identity to the republic and cannot fail to have a greater or less influence upon the ultimate destiny and stability of the Union itself." Such a statement was unexceptional at the time and the topic merits a closer geographical examination than it has generally received.

The problem of how to carve out new states from a generally undifferentiated expanse of territory was there from the first. The report of a committee chaired by Thomas Jefferson initiated formal debate on the matter. After important modifications Congress enacted in 1784 a set of "Resolutions for the Government of the Western Territory," which, after much further discussion, was superseded in 1787 by "An Ordinance for the government of the territory of the United States North west of the river Ohio." This Northwest Ordinance defined a set of procedures for the orderly expansion of the federation. These included a three-stage political process for the transition from territory to statehood:

1. Congress would first organize a formal territorial government under a minimal set of federal officials.
2. On reaching a population of 5,000 free adult males, local citizens could elect a territorial legislature and submit a list of candidates for a council; the federal government would appoint a governor and select the members for the council; this temporary government could then elect a delegate (nonvoting) to Congress.
3. When the territory had 60,000 free inhabitants it could be admitted to the Union "on an equal footing with the original States, in all respects whatever," and proceed to draw up a constitution and form a government (an appended provision stated that if it should be "consistent with the general interests of the Confederacy" the 60,000 requirement might be waived).

The Northwest Ordinance is justly famous for having provided such a process and for having thereby declared at the outset a constitutional equality between the original states and any new additions.

The ordinance also dealt with basic problems of geographical design that had been (and would continue to be) much debated:

1. Should a general geopolitical plan for the national territory be set forth at once, or should states be designed piecemeal only as each area became eligible for admission?
2. Although the existing states held the power of admission to the Union, should Congress also impose the exact boundaries of every unit, or was it more appropriate for a democratic republic (as was later argued in a typical case) "to adhere to the bounds asked by the people . . . who were there, who had settled the country, and whose voice should be listened to in the matter"?
3. Whatever the locus of decision, should some general standard be established as to size, shape, and geographical character of these additional units, or should there be allowances for markedly individual designs adapted to varied circumstances?

It would increasingly become apparent that of greatest importance to the political life of the federation were the corollaries of such decisions: how *many* new states should there be, and how *rapidly*, in what *sequence*, should they be added to the Union? We shall defer treatment of the full force of these latter questions and focus first on the topic of individual state design.

Jefferson's committee did produce a general plan for the geopolitical subdivision of the entire national territory (fig. 72). Various versions of such a framework soon appeared in map form and have received a good deal of attention from historians, but more from what they help reveal about their principal author than from their importance in shaping the federation. Jefferson's proposal for a dozen or more new states (as many as sixteen in some versions) alarmed most national leaders. Madison, among others, argued strongly against "multiplying the parts of the Machine" to such an extent: "We experience every day the difficulty of drawing thirteen States into the same plans. Let the number be doubled & so will the difficulty." General agreement that in its basic powers each new state should be equal to any other state did not mean that charter members were ready to commit themselves to share federal power so generously. The Northwest Ordinance declared that at least three, but no more than five, states should be created in that northern half of the western domain (compared with at least nine in Jefferson's proposals) and defined some specific boundaries. The first territory to complete the transition process to statehood was Ohio, admitted to the Union on March 1, 1803.

The three units defined for the southern part of the Northwest Territory offer a

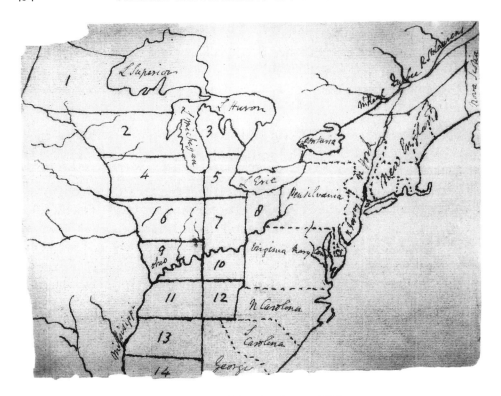

72. A Proposal for New States, 1784.

This is the so-called Jefferson-Hartley map, a copy by David Hartley of a sketch Jefferson made while in Paris, the original of which has disappeared. It is apparently a stage in the deliberations of the committee appointed to create a plan for the government of the Western Territory. It does not accord exactly with Jefferson's earlier proposals and is not what the committee ultimately reported, but it exhibits his strong predilection for many states and geometric boundaries. (Courtesy of the Clements Library, University of Michigan)

good indication of congressional thinking about the appropriate size and shape of new states. Ohio (c. 41,000 square miles), Indiana (c. 36,000), and Illinois (c. 48,000 within the limits specified in the ordinance) were general equivalents of the big states of Pennsylvania (c. 45,000) and New York (c. 50,000) but considerably smaller than the biggest—Virginia (c. 65,000). No general plan was adopted for the western territories south of the Ohio, but the result was generally similar. Kentucky (c. 40,000) and Tennessee (c. 42,000), admitted to the Union in the 1790s, were simply western extensions of Virginia and North Carolina, respectively, and not fully part of this newly defined process of evolution. The bisection of the remainder of the old Southwest Territory into Mississippi (c. 48,000) and Alabama (c. 52,000), together with the earlier definition of Louisiana (c. 48,000), confirmed the general standard that was often referred to in later debates over admissions.

The accession of these eight western states before 1820 offered an American substantive response to a well-worn topic in political philosophy: what is the appropriate extent of territory for a republic? That question lurked through all the crucial debates over the Constitution: "At the center of the theoretical expression of Anti-Federalist opposition to increased centralization of power in the national government was the belief that republican government was possible only for a relatively small territory and a relatively small and homogeneous population." The example of the Greek city-states and Montesquieu's familiar warnings against the dangers of "excessive size" were often cited. The new United States was in fact a bold experiment in the political form Montesquieu had decreed as best suited to such an extent of territory—a "confederate republic"; but such a creation must be "a society of societies," and therefore the principle was as applicable to the parts as to the whole.

The first report on the Western Territories declared "not less than one hundred, nor more than one hundred and fifty miles Square" as "a suitable extent of Territory" for these "distinct Republican States." Such a size (10,000–22,500 square miles) was toward the smaller end of the existing scale (for example, Maryland, 10,600; New Hampshire, 9,300; Massachusetts, 8,300). Jefferson's comprehensive plan, using two degrees of latitude and specified meridians, resulted in a set of states of approximately 27,600 square miles (similar to South Carolina, 31,000). It was generally agreed that these thinly settled frontier territories must be provided with effective governments, and Jefferson repeatedly argued that large states would have such dispersed populations, diversities of interest, and centrifugal tendencies as to require a government much stronger than would be desirable in a republican state. But for the most part, both local and national interests pressured toward larger and larger states. Local officials and citizens generally wanted as much territory under their control as possible, for they understood, quite rightly, that statehood fixed the areal framework of their future; however, they might be induced to accept a smaller size to avoid a lengthy delay in acquiring statehood and the multiplication of offices and self-government attendant therein. At the national level, representatives of the existing states, and especially senators, naturally tended to resist depletion of their own influence through excessive "multiplying the parts of the Machine"; they might, however, be very ready to multiply the parts of their own section—North or South—in response to the competitive pressures of party and national politics.

If the size of new states had profound implications for the federation as a whole, their shapes and specific boundaries had as profound an importance for state and local interests. The first three states admitted from the old Northwest Territory displayed several telling features: compact in shape, basically rectangular units modified by the use of major natural features as boundaries—the Ohio, Mississippi, lower Wabash, and Lake Erie. They also showed some calculated geopolitical adjustments from the original congressional design. The northern land boundary of all three was to be a latitudinal line drawn through the southernmost point of Lake Michigan. Since such a tangent would not ensure a usable frontage on the lake, Indiana was accorded a boundary set ten miles north of that point. That in fact gave Indiana a long, sandy strand but no effective harbor, and the territorial delegate from Illinois set out to ensure that his future state would suffer no such disadvantage. The original bill to create Illinois had set the northern boundary along the same line as that of Indiana. Nathaniel Pope, the delegate, immediately introduced an amendment to shift it to 42°30′N in order to gain "a coast on Lake Michigan," "the port of Chicago," and an interest in the opening of "a canal between Lake Michigan and the Illinois river," as well as to ensure the connection of the new state through the lakes with the "States of Indiana, Ohio, Pennsylvania, and New York" and thereby "afford additional security to the perpetuity of the Union." Apparently no rival interest or alternative emerged and this change was adopted without dissent. The enormous implications of that modest 41-mile extension and 8,500-square-mile addition for the future of the State of Illinois (and that of Wisconsin) would be difficult to calculate; the most immediate, even before the meteoric rise of Chicago, was the inclusion of Galena and a portion of the lead region; less obvious was the eventual inclusion of a broader segment of the western extension of Yankee settlement (and an attempt in 1840–42 by these northern counties to secede and join Wisconsin). A much more limited adjustment, complicated by initial dependence on an inaccurate base map, led to a protracted and bitter dispute between Ohio and Michigan over Maumee Harbor (Toledo).

The relative compactness of Ohio, Indiana, and Illinois (as originally proposed) stood in contrast to Kentucky and Tennessee, whose elongated forms stretching across a set of sharply differentiated regions reflected ancient colonial claims rather than a desirable model of state design. The use of the Ohio and Mississippi rivers as state boundaries emerged from some national geopolitical realities of the 1780s: the Ohio became the western divide between free states and slave states; the Mississippi was the western limit of United States territory. Although such great rivers and their valleys had a natural unity, they were more commonly seen as "natural" demarcations. Thus an early petition for the admission of Missouri stressed the need to "make the Missouri river the *centre*, and not the *boundary* of the State," and went on to deprecate "the idea of making the divisions of the States to correspond with the natural divisions [that is, great rivers] of the country." (The lower Mississippi had already been straddled by Louisiana, but as we have seen, that addition of the Florida Parishes was a geopolitical expediency made quite apart from discussions of boundaries.) Although a state centered on the river would seem to be a design made obvious by the reach of settlement westward into the hinterland of St. Louis, counterarguments favoring the lower Missouri as a boundary did arise. As always, the topic was enmeshed in a tangle of factions, each tailoring geographical "logic" to fit its own concerns. One interesting general concept emerged: the idea of creating a series of longer, narrower states—more "Tennessees," as one newspaper put it—so as to give a frontage on the Great River to every trans-Mississippi state. The steamboat was at this very time making river frontage an intensified concern and was a factor in an unusual alteration of Missouri's shape after statehood. It was originally bounded on the north, west, and south by geometric lines (except for the minor "boot heel" anomaly, attached, apparently, through the efforts of influential citizens of the New Madrid district); in 1835, Missourians petitioned to shift their state's northwestern limits to the Missouri River because that would provide a "natural boundary" separating Whites and Indians (the new territory to receive "emigrant Indians" was being formed west of the river) as well as "excellent water privileges and additional landings." This so-called Platte Purchase addition made the largest state in the Union (c. 66,500 square miles compared to Virginia's 65,000) even larger (c. 69,700).

The issues of appropriate size, shape, and geographical circumstance are further illustrated by the case of Iowa (fig. 73). The original petition from the Iowan convention defined an area approximately pentagonal and only slightly smaller than Missouri, bounded on the northwest by the lower Minnesota River and a line from the mouth of the Blue Earth River (Mankato) to the mouth of the Big Sioux (Sioux City). This design was endorsed by the Committee on Territories but encountered strong resistance in the House debate. Northern congressmen, alarmed at the implications of adding Texas, wanted to protect the possibility of carving a larger number of states out of these northwestern territories, and they succeeded in amending the bill to redefine a considerably smaller more rectangular Iowa, closed off from the Missouri River on the west and reduced in frontage on the Minnesota and Mississippi on the north. The admission of Iowa in this altered form was approved, but despite the strong attractions of statehood when (in the words of their delegate) the people of the territory "found that Congress . . . had given them mere arbitrary and artificial lines, cutting them off from those great rivers, they rose up almost as one man, and by an overwhelming [actually a modest majority] vote rejected" such terms. Such a rejection of statehood was unprecedented. Clearly, the major geographical issue for Iowans was their loss of the Missouri Slope, and in the following year they accepted the compromise offered by Congress of a state fronting broadly on both the Mississippi and the Missouri with a northern boundary along 43°30'N eastward from the Big Sioux River. Ten years later Iowa attempted unsuccessfully to emulate Missouri in adding a northwestern triangle through extension of its northern boundary all the way west to the Missouri River (nipping off the southeastern corner of what would become South Dakota).

Similar issues arose in the formation of Minnesota. Interests in St. Paul favored a

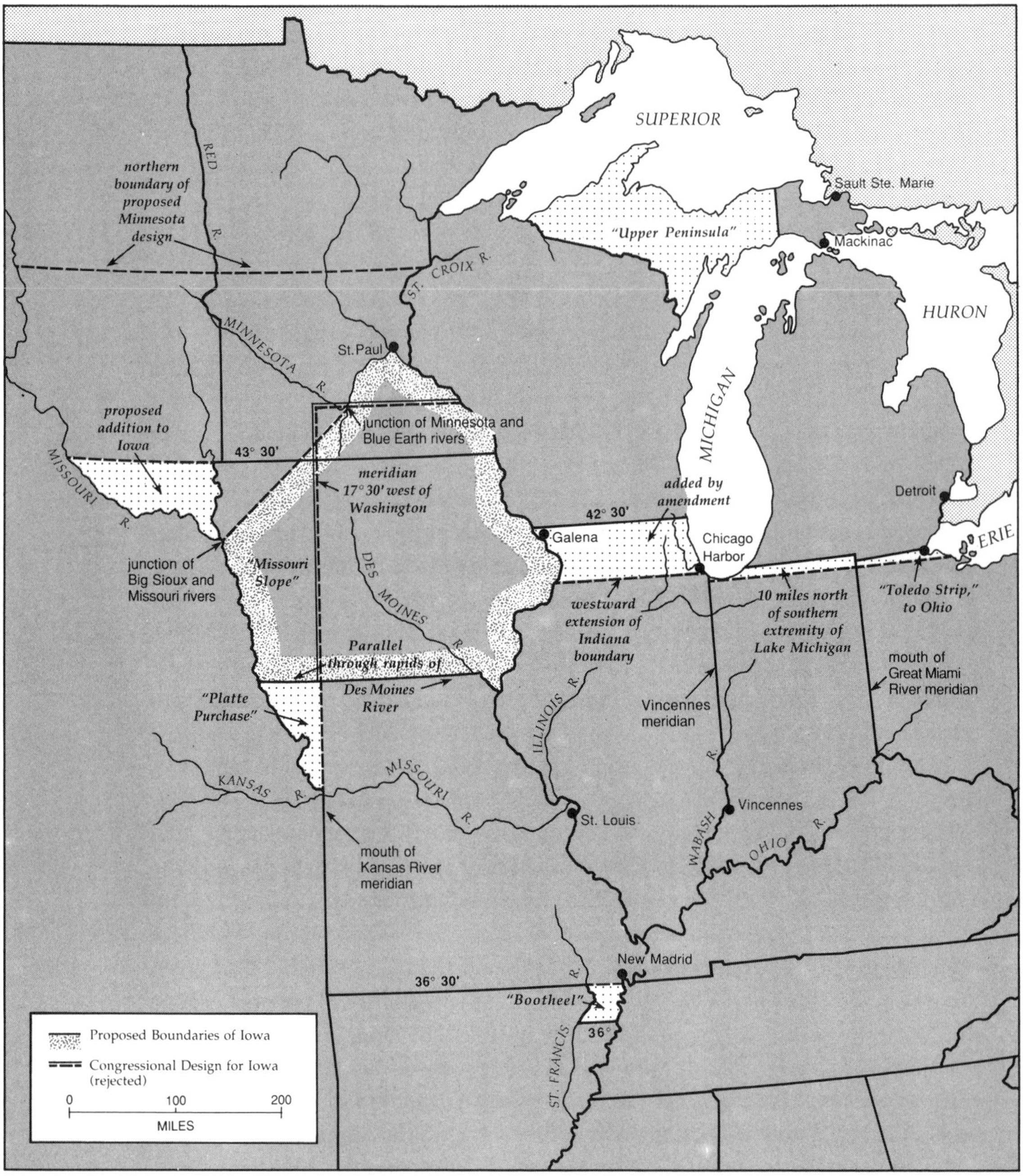
SUPERIOR
Sault Ste. Marie
"Upper Peninsula"
Mackinac
HURON
MICHIGAN
Detroit
ERIE
RED R.
northern boundary of proposed Minnesota design
ST. CROIX R.
MINNESOTA R.
St. Paul
junction of Minnesota and Blue Earth rivers
proposed addition to Iowa
43° 30'
MISSOURI R.
meridian 17° 30' west of Washington
added by amendment
42° 30'
Galena
Chicago Harbor
junction of Big Sioux and Missouri rivers
"Missouri Slope"
DES MOINES R.
westward extension of Indiana boundary
10 miles north of southern extremity of Lake Michigan
"Toledo Strip," to Ohio
Parallel through rapids of Des Moines River
"Platte Purchase"
ILLINOIS R.
Vincennes meridian
mouth of Great Miami River meridian
KANSAS R.
MISSOURI R.
St. Louis
Vincennes
WABASH R.
OHIO R.
mouth of Kansas River meridian
New Madrid
36° 30'
"Bootheel"
36°
ST. FRANCIS R.
Proposed Boundaries of Iowa
Congressional Design for Iowa (rejected)
0
100
200
MILES

73. Some Geographic Issues in State Formation.

state that reached north to Lake Superior and the Red River Settlement, encompassing the river routes and cart roads that focused on their thriving city at the head of Mississippi navigation. But another faction, mostly of newer immigrants of a different political persuasion and involved in agriculture and land speculations, was quite ready to give up all the northern wilderness for a state lying south of the Forty-sixth Parallel (or some close variant) and elongated between the Mississippi–St. Croix on the east and the Missouri River on the west (including the triangle Iowans had sought). Such a design would make the Minnesota Valley the main axis, and its proponents actually got the territorial legislature to approve a prospective shift of the capital (upon reaching statehood) from St. Paul to St. Peter. This competing design was only narrowly defeated by a set of complicated political maneuvers.

The case of Texas threatened all precedents as to size, shape, and geographical circumstance. Annexation and admission was bitterly contested on grounds relating to the most basic issues of the federation. Size and its corollary, number, were matters of great importance. Provisions for admission to the Union were drawn up on the assumption "that Texas was too large for a single state," and specified some sort of subdivision. Senator Benton's prominent bill, calling for the admission of "the State of Texas, with boundaries fixed by herself, and an extent not exceeding that of the largest State in the Union" (his own state, Missouri), with the remainder formed into a large territory, was an influential model. In the end, subdivision was optional rather than enforced: Texas was admitted as a single state, with provision for division into as many as four new states (with the consent of Texas) in the future. Texas was of course a special case: it had been an independent republic, and in fact for several years no one knew how big it actually was, for it continued to claim half of New Mexico. A compromise in 1850 fixed that boundary and thereby defined a state of approximately 267,000 square miles, and in that same year Congress admitted a California of about 169,000 square miles, more than double the size of Missouri. In both of these western cases there was, in addition to their extraordinary geopolitical history and circumstances, the contention that much of their territory was barren and mountainous and unlikely ever to be densely settled. A similar argument for departing from the general national standard had been put forth many years before by those who sought admission for an undivided Mississippi of nearly 100,000 square miles: "In its capacity for sustaining a *population* or commanding a *resource*, [it] will be greatly short of either [Virginia or New York], because a large extent of the southern section of territory is almost an uninhabited waste of pine barren, and because our climate is so oppressive that our population will never be much condensed, nor very efficient." Such a justification also became prominent in debates over the subdivision of the upper Great Lakes region.

The original design for Michigan statehood included the obvious block of land between Lakes Huron and Michigan plus the immediate hinterlands of Mackinac and Sault Ste. Marie, the only valued district to the north, making a compact state of about 45,000 square miles. Two issues intruded upon this seemingly simple plan, however. The principal of these was the long-festering dispute between the State of Ohio and Michigan Territory over what came to be called the Toledo Strip. In the 1830s this problem came to a boil (Michigan called out its militia), and because President Jackson and congressional leaders were eager to admit Michigan but placate Ohio, a compromise was offered whereby in return for giving up the Toledo Strip Michigan would be granted a large extension of territory in the far northwest, south of Lake Superior. That idea arose from a second issue, for whereas the original Michigan design was quite in line with the general scale intended for the region, if, in keeping with the Ordinance of 1787, the remainder of the Northwest Territory were formed into a fifth and final state (Wisconsin), it would be much larger. Thus the Committee on Territories proposed to solve both problems by reducing Wisconsin to a more appropriate size and consoling Michigan with that excision. Michigan spokesmen at first refused to consider such a trade, dismissing the proposed addition as a "sterile region . . . destined by soil and climate to remain forever a wilderness" (the great copper and iron deposits were as yet unappreciated), but they were eventually lured to accept it when sweetened by lavish grants of land and money from the federal treasury. In this way the most peculiar departure from common designs became fixed on the map. The specific terms of the Northwest Ordinance were later ignored when the western boundary of Wisconsin was drawn along the St. Croix rather than the uppermost Mississippi. The great size of Minnesota (c. 84,000) was excused on the grounds that it, too, contained so much useless country, and less good land than adjacent Iowa.

In the formation of states, Congress had the obligation not only of "making them of suitable and convenient size for the purpose of government," but also of having due regard for "the geographical affinities and dependence of its [sic] parts." Because a territory needed just 60,000 free inhabitants to become eligible, most of the filling in remained to be done and hence there must always be some uncertainty about "geographical affinities" and the nature of its "parts." Formed during an early stage in the expansion of settlement, these embryonic states typically developed from a corner or along the edge most accessible from older regions. In several cases a settlement district antedating the United States was encompassed, such as Detroit, Vincennes, Kaskaskia and the American Bottom, St. Louis, and Mobile, but not all of these served as principal nuclei for subsequent development. Ohio, Indiana, and Iowa grew from numerous early settlements along their great river borders. The division of the old Southwest into Mississippi and Alabama reflected the separate and rival interests of the Natchez and Mobile districts and the prospective commercial intercourse between Mobile and settlements along the Tennessee.

Changes in the geography of population distribution usually brought a shift in the location of the capital. This was usually a three-stage process: territorial government set up in some existing settlement on or near the border (Vincennes, Kaskaskia, St. Stephens, Natchez, St. Louis, Burlington); soon a removal to some point near the vanguard of settlement (as, in the above cases, Corydon, Vandalia, Cahaba, Washington, St. Charles temporarily, Iowa City); eventually a further shift to a location near the geographical center of the state (Indianapolis, Springfield, Montgomery, Jackson, Jefferson City, Des Moines). Alabama actually had four different capitals because Cahaba was virtually washed away by floods and the governor and legislature moved to Tuscaloosa in 1826. Most of the other states moved the capital once (Chillicothe to Columbus, Detroit to Lansing, Belmont to Madison, Arkansas Post to Little Rock); only Minnesota held to the initial territorial center (St. Paul), which remained the best natural focus for the state that eventually emerged.

Any move in location of such an important functional and symbolic place of course generated intense rivalries and speculation (and, most likely, corruption) and the more so when such a change was delayed until a large proportion of the state was already settled, as in Illinois, Iowa, and Michigan. Although the removal of the capital to a virgin site away from existing seats of commerce and political factions—following the example of the national federation—was often cited as an important principle bearing on such decisions, speculators wagered that any capital town would soon become a focus of roads, a commercial center, and a place of substantial growth. The capital was the most coveted prize, but there were others to contend for. Thus Iowa City received the state university as consolation for its loss, the former capitol providing a fine nucleus for a riverside campus (Tuscaloosa already had the university before it lost the capital to Montgomery). As the state developed, an array of institutions—armories, prisons and reformatories, insane asylums, schools for the deaf and dumb, schools for the blind, state fairgrounds, and other benevolent facilities and payrolls—would be allocated among contending towns and districts.

The eleven new states created out of the western national territory between 1803 and 1858 in general accordance with the procedures defined in 1787 (leaving aside Louisiana and those states created from Spanish and Mexican cessions) were designed to provide a rational geographical framework for republican government. Each state was of course unique in its location and character, and those individualities, modified through the years, would ever be significant in the operations of the federation, but for the moment we may focus on what they had in common, and do so through the example of a particular state. Indiana was created out of the Northwest Territory in May 1800 and evolved through the normal stages; on December 11, 1816, it was declared "to be one, of the United States of America, and admitted into the Union on an equal footing with the original States, in all respects whatever." Its shape was that of a compact rectangle modified to fit river boundaries on the south and southwest and a corner of Lake Michigan in the northwest (fig. 74). A special census taken in support of its petition for admission

74. Indiana as a Model.

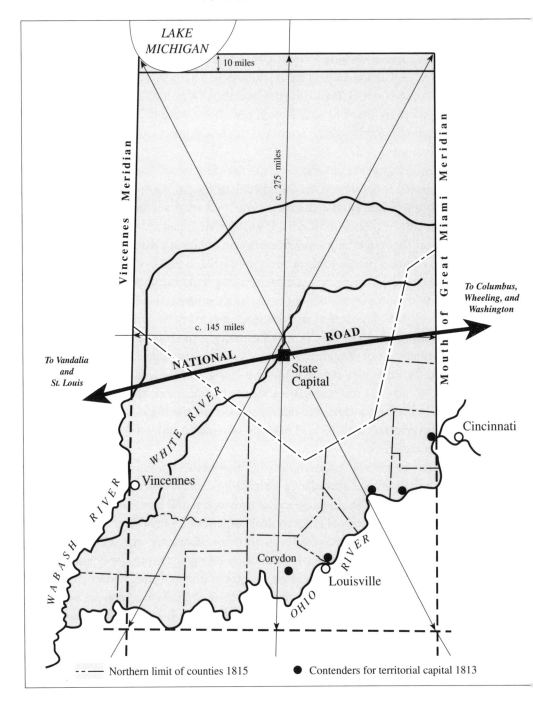

revealed a population of 63,897, and this was obviously rapidly increasing and spreading inland from the many landings along the Ohio River. The state constitution declared Corydon to be the capital until 1825, whereafter it would be moved to a permanent site selected by a special commission. In 1818 a federal Indian treaty opened all but the northernmost sector of the state, and the commission soon thereafter nominated a location on a level plain near the geographical center of the state; this site was approved in 1821, and the capital moved there in 1825.

The plan of this new town, drawn up by Alexander Ralston, was emblematic of the model geography of its day in many features (fig. 75). Ralston had been an Indiana resident for several years, but as a young Scottish surveyor he had assisted Pierre-Charles L'Enfant in laying out Washington and therefore had a strong sense of what a capital city should look like. He marked off a square-mile plat centered within the land reserved for the town and laid it out in one hundred square blocks (interrupted in the southeast by an angled strip of lots along a small stream); within the central four blocks he drew a circle; from this nodal circle and square complex he laid out avenues radiating in the cardinal directions and to the four corners of the town—and by implication to the edges and corners of the state. With the exception of Meridian, Market, and Washington, all streets of the grid were named after states of the Union. Government would of course occupy the center, but Ralston interestingly reserved the circle for the governor's house and placed the capitol and courts on nearby blocks. It might have been argued that in a republic the capitol, housing the elected representatives and offices of all three branches of balanced governmental power, rather than the home of the foremost executive, would have been more appropriate for this calculated point of centrality, accessibility, and visibility. In fact, no governor was willing to reside in the mansion provided at this focus, but it was locally understood that Ralston's intention was defeated not by any sense of inappropriate symbolism but by a rather more mundane kind of visibility: a circle has no back, and no governor's wife would tolerate the fact that "the family wash would have to be hung out to dry in plain view of all the town." Squares reserved for the government, commerce (the market), and religion expressed the routine acceptance of these as primary components of American civic order, but the details of that order were modified in practice because the first churches obtained lots directly on the circle rather than in the squares reserved for them near the outlying corners—they preferred to be at the crossroads rather than in embowered residential districts.

The very name of the place had a calculated classical ring to it, suggesting that it aspired to be a true city in size and activity as well as in formal design (although there had been strong efforts to name it Tecumseh). With Indiana's statehood Congress had agreed (as with Ohio previously) to reserve 5 percent of the net proceeds from the sale of federal lands "for making public roads and canals"; three-

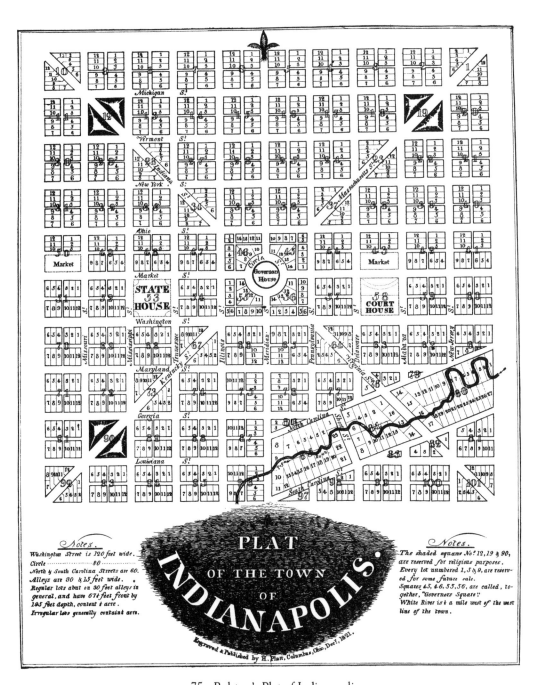

75. Ralston's Plat of Indianapolis.
(Courtesy of John W. Reps, from the Geography and Map Division, Library of Congress)

fifths of this income was to be spent by the state for internal improvements, two-fifths by Congress for the making of roads leading to Indiana. In 1827 the National Road was surveyed across the state, passing through Indianapolis along Washington Street (in keeping with Ralston's intention) and thereby balancing Indianapolis and Indiana on the new overland axis of the nation. Construction proceeded east and west from Indianapolis, and within a few years bridges were completed, the roadbed was macadamized, and the Great Western Mail had placed the capital of Indiana just sixty-five hours away from the capital of the United States.

Internally there was an analogous stage-by-stage subdivision of thinly organized territory into workable political areas. The territorial government had authority to create counties and designate their bounds and seats, and thirteen of these existed on the eve of statehood. The state constitution sought to regulate the scale of this process, stating that in the creation of a new county, the General Assembly shall not reduce the old county or counties from which it was taken "to a less content than four hundred square miles." Attempts to amend this to allow the creation of smaller counties in the hilly country bordering the Ohio were defeated. Similarly, county commissioners had authority to subdivide the county "into as many townships as the convenience of the citizens may require" and to alter the number and bounds of such areas as might be desirable. At this lowest level in the political hierarchy, township officials were charged with oversight of local schools, roads, fences, and drains.

Although the new state of Indiana was not an undifferentiated space, a tabula rasa, as a political space it closely reflected the abstract model of a constituent American republic. The integrity of that design was aided by the relatively uniform surface of so much of the area so that only modest adaptations to terrain and waterways deformed the relentless geometric symmetries of state, county, township, and capital city. Underlying that design, here as elsewhere over most of this West, was of course the rigid and comprehensive rectangularity of the township-and-range survey system imprinted upon all federal lands.

It is useful to consider state formations as both a *national* and a *federal* process, with powerful implications for the ongoing life of the United States. Here again surfaced the fundamental issue that arose so prominently during the formative years of the Union: Were states mere "districts of people," arbitrary compartments of convenient size within one homogeneous political society (as counties were within each state)? Or were states "organic societies" of particular peoples with a common local heritage, rooted in time and place, who by their own initiative elected to join as an equal but unique member of the Union? The Constitution spelled out the compromise reached in the formation of a federative structure of two sovereignties—state and national—co-existing with defined fields of authority. But of course, the specific human content and character of the parts and the whole were undergoing continuous alteration as populations grew and spread. The greatest internal challenge to the functioning of the United States was its rapidly and extensively changing human geography. Although every new state joined as an equal in terms of its sovereign authority, these new western states perforce differed in kind as political societies. For whereas in 1789 each of the thirteen states was in fact a preexisting sovereignty and in some significant degree a distinct organic society, these new additions were to an important degree arbitrarily defined pieces of thinly settled national territory shaped in congressional committees and debates. The most obvious exceptions were the sovereign Republic of Texas and those states formed around substantial captive populations, as Louisiana, and later New Mexico and Utah. For the rest, such older rooted populations as those at Mobile, Vincennes, Detroit, or St. Louis were much too small and weak to shape the character of the new encompassing state. All such places were soon swamped by the influx of Americans.

We may presume that in general it would be quite impossible for these new-comers to have the same sense of state allegiance as those rooted in older colonial societies of the seaboard. The Indianans or Alabamans of 1830 might be fervent boosters of the greatness of their young states, but it could not have quite the same meaning and power as the feelings of fourth- or fifth-generation Pennsylvanians or South Carolinians for their historic home ground. Such differences must surely affect in subtle (and not readily measurable) ways that special American balance between state and national allegiance. One might infer that these new Westerners would likely have a greater sense of national than state identity, a considerably stronger sense of being American than being Indianan or Alabaman. Such an assumption is strengthened by the evidence of so much continuing movement on the frontier, by the fact that so many Indianans or Alabamans of any one year would become Iowans or Texans a few years hence.

But any such reasoning about this dual allegiance of Americans is too hasty and simple, for it overlooks the crucial intermediate scale of such things. After all, migrants from the seaboard were not simply "Americans," nor were they simply Pennsylvanians or South Carolinians; they came from particular localities within deep-rooted regional societies. However willing, even eager, they may have been to leave that behind and start life anew in the West, they did not, could not, simply shed their basic cultural character. Whatever self-identity they might assume, they had been indelibly shaped in myriad ways by their social parentage. The vital human patterns of these new western states were formed by particular streams of migration and the particular deposits laid down. The United States was not only a nation and a federation, it was also, as always, a set of regional societies, and it was the changing human geography of these societies that was the most important dynamic in the fate of the nation and federation. And here, again, a critical feature in this geopolitical shaping of the United States was the fact that these state boundaries were set before the full pattern of regional societies would become apparent in these western lands. Thus congressional discussions focused much more on general standards of size and shape and showed a strong preference for simple geometric boundaries than on a careful drawing of lines so as to encompass similar peoples and exclude others. The consequences for politics at both state and federal level could not be readily foreseen; in some cases they could be very great, in others not. For example, if the land lying west of Georgia had been divided in half latitudinally so as to form two states elongated east-west following the pattern of Kentucky and Tennessee, the general character of these states would not have been markedly different from that of Alabama and Mississippi because the entire area was given a sufficiently common imprint by early migrations and the subsequent development of the cotton belt. But if the land lying directly west of Pennsylvania and Virginia had been divided latitudinally (say, along 40°N) and, given the long reach of that line, subdivided into eastern and western quarters (say, along 87°W, so as to give each of the northern states access to Lake Michigan), the resulting states would have become markedly, profoundly, different in character from Ohio, Indiana, and Illinois; the southern pair created by such a division (40°N) would have been two more "Kentuckys"—heavily dominated by Uplands Southerners, with Cincinnati and the Miami Valley a somewhat greater enclave than Louisville, while the northern pair would have been almost purely Yankee and Midland in cultural character. As it happened, the longitudinal division into three states set Ohio, Indiana, and Illinois in the path of three streams of migration that would fill them with diversity and tensions.

2. Expanding the Federation

The United States of America was a precarious structure from its beginning. The initial confederation was a makeshift alliance uncertain in number and extent; the Articles of Confederation had specifically reserved a place for Canada and the rebels had hoped to include Nova Scotia, Bermuda, the Bahamas, and the Floridas as well. When the bounds of the new republic were established by treaty in 1783, half of its territory was politically unorganized. Because such country was regarded as a vast area to be colonized and added to the union of states, a recurrent extension and reshaping was programmed into the future of this experimental geopolitical creation. As noted in *Atlantic America:* "If federalism by its very nature involves duality, compromise, and delicate balances among the territorial parts, the need to cope with so much more internal geopolitical change would surely keep this structure under heavy stress for some years ahead."

The first additions to the Original Thirteen were approved in February 1791, during the second year of George Washington's presidency of a redefined federal structure. Vermont and Kentucky were, in a sense, "natural" increments. Each was essentially a direct extension from an original colonial seaboard society, and each was a clearly bounded territory: the one a wedge created by the fixing of the international boundary (and the withdrawal of competing claims from New Hampshire and New York); the other a long-recognized transmontane reach of Virginia's charter (after relinquishment of its sovereign claims north of the Ohio River). That these two accessions should be paired to maintain the existing balance between Northern and Southern states had been mentioned during congressional considerations and years later would be cited as having established just such a precedent, but that principle was evidently given no prominence at the time.

The admission of Tennessee in 1795 brought the slaveholding and non-slaveholding states into even balance at eight each. There had been talk of creating two states out of this western extension of North Carolina, but that had arisen from internal geography, from the difficulties of communication between the eastern and western districts of such an elongated territory, rather than from the external implications of senatorial numbers. Sectional tensions certainly lurked in many congressional issues, as Washington had noted and warned against in his Farewell Address. Slavery had become an ominous presence at the Constitutional Convention and made the Southern states conscious of themselves as a distinct geopolitical section within the federation, at least with reference to that part of their human geography.

The Northwest Ordinance had specified that three to five free states be carved out of that quadrant, but there was no similar plan for the Southwest. It was obvious that there would be more states created from the lands west of Georgia, but the admission of Ohio in 1803 produced no anxious pressure from the South to restore the balance. That would not come until 1812 with Louisiana. In spite of the huge northern expanse of the Louisiana Purchase, the agitations of the time had been so focused on New Orleans and the lower Mississippi that this doubling of national territory tended to be viewed primarily as an addition to the South, and it generated loose talk about the need to annex Canada on the north to restore the equilibrium. The dismal results of the War of 1812 dampened such notions. The de facto paired admissions of Indiana and Mississippi, followed by the rather looser association of Illinois and Alabama, seem to have spurred no important discussion of larger geopolitical considerations (fig. 76). These cases, of course, involved territories already allocated to North and South. With these accessions, nine states had been added to the Original Thirteen, and slave states and free states were in balance with eleven each. Why, then, was the proposed addition of Missouri—and soon thereafter of Maine—in 1819 so explosive?

1850's			1840's		1830's	1820's	1810's			1800's	1790's			
36 OR	34 MN	32 CA	30 WI	28 IA	26 MI	24 ME	22 IL	20 IN		18 OH	16 VT	ORIGINAL	14	N
			TX 30	FL 28	AR 26	MO 24	AL 22	MS 20	LA 18		TN 16	KY 14	STATES 12	S
66	64	62	60	56	52	48	44	40	36	34	32	28	26	

Sequence and Sets of State Admissions
with number of senators per section

∫ paired admissions

	1860	1850	1840	1830	1820	1810	1800	1790	
	158	144	135	141	123	103	76	57	N
	(83)	90	88	99	90	78	65	48	S
	(241)	234	223	240	213	181	141	105	

House of Representatives
as reapportioned after each census

(but additional members added after each state admission)

76. Expanding the Federation.

The debates in Congress and in public forums leading up to the Missouri Compromise have long been accepted as a major landmark in American history. Specialists have explored the issues with great thoroughness, described important conditions of national life at that time, and offered plausible explanations for the intensity and portent of the episode. We shall focus on specific geographical dimensions of the matter—on why, thirty years after the Constitution, the contest over Missouri brought North and South, defined in terms of free and slave, to the fore as the primary internal geopolitical reality of the United States.

The intensity of this intramural battle was very likely heightened by a discernible change in the larger geopolitical context of the United States: the greater confidence and security felt after the end of a generation of European wars with which it had become entangled on sea and on land. From the first years of its life the "imperatives for survival of a marginal republic perched on the edge of a vast continent on the fringes of the European commercial system" had held together—none too firmly—the diverse and even clearly divergent regional interests of these

American states. As external dangers waned and the vigor of internal expansion strengthened, it was probably inevitable that the contest for the continent between competing sections would become more bold.

But the issue was directly related to the specific position of Missouri within the body of the federation. Although much land behind remained unoccupied, and important districts were still unceded by the Indians, in the broader view the westward-moving settlement frontier had reached the Mississippi River and all the intervening territories had been formed into states. Thus the proposed State of Missouri, with its 500-mile frontage on the Great River, lay athwart the future— the difficulty was that North and South alike saw it as an important part of the future of its particular section. Because those sections had become defined in terms of the exclusion or the admittance of slavery, there was no way for both to share a single territory.

The demarcation of the exact territorial line between slave and free had not been a recurrent issue because that boundary had been set as far west as the Mississippi by the Northwest Ordinance of 1787, before any competing transappalachian expansions. At that time all the territory bordering the Ohio River on the south was Virginian, all to the north was under federal jurisdiction, and the river, the central axis of the West, had been readily accepted as an appropriate division. This boundary, which was to become so fundamental in the affairs of the Republic, was as yet not so clear in detail or in daily life. Slaves lived on both sides of the line. Some of those north of the river stemmed from the old French settlements at Vincennes and Kaskaskia, others had been brought in by migrants from Virginia or Kentucky and held in bondage under some form of indenture that evaded the spirit if not entirely the letter of territorial laws. Emancipation was a gradual process even in the older states north of the Mason-Dixon Line, and aside from occasional court cases such status was not closely monitored.

Furthermore, there was no certainty that the Ohio River would remain the northern boundary of legal slavery. As Finkelman observed, while efforts were underway in Kentucky and Virginia, as well in the Northeast, "to abolish slavery gradually and painlessly; in Indiana [and Illinois] the legislature was attempting to introduce slavery gradually and surreptitiously" through various forms of bondage. There had been a strong movement to fix gradual emancipation into the new Kentucky Constitution of 1799, and even though that effort failed, there were repeated attempts to chip away at slavery in various bills and resolutions relating to importation, manumission, and so on. Across the Ohio there were efforts to reverse the situation; and explicit antislavery clauses in the constitutions of Indiana and Illinois did not dash hopes for change. The leading proponents were planters and speculators from south of the Ohio, the main source of immigration (both senators from Illinois at the time of these critical debates were slaveholders).

Opinion on the matter was not a simple reflection of origins, however; some Southerners had crossed the river specifically to get away from slavery, while not all settlers from the free states opposed it. William Newnham Blane was appalled to find, during his visit in 1822–23, that even some persons who acknowledged that slavery was a great curse (including some of his former compatriots around Albion) supported making Illinois a slaveholding state. Their motive was to lure wealthy Southern planters and drive up the price of land so they could sell out at a good profit and move further west. The call for a convention to make such a change was defeated in a statewide vote the next year.

Slaves were part of the visible scene throughout the Ohio Valley because the movement of owners and their slaves as travelers or sojourners was essentially unhampered. The Ohio was the great highway and Cincinnati a great commercial and cultural center for Northerners and Southerners alike, and land routes across southern Indiana and Illinois were the direct pathways to St. Louis. Security of property in transit was upheld as a matter of course; recognition on the part of Northern states of such slaves as property was a matter of comity, the courtesy given to the laws of another jurisdiction, a reciprocity indispensable in a union of equal states. Thus a Virginia planter might take his large entourage of family and slaves to Cincinnati (or New York City) and stay for weeks or months en route to Louisiana or Texas. Only later was this mutual respect of laws undermined.

Thus, the Ohio River was a boundary, but the Ohio Valley was a borderland— and so was Missouri. Those overland roads converging on St. Louis brought North and South into focus on the same territory. The proposed state lay directly west of both Illinois and Kentucky and thus allowed each side in the congressional debate to point to the simple logic of geography—"cast your eye on the map, sir"—the one side noting that "Missouri lies in the same latitude as Illinois and Indiana; its soil, productions, and climate are the same, and the same principles of government should be applied to it"; the other noting that Missouri lay almost entirely south of the Mason-Dixon Line, that "a part of Kentucky, Virginia, and Maryland were as far north as the northern boundary of the proposed state" (not entirely true). It was, of course, the southwesterly trend of the River Ohio that made Missouri appear to be an extension both of the Northwest and of Virginia. It was in fact as well as inference a frontier for both, but the most critical feature was the presence of more than 10,000 slaves already resident in Missouri in 1819, the result, very largely, of a decade or more of Southern colonization (fig. 77).

The controversy over this next phase in expansion of the federation was ignited by a New York congressman with an amendment to prohibit any further introduction of slaves into Missouri and to program the gradual emancipation of those born into slavery after statehood. The House, dominated by a newly self-confident North ("we now have the numerical force; we have a majority of ten or fifteen in

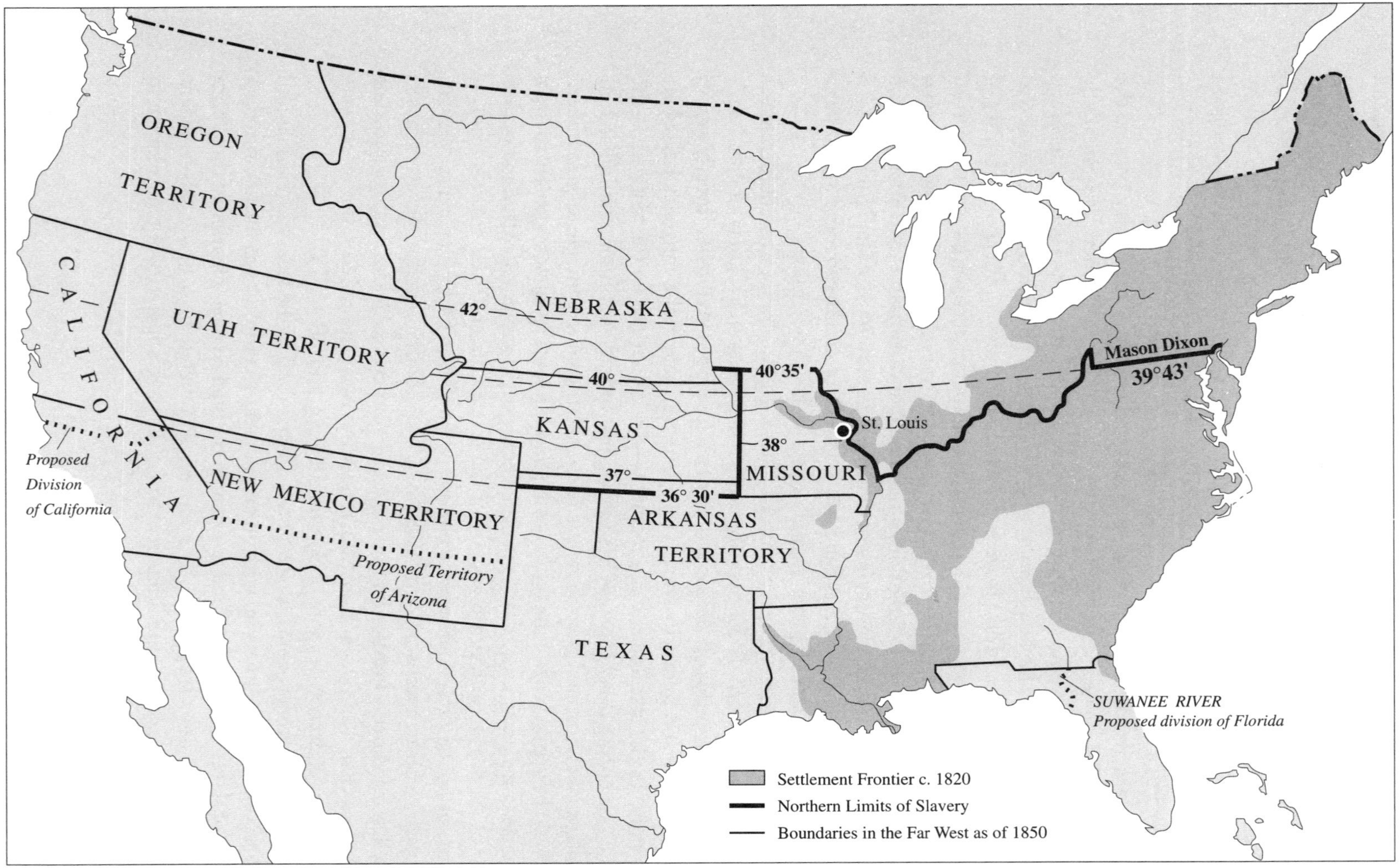

Mason Dixon
39°43'

SUWANEE RIVER
Proposed division of Florida

St. Louis

40°35'
38°
MISSOURI

36° 30'
ARKANSAS
TERRITORY

37°

NEBRASKA
40°

KANSAS

42°

TEXAS

OREGON
TERRITORY

UTAH TERRITORY

NEW MEXICO TERRITORY

Proposed Territory
of Arizona

CALIFORNIA

Proposed
Division
of California

Settlement Frontier c. 1820
Northern Limits of Slavery
Boundaries in the Far West as of 1850

77. Limiting Slavery.

the representation on this floor"), repeatedly approved these measures; in the Senate a united South together with a few other votes (such as those of the senators from Illinois) ensured repeated defeat. Attempts to unite Maine and Missouri into a single admissions bill failed to resolve the impasse. Introduction of a bill to organize Arkansas Territory broadened the areal focus and may have led to the eventual compromise. The failure of Northern congressmen to support an amendment to exclude slavery from that proposed territory seemed to point to the possibility of a trade: if Northerners would accept Missouri as a slave state, Southerners might agree to accept the southern boundary of Missouri (36°30'N) as the northern limit of slavery in the remaining western territories (at the time, Arkansas extended west to the 100th Meridian, the treaty boundary with Spanish Mexico); Maine would be admitted to maintain the balance of power in the Senate. As the tedious negotiations on such a resolution proceeded there were attempts by Northerners to reduce what they saw as the anomalous northerly reach of slaveholding Missouri. Proposals to divide Missouri into two states along the Missouri River, or along 38°N, or to shift its northern boundary southward to 39°N (from 40°35') all failed. A precarious compromise was achieved in March 1820: Maine was admitted; Missouri was authorized to form a constitution and state government; after further contrived ambiguities relating to its constitution, Missouri joined the Union of States in August 1821.

One geographical question arising from the Missouri Compromise is why the South accepted 36°30'N as a northern limit of slavery in the western territories. That particular line first appeared west of the Mississippi in 1808 as the arbitrary northern boundary of a newly created District of Arkansas (within the Territory of Louisiana). It was a projection across the river of the Kentucky-Tennessee boundary and thus positioned only a short distance below the mouth of the Ohio River. Still, it was entirely south of Kentucky, so why did not Southerners insist on a more northerly division, say 38°N, more nearly midway between the most southerly point of the free states (Illinois) and the Mason-Dixon Line, and more nearly a bisection of the land between the northern wilderness of the upper Great Lakes and the Gulf Coast? Historians have concluded that the compromise decision was not the result of any close geographic assessment. The opening salvo did declare that the debate was about the future millions who would populate the vast western lands rather than about the few thousand settlers then present, but surprisingly little attention was devoted either to the supposed qualities of the country or to the areal proportions resulting from proposed divisions. As noted earlier, information was still very sketchy; the journals of Lewis and Clark described many attractions along the upper Missouri but uncertainties remained; the Long Expedition had not yet filed its report on "the Great Desert," and the trail to Santa Fe was not yet open. Regional agricultures were occasionally mentioned in debate, and it was pointed out that both of those famous Southern staples, tobacco and cotton, were grown in Missouri, but these were not decisive. The issue was argued and resolved on complex legal and simple geopolitical grounds. Southerners felt themselves suddenly under siege and therefore united in their determination to get Missouri into the Union as one of their own. They could (and later would) rationalize that the prohibition of slavery north of 36°30′N applied only to *territories* and not necessarily to future states. It was generally assumed that whatever the character of the country might be, at least one more tier of states to the west would eventually be formed.

The prolonged agony of this decision making brought into the open all the incendiary issues and divisive forces that would lead to a disintegration of this shaky federation forty years later. For the time being, we shall focus on the admission of new states with reference to this newly exposed division and hardening of lines between North and South.

In spite of the impact of the Missouri Debate and of a number of other major events bearing upon basic contentions, the next additions to the Union, fifteen years later, added little to the tension. Each of these incipient states, Arkansas and Michigan, was an integral part of its section, its character already firmly determined, and no boundary or borderland between slave and free was involved (Arkansas having been contracted eastward to its present limits in 1828). Senatorial power was the only concern, and there were complaints that Michigan was being held hostage by the South to ensure the admission of Arkansas—as in fact it was, so that Congress could in due course be "delivered of twins" (authorizing both to proceed toward statehood).

Any satisfaction with the relative ease of this tandem action was soon beclouded by the appearance of an independent Republic of Texas knocking at the door. Such a large addition to the South would obviously cause great concern in the North, and immediate annexation was thwarted. When the topic reappeared in 1844–45 there were intense efforts to subdivide Texas into free and slave states or territories. Senator Benton's bill would have prohibited slavery west of 100°W and provided for two free states as well as three slave. Pairing as a device for preserving the balance of power received unprecedented recognition in a bill sponsored by Senator William Haywood of North Carolina to annex Texas, lump it with all United States territory south of 42°N, divide that amalgamation in half at 34°N to form two territories ("Nebraska" and "Texas"), and provide "for the future formation in said Territories of at least two States, and if more than two, then of four States, and if more than four, then of six States," and, further, that one-half of the number formed be from the northern territory and hence free, the other one-half from the southern and hence slave. Texas was eventually brought into the Union by a political maneuver that avoided direct sectional confrontation. Its special defined privilege of subsequent subdivision was not exercised, in part because of fears over opening an internal issue over slavery. There were inevitable cries of alarm over the addition of such an outsized unit. Senator Choate of Massachusetts declared: "Everything has been changed. An empire in one region of the country has been added to the Union. Look east, west, or north, and you can find no balance for that." The question of Texas had produced numerous references to a logical makeweight. Petitions from citizens in New York and Michigan stating that "the proposed acquisition of Texas . . . will make the annexation of Canada indispensible [sic] to the just balance and equipoise of the Union" were denounced by Southerners as a ruse to thwart the addition of Texas—which they probably were. In spite of a few outspoken expansionists, there was no sectional or national pressure toward such an end. Rather, settlement of chronic boundary disputes with Great Britain brought a newly defined American Oregon into these federal calculations.

Even before Texas and Oregon were formally within the fold, another very careful pairing had encountered trouble in Congress. In 1844 the House Committee on Territories recommended that the admission of Florida and Iowa be considered in a single bill. This proved unacceptable; the two were separated and each was challenged and modified before approval. As already noted, Northern congressmen reduced Iowa in size to preserve more room for future states to the north and west, but the people of Iowa rejected that design and later accepted the compromise of their present boundaries. The proposed Florida constitution was routinely attacked for its provisions regarding slavery and the exclusion of free Blacks, but a special geopolitical proviso in the admissions bill allowing for future subdivision into two states became the main topic of debate. There was an obvious historical basis for such a division. The British had governed the area as two colonies, the treaty of annexation had recognized these, and the initial American military government was so organized, dividing West Florida from East Florida along the Suwanee River (the Apalachicola River had earlier served, but half of the former West Florida had already been allotted to Alabama, Mississippi, and Louisiana). There were so few Whites that Florida was later organized under a single territorial government, but as settlement expanded memorials for a division responsive to the divergent interests of the two parts became frequent. The territorial delegate carefully instructed his congressional colleagues in the geographical realities of the case ("here [he] held up a map of the United States, showing the long peninsula of Florida, running out between the Gulf and the Atlantic"), but after considerable debate the proviso for eventual subdivision was stricken from the final statehood bill.

The huge additions to the national territory in the 1840s reopened and compounded the import and difficulties of these geopolitical issues. What access would

North and South have to the western half of this transcontinental republic? Some Northerners, confident of their increasing power and angered at the covert addition of Texas, moved to exclude slavery from all territory acquired from Mexico. This "Wilmot Proviso" was bitterly denounced by the South. An obvious counterplay was to restrain the central government from imposing any such restriction and to allow the people of each territory and incipient state to decide for themselves—"popular sovereignty," as it came to be called. Some Northerners were quite willing to leave the matter open in this legal sense because they were confident that slavery would be contained by a higher power, as Daniel Webster declared in a famous speech: "Now, as to California and New Mexico, I hold slavery to be excluded from those territories by a law even superior to that which admits and sanctions it in Texas. I mean the law of nature, of physical geography, the law of the formation of the earth." Such lands were entirely too rugged and barren to make "African slavery, as we see it among us," attractive, or even possible. Provisos against it in such a land were as "senseless" as would be one "to protect the everlasting snows of Canada from the foot of slavery," should that land be annexed ("we hear much of" that). But to the more strident partisans on either side it was not the actual geography that was important but the abstract geography: should any kind of territorial demarcation be laid down?

An obvious compromise between extreme positions was to extend the 36°30′N line of separation to the Pacific. Greatly alarmed at the strength and vehemence of antislavery advocates, many in the South were ready to reaffirm this twenty-five-year-old limit, even though the southern portion of such a division was hardly one-quarter of the area in contention. Even this limited geographical share was soon jeopardized by a California constitutional convention prohibiting slavery within the generous bounds of that proposed state. (The admission of Wisconsin in 1848 had restored the North-South balance at fifteen each.) The precarious Compromise of 1850, as finally enacted in a series of bills, provided for the admission of California as a free state, imposed a western boundary upon Texas, and organized Utah and New Mexico as territories. By it and other acts the possibilities for slavery in these new territories were deliberately left uncertain, and control of such decisions inevitably became a major concern of the more extreme proponents on either side. Of particular interest, with reference to state formation and senatorial balance, were the attempts by Southern interests to organize a Territory of Arizona out of the southern half of New Mexico and to promote the subdivision of California so as to create a new territory and eventual state from southern California. Both movements were eventually approved, but too late to affect larger issues or survive the cataclysm that ensued.

The next crisis developed from the attempt by Senator Stephen Douglas of Illinois, powerful Democratic party leader and chair of the Committee on Territories, to ease Southern discontent by removing the 36°30′N limit and allowing the issue of slavery in Kansas and Nebraska to be resolved by local popular vote. Pressures to open this next westward tier of the Louisiana Purchase were becoming severe. The collapse and compression of the elaborate Indian protectorate that stood in the way were regarded as inevitable and desirable. The division (along 40°N) of the area into Kansas and Nebraska territories reflected the significance of the Kansas and Platte river valleys for Pacific railroad routes, the one leading west from St. Louis, the other from Chicago. (The southern boundary of Kansas was set at 37°N rather than 36°30′N to avoid splitting the Cherokee Reserve.)

Because Kansas lay directly west of Missouri, Southern leaders assumed that it could be quickly occupied with sufficient sympathetic population to ensure a favorable decision in the critical initial phase of territorial government. The result, however, was civil war, minor in scale but magnified in nationwide publicity as a contest between two militant invading forces, each determined to save Kansas for their side. It was in part a calculated confrontation initiated in typical Yankee fashion by an emigrant aid society dedicated to ensuring a shaping morality (as well as profits from land sales): "Dot Kansas with New England settlements, and no matter how heterogeneous the great living mass which flows into the Territory may be, it will all eventually be moulded into a symmetrical form." Under their leadership several thousand colonists (mostly from the western states) were assisted and a number of towns (notably Lawrence, Topeka, and Manhattan) were founded, but the great bulk of settlers came on their own and decisions on slavery were enmeshed in a welter of local issues and personalities. Pressure from President James Buchanan to have Congress recognize a proslavery Kansas constitution provoked great bitterness and rejection; subsequent popular rejection by Kansas settlers ended any prospect of immediate statehood and, more ominously, essentially ended Southern hopes of maintaining the sectional balance of power in the Senate. In the complicated political maneuvers of the time the admission of a presumed slaveholding Kansas in tandem with a free Oregon or Minnesota had been mentioned. By 1859 both of these Northern states had been added, but Kansas, the bloody borderland, had been blocked. As noted with reference to the larger context of American expansion, Southern hopes and various presidential efforts to obtain Cuba and additional states of Mexico during these same years failed (as did proposals to annex Hawaii). By 1860, therefore, there were thirty-three states, of which eighteen were free and fifteen slaveholding.

The Civil War remains the great watershed in American history. We tend to be so traumatized by that awesome bloodletting that the insistent question is always: Why did the Union fail? But a broader perspective on such geopolitical matters might first pose the question: How could it have held together for so long under such dynamic circumstances? For the rapidity and scale of expansion of the American federation during the first half of the nineteenth century were, and remain, unprecedented in world political history. Before California was admitted at mid-century, fourteen new states had been added to the sixteen-state Union of 1800. Such a near-doubling was certainly in defiance of some cogent expectations and discernible tendencies. Suffice it to recall Madison's warning about the difficulties inherent in "multiplying the parts of the Machine," Tocqueville's declaration of the well-grounded principle that confederations "have a natural tendency to dismemberment," and Boorstin's modern observation that "the tendencies of American political life were centrifugal—expressed in the American Revolution and in the secessionist tradition which long survived the Revolution."

Basic to the success of such geopolitical enlargement was the absence of any strong power or large body of alien people in its path. Indians were expelled or reduced to impotent remnants. The Louisiana French were quickly encompassed by Anglo-Americans and incorporated without serious stress on the overall structure or on the sectional society of which they became a part. Basic also was the adoption, before expansion, of a simple and orderly system for new jurisdictions to proceed through territorial phases to statehood on equal terms with all preexisting states. As Boorstin has emphasized: "The successful application of this notion of a predictable, gradual, step-by-step progress toward self-government and national involvement is one of the marvels of American history." The immense uniformities of the North American setting of this drama must also be taken into account. Beyond the Appalachians pioneers could advance along broad fronts, carrying their forms of society latitudinally deep into the heart of the continent. The only important uplands encountered, the Ozarks, were readily occupied as an attractive repetition of the southern Appalachians. This relative emptiness and uniformity of the vast interior hinterlands of the Atlantic seaboard societies gave those who would decide how to partition it into new units by the "Add-a-State" plan a remarkable range of options.

Because the most fundamental geopolitical issue divided the federation into two sections, and because these sections were in a position to expand their settlements westward from their seaboard source regions concomitantly, parallel, with equal facility and general prospects, the pairing of state accessions became an obvious means of preserving the basic geopolitical symmetry of the structure. Such a practice was informal, never fixed, and indeed often denied; as late as 1850 Senator Douglas insisted that any conscious pairing of states "to preserve an equilibrium . . . was a new doctrine, broached for the first time during the last few days," but such a stratagem in debate could not counter nearly sixty years of evidence covering at least six sets of admissions and additional proposals. Again, in broader perspective, one can only marvel at the extent to which such a policy was possible. Congressional adherence, without any firm rules, to a general standard as to size and shape of these new units was surely an important, if generally unrecognized, feature of this geopolitical history.

These more or less simultaneous sequential accretions to North and South worked reasonably well for several decades. In Frederick Jackson Turner's memorable characterization, these "rival societies . . . were marching side by side into the unoccupied lands of the West, each attempting to dominate the back country, the hinterland, working out agreements from time to time, something like the diplomatic treaties of European nations, defining spheres of influence, and awarding mandates [trusteeships], such as in the Missouri Compromise, the Compromise of 1850, and the Kansas-Nebraska Act." But these "treaties" were a mark of strain. What put the overall structure recurrently in jeopardy was not so much the balancing of the two expanding parts but the setting of the boundary between them. Although there had been much interpenetration and mixing of migration streams in the Ohio Valley, a boundary had been fixed through that borderland at an early stage. Northerners were naturally attracted to the idea of extending some such line across later-acquired western territories, whereas Southerners argued that these vast additions were a national patrimony that should be shared without geographical restrictions. The dispute flared in 1819 because Missouri was already a borderland occupied by settlers from both sections in a pattern that severely limited the options for congressional reshaping of the incipient state. Had most of the slaveholders been south of the Missouri River there would surely have been a stronger effort to make that major stream the northern boundary of any slave state in this sector. Had that been done, the Kansas River would have provided a line for the further extension westward, thereby dividing North and South in closer approximation to the Mason-Dixon Line across the main continental body of the federation.

The bloody confrontation in Kansas was a catalytic shock because it demonstrated that without a clear legal line of separation between these two competitive expansions the friction generated along their overlapping edges would ignite and cause an explosion, endangering the whole. By that time it had become starkly apparent that pairing and imperial expansion, which had been promoted as means of defusing conflict, had simply extended the reach and enlarged the arena of confrontation. As Bright summed it up: "Continuous westward expansion kept reopening the sectional argument over the extension of slavery and the balance of power at the center. Compromise thus had a tendency to hemorrhage on the open frontier."

By 1850 Southern hopes for maintaining that balance were fading. The system of paired admissions was not necessarily at an end, but parity in the Senate was no longer ensuring sufficient protection of Southern interests, as Calhoun spelled out in his final great pronouncement. "The Union is in danger," he said, not just because of "the agitation of the slavery question" but, more fundamentally, because "the equilibrium between the two sections of the Government, as it stood when the Constitution was ratified, and the Government put in action, is destroyed." The North had attained "a preponderance over every department of the Government by its disproportionate increase of population and States." If Calhoun's explanation for this unbalance was disingenuous (equal access to all territories and equal power over national revenues would have allowed the South to have obtained an equal share of immigration and industry), the size and trend of population growth in the North was apparent to all. The South had not yet fallen behind in the Senate, but it was surely losing ground in the House (by a margin of 88 to 135 at that time). Such a decline was not precipitous (the South held 46 percent of the seats in 1790–1800, compared to 39 percent in 1840 and 38 percent after the 1850 reapportionment), but everything indicated that it was inexorable. What really gave importance to these figures, of course, was the accelerating trend toward polarization, toward North and South as geographical voting blocs.

Calhoun's diagnosis involved more than such numbers. He decried an assumption of powers by the central government over the member states that had changed the basic character of the polity "from a Federal Republic, as it originally came from the hands of its framers . . . into a great national consolidated Democracy." After a review of how this had taken place and how the many "cords that bind the States together" were beginning to snap, he declared that the only way to save the Union was for the North to "cease agitation of the slave question," fulfill faithfully the fugitive slave law, give the South "equal right" to acquired territories, and join in amending the Constitution to "restore to the South . . . the power she possessed . . . before the equilibrium between the sections was destroyed"—in other words, with reference to this last admonition, to reverse the political impact of the continually changing human geography of this complex confederation.

Nearly twenty years earlier Tocqueville had assessed the prospects of this Union. He foresaw mounting difficulties from the increase in the number of states, "the continual displacement [westward] of its internal forces," the differential growth and precipitous pace of change, and he described as a possibility inherent in such structures precisely the alteration Calhoun asserted as having taken place during the intervening years: "States form confederations in order to derive equal advantages from their union. . . . If one of the federated states [or sections] acquires a preponderance, sufficiently great to enable it to take exclusive possession of the central authority, it will consider the other states as subject provinces and will cause its own supremacy to be respected under the borrowed name of the sovereignty of the Union." Viewing the United States with his usual breadth and discernment, Tocqueville emphasized that all sections were growing in population and wealth "more rapidly than any kingdom in Europe" and that much of the South's complaint was a rather natural expression of envy and suspicion at the relatively greater increases in the North. The changes were real enough and the feelings understandable, but he thought the remedy proposed by extremists—and logically appropriate to federations—was contradictory to their best interests: "The inhabitants of the Southern states are, of all Americans, those who . . . would assuredly suffer most from being left to themselves; and yet they are the only ones who threaten to break the tie of the confederation."

Such threats had welled up in the 1830s over Nullification and Indian Removal; they were not entirely new then and they would reappear and grow more strident in later years, revealing the United States of America as a great paradox: a growing, prospering, ever-expanding federation was a turbulent, weakening, and foundering federation.

3. The Idea of Separation

The United States of America was a geopolitical experiment. That it might not succeed, that such a conglomerate might not hold as a constitutional federation, was acknowledged by various leaders and commentators from the beginning. In his first term as president, George Washington "expressed his fear that there would be ere long, a separation of the union," and that possibility—fearsome or not, depending upon one's stance and interests—kept reappearing as a topic of active discussion.

In the early years of the Republic such talk was not necessarily considered to be alarming or unpatriotic. It might seem logical that a union formed voluntarily among a diversity of states to achieve certain ends could be dissolved as a whole or in part if it was demonstrably ineffective toward, or, worse, incompatible with, achieving those ends. Under appropriate circumstances, voluntary separation might be both practicable and legal. Yet, such a basic issue involved much more that practicalities and law, for emotions were bound into this creation. It had been born in bloodshed and designed after intensive debate on the most basic principles of government; it was a proud achievement, world-famous, and was surely an experiment worthy of the most serious and sustained trial.

There was also a commonsense bias in favor of hanging together even under discomfiting internal stress. After all, as Thomas Jefferson pointed out to some restive Southerners in 1798, "an association of men who will not quarrel with one another is a thing which never yet existed, from the greatest confederacy of nations down to a town meeting or vestry." Thus, even though he acknowledged that for the time being "we are completely under the saddle of Massachusetts and Connecticut, and that they ride us very hard, insulting our feelings, as well as exhausting our strength and substance," he warned of the grave danger, the foolishness, of what might seem to be the logical remedy:

If on a temporary superiority of the one party, the other is to resort to a scission of the

Union, no federal government can ever exist. If we rid ourselves of the present rule of Massachusetts and Connecticut, we break the Union, will the evil stop there? Suppose the New England States alone cut off, will our nature be changed? Are we not men still to the south of that, and with all the passions of men? Immediately, we shall see a Pennsylvania and a Virginia party arise in the residuary confederacy, and the public mind will be distracted with the same party spirit. . . . If we reduce our Union to Virginia and North Carolina, immediately the conflict will be established between the representatives of these two States, and they will end by breaking into their simple units.

And so Jefferson cautioned patience, until the tide turns and things begin to move more favorable to one's programs and principles. They soon did, of course, with Jefferson in the presidency, and so strongly as to drive some of his New England adversaries to despair and cause *them* to think of separation.

New England Federalists became alarmed by the philosophical and geopolitical changes so quickly apparent in the new administration. They perceived Jeffersonian concepts of "liberty" to be "license," of "democracy" to be "Jacobinism," threatening to replace deeply held ideas of social order with the chaos and tyranny so frighteningly on display in France. Furthermore, the Louisiana Purchase and the rapid growth of Kentucky and Tennessee seemed certain to make their region increasingly impotent and marginalized: "The balance of power under the present government is decidedly in favor of the Southern States; nor can that balance be changed or destroyed. The extent and increasing population of those States must for ever secure to them the preponderance they now possess." As to how to rid themselves of the source of these dangers, of "the overbearing influence of Virginia," "of negro Presidents and negro Congresses" (referring to those elected on the basis of the three-fifths rule in counting the slave population in proportional representation), a Massachusetts senator declared: "The principles of our Revolution point to the remedy,—a separation"; and a prominent Connecticut Federalist concurred: "I have no hesitation myself in saying [privately] that there can be no safety in the Northern States *without a separation from the confederacy.*"

In the discussions among this small group of leaders, Massachusetts and Connecticut were seen as the obvious core area, and these together with the other New England states the minimal grouping, with New York as highly desirable (indeed, the "centre" of the ideal Northern Confederacy), Pennsylvania ("at least east of the Susquehannah") as a possible addition, and perhaps even the adjacent British colonies ("with the assent of Great Britain"). Such designs, set forth in 1804, assumed the eventual secession of the Mississippi Valley because of naturally divergent orientations and interests.

The initial flurry of such talk waned, only to wax again with the severe impact of the Embargo Act of 1807 on American commercial interests, and was soon reinforced by the debates over creating a State of Louisiana, which produced Josiah Quincy's strident warning in Congress that admission would be "virtually *a dissolution of the Union*" and make it "the *duty of some to prepare* for separation, amicably if they can, *violently if they must.*" Open warfare with Great Britain fanned such feelings and fears, for New Englanders found themselves seriously endangered by a war they had bitterly opposed. By the time an irregular group of delegates gathered at Hartford in December 1814, to seek some remedy for their tribulations, British forces occupied much of the Maine coast, Boston itself seemed threatened, and it was considered likely that the British would capture New Orleans and West Florida, with surely profound ramifications upon the Western states and territories. Thus, some felt a real urgency to "rescue from ruin at least some portion of our beloved country." In spite of much more open talk by now of a separate peace and secession, the *Convention Report* was more conservative, focusing on constitutional revision as a means of redress for the perceived inequities among regions. But this political movement was abruptly aborted when those delegated to present its resolutions to President Madison arrived on the day all of Washington was celebrating news of the war's end; Jackson had devastated the British at New Orleans, the Union was secure, and these New England dissensions now seemed not only an embarrassment but scandalous, indeed traitorous (there had been a conversation with the British commander at Halifax)—as defensive Southern congressmen would never let their Yankee colleagues forget in the rancorous debates ahead.

New England separatism was terminated not only by this abrupt change in the international situation but by changes in human geography and regional perceptions. New England was industrializing; Upstate New York, heavily colonized by Yankees, was emerging into prosperity; great canals were under construction; Ohio and the West now beckoned more clearly as a rich realm for colonization, evangelism, and commercial development. The collapse of the Federalist party and the search for new political alignments was undergirded by the extension and elaboration of geographic networks giving sinew and substance to a broader North.

It had been understood from the beginning, as Madison had noted during the constitutional debates, that "the great division of interests in the U.S. . . . lay between the Northern & Southern" states, but that fundamental pattern only came starkly to the surface in the Missouri controversy. A long sequence of votes on various bills and amendments relating to slavery revealed, time after time, an almost complete geographic separation into North and South. At the outset the slave states proved solid except for an occasional defection by a senator or representative from the borderlands of Delaware or Maryland; there was always a scattering of Northern votes in support of the Southern position, in some cases from obvious sympathy with the interests of slaveholders (as in southern Illinois), but mostly from a search for accommodation of conflict and defusing of so explosive an issue. As this confrontation intensified spokesmen on each side openly referred to the collapse of the Union, most notably in the vehement exchange between Thomas Cobb of Georgia and James Tallmadge of New York (whose amendment had sparked the battle). "If we persist, the Union will be dissolved," warned Cobb, "we have kindled a fire which [with] all the waters of the ocean cannot be put out, which seas of blood only can extinguish"; to which Tallmadge retorted: "Sir, if a dissolution of the Union must take place, let it be so! If civil war, which gentlemen so much threaten, must come, I can only say, let it come!" The Missouri Compromise papered over this alarming fissure, but its ominous presence was now a fixture in American politics. As Glover Moore concluded, "The Missouri Controversy was the first occasion on which all of the strands in the fabric of North-South sectionalism were brought together and paraded before the public in magnitudinous proportions. . . . Without an arrangement similar to the one actually made, the Union would have disintegrated before the 1820s were half over." Just what pattern such a disintegration might have taken cannot be readily inferred from debates and votes in Congress (the general public was not yet much aroused) or from the human geography of the time, since developments in the West were still very uneven and rapidly changing. Henry Clay's prediction that the country would soon become divided into three separate confederations, North, South, and West, must have seemed a realistic possibility in 1819, without much thought given to actual geographical definitions.

The strongest voice of the South in this first great confrontation was that of Virginia, the historic leader and primary seat of Southern political influence in the nation—and thereby the chief focus of Northern strategy and critique. The vigor of the Virginian response no doubt reflected some insecurity in its longposition of dominance, arising not only from broader geopolitical trends but from internal pressures of emigration and economic stagnation, and especially from a determination to ensure unrestricted access to its furthest western frontier in Missouri.

The next major dissension, and overt threat of secession, sprang from a different corner of the South. South Carolina was of course another important American nucleus, distinct in its colonial origins, economy, and sociopolitical character. Relatively small in population and area, it could never routinely exert anything like the power of Virginia in national politics, but it made itself heard, if not heeded. For the first generation or so South Carolinians were strong, even militant, supporters of the Union, especially with reference to external enemies. As the national situation changed in the 1820s, so did South Carolina's stance regarding national policies.

The tariff was the ostensible issue in this new confrontation. Designed to aid American manufacturers, it was, unavoidably, a geographically divisive instrument and tended to be viewed by its opponents as no more than that: a penalty upon the South to reward the North. Economic stringencies, peculiarly severe in South Carolina, intensified opposition to a proposed increase in this form of taxation, but there was much more at stake. As John Calhoun confessed in a letter of 1830: "I consider the Tariff, but the occasion, rather than the real cause, of the present unhappy state of things. The truth [could] no longer be disguised, that the peculiar domestick institutions of the Southern States" were under threat from an interfering central government. That truth had of course been exposed in the controversy over Missouri, wherein a South Carolina senator had openly declared that the main issue was not any specific territorial allocation but "keeping the hands of Congress from touching the issue of slavery." In Southern minds the tariff and slavery were linked in contentions over the nature of the federal compact. The South Carolina tactic was "nullification," a doctrine declaring the right of a sovereign member state to intervene and prevent the enforcement within its jurisdiction of federal laws that it deemed to be in excess of the powers delegated by the Constitution to the central government. The ultimate objective was to ensure state control over its "peculiar domestick institutions."

The matter came to a head following a statewide electoral campaign in 1832, but its fervent supporters had misjudged the response expected from a Southern (indeed, native South Carolinian) and slaveholding president. Andrew Jackson declared forthrightly that the Union would be preserved intact, that such defiance would be put down by armed force if necessary; and Congress provided special help for doing so. After a flurry of saber rattling on both sides, a hasty compromise was reached involving a modest reduction in the tariff but no retreat by the federal government from its asserted powers.

The most remarkable thing about this brief, aborted movement was that it was the action of a single state, one unit among twenty-four—no other state proffered a gesture of support. If secession were to be recognized as a logical, legal remedy, appropriate to a voluntary association of sovereign parts, there was nothing geographically impracticable about such a move by a compact seaboard state with its own prominent cultural and commercial center, as Charleston obviously was (although the longer-term prospects of such a limited entity were surely another matter). But if such a separation were to be construed as an illegal revolt against the whole to be put down by force, it would seem suicidal for a South Carolina to attempt. That an apparent majority of South Carolina voters were willing to run "the risk of provoking an American civil war" suggests that they anticipated something intermediate of these extremes: that the central government would yield on the specific issue and separation would not be necessary; or that suppression by arms would never actually be undertaken and a de facto separation would be allowed; or that if it came to war, or even the very real threat of war, a large part of the South would be forced by the critical issue at stake to align itself with South Carolina. It is, of course, our knowledge of subsequent events that gives a broader significance to this singular action by this particular state.

Historians have sifted and assessed the factors that combined to produce this intransigence of South Carolina. That so many of these—economic distress, demographic stagnation, slave rebellions, and dread fear of abolitionism—were apparent in other areas of the South, makes the lonely stance of South Carolina all the more notable. The special combination and intensity of these pressures in the Carolina case is clear, but they only underscore the deep-rooted distinctiveness of this regional society and foreshadow what a powerful role it would play in the developing crisis of this federation despite its small—and ever-smaller relative— size.

Backing down on nullification produced such severe strains within South Carolina as to threaten local civil war and intensified the militancy of those determined to protect their slave properties and social system at all costs. There followed a major strengthening of the state militia and fortifications, and "the most thoroughgoing repression of free thought, free speech, and a free press ever witnessed in an American community," including prohibition of the teaching of reading to, or access to literature by, slaves and interruption of United States mail services to intercept abolitionist or other incendiary literature. There were also greater efforts to rally support in other states for the regional cause as defined by South Carolinians.

During the next twenty-five years, a great many strands, varied in source, weight, and coloration, became interlaced to form ever-clearer patterns of Southern sectionalism. Here only a few of the bolder threads and major motifs will be noted. Political economy provided a basic theme and the Panic of 1837 a strong impetus. In that year some Augusta merchants invited others in the South to gather for discussion of common problems. Only a few from Georgia and South Carolina showed up, but they generated the momentum for three subsequent meetings (the last of which was held in Charleston), which attracted as many as two hundred delegates from eight states to consider (as one of their formal resolutions put it) how "to throw off the degrading shackles of our commercial dependence." It was tirelessly reiterated that whereas the Southern states produced three-quarters (in value) of United States exports, scarcely one-tenth of the merchandise imported in America came directly to Southern ports. Much attention, therefore, was given not only to the chronic issue of tariffs but to the need to establish a line of ships to carry on direct trade with Britain and Europe. Nothing tangible came of this or other economic proposals, but a larger geopolitical purpose may have been served. John Quincy Adams, upon reading the proceedings of the first Augusta conclave, recorded that he believed it to be the "germ of a Southern

Convention, with South Carolina at its head, which is to divide this Union into a Northern, a Southern and a Western Confederacy, with Texas and a fourth part of Mexico annexed to the confederacy of the South." Adams was dead set against the annexation of Texas, and he assumed that this whole movement had been engineered by his old adversary Calhoun to thwart Northern efforts to curb the power and spread of slaveholders.

The senator from South Carolina was not in fact much involved at that stage, but became so, rather reluctantly, a few years later when he was elected to preside over a much larger and more impressive gathering in Memphis. Here, before nearly six hundred delegates from seventeen states, he set forth an extensive program for internal improvements designed, primarily, to bind the South and West together. The famous "strict constructionist" defined a role for federal aid in this scheme by treating the Mississippi River system as a national waterway, "a great inland sea," as it were, which the central government had as much right and duty to protect and improve as it did American seacoasts. Having gathered, as one historian put it, "to beatify the Mississippi Valley under federal auspices," the convention happily elaborated Calhoun's proposals into a vast program for development. Envisioning such a role for Washington might seem antithetical to nullification and secession, but the regional designs specified or implied had major geopolitical implications that other sets of interests were not long in countering. Subsequent commercial conventions in St. Louis and Chicago denounced the Memphis prospectus as divisive and illogical and offered very different views of regional orientations. Though powerless in themselves to undertake, or even promote at all effectively, anything of substance, these rallies exposed the uncomfortable fact that Southern definitions of a Greater South cut across and became entangled with competing definitions of a Great West—and, increasingly, a Greater North.

In the aftermath of Texas annexation and the Mexican cessions, concern for the *political* dimensions of political economy intensified. While congressional leaders struggled to formulate some sort of compromise legislation, a small coterie of secessionists, mainly from South Carolina and Mississippi, sought a more militant stance and set out to foster a fervent Southern nationalism. Under their prompting, delegates from most of the Southern states met in Nashville in June 1850, and another meeting was held in November, but congressional acceptance of the Compromise of 1850 undermined, and the opposition of Southern Unionists directly thwarted, the organizers' hopes for a concerted Southern ultimatum. Plans for a more formal Southern congress to meet in 1851 were abandoned. David Potter observed that while "the actual danger of disunion in 1850 remains a matter of controversy among historians," it seems clear that "the idea of secession as a possible recourse first won widespread acceptance in the South during the prolonged deadlock of 1846–1850"; he further noted that an analysis of the voting suggests that no real compromise between the sections was actually effected and the whole affair might better be called the "Armistice of 1850."

Common commercial interests, under pressure of the rapidly changing geography of the nation, especially the extension of railroads, industrialization, and the great strategic issue of a railroad to the Pacific, led to a series of nine Southern Commercial Conventions during the years 1852–59 (a tenth, scheduled to meet in Atlanta in 1860, was canceled). Attended by hundreds and sometimes more than a thousand delegates from all across the South (and often a sprinkling from adjacent Northern states as well), these open, sprawling affairs are difficult to assess. The delegates were variously appointed by governors, mayors, city councils, boards of trade, and citizen meetings, and were not necessarily representative of broad public feeling on any topic. Like earlier gatherings, these conventions were long on speeches and resolutions, but with little discernible influence upon public policies or private undertakings. By meeting in a different city each time, issuing reports, and receiving a good deal of publicity, they surely played an important, if unmeasurable, role in fostering a greater sense of common regional problems and of growing sectional divisions within the nation. Yet, they also displayed a South riven with competing interests and conflicting strategies. Some of these were obviously geographical, such as those between rival ports; others were more political or philosophical, though not unrelated to such basic variations in the human surface as the proportions of Blacks and involvement in slavery. Much the most prominent division was that between Unionists (who saw the Constitution, narrowly interpreted, as their best defense) and secessionists (who despaired of adequate protection from any central government). Furthermore, there was clearly a shift in emphasis and agenda through these years toward a more radical, confrontational Southern stance on basic federal issues. Thus, what began at Baltimore as an almost purely commercial meeting (and one so biased in its promotion of Baltimore as the natural premier port for all sections to make some delegates wonder if it was really a *Southern* convention at all), had moved two years later, in the Charleston meeting, to focus on the imperative need for the Southern states to build a Pacific railroad to ensure their geopolitical position on the continent, and, two years after that, in Savannah, had added reopening of external slave trade to its agenda. By 1857, James De Bow, the Charleston-born publisher whose *De Bow's Review* (published in New Orleans—but printed in New York!) had become a powerful voice for the Southern cause, regaled the Knoxville convention with a grand vision of the South benignly separated from the Union and assuming "her stand among the nations" in "the rank of a first class power."

The idea of peaceful secession remained alive through all the threatening rancor of these years. Amid a widely publicized address of 1839 celebrating the "Jubilee of the Constitution"—a rhetorical occasion, surely, for celebrating the *Union*—John

Quincy Adams, former president and current congressman from Massachusetts, saw fit to declare:

> If the day should ever come (may Heaven avert it!) when the affections of the people of these States are alienated from each other, when the fraternal spirit shall give way to cold indifference, or collisions of interest shall fester into hatred, the bonds of political association will not long hold together parties no longer attracted by the magnetism of conciliated interests and kindly sympathies; and far better will it be for the people of the disunited States to part in friendship from each other than to be held together by constraint. Then will be the time for reverting to the precedents which occurred at the formation and adoption of the Constitution, to form again a more perfect Union by dissolving that which could no longer bind, and to leave the separated parts to be reunited by the law of political gravitation to the centre.

A few years later a telling example of such a separation within an important institution was on display. During these same decades of national expansion, growth, and tension the Methodist Episcopal Church had become the largest religious denomination in the United States. Spreading rapidly into every region from its foundations in the Delaware-Chesapeake border zone, it was now the most national in distribution, active in virtually every county, and proportioned in membership North and South, in White and Black, and in slaveholders, non-slaveholders, and abolitionists, not unlike that of the total population. Coeval and coextensive with the Republic, organized into many regional conferences whose bishops met periodically in General Conference to determine overall policy, the Methodist church was therefore of special interest with reference to the geopolitical implications of the deep moral contest reverberating in the United States. The first fracture appeared in the early 1840s when Methodist abolitionists, failing to win support from the church as a whole, began to secede as congregations to form the Wesleyan Methodist Church. Numerically this was a distinctly minor movement, rooted in the Yankeelands of Upstate New York and Michigan, but in 1844 the national church became so deadlocked over the issue of slavery in another guise that it was reluctantly proposed that a "constitutional plan for the mutual and friendly division of the Church" was the only solution. Such a Plan of Separation was approved by a great majority (135–15) and was followed by organization of the Methodist Episcopal Church, South, at a special convention in Louisville in 1845.

This "spirit of brotherly separation quickly evaporated," however, and the two bodies were soon in bitter contention (in 1848 the Northern church repudiated the separation agreement, but to no practical effect). Much the greatest difficulty was geographical: setting "the line of division" between the two bodies. The separation plan had specified that affiliation in the border zone should be by major vote in "the societies, stations, and Conferences," and once a fixed line was established (as already the case between the Methodist churches of Canada and the United

States), the two churches would respect one another's territory. But such rulings were ambiguous and without force, and the separation was engulfed in confusion and rivalry. Whereas the M.E. Church, South, moved quickly to make itself coextensive with the slaveholding states, six conferences of the undivided church had overlapped that critical boundary, and popular feelings on slavery and allegiance varied greatly from district to district through a broad border zone extending from Delaware and Maryland through the Ohio Valley and across Missouri into the Indian Territory. Thus conferences, districts, and even single congregations got torn apart, cities were separated from hinterlands (as St. Louis from most of Missouri), sets of competing officials were installed by rival bodies (as in the Kanawha District, claimed by both the Ohio and Kentucky conferences), and aspirations for a "mutual and friendly" separation faded into festering antagonisms.

This snapping of ecclesiastical bonds by "the explosive effect of slavery agitation" was emphasized by Calhoun in his impassioned last speech in Congress. The members of the Methodist church, he said, were "now arrayed into two hostile bodies," the Baptists likewise, and the Presbyterians very nearly so. His reference to the sundering of these nationwide organizations (the largest denominations in America) was no mere rhetorical flourish. He pointed to them as early warning systems, because these great religious bodies were some of the "most important cords which bind these States together in a common Union." So indeed they were, and it now seems that not only were they symptomatic of national stress, they were active agencies of union and separation. By their actions and justifications they helped shape the developing patterns of sectionalism and confrontation—and helped sustain the self-image and morale of their society; as Goen has stated, they "encouraged the myth of 'peaceable secession,' established a precedent of sectional independence, reinforced the growing alienation between North and South by cultivating distorted images of 'the other side,' and exacerbated the moral outrage that each section felt against the other." If not all historians would go so far as those students of American religion (and some commentators of the time) who maintain that "the split in the churches was not only the first break between the sections, but the chief cause of the final break," they would not deny that the churches were deeply important in shaping the course of these momentous events.

If such moral and philanthropic bodies found negotiated separation to be a confounding and embittering process, what prospect was there that the whole American society could manage it? By midcentury that possibility seemed dim indeed, and for some of the same reasons. "Peaceable secession! Peaceable secession! The concurrent agreement of all members of this great republic to separate!" an incredulous Daniel Webster thundered in Congress;

> Why, what would be the result? Where is the line to be drawn? . . . Sir, I may express myself too strongly perhaps, but there are impossibilities in the natural as well as in

the physical world, and I hold the idea of a separation of these States, those that are free to form one government, and those that are slave-holding to form another, as such an impossibility. We could not separate the States by any such line, if we were to draw it. We could not sit down here to-day and draw a line of separation that would satisfy any five men in the country. There are natural causes that would keep and tie us together, and there are social and domestic relations which we could not break if we would, and which we should not if we could.

Where to draw the line?—an obvious, looming, insistent issue. Few Southerners wanted to talk about it, but a good many Northerners were eager to use it as a club to beat down the very idea of secession. One great geographical reality was the discordance between the firm juridical boundary separating free from slave states and the day-to-day functioning of the nation's ordinary economy and society. There might be a growing polarization of extremists on either side, but actual separation could never be a simple parting. As Mr. Vinton of southeastern Ohio put it, as early as 1845:

Massachusetts and South Carolina, [as] the North and the South, might, for aught I know, find a dividing line that would be mutually satisfactory to them; but, sir, they can find no such line to which the western country can assent, where would you draw it? Would you make the Ohio the boundary . . . ? Can the people on either side of the Ohio consent to that? . . . Lay now the map of the country before you; look, sir, at the wonderful net-work uniting the West with the North and the South and let any northern or southern man tell me where he would begin the work of . . . destruction.

His warning had been sounded even more forcefully by Mr. Hardin of Illinois:

The great natural outlet for our commerce is the Mississippi river; and let me tell southern gentlemen who have pictured in their imagination that El Dorado—a southern confederacy—that the free states situate on the Ohio and Mississippi will never permit the mouth of that river to belong to any government than their own . . . not all the united chivalry of the South would ever be able to hold it against the combined forces which would be concentrated to open that great outlet of our commerce.

Five years later Daniel Webster pointed to the same in his dismissal of the very idea of peaceable secession:

Well, now, Sir, I beg to inquire what the wildest enthusiast has to say on the possibility of cutting [the Mississippi] in two, and leaving the free States at its source and on its branches, and slave states down near its mouth, each forming a separate government? Pray, Sir, let me say to the people of this country, that these things are worthy of their pondering and of their consideration. Here, Sir, are five millions of freemen in the States north of the river Ohio. Can any body suppose that this population can be severed, by a line that divides them from the territory of a foreign and alien government, down somewhere, the Lord knows where, upon the lower banks of the Mississippi?

The situation was no simpler east of the Appalachians. Delaware and Maryland were slave states, but both were deeply bound into the Northern economy and society. By 1850 almost half of Maryland's Black population were already free, as were seven out of eight in Delaware. Calhoun, in calculating Southern strength, admitted that "Delaware had become doubtful as to which section she properly belongs." As for Maryland, slavery was very largely confined to its southern tobacco counties, and although sympathy for the Southern cause was much more widespread, casual Southern assumptions that Baltimore would become the "New York of the South" were geopolitically naive and not supported by Maryland businessmen. And what about the capital of the United States in the event of separation? With reference to local customs and laws Washington might be a Southern city surrounded by Southern states, but it was surely obvious that the central government of the United States was not going to hand the District of Columbia over to a Southern confederacy. Would it allow the Potomac to become an international boundary—with the capital in easy sight and range of the guns of a foreign power? If not, would Virginia voluntarily give up its northern counties to provide a buffer?

In the rancorous debates over the fugitive slave law Unionists pointed to the contradiction inherent in the very idea of secession as a protection of slavery: if an international boundary were created, there would be no fugitive slave law to the north of it, and the lure of such an inviolable sanctuary would drain the South of its most valued property. The scenario was sketched (at much greater length than this excerpt) by Horace Mann of Massachusetts in 1850:

> First, as to the recovery, or non-recovery, of fugitive slaves, which is one of the alleged provocatives of dissolution. Take a map of the southern States and spread it out before you. Although they cover an area of about nine hundred thousand square miles, . . . only an insignificantly small portion of this vast extent lies more than two hundred fifty miles from a free frontier. . . . An outside belt or border-region of the slave States, no part of which shall be more than one hundred miles from a free frontier, would embrace nearly one-half of their whole area, and, as I suppose, much more than one-half of their slave population [he included the seacoast as a "free frontier"]. What is to prevent the easy escape of slaves living within these limits? While God sends nights upon the earth, nothing can prevent it. . . . The Mississippi and Ohio Rivers, where they border upon free States, will be alive as with shoals of porpoises. Remember, there is no Constitution of the United States now. That you have broken. The free States are therefore absolved from all obligation to surrender fugitives.

From this time on, the terribly divisive complications of maintaining an internal boundary between slave and free sectors of the federation and the ominous anticipated consequences of converting it into a line of sovereign separation could never be banished from political thought. Ten years later, in December 1860, Senator James Green of Missouri introduced a resolution in Congress "for establishing an armed police force at all necessary points along the line separating the slaveholding from the non-slaveholding States, for the purpose of maintaining the general peace between the States; of preventing the invasion of States by citizens of another; and also for the efficient execution of the fugitive slave laws." It was referred to the Judiciary Committee.

Such geographical realities made *any* process of separation an ominous prospect, and it is not surprising that only ardent Unionists wished to discuss such hard questions. During all these years of intensifying agitation, those committed to secession, or even the threat of secession, were almost entirely from the cotton states of the Lower South, and they studiously ignored this fundamental issue. One finds no reports of special committees, societies, or parties detailing where the division should be, no maps showing proposed confederacies and lines of separation. The issue would have to be faced by the "border states"—giving a darker portent to that well-established geographical term. It was in these states, in Virginia and Maryland, in Kentucky and Missouri, that one finds the most agonizing ambiguities of the time: deep sympathy with the Southern cause, deep fears of separation, and fervent hopes that some sort of compromise could be patched together once again.

Compromise depended upon Congress and the Executive, upon national politics and major parties. Political parties had undergone great changes from the singular situation of 1820, when the collapse of the Federalist party (that "half-way house between the European past and the American future") allowed President James Monroe to run for reelection unopposed. The major patterns were the emergence of the Democrats and Whigs as competing national parties in the 1830s, followed by new disintegrations and realignments into Democrats and Republicans in the 1850s. There were many important developments in the very nature of American politics during these years, in the organization of parties, in the methods and style of campaigning, in the formation of interest groups and the kinds of issues in contention, but we must keep our focus on the most general of geographical patterns.

Amid the debates on Missouri (in the very year that Monroe would later be almost unanimously reconfirmed into office), Congressman Charles Kinsey of New Jersey commented: "Few gentlemen have risen . . . without deeply lamenting (and I think with great reason) the existence of parties, designated by geographical lines and boundaries. I also depreciate it, as being a division of the Union into parties so equal in number, wealth, intelligence, and extent of territory." He was of course referring to the North-South sectionalism that had welled up and broken through the surface of nationwide party and electoral patterns. The emergence of two major parties vigorously contending for office in every region soon eased such fears for a time. From 1828 onward every president was elected by a majority in both sections. Yet each party was an insecure coalition, spanning North and South but primarily based in one section. Thus the Jacksonian Democrats were basically a Southern party, with strong extensions in the agrarian West and alliances with certain political machines in the urban North; whereas the Whigs were solidly based in the Northeast, with strong support from merchants, bankers, and some commercial farming interests throughout the South and West. But the increasingly strident confrontations over slavery strained these coalitions so severely that the Whig party disintegrated and the Democrats lost some of their Northern support. By 1855 the "most dangerous divisions of the people"—those that followed "geographical lines"—began to appear with new force. As measured by a sequence of congressional elections and the presidential ballot of 1856, the results remained somewhat muddled. There was the complication of the ephemeral American (Know-Nothing) party and considerable shifting of the major party borderlines in Pennsylvania, Ohio, Indiana, and Missouri. In the presidential election of 1856, Buchanan (Democratic) carried these four states and New Jersey as well as the entire South, while Frémont (Republican) carried only the remaining Northern states (and not including California).

That the contest of 1860 would be fought by a set of sectional parties was foretold in the disintegration of the Democrats at their national convention. Unable to reconcile (after fifty-seven ballots) the Southern (incipient secessionists) and Northern (strong Unionists) delegates with a single platform, the convention broke up and each contending faction reconvened to nominate its own candidate for president: Breckinridge of Kentucky (Southern Democrats) and Douglas of Illinois (Northern Democrats). Meanwhile, the Republicans had nominated Lincoln, but a new political group calling itself the Constitutional Union party, made up primarily of conservative Whig and American party remnants, selected Bell of Tennessee as their candidate. The results of the national election clearly revealed a threefold geographical division: North (Lincoln), South (Breckinridge), and Border (Douglas and Bell). Lincoln carried every nonslave state (including California and Oregon) and not a single Southern state (he was not even on the ballot in ten states). Douglas won only Missouri; Bell carried Kentucky, Tennessee, and Virginia (and missed carrying Maryland by just 522 votes); Breckinridge took the rest of the South. If political parties were indeed the "connective tissue" of the nation, something alarming had happened to the body politic.

Six weeks after the election, on December 20, 1860, South Carolina formally declared its secession from the Union. The concept of voluntary withdrawal, of legal separation, so long discussed and increasingly threatened, had been set in motion. The vivisection of the national body had begun, but how far and along just what lines the incision might reach, how deeply it might cut, how much might be severed, what risks there might be for continuing life in the severed parts, or for stitching them back together, restoring the whole and healing the wound, was all quite unpredictable.

4. Disintegration

The historian Don E. Fehrenbacher emphasized the need to be precise about "southern" secession: "The South, of course, did not secede. It was South Carolina that did so—South Carolina alone, followed in order by Mississippi, Florida, and Alabama; then Georgia, Louisiana, and Texas." It took forty-two days to complete that phase of secession. Eight days later, on February 8, 1861, representatives convened in Montgomery to form the Confederate States of America, and two days after that they elected Jefferson Davis as president. The formation of this new "South" was therefore the result of a sequence of formal processes undertaken separately by each of seven states. It was not impelled by any clash, or even threat of clash, with Northern forces, and it did not directly result in any such thing. It was initiated in response to a routine democratic national election, and it was all completed before Abraham Lincoln took office. It was, in short, a peaceable secession.

There were certainly those who had hoped and worked for "Southern secession" rather than this sequence of state actions that actually ensued. South Carolinians, especially, were aware of the dangers of single-state initiatives. In December 1859 they had sent an official commissioner to seek the cooperation of Virginia in convening representatives from all the slave states to consider a common strategy. The Virginia legislature listened but gave no support; attempts to convene a meeting in Atlanta in the summer of 1860 fared no better. In October, on the eve of the national election, the governor of South Carolina wrote to all Southern governors on the need to coordinate their actions if Lincoln were elected, but most responded that such a result would not in itself be sufficient cause for secession. In spite of the long intensifying threat of Southern separation, "Southern consensus ended abruptly at the point of transition from generalities to specifications." There was deep disagreement over secession as an appropriate remedy, over the right time to secede if it were to be used, and just how to proceed once the time had come to do so. Secession, therefore, was a difficult, divisive topic in each state, and the question of separate or concerted ("cooperationist") action among the states was an explicit issue in most. Simply to say that South Carolina took the lead masks the intense struggle within that most radical of states over policies, strategies, and timing.

Once a decision was reached, the influence of South Carolina in creating a

Southern confederacy was surely very great, if not readily measurable. It sent official agents to other states and to Washington to promote a common Southern response, and the fervor generated in its own internal contest was rapidly applied beyond its borders. The shrill advocacy of secession by so many of its political leaders and editors was heard across the Lower South, and it enjoyed a special receptivity. A good many of the ardent secessionists in the other states had some connection with South Carolina. Some were migrants from the state that had sent a higher proportion of its population westward than any other (in the Mississippi secession convention natives of South Carolina outnumbered those of Mississippi). Of special significance, as mentioned earlier, were the many prominent persons—governors, judges, lesser officials, and local leaders—who had received training in South Carolina. Of course, not all these migrants, graduates, and trainees were avid secessionists, but it is generally agreed that this widespread South Carolinian permeation of the Gulf states, together with the pressures applied by its example and exhortation, was fundamental to the creation of this new federation of American states.

The geographical patterns of relative support of secession are impossible to define with any precision. Votes were recorded in every state, but the varied nature of the state conventions, of the selection of delegates, and of the way the issue was presented for decision muddies the waters. Only in Texas was a direct popular vote taken and that in the form of a referendum on a secession ordinance already enacted by the Texas convention—and after six states had seceded. Secession was a highly emotional issue and was propelled by powerful waves of enthusiasm, accompanied by many prods of intimidation from a variety of militia, "Minute Men," and other local groups. Unanimously endorsed at the South Carolina convention, it gained momentum with each successive state declaration and with declining hopes for compromise in various Washington negotiations. At each point of decision the basic question for many people was not whether to separate but when to do so. It seems likely that a majority of the people of the Lower South were opposed to secession in November 1860, but the desire to leave the Union developed strongly during the next two months.

Although we cannot offer a map showing diffusion of the idea of secession, detailed analyses by historians provide a general sense of where support for and opposition to the idea were most strongly expressed at the time of decision in each state. The main area of opposition took the form of a large "embayment" on the northern border extending from the red-clay counties of northern Georgia southwesterly deep into Alabama and curving back across the sand hills of northeastern Mississippi; the Red River Valley in northern Texas formed a western outlier of similar stance. The eastern portion of this embayment included the southern end of the Appalachians, and throughout it was in general an area of relatively few slaves. Much of it (including the Texan outlier) had been settled primarily out of Tennessee, and its antisecessionism presumably reflected a legacy of strong Jacksonian support for the Union. The most obvious additions to the map of opposition were some of the heavily German counties of central Texas and a block of counties in the piney woods of south-central Georgia—yet many counties similar in character to the Georgia woods in Florida, Alabama, and Mississippi were strongly secessionist.

And indeed the obverse pattern is considerably more complex. Joseph Sitterson's conclusion about the later vote in North Carolina applies equally well to its forerunners: "A secession county was likely to be a slaveholding county, but a slaveholding county might not necessarily be a secession county." There *was* a general correlation: the main cotton- (and rice-) producing districts from South Carolina westward across the Black Belt, Mississippi floodplain, to the western reaches of the plantation system along the Brazos and Colorado were predominantly secessionist. But there were many punctuations and variations. Voting in the Georgia Piedmont displayed a mosaic of counties on either side of the issue. Most of the "town counties" in Georgia voted for secession, as did Mobile, while Natchez and Vicksburg conspicuously did not. The New Orleans delegation was strongly for immediate secession, yet many of the great sugar planters were against it (they were thriving under tariff protection) as were probably a majority of all French Louisianans. So many factors were involved; so much confusion and uncertainty apparent. In many a county—probably most—the local establishment composed of a small oligarchy of large landowners, younger aspiring planters, and lawyers dictated the outcome, but some of these elites, including some prominent public men in the South, were deeply convinced that secession would prove disastrous. Recent party affiliation was an unreliable indicator; some Whigs continued to adhere to the Union as the best hope, many others became swept up in the movement for separation.

It must be reiterated that a vote against secession was a decision only for that moment. Any change in the conditions of the developing confrontation between section and nation might quickly alter these patterns. Southern response to any perceived Northern coercion would expose rather more clearly the really fundamental cultural geography of America.

However difficult it might be—then or now—to decipher patterns and motivations, the fact is that by early February 1861, seven states had formed a new confederacy. Extending from the Atlantic to the Rio Grande, it was a geopolitical entity of 563,678 square miles with a population of 5 million. Just under one-half (47.3 percent, by the 1860 census) of these people were slaves (fewer than 40,000 Blacks were free). It was a contiguous block of states and, except for that northern embayment that was oriented to the Tennessee River or to Memphis, its new boundaries did not cut through closely integrated areas. Internally, however, it was far from being a coherent geographical structure, a fact dramatized by Jefferson Davis's journey from his home near Vicksburg to his inauguration in Montgomery. The two cities lay less than 300 miles apart, along a direct east-west road, but Davis, hastening by rail, had to travel north into Tennessee, thence across northern Alabama to Chattanooga, south to Atlanta, and from there southwesterly to Montgomery, a distance of 850 miles around three and one-half sides of a square on half a dozen railroads (and three different gauges). No railway trunk lines bound these states together because there was little traffic to be served by such links. The great devotion to cotton had provided a powerful common interest for these states (it had become common, locally and at large, to refer to them as "the Cotton States") but little basis for any substantial trade among them. Thus, the circulation systems—by water and rail—of this new confederacy were markedly compartmentalized, focusing on five main ports: Charleston, Savannah, Mobile, New Orleans, and Galveston. However serviceable for an export economy, such a set of separate systems would appear to limit severely the geopolitical efficiency of this new creation. As Davis's trip displayed, travel even between the capitals of adjacent states was an indirect, time-consuming affair. It took five rail lines to get from Columbia to Milledgeville, for example, while the minor Florida system, Texas, and most of Louisiana had no rail connections at all with other states. Postmortems on the Confederacy usually identify a jealous regard for states' rights, resulting in a bristly independence of each member, as a major weakness of this political system. Such separation within was foreshadowed and undergirded by its routine functional geography.

The geopolitical character of this seven-state confederation was little discussed at the time both because its leaders and supporters assumed that it would soon become much larger by the addition of other Southern states and because those who opposed the very idea of such a separate confederacy assumed that it was a means and not an end, a tactic to coerce the federal government into acceptance of Southern demands for more explicit protection of Southern interests. As for the first group, the spread of the secessionist movement was halted, just as the Confederacy was being formed, by the decision of Virginia to remain in the Union, the overwhelming defeat of secession in Tennessee, and the narrower victory of Unionists in Arkansas and Missouri. As for the second group, the creation of the Confederate States of America changed the central issue of the sectional conflict from slavery to secession and thereby raised the stakes enormously. An awesome set of unprecedented decisions had to be faced: How should the federal government of the United States respond? How should the individual states (as sovereign republics within the federation) respond?

The results must be understood within the context of that peculiar American interregnum between the election of a new president and administration in early November and their actual assumption of office in early March. During that four-month interval the ship of state drifted. Buchanan, the lame-duck president, fearing disaster, was unwilling to accept secession but was openly sympathetic to the South and unwilling to risk coercion against it; Lincoln, the elected leader, was without formal power and unwilling to declare a policy until he had formed a cabinet and taken office. Lincoln did state his belief in an inviolable Union, but he clearly wished to avoid a confrontation. At this stage he considered secession to be the work of an extremist minority, a conspiracy that could with patience be exposed and quelled.

Such an environment spurred the search once again for some patchwork compromise. Putting the blame on antislavery agitation, Buchanan called for an "explanatory amendment" to the Constitution to specify protection of slaveholders' rights of property. The Senate and the House, following the example of 1850, appointed special committees. What hope there was seemed to rest on the border states. Governor John Letcher of Virginia had so indicated; ex-President John Tyler, Virginia's most illustrious son, called for a special border state convention; the Virginia Assembly endorsed the general intent but broadened the invitation to all states to send delegates to what became known as the Washington Peace Conference, to begin on February 4, 1861. Twenty-one states (all except the seceded South and Arkansas, Michigan, Wisconsin, California, and Oregon) sent delegations. All of these deliberating bodies focused primarily on the Crittenden Plan, a set of resolutions offered by the Kentucky senator that would reestablish the 36°30'N Missouri Compromise line and explicitly affirm various protections of slavery. Many Northerners were quite ready to accept such a division. Before these emergency sessions were over the free state of Kansas had been admitted and the Territories of Colorado, Dakota, and Nevada (with no specification about slavery) created with little controversy. It seemed that the South would probably gain only New Mexico, where it was assumed slavery would never flourish. At the conference a provision was added to halt any further acquisition of territory (except for strategic stations, depots, and transit routes) without the concurrent majority of the senators from the two "classes" of states, slaveholding and nonslaveholding. But all of these efforts came to naught. No national leadership was exerted, debate was desultory; too many minds were made up, too many people had lost hope.

"The question," said an Ohio representative, "was not merely what will keep Virginia in the Union, but also what will bring Georgia back" (like many others, he despaired of South Carolina). Many people thought that keeping Virginia in was in itself the best hope of bringing Georgia back. So long as the great prestigious mother-of-presidents remained in the Union, secession would spread no farther and some sort of "voluntary reconstruction"—re-union—of the federation might be possible. In such a view, holding the border states in the Union was absolutely essential; they were "in destiny as in position, . . . the real Keystone of the Arch of the Union." A more radical alternative was the creation of a Border State Confederacy. The governor of Virginia predicted such a thing in December 1860, should the Lower South secede. At the least, such a formation would serve as a buffer between the extremists of North and South (between "the wickedness of Northern fanaticism and the intemperate zeal of secession"), a holding action to prevent warfare until some basis of settlement, peaceable secession or peaceable reunion, could be found. Senator James Pearce from Maryland's Eastern Shore spoke for many when he said: "I have no idea that this Union can be maintained or restored by force. Nor do I believe in the value of a Union which can only be kept together by dint of a military force." There were discussions among governors, proposals for conventions, and a flurry of calls for some kind of bold initiative from this sector of the country: "The Central States, and the great Northwest, must take the matter into their own hands. North Carolina, Virginia, Kentucky, Tennessee, with Pennsylvania, New Jersey, and other States near them, must unite with Ohio and the Northwest to save the country. They have the power to do it—they must do it." So said a Virginia delegate to the Peace Conference. But he offered no plan; the power of such a coalition was only that of a buffer and a deterrent to Northern attack. Nevertheless, he spoke from the heart, for he was from the Kanawha Valley and plainly saw the fearful prospect that these states might become a bloody battleground on "the long frontier between two foreign nations." Southern Unionists clung to the hope that time was on their side, that fervors would fade, that the new Confederacy would flounder, that Unionist politicians would gain firmer hold upon key states, that some new Union-saving plan could be formulated at a border state conference in Frankfort, Kentucky, scheduled for late May.

In his inaugural address, in a capital city bristling with bayonets for his protection, Lincoln clearly stated his interpretation of the case: "The Union of these States is perpetual, . . . [therefore] no State, upon its own mere motion, can lawfully get out of the Union." Secession ordinances were "legally void," and any "acts of violence, . . . against the authority of the United States, are insurrectionary or revolutionary." During the interval between Lincoln's election and assumption of office, the seceding states had taken over customhouses, arsenals, the Pensacola navy yard, and forts at Savannah, Mobile, and the mouth of the Mississippi. These essentially ungarrisoned posts had been turned over by caretakers without resistance. However, three important points remained under federal control: Fort Taylor (Key West), Fort Pickens (Pensacola), and Fort Sumter (Charleston). It was the attempt to send supplies to the last that prompted the South on April 12 to begin bombardment and force the surrender of the United States garrison. No blood had been shed, but the assault on Fort Sumter by the most radical of the seceding states was at once dramatic and symbolic, and it galvanized the North; Lincoln's subsequent call for troops to suppress this insurrection galvanized the Upper South. On April 17, Virginia seceded from the Union; three weeks later Arkansas and Tennessee followed, and two weeks after that, North Carolina. The Confederate States of America now numbered eleven, its area was ostensibly augmented by more than 200,000 square miles, its population by more than 4 million. On May 20, its capital was moved from Montgomery to Richmond.

Lincoln's call for troops "dissolved the Union" and "as by a stroke of lightning, made the North wholly North and the South wholly South," said a North Carolina Unionist editor with some shock and sadness. It was soon evident, however, that in spite of this sudden and decisive change the actual split and conformation of the two parts would not be so simple. Unlike the first phase of disintegration, the residual United States was not going to come apart neatly at the seams along existing state boundaries, and certainly not along that long juridical divide between slaveholding and nonslaveholding states. Rather, over the next few months the United States would be ripped apart, jaggedly, along lines determined primarily not by formal votes for or against secession but by local militias, guerrilla bands, and armies. Two days after Virginia's secession, mobs attacked a Massachusetts regiment marching between railroad stations in Baltimore en route to Washington, with loss of life on both sides. Officials of Maryland, with its deeply divided constituencies and positioned in the most imperiled sector of the borderlands, desperately sought to remain neutral. But while the legislature convened in Frederick to declare such a policy, federal forces had already occupied Annapolis and moved to secure the national capital. The president of the Baltimore & Ohio offered his railway's services to the Union immediately after the attack on Fort Sumter. Although local militia and police had burned all the bridges leading from the North into Baltimore, three weeks later federal troops occupied the city unopposed. Maryland and Delaware were bound into the Union by the firm stance of a few leaders (the Duponts ended powder sales to the Southern states after Sumter) backed up by the quick movement of external forces securing strategic trunk lines.

Federal troops also crossed the Potomac to occupy Alexandria and secure the southern approaches to Washington, but a more severe and permanent division of Virginia was in the making. Delegates from the northwestern corner of the state returned from the secession convention determined to secure by other means what they had failed to accomplish with their Unionist votes. In Wheeling, especially, vexations over a "far off" Richmond and a planter oligarchy were long-standing: "We are as much two people . . . [as] those living on two sides of the Alps . . . the God of Nature made us a part of Pennsylvania, while the surveyors, by accident or design, made us a part of Virginia." In May, delegates from twenty-five western counties voted to request approval from Richmond to create a new state. Such benignity soon gave way to stronger action. Once the Virginian people had formally endorsed secession, Union regiments from Ohio crossed the river at Wheeling and Parkersburg and with the help of local militia moved eastward into the mountains against only scattered opposition. Subsequently, at a second Wheeling convention delegates from thirty-nine counties were emboldened to declare that their main goal was not "to create a State, but to save one," and they organized "The Restored Government of Virginia" and proceeded to elect a governor and new members of Congress. Once this action was recognized by Lincoln there was, formally, a Virginian government in the Union as well as a Virginia in the Confederacy.

The legislature of this new government soon gave formal consent to begin the creation of a new state out of northwestern Virginia. In May 1862, it approved a design composed of a block of forty-eight counties, with provision for up to three more (Jefferson, Berkeley, and Frederick, occupying the northern end of the Shenandoah Valley) to be added if approved by voters in each county (the first two acceded; no vote was ever taken in Frederick). A proposal to extend this eastern Potomac corridor to Fairfax County, opposite Washington, D.C., with a further addition of Accomack and Northampton counties on Virginia's Eastern Shore (these latter presumably to ensure direct access to the Atlantic bypassing Norfolk) was defeated. More persistent were repeated attempts to include the entire Great Valley. As it was, the forty-eight-county unit enclosed a large area on the south that was far from sympathetic to this separation from the Old Dominion and was not yet under the control of federal forces. Debated in Congress in June and July, the West Virginia bill was not approved and signed by Lincoln until December. A requirement that a convention be held to formalize gradual emancipation further delayed admission of this new state until June 1863. The capital was awarded to Wheeling, chief source of this movement and the most secure place in a dangerous borderland. Having completed this bit of legal legerdemain the federal government of Virginia shifted its headquarters to Alexandria.

Farther west in the Ohio Valley there were indications of similar possibilities but with a different balance of forces. Lincoln's call for troops was firmly rejected by the governor of Kentucky, and it even prompted a flurry of secessionist meetings in southernmost Illinois. While volunteers from both sides of the river began to head for Confederate or Union recruiting offices, Kentucky officials struggled desperately to dampen the dangers of their long borderland position and to avoid the chaos of local wars. The strong Southern sympathies of the governor and many officials were offset by the strong Unionist feelings of much of their citizenry, especially in the eastern and central hill country. The governor turned this impasse into a formal declaration of neutrality and negotiated with neighboring governors and generals on either side to respect Kentucky's position. Lincoln tacitly accepted such a stance for a while as a means of holding Kentucky in the Union. Later in 1861 when Confederate forces from Tennessee moved into strong prosecessionist western Kentucky, delegates from sixty-five counties convened at Russellville, passed an ordinance of separation from the Union, and organized a government (with a capital at Bowling Green); on December 10, 1861, the state was officially added to the Confederacy. Thus Kentucky was also formally in both camps. If the state eventually proved to be quite strongly Unionist, the pattern of allegiance was blurred: "Every county sent men into both the Union and the Confederate armies. Only the proportions varied."

Such division and ambivalence was apparent even more deeply in the South. After the Tennessee legislature had declared the state's independence and formed a political league with the Confederacy, East Tennessee rejected secession by a strong popular vote and delegates gathered in Greeneville to consider forming a new state. As in Virginia, there were plenty of old complaints about the indifference of the planter aristocracy in the rich capital region, but East Tennessee had also been feeling a marked loss of power from the recent and rapid rise of Memphis and the western cotton counties. There was strong Unionist leadership in the area, and the more extreme were ready to follow the urging of the leading Knoxville paper and declare independence as the new State of Frankland—or some other name. Moderates prevailed long enough to send a commission to Nashville to seek legislative consent for a separate state. Failure to get anywhere with that formal approach soon led to local harassment of the Confederate army. These troops had been hastily dispatched to guard the vital Virginia & Tennessee Railroad, the only trunk line of the Upper South, and it was the presence of such forces that produced an outcome different from that of Virginia: "East Tennessee, like trans-Allegheny Virginia, in effect and in spirit seceded from the remainder of the state when the state seceded from the Union. Tennessee did not divide into two states only because no federal army could aid East Tennessee Unionists early in the war."

Missouri, the focus of the first great irruption of North-South contentions forty years earlier, also quickly displayed its character as a true border state. A strongly secessionist governor seated in a generally pro-Southern district hoped to carry the state quickly into the Confederacy. But much of St. Louis and the German counties, as well as some of the Ozark districts, were populated by determined Unionists, and the delegates' decision to move the special convention from Jefferson City to St. Louis was probably as decisive as it was symbolic in holding Missouri in the Union. A clash of arms over control of the St. Louis arsenal ignited a civil war that would continue with wide-ranging bloody effect throughout the years of the larger conflict. The governor and his main forces retreated to the southwest, where at Neosho, in late November, a remnant of the legislature declared secession, and thus Missouri, too, was formally admitted to the Confederacy.

Having lost the battle for Kansas some years ago there was no attempt to organize a government there, but opportunities beckoned farther to the south and west. As early as January 1861, a Georgian was urging that the Southern Indian nations be converted into "an invaluable arm of defense—into cossacks of the Don & Volga." Later that year a Confederate commissioner negotiated treaties with the Choctaws and Chickasaws, the Creeks and Seminoles, and, eventually, the Cherokees. Each of these three groups was accorded a delegate to the Confederate Congress, and the treaty with the Choctaws and Chickasaws stated that they might eventually seek admission as a state, a unit that might also embrace any one or all of the other three "civilized nations." The Indians were to provide troops for local support of the Southern cause; in return, the Confederacy agreed to assume all federal annuities and obligations. Treaties of peace and protection were also signed with a motley of eleven other emigrant and local "tribes and bands" residing in the Washita country on lands leased from the Choctaws and Chickasaws.

While securing this flank of their domain, Southerners also reasserted their claim to lands beyond Texas. Texan ranchers and suppliers were thinly scattered all along the southern trail to California. Agitations to detach this corridor from New Mexico and a remote Santa Fe had begun soon after the Gadsden Purchase. In 1860 such a design seemed near fruition; foundering in sectional politics, it was revived the next year at a convention in Mesilla, backed by Texas cavalry, and in March 1862, formally added to the Confederacy as the Territory of Arizona. Long-standing Southern expansionist dreams of a portal on the Pacific at San Diego or Guaymas now seemed much nearer realization (a school geography book published in Atlanta in 1862 denoted all the land between 40°N and 25°N as the appropriate field for Confederate aspirations). The Confederate Constitution (unlike that of the United States) specifically declared that "the Confederate States may acquire new territory" and that new states might be formed and admitted from such acquisitions, but in fact Arizona would prove to be the final unit added to the secessionist structure.

As the foregoing suggests, defining just what constituted the Confederate States of America is not quite as simple as the standard maps in our textbooks and history atlases imply. These almost invariably show a solid block of eleven states, conforming to those over which the Confederacy had, initially, firm control—and to those formally charged with rebellion by the North. The geopolitical realities were rather more complex (fig. 78). There was, of course, the difference between aspiration and actuality—and, further, between various forms of actuality. Behind the presiding officer's chair at the convention in Charleston in December 1860 was suspended a special "banner of secession" depicting an arch formed by the seals of the fifteen slave states. Such was clearly the hope of those envisioning a new Southern republic. The first two phases of secession brought only eleven of those states into the Confederacy. However, the official flag adopted in October 1861

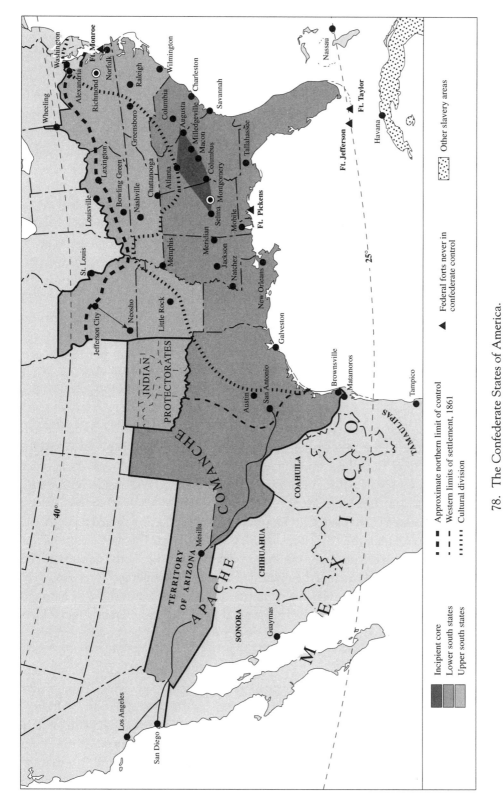

78. The Confederate States of America.

"Cultural division" refers to the generalized boundary between the Upper South and Lower South (after Jordan).

Incipient core
Lower south states
Upper south states

- - - - Approximate northern limit of control
- — - — Western limits of settlement, 1861
· · · · · · Cultural division

▲ Federal forts never in confederate control

Other slavery areas

featured thirteen stars, declaring claim to Kentucky and Missouri, which did join (in the contrived manner described) later that year. Allocation of seats in the Confederate Congress to delegates from these thirteen states, with the addition of seats for Indian Territory and Arizona, would seem to define the official territorial bounds asserted by this new federation. It should also be noted that, although they had given up on Delaware, members of the Confederate Congress were not ready to abandon a Maryland seized from them by federal forces, and so they passed a resolution to make no peace treaty with the United States without providing for Maryland to choose freely whether it wished to join the Southern Confederacy.

A map published in London during the war offered a clear depiction of aspirations and actuality. It showed the "Territory *claimed* by the Confederation" as encompassing all of the slave states except Delaware, plus Indian Territory and the whole of the original New Mexico (which Southern troops briefly held); it also marked the "Territory in the *Military possession* of the Confederates in 1861." The discordance between that de facto division and the northern limit of territory claimed—the whole of Maryland and large parts of Virginia, Kentucky, and Missouri—provides one useful definition of the borderland. But that critical geographical zone was much broader and more complex than that. We need to see it in relation to some deeper patterns of American life; its relation to cultural as well as to political lines.

In the prelude to secession it was not unusual for those who deplored the avid intensification of the crisis to imply that all of the country lying between Massachusetts and South Carolina was a borderland: a broad belt of reasonable, nonbelligerent people who disdained the shrill extremists on either side (in the early stages of the war, Lincoln's principal general, George McClellan, stated privately that "he detested both South Carolina and Massachusetts, and should rejoice to see both States extinguished"). Insofar as Massachusetts was the main seat of abolitionism and "Yankeeism" (in its narrowest definition) and South Carolina of "fire eaters" who asserted the moral goodness of slavery and fomented secession, there was some truth in such a view. Such antitheses were rooted in the very nature of these primary regional societies. In a general sense the seven-state original Confederacy that spread across the Lower South was matched by Yankee-dominated lands extending out of New England across six states on the north. Recognition of this "extreme" North and "extreme" South (in political as well as locational terms) defines an intermediate belt of country, in places several states wide. This broadest of borderlands was bisected by the northern legal limits of slavery. Although slavery provided the most notorious distinction between North and South, and the local presence of slavery was by now a sure mark of "Southernness," it was not in itself sufficient to define or indicate the extent of Southern culture. For that, we must refer again to the deposits laid down by those early streams of migration into transappalachia and recall how those westering Southerners left their imprint strongly upon southern Ohio, Indiana, and Illinois. Those three states thereby stand out as a special category within this borderland complex as geopolitical entities deeply split within themselves between a strongly Yankee Republican north and a strongly Southern Democratic south, a pattern punctuated by the more complex cities (such as Cincinnati and Chicago) and separated by a more varied and less engaged Midland belt (itself punctuated at many points by the presence of Quaker abolitionists). The chronic intrastate contentions arising from these different political cultures had now become magnified and concentrated on matters of vital importance. In these states "copperhead" politicians and editors, sympathetic with Southern complaints, antagonistic to special war measures, willing to search for peace even at the cost of acceding to Southern secession, were especially prominent. A kind of mirror image of this pattern was displayed in the strongly Unionist areas within the slave states. Such a stance did not represent "Northernness" (except, in part, in such border cities as Wheeling, Louisville, and St. Louis) but rather the painful dilemma of so many Upper Southerners trying to ride two horses at once: to defend slavery as a routine component of their regional culture (even if they were not directly involved with it) and to remain in a great Union they had helped create and develop. Their allegiance was manifest in many ways: in the representatives sent to the Thirty-seventh United States Congress (1861–63) from eight districts of Virginia and Tennessee as well as from all districts of Maryland, Kentucky, and Missouri; in local harassment of Confederate "occupying" forces; in resistance to Confederate conscription, taxes, and other policies. In some areas such opposition might be entirely passive but no less resolute: "Confederates never effectively controlled parts of the Quaker Belt in North Carolina." These Unionist areas were part of a mosaic of sharply contrasting colorations, scattered among districts strongly committed to the Confederate cause, revealing a general but fuzzy and distorted picture of the uneven incidence and intensity of slavery in the Upper South.

Taken together these dissident and ambivalent areas of North and South define the traumatic zone of this ragged vivisection (fig. 79). And perhaps the best indication of the breadth of the tear in the body politic were the thousands of young men who crossed the Ohio River or left other Northern-held lands and headed south to join the Confederate army and the thousands who fled north from the seceding states to join the Union forces (more than 30,000 from Tennessee). It was a profound sorting that affected not only districts, towns, and countrysides but clans and families, and it took place from the Atlantic seaboard to the Plains (where the Cherokee, Creek, and Seminole nations each split and sent men to both sides). Finally, the ugliest wound in this American trauma, the narrower borderland that equaled anyone's worst fears, was soon defined by guerrilla bands,

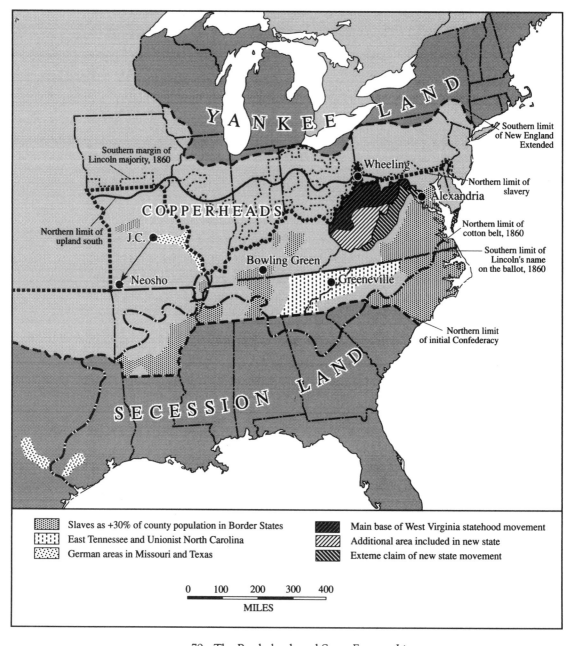

79. The Borderlands and Some Fracture Lines.

bushwhackers, barnburners, looters, and assassins who ravaged every district of divided or contrary allegiances from western Virginia to eastern Kansas. For the unfortunate citizens of those areas the failure of peaceable secession brought not just war but chaos.

Maps cannot convey the pain and suffering attendant upon the disintegration of the United States, but our search for a geographical definition of the borderlands can at least suggest how we must surely have something more than a simple map of North and South, of a Mason-Dixon Line (even as a shorthand term), of the Union and the Confederacy as two entities, if we are to have any sense at all of what "secession" meant in this complicated geopolitical structure during its unprecedented crisis.

5. Geopolitical Alternatives

Federalism is a geopolitical device for dealing with basic differences among a set of states associated under a common government. Voluntary federal structures necessarily involve negotiating an acceptable balance of power among the member states. Subsequent alteration of the actual or perceived patterns of such power will likely put the structure under some strain. Should such changes become viewed as major and threatening to some state or group of states the stress may become severe and the pressure for restructuring very great.

In the United States the Constitution had resolved the problem of how large and small states could live together under the same government, but as one congressman put it in 1861, the Founding Fathers "seem wholly to have overlooked the danger of *sectional combinations* [among states] . . . to the injury and oppression of other sections. . . . In like manner, too, they seem to have utterly underestimated *slavery* as a disturbing element in the system." Those men of course could not have foreseen "the vast extent and diversified interests and institutions of the several States" that would make "the existence of sections a fixed fact." There had in fact been some awareness of such problems in that formative time, and the first hint of strain and a proposal to alter the structure was not long in appearing. In 1815 the legislatures of Massachusetts and Connecticut sought a constitutional amendment that "the same person shall not be elected to the President of the United States a second time, nor shall the President be elected from the same State two terms in succession"—an obvious attempt to curb the influence of the largest state and end the "Virginia dynasty."

The first serious pressure for redefinition of the federal "compact" was Calhoun's "concurrent majority" proposal in which the states would be grouped into two classes—North (nonslaveholding) and South (slaveholding)—and Senate approval by both classes of all important sectional legislation would be required. The concept of a dual executive was also discussed. Although politically impossible to adopt at the time, there was nothing inherently unworkable about such dual structures. With typical hyperbole (and dubious analogy), a South Carolina leader noted that "the Roman republic, with its two consuls, so far from proving an impracticable government, lasted five hundred years."

A federation of two large parts was especially vulnerable to scission because most any considerable sociocultural difference could be magnified and hammered as a wedge of separation. During the dispiriting search for compromise after the first phase of secession, Clement L. Vallandigham, Democratic representative from Dayton, Ohio, offered a set of resolutions for the radical restructuring of the workings of the American federation that focused directly on this feature. On February 20 he admonished the House on the stark reality: "Secession has been tried and has proved a speedy and terrible success. The practicality of doing it and the way to do it, have both been established." Thereby the "grandest and the saddest" revolution of modern times was under way and "something searching, radical, extreme, going to the very foundations of government, and reaching the seat of the malady, must be done, and that right speedily, while the fracture is yet fresh, and re-union is possible." The malady was not slavery as such (only a small vociferous minority advocated immediate emancipation) but the relentless pressure of a majority section upon a minority section. The confrontation of a North and South defined in terms of a "moral and political principle" had doomed the federal Union. The only hope was to alter that binary pattern without impinging on the principles bound into it. Vallandigham's solution was "to multiply the sections, . . . efface the [simple] slave-labor and free-labor division, . . . diminish the relative power of each section. And . . . prevent combinations among these sections." He therefore proposed the creation of four "grand sections": North, West, Pacific, and South—"all of them well known or easily designated by marked natural, or geographical lines and boundaries" (which he defined). On demand of one-third of the senators from any one section a concurrent majority from each of the four sections would be required to pass legislation. Similarly, the president and vice-president must obtain majority support from electors within each section. Other provisions related to terms of office, property rights (without direct mention of slavery), and rights of secession (which he sought to formalize—and discourage).

Vallandigham was an intense partisan. He took pride in his border state antecedents, was sympathetic with Southern interpretations of the Constitution, and was deeply committed to finding some peaceful solution—he would soon emerge as the most outspoken, adamant "copperhead," calling throughout the war for peace (and suffering arrest and exile). It is not at all surprising that his proposal was ignored by Congress and derided by Republicans. Some reports misrepresented him as advocating the division of the United States into four independent republics (a familiar idea, set in motion some months before by the aged General Winfield Scott). There is little need to analyze such a stillborn proposal, but we may at least recognize it as a serious response to the American geopolitical crisis. Anticipating that his design would be considered too complex and clumsy, Vallandigham reminded his colleagues that in 1789 many considered the present system, with its bicameral legislatures, three branches of government, and careful separation of powers, to be so. Complexity was inherent in the very nature of, in the very need for, federations—in the kinds of geopolitical problems that called forth such political constructs. From our late twentieth-century perspective, looking back on, say, a Canada, Union of South Africa, Yugoslavia, Belgium, Soviet Union, Republic of India, early Pakistan, Vallandigham's four-sectioned United States does not seem quite as bizarre and awkward as it must have appeared in 1861. It was ephemeral because it was then too late to reshape and contain American emotions within sectional compartments—and because the American federation was giving way to the American nation.

Failing to achieve internal reform, secession becomes an obvious alternative for a province or larger part that feels itself to be a minority unjustly suffering within a union. Ireland was a commonly cited example of the plight ("represented nominally, but really . . . powerless"), but Southern leaders insisted that unlike that unhappy land the South was not trapped in a "compulsory union" but could exercise a perfectly legal as well as moral right of separation. Just how many officials really believed that peaceable secession was possible will never be known (Jefferson Davis later said he was one of the few Southerners "who regarded secession and war as inevitably connected"), but the new Confederacy proceeded as if it were possible. Its Provisional Constitution provided for immediate negotiations with the United States "to adjust everything pertaining to the common property, common liabilities, and common obligations of that Union, upon the principles of right, justice, equity, and good faith." They clearly envisioned two confederacies coexisting and proceeding "in security upon their separate lines of progress and civilization"—as, indeed, the United States and an emergent Canadian confederation would soon be doing.

Because a federation consists of an articulation of two distinct levels of governments, national and state (or provincial), each fully operative within prescribed limits on the same territory and body of citizens, seceding states were complete governments, with a governor, legislature, courts, and militia already in place. Joining together, the Confederate States could immediately and confidently claim that they constituted "an independent nation, *de facto* and *de jure,* and possess a government perfect in all its parts, and endowed with all means of self-support." On that basis they sent commissioners to Washington to negotiate the details of a peaceful separation.

As Tocqueville had pointed out thirty years earlier, should the United States split "not only would they diminish the strength they now have against foreigners, but they would create foreign powers upon their own territory." Thus, the Southern Confederacy not only must take control of those customshouses and military posts already within the bounds of its member states (which it attempted to do) but must eventually erect a system of such facilities at key points along its new northern border. There was no immediate move to construct such a system because the location of that border was uncertain, awaiting the secession of more states. One geopolitical consequence, however, was immediately apparent and of major concern: the imposition of an international boundary across the lower Mississippi River. When the governor of Mississippi erected artillery batteries at Vicksburg and ordered that all vessels be stopped for inspection it provoked a furious reaction upriver—some calling it an act of war. Northerners had long warned that absolutely no interference with commercial navigation on that great artery would be tolerated. Henry Clay's resounding declaration of 1850, "Never, never, never, shall we who occupy the broad waters of the Mississippi and its upper tributaries, consent that any foreign flag shall float at the Balize [the entrance] *or upon the turrets of the Crescent City*—NEVER, NEVER," was now repeated in general refrain and feeling by a large chorus. Senator Douglas of Illinois, characteristically, left an opening: "We can never acknowledge the right of a State to secede and cut us off from the Ocean and the world, without our consent." The Confederate States moved quickly to defuse the situation so as to obtain that consent. The surveillance was soon lifted, and on February 25 the Congress stated that "the peaceful navigation of the Mississippi River is hereby declared FREE to the citizens of any of the States upon its borders, or upon the borders of its navigable tributaries." Nevertheless, the Mississippi remained a stark geographical issue that strongly affected Northern, especially Northwestern, opinion. Here was the one obvious place where secession of the Lower South seemed to threaten in fact and in principle the basic interests of nearly all the Western states. Such fears undermined inclinations to avoid war at any cost. As one historian put it: "Paradoxically, then it was the interest most involved in the Southern route that was most intent that New Orleans should not be controlled by a foreign power. If Southern Ohio, Indiana, and Illinois could not secede with the South, then the South should remain in the Union with them."

Aside from this reappearance of the Mississippi problem (fifty-eight years after the Louisiana Purchase) there was nothing in the human geography of the time to make a peaceful separation of the original seven-state Confederacy particularly difficult. The probable addition of at least lowland Arkansas to that new entity would have made this South nearly coincident with the Cotton States (encompassing 93 percent of American production), noticeably discordant only in the exclusion of Memphis and southwest Tennessee. It would also have included all of the sugar and nearly all of the rice lands (excepting only the Cape Fear district) and thereby would have been very much the Plantation South—one telling measure: it included all but 6 (all in Virginia) of the 105 counties or parishes wherein the average number of slaves per slaveholding was fifteen or more. Whatever the variety of people and farming systems within, such an eight-state Lower South had a very considerable basis for self-definition as an incipient national state. In a narrow view, such a separation might appear to be geopolitically feasible and even attractive to both parties (assuming resolution of the Mississippi problem).

On the other hand, acknowledging Lincoln's commitment to the integrity of the Union, Don E. Fehrenbacher made the interesting observation that perhaps "seven was the optimum number of secessions for starting a civil war." As he explained: "If only three or four states had seceded, such a feeble effort might well have ended peacefully in failure, whereas if twelve or thirteen states had seceded before Lincoln's inauguration, such a formidable movement might well have ended peacefully in success. . . . [Thus] it may be that Virginia's initial failure to secede was as much a cause of war as South Carolina's headlong leadership in the secession movement." Support for such a speculation might be found in a private comment by Lincoln early in the war: "I think to lose Kentucky is nearly the same as to lose the whole game. Kentucky gone we cannot hold Missouri, nor, as I think, Maryland. These all against us, and the job on our hands is too large for us. We would as well consent to separation at once, including the surrender of the capital." That indicates secession of all the slave states (except, perhaps, Delaware) as creating the line of division—commonly referred to as the Mason-Dixon Line—but knowing how raggedly the nation was in fact ripped asunder, it is difficult to imagine how any essentially peaceful separation could have been negotiated without departing from simple state boundaries. Would the Baltimore & Ohio counties of Maryland and Virginia or St. Louis and the German counties of Missouri have been handed over to a Southern Confederacy without a battle? One obvious response to the problem would have been a county-by-county plebiscite (under neutral international supervision?). As our examination of the borderland has shown, there would have been great geopolitical complications, but of course we can never know what pattern such a process might have produced, for the context would have been critically different: a ballot on geopolitical affiliation with a new entity, one-half of the United States, North or South, with both sides pledged against war. Such considerations are a useful reminder that the problems of antagonistic populations and state formation and of the disintegration of empires and confederations were not a peculiarly American experience and that war was not the only alternative, even though local strife might be very difficult to avoid. Plebiscites, the redrawing of boundaries, enclaves and exclaves, population uprootings and transfers, internationalization of strategic points and passageways—as well as war—were part of the European scene in that century, as in our own.

Continuing to speculate on peaceful secession, we may note the paradox that the enlargement of the Confederation weakened the South as an incipient nation. To add the Upper Southern states complicated the internal character of the new formation, diluting the dominance of the slaveholding Plantation South and increasing the tension between important regions within. In the years leading up to secession persons in Virginia and other border states had wondered whether to be "the South of the Northern confederacy would not be more preferable . . . than [to be] the North of a Southern confederacy," and the question was often phrased in disdainful terms: "Who can contemplate Virginia as the tail of a Southern Confederacy, standing as a guard, and playing patrol for 'King Cotton'?" Resentment against an intemperate South Carolina and the arrogance of the Lower South in breaking up the Union and forcing a terrible choice upon others was laced all through the Upper South. Such feelings, grounded in basic regional differences in character and position, would surely have complicated the development of Southern unity. Nevertheless, the very fact of secession demonstrated that there was a basis for developing a national cultural identity.

An overview of the geography of an independent South (composed, more or less, of the eleven fully seceded states) displays some of the features, difficulties, and possible responses to the challenge of nation-building. In terms of population there were no gross imbalances in this confederation. Virginia was the most populous state but could be balanced by most any pair of the older Lower South states. The White populations of the Upper and Lower South were about equal; in terms of totals the ratio was about forty to sixty. The most westerly states were of course growing at the expense of the older Atlantic seaboard; there was room for much local expansion within the Mississippi floodplain (at the cost of heavy reclamation), but Texas was the great frontier for general colonization and it was a frontier for both sectors of the South, with the trails across Arkansas from Tennessee as heavily traveled as those across Louisiana from the Gulf States.

Certainly at its beginning this was a very loosely articulated geographical structure without much hint of some common national features. Not only were the Upper and Lower South barely linked in any functional sense, but each of these broad divisions was distinctly compartmentalized into more local patterns of circulation, each focused on a major port. That such a set of discrete and divergent orientations posed severe restraints on many aspects of incipient national life was readily apparent. The only semblance of a trunk line to bind these parts together was the Virginia & Tennessee Railroad connecting at Chattanooga with the Charleston and Memphis line. There was nothing comparable along the arc of the Coastal Plain or Piedmont. Under the pressures of national defense, a Confederate government, though desperately short of labor and materials, gave high priority to building rail connections between Danville, Virginia, and Greensboro and between Meridian and Selma (leaving the Selma-to-Montgomery section to be served by steamboats). Many more such links would be needed to transform a set of disparate and defensive state networks into a national system, but of course this could eventually be done. The great pivotal points of such a system had already appeared in the relatively new cities of Chattanooga and Atlanta. And perhaps the faint outline of a core area of this Southern nation began to emerge as a result of the emergency policies of the Confederate government in answering the sudden need for many kinds of materials. By direct or indirect government sponsorship, an array of major arsenals, powder works, rolling mills, textile mills, shoe factories, and quartermaster and commissary supply centers were constructed or expanded. As the premier industrial city, Richmond was an obvious choice for some of these initiatives, but it was also dangerously exposed and eccentric within the main body of the nation. Although pressure from state interests and the need to make use of every existing facility led such assistance to be widely dispersed, there was also a discernible emphasis upon a particular set of localities that together formed a relatively coherent nucleus in a safe and central region. That area may be defined as a sort of obtuse triangle extending from Augusta through Macon, Columbus, and Montgomery to Selma, with its apex at Atlanta. Here were concentrated some of the largest armories, workshops, factories, and distribution centers. This area included some of the richest cottonlands of the quintessential Plantation South, but it also drew on new industrial resources. Selma's important foundries (operated primarily by German immigrants) had begun to tap the rich hematites of Red Mountain, where Birmingham would later emerge as the "Pittsburgh of the South." With ready access by rail and waterways to the Atlantic and the Gulf of Mexico, this area was well positioned to become a major nucleus within the nation as a whole.

The shift of the capital of the Confederacy from Montgomery to Richmond had been a controversial move, generally understood as part of the price paid for Virginia's secession. Once war was under way in earnest the advantages in having the seat of government in such a forward position near the zone of battle became obvious. But there were also obvious risks and disadvantages of such an eccentric location for the conduct of ordinary national business, and there was considerable speculation as to where the future and permanent capital of the South should be. Had peace prevailed, there would almost certainly have been a bitter and divisive battle over that issue—a problem inherent in new federations that are not dominated by one powerful state or city. Civic leaders pushed Atlanta as a strong contender, and with good reason. Its pivotal position within the nation as a whole was unrivaled. It was a high, healthy location (a major consideration), and it was a new city unfettered to powerful Low Country or Black Belt planter oligarchies. Rivalries among the several states for such a prize would be severe, but here, too, Atlanta had an advantage in the reputation of Georgia as a solid, much less politically contentious or culturally pretentious state than South Carolina or Virginia. Of course, geopolitical decisions do not necessarily accord with such obvious geographical features. Still, Atlanta made a good impression on a lot of sojourners and travelers, as Lieutenant Charles C. Jones, Jr., reported to his father in the summer of 1862:

> Atlanta exhibits more signs of life and energy than any other city in Georgia. You would be surprised at the immense quantity of sugars, tobacco, etc., etc., there stored. Real estate has advanced to an enormous extent, and the probability is that when peace and happiness are again restored to our now distracted country, that the future of the city will be very bright. It contains now a population of some seventeen thousand, and great improvements are constantly progressing. Fine stores with iron and granite fronts. Neat residences meet the eye on every hand. But a few years since, Atlanta was regarded as the home only of speculators, railroad hands, businessmen, demireps and rowdies; but the tall spires of newly erected churches, frequent schoolhouses, and the increasing comforts of private residences, and the permanency of stores and public buildings give ample token that the rude infancy of this busy place has been superseded by an age of quiet, maturer civilization. It is even rumored that Atlanta may be selected as the future and permanent capital of our Confederacy; but of course this is simply a matter of speculation.

Without extending these simple geographical speculations to imagine other patterns of development in agriculture, industry, and commerce, and in the growth of cities and hinterlands, it is perhaps worth asserting that had the South entered into independence without severe trauma—without blockade, without the exodus of thousands of Northern entrepreneurs and engineers, artisans and teachers, and without loss of reasonably open access to Northern American and British markets—there would seem to be nothing inherently improbable about its continued economic viability; by world standards it was a prosperous nation, providing a relatively high standard of living to its property-owning population—until overtaken by the international abolition movement. One can imagine a South becoming something like an Argentina, a New World patriarchal agrarian society, ostensibly and assertively independent but in critical ways a de facto economic province in an expanding British commercial empire.

Although there is a large literature on Southern nationalism and the aspirations of an independent South, it is hard to find any comment at all on the prospects for a Northern nation—that is, for a residual North, shorn of the South. The reason is obvious enough: for Northerners such a creation would come as an unwelcome consequence, a failure, rather than as a programmed objective. Only when Southern secession was well under way and peaceful negotiation seemed to be the only rational alternative to a terrible war of conquest did such a thing seem at all imaginable. A flurry of editorials in Northern newspapers in that alarming winter of 1861 brought the prospect to the fore. Though all lamented such an outcome, even some Republicans saw nothing catastrophic in it:

> Suppose there is a peaceful separation by general consent, the terms of which are fixed by a national convention, since Congress has no power under the constitution to provide for so anomalous a state of things; suppose that all the slave states that are really attached to the institution by prejudice or interest go with the cotton confederacy, leaving only Delaware, Kentucky and Missouri, and perhaps a new state formed from western Virginia, in the present Union. In wealth, resources, moral and physical strength, more than two-thirds of the Union will remain. All connection with slavery and all responsibility for it will almost immediately be removed by purging the adhering slave states of the last remains of the institution. The constitution may then be relieved of all recognition and support of slavery, and we shall have a republic in reality as well as in name. It is the sheerest folly to suppose that we cannot go on as strongly and prosperously without the slave states as with them. And, except in the mere matter of extent of territory, we should have lost almost no element of power and national influence, while we should be relieved of a source of weakness and fear growing out of a servile and dangerous population of four millions, which would compensate for many items of loss.

The moderate Ohio lawyer Rutherford B. Hayes (who would fight heroically as a soldier and later become governor and then president) confirmed that opinion in his diary in January 1861: "Twenty millions in the temperate zone, stretching from the Atlantic to the Pacific, full of vigor, industry, inventive genius, educated, and moral; increasing rapidly by immigration, and, above all, free—all free—will form a confederacy of twenty states scarcely inferior in real power to the unfortunate Union of thirty-three States which we had on the first of November."

Even after Lincoln assumed office, separation seemed the only sensible solution to some of his supporters:

> The "current events and experience" by which he promised to be guided, must, we are convinced, soon lead him to lend the whole influence of his Administration to the accomplishment of the peaceful separation of the disaffected from the adhering States of the Union; and in doing this, it may be necessary . . . to mortify exceedingly the national pride, which as a people we have cultivated to an extraordinary degree. . . . The dream of an ocean-bound republic, which has been so grateful to Young America, we yet hope to see realized; but in the meantime there is room for several flourishing nations on this continent; and the sun will shine as brightly and the rivers run as clear—the cotton fields will be as white and the wheat fields as golden—when we acknowledge the Southern Confederacy as before. We would not undervalue the Union. It has ministered to our national pride, as well as to the prosperity of the whole country. But when it is gone, we will still have our fruitful and inviting soil and clime—our seats and channels of commerce—and the unequaled capacity of the people for productive labor.

Such confidence in the continuing viability and prosperity of the North was unexceptional. In spite of the many fulminations over the Mississippi, a Cincinnati (Republican) paper underscored the newer realities of American commercial geography:

> An immense majority of the people of the Northwest doubtless believe that the loss of the command of the mouth of the Mississippi would be a tremendous misfortune. We undertake to maintain that practically the people of Ohio, Kentucky, Indiana, Illinois, and all the rest of the great Northern Mississippi Valley States, are more interested in the management of the four great Railroads to the seaboard, and of the Erie Canal, than they are in any possible proceeding at the mouth of the Mississippi. . . . The proportion of the products of the Northern States of the Mississippi Valley that are exported by way of New Orleans, is not more than *one tenth* of the aggregate.

The absence of comment in such literature on any other geographical issue (except occasional mention of the national capital, should Maryland secede) may be taken as implicit recognition of any residual North as a coherent geographical system that could readily survive even so large an excision. High priority could be given to enlarging existing thoroughfares ("the great canals of New York and Illinois") rather than to desperately patching together a bare semblance of a system.

Indeed, some saw removal of the South as opening the way for a Greater North. It was a common delusion of American commentators that the British American colonies would come knocking on the doors of a United States shorn of the South and slavery. Thus William Seward was quoted as stating: "For every State that goes out one must come in, and so I look upon Rupert's Land and Canada, and I am able to say 'It is very well; you are building excellent States to be hereafter admitted into the American Union'"; he fixed the capital of this great Northern Confederacy at or near St. Paul. A Toronto paper responded by saying that "the annexation will be in the other direction" and pointed to a strong feeling in Upper Canada that a political connection with New York "is the natural one."

Yet, it was far from certain that peaceable secession would result in just two confederacies, North and South. Once dismemberment began there was no way of knowing where it might stop. When a union of thirty-three states begins to come apart the possible patterns might seem almost kaleidoscopic. Echoing Thomas Jefferson, William Grayson had warned fellow Southerners in 1850: "Once break up the present Confederacy and the principle of voluntary cohesion is gone forever. In this as in every other movement of change or revolution men never go back." Would a new Southern union organized by the most vociferous states' rights proponents likely endure? If it began to falter would not Texas be strongly tempted to resume its independence? Because outside the South—and chiefly the Lower South—there had been no political movements dedicated to the creation of separate confederacies, speculation ran free, unanchored by any existing designs. Many thought the outcome of secession would be several, even "half a dozen Confederacies." A Pacific republic seemed an obvious geographical entity, and the same kind of loose logic of distance, size, and common interests suggested the likelihood of an independent Northwest. A good many voices predicted, even promoted, dismemberment of the North so as to exclude New England, because surely no other state would want to remain associated with the "Yankee States"— or, in the more colorful language of the day, with "the fanatical, abolitionized, canting, hypocritical New England States." There were those in Albany who questioned whether New York would wish to remain in the same Senate "with the petty New England States," but the more radical proposition, advanced by the mayor, some leading merchants, and at least one local congressman (and heartily endorsed by *De Bow's Review*), was a metropolitan separation from the state—and perhaps the nation—to form a free city-state, such as enjoyed by Hamburg and Bremen in the loose German Confederation (the obvious example of the time). Rather more bizarre was the proposal by several New Jersey politicians and editors that their state secede so as to serve as the industrial center for the South.

Such statements do not represent serious political movements. They are the pronouncements of individual editors and politicians during a terribly confused and alarming time when a familiar world seemed to be dissolving. There is no way of knowing how much support such ideas might have gathered or what others might have appeared had peaceable secession continued as a process. They are of interest in revealing some public ideas about the regional structure of North America and in illustrating the kind of geopolitical speculation unleashed by the shock of actual secession.

They are also a reminder that just as many voices had opposed the relentless expansion of the United States across North America, so many opposed preserving American unity by force of arms. And just as we cannot assume that those critical of expansion were any less patriotic, any less interested in having a strong, secure, and prosperous United States, so we cannot assume that those opposed to the forceful reunification of the country were any less patriotic or less interested in the longer-term prospects for life, liberty, and the pursuit of happiness as Americans— whether Northern Americans or Southern Americans. Just as there was no law of nature shaping the United States into a transcontinental republic, so there was no such law undergirding its continued existence as a single nation. There is no compelling geographical reason why there should not have been three great confederations—South, North, and Canada—spanning the continent rather than two, or, indeed, any of the variations considered at the time.

These speculations were abruptly quelled by the outbreak of hostilities, and in the North the image and the goal of unity assumed complete dominance. In his inaugural address Lincoln had spoken eloquently of the futility of separation as a cure:

> Physically speaking, we cannot separate. We cannot remove our respective sections from each other, nor build an impassable wall between them. A husband and wife may be divorced, and go out of the presence, and beyond the reach of each other; but the different parts of our country cannot do this. They cannot but remain face to face; and intercourse, either amicable or hostile, must continue between them. Is it possible, then, to make that intercourse more advantageous, or more satisfactory, *after* separation than *before*? Can aliens make treaties, easier than friends can make laws? Can treaties be more faithfully enforced between aliens, than laws can among friends? Suppose you go to war, you cannot fight always; and when, after much loss on both sides, and no gain on either, you cease fighting, the identical old questions, as to terms of intercourse, are again upon you.

After a year and a half of war, in his annual message to Congress, he used exactly the same illustration and elaborated upon his sense of the compelling fundamental geography of the case:

> A nation may be said to consist of its territory, its people, and its laws. The territory is the only part which is of certain durability. "One generation passeth away, and another generation cometh, but the earth abideth forever." It is of the first importance to duly consider, and estimate, this ever-enduring part. That portion of the earth's surface which is owned and inhabited by the people of the United States, is well adapted to be the home of one national family; and it is not well adapted for two, or more. Its vast extent, and its variety of climate and productions, are of advantage, in this age, for one people, whatever they might have been in former ages. Steam, telegraphs, and intelligence, have brought these, to be an advantageous combination, for one united people. . . .
>
> There is no line, straight or crooked, suitable for a national boundary, upon which to divide. Trace through, from east to west, upon the line between the free and slave country, and we shall find a little more than one-third of its length are rivers, easy to be crossed, and populated, or soon to be populated, thickly upon both sides; while nearly all its remaining length, are merely surveyor's lines, over which people may walk back and forth without any consciousness of their presence. No part of this line can be made any more difficult to pass, by writing it down on paper, or parchment, as a national boundary. The fact of separation, if it comes, gives up, on the part of the seceding section, the fugitive slave clause, along with all other constitutional obligations upon the section seceded from, while I should expect no treaty stipulation would ever be made to take its place.
>
> But there is another difficulty. The great interior region, bounded east by the Alleghanies, north by the British dominions, west by the Rocky mountains, and south by the line along which the culture of corn and cotton meets, and which includes part of Virginia, part of Tennessee, all of Kentucky, Ohio, Indiana, Michi-

gan, Wisconsin, Illinois, Missouri, Kansas, Iowa, Minnesota and the Territories of
Dakota, Nebraska, and part of Colorado, already has above ten millions of people,
and will have fifty millions within fifty years, if not prevented by any political folly or
mistake. It contains more than one-third of the country owned by the United
States—certainly more than one million of square miles. Once half as populous as
Massachusetts already is, it would have more than seventy-five millions of people. A
glance at the map shows that, territorially speaking, it is the great body of the
republic. The other parts are but marginal borders to it, the magnificent region
sloping west from the rocky mountains to the Pacific, being the deepest, and also the
richest, in undeveloped resources. In the production of provisions, grains, grasses,
and all which proceed from them, this great interior region is naturally one of the
most important in the world. Ascertain from the statistics the small proportion of the
region which has, as yet, been brought into cultivation, and also the large and rapidly
increasing amount of its products, and we shall be overwhelmed with the magnitude
of the prospect presented. An[d] yet this region has no sea-coast, touches no ocean
anywhere. As part of one nation, its people now find, and may forever find, their way
to Europe by New York, to South America and Africa by New Orleans, and to Asia by
San Francisco. But separate our common country into two nations, as designed by
the present rebellion, and every man of this great interior region is thereby cut off
from some one or more of these outlets, not, perhaps, by a physical barrier, but by
embarrassing and onerous trade regulations.

And this is true, *wherever* a dividing, or boundary line, may be fixed. Place it
between the now free and slave country, or place it south of Kentucky, or north of
Ohio, and still the truth remains, that none south of it, can trade to any port or place
north of it, and none north of it, can trade to any port or place south of it, except
upon terms dictated by a government foreign to them. These outlets, east, west, and
south, are indispensable to the well-being of the people inhabiting, and to inhabit,
this vast interior region. *Which* of the three may be the best, is no proper question.
All, are better than either, and all, of right, belong to that people, and to their
successors forever. True to themselves, they will not ask *where* a line of separation
shall be, but will vow, rather, that there shall be no such line. Nor are the marginal
regions less interested in this communications to, and through them, to the great
outside world. They too, and each of them, must have access to this Egypt of the
West, without paying toll at the crossing of any national boundary.

Our national strife springs not from our permanent part; not from the land we
inhabit; not from our national homestead. There is no possible severing of this, but
would multiply, and not mitigate, evils among us. In all its adaptations and aptitudes,
it demands union, and abhors separation. In fact, it would, ere long, force reunion,
however much of blood and treasure the separation might have cost.

Our strife pertains to ourselves—to the passing generations of men

In such a view geography points the way; there is a logic in the land, if only the
people heed it, but the response remains a matter of choice. The really decisive

concept is that of a *national homestead* for a *national family.* Of course there was a North and a South, differing in forms of economy, ways of life—indeed, even "two civilizations"—yet there was something greater, more fundamental, and more powerful: an American nation, grounded in an American culture, focused on American ideals, powered by the aspirations and energies of tens of millions present and the generations to come.

That there was in fact a Southern nationalism was by then amply apparent from the armies in the field and the blood already shed. But there was no counterpart Northern nationalism—nationalism indeed, but not at the same scale or meaning. For whereas the South could regard the war as a case of two halves of the United States fighting over mutual recognition and where to draw the line of separation, for the North the war was the onerous responsibility of the leaders of the national family to restore peace and wholeness within the national homestead. The nationalism of the South was a regionally based protective movement; the nationalism of the North was a self-proclaimed expansive American movement.

In structural, constitutional terms, it was a contest between two concepts of federalism, between a state-centered compact and a nation-centered perpetual union, and this difference was expressed in the official title each side gave to the struggle: the War between the States (South) and the War of the Rebellion (North). In central objective that contrast might better be stated as the War for Southern Independence and the War of National Unification. In experience and memory it would become seared on the American soul as that most painful of all struggles: the Civil War.

6. Conquest and Emancipation

In one of his large and rich studies of America's great convulsion, Allan Nevins stated forthrightly: "It was a war over slavery *and* the future position of the Negro race in North America." Even as we acknowledge another historian's observation that "the academic controversy over the causes and character of the American Civil War seems as irreconcilable as the divergent viewpoints in the sectional controversy of the 1850s," it is impossible to avoid the basic truth—even if it is not of course the whole truth—of Nevins's assertion. The simplest test of the proposition is to try to imagine the irruption of such a massive conflict had there been no slavery and no presence of Blacks in something like their actual proportions and position within the American Union.

Nevins's statement does not assert a direct *cause,* and we should be wary of studies that purport to offer such an explanation; as Fehrenbacher warns: "What caused the Civil War is not a single historical problem but rather a whole cluster of problems, too numerous and complex to be incorporated into any single model of historical interpretation." Slavery did not cause the war, but it so permeated the issues that it must be seen as the root of the conflict. Our special geographic perspective leads to a similar kind of conclusion: although we may be certain that geography did not cause the war—and it must not be reified as an active force—it is just as certain that plausible interpretations of this vast drama must be grounded in a cluster of geographic conditions that impinged upon the developing crisis.

1. *The United States was divided approximately equally into blocs of states forming two distinct kinds of territory, slave and free, within the one overall national structure.* It was the only such case extant. Brazil, the only other large national slave society, had no such internal partition. (The crucial difference between the United States and the common imperial pattern of a European state with slavery confined to overseas colonies was made clear in the 1830s when a home country parliament and administration imposed emancipation on their small, distant, and distinctly subordinate West Indian colonies.)

   a. The formal geographical boundary between the free and slave territories was defined very early along a clear east-west line across the entire breadth of the national territory.

   b. Huge territorial additions to the United States recurrently reopened the topic of extending this geographical line of separation. This issue provoked intense geopolitical disputes that were resolved by complex and ambiguous compromises, which proved unstable.

   c. There was no attempt to convert this internal boundary into a formal barrier, a patrolled line of controlled movement, or to inhibit in any way the free functioning of the general commercial and social systems of the nation, *except* for the movement of Blacks between these two sectors, as manumitted persons, as fugitive slaves, as repossessed slaves, or sometimes simply as free Blacks in routine jobs (as in attempts to prohibit Black sailors in Northern vessels from landing or having any contact with local Blacks, slave or free, in Charleston and other Southern harbors); and this exception was fraught with complications and controversy.

2. *The United States expanded westward along a broad front extending with equal vigor the populations and economies of its several sectors and preserving the initial North-South balance without disruptive strain.*

   a. Expansion was primarily a spread out of four regional societies of the Atlantic seaboard. The distinctive characteristics of these several societies were deep-rooted and not anchored on the simple presence or absence of slavery (which had been present in all during the colonial period). The result was a regional patterning of peoples and political cultures that expressed much more complex sets of interests and did not conform to the internal boundary between the slave and free halves of the nation.

b. When the issue of the extension of slavery irrupted at the national level, concurrent initial expansion allowed new states to be admitted more or less as pairs, so that the sectional balance of senatorial representation was maintained into the 1850s.

3. *The North and the South were not primary regions of the United States.* They were made possible by the developing patterns of human geography, but they were created in part by conscious effort and took on shape and substance through the unfolding of events. Regional differences became magnified, narrowly focused, and essentially redefined through the agitations of dedicated ideologists.

    a. Abolitionists represented but one facet of moralistic political culture. Geographically this movement was almost entirely confined to Yankee and Quaker areas and in its more extreme forms represented only a small minority of such peoples.

    b. Apologists of slavery as a positive form of modern society represented but one facet of a hegemonic political culture. Geographically this movement was most deeply rooted in South Carolina, largely confined to major plantation areas and probably supported by a relatively small minority of Southerners.

    c. In the clash of the ideologies, selected regional differences became magnified into caricature, giving "a false clarity and simplicity," and undergirding the polarization in public perceptions (then and thereafter) of two distinct societies:

Yankee	Cavalier
industrial	agrarian
entrepreneurial	paternal
individualistic	familial
materialistic	organic
progressive	conservative

4. *The most critical, fundamental geographic feature was the distribution and proportion of Blacks within the total population of the South.* Because Blacks were a majority or large minority over so much of the region, Southern Whites assumed that any basic alteration in the legal and caste structure would destroy Southern society. Therefore, even those who regarded slavery as an evil (perhaps a majority) accepted it as an inherited burden that must be carried until White Southerners themselves found some way out.

    a. No program for abolition or even gradual emancipation was considered feasible: colonization programs demonstrated the impossibility of large-scale deportations; to accept Blacks as local citizens would destroy White political dominance; to convert them into a peasantry would require a major redistribution of property; to transform them into wage-laborers would create an undisciplined and seasonally redundant body that would become an intolerable burden and threat to White communities.

b. The history of Santo Domingo and the presence of Black Haiti were a constant reminder of the terrifying possibility of Black revolt and revenge.

5. *The peculiar dual character of the United States, divided between areas of slavery and of nonslavery, was maintained by its federal structure.* Slaves defined as a species of property were under the jurisdiction of the individual states and not of the central government. When lagging population growth began to undermine the political power of the South, the weaker section feared that this interpretation of jurisdictions would be altered so as to threaten its vital interests. After the early failure of nullification, the South sought protection in drastic geopolitical alterations of the federal structure.

a. Proposals for an internal restructuring of power, such as Calhoun's "concurrent majority" and Vallandigham's four-sections concept, failed to gain support.

b. South Carolina's initiative in peaceful secession succeeded in creating a new seven-state confederation, but none of these actions was accepted as legitimate by the United States central government.

c. The inherent geographic complication of federally garrisoned facilities within the bounds of seceding states was not resolved peacefully.

d. Secession of states in the Upper South threatened to convert the long-standing slave-free interstate boundary into an international boundary. The central government was unwilling to accept that line of separation or any negotiated alternative line and undertook the task of forceful total reunification of the United States.

This very selective review makes no attempt to cover all the issues of this crisis. We are not searching for cause but only trying to illuminate certain geographical aspects. Wars are caused by human actions, by decisions, usually of very limited intent, whose results cannot be controlled or foreseen. Just as in the case of the American War of Independence, we can readily identify an incremental dynamic of action and reaction building from the local moves of small cadres of people (as at Fort Sumter) into a massive confrontation and convulsion.

The American Revolution and the conflict of 1861–65 were both civil wars, but they differed in important respects. In a general typology of internal war, we may categorize the first (following Lee Benson) as a *colonial-imperial revolution* and the second as a *separatist-national revolution.* In the first, a narrow and localized internal quarrel evolved into a much larger movement by which, without the intent of doing so, a set of physically detached and semi-autonomous provinces broke loose from superintending authority and began the creation of a new nation. In the second case, according to Benson, a small group of Southern Nationalists deliberately set about to induce secession and form a new confederation. In that view, as one of the ideologists of the time put it, Southerners sought to become "a nation among nations" rather than continue as "a nation within a nation."

Insofar as the conflict between North and South may be regarded as a contest between two nations, it was an encounter between nationalisms that were similar in type but quite unequal in depth and task. Both movements became expressions of a romantic nationalism then current that asserted an emotional bond of people and territory ("Blut und Boden," to use a fervent Germanic rendition) as fundamental and indivisible, the essential basis for the political state. The rival concepts of "America" and "the South" both generated powerful emotional responses, but they were grounded in critically different geopolitical experiences. Not only was American nationalism supported by a now avidly fostered cult of Union, it was grounded upon nearly eighty years of profound political experience during which all regions, southern as well as northern, had vastly expanded and prospered. Northern leaders could therefore define their task as one of quelling an irrational and intemperate act of destruction.

In contrast, although Southern nationalism was built upon an idealization of a deep-rooted regional society, it was a new, untried substitution. It had to break the bond of the allegiance so long given to a huge and famous geopolitical unit that Southerners themselves had helped mightily to create. Southern leaders had to convince their people that it was no longer tolerable to be Southern and American within the same geopolitical framework. Furthermore, although the commitment to defend slavery as a legal institution was an important bond, there had been no experience of any formal association of any set of these states as a constituent political body within the United States. The obvious precedent, of course, was the creation of the United States, and the new confederacy assiduously modeled itself on that example, but its militancy about states' rights ran counter to the idea of a firmly united association (Jefferson Davis was scolded for occasionally referring to the Confederacy as a "nation"). Southern nationalism was clearly too shallow and uneven, especially in the states of the Upper South, to produce anything like equal allegiance to the asserted objectives. And in fact it is a rather gross simplification and exaggeration to regard it as having been "a nation within a nation" (as compared, for example, with the French in the developing structure of Canada)—such a description would become more appropriate after the war than on the eve of it.

Yet, American nationalism, even within the remnant North, was far from solid and simple over all areas either, as the protracted conflict would reveal. Once armies were in the field, the South had the advantage of declaring that its very life was at stake. Southerners saw themselves as underdogs, fighting an imperialism bent on destroying Southern society and remaking it in the despised image of the North. Their motives were clear, their purpose defensive, their objectives limited.

Northerners, in contrast, had little obvious reason to fear for their homes and their way of life, and had to be given reason for invading the South. The need to put down rebellion and preserve the Union might seem worthy general objectives, and recovering control over the Mississippi and preventing any international boundary being laid down across old trafficways might seem valuable and practical objectives, but support for such things was vulnerable to questions of cost and end results: Was it worth tens—and eventually hundreds—of thousands of lives? And would not a Union put back together by force be more like a despotism than a proper American polity? Hence the need for a cult of Union, cultivating an allegiance to something higher, more ethereal, spiritual, than a mere politically engineered state; "Union" therefore must connote more than mere unity, it had to stand for liberty, popular government, the rule of law—all those things that its propagandists claimed were threatened by the act of secession and under assault by the attack on Fort Sumter.

These differences in situations and objectives shaped the contrasting grand strategies of the two sides. The South sought formal recognition of its existence as a separate independent state. It needed to defend itself against destruction, but it had no need to conquer the North. Its best hope was to so magnify the costs of war for the North as to induce a negotiated peace. Its best strategy was to carry the war quickly into the North: to seize or lay siege to Washington, invade Pennsylvania, threaten Philadelphia, occupy ambivalent Maryland—hence the significance of the battles of Bull Run, Antietam, Gettysburg. Simultaneously, the leaders of the Confederacy sought European support and recognition so as to procure vital supplies, obtain endorsement for their cause, and enhance their stature—hence the hope in cotton for the mills of Britain and France as a trump card (fig. 80).

For the North the situation was very different. Having failed to prevent secession, it was faced with somehow forcing a reunification. If an initial mobilization or battle did not sober the South by the prospects of protracted war, then a conquest must be undertaken. The most vulnerable parts of the South were its capital and its coasts (for it had almost no navy). If Richmond could be quickly captured and all the main Southern harbors blockaded, the futility of the rebellion might be made apparent.

But grand strategies could not be readily implemented. Neither side had much of an army to begin with. The total strength of the United States Army at the time of the firing on Fort Sumter was only 16,000, mostly deployed in imperial outposts in the Far West. In the ensuing scission a considerable portion of these officers and men elected to serve the South. State militias could be hastily assembled and volunteers signed up, but it would take time to train and equip these much enlarged units. Furthermore, as some of the more astute civilian critics would note, the military mind was not primarily focused on offense. At West Point officers were taught first of all to protect their forces, to dig in, erect defenses, and establish clear

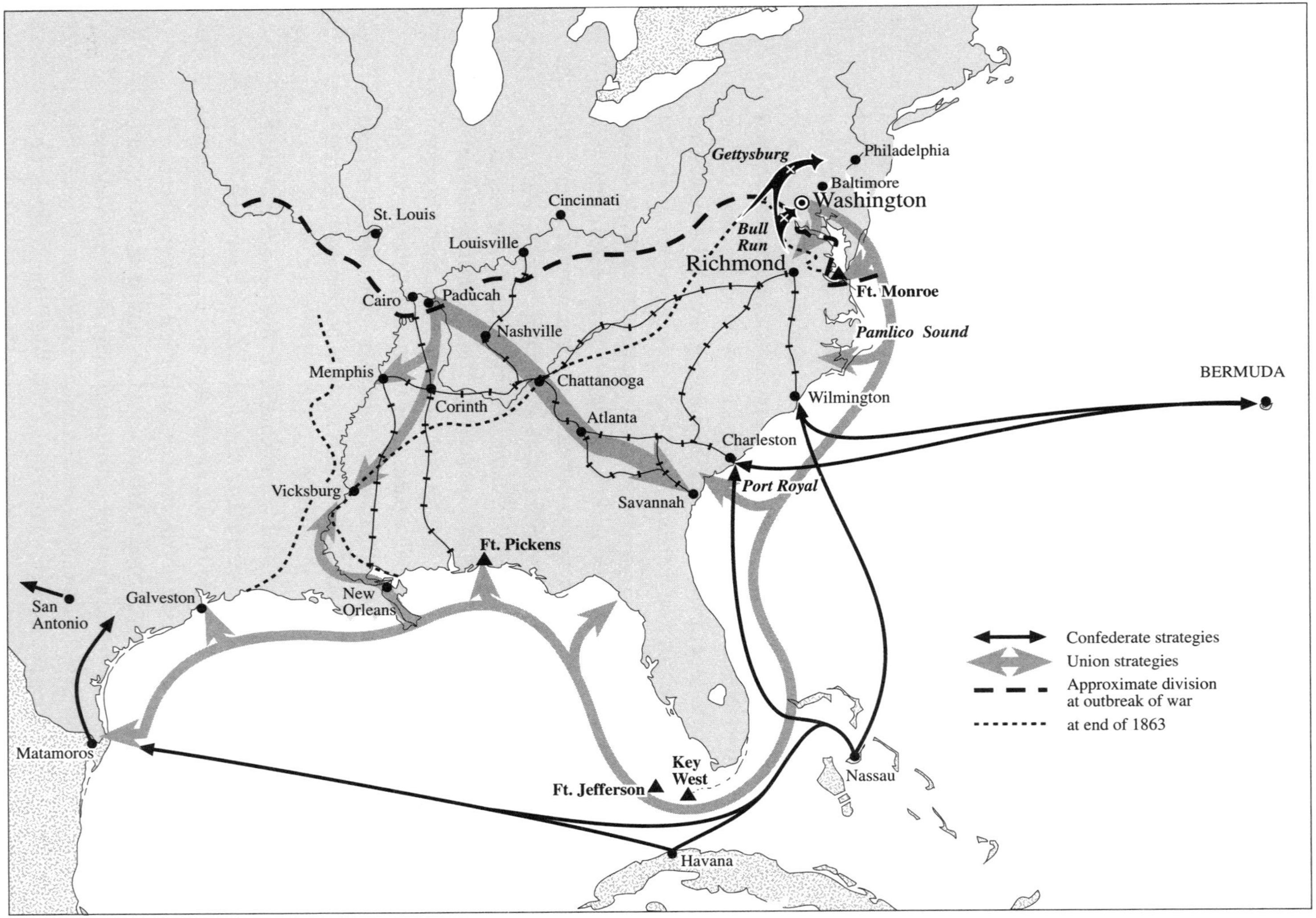

BERMUDA

Philadelphia
Baltimore
Washington
Ft. Monroe
Pamlico Sound
Gettysburg
Bull Run
Richmond
Cincinnati
Wilmington
Charleston
Port Royal
Savannah
Chattanooga
Atlanta
Nashville
St. Louis
Louisville
Paducah
Corinth
Cairo
Memphis
Vicksburg
New Orleans
Ft. Pickens
Key West
Ft. Jefferson
Havana
Nassau
Galveston
San Antonio
Matamoros

Confederate strategies
Union strategies
Approximate division
at outbreak of war
at end of 1863

80. General Strategies.

lines of demarcation between belligerents; only after that had been done might a judicious maneuvering against the opposing forces be undertaken. Thus, in the North especially, there was an incongruity between geopolitical and military priorities. Lincoln and some of his civilian advisers saw an urgent need not only to hang onto the immediate border states but to thrust into the southern Appalachians and Piedmont so as to "nourish and protect the Union sentiment, and create and strengthen a national feeling counter to Secession." In his first annual message to Congress, Lincoln stated, "I deem it of importance that the loyal regions of East Tennessee and western North Carolina should be connected with Kentucky, and other faithful parts of the Union, by railroad." He urged that a line be run from a railhead in the Bluegrass toward Cumberland Gap or Knoxville as soon as possible. But generals, understandably, preferred to use or destroy railroads rather than build them, and it was nearly two years before any substantial Union army reached East Tennessee.

But we must understand that no American general had ever been faced with— or trained to anticipate—war on these terms: on such a massive scale and within his own country. The coordinated movement and provision of large forces over long distances was a formidable challenge, greatly aided in some regions by the new instrument of the railroad but impeded in most by stretches of rough country, thick woods, and innumerable rivers. Nor were armies used to living off the local countryside; they became adept—and increasingly ruthless—in doing so, however, and that could make even a stationary army defending its own territory and people a heavy burden. For example, on the eve of Gettysburg, Colonel Arthur Freemantle, an English observer with Confederate general James Longstreet's forces, recorded an ancillary motivation for the Confederation invasion of Pennsylvania: "Ewell, after the capture of Winchester, has advanced rapidly into Pennsylvania and has already sent back great quantities of horses, mules, wagons, beeves, and other necessities. He is now at or beyond Carlisle, laying the country under contribution and making Pennsylvania support the war instead of poor, used-up and worn-out Virginia." Thus, while presidents and politicians fumed with impatience and near despair, generals (and especially Northern generals, who increasingly knew that time was on their side) tended to move with caution and deliberation.

Both sides, furthermore, were beset by differences and doubts about objectives. Although Jefferson Davis had not been an avid secessionist while serving in the United States Senate (he had been willing to accept the Crittenden Plan), from the moment he became president Davis insisted that re-union with the United States was "neither practicable nor desirable," and he worked resolutely for Southern independence as the sole objective. Yet it was obvious that many Southerners, including some in high offices, regarded secession as a drastic strategum to force the

North into renegotiating the terms of Union. Such "re-construction" (as it was then called) must ensure the continuance of slavery but, at least as important, must somehow formally recognize Southerners as fully respected and valued co-founders and partners in the Union. As David Potter concluded, "Southern nationalism was born of resentment and not of a sense of separate cultural identity"; thus, it was quite possible to regard the initiation of war as a means of getting back into the Union on better terms. (The recurrent agitations—and threat of secession—by the province of Quebec, and the stance of French Canada in general, for similar explicit recognition within the Canadian confederation offers a useful modern analogy; of course, there is nothing in that case akin to slavery, but the resolute "Frenchness" and minority position have engendered strong and volatile feelings on both sides.)

In the North the very idea of a war of conquest was challenged from the first. It was political as well as military conservatism that brought forth the "Anaconda theory" of squeezing and suffocating the South without the need for major assaults and invasion, and at every new stage of the conflict there were pressures for an armistice and negotiation, whether for re-union or separation. In the presidential election of 1864 the platform of the Democratic party called for an armistice and peace convention to search for a means of restoring the union (the party's nominee, General George McClellan, however, repudiated that plank and called for a continuance of the war). Thus, on neither side were the issues as clear nor the support as firm as the leadership and propaganda asserted (and army desertions were a chronic and serious problem for both sides).

Once the initial thrusts were blunted and stalemated in northern Virginia and each side was forced to commit large armies to protect its capital, broader strategies were tested. Prolonged war would render the naval blockade ever more important, for the South would likely become seriously short of arms, munitions, medicines, and much else. This interdiction was not an easy task, but not quite as formidable as the map might suggest. The coastline stretched for 3,500 miles, but not all of it was equally significant. Florida and Texas were lessened in importance by their lack of railroad connections with other parts of the South. On the Atlantic coast, the federal government retained hold of mighty Fort Monroe on the north side of Hampton Roads, guarding the approaches to Norfolk (but Confederate batteries upriver threatened shipping to Alexandria and Washington), and of Key West and Fort Jefferson (the latter an enormous, but uncompleted, fortress on a tiny islet sixty miles to the west) together guarding the Florida Straits and the approaches to Havana. In between, the North soon seized the great anchorage of Port Royal in the Sea Islands just north of Savannah and the Cape Hatteras–Pamlico Sound waters in North Carolina. These two became large supply and repair bases for the blockade fleet. But the North failed to capture Wilmington and Charleston, and these became the main portals of whatever commerce could slip through the federal patrols. Blockade-running became a spirited, dangerous, and systematized adventure. Bermuda and the Bahamas (and to a lesser extent, Havana) were the key junction points between capacious ocean vessels (largely British) and the smaller, faster blockade-runners that hugged the coasts on moonless nights, while the wharves of St. George and Nassau were piled high with bales of cotton, the standard Southern currency. In the Gulf of Mexico the North held onto Fort Pickens at Pensacola, occupied Ship Island off Biloxi, and in April 1862 forced the downriver defenses and captured New Orleans, the South's largest city, port, and banking center. In the later desperate stages of the war, the South made much use of Matamoros because the North could not legally impede British ships from calling at that Mexican port (cargoes were actually lightered ashore at Bagdad at the mouth of the Rio Grande). Such goods could then be readily taken across the river but faced long wagon hauls across a desolate area and could only serve the severed southwest.

The capture of New Orleans and extension of its hold to Baton Rouge was the southern end of the North's campaign to gain control of the Mississippi River and cut the South in two. Union forces moved south by land and by water from Paducah and Cairo and encountered no strong opposition until they neared Corinth, Mississippi, the key railroad crossroads of the region. After heavy fighting at Shiloh, they soon occupied Corinth and Memphis and later moved on to lay siege to Vicksburg. Although Vicksburg and Port Hudson held out for a year, the connection between the main body of the Confederacy and its Transmississippi Department was now so narrow and precarious that it generated rumors that these westernmost states would defect and sue for peace.

Simultaneous with the thrust downriver was another southeastward from the lower Ohio into Tennessee. Designed first of all to ensure that Kentucky stayed in the Union, this campaign soon resulted in the occupation of Nashville and control of the richest districts of this border region. Rather than drive directly eastward to relieve, belatedly, the beleaguered Unionists of East Tennessee, as Lincoln had originally urged, the next military objective now seemed clear: to capture Chattanooga, the trunk-line crossroads of the South. That proved to be arduous, long delayed by the need to counter Confederate forays into Kentucky and even across southern Indiana and Ohio (Morgan's cavalry raid from Corydon to Buffington Island, skirting—and scaring—Louisville and Cincinnati), and accomplished only in the autumn of 1863 at the awful cost of battles at Chickamauga and Chattanooga. After months of recuperation of badly mauled armies, Sherman began his move on Atlanta, occupied the city by mid-summer, and then undertook his famous-infamous (and virtually unopposed) march across the Southern heartland to Savannah and the sea, essentially completing the decisive central segment of this grand strategy and sealing the fate of the remnant Confederate forces on the eastern seaboard.

The Southern response to this Northern strategy was effective only in extracting an horrendous toll and prolonging the struggle far beyond all expectations. The Confederates' defense of Richmond was stalwart until the end, but their great counteroffensives into the North were costly failures (Antietam and Gettysburg), halted before they could reach into Northern vitals (but not before their cavalry made alarming forays almost to Harrisburg, to York, and to Wrightsville on the Susquehanna, causing the local federal guard to set fire to the long bridge connecting to Columbia). The sequential contractions and sunderings of the Southern domain, the tightening of the blockade, the irreplaceable drains upon Confederate manpower and resources condemned even the most valiant effort to failure—assuming the North persevered despite even larger expenditures of men and materials.

The ability of Southern armies in battle was never in doubt, but the pressures of combat had an ambivalent effect on the Confederacy's ability and commitment to wage war. On the one hand, the early stages of open conflict energized the new polity in a common cause, under central leadership. A national army, mobilized from a thousand localities, fought under a national banner symbolizing to themselves, as to all the world, a new unity. On the other hand, the Confederacy was seriously handicapped by defection and defiance from within. Allegiance to the cause of separation and independence was highly uneven, and failure to secure that goal within a short time soon began to magnify dissensions. The recalcitrant region centered on East Tennessee and western North Carolina fostered secret societies that spread subversion into neighboring areas of Virginia, Alabama, and Georgia; there were strong pockets of defection elsewhere (especially in mountainous Arkansas and German Texas) sheltering deserters and defying Confederate decrees. Most telling, perhaps, was the rising resentment of so many Southern Whites over "a rich man's war and a poor man's fight," a class consciousness stimulated by severe inequities in conscription, rampant economic speculations, and what came to be considered despotic rule under planter-politicians. State governments resisted central authority and jealously asserted their prerogatives. The planters themselves were sometimes the strongest opponents of Richmond leadership. For them, the war was certainly over slavery, and they feared that a Confederate government might ultimately interfere with their vital interests as many had been certain Washington would. Once they determined that Richmond could not protect them, as was early the case in Louisiana and parts of Mississippi, they "chose homestead over homeland," as one historian phrased it, and readily responded and adapted to approaching and occupying Union forces in hopes of saving their property and position. Some of these men had been Unionists all the while, "Whig planters," but it would probably be more accurate to say that for all such people "their homestead was their homeland"—in the sense that loyalty to plantation, county, and local region was stronger than commitment to some broader abstract South—or Union (and had situations been reversed and had Southern forces firmly occupied the southern parts of Ohio, Indiana, and Illinois, the same might well have been true of major property-holders in the North).

As the exigencies of the war brought demands from Richmond for even greater centralization and sacrifices, the brittleness and shallowness of Southern nationalism became more apparent, and it did not survive the war—at least in anything like what it had aspired to be. It is an important paradox that the bitter experience of war and defeat and the imposition of radical social change sharply intensified and solidified a Southern sense of regional identity and common purpose, but Southern nationalism in the former geopolitical sense was dead—as attested by the absence of guerrilla resistance to federal military forces (despite Jefferson Davis's call for exactly that in his final address "To the People of the Confederate States of America," issued from Danville, Virginia, his temporary capital following the evacuation of Richmond), the absence of mass exodus and governments in exile or of any significant voices continuing to speak for separation or autonomy (fig. 81).

Secession was dead, and so was slavery. The demise of slavery was intricately connected to the progress of the war and was little less complicated and protracted. Formal proclamations and legislations were many and piecemeal, and all the while slavery was collapsing and shrinking internally through the actions of Blacks and Whites in localities all across the South. In April 1862, Congress emancipated slaves in the District of Columbia (with provision for compensation to owners), and three months later it abolished slavery in all the formal territories (except Indian Territory). Lincoln's famous Emancipation Proclamation, issued in September to take effect January 1, 1863, applied only to those "persons held as slaves within any state, or designated part of a state, the people whereof shall be in rebellion against the United States," and specifically excluded those in the loyal border states, in West Virginia, and in seven counties of Virginia and thirteen parishes of Louisiana under Union occupation. Late in the war Maryland and Missouri abolished slavery, as did (or soon thereafter) the various Unionist governments set up in the partially conquered states. By the time the Thirteenth Amendment, formally abolishing slavery throughout the United States, was ratified in December 1865, human bondage was still legal only in Delaware, Kentucky, and in parts of Indian Territory (the Cherokees had ended it in 1863).

But such formalities give little sense of the real dynamics of emancipation, which was driven by the actions of thousands of individuals to escape bondage and of thousands more to receive and shelter them (however reluctantly and minimally). As soon as war broke out Blacks began to find new ways to freedom. Some

81. Richmond, April 1865.
Andrew Joseph Russell's photograph of Jefferson's famous capitol standing starkly above a devastated city and the rubble of war in the foreground seems a powerful image of the destruction of the Confederacy. In fact, the city had not been destroyed by Union forces but set aflame as it was being evacuated to keep valuable munitions and stores from falling into the hands of the enemy. Arson and looting by a frantic and hungry population spread the damage. (Courtesy of the Virginia Historical Society)

of the slaves impressed to labor on fortifications around Norfolk sneaked away, and the Union commander at nearby Fort Monroe was faced with what to do with the growing numbers of men, women, and children who appeared at his gates. He declared them to be "contraband," seized from disloyal owners, a concept soon formalized by Congress in a Confiscation Act, which became in effect, if not technically, a means of emancipation. The number of such refugee points multiplied as Northern forces occupied footholds along the coast and armies began to move into Confederate territory in the West. Slaves escaping from Unionist masters in loyal territory created rasping political and practical problems for officials but also an increasing reluctance to return them. In time the North began to recruit such Blacks into service, first as labor battalions, eventually as armed troops, and all the while they were being employed, often informally, as servants, cooks, laundresses, grooms, and much else by individual officers, soldiers, and sutlers. On the other side, the Confederate government began to requisition large numbers of slaves to meet urgent demands for labor, despite the strong protests of owners who insisted that they were more than ever needed at home. Such disruptions caused and aided more Blacks to flee, and slaveowners, trying to stem depletions from both escape and impressment,

> moved frenetically about the South. The removal of slaves that began as a trickle in the first year of the war turned into a flood in the second half of 1863. Many slaveholders along the eastern seaboard from Virginia to Florida had already refugeed their slaves inland, and those along the northern borders of the Confederacy headed south. After Union forces gained control of the Mississippi River, masters refugeed their slaves from the valley—those on the east bank generally moving to Alabama and Georgia, those on the west going to Texas. The movement uprooted thousands, indeed hundreds of thousands, of slaves. . . . Wartime refugeeing altered the geography of black life and, contrary to its design, added momentum to slavery's decline.

These many dislocations accelerated the loosening up of the whole traditional system. The ever-heavier drain of White males from the countryside diminished supervision and security while the ever-heavier pressures of subsistence and even survival brought an ever-greater need for Black labor and skills. Readily perceiving such changes, slaves increasingly worked as they pleased, bartered their services, defied orders and threats, roamed the countryside, ransacked storehouses, and everywhere "took advantage of the possibilities created by the war to unbind their shackles." In areas conquered where planters had fled and large numbers of Blacks remained, as at Port Royal and eventually (after Sherman's march) the entire Sea Island coast south of Charleston, local Union officials, struggling with how to handle a pressing and undefined situation, sold or allocated plots of land to freed slaves, while in many other places Blacks simply occupied tracts of abandoned property.

The collapse of slavery was contagious and chaotic, spreading inwardly upon the Confederacy, highly uneven in its course (and meeting some of its stiffest resistance in areas of Kentucky, which had never been treated as a rebel state), but altering the social geography even of its strongest redoubts: "At the end of war, the last remnants of the Confederate heartland—crowded with refugeed slaves—contained a considerable portion of the South's antebellum slave population. The liquidation of bondage in these areas would await the postwar arrival of the Union army of occupation and the agents of the newly established Freedmen's Bureau. But even before the fighting ceased, wartime events had abolished slavery in all but name in much of the Confederacy." The mere installation of that army of occupation would do little to end the turmoil and tension endemic in the land, as many a report would soon testify. As Carl Schurz, after a tour of investigation at the behest of President Johnson, summarized in late 1865: "The general government of the republic has, by proclaiming the emancipation of slaves, commenced a great social revolution in the south, but has, as yet, not completed it. Only the negative part of it is accomplished."

Secession and slavery were dead, but that inexorable corollary, "the future position of the Negro race in North America," stood starkly unresolved, a formidable and desperately unwanted problem that the country was ill-prepared to handle. The war was over, but the revolution had just begun.

7. Empire, Nation, Federation: Geopolitical Contentions

In the spring of 1865 the war was over—and suddenly there was a new American empire. Secession had been subdued, but the Union was not thereby restored. The states that had been officially declared to be in rebellion remained on the map as before (with one important exception), but they were not once again equal members of the federation. Quite the contrary—they were under military occupation and governance.

This captive area was divided into four military "divisions" (Atlantic, Gulf, Mississippi, Tennessee), each of which was composed of one or more departments coextensive with individual states. There was no mistaking the imperial character of this realm. It was ruled by assigned agents: army officers and federal officials, including, especially notable, those representing the new Bureau of Refugees, Freedmen, and Abandoned Lands, which had been set up as a division within the War Department under General O. O. Howard to deal with specific problems of this captive territory. And, like most new empires, it was not a tranquil realm. Imperial service is often dangerous work. As Carl Schurz reported after his late summer reconnaissance: "All organized attacks upon our military force stationed in the south have ceased, but there are still localities where it is unsafe for a man wearing the federal uniform or known as an officer of the government to be abroad outside the immediate reach of our garrisons."

How to rationalize this new conquest and, more immediately, how to manage these captive peoples was the task facing the U.S. government. For the moment, it was applying a form of direct rule. Each military governor relied basically on martial law but tried to disturb local customs as little as possible, except with respect to a set of changes imposed by central authority. Valuable experience had been gained from the rule of areas conquered during the course of the war, but at that time the progress of armies was always foremost, and this peacetime occupation posed new problems. As is generally the case, the imperial power sought the cooperation of local elites but, at least at the outset, did not want to deal with those who had been obvious enemies. There was therefore a search for Southern Unionists, the insistence on oaths of allegiance, and the management of elections for "loyal" citizens, resulting in a species that later generations around the world would come to call "puppet governments."

Such arrangements were recognized at the time as expedient and temporary, a necessary imposition during a period of transition. But transition to what? The complicating fact was that the war had come to an end without an established policy about what was to happen next. To use a later American cliché, the North had won the war but had no clear idea about how "to win the peace." There was no obvious guide or model. The Constitution contained no provision for secession or re-union, there was no practical experience to draw upon, and the political forces that had combined to defeat the South were deeply divided as to what the war had been about and what larger purpose it should be made to serve.

The topic of "reconstruction" (as this process and era came to be called) is one of the most complicated and controversial in American history. It is a tumultuous, factionalized, emotional, and profoundly important issue—among its historians as well as among the leaders and people of the time. In this, as in so many topics, we must maintain our rather distant stance and angle of vision and avoid being drawn into the maelstrom of competing personalities, interests, and the full sweep of events. Our geopolitical perspective suggests a useful simplification of the basic policy alternatives for dealing with this problem: to view it in terms of three competing formulations, which we can appropriately identify as federal, national, and imperial, and consider in turn.

If the main objective of the war was to deny secession as an option for any member state of the Union, then the primary objective of the peace was to restore the Union to its full complement of equal states, to put the structure back in working order as soon as practicable. That meant getting state governments back in power as de jure republics. These must of course be loyal, but a simple oath of allegiance to the United States by candidates and voters would serve and would be, as well, an implicit admission of defeat and an end to any further idea of secession.

Many variations from this simplest concept of restoration, while still adhering to the primacy of the federal structure, were of course possible. There might be some geographic modification of the original states. A West Virginia, created during the war, was an obvious, insistent case. Should there be an East Tennessee—which had been so earnestly sought by loyal Unionists and only thwarted by the exigencies of war? And could a South Carolina, so generally considered in the North to be the instigator of this bloody trauma, be simply welcomed back into the Union it had so rashly tried to destroy, or should it be divided or amalgamated in some way so as to ensure that it would never again be a part that could challenge the whole? To raise such questions complicates and begins to compromise the very idea of restoration and carry us more toward "reconstruction" of the Union.

Lincoln's program, as it evolved, was basically in keeping with this federal formulation. If, as he always maintained, the Union was perpetual, then secession was illegal, an aberration that could be wiped out and the states restored to their proper practical relations. In 1862 he sent the assertively loyal Tennessean Andrew Johnson back to Nashville as military governor with general instructions to return Tennessee to the Union as soon as practicable. Johnson proceeded to build up his own party, arrest opponents, suppress opposition newspapers, defy laws, and eventually manage the election of a representative (but the Congress refused to seat him). Lincoln initiated similar attempts in other occupied states and in 1863 issued a Proclamation of Amnesty and Reconstruction, later adding refinements as to how this process of restoration was to work. The most controversial item of "this desperately simple document" was his specification of 10 percent of the number who had voted in the presidential election as of 1860 sufficient participation ("a tangible nucleus") for the initiation of a loyal government; the most important geopolitical feature was his recommendation that "the name of the State, the boundary, the subdivisions, . . . as before the rebellion, be maintained" (his proclamation was directed to ten states only, and omitted Virginia). Although Lincoln might have referred at times to the "main question" of the war as "a perplexing compound—Union and Slavery," he was famously forthright in declaring emancipation to be secondary: "My paramount object . . . is to save the Union. . . . If I could save the Union without freeing any slave I would do it, and if I could save it by freeing all the slaves I would do it; and if I could save it by freeing some and leaving others alone I would also do that."

As noted, Lincoln began with the last of these alternatives, freeing only those slaves under rebel control. Furthermore, at the outset he hoped to ameliorate the impact of emancipation upon Whites by fostering extensive colonization of "persons of African descent" in some other country. The secretary of State sent out a circular seeking prospects for such American-sponsored colonies and received expression of interest from Colombia, Ecuador, Liberia, and Haiti. Two formal proposals were accepted. The one in the Chiriqui district of the Panamanian sector of Colombia was soon withdrawn in the face of Costa Rican claims upon the area; the other, on the Ile à Vache off the south coast of Haiti, resulted in the shipment of 453 American Blacks—and the return a year later of the remnant that had survived. Both schemes were land promotion frauds, and the eagerness of Lincoln to try them simply underscored the persistent, preposterous, and pernicious American interest in getting rid of its Black population. Once the Emancipation Proclamation was issued, its acceptance became a requirement for state restoration in the Union; Lincoln was pressured to accept limited enfranchisement of Blacks, and he supported some form of freedmen education, but he never offered a program to deal with the social change wrought upon the South.

Various congressional plans (vetoed) and that of Lincoln's successor (the same

Andrew Johnson) were generally similar in seeking to get the Southern states back into normal functioning order as soon as practicable. A common way of representing their perdurable status was to refer to the national banner that had flown all through the war: "Sir, the flag that now floats on the top of this Capitol bears thirty-six stars. Every star represents a State in this Union. . . . We entered the [Southern] States to save them, not to destroy them."

If the objective of the war was not only to deny secession but to abolish slavery as an archaic labor system unsuitable to a modern state and a cripplingly divisive problem in national politics, then the primary objective of the peace must be to reconstruct the Union so as to foster a more effective integration of its parts and make the South conform more closely with the dominant social patterns of the nation. The Thirteenth Amendment ensured a minimal uniformity; helping the South to work out some sort of alternative wage-labor system would set it on the road to further conformity, while extensions of railroads and various other systems of integration would ensure a greater efficiency and harmony of the whole. The South would surely remain a distinctive domain, but it must become more like the West: a convergent rather than a divergent region, ever-more fully participating in the continuous development of the United States as a prospering republic of free men—as an American nation.

The emancipation of slaves and the proposed Fourteenth Amendment provided the groundwork for such a program. The amendment declared the nationalization of citizenship and the basic equality of rights and protection of the laws for all citizens (it also legalized the exclusion from office of particular classes of persons involved in the rebellion). Ratification of this proposal became another essential condition for state reinstatement. By 1867 only Tennessee had done so. The very role of the central government in defining such things was itself a powerful exhibit of the ascendancy of national over federal dimensions of political power. In the words of Richard Bensel, "The secession of the South and the decision of the North to attempt military reunification produced an *explosive expansion* of central state authority." Under the president as commander-in-chief, basic laws were suspended, federal procedures were abandoned, and new instruments, such as a national banking and currency system, national taxation (and a Bureau of Internal Revenue to collect it), the expanded jurisdiction of federal courts, and national conscription for the armed forces, were created to deal with the emergency. Such developments made it clear that no power could literally "restore" the Union—too much had changed in substance and spirit for that (and the Confederate States had undergone a generally analogous experience). There was much concern and many proposals for how to aid the South in the transition from slavery to some sort of new labor system. Insofar as these looked toward creating conditions akin to those in the North they reinforced this national approach to reconstruction; and of course it was assumed that the South would now be much more open to industrial and commercial developments that would routinely strengthen national integration.

If the objective of the war was not only to deny secession and to abolish slavery but to punish the South for its arrogant rebellion and to alter the basic structure of that society so as to ensure that the legacy of slavery might be quickly overcome and all of the region's people, Black and White, might enjoy the same basic civil rights, then the South must be kept under Northern authority and tutelage for some considerable period of time as a subordinate province—a formal, institutionalized imperial relationship. Such punishment and remolding might require some drastic measures: redrawing of state boundaries, expulsions of intransigents, confiscation of lands, removals and relocations, colonization of select areas by Blacks and local loyalists or Northerners, central control of key agencies and facilities. It would of course be a case of imperialism in a worthy cause (and neither the first nor certainly the last to claim such justification): to work a social revolution so as to establish (as one proponent phrased it) "a Christian civilization and a living democracy amid the ruins of the past."

There were very strong voices in support of some such imperial program. As might be expected, those long in the struggle against the "Empire of Slavery" tended to be emphatic about the new situation and the need. Speaking at the ceremony restoring the flag over Fort Sumter, Henry Ward Beecher declared it to be "the flag of sovereignty. The nation, not the States, is sovereign. Restored to authority, this flag commands, not supplicates." And in another of his many expositions during the war he had made clear the agenda for such command in this case: "We are to have charge of this continent. The South has been proved and found wanting. She is not worthy to bear rule. . . . This continent is to be from this time forth governed by Northern men, with Northern ideas, and with a Northern gospel. . . . We hold the vitalizing principles of national life." As in standard imperial practice, Yankees were to be the "ethnic elite," the "aristocracy" of imperialism.

Such ideas were formally proposed in Congress. The Radical Republicans insisted that the rebel states were "conquered communities"; as states they had committed suicide and were now simply a group of "geographical divisions of the Republic whose people are wholly without any valid civil government, and without any constitutional power to frame such government; . . . they are necessarily Territories of the United States." George W. Julian of Indiana (from the Quaker district around Richmond), in a speech published as "Regeneration before Reconstruction," argued at length against "an easy and quick return" of these units to the Union. They needed to be placed under "the strong arm of power, outstretched from the central authority here in Washington" and undergo "years of careful pupilage" (a "probation"; "a well-appointed political *purgatory*") to train them up "in the way they should go." Meanwhile, these territories must be helped to "*grow*" into states by "making it safe for the freedmen of the South, safe for her loyal white men, safe for emigrants from the Old World and from the northern States to go and dwell there; safe for northern capital and labor, northern energy and enterprise, and northern ideas to set up in peace."

"Territorialization," placing these former states wholly under congressional control, would open a whole range of possibilities already being voiced, such as redefine names and boundaries (one congressman wanted the names South Carolina and Georgia erased from the map; early in the conflict, the secretary of War, obsessed with the security of the national capital, had recommended "a reconstruction of the boundaries of the States of Delaware, Maryland, and Virginia"); permanently confiscate planter properties (take 400 million acres from the wealthiest 10 percent and distribute them to freedmen); "drive the nobility" ("seventy thousand proud, bloated, and defiant rebels") into exile; create Black colonies in South Carolina, Georgia, Florida, and Texas (or carve out a new state for that purpose from this last); give Blacks privileged access to public lands (a Southern homestead act); set up educational systems under national oversight for Blacks. In short, as Thaddeus Stevens, the most powerful leader of such interests, declared: "The whole fabric of southern society *must* be changed."

These three formulations are, we must remember, simplifications to provide perspective to this complex affair. And they were not mutually exclusive; they could be combined selectively in various forms and with differing emphases. The contest for control over the treatment of the defeated South was of course a contest for control of the victorious nation and was thus an intense struggle among an array of personalities and party factions. In March 1867, Congress passed the Reconstruction Act, which represented some basic elements of the "national" version of these model policies. The South remained divided into five military districts, but this was clearly to be temporary. State boundaries would remain unchanged (except for West Virginia), and these units were given directions on how to form a nucleus of republican government, write a new constitution providing minimal manhood suffrage, and ratify the Fourteenth Amendment. Passed over President Johnson's veto, the act represented a defeat for those (like Johnson) who had urged a rapid restoration of the federal union, and it was far less stringent and comprehensive than the radical imperialists had demanded. But it left much undecided. It was obviously but one step in a larger process—and that process now moves beyond our view for the time being. To trace the reintegration of the South into the federation and the nation it will be better to enlarge our perspective so as to bring the whole of transcontinental America into the picture—as we shall do in Volume III.

However intense the controversy and uncertainty over how best to shape the future of the United States might be, some important changes wrought by this immediate past were starkly apparent. Before we shift our focus once again, some important geopolitical results of this Second American Revolution should be summarized.

1. *The South had become a formal subordinated province.* Reconstruction policies applied to a designated set of former rebel states, creating a new internal geopolitical differentiation. It was of course a direct legacy of the former reality of the Confederate States of America, and it replaced the long-standing distinction of slave states and free states. How long this formal unequal relationship would last was uncertain; that depended upon the definition of Northern demands as well as upon Southern responses. It was already clear, however, that readmission to full and equal status would be done state by state rather than on the basis of the provincial set of states as a whole.

2. *Southern sectionalism had been sharpened and intensified.* The South had been beaten and battered and left impoverished. Not only had nearly all the battles been waged on Southern soil and broad areas been ravaged by Northern invaders, much of the Southern countryside had been picked clean by Southerners themselves under pressures of survival. Such conditions could be repaired in time and a new regional economy established, but the South had been irrevocably altered and embittered by the devastating assault upon its social system. Union conquest, occupation, and sociopolitical decrees seemed to confirm a North driven by that "lust of empire" that Jefferson Davis would claim (in his memoirs) had "impelled them to wage . . . a war of subjugation" against "their weaker neighbors." Carl Schurz reported "an *utter absence of national feeling*" for "the great republic" on the part of Southern Whites.

If the South was now far weaker than before in all material resources, it was far from impotent in this new phase of the interregional contest. While Southern Blacks sought desperately for some bit of land as a basis for family support and community survival, White Southerners were implacable in their determination to reconstitute and enforce White supremacy at all costs. They proceeded on the firm conviction that "the blacks at large belong to the whites at large" and did everything possible to keep Blacks as a subordinated laboring caste. The result of this collision of aspirations within the Southern population was deep enmity, intimidation, persecution, bloody riots, wanton killings, dislocations—a chaos in the countryside that the imperial power was unable or unwilling to halt. Southern Whites were united in seeking a quick end to imperial supervision and control over their local affairs (foretelling the "Solid South" of later congressional history). It should be noted that this newly self-conscious South included all areas affected by the revolution in race relations and thus extended beyond the occupied states, especially into Kentucky and Maryland.

3. *The Union would probably be restored using the same federal parts—except for West Virginia.* That was not absolutely certain, but in spite of some radical talk, congressmen were naturally very wary of tampering with the territorial integrity of states. Lincoln was certainly against doing so ("the division of a state is a dreaded precedent"), and he accepted the scission of Virginia only because it was a wartime expedient that strengthened the cause of restoring "the national authority throughout the Union." It was an action initiated and consolidated by western Virginians themselves and once accomplished could not be reversed without breaking faith with those who had fought hard and risked much in support of the Union. (After the war, Virginia made a gesture to nullify this internal secession and tried harder to obtain the return of Jefferson and Berkeley counties—the end of the "panhandle.") An analogous potential in East Tennessee was not effectuated because Union armies conquered West and Middle Tennessee well before they got hold of the eastern region. By seizing hold of Nashville so early in the war, national and local Unionist efforts were directed toward restoring the entire state of Tennessee to the Union rather than merely a severed loyalist part. Serious proposals by some Texans in 1866 for a subdivision of their state were quite a different matter, reflecting the peculiar prerogatives specified in the annexation agreement.

Territories, by contrast, had always been fair game for congressional reshaping, and the Confederate Territory of Arizona was completely redesigned shortly after its conquest (its existence had never, of course, been recognized by the United States). The latitudinal division of the original New Mexico Territory was an older concept, supported by local interests scattered along the southern route to California. At the outset of the war Confederate cavalry from Fort Bliss at El Paso ranged west as far as Tucson and in the next year marched north to Albuquerque and Santa Fe. However, they were soon driven out by the threat of superior Union forces converging from Colorado and California, and acting in conjunction with Santa Fe interests, Congress now divided the original territory longitudinally along 109°W to form an Arizona and a New Mexico directly opposite the Confederate bisection. These would long remain territories, open to further modifications.

4. *The United States was, first of all, a nation.* That was the compelling fact, however long it might take to restore the Union. Historians like to point to the shift in common usage from the United States *are* to the United States *is*, or to trace the change in Lincoln's use of words: in his inaugural address he referred to the Union twenty times, with no mention of the Nation; at Gettysburg he referred to the Nation five times, with no mention of the Union; in his second inaugural

address, in 1865, he spoke of the South as seeking to dissolve the Union and of the North as determined to preserve the Nation. Such rhetoric was an important part of the reality of nationalism. To speak of the Union as being "perpetual" gave emphasis to a past as well as to a future, to the values of the historic community as well as to the principles for sustaining a republic. Such an appeal to the bonds of tradition, territory, and society was of course the basis of Southern nationalism, but under the sudden, unexpected pressures of war it emerged with new force at a new scale in the North. Secession had demonstrated the weakness of federalism, the dangers of state power, and the need for stronger central government. The suppression of that formidable rebellion had fostered a degree of organization, integration, and centralization beyond anything known before the war. Henceforth the United States would increasingly function more as a national network of interests than as a loose federal system of states.

5. *The American Core was magnified in power and prospects.* The war had been a great stimulus to economic development in both sections (though to what degree and whether they would have prospered even more without war remain controversial topics). But whereas Southern industry and infrastructure now lay in ruins and bankruptcy, the North was poised to build upon an unimpaired surge of wartime growth. Northern agriculture had prospered on the basis of unprecedented export as well as national demands. Machinery sales soared (as did the use of female labor in the fields); two and a half million acres were taken up under the new Homestead Act (1862), with migrants from the border states seeking a safe haven in the West offsetting in some degree a reduction in foreign settlers; and marketing facilities (such as grain elevators and union stockyards) greatly improved. Nearly every kind of industry had prospered on wartime orders (furthering the initiatives of the 1850s), new ones had appeared (such as petroleum refining), and new resource areas had been tapped (salt and iron ore in Michigan). City growth had been uneven (Chicago had added 70,000 in five years and surpassed a nearly stable St. Louis), but civic improvements in the form of sewage and water systems, gas lights, paved streets, and streetcar services were common to all the larger and many of the smaller centers. All of this was concurrent with improvements in internal transportation (in contrast to the merchant marine, which was heavily depleted and never recovered). Nearly 5,000 miles of new railroad were constructed, including a major extension from the New York & Erie (by the Atlantic & Great Western) to Cleveland and Cincinnati, establishing a single-gauge connection all the way between New York City and St. Louis. More important than extensions of track were improvements in service, such as consolidation of companies, conformity of gauges, fast freight services, and sleeping car and express companies. Northern experience in railroad operations—the coordination of thousands of workers in

many different tasks spaced along hundreds of miles of a system—had provided invaluable lessons for the sudden challenge of equipping, transporting, and supplying hundreds of thousands (and, in total, 2.5 million) of men in arms, and much more had been learned and new systems applied "towards the achievement of functional nationality."

The most intense pressures for infrastructural improvement focused on the main axis of the core and trunk-line connections to Chicago and other western cities. One of the most obvious changes was the transformation of Washington from a federal into a national capital. The war caused a massive influx, a doubling of population, and a great diversification of interests and prospects. Nathaniel Hawthorne gave readers of *Atlantic Monthly* a vivid portrayal as measured by those who crowded the Willard Hotel ("much more justly called the centre of Washington and the Union than either the Capitol, the White House, or the State Department"):

> It is the meeting-place of the true representatives of this country—not such as are chosen blindly and amiss by electors . . . , but men who gravitate or are attracted hither by real business, or a native impulse to breathe the intensest atmosphere of the nation's life, or a genuine anxiety to see how this life-and-death struggle is going to deal with us. Nor these only, but all manner of loafers. Never, in any other spot, was there such a miscellany of people. You exchange nods with governors of sovereign states; you elbow illustrious men, and tread on the toes of generals; you hear statesmen and orators speaking in their familiar tones. You are mixed up with office-seekers, wire-pullers, inventors, artists, poets, prosers, (including editors, army-correspondents, attaches of foreign journals, and long-winded talkers), clerks, diplomats, mail-contractors, railway directors, until your own identity is lost among them.

The city was jammed with war materials and encampments, hospitals and refugees. Enlarged and efficient links with other parts of the country assumed vital importance, and most especially those with New York City. The direct rail connection was swamped with traffic, the alternative Allentown-Harrisburg-York route was pressed into through service, and there arose a strong movement to get the federal government to build or subsidize a high-capacity direct line between the two national capitals (bypassing Philadelphia, where local interests had blocked direct connections between existing routes). Such a controversial project was not undertaken, but by the end of the war most of the existing lines had been double-tracked, and a bridge across the Susquehanna was under construction. These improved facilities (and a railroad bridge across the Potomac) and the influx of Northern businessmen gave rise to visions of Washington as a commercial base, the portal to a South that would be redeveloped and integrated far more firmly into the national system.

These functional geographic transformations were symbolized in the physical transformation of the Capitol itself. A much-needed enlargement had been initiated in 1850 (under Senator Jefferson Davis's Public Building Commission), but the design was repeatedly altered in scale and concept so that "a building which had been merely the outdated seat of American government became a symbolic embodiment of the American Union." At Lincoln's first inaugural ceremony, on the Capitol steps, the new dome stood half-completed amid the scaffolding and cranes, and the widely distributed photographs of the event might easily lead the imagination to think of it as a symbol of a Union decapitated by secession; at his second inaugural, in 1865, it stood completed (on the outside) and could be taken not only as assurance that the Union would survive but that a Nation had come of age. The great victory celebration (fig. 82) was held in May with a Grand Review of 200,000 soldiers marching on Pennsylvania Avenue among the flags and bunting and flowers and bands and masses of spectators: "At the end of the avenue the Capitol was almost overpowering in its splendor. It loomed far taller than anything in the whole countryside; its whiteness dazzled the eye. Hundreds of thousands of Americans were brought to Washington by the war. Most of them would never visit the city again, but the triumph and tragedy of what they had lived through was unmistakably summed up in the memory of the dome."

Amidst the euphoria and relief associated with that celebration of the nation there were also symbols and plenty of tangible evidence in this newly magnified capital that the war had indeed been fought over the other part of "that perplexing compound—Union and Slavery." Washington had become a powerful magnet for freedmen. The Black population soared from 14,000 to nearly 40,000, with thousands more encamped in government villages in the Virginian environs. The physical and social conditions wrought by the war upon the city as a whole were widely deplored, and the plight of the Blacks was considered by many to be a national scandal. The sudden decline in wartime business and uncertainty about the future, the limited power (and the strong Southernness) of civic leadership, and the general indifference of Congress to the special problems of the District produced a sense of crisis and considerable despair. But there were also those who regarded Washington as a crucial testing ground for the social revolution and were determined to carry it forward. Thousands of Black soldiers had marched in that victory parade, and Black leaders and churches and societies joined with Whites in furthering the work of the Freedmen's Bureau and many other agencies and causes. Under intense lobbying Congress had enacted an education bill, and in May 1865 a row of small frame houses in the shadow of the Capitol became the city's first Black public school. Schools, like much else, were racially segregated, but by 1867 there were more than 3,000 Black pupils, and in that year a charter was issued and federal funds were appropriated to establish Howard University (named for the general in

82. A Nation Triumphant, May 1865.
(Courtesy of the Junior League of Washington)

83. Freedman's Village, Arlington, Virginia.
After slavery was abolished in the District of Columbia in April 1862, Blacks began to pour in from nearby Virginia and Maryland. Within a year the government was constructing thousands of simple standardized houses, like these sketched by A. R. Waud for *Harper's Weekly*, as temporary accommodations. (Courtesy of the Junior League of Washington)

charge of the Freedmen's Bureau) as an institution expressly dedicated to biracial education and primarily intended to produce generations of Black leaders (fig. 83). These were surely positive signs in the nation's capital; how symbolic they might be for the nation as a whole remained utterly uncertain.

At the cost of 620,000 lives, four years of war had determined that the United States of America would be one federation instead of the parent of two. The Union had been saved and the Nation reinforced, but perplexing new problems had been produced: what to do with a captive province and with a freed people—four million newly freed and landless people. If the national flag with its thirty-six stars on a field of blue seemed to confirm the eventual restoration of the federation, the meaning of the maxim on the other national banner—*E Pluribus Unum*—seemed less clear and more deeply controversial than ever before.

PART FOUR
CONTEXT:
THE UNITED STATES IN NORTH AMERICA
CIRCA 1867

The unuttered truth was that three great powers, each in its own way, were recognizing the fact of the supremacy of the United States in America, and were withdrawing from the North American continent.

W. L. Morton

Prologue

The year 1867 has little visibility in the usual panoramas of American history. It features no memorable event, it marks no important beginning or ending. The purchase of Alaska was a surprise rather than the fruition of some protracted national effort, and it was considered so marginal in value as to be the subject more of derision than satisfaction. Our featured year falls two years after the victory of those forces that fought to put North and South back together; it comes two years before the conclusion of the herculean effort to bind East and West with iron bands. At the time, the United States was, understandably, immersed in the unprecedented problems of the post–Civil War era. But our geographical perspective insists that we try to see things in their larger setting—in areal context, in relation to their surroundings—and once we step back and take a more fully continental view, the movements and events of 1867 take on considerably greater interest.

The withdrawal, in varying ways and degrees, of the three largest European imperial systems from their holds upon huge areas in North America is surely a change worth noting. It affected all the great borderlands and redefined just what kind of neighbors the United States would have on this continent. Furthermore, the residual, insular area of European colonies was also altered internally in important ways just as that tropical sector was taking on new geopolitical importance for the United States.

What follows, therefore, is not at all a geographical summation of the United States as of about 1867 but a widening of our lens to include these adjacent areas and peoples and the identification of a few more landmarks

on the particular map of the past we are constructing for the modern traveler.

1. Continental America

Near the end of the war, in his annual message to Congress and the nation,
Abraham Lincoln pointed to the larger context of American development: "It is of
noteworthy interest that the steady expansion of population, improvement and
governmental institutions over the new and unoccupied portions of our country
have scarcely been checked, much less impeded or destroyed, by our great civil war,
which at first glance would seem to have absorbed almost the entire energies of the
nation." But of course presidents tend to paint a bright picture on such occasions,
and many persons more closely involved in "new and unoccupied portions" of the
country had a rather darker view of their situation. A year later the secretary of the
Interior offered a quite different summation of their recent experience: "Our defenceless frontier settlements were harassed; the communications between the
Mississippi valley and our possessions on the Pacific seriously interrupted; emigrant
and Government trains assailed; property of great value destroyed, and men,
women, and children barbarously murdered." But of course such public officials are
prone to exaggerate in hopes of wheedling more funds from a niggardly Congress.

Actually, there was a good deal of truth in both statements—and therein lay the
cause of much of the trouble. Population and governmental institutions had indeed
continued to expand—which meant, as always, relentless pressures and wanton
trespasses upon Indian lands and resources. And the depletion of frontier garrisons
and abandonment of some posts had opened new opportunities for Indian retaliation. Losses had been considerable, and White settlement had even retreated in
several sectors. The Sioux struck at New Ulm and sent panic along the Minnesota
frontier; Cheyennes, Arapahoes, and Kiowas harassed travelers and hunters on the
plains; the chaotic civil war within and among various groups of Indians and
Whites devastated Kansas and the Indian Territory; the Comanches raided almost
at will deep into central Texas; Navahos laid siege to New Mexican settlements;
while various Apache bands made Anglo life along the southern border highly
hazardous. In return, frontier militias vented their wrath upon any Indians within
reach, as in the Sand Creek massacre of Arapahoes in Colorado, and Kit Carson
and a band of volunteers (under U.S. Army authority) defeated the Navahos,
destroyed their fields and flocks, and marched nearly 9,000 of them into captive
exile on a Pecos Valley reservation.

At the end of the Great War the Union army was rapidly reduced from a million
men to a standing force of 50,000, and most of these were deployed to the western

frontiers to secure the outposts of empire and sustain "that steady expansion of population and improvement" that had been so central to the purpose of American government. Now-famous generals (such as Sherman, Sheridan, and Pope) undertook the very different, in some ways more difficult, task of policing and punishing (and for at least some of these officers it was a more distasteful task, for they expressed some genuine sympathy for beleaguered Indians who were compelled to steal or starve). Beyond protecting the main districts of settlement, the principal general strategy was to create "for our people exclusively the use of a wide belt, east and west, between the Platte and the Arkansas, in which lie the two great railroads, and over which passes the bulk of travel to the Mountain territories."

Such a program was an admission that the United States, for all of its great geopolitical position and power, was not as yet an effective transcontinental nation or federation. Large areas of the Great Plains and Far West were unsecured and unorganized, and the sinews of empire and nation were extremely thin and tenuous. The two railroads referred to in this report of November 1866 were still slowly advancing across the plains: the Union Pacific was just starting up the North Platte, 270 miles west of Council Bluffs (which was itself not yet connected by rail across Iowa); the Eastern Branch (Kansas Pacific) had only reached Fort Riley, 135 miles west of Kansas City. On the Pacific side, the Central Pacific was still blasting its way up the western slope of the Sierras, leaving a gap of more than 1,300 miles yet to be built. Meanwhile, the several western areas of settlement were being served by freighting teams and stagecoaches but always at some risk; an attempt, under military protection, to open a new road to the Montana mines by way of the Powder River brought a sharp attack from the Sioux, and the army was too weak to respond.

The eventual outcome, of course, was never in doubt. Those converging railroads were simply one key instrument of a polity and people that were relentless in their advance from the east and the west. Only the timing of the defeat and place of disposal of the many as yet unsubdued Indian peoples in between remained uncertain. There could be no real doubt that the United States would soon become, at the very least, a fully transcontinental power.

2. The Northern Borderlands

There were, as always, other peoples as well who had good reason to care about just what the nature and extent of that American power would be. British North Americans could take satisfaction that their aggressive neighbor gave them little polemical notice following the various fixations of a transcontinental boundary in the 1840s, and in the 1850s the Canadas, especially, grew concomitantly and in many ways integrally with the larger systems to the south. As in the United States, there was a surge in immigration from famine-ravaged Ireland, but unlike the United States, other British, and especially Scots were also prominent (while Germans were very few). Coming up the St. Lawrence, the majority docked in Montreal and moved on to the industrial towns and agricultural areas of Canada West. The fertile "peninsula" of good farmlands was soon completely taken up, and unwilling to accept an end to such pioneering progress, the government built a series of "colonization roads" and offered land on easy terms to lure settlers north-ward into the rocky wilderness of the Laurentian Shield. Few, however, could be attracted to such lands while the fertile prairies of Iowa and Minnesota were available, and the number of immigrants (and younger Canadians) moving on to beckoning opportunities in the United States became even larger than usual. By 1860, also, New England mill towns were becoming a routine outlet for the demographic pressures of large French families in Canada East, and perhaps 50,000 now resided south of the border. Commercial as well as migration links were greatly elaborated. The old Laurentian axis was still important, but in Canada West the ties with New York were more so. Toronto, at 45,000, was just half the size of Montreal, but it was clearly the leading center of the most vigorously developing region.

The basic geopolitical problem of Laurentian America, however, had only worsened, in part because of these developmental trends. In defiance of the 1841 design of a United Province, Canada was functioning, in effect, as a federation of two parts. The chronic English-French impasse had produced an unstable hyphe-nated politics, a de facto dual leadership with every administration a delicately balanced coalition of English and French, requiring endless personal negotiations and shifting in venue every few years between Toronto and Quebec. As the balance in actual population and prospects tipped increasingly in their favor, leaders in Canada West called ever-more loudly for some major revision of this frustrating partnership.

Incipient changes much farther west had an important bearing on the matter. Anticipation of the expiration in 1859 of the Hudson's Bay Company's monopoly license over Rupert's Land and the Northwest generated competing formulations for the governance and control of these vast lands and resources. Toronto and associated business interests began to work for outright annexation to Canada, some British colonial officials tended to think in terms of a separate Crown colony (such as Vancouver Island), local peoples were much divided and uncertain. Political leaders were agreed, however, on one thing: the need to counter the vigorous American activities in the borderlands. In the late 1850s several scientific expeditions were sent out, the most important being that led by the geologist H. Y. Hind, sponsored by Toronto interests, and one sponsored by the Royal Geographical Society (with Colonial Office subsidy) under Captain John Palliser. Of principal concern were the settlement prospects on the great plains broadening westward from Red River and the feasibility of trafficways east to Canada and west to the Pacific. The sponsors of these investigations were well aware of official U.S. explorations for a railroad route from Lake Superior to Puget Sound, initiated in 1853 under the direction of Isaac Stevens, governor of newly created Washington Territory. Like that of Stevens, these British assessments drew upon the very reassuring climatology of Lorin Blodget, whose maps showed summer isotherms curving far northward, defining temperatures as warm in the Saskatchewan country as in Toronto and New York. Extensive reconnaissance delimited the northern reach of the arid high plains (known thereafter as Palliser's Triangle), but between that steppe zone and the great northern forest lay a prairie and parkland belt of great fertility eminently suited for agriculture and stock raising. In London, Colonial Secretary Sir Edward Bulwer Lytton waxed eloquently upon the possibilities, inviting his colleagues "to see, in the settlement of the Red River, a nucleus of a new colony, a rampart against any hostile inroads from the American frontier, and an essential arch, as it were, to that great viaduct by which we hope one day to connect the harbours of Vancouver Island with the Gulf of St. Lawrence." His endorsement of a new colony in this interior was in line with Palliser's conclusion that the southerly wedge of the great Shield constituted such a formidable barrier that it would not be feasible to annex this West to Canada.

The Canadians of course stressed the "great viaduct" (railroad) part of the vision and put their case for a union built around an expanded Canada to the Colonial Office. In the throes of economic depression in 1857, however, Canada was decreed to be too weak, debt-ridden, and unstable to carry such a structure.

Years of wrangling had failed to resolve the festering problem of a permanent location for the government, and in desperation Canadians turned to Queen Victoria for a decision. Her choice (following the recommendations of her governor-general) in 1857 of Ottawa over five other contenders (Hamilton, Toronto, Kingston, Montreal, Quebec) was a deep disappointment in Canada West and only spurred further efforts to stake out a claim to new frontiers. Toronto businessmen formed a new company to place a line of steamships to connect their Northern Railway at Collingwood on Georgian Bay with ports on Lake Superior.

Such a strategy was impelled by a real anxiety over the surge of colonization in Minnesota and the talk of St. Paul expansionists. By 1859 Americans had a steamboat on the Red River, further strengthening the superiority of the U.S. trafficway over any Canadian route. Lytton's reference to the need for a "rampart against any hostile inroads" from the Americans was prompted by even more alarming developments farther west. The discovery of placer gold on the Fraser River brought a sudden influx from all parts of the American Far West. In July 1858 the Colonial Office created the formal mainland colony of British Columbia and added it to the responsibilities of James Douglas, governor of Vancouver Island. Thus, for the time being both colonies were administered from Victoria, although a future capital was surveyed on the banks of the lower Fraser at New Westminster. The gold resources did not prove to be another California, but a sequence of minor discoveries kept luring prospectors and their suppliers ever-further inland. Victoria and British Columbia thereby emerged as part of a Pacific world, linked closely with Oregon and Hawaii and focused on San Francisco. Even so, important continuities remained, for prominent within those commercial networks were Scots merchants and shippers with comfortable ties to the Hudson's Bay Company and to Britain.

The outbreak of an enormous civil war in the United States reverberated quickly and ominously upon British North America. Tensions arose over (what can now be seen as) a host of petty episodes and misinterpretations: confrontations with Great Britain over Confederate movements and commerce on the high seas; the activities of Southern agents and sympathizers operating along the northern border, intriguing with copperheads, and conducting small raids into the Northern states; the imposition by the United States of passport requirements to counter such activities; the sudden presence of an enormous United States military force and an upsurge of the usual loose American talk about annexing these British colonies as a form of compensation or an obvious next step in continental consolidation—such things generated strong feelings and fears north of the border. The difficulties of trying to rush several thousand British troops from Halifax to the St. Lawrence by way of the Madawaska in midwinter underscored the need for interregional railroad connections. Detailed plans were drawn up for a set of elaborate fortifications ringing the Laurentian cities and for gunboats on the borderland lakes and rivers. British imperialism, however, was in one of its strong commercial rather than military phases (a Little England stance), and it had more important concerns elsewhere. Furthermore, especially as the outcome of the American war became more obvious, Britain wanted not only to reduce its costs but to lower its visibility on the North American continent so as to reduce the possibilities for tensions with this much-magnified American power. All these things seemed to point toward the need for greater British North American cooperation and self-reliance and thus gave fresh impetus to the idea of a wider union.

In September 1864 a conference at Charlottetown originally called to deal with problems common to Prince Edward Island, New Brunswick, and Nova Scotia was enlarged to include the Canadas. Initial discussions were so promising that the delegates reconvened a month later in Quebec (with Newfoundland now represented) and drew up a long set of resolutions for the creation of a formal federation. There ensued a period of debate and discussion in the several colonial legislatures, newspapers, and various forums. During this time new pressures welled up in the borderlands. In 1865 the United States gave formal notice that neither the commercial Reciprocity Treaty nor the treaty limiting armaments on the Great Lakes would be renewed, there was a series of local raids and provocative plots upon British American soil by the militant Irish-American Fenian Brotherhood, and American congressmen not only talked about annexation, but one of them, Nathaniel Banks of Massachusetts, submitted a bill in July 1866, "establishing conditions for the admission of the States of Nova Scotia, New Brunswick, Canada East, and Canada West, and for the organization of territorial governments"; it was referred to the Committee on Foreign Affairs. Banks was probably more interested in courting the local Anglophobic Irish vote than in realizing actual annexation, and there was no serious political response to the topic, but British Americans had little reason to be complacent about such things. Their leaders could make ready use of such fears even if they did not share them. Later that year delegates from those four colonies met in London to negotiate a new relationship with the Crown (Newfoundland and Prince Edward Island having decided not to participate). On March 31, 1867, a new British North America Act creating a Confederation was signed by Queen Victoria and the Dominion of Canada was officially proclaimed, to come into effect on July 1, 1867 (fig. 84).

The United States now had a new neighbor. The character of the borderland had been altered, and it is important to get at least a general geopolitical sense of what had been created. Although *confederation* was the official term of reference, this new superstructure provided a rather strong central parliamentary government (the American civil war being presumed to have demonstrated the folly of a weak center) under the oversight of a Crown-appointed governor-general, consisting of a popularly elected House of Commons, apportioned federally by population (initially in a ratio of Ontario 82, Quebec 65, Nova Scotia 19, New Brunswick 15), and a Senate (apportioned among these provinces at 24–24–12–12) whose members were chosen and appointed for life by the governor in council and whose powers were much more limited. Each province was to have its own legislature, with control over designated local affairs. English and French were given equal official standing in Parliament (and in the legislature of Quebec—to protect the English-speakers of Montreal) and in the courts and official records of Canada (and Quebec). Ottawa was the capital, with the new buildings constructed for the old Canada United to serve as the seat of the new Dominion.

It was a shaky structure from the start, a union of historic units markedly different in origins, interests, and prospects. It took its name (without opposition) from the old Laurentian provinces that had been reluctant bedfellows for so many years. These two original Canadas provided the firm foundation of the new structure, for once unyoked from one another within a single polity, these old rivals

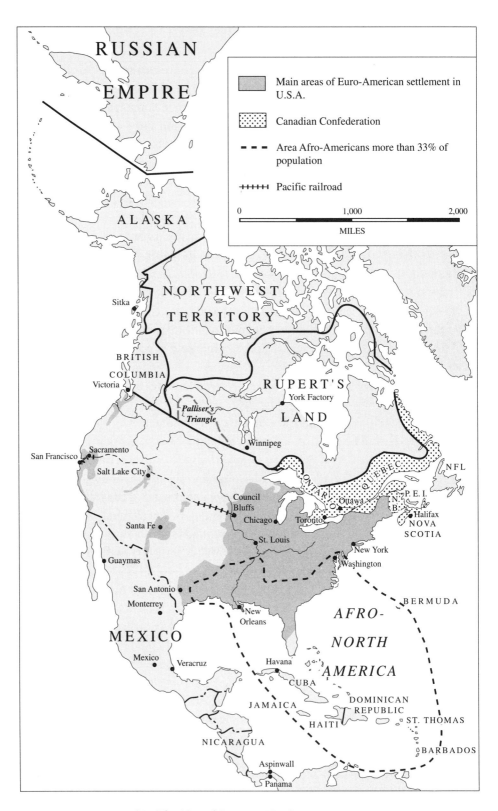

84. The United States in North America, 1867.

found much to their liking in the new arrangement. The French were now firmly in charge of their own province and thus in a position to nurture and protect their primary national culture: their language, religion, education, and civic institutions. The English presence in Montreal was a chronic internal issue for both peoples, but the wider possibilities of confederation drew the strong support of business leaders. As Alexander Galt, one of the architects of union, assured a Sherbrooke audience: "When we extend the boundaries of our Empire to the countries bordering on the Saskatchewan and the Rocky Mountains, the whole wealth of that great country must pour down the St. Lawrence and stimulate the industry of the cities of Lower Canada." Of course, the leaders of newly named Ontario (rather than "Toronto," an alternative proposal) saw themselves in an even more advantageous position: no longer in tandem with the French downriver, free to concentrate on augmenting an already dominant role, "wherever he looked the Upper-Canadian patriot saw in Confederation an alluring prospect of wider opportunities for the abounding energies and ambitions of the dynamic, forward-looking, English-speaking Protestant people of Ontario."

Ottawa seemed, to some at least, well positioned to serve these conceptions of a greater Canada: a new city (superimposed on a lumber town) poised on the cultural boundary and detached from the chronic urban jealousies of the Laurentian axis but on the old route west that would, it was assumed, soon be laid with rails to the Pacific (but at the time was connected only by a backwoods branch line from Prescott).

But the view from other provinces was very different. It has been common to attribute the widespread opposition to the new union in the Maritimes to a characteristic parochialism and political conservatism. As in the United States case, Canadian anti-federalists tend to be categorized as persons of small minds who could not grasp the larger continental concept. There was evidence to support such a view, but it was surely more complicated than that. As recent assessments have suggested, much of the opposition was directed not at the general idea of a wider union but at the specific design of this one that seemed likely to put these much smaller and circumscribed provinces at serious disadvantage in their association with the central Canadas and a developing West. Some of the supporters of the original Charlottetown conference wished to form a regional union of at least some of these Atlantic colonies as a prelude to negotiating a place on better terms and as a more substantial unit within the federal structure. Given the powers granted to the central parliament, there was ample reason for such geopolitical concerns.

Other divisive and divergent geographical issues were exposed by the debates over this new grand design. Many New Brunswick businessmen could see no advantage in union. For years they had sought help in building railroads, but the Intercolonial promised by the Confederation was committed to a route as distant as possible from the American frontier and would thus cut across the thinly populated eastern border counties remote from the settlements, capital, and port of the Saint John Valley. Local interests had focused on getting help to complete the Western Extension to bind the Shediac–Saint John fragment of the European and North American Railway (an old, grandiose scheme for a set of fast trains and steamships linking London, Ireland, Halifax, New York, and Canada) with Maine, seeing closer links with American commerce as preferable to being taxed to further the aspirations of a distant Ontario. It took pressure from London (concerned not so much with New Brunswick itself but with the need to have a land connection between Nova Scotia and Canada) to bring New Brunswick into the Confederation.

Nova Scotia was a more complex case. A society long riven with local and group loyalties and jealousies arising from its complicated history on a complicated peninsula, it was now being altered by the moving tide of Scottish and Irish immigration: "A Celtic and Catholic element, unsettling and pervasive, was seeping through the ancient province, upsetting its Yankee ways, challenging its British stolidity, making it a Nova Scotia indeed." The old ties to Boston and New England remained but were weakened by various economic and political developments of midcentury. By continental standards Halifax may have been a small city (under 30,000), but Haligonian society had "a metropolitan tincture" because, as W. L. Morton has so well depicted, it was an important center in a much larger world:

> In Halifax, as in Quebec, the morning and evening bugles, the thud of the noon-hour cannon, and the warships riding dark and silent in the harbour beneath the citadel, signalled the martial character of the garrison city. And as in Quebec, the presence of the military and the navy brought into the life of the provincial capital an influential stream of metropolitan manners and metropolitan connections. Halifax was kin to Portsmouth and Plymouth, as much as to Montreal or New York. . . . [and] the great world, the place of emulation and eminence, was in London.

The need to conjoin this Atlantic station and province with the western colonies was not altogether self-evident to Nova Scotians. So far the links had been mainly imperial rather than commercial, for the position of Halifax as the easternmost ice-free outpost on the mainland was far less commanding in economic terms. Portland, Boston, and especially New York provided more efficient access to the North American interior than Halifax ever could. Nova Scotia was nudged into the Confederation by an emphasis on larger geopolitical concerns bedecked with visions of vast commercial and industrial opportunities and an explicit constitutional guarantee of "a railway connecting the River St. Lawrence with the City of Halifax . . . with all practicable speed" (it took nine years), and it was such a controversial move that the terms of association (relating to subsidies) had to be negotiated and sweetened two years later to keep it in.

These two Maritime provinces came into union with the Canadas haltingly because "they had been sure neither of its wisdom nor of their welcome," and the rejection of union by the island colonies of Newfoundland and Prince Edward Island was a more blatant display of how ambivalent this sector of Atlantic America was to the larger continental concept—at least as it came to be defined in Quebec and London.

As for the new West, despite the work of a few Canadian protagonists in the new town of Winnipeg, the majority opinion in the Red River Settlement and especially among the métis of Assiniboia was strongly against being simply handed over to Canada by London decree. Nevertheless, that is what happened. An initial committee report on the overall prospects for the interior had recommended that the Hudson's Bay Company's license be renewed in the northern regions unsuitable for colonization but that the fertile open country be annexed to Canada in preparation for development. No such decision was made at the time, but a succession of colonial secretaries held to Canadian succession as the simplest—and cheapest—solution, and as the new Confederation came into being, the Crown gave it the task of negotiating the transfer of title to all (not just the northern parts) of Rupert's Land and the Northwest from the Hudson's Bay Company and of assuming governmental responsibilities for that entire area, extending from Labrador to the Rockies and the Arctic seas. The mode of incorporating specific territories into the structure of the new union was left to Ottawa. When officials of Canada gave no indication that they would consult with the people of Red River nor recognize local governments that had sprung up in a decade of official neglect, suspicions and fears arising especially from uncertainties about land titles and métis rights and privileges intensified. Nothing was yet fixed in 1867, but it appeared as if this West would be simply annexed as a subordinate territory to be managed and manipulated entirely from Ottawa—an imperial relationship.

The leaders of Confederation clearly envisioned their new creation as the eventual successor to all British North America, a dominion from sea to sea (the term itself is said to have been suggested by Psalm 72), and they immediately set out to entice Prince Edward Island, Newfoundland, and British Columbia into the fold and to lay plans for the acquisition and subdivision of the vast Hudson's Bay Company realm. Other than their own fresh experience, there was neither precedent nor process defined for the mode of such geopolitical expansion. There was, of course, always on view another model of federation with long experience in the formation and admission of new units. By this date the American side of this western borderland had been organized into the State of Minnesota and the Territories of Dakota, Montana, Idaho, and Washington. Such territories were states in embryo that could confidently expect that at an early, critical stage in their development they would routinely be admitted into the Union "on an equal footing" with all the other states. Residents of western British America were well aware of that policy and many were attracted by its essential features; there was talk of annexation to the United States as preferable to being given to Canada, or, as some emphasized, to Ontario. During these uneasy months, Senator Alexander Ramsey of Minnesota sought to intercede on behalf of those residents with an alternative future. Asserting that most of these westerners would prefer admission to the American Union, he introduced a resolution in Congress on December 9, 1867: "That Canada, with the consent of Great Britain, shall cede to the United States the districts of North America west of longitude 90° [a line just west of Fort William, and of the easternmost tip of Minnesota] on the conditions following . . . ." These conditions included United States payment of $6 million to the Hudson's Bay Company to discharge all claims; U.S. assumption of up to $2 million of the public debt of British Columbia; further American aid for the construction of the Northern Pacific Railway; and explicit provision that "the northwest territory shall be divided and organized into Territories of the United States, not less than three in number."

Routinely referred to the Committee on Foreign Relations, the Ramsey resolution disappears from view, but it was not an ephemeral thing to the Confederation builders of Canada. For just when they took a giant step toward redefining the geopolitical character of North America, the United States did likewise. Within hours after Queen Victoria had signed the British North America Act initiating the Dominion of Canada, U.S. Secretary of State William H. Seward signed the treaty transferring the whole of Russian America to the United States for the sum of $7.2 million. That the United States had once again accessioned a huge territory by benign purchase made the subsequent proposal of Senator Ramsey appear to Americans as routine and inoffensive (though they might have understood that an offer of just $8 million for the western half of British America after paying nearly that much for a widely disparaged Alaska could have seemed insulting).

These enormous territorial transactions—the creation of a Canadian Confederation empowered to annex and organize most of British North America and the purchase of Alaska—were closely related in more than mere timing. On one side, Confederation was seen as the means of consolidating a British sea-to-sea hold on northern America in the face of an endemic U.S. expansionism; on the other, the transfer of Alaska was regarded as a means of thwarting a possible British seizure of a vulnerable territory valuable to a world maritime power. Both cases were much more complex than that, but these broadest of geopolitical issues were prominent in the minds of many of the leaders involved. The earliest intimation of such Russian concern and a possible transfer of its American possessions to the United States appeared in 1854 during the Crimean War, which pitted Russia against Britain and France, and the decisive pressure came ten years later, when the czar had good reason to be greatly concerned about a general war with those western powers over Balkan and Mitteleuropa issues. As the head of the czar's navy emphasized, "Russia must endeavor as far as possible to become stronger in her center, in those fundamentally Russian regions which constitute her main power in population and faith." Alaska was a remote fringe, indefensible—against current *American* interlopers (fishermen, whalers, traders) as well as eventual American expansionists ("following the natural order of things," America was bound "to possess the whole of North America")—and unprofitable (the Russian-American Company was generally regarded in St. Petersburg as a corrupt and moribund operation). Furthermore, in 1860 the Treaty of Peking opened up new opportunities in the Russian Pacific. By confirming the Russian hold upon the Amur and Ussuri territories and providing for commercial access to Peking, Vladivostok became the obvious base for the Pacific fleet, China emerged as the great focus of attention, and Russian America faded into an attenuated fringe.

Acquisition of Alaska did not result from the kind of American imperial aggression exhibited in the case of, say, Mexico or Oregon. The initiative came from Russia (a fact carefully disguised in the diplomatic negotiations), the treaty obtained by Seward was sprung as a surprise on the president, his cabinet, and Congress, and it was passed only after intensive lobbying. Americans were still absorbed in domestic issues. Impeachment and Reconstruction dominated and embittered political life, and few leaders had time for or interest in the acquisition of distant and detached territories. Proponents hastily patched together all the favorable reports and opinions they could find on the resources and the strategic significance of Alaska, but little was actually known about such resources and relatively few persons responded avidly to the grand global visions outlined in strategic prospects; an active commercial interest in Alaska as a land route for an American-Eurasian telegraph line had suddenly collapsed on the successful completion of a transatlantic cable in 1866.

One of the most appealing features of the Alaska treaty, emphasized by Charles Sumner, a key figure in the debate, was the fact that "by it we dismiss one more monarch from the continent." The spread of republicanism over North America was widely accepted by Americans as an appropriate and undeniable goal. A few days before the Dominion of Canada was proclaimed, Congressman Nathaniel Banks of Massachusetts offered a protesting resolution:

> That a confederation of States on this continent, extending from ocean to ocean, established without consulting the people of the Provinces to be united, and founded upon monarchical principles, cannot be considered otherwise than in contravention of the traditions and constantly-declared principles of this Government, endangering its most important interests, and tending to increase and perpetuate embarrassments already existing between the two Governments immediately interested.

After some argument as to its accuracy (the Confederation had been approved by the elected legislatures of the provinces) and its futility, the resolution passed. Few Americans, in Congress or otherwise, seemed to have had much interest in the matter, but the British took such sentiments seriously. Canadians had proposed that their new creation be called "the Kingdom of Canada," but Lord Monck, the governor-general, raised the objection that such an imprint on the continent would needlessly "open a monarchical blister on the side of the Americans," and they reluctantly switched to "Dominion" as less rasping.

In his speech from the throne at the opening session of the first Parliament of the new Confederation, Lord Monck offered his congratulations on the creation of a structure "which has laid the foundation of a new nationality." His use of the term was much remarked upon at the time. It seemed as if the admonition of Lord Durham had finally been heeded: the British North American colonist was being given "some nationality of his own," and "these small and unimportant communities" were being elevated into "a society having some objects of a national importance." It was a theme perfectly suited to the "design clearly seen and strongly held" by Sir John A. Macdonald, the first premier; as Morton succinctly put it: "Macdonald proposed to make a nation on the northern half of the continent which, as a member of the Empire, would perpetuate British institutions in America for all time to come." It would, of course, take time, and at the outset Canada was "a nation projected rather than a nation formed" (fig. 85).

Durham's remarks had been pointed toward the need to form a more substantial and vitalized polity to withstand the absorptive power of the United States. His words had lost none of their pertinence for the succeeding generation. Indeed, the general lack of any intense American interest in or response to the creation of the Canadian Confederation was due in considerable part to a complacent assumption that it would not make much difference in the long run. As *Frank Leslie's Illustrated News* commented, the United States could remain indifferent because of an "implicit confidence . . . in our own powers of absorption, and the belief that sooner or later—the exact time being unimportant—all the populations on the continent, whatever their present condition, must gravitate towards our political system, and ultimately be merged in it." A Canadian historian notes, "This fantasy acquired a certain theoretical dignity in the term 'political gravitation'"—a term coined long before by John Quincy Adams with reference to Cuba. The addition of Alaska added a further "natural" geographic imperative; as the New York *World* put it in April 1867: "A gap in our possessions on the Pacific Coast will always be an eyesore to the nation, whose sense of symmetry will be offended by the ragged look of the map"—and thus the need to annex British Columbia. Such a perspective and conviction allowed Senator Sumner, chairman of the Foreign Relations Committee, to peddle the Alaska treaty as "a visible step in the occupation of the whole North American continent" as if such a "manifest destiny" were a wholly benign,

85. Ottawa: The New Capitol of the New Confederation.
Views of Ottawa—like views of Washington—almost invariably focus on the central buildings
of government seated in handsome grounds on their commanding heights—in the case of
Ottawa on the bluffs overlooking the boundary river between the two earlier Canadas. This
photograph (c. 1866) offers a more telling picture, suggests W. L. Morton: "The Parliament
Buildings, one of the great expressions of the Gothic Revival [—so unlike Washington—], rise
above the shanty town of Ottawa, as the Confederation rose out of the provincial politics of the
colonies." (Courtesy of the National Archives of Canada, C-6998)

beneficent, and natural process to be welcomed by all. It was in the face of such
prevailing assumptions on the part of their powerful neighbor that the British and
the French of Canada could find common cause and both seek "la survivance" in
the framework of Confederation.

Thus, the northern borderlands of North America had been further extended
and redefined. The character and meaning of the elongated boundary line remained uncertain in several respects, but important changes were apparent. Two
great imperial systems had withdrawn from the continent, the one completely and
the other by major reductions in its powers and positions. The Russians had
unhesitatingly turned over their American realm to the one great indigenous
power of the continent. Britain had calculatingly empowered a set of its colonial

offspring (including an old adopted captive) to sustain a continued presence and a counter to that indigenous power. Although Americans did not have—nor would ever have—much understanding of the nuances of British imperial devolution, the creation of the Dominion of Canada would eventually be regarded as one of the great exhibits of the British genius, sharpened by the experience of the American Revolution, for gradual adjustment to changing realities (as W. L. Morton commented—with some bitterness as a native Manitoban—regarding the decision to assign to Canada the task of negotiating with the Hudson's Bay Company: "One of the greatest transfers of territory and sovereignty in history was conducted as a mere transaction in real estate"). And so two sovereignties persisted in this transcontinental borderland, both profoundly changed. One was a callow, shaky, experimental structure, as yet uncertain in extent or character, but drawing upon several of the oldest European systems and implantations in North America. The other was a forcibly restored Union, powerful and expansive, certain to fill out its existing continental framework, and destined—so many of its leaders and people said—to include a great deal more.

3. Hispanic Borderlands

In early 1861, the liberal regime in Mexico, triumphant but bankrupt after three years of civil war, turned to the United States for help and example. The reform-minded President Benito Juárez sent an emissary to President-elect Abraham Lincoln in Springfield to affirm amicable relations, invite American investment, and seek loans to fend off European powers clamoring for the repayment of debts. American expansionist appetites were not forgotten, but liberal leaders tended to blame the cessions of 1848 and 1853 on corrupt and archaic Mexican institutions and officials, and they were ready to try another tactic. "The best means of impeding annexation," stated their young emissary, "is to open the country to the United States, conceeding [sic] them all reasonable privileges, with the objective of making annexation unnecessary and undesirable." Such a stance was generally compatible with the new administration in the United States, and Secretary of State Seward's policy sought a stable Mexico under liberal control while warning that government against Southern expansionists. Nevertheless, the voracious American appetite could not be quelled. The U.S. minister negotiating a set of treaties with Mexico relating to postal services, extradition (as a weapon against border raids), and loans sought to include the annexation of Baja California and a lien on Chihuahua, Sonora, and Sinaloa as security for the money. This generated strenuous debates in the American president's cabinet and the Senate committee. The loan treaty was eventually presented—and rejected—without these territorial provisions, but the acquisition of Baja California kept cropping up in subsequent negotiations.

With the outbreak of civil war in the United States, the Confederate government sent rival agents to curry Mexican favor, hoping for at least neutrality, if not
recognition. In spite of reassurances from these Southerners, the Mexican government was cool to their cause and appropriately skeptical of their intentions (the
principal Confederate agent cautioned his Richmond superiors not to be misled by
his diplomatic language to the Mexicans, for "no one is more impressed than the
writer with the great truth that, *Southward* the Star of Empire takes its way"). The
Confederates soon turned to dissident Mexican conservatives and European monarchical interventionists as more natural allies.

Mexico's suspension of payment on foreign debts together with continued concern about American designs upon the country (and, for the moment, American
preoccupation with its internal conflict) emboldened Great Britain, Spain, and
France to join in a military expedition to seize Veracruz (the leading port and
customs station) and extract payment. Soon after attaining that foothold, however, disagreement over the purpose and mode of this intervention caused Britain
and Spain to withdraw and exposed the larger designs of Napoleon III. His motives
were complex, arising from conditions in France and Europe as well as opportunities discerned abroad, but he openly sought to reestablish a strong position "in
the center of America" to block the United States from expanding and dominating
the countries and commerce of Hispanic America and the Caribbean. He assumed
that *Latin* Americans would be strongly attracted to French leadership in creating a
global commercial network in competition with the British. The French poured in
more than 30,000 troops and after long sieges and bloody battles drove the Juárez
government from Mexico City. A cooperative clique of Mexican monarchists
agreed to invite Napoleon's choice, young Archduke Ferdinand Maximilian of
Austria, to assume the throne, which he did in April 1864. The refugee Juárez
government was then seated in Monterrey, but though harassed and pushed from
one city to another in the northern provinces, it continued to be recognized by the
United States as the legitimate government of Mexico. Meanwhile, European
states had recognized Maximilian, and Confederate agents and opportunists
sought to further their interests with these insurgents. One of the more elaborate
plans, presented to Napoleon III in Paris by former senator William Gwin of
California, sought to create a large immigrant colony of miners and farmers in
Sonora and Chihuahua; this was soon countered by a French scheme to establish
thousands of French soldier-colonists in the northern Mexican states as a barrier to
American infiltration and a protection of Maximilian.

Little was accomplished before the Confederacy, and Maximilian's Mexico
began to crumble. The United States had in various ways announced its opposition
to any such monarchical imposition, and once its own war was over, both popular
and official pressure was intensified (General Grant publicly stated that "he did not
consider the Civil War completely terminated while the French remained in

Mexico" and ordered 50,000 troops to the Rio Grande). Most leaders in Washington, however, did not want to add any such foreign complication to the immense tasks facing the nation. The critical feature was the work of the Mexicans themselves. It was now clear that the imperial regime had little popular support, the Juárez government had doggedly persevered and was in control of the northern states, and Napoleon's vainglorious scheme was proving to be painfully expensive. The French decided to withdraw, but Maximilian, quite misguided about his popularity, elected to remain. For a brief interlude, a major infusion of support from the defeated Confederacy seemed possible. A month after Appomattox, before Union officers arrived to disarm and disband Confederate forces in the Transmississippi Department, a group of officers and political leaders met in Marshall, Texas, to organize an army of 15,000 to march into Mexico in support of the monarchists. Various delays (and the failure of Jefferson Davis to reach them) undermined the scheme, but a few thousand, including several generals and former governors, did march across Texas to Monterrey, where they were received by an imperial Mexican official. By the time the leaders of this band got to Mexico City, Matthew F. Maury, who had served as a Confederate agent in Europe, had arrived there and was busy arranging for the establishment of Confederate colonies in Mexico. Maximilian named Maury commissioner of immigration, and by December 1865 Maury was setting up agents in the Southern states and larger northern American cities to publicize the availability of choice lands at nominal cost and to point to a number of colonies already under way. The main focus was to be on a series of new civil and military settlements spaced along the corridor of the uncompleted railroad between Veracruz and the capital. The principal one, Carlota (named for Maximilian's wife), flourished momentarily from the sudden infusion of American capital and energy, then faded away as these exiles fled a resurgent Juarista Mexico or simply drifted back to home ground. In fact, only a few thousand Americans came into Mexico at this time, and few of these even attempted to settle in as colonists. In the wake of the first Confederate exodus from Texas, Union forces occupied every port and border crossing to prohibit such emigration. In the larger view we can see such movements as episodic expressions of the traumas and uncertainties on both sides of the border, and they faded quickly as order was reimposed in each country.

In May 1867, Maximilian surrendered to Mexican forces (augmented by a few thousand Americans, mostly former Union troops recruited by the promise of good pay and land bonuses); in June, he was tried and executed; on July 15, the republican government was reinstalled in the National Palace, and in October, Benito Juárez was elected to a third term. Although more than 100,000 lives had been lost (including 25,000 French and other European soldiery) and the country was bankrupt and in a shambles, historians today look back on this violent experience as a turning point: "Modern Mexican history begins with the liberal victory of 1867. In a very real sense the republic became a nation." That in itself would be a major change in this tumultuous borderland, and, at a different scale, other changes were also under way: American promoters and investors were besieging the Mexican government for concessions to build railroads, establish steamship lines, open mines (already obtained for the rich Nacozari ores of Sonora), and tap the oil resources of Tabasco. Given the general attitude and the desperate needs of the Mexican regime, it seemed likely that a new phase in borderland relations was under way. To many Americans it also seemed likely that such concessions surely presaged further geopolitical changes. As American agents repeatedly assured congressional committees: "We will have a hold in the future on Mexico, by settling all her immense vacant lands with our people" and "in the course of time . . . the border states . . . will . . . segregate in due order of gravitation, peacefully into the American Union." Confidence in such benign expansionism was quite unaffected by the fact that for the moment—all through the 1860s—most of the boundary zone was dominated by the Apaches.

Havana, too, became crowded with Confederate officers and politicians, planters and professionals, some with their Black slaves in tow. This cosmopolitan colonial city was of course long used to political exiles, and there were plenty of Anglo-American residents of Southern sympathies to aid in the welcome. On the surface Cuba might seem a relatively stable and prosperous place, but tensions were endemic throughout the Spanish Antilles, and the North American struggle had intensified them. The population was nearing 1.5 million, and the island now produced 40 percent of the sugar entering the world market, but the increasing dominance of "the semimechanized, capitalistic, export-oriented sugar plantation" had made the whole system and society more rigid and vulnerable. Field labor was becoming a problem. Imports of African slaves had nearly ceased, and some planters had turned to importing indentured laborers from China. The forced abolition of slavery in the United States reverberated loudly across city and countryside. Liberal leaders had long called for emancipation, with compensation to the owners, and the collapse of the Louisiana sugar industry and huge economic losses of those American planters was a powerful example, yet, like its recent Anglo-American counterpart in the Cotton Kingdom, the ruling oligarchy could see no way to change the system without wrecking the economy and endangering society. Cuban reformers, at home and abroad, differed on how to advance their cause. Some continued to look to the United States for help, though few now openly supported eventual annexation. Spain's attempts to reassert its imperial power, as in its brief joint venture into Mexico, reassumption of authority over the Dominican Republic, and pressures applied upon various South American states, generally reinvigorated nationalism in the remnant American colonies. In 1866 the new Republican Society of Cuba and Puerto Rico, founded in New York, demanded "independence for the Spanish Antilles, and the absolute liberty for all its inhabitants without distinction of race or color." Minor uprisings in Puerto Rico warned of the possibility of explosive change.

The confused situation on the island of Hispaniola attested more directly to the smoldering instabilities in this borderland. In 1843 a creole uprising had liberated the eastern (Hispanic) half of the island from Haitian forces. The newly established Dominican Republic (but commonly referred to as Santo Domingo for long after) had plenty of reason to regard Haiti as its main foe and looked to foreign powers for aid and protection. The Haitians, too, had ample reason to be obsessed with their own security and feared that any foreign presence anywhere on the island might lead to attempts to conquer and reenslave them, and they repeatedly invaded the Hispanic sector to forestall any such possibility. Both states were thus ruled by dictators under a constant state of emergency. In 1861 the Dominican president requested Spain to reassume sovereignty over his bankrupt country and provide protection (and money). Spain did so, but within a few years Dominican resistance to, and the spiraling costs of, such imperial rule caused Spain to withdraw and a new local leader to turn elsewhere for succor. There ensued a remarkable attempt to lure a reluctant United States into annexing the country.

American geopolitical interest in the island was not new. In 1846 a naval officer had been sent to assess the long embayment of Samaná as a possible West Indian base, and official negotiations for the lease of that area were held in 1853 (prompting another Haitian invasion). By that date American concerns were prompted by the new strategic importance of routes to California, as well as by outright expansionism and a muddle of more personal interests. The initiatives of the 1860s were generated largely by a few individuals. A small clique of resident American speculators connived with a corrupt dictator to engineer at least the sale or lease of Samaná Bay (for a large payment), at most the annexation of the entire country as a formal territory of the United States (with assumption of its debts and a large payment for title to a long list of national facilities). Such an audacious plot would require skillful lobbying in Washington, but the overture was sufficient that Secretary of State Seward paid a brief visit to Santo Domingo in January 1866. The topic was kept alive and three years later would receive a great boost from the avid support of the new American president, Ulysses S. Grant.

4. The Afro-American Archipelago

Seward was certainly interested in the possibility of obtaining Samaná Bay, but his stop was very brief because he was en route to inspect a better prospect he was already quietly negotiating for: the Danish West Indies. This remnant of seventeenth-century sugar and slave trade days consisted of three main islands and many small ones within the larger Virgin Islands group. Lying fifty miles east of Puerto Rico they were pivotal between the Greater and Lesser Antilles and strategic to several main passageways through this insular screen. They commanded not only "the best position," according to a Navy Department report, but "the best island, that of St. Thomas, is well-known to many officers of our Navy as having a fine harbor, capacious, secure, and easy of ingress and egress" (fig. 86). Seward had initiated the idea, and Denmark agreed to sell only after a long negotiation over the price and provisions for an island plebiscite, together with the pressures from its deteriorating European situation (in 1866 the king of Denmark had been closed out of Schleswig and Holstein by an aggressive Prussian-dominated German con-

86. St. Thomas, Danish West Indies, c. 1843.

The capacious sheltered harbor that so interested American officials is readily apparent in Walford Thomas Bellairs's depiction of this cosmopolitan crossroads. At the center a Danish flag hangs limply over the large fortress of seventeenth-century slave-trading days, when St. Thomas thrived more as a neutral and free-haven marketplace amid contending imperial systems than as a substantial center of the African trade. (Courtesy of the I. N. Phelps Stokes Collection, Miriam & Ira D. Wallach Division of Art, Prints and Photographs, the New York Public Library, Astor, Lenox and Tilden Foundations)

VIEW OF THE TOWN OF ST THOMAS,
in the West Indies
taken from the Residence of P. Van Heerden Esq.
From a Sketch by Lieut. W. T. Bellairs R.N.

federation). A treaty to transfer the islands, excepting St. Croix (which lies somewhat apart), to the United States for $7.5 million was signed by the two nations in October 1867. There was little support in Congress or among the public for such a purchase, however. The House served notice that it would not likely vote the money, and the treaty was simply set aside by the Senate and, despite the Danish minister's urgent lobbying, eventually died.

The United States did not add these small islands to its territories at this time (as it would do fifty years later) for many reasons. Suffice it to note that it was an extremely contested period in domestic politics, and Seward, who had so personally and closely managed the affair, had many enemies. Furthermore, it was easy to ridicule the price for two small islands when a few months earlier Seward had obtained the whole of Alaska for less. That the United States would be not only purchasing a valuable harbor but conferring its citizenship on 15,000 Blacks (or 40,000 if they also took St. Croix) does not seem to have been a major issue in the debates over the Danish West Indies. Such a small population separated at such a distance presumably would cause no disturbance to the national society. The concurrent proposal to take over the Dominican Republic did, however, give some pause: "It may be convenient to have a naval station in the West Indies," said *Harper's Weekly,* "but is it wise to buy it by adding to our population nearly a million of creoles and West Indian negroes, and by the assumption of nobody knows what debts and liabilities" (actually a gross exaggeration of the population; official figures of the time gave about 600,000, whereas modern studies suggest no more than half that). Such comments remind us again of that great geocultural pattern that Anglo-Americans tend to overlook: the existence of a large Afro-American world, within which the Black population of the United States constitutes only the northern sector (see fig. 84). Even though that "world" was not a coherent and closely interactive context for the Blacks themselves and there were marked differences in sociopolitical character between the mainland and the islands, there were important reverberations between these two broad sectors.

While the United States was emancipating nearly 4 million slaves amid the chaos of a bloody civil war, the northern European colonial powers were just completing the peaceful emancipation of well more than a million slaves in tropical America. After a long and famous agitation, abolition was put into effect in all British colonies on August 1, 1834. The concurrent movement in France had to await the political revolution of 1848; Denmark also ended slavery in that year, while the Dutch gave way grudgingly in 1863. Thus, when the United States was struggling to formulate a postwar program of "reconstruction," post-emancipation programs had been in operation for more than thirty years in some islands. In spite of crucial differences, there were also some obvious broad similarities between the two situations: in each case emancipation was imposed upon local societies by external powers; as might be expected, the planters everywhere hoped to continue their production system and social position with minimal adjustment, and impelled by racial prejudice and fears, central governments and local officials offered considerable help in support of such continuity. The British provided £20 million in compensation to slaveowners (£3 million of which was applied to Cape Colony and Mauritius), but in spite of the pleas of abolitionists, no compensation was paid to ·the slaves themselves. In fact, the act that abolished slavery did not fully emancipate the slaves but rather converted them for a period of four to six years into "apprentices," compelled to work most of their time without pay for their former owners. The avowed intent was to ensure continuity in economy and prepare slaves for life as docile, hardworking wage laborers. The results varied greatly, reflecting the very different human geographic situations. In Bermuda, where there were no plantations, the local assembly simply dismissed the apprentice system as a nuisance and immediately emancipated all slaves. In the Bahamas, apprenticeships were mainly imposed on newly arrived Africans deposited there from captured slave ships, as a means of "civilizing" them. But almost everywhere else this program for a formal transition from slavery to freedom was tried, and the starkly different results in two of the foremost sugar-producing islands is instructive.

Barbados became "the outstanding example of continuity" for the simple reason that the freed Blacks had little alternative. There was no unused land available to them on that densely populated, intensively cultivated small island, and they remained dependent upon the planters for wages and subsistence (mostly from plots assigned to them by the owners). In Jamaica the planters also tried their best to maintain the estate system with minimal change but had little success. Sugar production was confined to the richest of the intermittent coastal lowlands, there was much unoccupied land, and the freed slaves quickly moved in upon it, disdaining the harsh drudgery of the canefields. "Long before the end of the period of apprenticeship (1838), Jamaican slaves were producing not only most of their own subsistence but also an astonishingly large surplus of foods, the bigger part of which ended on the tables of free peoples, including the planters themselves." As more and more labor-short, debt-ridden estates were abandoned, most of those lands were also occupied, often through the philanthropy of Baptist missionaries who sponsored many "free villages." Thus, within a short while Jamaica was transformed from a premier sugar colony worked by more than 300,000 slaves into what was primarily an Afro-American "peasant society" (the term takes on special meanings in the West Indies) with a few residual enclaves of European-owned plantations. In 1866, after having been frightened into a brutal and much-criticized response to a small rebellion, the beleaguered ruling White oligarchy voted to dissolve the local assembly and turn the colony back to the queen—just the reverse of the concurrent political change in Canada—and eventually several of the other island governments did the same.

Such contrasting developments were also to be found among the lesser islands and added to the already-marked diversities and dynamics of this chronically tumultuous world. While Jamaica and some of the other more mountainous islands were being transformed into Black peasant societies, White planters were busy expanding sugar production on the fresh lands of Trinidad, British Guiana, and Surinam and had begun their worldwide search for cheap and tractable labor. Because newly freed West Indians had generally resisted such labor recruiters, indentured immigrants from Madeira, Mauritius, India, Java, and China were already present. And continuing through these years were the utterly divergent developments of the two largest island societies of the West Indies, making Windward Passage, the narrow strait between them, a sociopolitical fault line of ominous tension. On the west lay Cuba, the last great bastion of Spanish imperialism and slavery, with its enormous prospering and expanding sugar production system, and all the while, fifty some miles across the water to the east lay Haiti, the only independent Afro-American state, now formally recognized by the great powers (and, importantly, by the Vatican). Now wholly a peasant society, it was the only place where a once enormously prosperous sugar industry had been completely destroyed. Haiti was ruled by a militantly defensive dictatorship (Whites were prohibited from owning land), but its tiny educated elite reached out to assert the aspirations of all Afro-America, proclaiming a Black ideology of equality and dignity in the world.

For the moment the United States was too obsessed with internal problems to pay much attention to this scattering of minor colonies and singular state. Yet the very nature of the greatest of those problems displayed the Republic as part of that larger world. The drastic, chaotic upheaval that Americans were now forced to deal with—the question of what to do with 4 million former slaves, with thousands of bankrupt planters, with vital contradictory demands for land and labor, with "the future position of the Negro race in North America"—exhibited the United States as but the northern half of an Afro-American World wherein abolition and emancipation, national programs and uncontrollable consequences, contradictory basic interests between Blacks and Whites, cultural philosophies and their propagation were already variously on view in the southern, insular half of that world. It is in such terms, more basic than a geopolitical interest in a few naval bases, that this long, thin archipelago curving nearly 2 thousand miles across the tropical seas continues to be part of the essential, intelligible field for our perspective on the shaping of America.

And yet, though it is important to see this Afro-America as a vast geographic pattern encompassing more than 6 million Blacks and to recognize the problems, processes, and historical movements common to that whole, we must, as always, note the human geographic differences within it as well. With its 4.5 million Blacks, the United States was much the largest sector of that Afro-America, yet, quite in contrast to those on the islands, these millions were locked into the body of a powerful nation and federation and, by all evidence, seemed destined to be a marked minority subordinated within an assertively ever-stronger White society.

5. A Wider Presence

"The display of the flag of the Union in foreign parts and in distant seas" serves as "an admonition of the naval power of the Republic," stated Secretary of the Navy Gideon Welles in December 1866, and he was pleased to report that in the aftermath of wartime reductions American foreign squadrons had all been re-established. He detailed the distribution of sixty-eight armed vessels among seven squadrons assigned to cruise particular portions of the Global Sea, covering to-gether all but the Indian Ocean. During the course of the year these vessels had "visited nearly every principal port of the world"—and a great many minor ones. Some calls were occasions of foreign receptions and festivities that reinforced amicable diplomatic relations, but the principal purpose of this fleet was to protect American shipping and to declare implicitly that the United States "would be prompt and efficient in vindicating the rights and interests of our countrymen" wherever they might be.

American ships had been plying and patrolling the high seas for many years, but signs of important changes were now apparent. Most obvious was the rapid increase in steam-powered vessels. The Civil War had dramatically emphasized a new geographical reality: the need for coal at convenient intervals on any cruising course. Union warships on blockade and patrol against commerce raiders had often depended on and had difficulties in procuring supplies from foreign ports. Secretary of the Navy Welles commissioned an inquiry into the matter, and the ensuing report of 1866 spoke of the new era in world communications, in which speed was important and time valuable, and predictably stressed the need to have "our own *coaling stations*" (supplied with our "best quality of anthracite coal") at intervals of "seven to ten days steaming" as "colonies under our own flag." Priority should be given to the West Indies, and it was the admiral-author of this report who nomi-nated St. Thomas as eminently eligible.

Although Gideon Welles did not prove to be a vigorous advocate of such acquisitions, a fellow cabinet member, William H. Seward, saw such objectives as perfectly in accord with his geopolitical visions. This energetic New Yorker, secre-tary of State from 1861 to 1869, has been characterized as "an expansionist of hemispheric voracity," but there was a system and selectivity to Seward's appetite that differentiated him from the more rabid "manifest destiny" types so prominent in the 1840s and 1850s. In general, as we have seen, he believed strongly in the benign power of cultural diffusion and "political gravitation" on the continent—in the power of republican principles, democratic institutions, and material prosperity to induce among neighboring peoples and politics an ever-closer convergence with the United States. More than this, however, Seward saw the United States as destined to be a center of world power, a great source of expanding commerce, and a primary seat of transoceanic globe-girdling networks. Such developments were already well under way, and he argued the need for appropriate geopolitical support.

Creating an effectively transcontinental nation was the first priority. As a senator Seward had been a vigorous advocate of a Pacific railroad, and as secretary of State he gave much attention to securing American dominance over isthmian sea routes. In addition to negotiating for a West Indian base, he obtained a freedom of transit treaty from Nicaragua and prodded American capitalists to take serious interest in a Panama canal (American warships were always present off each terminus of that route, "prepared to give assistance and protection to the immense numbers of our countrymen, and the vast wealth crossing the Isthmus"). Seward was especially interested in China and the Pacific. He would have dearly loved to have obtained the Hawaiian Islands but deferred action in the face of political opposition and public indifference. Some American initiatives in that realm were undertaken. The postmaster general negotiated a contract with the Pacific Mail Steamship Company to build four vessels and commence, by January 1, 1867, monthly service between San Francisco, Honolulu, and Hong Kong. In 1866 the newly reorganized Hydrographic Office of the Navy Department began intensive study of the northern Pacific, and in the following year an American naval officer took possession of Midway Islands, an uninhabited set of atolls 1,300 miles west of Honolulu, a potential outpost in the central Pacific opposite the long reach of the Aleutians far to the north. In spite of Seward's tireless and skillful efforts, this tiny speck in the vast ocean and that huge but remote and marginal expanse in the boreal extremities of the continent were the only additions to U.S. territory at this time.

For all this far-ranging display of the flag and talk of Seward and other visionaries about America as an emergent world power, the United States remained in many ways a detached provincial outlier of the centuries-old seats of major power. Not only was its navy a relatively limited force fit for little more than coastal defense and police work, but those in charge seemed to look inward and backward, preferring wood and sail and actually prohibiting any routine use of coal and steam as an economic waste. This stance reflected not merely governmental austerity but, more basically, a confident reliance on the sufficiency of the great ocean moats, a *continental* strategy responding to the recession of the European imperial presence (and therefore of the likelihood of territorial disputes), and a general disinterest in extracontinental expansions.

Even more telling was the marked decline in the relative position of the American merchant marine. The war had disrupted normal services and taken a heavy toll of ships, but more important was the failure of the usually enterprising Americans to compete effectively for the North Atlantic trade. The famous American clipper ships had reached their apogee in the 1850s concurrent with a generation of experiments with steam-powered oceangoing vessels. While America was engulfed in war, improvements continued to be made in Europe, so that by the later 1860s iron-hulled steamships with screw propellers were setting new standards for speed, comfort, capacity, and regularity of service. British companies dominated the North Atlantic run (and most others), but German and French firms were strong competitors. The economics and profitability of the premier passenger services were much debated and mail subsidies were perhaps critical. It was especially revealing, therefore, that the postmaster general recommended that rather than subsidize an American carrier, foreign companies be encouraged to bid for U.S. mail contracts on the North Atlantic run. His reasoning invoked the old governmental difficulty of making geographic choices among competitors: to choose a single American port would cause an outcry from others (and could not provide the most efficient service); to select several ports and companies would cost too much (and create a bad precedent of spreading favors). In larger perspective we can again recognize a distinct Continental America at work here. Americans had been in the forefront of the development of steam propulsion on water and on land, and their immense system of inland waterways and railroad services was unparalleled in scale and rapidly expanding within—and soon across—North America. But the nation could not generate anything like the same interest in oceanic services. Unlike canals and railroads, shipping could not be closely tied to land speculation and population growth. The famous Yankee fleet was a regional specialization and could not attract national support. It was generally agreed that continued involvement in the fishery and expanding coastwise services (reserved by law to American vessels) should be enough to sustain a considerable merchant fleet. America would grow to greatness within its own continent.

In fact, however, American development was, as always, deeply, variously, and essentially bound up with Europe. In spite of its great expanse and intrinsic power, this Continental America depended heavily on Europe for capital and many industrial goods, and the great bulk of its exports were raw materials and foodstuffs sent to the central market of the world economic system. Henry Carey's rhetorical complaint, voiced in the summer of 1867, carried a ring of truth: "I pray you now to take up a railroad map of the Union, and mark the fact that all our great roads are merely spokes of a wheel whose hub is found in Liverpool." And it was still being vitalized by the influx of Europeans. After a brief slackening at the start of the war, the human tide across the Atlantic was running as strongly as ever and had received a special welcome from Abraham Lincoln: "I regard our emigrants as one of the principal replenishing streams which are appointed by Providence to repair the ravages of internal war, and its wastes of national strength and health." A special "Act to Encourage Immigration" established a commissioner and program of promotion (including exemption from military service until the newcomer applied for citizenship). In 1865–67 more than three-quarters of a million Europeans arrived, with Germany contributing the largest number. (Competition for the carriage of such volumes was a major spur to European shipping companies.) And, as always, much more than mere numbers were important. The impact of this immigration must be measured in terms of the kinds of people who elected to come, their motivations and objectives, their national, ethnic, linguistic, and religious identities, their talents and energies, their skills and professions, the ways they continuously altered the content of American society and challenged its powers of assimilation. And there was, all the while, an intensifying traffic in ideas, in cultural diffusions resulting in adoptions and adaptations, imitations and innovations, complicating the ever-lively topic of America's self-identity as a people, a nation, a culture. Whatever the measure of such things might yield, whatever the balance of forces might be, there was no question that the United States was a continuation as well as an invention, the most vigorously creative offspring in a relentlessly expansive Neo-European World.

Such things demand attention in any geographical perspective on the shaping of America, but this can better be given with a wider lens and a shift in stance—even a short step back in time—so as to bring both different details and broader patterns into focus. These can then be traced through the emergence of a fully transcontinental—and transoceanic—America.

Sources of Quotations

PART ONE

p. 4 Jefferson, *Writings*, vol. 8, 3
p. 6 Jefferson, *Writings*, vol. 5, 225
p. 6 Spanish governor: Robertson, *Louisiana*, 297
p. 7 "northern boundary of the 'Mississippi interest'": Whitaker, *Mississippi Question*, 153
p. 7 "rival port of Natchez": Whitaker, *Mississippi Question*, 147
p. 9 Jefferson, *Writings*, vol. 5, 219, 472–73
p. 9 "Nature has decided": Jefferson, *Writings*, vol. 5, 219
p. 10 "There is on the globe": Jefferson, *Writings*, vol. 8, 144
p. 10 Livingston: *Annals of Congress*, 2d Cong., 2d sess., 1070
p. 11 "not sanguine": Jefferson, *Writings*, vol. 8, 229
p. 13 White (Delaware), "new, immense, unbounded world": *Annals of Congress*, 8th Cong., 1st sess., 33–34
p. 13 Breckinridge: *Annals of Congress*, 8th Cong., 1st sess., 60
p. 14 Jefferson, *Writings*, vol. 8, 344
p. 14 "inhabitants would readily agree": Madison, *Annals of Congress*, 7th Cong., 2d sess., 1106
p. 14 "be so unwise as to prefer": Wright (Delaware), *Annals of Congress*, 8th Cong., 1st sess., 44
p. 14 Adams: quoted in Brown, *Constitutional History*, 130
p. 14 treaty declaration on "inhabitants of the ceded territory": Brown, *Constitutional History*, 65
p. 14 amalgamate with Americans: Jefferson, *Writings*, vol. 8, 250
p. 15 "I propose . . . enlisting 30,000 volunteers": Jefferson, *Writings*, vol. 9, 9–10
p. 17 Dargo, *Jefferson's Louisiana*, 171, 174
p. 17 Quincy: *Annals of Congress*, 11th Cong., 3d sess., 524ff.
p. 22 "to ever consider themselves the equal of whites": quoted in Crété, *Daily Life*, 80
p. 23 Humboldt, *Cuba*, 98
p. 26 congressional committee on East Florida: *Annals of Congress*, 7th Cong., 2d sess., 373
p. 28 "Creek troubles": Cotterill, *Southern Indians*, 181
p. 28 Jackson to Monroe: quoted in Tebeau, *History of Florida*, 110
p. 29 Adams: quoted in Bailey, *Diplomatic History*, 172
p. 32 Jefferson on Cuba: *Writings*, vol. 9, 251, 252, 125
p. 33 Humboldt, *Cuba*, 110
p. 34 Adams on Cuba: *Writings*, vol. 7, 372–73
p. 41 "pass and repass by land or inland navigation": quoted in Burt, *United States, Great Britain and British North America*, 146
p. 44 boundary "non-existent in . . . daily life": Hansen, *Mingling*, 73
p. 44 boundary "all but disappeared": Williamson, *Vermont in Quandary*, 242
p. 44 Burt on "American" character of movement: *United States, Great Britain and British North America*, 183
p. 45 "far from rejecting all things American": Errington and Rawlyk, "Loyalist-Federalist Alliance," 160–61
p. 46 need to "cut off the communication between foreign nations and the Indians": Mr. Findley (Pennsylvania), quoted in Pratt, *Expansionists of 1812*, 21
p. 47 Jefferson, *Writings*, vol. 9, 366
p. 47 "defended by only a few regular soldiers": Craig, *Upper Canada*, 67
p. 47 "Tory revolt": Stagg, *Mr. Madison's War*, 262
p. 47 British army "were eating beef provided by American contractors": Sir George Prevost, quoted in Burt, *United States, Great Britain and British North America*, 322
p. 47 "trunk" and "the leaves and branches" of British power: Burt, *United States, Great Britain and British North America*, 325

p. 50 Brebner, *North Atlantic Triangle*, 92

p. 50 "speedy settlement of the Colony": quoted in Craig, *Upper Canada*, 124–25

p. 51 Thomas Rolph: quoted in Tomkins, "Understanding Ourselves," 77–78

p. 52 Montreal as "the heart of the country": Governor Dalhousie, quoted in Creighton, *Empire of the St. Lawrence*, 214

p. 52 "conscious symbols of British Protestant authority": Harris and Warkentin, *Canada before Confederation*, 103

p. 53 "It was a dazzling conception": Craig, *Upper Canada*, 105

p. 54 Kingston, that "sober, granite town": Roberts, *Montreal*, 177

p. 54 "If the British Government intends to maintain its hold": *Durham Report*, 291, 294

p. 55 "the deadly animosity": *Durham Report*, 16

p. 55 "It is to elevate them from that inferiority": *Durham Report*, 292

p. 55 on the example of Louisiana: *Durham Report*, 299, 303

p. 56 "the great natural channel of the St. Lawrence": *Durham Report*, 319

p. 56 Creighton, *Empire of the St. Lawrence*, 334

p. 56 "two totally different traditions of vernacular architecture": Harris and Warkentin, *Canada before Confederation*, 94

p. 57 "influence of the United States surrounds": *Durham Report*, 311

p. 57 "there was nowhere any substantial group": Brebner, *North Atlantic Triangle*, 144

p. 57 "the determination not to be American": Tomkins, "Understanding Ourselves," 77

p. 57 "that they were more British than they actually were": Brebner, *North Atlantic Triangle*, 143

p. 57 Bell, "Loyalist Tradition," 30

p. 58 "If we wish to prevent the extension of this influence": *Durham Report*, 311–12

p. 58 "American Revolution created not one country, but two": Bell, "Loyalist Tradition," 22

p. 59 Louisiana "but little known": *Annals of Congress*, 8th Cong., 2d sess., 1504

p. 59 Allen, *Passage Through the Garden*, 55

p. 63 "plains rich in meat": Morton, *Manitoba*, 39

p. 65 Jefferson, "to find the shortest and most convenient route": Jackson, *Letters . . . Lewis & Clark*, 669

p. 65 Jefferson's instructions to Lewis: Jackson, *Letters . . . Lewis & Clark*, 61

p. 65 Lewis's report to Jefferson: Jackson, *Letters . . . Lewis & Clark*, 319–22

p. 67 St. Louis newspaper report: Rollins, *Oregon Trail*, lxvii

p. 68 "bounds drawn with . . . magnificent freehand": Morton, *Manitoba*, 45

p. 71 "because of their immense power": Jackson, *Letters . . . Lewis & Clark*, 166

p. 71 Billington, *Westward Expansion*, 385

p. 73 "more like a geographer than a fur trader": Gabriel Franchère, quoted in Meinig, *Great Columbia Plain*, 50

p. 74 "Westward of the Stony Mountains": from 1818 Convention, quoted in Van Zandt, *Boundaries*, 21

p. 75 "cause an exploring expedition" proposal: *Register of Debates in Congress*, 20th Cong., 2d sess., 153

p. 75 Brown, *Historical Geography*, 369

p. 76 Pike and Long on the "Great Desert": quoted in Goetzmann, *Army Exploration*, 43

p. 78 Jefferson, *Writings*, vol. 8, 249

p. 78 "expansion with honor": Berkhofer, *White Man's Indian*, 134

p. 78 on John Sevier: Mooney, *Historical Sketch*, 219

p. 78 More, *Utopia*, 67; initial reference from Fried, "Land Tenure, Geography and Ecology"

p. 78 Washington: *Writings*, vol. 27, 138; in Meinig, *Shaping of America*, vol. 1, 408

p. 79 Jefferson: *Writings* (1803), vol. 8, 194

p. 80 Jefferson to Northwest chiefs: *Writings*, vol. 8, 234

p. 80 "to promote civilization among friendly Indian tribes": *Am. St. P.: Indian Affairs*, vol. 2, 325

p. 80 Prucha, *Great Father*, vol. 1, 146

p. 81 Monroe, "no tribe or people have a right to withhold": quoted in Prucha, *Great Father*, vol. 1, 149

p. 81 Monroe's proposal for removal: *Niles National Register*, vol. 27, 237

p. 83 Algonkian movement to keep "out of the meshes of the settled life": Spicer, *Short History*, 77

p. 86 Cherokee chiefs, Calhoun's warning, and Cherokee reply: Am. *St. P.: Indian Affairs*, vol. 2, 473, 474

p. 88 Jackson, Indian tribes "are a conquered & dependent people": quoted in Abel, "Proposals for an Indian State," 385

p. 90 "to gain possession of the blacks among them": Hudson, *Southeastern Indians*, 465

p. 90 American general on Seminole War: Prucha, *Great Father*, vol. 1, 232

p. 92 Vinton (Ohio): *Gales & Seaton's Register of Debates* (February 20, 1828), 1579

p. 92 War Department commission to "examine the country": S. Doc. 512, 23d Cong., 1st sess., quoted in Garver, "Role of U.S. Army," 198, 200

p. 96 "inroades and depredations": Agnew, *Fort Gibson*, 55, 73

p. 96 "intestine wars between the several tribes": Cherokee treaty, in Mooney, *Historical Sketch*, 119

p. 97 "the United States guarantee": Shawnee treaty, in Kappler, *Indian Affairs*, 333

p. 99 all quotations illustrating federal government commitments: Kappler, *Indian Affairs*

p. 101 "in common parlance" referred to as "the Frontier": Juricek, "American Usage of the Word 'Frontier,'" 24, quoting George Catlin

p. 102 "open a wide sweep of country": Indian Commissioner Orlando Brown (1849), quoted in Garver, "Role of U.S. Army," 472

p. 102 "experiment . . . had 'measurably failed'": Indian Commissioner George Manypennny (1853), quoted in Garver, "Role of U.S. Army," 468

p. 103 Indian titles to lands "had no foundation in antiquity": Abel, "Proposals for an Indian State," 412

p. 103 "discordant to the feelings of the people of the United States": Miner and Unrau, *End of Indian Kansas*, 14–15

p. 104 on naming Fort Vancouver: Governor Pelly to Canning (December 9, 1825), in Merk, *Oregon Question*, 29

p. 104 "surprising difference between the climates": Powell, *Hall J. Kelley*, 16

p. 104 "a climate much like England": Marcus Whitman, quoted in Gibson, *Farming the Frontier*, 130

p. 105 "the whole looks like a very neat and beautiful village": John Townsend (1832), quoted in Gibson, *Farming the Frontier*, 34

p. 108 on Kelley's "General Circular": Powell, *Hall J. Kelley*, 70ff.

p. 109 Wyeth, "the Americans are unknown as a nation": *Report of the Committee on Military Affairs* (1843), 27th Cong., 3d sess., H. Doc. 31, 13

p. 110 "the germe of a great State": *Report of the Committee on Military Affairs* (1843), 27th Cong., 3d sess., H. Doc. 31, 4–6

p. 110 "overcharged pictures of fertility": Rich, *Letters of McLoughlin*, vol. 2, 226

p. 110 directors to McLoughlin, "We consider it of the utmost importance": Galbraith, *Hudson's Bay Company*, 208

p. 111 instruction to Wilkes "to direct your course to the Northwest Coast": Wilkes, *Narrative*, vol. 1, xxvii

p. 111 "influx of strangers to the Columbia": London office to McLoughlin (31 December 1839), in Merk, *Oregon Question*, 246

p. 111 on the "terrors of the bar of the Columbia": Wilkes, *Narrative*, vol. 4, 293

p. 113 St. Louis newspaper quotations: "Documents Relating to Oregon Emigration"

p. 113 on the Methodist mission: Loewenberg, *Equality on the Oregon Frontier*, 234

p. 114 Melish on the Forty-ninth parallel: *Geographical Description*, 23

p. 115 Slacum on Puget Sound: *Memorial* (1837–38), 25th Cong., 2d sess., S. Doc. 2, 17

p. 115 Wilkes, "the entrance to the Columbia is impracticable": *Narrative*, vol. 5, 144

p. 117 "boundary that the finger of nature . . . pointed out": Merk, *Oregon Question*, 103

p. 120 "encroaching spirit of the U.S.": Earl Grey, colonial secretary, quoted in Galbraith, *Hudson's Bay Company*, 283

p. 122 British visitor on St. Paul as "the best specimen": Gluek, *Minnesota and the Manifest Destiny*, 99

p. 124 "The most indispensable condition for the security": Classen, *Thrust and Counterthrust*, 80

p. 125 Acadians as "fugitives," "neutrals," etc.: quoted in Classen, *Thrust and Counterthrust*, 18–19

p. 125 Maury on Upper Canada as a "dangerous . . . thrusting of foreign territory" and British response to "lust of the United States": Merk, *Oregon Question*, 69, 71

p. 126 "ingrained resistance to the United States": Careless, *Union of the Canadas*, 130

p. 130 "one of the greatest break-throughs": Sauer, "Personality of Mexico," 363

p. 133 Mora, comparison of United States and Mexico: Hale, *Mexican Liberalism*, 206

p. 134 United States had "no absolutely national character": Brack, *Mexico Views Manifest Destiny*, 23

p. 134 "Humboldt's book changed the concept of Mexico": Schmidt, *Roots of Lo Mexicano*, 17–18

p. 135 Clay, "carried Yankee ingenuity to its extreme": Weber, *Mexican Frontier*, 12

p. 135 "If we do not take the present opportunity to people Texas": Timmons, *Tadeo Ortiz*, 15

p. 138 Indians "better armed, better mounted": Weber, *Mexican Frontier*, 86

p. 138 Indians "like balls in a row": Weber, *Mexican Frontier*, 100

p. 142 San Francisco Bay "the most convenient, capacious": Prevost, quoted in Johansen and Gates, *Empire of the Columbia*, 116

p. 143 Wilkes on San Francisco Bay and California: *Narrative*, vol. 5, 152, 172

p. 144 Thompson, "It will be worth a war": *Recollections*, 235

p. 145 on San Francisco, "if these should be turned against us": Buchanan to Slidell, S. Ex. Doc. 52, 30th Cong., 1st sess., 1848, 79

p. 145 "Mexico has passed the boundary": Pletcher, *Diplomacy of Annexation*, 385

p. 145 "never any question that Polk regarded permanent possession": Pletcher, *Diplomacy of Annexation*, 422

p. 146 "the territorial cessions were like an amputation": Pletcher, *Diplomacy of Annexation*, 566

p. 147 "a large part of the American public was blundering": Pletcher, *Diplomacy of Annexation*, 551

p. 147 resolution "that the present war with Mexico should not": *Cong. Globe*, 30th Cong., 1st sess., 21 December 1847, 61

p. 150 New Mexicans as members of "the Mexican family": General Pacheco, 30th Cong., 1st sess., 1848, S. Ex. Doc. 52, 342

p. 150 "an inconsiderable portion of the Mexican people": Polk, in Richardson, *Messages and Papers*, vol. 4, 2391

p. 150 amendment to exclude "the State of New Mexico": S. Ex. Doc. 52, 30th Cong., 1st sess., 1848, 22

p. 150 Trist, arrangement "would inevitably give rise . . . to the old Mississippi question": S. Ex. Doc. 52, 30th Cong., 1st sess., 1848, 198

p. 154 Yucatán envoy suggested "dominion and sovereignty" and "vicinity to Cuba": *Cong. Globe*, 30th Cong., 1st sess., 29 April 1848, 709

p. 155 Polk, "I am decidedly in favour of purchasing Cuba": Rauch, *American Interest in Cuba*, 71

p. 155 Spain "would prefer seeing it sunk in the Ocean": Rauch, *American Interest in Cuba*, 97

p. 155 Buchanan, "We must have Cuba": Rauch, *American Interest in Cuba*, 98

p. 155 Everett, "The island of Cuba lies at our doors": S. Ex. Doc. 13, 30th Cong., 2d sess., 1852, 17–18

p. 157 "the safety of the South": Rauch quoting *De Bow's Review*, in *American Interest in Cuba*, 290

p. 157 Ostend Manifesto, "on the very same principle": H. Ex. Doc. 93, 33d Cong., 2d sess., 1854, 129, 131

p. 159 Polk on New Mexico and Upper California: *Cong. Globe*, 30th Cong., 1st sess., 6 July 1848, 901

p. 159 De Bow, *Statistical View*, 32

p. 159 Taylor, "California and Oregon were too distant": Polk, *Diary*, vol. 4, 375

p. 160 "Can any legislator seriously think": Tracy (New York), *Annals of Congress*, 17th Cong., 2d sess., January 1823, 597

p. 160 Adams: quoted in Pomeroy, *Pacific Slope*, 58

p. 160 California's position "is a delicate one": McCorckle, *Appendix, Cong. Globe*, 32d Cong., 1st sess., August 30, 1852, 1081

p. 161 Pierce, "The apprehension of dangers from extended territory": Richardson, *Messages and Papers*, vol. 4, 2731

p. 161 "the accursed question of slavery": a "distinguished Southerner" in *De Bow's Review* (1849), quoted in Russel, *Improvement of Communication*, 26

p. 168 "Malta in the centre of the Pacific": quoted in Pletcher, *Diplomacy of Annexation*, 424

p. 168 British consul on "the tide of Emigration": Kuykendall, *Hawaiian Kingdom*, 384

p. 168 American missionaries, "the Hawaiian Islands are already a virtual colony" and "the native Hawaiian race would be trampled in the dust": quoted in Phillips, *Protestant America and the Pagan World*, 130–31

p. 171 cry out against converting "the Republic which our fathers created for us into an Empire": *American Whig Review* (7 May 1848), quoted in Horsman, *Race and Manifest Destiny*, 245

p. 174 "no prospect of a numerous and speedy immigration," H. Misc. Doc. 40, 34th Cong., 3d sess., 1857, 1

p. 175 Charles Conrad on inducing New Mexicans to remove traders, and response: *Missouri Republican* (April 18, 1853), cited in Sunseri, *Seeds of Discord*, 86

p. 177 "aristocracy and empire [are] naturally linked": Thornton, *Doctrines of Imperialism*, 40

p. 179 French historian: Debouzy, "American History in France," 546

p. 180 Jefferson, "When we shall be full on this side": *Writings*, vol. 8, 243

p. 180 "domestic dependent nations": Justice John Marshall, quoted in Prucha, *Great Father*, vol. 1, 209–10

p. 181 to bring "a deputation of their chiefs through . . . our country": McKenney, "Report" (1828), 94

p. 182 Berkhofer, *White Man's Indian*, 138

p. 183 Tocqueville, *Democracy*, vol. 1, 369

p. 184 Treaty of Greenville: Smith, "Land Cession Treaty," 96

p. 185 Lincoln, "You know it is not always possible for any father": *Collected Works*, vol. 6, 152

p. 185 Sheehan, *Seeds of Extinction*, 275

p. 188 treaty phrases from various documents: Kappler, *Indian Affairs*, vol. 2

p. 188 "a degree of independence [as an enclave]": Satz, *American Indian Policy*, 54–55

p. 189 *Durham Report*, 38

p. 189 Gilpin, "the Anglo-Saxon is pushing aside the Frenchman": quoted in Horsman, *Race and Manifest Destiny*, 209

p. 189 Census schedules: De Bow, *Statistical View* (1854), 15, 62; *Preliminary Report on the Eighth Census 1860* (1862), 135

p. 190 "half breeds and mongrels": Charleston newspaper, quoted in Pletcher, *Diplomacy of Annexation*, 456

p. 190 Horsman: annexation "primarily an argument not about territory": *Race and Manifest Destiny*, 236

p. 190 Buchanan on Cuba: quoted in Rauch, *American Interest in Cuba*, 83

p. 191 Merk, "a national reluctance to add peoples of mixed blood": *Manifest Destiny and Mission*, 227

p. 192 Thornton on German expansionism: *Doctrines of Imperialism*, 78

p. 192 Mason, *Patterns of Dominance*, 337

p. 192 Royce, *California*, 119

p. 193 Indian agent to Potawatomies: Murphy to Council of Potawatomies (April 19, 1858), quoted in Miner and Unrau, *End of Indian Kansas*, 84

p. 193 Warner, "Will it be said that the land is not broad enough": Minority Report (1852), reprinted in part in Heizer and Almquist, *Other Californians*, 75

p. 195 Horsman, "Enlightenment did not mean cultural pluralism": *Origins of Indian Removal*, 4

p. 195 Houston, "love of domination": quoted in Horsman, *Race and Manifest Destiny*, 214

p. 195 Tocqueville, *Democracy*, vol. 1, 452

p. 197 Monroe on Cuba: *Writings*, vol. 6, 312

p. 200 "nature has fixed limits": Tracy (New York), *Annals of Congress*, 17th Cong., 2d sess., January 1823, 598

p. 202 Benton, "magnificent parallelogram": *Cong. Globe*, 30th Cong., 2d sess., 7 February 1849, 473

p. 203 Billington, *Westward Expansion*, 4th ed., 11

p. 203 Hietala, *Manifest Design*, 272

p. 203 Jefferson on Florida settlement: *Writings*, vol. 5, 316

p. 204 Jefferson, "although effected by their own voluntary sales": *Writings*, vol. 8, 194

p. 205 Buchanan on Cuba: in Richardson, *Messages and Papers*, vol. 4, 3041

p. 205 Mexican commissioners, "It was a new experience": quoted in Callahan, *American Foreign Policy in Mexican Relations*, 175

p. 205 Brack, *Mexico Views Manifest Destiny*, 179

p. 205 DeVoto, *Course of Empire*, 411

p. 207 Clay: *Annals of Congress*, 11th Cong., 3d sess., 63

p. 208 U.S. commissioner in Hawaii: quoted in Kuykendall, *Hawaiian Kingdom*, 404

p. 209 Weber, *Mexican Frontier*, 276

p. 211 Adams, *Memoirs*, vol. 4, 439

p. 211 O'Sullivan on "manifest destiny": *New York Morning News* (27 December 1845), quoted in Weinberg, *Manifest Destiny*, 145

p. 211 Everett: S. Ex. Doc. 13, 32d Cong., 2d sess., 1852, 19, 21

p. 211 Guyot, *Earth and Man*, 276, 16, 302

p. 212 "Our people, with a spirit of enterprise unparalleled": Bowlin (Missouri), *Cong. Globe*, 28th Cong., 2d sess., 1845, 97

p. 212 Jefferson on "the elder and the younger son": *Writings*, vol. 8, 243

p. 213 Adams: quoted in Cook, *Flood Tide of Empire*, 515

p. 213 "our India is south of us": senators quoted in Olliff, *Reforma Mexico*, 28

p. 214 "insane thirst" for territory as "the great American disease": Alabaman supporter of Calhoun (1847), quoted in Fuller, *Movement for Acquisition of all Mexico*, 65

p. 217 Wolf, *Europe and the People without History*, 6

p. 217 Boorstin, "not the 'manifestness'": *Americans: The National Experience*, 274

p. 217 Hietala, "anxiety, not optimism," . . . "territorial expansion would encourage nationalism": *Manifest Design*, 262, x

p. 218 Boorstin, "The continental extent of the nation": *Americans: The National Experience*, 274

PART TWO

p. 222 "I invite you to go to the West . . . the American multiplication table": Kennedy, *Appendix, Cong. Globe*, 29th Cong., 1st sess., January 10, 1846, 211

p. 223 "one of the great immigrations": Rohrbough, *Trans-Appalachian Frontier*, 158

p. 224 "the 'geology' of settlement": Elazar, *Cities of the Prairie*, 153ff.

p. 225 "designed by nature for the grand emporium of the Western world": Wyckoff, *Developer's Frontier*, 180–81

p. 229 "well-proportioned with prairie and timber": McManis, *Initial Evaluation . . . Illinois Prairies*, 46

p. 232 "the Alabama Feaver rages": quoted in Rohrbough, *Trans-Appalachian Frontier*, 196

p. 234 Newton, "When in 1811, Hidalgoist Bernardo Gutierrez": in Mitchell and Newton, "Appalachian Frontier," 58

p. 234 Southern expansion as "dispersal and reassembling of the same families": Parkins, *The South*, 118

p. 234 "the typical East Texan derived from": Lathrop, "Migration into East Texas," 201

p. 236 "Though they have generally good houses": Flint, *Recollections*, 76

p. 236 "from the first discovery . . . , one master passion": Barbour, H. Rept. 231, 19th Cong., 1st sess., 1826, in *Am. St. P.: Indian Affairs*, vol. 2, 647

p. 237 Hulbert, *Where Rolls the Oregon*, vol. 3, 36

p. 239 Blodget, *Climatology*, 455

p. 240 "One acquires as he proceeds westward": John Alonso Clark, *Gleanings by the Way* (1842), quoted in Jakle, *Images*, 119

surveyor's instructions: Hinsdale, *Old Northwest*, vol. 2, 257–58

p. 243 Faragher, *Sugar Creek*, 61

p. 244 Iowa settlers in 1838: Dick, *Lure of the Land*, 261

p. 244 Preemption Act as "merely declaratory of the custom": Senator Scott (Indiana), quoted in Turner, "Significance of the Frontier," in *Frontier and Section*, 54

p. 244 Iowa editor: *Charles City Intelligencer* (September 1, 1859), quoted in Hibbard, *History of Public Land Policies*, 223

p. 246 Jordan and Kaups, *American Backwoods Frontier*, 247

p. 246 "I had been reared . . . in the pleasure of frequent changes of country": quoted in Rohrbough, *Trans-Appalachian Frontier*, 201

p. 248 Wade, *Urban Frontier*, 1

p. 249 Rohrbough on Michigan: *Trans-Appalachian Frontier*, 371

p. 249 "If the plethora of town making did not cease": Buley, *Old Northwest*, vol. 2, paraphrasing *Miner's Free Press*, Mineral Point, September 1, 1837

p. 253 Boorstin, *Americans: The National Experience*, 153

p. 254 "It is . . . plain that the religious and political destiny of our nation": Beecher, *Plea for the West*, 11

p. 255 "in new areas denominational leaders read maps": Butler, *Awash*, 275

p. 255 "revival of revivalism": Ahlstrom, *Religious History*, 435

p. 256 Dykstra, *Cattle Towns*, 3–4

p. 256 Doyle, *Social Order*, 62–63

p. 258 Jefferson's observations: letter to William Ludlow, September 6, 1824, *Writings* (Library of America ed.), 1496–97

p. 258 Turner: "Significance of the Frontier," in *Frontier and Section*, 43, 37

p. 259 Hofstadter: "Turner and the Frontier Myth," in Billington, *Frontier Thesis*, 101

p. 264 Sauer, "good drama but . . . not our history": "Homestead and Community on the Middle Border," *Selected Essays*, 61

p. 264 "eternal pluralism of history": Sauer, "Historical Geography and the Western Frontier," *Land and Life*, 49

p. 264 "Amongst all the columns of emigration," etc.: Chevalier, *Society, Manners, Politics*, 111, 109, 111, 113, 114

p. 264 "vast empire . . . innumerable villages," etc.: Dwight, *Travels*, vol. 4, 370

p. 265 Dwight on New Hartford: *Travels*, vol. 3, 123

p. 265 Dwight on New York as a colony of New England: *Travels*, vol. 3, 186

p. 266 Martineau on road to Buffalo, *Society in America*, vol. 1, 139

p. 268 "Some Milk 30 or 40 cows": Lawrence and Branz, *Flagg Correspondence*, 9

p. 268 "There is more grass": quoted in Power, *Planting Corn Belt Culture*, 92

p. 268 Dwight, "included a proportional number of mechanics" and enterprising businessmen: *Travels*, vol. 3, 373, 372

p. 268 on Yankee propensity "to form villages": Flint, *Recollections*, 44, 45

p. 269 Turner on New York and New England: *United States*, 98, 99

p. 272 Martineau on the New England states, *Society in America*, vol. 1, 216
"an established elite who often inherit": Elazar, *American Federalism*, 93

p. 277 Bishop Asbury's remarks on Nashville: quoted in Goodstein, *Nashville*, 57

p. 277 "Celtic cowlords": Newton in Mitchell and Newton, "Appalachian Frontier," 56

p. 278 Flint's remarks on Virginians: Flint, *Recollections*, 72, 74

p. 279 Blount on Western man: quoted in Goldstein, *Nashville*, 5

p. 279 Jefferson's design for the West: letter to John Tyler, May 26, 1810, *Writings* (Library of America ed.), 1225–26

p. 281 "almost exclusively from Pennsylvania": Conlin, *Simon Perkins*, 100–101

p. 281 Chevalier, *Society, Manners, Politics*, 120, 124

p. 282 Tocqueville, *Democracy*, vol. 1, 422

p. 282 De Bow on values of the commercial town: quoted in Wiebe, *Opening of America*, 293

p. 282 Murrin, "Roof without Walls," 347

p. 283 on the Illinois Central changing the "political physiognomy": Parker, "Northwest to Mid-West," 28, quoting *New York Evening News* (September 2, 1858)

p. 284 Cayton and Onuf, *Midwest and Nation*, 89–90

p. 286 "an extraordinary burst of wealth": Kennedy, *Architecture, Men, Women, Money*, 162

p. 286 Kennedy on Natchez planters: *Architecture, Men, Women, Money*, 367–68

p. 287 on transformation of Mobile: Kennedy, *Architecture, Men, Women, Money*, 249

p. 289 "a perfect waste . . . washed into Gullies": Eaton: *Growth of Southern Civilization*, 42–43

p. 289 "after taking the cream off their land": Eaton, *Growth of Southern Civilization*, 41

p. 289 Rothstein on Natchez planters: "Antebellum South as a Dual Economy," 382

p. 291 "The large planters—the one-thousand-bale planters": Adkins, "Geographic Base of Urban Retardation," 39, quoting *Mississippi Free Trader* (April 14, 1842)

p. 291 "Confederate flag never flew officially": Kennedy, *Architecture, Men, Women, Money*, 403

p. 291 on Wade Hampton I: Kennedy, *Architecture, Men, Women, Money*, 274

p. 291 "the center of civic life": Newton, "Settlement Patterns as Artifacts," 339

p. 292 "brittle, gay, showy style of life," etc.: Dunn, "English Sugar Islands," 58

p. 292 De Bow, *Statistical View*, 38

p. 295 Green, *Role of the Yankee*, 39

p. 296 "the significance of race . . . can scarcely be exaggerated": Litwack, "Trouble in Mind," 317

p. 298 "instead of being challenged where it prevailed": Potter, *Impending Crisis*, 49

p. 298 remarks of Stone: *Appendix, Cong. Globe*, 28th Cong., 2d sess., January 24, 1845, 225

p. 298 Texas would "act as a safety valve": Walker letter, reprinted in Merk, *Fruits of Propaganda*, 234

p. 298 remarks of Miller: *Appendix, Cong. Globe*, 28th Cong., 2d sess., February 25, 1845, 354

p. 299 "Diffusion is about as effectual a remedy": quoted in Olson, *Baltimore*, 68

p. 299 remarks of Barbour: *Annals of Congress*, 16th Cong., 1st sess., February 1, 1820, 326

p. 299 remarks of Jefferson Davis: quoted in Potter, *Impending Crisis*, 37

p. 299 "menace of Negro immigration": Woodson in Rudwick, *Free Blacks*, 71

p. 300 "to prevent free negroes and mulattoes from coming to and settling": Rudwick, *Free Blacks*, 142

p. 300 delegate of Iowa, "the whole black population of the Union": quoted in Berwanger, *Frontier against Slavery*, 33

p. 300 remarks of Wilmot: quoted in Berwanger, *Frontier against Slavery*, 125–26

p. 301 Ohio representative, "I sympathize with them deeply": quoted by Litwick in Rudwick, *Free Blacks*, 150

p. 301 Kentucky Abolition Society petition: Resolution No. 395, 14th Cong., 1st sess., *Am. St. P.: Misc*, vol. 2, 278

p. 301 Indian territory as "the entering wedge": *Niles National Register* (May 5, 1838), 156

p. 301 Duer's proposal and responses: *Cong. Globe*, 30th Cong., 1st sess., May 18, 1848, 778, 727, 730–31

p. 301 Jefferson: letter to the governor of Virginia, November 24, 1801, *Writings*, vol. 8, 104–5

p. 304 "drew its strength from humanitarianism and fear alike": Pease and Pease, *Bound with Them in Chains*, 9

p. 304 colonization as White scheme to "expel the colored man entirely," and "We do not mean to go to Liberia": Douglass in Hill and Kilson, *Apropos of Africa*, 39

p. 304 Berry and Blassingame, "judging by the letters received": *Long Memory*, 400

p. 305 Jefferson on West Indies: letter to governor of Virginia, November 24, 1801, *Writings*, vol. 8, 105

p. 305 Blair's proposal: quoted in Nevins, *Emergence of Lincoln*, vol. 2, 164–65

p. 307 "Like other apparent panaceas": Friedman, *Inventors of the Promised Land*, 253

p. 311 Merk on "the concept of a society": *Fruits of Propaganda*, 119–20

p. 311 Gallatin, *Report*, 8

p. 312 Merrimack Canal as "greatest work of its kind": Gallatin, *Report*, 50; as "important . . . all out of proportion": Vance, *Capturing the Horizon*, 112

p. 313 Gallatin on the need to sponsor "a number of local improvements": *Report*, 68

p. 316 Vance on "misfit of entrepôt": *Capturing the Horizon*, 108

p. 321 "Erie Canal that assured . . . an American Canal Era" and New York as "only part of America where a comprehensive system": Vance, *Capturing the Horizon*, 128, 126

p. 321 tonnage on Pennsylvania Mainline and on the Erie: Vance, *Capturing the Horizon*, 132

p. 323 "of all the elements of the prosperity of the West": *Memorial of a Number of Citizens*, 28th Cong., 1st sess., S. Ex. Doc. 179, 18

p. 323 to win "western independence" from "Pennsylvania and Maryland waggoners": quoted in Hunter, *Steamboats*, 21

p. 324 "Charleston enterprise to save Charleston": Wallace, *South Carolina*, 377

p. 324 Baltimore merchants: quoted in Vance, *Capturing the Horizon*, 270

p. 325 "railroad craze . . . superimposed on the canal mania": Hill, *Roads, Rails, and Waterways*, 99

p. 325 a "new Northwest Passage": Vance, *Capturing the Horizon*, 280

p. 328 "Great Southern & Southwestern Mail Route": Davis, *Southern Railway*, 110

p. 330 on Canadian strategies: Glazebrook, *History*, 159, 162

p. 330 Andrews, *Report*, 9

p. 334 Lacock: *Report of the Committee on Roads and Canals* (February 17, 1817), 14th Cong., 2d sess., S. Doc. 429, 425

p. 336 "almost from the first morning two distinct rail systems": Vance, *Capturing the Horizon*, 265

p. 337 Great Western Railway "at the most advantageous distance": [Redfield] Report, quoted in Armroyd, *Connected View of . . . Internal Navigation*, 587

p. 338 "conservative metropolitan capitalists": Baer, *Canals and Railroads of Mid-Atlantic States*, 10

p. 339 Calhoun, facts of "the late war": *Report of Sec. of War* (1819), 15th Cong., 2d sess., H. Doc. 462, 534

p. 339 to connect the "seat of the General Government to . . . two frontiers": *Debates*, 21st Cong., 1st sess., 23 March 1830, 630

p. 341 Calhoun, "Opposed in principle to a large standing army": *Report of Sec. of War* (1819), 15th Cong., 2d sess., H. Doc. 462, 534

p. 341 Kentucky and Tennessee "have no frontiers of their own": Blair (Tennessee), *Debates*, 21st Cong., 1st sess., 24 March 1830, 658, 9

p. 341 C & O Canal "peculiarly national": Hemphill, *Report of the Committee on Roads and Canals*, in *Gales & Seaton's Register of Debates*, 18th Cong., 2d sess., 1825, vol. 1, 78

p. 342 "to facilitate the administration of Government": *Report upon a National Road, Washington to New Orleans* (1826), 19th Cong., 1st sess., H. Doc. 156, 24

p. 342 in "a political system of confederate Governments . . . any thing calculated to facilitate . . .

intercourse between . . . States": *Report upon a National Road, Washington to New Orleans* (1826), 19th Cong., 1st sess., H. Doc. 156, 23–24

p. 342 "to connect the seat of the Federal Government, by the shortest lines": *Surveys* (1827), 19th Cong., 2d sess., H. Report 102, in *New Am. St. P.: Transp.*, vol. 2, 213

p. 342 "through the capitals of the States south of Washington": Committee on Roads and Canals (1828), 20th Cong., 1st sess., H. Report 270, in *New Am. St. P.: Transp.*, vol. 2, 248

p. 342 Calhoun on steamboats: *Report of Sec. of War* (1819), 15th Cong., 2d sess., H. Doc. 462, 534

p. 342 Carson, "What! bring men from the State of Ohio . . . ?": *Debates*, 21st Cong., 1st sess., March 25, 1830, 670

p. 342 Carson, the railroad "a system of road intercommunication": *Debates*, 21st Cong., 1st sess., March 25, 1830, 669

p. 343 Gaines, railroads as "greatest improvement or discovery known to military history": letter, February 20, 1835, published in Gaines, *To the Young Men*, 67

p. 343 Gaines, "A System of Rail Roads": caption of map, reproduced in Silver, *Gaines*, 245

p. 345 Gaines on Memphis: letter to Secretary of War John Bell, August 31, 1841, "Correspondence . . . relating to . . . Western Armory"

p. 346 quartermaster general, "I can safely say that the rivers, canals, and railroads": H. Ex. Doc. 48, 34th Cong., 3d sess., 1857, 2

p. 346 on steamboats and mail service: *Mail—New York to New Orleans Irreg.* (1840), 26th Cong., 1st sess., H. Doc. 159, 4

p. 346 "if God were suddenly to call the world to judgment": Domingo Faustino Sarmento, quoted in Ward, *Railroads and . . . Character*, 106

p. 347 towns "were no longer spatially individual": Schivelbusch, *Railway Journey*, 197

p. 348 Calhoun: "We are great, and rapidly . . . growing": *Debates*, 14th Cong., 2d sess., February 4, 1817, 854

p. 348 removing "the ancient doubt . . . as to . . . enlarging the sphere of Republican Government": *Surveys* (1827), 19th Cong., 2d sess., H. Report 102, in *New Am. St. P.: Transp.*, vol. 2, 217

p. 348 "give to the republic one national heart and one national mind": *Hunts Magazine* 4 (1841), quoted in Hunter, *Steamboats*, 28

p. 348 Yates on railroad and union: *Appendix, Cong. Globe*, 32d Cong., 1st sess., April 23, 1852, 476

p. 349 had better "encircle South Carolina": Carson, *Debates*, 21st Cong., 1st sess., March 25, 1830, 670

p. 349 Madison's warning on "enlarging federal power": quoted in Larson, "'Bind the Republic Together,'" 370

p. 349 "not so much as a design for a [transportation] system": Larson, "'Bind the Republic Together,'" 374

p. 349 "it mattered absolutely . . . who designed and constructed the roads and canals": Larson, "'Bind the Republic Together,'" 366

p. 350 "one grand, magnificent, consolidated empire": Robertson, *Debates*, 14th Cong., 2d sess., February 4, 1817, 866

p. 350 "the worst feature in the conduct of the [federal] government": Blane, *Excursion*, 39

p. 350 "an island in the heart of the Union": Committee on Roads and Canals, H. Doc. 526, 17th Cong., 1st sess., 1822, 935

p. 351 Calhoun, "The interest of commerce and the spirit of rivalry": *Report of Sec. of War* (1819), 15th Cong., 2d sess., H. Doc. 462, 535

p. 351 "The South . . . to compete with eastern cities": Blanding, address to citizens of Charleston, quoted in MacGill, *History of Transportation*, 427

p. 351 Barbour, "too lofty a magnanimity": *Debates*, 21st Cong., 1st sess., March 23, 1830, 651, 650

p. 352 "impossible to foresee all the channels": Hemphill, *Debates*, 21st Cong., 1st sess., March 23, 1830, 638

p. 352 new cities "spring up amidst the forests": Trollope, *Domestic Manners*, 308

p. 353 Hall on Rochester: quoted in Mau, *Development of Central and Western New York*, 270–71

p. 353 "the forces of geography fundamentally determined": Glaab and Brown, *History of Urban America*, 72

p. 354 Cooper, *Guide in the Wilderness*, 17–18

p. 355 once "capital and population": Henry Ruffner (1838), quoted in Schwab, *Travels in the Old South*, vol. 2, 344

p. 357 town "near the Junction of the Ohio and Mississippi": *The Illinois Wabash Land Company Manuscript*, quoted in Reps, *Making of Urban America*, 350

p. 357 "Town of America": Wade, *Urban Frontier*, 31

p. 361 "an isthmus of dry and level land," etc.: Abbott, *Boosters and Businessmen*, 173, 175

p. 362 Gilpin on "Centropolis," etc.: Glaab, "Visions of Metropolis," 24

p. 363 "our great central lake": Scott, "Internal Trade," 38

p. 364 "what a revolution must follow": quoted in Hunter, *History of Industrial Power*, 102

p. 366 "you can easily trace": William Henry Milburn, *The Pioneers, Preachers, and People of the Mississippi Valley*, quoted in Strauss, 153

p. 369 "Norfolk, Charleston . . . are but suburbs": Charleston *Mercury* (November 4, 1860), quoted in Goldfield, *Urban Growth*, 257

p. 369 "like imperial states": Wade, *Urban Frontier*, 336

p. 369 Lukermann, "Empirical Expressions of Nodality," 43

p. 370 Olson, *Baltimore*, 66

p. 370 "a municipal environment dedicated": Conzen, "Morphology," 135

p. 370 city "treated not as a public institution": Mumford, *City in History*, 426

p. 371 "Around 1850 . . . the sky . . . grew darker": Tunnard and Reed, *American Skyline*, 67

p. 371 Mumford, *City in History*, 461

p. 375 "Until we manufacture more": *Boston Gazette*, quoted in Henretta et al., *America's History*, 262

p. 375 Congress requesting report on "manufactures": H. Report 31, 2d Cong., 1st sess., 1791, in *Am. St. P.: Finance*, vol. 5, 123

p. 375 Cochran, *Frontiers*, 82

p. 375 Gallatin: excerpt in North and Thomas, *Growth of American Economy*, 180

p. 375 Jefferson: "Notes on the State of Virginia," Query VIII, *Writings* (Library of America ed.), 212

p. 376 "nation's nursery of manufacturing": Vance, *This Scene of Man*, 341

p. 378 Springfield Armory as "a world leader": Hounshell, *From American System to Mass Production*, 32

p. 378 Hounshell quotation: *From American System to Mass Production*, 43

p. 382 "urban America . . . almost wholly dependent upon wood": Hunter, *History of Industrial Power*, 409

p. 384 on smoke at Pittsburgh: various travelers quoted in Jakle, *Images*, 135–36

p. 386 "coal, iron, and clothing businesses . . . intertwined": Cochran, *Frontiers*, 112

p. 390 "In Philadelphia by 1810": Cochran, *Frontiers*, 73

p. 391 "mutual wants . . . one of the strongest links": Hamilton, "Manufactures," 134

p. 391 "retard or prevent the population of the Western Wilderness": memorial attached to [Coxe], "Essay on Manufacturing Interest," v

p. 391 "conversion of this extensive wilderness": Hamilton, "Manufactures," 134

p. 392 artists and manufacturers of Philadelphia statement: in memorial attached to [Coxe], "Essay on Manufacturing Interests," v

p. 392 manufacturing suitable for "large districts," etc.: Hamilton, "Manufactures," 129

p. 392 on New Jersey: Hamilton, "Prospectus of SEUM," 146

p. 392 "appeared prudent to take a position": Coxe, "Observations" (1792), reprinted in Folsom and Lubar, *Philosophy of Manufactures*, 115

p. 393 "an auxilliary to Philadelphia": Coxe, *View of the United States*, 394

p. 393 "first true mill town": Dunwell, *Run of the Mill*, 19

p. 393 Clay, "others may prefer the cloths": speech (1810), reprinted in Folsom and Lubar, *Philosophy of Manufactures*, 170

p. 393 Slater, "extended his power over as many phases of his workers' lives": Dunwell, *Run of the Mill*, 24

p. 393 Dunwell on Lowell: *Run of the Mill*, 35

p. 395 "circulating current from the healthy and virtuous population": John Amory Lowell (1856), quoted in Boorstin, *Americans: The National Experience*, 29

p. 395 "machine in the garden": Marx, *Machine in the Garden*

p. 395 "widely distributed . . . at salubrious spots": Edwart Everett (1830), oration reprinted in Folsom and Lubar, *Philosophy of Manufactures*, 285

p. 395 "many of these early factory towns appeared to be peaceful": Tucker, *Samuel Slater*, 15

p. 396 Wallace on "the reliable steam-driven factory": *Rockdale*, 293

p. 397 Slater, "If the people of this country": excerpt of essay reprinted in Kulick et al., *New England Mill Village*, 12

p. 398 "clearly developed a native technical tradition": Stapleton, *Transfer of Early Industrial Technologies*, 30

p. 398 "intensely dynamic reciprocities": Clark, *History*, 233

p. 398 "two rapidly advancing cultures": Cochran, *Frontiers*, 13

p. 398 "Europe modified industrialism to fit": Cochran, *Frontiers*, 128

p. 399 Chief Justice Marshall, quoted in Potter, *Impending Crisis*, 7

p. 399 Smith on "the term National": *Debates*, 14th Cong., 2d sess., April 11, 1828, 645

p. 399 Washington on *one Nation*: in Meinig, *Shaping of America*, vol. 1, 406

p. 399 Murrin, "in the architecture of nationhood": "A Roof without Walls," 347, 346

p. 400 Gallatin, "They are more American": quoted in Dangerfield, *Awakening*, 4

p. 400 Jeffersonian triumph initiated "a movement that was national in scope": Appleby, *Capitalism and a New Social Order*, 78, 47

p. 401 distribute newspapers as necessary cost "to help the . . . republic cohere" and "development of postal policy . . . one of the clearest examples": Kielbowicz, *News in the Mail*, 36, 182

p. 401 North Carolina representative on "poisoned sentiments of the cities," and Seward, "to denationalize this Union": quoted in Kielbowicz, *News in the Mail*, 86–87, 88

p. 401 on importance of federal postal system: Kielbowicz, *News in the Mail*, 183

p. 404 President Polk on "serious objections to . . . consolidating tendency": quoted in Short, *Development of National Administrative Organization*, 213

p. 405 Flint, *Recollections*, 188

p. 405 "the grid objectified national . . . order": Stilgoe, *Common Landscape*, 106

p. 405 "no universally acceptable image of what an American capitol should be": Hitchcock and Seale, *Temples of Democracy*, 48

p. 405 Stephen Hills's "marriage of dome, rotunda": Hitchcock and Seale, *Temples of Democracy*, 63

p. 405 "bank had scattered twenty-six": Craig, *Federal Presence*, 50

p. 406 Greek Revival, "columns could be added at will": Craig, *Federal Presence*, 50

p. 406 "towns everywhere clamored": Craig, *Federal Presence*, 163

p. 407 Smithsonian as "antidote to the . . . grid": Craig, *Federal Presence*, 91

p. 409 De Bow on categories of population: *Statistical View*, 39

p. 409 Kettner, "Those citizens who created the Union": *Development of American Citizenship*, 328

p. 409 Taney's opinion resting "on the social fact of prejudice": Kettner, *Development of American Citizenship*, 328

p. 409 "synthetic Anglo-Saxonism": Wiebe, *Segmented Society*, 93

p. 411 "education for assimilation": Kaestle, *Pillars of the Republic*, 72, 76

p. 411 "America had schools, but . . . not . . . school systems": Kaestle, *Pillars of the Republic*, 62

p. 411 Zelinsky on American education: *Nation into State*, 148

p. 412 Elson on New England as "schoolmaster": *Guardians*, 7

p. 412 textbook authors "emphatically believed" in "national character": England, "Democratic Faith," 191

p. 412 "that the law of history" and New England as the "measuring rod": Elson, *Guardians*, 258, 173

p. 412 on Bancroft's history: Nye's introduction, in Bancroft, *History of the United States*, xxii, xix

p. 412 on tendency "to treat all of American history as a gloss": Nye, *Society and Culture*, 113

p. 413 "invention" of George Washington: Zelinsky, *Nation into State*, 30

p. 413 Constitution as "the sacred document": "Providence in American History," *Harper's* 14 (1858), quoted in O'Brien, *God Land*, 37

p. 413 "despite the competition . . . all the denominations identified with the nation": Wood, in Bailyn et al., *Great Republic*, 294

p. 413 parallel development "evolved a myth of the American Christian past": Butler, *Awash*, 285

p. 413 Butler on "religious syncretism and creativity" and "Americans who shared a common religiosity": *Awash*, 255–56

p. 414 "landscape sacralization": Butler, *Awash*, 270

p. 414 "They not only furnished millions of people with": Goen, *Broken Churches*, 63

p. 415 Cincinnati writer, "a steamboat, coming from New Orleans": *Western Monthly Review* (1827), quoted in Turner, *Rise of the New West*, 87

p. 415 *Godey's* "became a household standard": Nye, *Society and Culture*, 369

p. 415 "the publishing industry by the 1830s" and "no nation . . . was so thoroughly covered by the press": Nye, *Society and Culture*, 371, 368

p. 416 New York as the "nation's newsbroker": Swarzlose, *Nation's Newsbrokers*, 211

p. 416 "Everything of interest occurring in any part of this country": Prescott, *History, Theory, and Practice of the Electric Telegraph* (1860), 385, quoted in Swarzlose, *Nation's Newsbrokers*, 233

p. 416 "surprisingly, few individuals in either North or South": Kielbowicz, *News in the Mail*, 114

p. 416 Zelinsky, *Nation into State*, 247, 221

p. 417 Pollard, "It was Yankee orators": selection from *The Lost Cause*, reprinted in Rozwenc, *Causes of the American Civil War*, 52–53

p. 418 Parker, "Like some complex sea organism": "Northwest to Mid-West," 5

p. 418 Tocqueville, "The United States has no metropolis": *Democracy*, vol. 1, 299–300

p. 421 Hall on Boston and New England: *Organization of American Culture*, 101 (also 68), 90, 92, 122

p. 423 Johnson on London: Boswell, *Life of Johnson* (September 30, 1769)

p. 423 Flint on Natchitoches: *Recollections*, 365–67

p. 425 "here every farmer . . . may become a freeholder": Caleb Atwater, a Yankee Ohioan in 1829, quoted in Jakle, *Images*, 120

p. 425 West as the "body of the American eagle": Jesup W. Scott, quoted in Abbott, *Boosters and Businessmen*, 204

p. 426 "deep American optimism": Abbott, *Boosters and Businessmen*, 207

p. 426 homes as "an index of progress": Cohn, *Palace or Poorhouse*, 51

p. 427 New Mexican memorial to Congress: H. Misc. Doc. 40, 34th Cong., 3d sess., February 9, 1857, 1

p. 428 Madison on center of population: McCoy, "James Madison and Visions of American Nationality," 228

p. 428 Tocqueville on "civilization of the North," *Democracy*, vol. 1, 422

p. 428 Grattan on national character: *Civilized America*, vol. 1, vii–viii

PART THREE

p. 432 Vinton on the formation of new states: *Appendix, Cong. Globe*, 28th Cong., 2d sess., February 11, 1845, 330

p. 432 Northwest Ordinance: Taylor, *Northwest Ordinance*, 31–77

p. 433 "to adhere to the bounds asked by the people": *Cong. Globe*, 28th Cong., 2d sess., February 10, 1845, 269

p. 433 "multiplying the parts of the Machine": Onuf, *Statehood and Union*, 56

p. 435 "At the center of the theoretical expression of Anti-Federalist opposition": Kenyon, "Men of Little Faith," 6

p. 435 on Montesquieu: Richter, *Political Theory*, 237

p. 435 report on the Western Territories: *Journals of Cont. Cong.* 30 (1786): 132–33

p. 436 Pope on Illinois boundary: Buck, *Illinois in 1818*, 225

p. 436 on the boundaries of Missouri: Shoemaker, *Missouri's Struggle for Statehood*, 40

p. 437 on Platte Purchase: *H. Doc. 107* (January 28, 1835), 1

p. 437 on Iowan rejection of statehood: *Appendix, Cong. Globe*, 29th Cong., 1st sess., June 8, 1846, 668

p. 439 "Texas was too large": Haywood, *Appendix, Cong. Globe*, 28th Cong., 2d sess., February 14, 1845, 159

p. 439 Benton's bill: *Appendix, Cong. Globe*, 28th Cong., 1st sess., June 10, 1844, 702–3

p. 439 on an undivided Mississippi: Carter, "Territory of Mississippi," 709

p. 440 northern addition as a "sterile region": Dunbar, *Michigan*, 314

p. 440 congressional obligation of "making [states] of suitable . . . size," etc.: Vinton, *Cong. Globe*, 28th Cong., 2d sess., February 11, 1845, 330

p. 441 on Indiana admission: Kettleborough, *Constitution Making*, 132

p. 443 on "the family wash": *Indianapolis Remembered*, 87

p. 445 on the size of Indiana counties: Kettleborough, *Constitution Making*, 118

p. 447 Meinig, *Shaping of America*, vol. 1, 395

p. 449 "imperatives for survival": Bright, "The State in the U.S.," 128

p. 450 "to abolish slavery gradually and painlessly": Finkelman, *Imperfect Union*, 92–93

p. 451 "cast your eye on the map, sir": Taylor, *Annals of Congress*, 15th Cong., 2d sess., 1819, 1224

p. 451 Taylor, "Missouri lies in the same latitude as Illinois" and Scott, "a part of Kentucky . . . as far north as": *Annals of Congress*, 15th Cong., 2d sess., 1819, 1172, 1202

p. 451 "we now have the numerical force": Whitman, *Annals of Congress*, 15th Cong., 2d sess., 1819, 1279

p. 454 Haywood's bill on Texas: *Appendix, Cong. Globe*, 28th Cong., 2d sess., February 14, 1845, 154

p. 455 "here [he] held up a map": Levy, *Cong. Globe*, 28th Cong., 2d sess., 1845, 275

p. 456 Webster, "Now, as to California": *Cong. Globe*, 31st Cong., 1st sess., March 7, 1850, 480–81

p. 457 "Dot Kansas with New England settlements": Thomas H. Webb, secretary of emigrant aid society (1854), quoted in Davis, *Kansas*, 47

p. 458 Tocqueville, confederations "have a natural tendency": *Democracy*, vol. 1, 400

p. 458 Boorstin, "the tendencies of American political life": *Americans: The National Experience*, 427

p. 458 Boorstin, "The successful application of this notion" and "Add-a-State" plan: *Americans: The National Experience*, 422, 425

p. 458 Douglas, "to preserve an equilibrium . . . a new doctrine": *Appendix, Cong. Globe*, 31st Cong., 1st sess., March 14, 1850, 374

p. 459 Turner, "rival societies . . . marching side by side": "Significance of the Section," in *Frontier and Section*, 118

p. 459 Bright, "continuous westward expansion": "The State in the U.S.," 132

p. 459 Calhoun: *Cong. Globe*, 31st Cong., 1st sess., March 4, 1850, 451–55

p. 460 Tocqueville, "States form confederations," etc.: *Democracy*, vol. 1, 404, 419, 418

p. 461 Washington "expressed his fear": Jefferson, *Writings*, vol. 1, 192

p. 461 Jefferson, "an association of men who will not quarrel": letter to John Taylor, *Writings*, vol. 7, 263–66

p. 462 "The balance of power . . . is decidedly in favor of the Southern States": Griswold to Wolcott, in Adams, *New-England Federalism*, 356

p. 462 "the overbearing influence of Virginia": Griswold to Wolcott, in Adams, *New-England Federalism*, 354

p. 462 "of negro Presidents and negro Congresses": Pickering to King, in Adams, *New-England Federalism*, 351

p. 462 "The principles of our Revolution point to the remedy": Pickering to Cabot, in Adams, *New-England Federalism*, 339

p. 462 "I have no hesitation myself in saying": Griswold to Wolcott, in Adams, *New-England Federalism*, 356

p. 462 on geographical design of Northern Confederacy: Adams, *New-England Federalism*, 341, 345

p. 463 Quincy's warning: *Annals of Congress*, 11th Cong., 3d sess., 14 January 1811, 524ff.

p. 463 "rescue from ruin at least some portion": Adams, *New-England Federalism*, 321

p. 463 Madison on "the great division of interests": Potter and Manning, *Nationalism and Sectionalism*, 88

p. 464 Cobb, "If we persist, the Union will be dissolved" and Talmadge, "Sir, . . . let it be so!": *Annals of Congress*, 15th Cong., 2d sess., 1819, 1204

p. 464 Moore, *Missouri Controversy*, 342, 350

p. 465 Calhoun, "I consider the Tariff, but the occasion": Freehling, *Prelude to Civil War*, 257

p. 465 "keeping the hands of Congress from . . . slavery": Freehling, *Prelude to Civil War*, 109

p. 465 "the risk of provoking an American civil war": Freehling, *Prelude to Civil War*, 259

p. 466 "the most thoroughgoing repression": Freehling, *Prelude to Civil War*, 308

p. 466 Adams on Southern Convention: Wender, "Southern Commercial Conventions," 28

p. 467 "to beatify the Mississippi Valley": Wender, "Southern Commercial Conventions," 59

p. 467 De Bow's classification: *Statistical View* (1854), 37–38

p. 467 Potter on "the actual danger of disunion": *Impending Crisis*, 122

p. 468 De Bow on the South assuming "her stand among the nations": Wender, "Southern Commercial Conventions," 187

p. 469 Adams, "If the day should ever come": quoted in Fowler, *Sectional Controversy*, 75

p. 469 "constitutional plan for the mutual and friendly division": Sweet, *Methodism in American History*, 249

p. 469 "spirit of brotherly separation quickly evaporated," Ahlstrom, *Religious History*, 663

p. 469 separation by vote in "the societies, stations, and Conferences": Sweet, *Methodism in American History*, 249–50

p. 470 Calhoun on "the explosive effect of slavery agitation": *Cong. Globe*, 31st Cong., 1st sess., 3 April 1850, 453

p. 470 "the split in the churches was not only the first break . . . but the chief cause": Sweet, quoted in Ahlstrom, *Religious History*, 673

p. 470 Goen, *Broken Churches*, 13

p. 470 Webster, "Peaceable secession!": *Cong. Globe*, 31st Cong., 1st sess., March 7, 1850, 482

p. 471 Vinton, "Massachusetts and South Carolina": *Appendix, Cong. Globe*, 28th Cong., 2d sess., February 11, 1845, 333

p. 471 Hardin, "The great natural outlet": *Appendix, Cong. Globe*, 28th Cong., 2d sess., January 15, 1845, 277

p. 471 Webster: *Cong. Globe*, 31st Cong., 1st sess., March 7, 1850, 482–83

p. 472 Calhoun, "Delaware had become doubtful": *Cong. Globe*, 31st Cong., 1st sess., April 3, 1850, 451

p. 472 Baltimore as "New York of the South": Clingman (North Carolina), *Cong. Globe*, 31st Cong., 1st sess., January 22, 1850, 204

p. 472 Mann, "First, as to the recovery . . . of fugitive slaves": *Appendix, Cong. Globe*, 31st Cong., 1st sess., February 15, 1850, 221–22

p. 473 Green, resolution "for establishing an armed police": *Cong. Globe*, 36th Cong., 2d sess., December 5, 1860, 8

p. 473　Federalist party, "half-way house": Henry Adams, quoted in Henretta et al., *America's History*, 281

p. 473　Kinsey, "Few gentlemen have risen": *Annals of Congress*, 16th Cong., 1st sess., March 2, 1820, 1583

p. 474　"most dangerous divisions of the people . . . geographical lines": Clingman (North Carolina), *Cong. Globe*, 30th Cong., 1st sess., December 22, 1847, 66

p. 474　political parties as "connective tissue": Boorstin, *Americans: The National Experience*, 430

p. 475　Fehrenbacher on Southern secession: *South and Three Sectional Crises*, 5

p. 475　"Southern consensus ended abruptly": Potter, *Impending Crisis*, 485

p. 477　Sitterson, "A secession county was likely to be": *Secession Movement in N.C.*, 224

p. 478　"the Cotton States": Kennedy, *Border States*, 3

p. 479　"The question was not merely what will keep Virginia in": Vallandigham (Ohio), *Appendix, Cong. Globe*, 36th Cong., 2d sess., February 20, 1861, 241

p. 480　Border States as "the real Keystone of the Arch": Louisville *Daily Journal* (December 4, 1860), in Dumond, *Southern Editorials*, 304

p. 480　Pearce, "I have no idea . . . Union can be maintained . . . by force": Wright, *Secession . . . Middle Atlantic States*, 41

p. 480　"Central States . . . must take the matter into their own hands": Summers, in Chittenden, *Report of . . . Conference . . . Held at Washington*, 155

p. 480　Lincoln, "The Union of these States is perpetual": Inaugural Address, March 4, 1861, in *Collected Works*, vol. 4, 264

p. 481　Lincoln's call has "dissolved the Union": *North Carolina Semi-Weekly Standard*, Raleigh (May 8, 1861), in Crofts, *Reluctant Confederates*, 333

p. 481　"We are as much two peoples . . . two sides of the Alps": Wheeling *Daily Intelligencer* (December 28, 1860), quoted in Perkins, *Northern Editorials*, 898

p. 483　"Every county sent men into both": Smith, *Borderland*, 308

p. 483　"East Tennessee, like trans-Allegheny Virginia . . . seceded": Crofts, *Reluctant Confederates*, 344–45

p. 484　Indians as "invaluable arm of defense": Coulter, *Confederate States*, 49

p. 484　Confederate Constitution, Article IV, Sec. 3: Vandiver, *Basic History Confederacy*, 114

p. 486　London map: "Map of the United States showing the Territory in Possession of the Federal Union, January, 1864," Bacon & Co., 48 Paternaster Row, London

p. 486　McClellan, "he detested both South Carolina and Massachusetts": Welles, *Diary*, 107

p. 489　Founding Fathers "seem wholly to have overlooked": Vallandigham, *Appendix, Cong. Globe*, 36th Cong., 2d sess., February 20, 1861, 236

p. 489　Massachusetts and Connecticut proposed constitutional amendments: S. Rept. No. 397, 14th Cong., 2d sess., January 17, 1816, 283

p. 490　"the Roman Republic, with its two consuls": Memminger, *Address before . . . Authorities of Virginia*, 40

p. 490　Vallandigham, "Secession has been tried and proved . . . a success" and four-sections proposal: *Appendix, Cong. Globe*, 36th Cong., 2d sess., February 20, 1861, 242–43

p. 491　Ireland "represented nominally, but really . . . powerless": Clingman (North Carolina), *Cong. Globe*, 36th Cong., 2d sess., April 12, 1860, 3

p. 491　"one of the few who regarded secession and war as inevitably connected": Davis, *Rise and Fall*, 316

p. 491　Provisional Constitution, "to adjust everything pertaining to the common": Davis, *Rise and Fall*, 244

p. 491　two confederacies coexisting "in security upon their separate lines": New Orleans *Daily Picayune*, March 17, 1861, quoted in Dumond, *Southern Editorials*, 489

p. 491　The Confederate States constitute "an independent nation": Davis, *Rise and Fall*, 676

p. 492　Tocqueville, "not only would they diminish the strength . . . they would create foreign powers": *Democracy*, vol. 1, 405

p. 492 Clay, "never, never, never": quoted by *Chicago Daily Tribune* (February 25, 1861), in Perkins, *Northern Editorials*, 558

p. 492 Douglas, "we can never acknowledge the right . . . to secede and cut us off": quoted in Williams, *Roots of Modern American Empire*, 101

p. 492 "the peaceful navigation of Mississippi hereby declared FREE": Davis, *Rise and Fall*, 245

p. 492 "Paradoxically, then it was the interest most involved in the Southern route": Parker, "Northwest to Mid-West," 29

p. 493 Fehrenbacher, "if only three or four states had seceded": *South and Three Sectional Crises*, 5

p. 493 Lincoln, "I think to lose Kentucky": letter to Browning, September 22, 1861, quoted in Smith, *Borderland*, 294

p. 494 "South of Northern confederacy . . . preferable than North of Southern": Richmond *Enquirer* (May 25, 1858)

p. 494 "who can contemplate Virginia as the tail of Southern Confederacy": Alexandria *Gazette* (December 15, 1860); both quoted in Goldfield, *Urban Growth*, 255, 253

p. 496 "Atlanta exhibits more signs of life and energy": Myers, *Children of Pride*, vol. 2, 937

p. 497 "Suppose there is a peaceful secession by general consent": Springfield (Massachusetts) *Daily Republican* (February 23, 1861), in Perkins, *Northern Editorials*, 358

p. 497 Hayes, "Twenty millions in the temperate zone": quoted in Hess, *Liberty, Virtue and Progress*, 22

p. 497 "The 'current events and experience' by which he promised to be guided": Cincinnati *Daily Commercial* (February 23, 1861), in Perkins, *Northern Editorials*, 375

p. 498 "An immense majority of the people of the Northwest doubtless believe": Cincinnati *Daily Commercial* (January 25, 1861), in Perkins, *Northern Editorials*, 547

p. 498 Seward, "For every State that goes out one must come in": quoted by *New York Herald* (February 1, 1861), in Perkins, *Northern Editorials*, 409

p. 498 Grayson, "Once break up the present Confederacy": Barnwell, *Love of Order*, 130

p. 499 "half a dozen Confederacies": New Albany (Indiana) *Daily Ledger* (November 21, 1860), in Perkins, *Northern Editorials*, 384–85

p. 499 "the fanatical, abolitionized, canting, hypocritical New England States": New Albany *Daily Ledger* (November 21, 1860), in Perkins, *Northern Editorials*, 385

p. 499 that New York not remain "with the petty New England States": Albany *Atlas and Argus* (November 22, 1860), in Perkins, *Northern Editorials*, 388

p. 500 Lincoln, "Physically speaking, we cannot separate," etc.: "Annual Message to Congress" (December 1, 1862); Lincoln, *Collected Works*, vol. 5, 527–29

p. 502 Nevins, *Emergence of Lincoln*, vol. 2, 471

p. 502 Fehrenbacher, "What caused the Civil War": *South and Three Sectional Crises*, 4

p. 504 "a false clarity and simplicity": Potter, *Impending Crisis*, 43

p. 506 Southerners sought to become "a nation among nations": Henry Timrod in "Ethnogenesis" (1861), quoted in Rozwenc, *Causes of the American Civil War*, 149

p. 509 Lincoln, to "nourish and protect . . . the loyal regions": annual message to Congress, December 3, 1861, in *Collected Works*, vol. 5, 37

p. 509 Freemantle on Confederate invasion of Pennsylvania: quoted in Mosby, *Stuart's Cavalry*, 101

p. 509 Davis, reunion "neither practicable nor desirable": *Rise and Fall*, 234–35

p. 510 Potter, "Southern nationalism was born of resentment": *Impending Crisis*, 469

p. 512 "chose homestead over homeland": Powell and Wayne, "Self Interest and the Decline of Southern Nationalism," in Owens and Cook, *Old South*, 45

p. 513 application of Emancipation Proclamation: Lincoln, *Collected Works*, vol. 6, 28–30

p. 515 slaveowners "moved frenetically about the South": Berlin et al., *Freedom*, 675–76

p. 515 slaves "took advantage of the possibilities": Berlin et al., *Freedom*, 680

p. 515 "At the end of the war, the last remnants": Berlin et al., *Freedom*, 682

p. 516 Schurz, "The general government of the republic": *Report*, 38

p. 516 Schurz, *Report*, 7

p. 518 "this desperately simple document": McPherson, *Battle Cry*, 699

p. 518 Lincoln on "name of the State, the boundary": *Collected Works*, vol. 7, 55

p. 518 Lincoln, "perplexing compound—Union and Slavery": letter to Charles D. Drake, October 5, 1863, *Collected Works*, vol. 6, 500

p. 518 Lincoln, "My paramount object . . . to save the Union": letter to Horace Greeley, August 27, 1862, *Collected Works*, vol. 5, 388

p. 519 "Sir, the flag that now floats": Doolittle (Wisconsin), *Cong. Globe*, 39th Cong., 1st sess., December 12, 1861, 26

p. 519 Bensel, *Yankee Leviathan*, 2

p. 520 "a Christian civilization": Julian (Indiana), *Appendix, Cong. Globe*, 39th Cong., 2d sess., January 28, 1862, 78

p. 520 "the flag of sovereignty": Beecher, *Patriotic Address*, 679

p. 520 "We are to have charge of this continent": Beecher, *Home Missionary* (1863), quoted in Power, *Planting Corn Belt Culture*, 11–12

p. 520 "geographical divisions of the Republic" and subsequent quotations: Julian (Indiana), *Appendix, Cong. Globe*, 39th Cong., 2d sess., January 28, 1862, 79, 78

p. 521 secretary of War, "reconstruction of the boundaries": *Report* (December 1, 1861), Ex. Doc. 1, 37th Cong., 2d sess., 13

p. 521 "drive the nobility" into exile: Stevens (September 6, 1865), as quoted in Bensel, *Yankee Leviathan*, 354 n 82

p. 521 Stevens, "whole fabric of southern society": quoted in Foner, *Reconstruction*, 236

p. 522 Davis, "lust of empire": *Rise and Fall*, 229

p. 522 Schurz, "an *utter absence of national feeling,*" *Report*, 13

p. 522 "the blacks at large belong to the whites at large," Schurz, *Report*, 24

p. 525 Hawthorne on Washington: quoted in Froncek, *Illustrated History*, 224

p. 526 "a building which had been merely the outdated seat": Hitchcock and Seale, *Temples of Democracy*, 123

p. 526 on the Grand Review, "At the end of the avenue": Hitchcock and Seale, *Temples of Democracy*, 146

PART FOUR

p. 532 Lincoln, "It is of noteworthy interest": annual message to Congress, December 6, 1864, in *Collected Works*, vol. 8, 145

p. 532 "Our defenceless frontier settlements": "Report of the Sec. of the Interior," *Appendix, Cong. Globe*, 39th Cong., 1st sess., December 4, 1865, 29

p. 533 to create "for our people . . . the use of a wide belt": Report of Lt. Gen. W. T. Sherman, November 5, 1866, in *Report of the Sec. of War*, in *Appendix, Cong. Globe*, 39th Cong., 2d sess., November 14, 1866, 20

p. 535 Lytton, "to see, in the settlement of the Red River, a nucleus": quoted in Morton, *Critical Years*, 39

p. 537 Banks, a bill "establishing conditions for the admission of": *Cong. Globe*, 39th Cong., 1st sess., July 3, 1866, 3548

p. 539 Galt, "When we extend the boundaries of our Empire": quoted in Underhill, *Image of Confederation*, 8

p. 539 "wherever he looked the Upper-Canadian patriot saw": Underhill, *Image of Confederation*, 5–6

p. 540 "A Celtic and Catholic element, unsettling and pervasive": Morton, *Critical Years*, 46

p. 540 Morton on Halifax: *Critical Years*, 45

p. 541 "they had been sure neither of its wisdom nor of their welcome": Stevens, *Canadian National Railways*, 194

p. 542 Ramsey resolution, "That Canada, with the consent of Great Britain": *Cong. Globe*, 40th Cong., 2d sess., December 9, 1867, 79

p. 543 "Russia must endeavor . . . to become stronger in her center" and "following the natural order of things": quoted in Jensen, *Alaska Purchase*, 15, 14

p. 543 Sumner, "by it we dismiss one more monarch": Jensen, *Alaska Purchase*, 89–90

p. 543 Banks's resolution, "that a confederation of States": *Cong. Globe*, 40th Cong., 1st sess., March 27, 1867, 392

p. 544 "open a monarchical blister": quoted in Morton, *Critical Years*, 212

p. 544 Monck, "which has laid the foundation": quoted in Underhill, *Image of Confederation*, 1

p. 544 Morton on Macdonald: *Canadian Identity*, 45, 46

p. 544 *Frank Leslie's Illustrated News* comment: quoted in Stuart, *United States Expansionism*, 244

p. 544 "This fantasy acquired a certain theoretical dignity": Stuart, *United States Expansionism*, 209

p. 544 New York *World*, "A gap in our possessions": quoted in Bailey, *Diplomatic History*, 402

p. 544 Sumner, "a visible step in the occupation of the whole": quoted in Jensen, *Alaska Purchase*, 89

p. 546 Morton, "one of the greatest transfers of territory": *Manitoba*, 117

p. 546 "The best means of impeding annexation": Schoonover, *Dollars over Dominion*, 19

p. 547 Confederate agent, "no one is more impressed . . . that, *Southward*": Schoonover, *Dollars over Dominion*, 37

p. 547 Grant, "he did not consider the Civil War completely terminated": Schoonover, *Dollars over Dominion*, 221

p. 549 American agents, "We will have a hold in the future on Mexico" and "in the course of time . . . the border states": from two reports quoted in Schoonover, *Dollars over Dominion*, 62, 67

p. 549 "the semimechanized, capitalistic, export-oriented sugar plantation": Scott, *Slave Emancipation*, 14

p. 550 "independence for the Spanish Antilles": Knight, *Slave Society in Cuba*, 151

p. 551 "the best island, that of St. Thomas": quoted in Tansill, *Purchase of West Indies*, 36

p. 552 "It may be convenient to have a naval station": *Harper's* (February 27, 1869), quoted in Bailey, *Diplomatic History*, 393

p. 553 Barbados as "the outstanding example of continuity": Galloway, *Sugar Cane Industry*, 149

p. 553 "Long before the end of . . . apprenticeship": Mintz, *Caribbean Contours*, 134

p. 555 "The display of the flag of the Union in foreign ports": *Appendix, Cong. Globe*, 39th Cong., 2d sess., December 3, 1866, 38

p. 555 Navy report on need to have "our own *coaling stations*": Tansill, *Purchase of West Indies*, 35–36

p. 555 Seward, "an expansionist of hemispheric voracity": Bailey, *Diplomatic History*, 392

p. 556 warships off Panama "prepared to give assistance and protection": *Report of Sec. of the Navy, Appendix, Cong. Globe*, 39th Cong., 2d sess., December 3, 1866, 40

p. 557 Carey, "I pray you now to take up a railroad map": *Misc. Works*, vol. 2, 10

p. 558 Lincoln, "I regard our emigrants as . . . replenishing streams": annual message to Congress, December 6, 1864, in *Collected Works*, vol. 8, 141

Bibliography

The following list of works used in the preparation of *Continental America* is divided according to the four parts of the text. Of course, some items were pertinent to more than one part, but these are listed only where first used. I have, at the outset, also noted a few books and references of more general utility.

Other materials essential to such a work in historical geography deserve mention in kind even if too specialized or inaccessible or, in some cases, too well known, to warrant separate listing. The most important are a large number of maps of many kinds, old and new, some in atlases, most in separate sheets, accumulated in the course of teaching and writing over many years. Some of the most useful are copies of maps in the National Archives or the Library of Congress, and many others were perused and notes taken on visits to these voluminous collections. I should like to think that the reader would soon sense that every page of this book was written with an array of maps immediately at hand.

Many standard federal government documents, especially abstracts of decennial censuses, annual reports of departments, topical papers collected in the two *American State Papers* series, and the sequential volumes of sessions and debates in Congress constitute another important topic, have usually been cited only when drawn upon for direct quotations. Finally, the state guidebooks produced by the Federal Writers' Project of the Works Progress Administration in the late 1930s and early 1940s (some of which have been reprinted) are too numerous and well known to require separate listing. Over the years I collected an almost complete set of these rich lodes of information on localities and have consulted them on countless details.

GENERAL

Bailyn, Bernard, David Brion Davis, David Herbert Donald, John J. Thomas, Robert H. Wiebe, and Gordon S. Wood. *The Great Republic: A History of the American People.* Vol. 1. 2d ed. Lexington, Mass.: D. C. Heath, 1981.

Boorstin, Daniel J. *The Americans: The National Experience.* New York: Random House, 1965.

Conzen, Michael P., ed. *The Making of the American Landscape.* Boston: Unwin Hyman, 1990.

Deák, Gloria Gilda. *Picturing America, 1497–1899: Prints, Maps, and Drawings Bearing on the New World Discoveries and the Development of the Territory That Is Now the United States.* 2 vols. Princeton: Princeton, Univ. Press, 1988.

Furnas, J. C. *The Americans: A Social History of the United States, 1587–1914.* New York: Capricorn, 1971.

Garrett, Wilbur E., ed. *Historical Atlas of the United States.* Washington, D.C.: National Geographic Society, 1988.

Henretta, James A., W. Elliot Brownlee, David Brody, and Susan Ware. *America's History.* Chicago: Dorsey Press, 1987.

Kagan, Hilde Heun, ed. *The American Heritage Pictorial Atlas of United States History.* New York: American Heritage, 1966.

Kerr, D. G. G. *A Historical Atlas of Canada.* Toronto: Thomas Nelson & Sons, 1961.

Martis, Kenneth C. *The Historical Atlas of Political Parties in the United States Congress, 1789–1989.* New York: Macmillan, 1989.

Miller, Theodore R. *Graphic History of the Americas.* New York: John Wiley & Sons, 1969.

Mitchell, Robert D., and Paul A. Groves, eds. *North America: The Historical Geography of a Changing Continent.* Totowa, N.J.: Rowman & Littlefield, 1987.

Paullin, Charles O., and John K. Wright. *Atlas of the Historical Geography of the United States.* Washington: Carnegie Institution, 1932.

Ristow, Walter W. *American Maps and Mapmakers: Commercial Cartography in the Nineteenth Century.* Detroit: Wayne State Univ. Press, 1985.

Rooney, John F., Jr., Wilbur Zelinsky, and Dean R. Louder, eds. *This Remarkable Continent: An Atlas of United States and Canadian Society and Culture.* College Station: Texas A&M Univ. Press, 1982.

Schwartz, Seymour I., and Ralph E. Ehrenberg. *The Mapping of America.* New York: Harry N. Abrams, 1980.

Van Zandt, Franklin K. *Boundaries of the United States and the Several States.* Geological Survey Bulletin 1212. Washington, D.C.: Government Printing Office, 1966.

PART ONE

Abel, Annie H. "Proposals for an Indian State, 1778–1878." *Annual Report of the American Historical Association* 1 (1907): 89–104.

Abernathy, Thomas P. *The South in the New Nation, 1789–1819.* Baton Rouge: Louisiana State Univ. Press, 1961.

Adams, John Quincy. *Memoirs of John Quincy Adams.* Vol. 4. Ed. Charles Francis Adams. Philadelphia: J. B. Lippincott, 1875.

———. *Writings of John Quincy Adams.* Vol. 7, 1820–1823. Ed. Worthington Chauncey Ford. New York: Macmillan, 1917.

Agnew, Brad. *Fort Gibson: Terminal on the Trail of Tears.* Norman: Univ. of Oklahoma Press, 1980.

Allen, John Logan. *Passage through the Garden: Lewis and Clark and the Image of the American Northwest.* Urbana: Univ. of Illinois Press, 1975.

Allin, Cephas A., and George M. Jones. *Annexation, Preferential Trade and Reciprocity.* Toronto: Musson, [1912].

Allworth, Edward, ed. *Central Asia: A Century of Russian Rule.* New York: Columbia Univ. Press, 1967.

Almonte, Juan N. "Statistical Report on Texas." *Southwestern Historical Quarterly* 28 (1925): 177–221.

Armstrong, F. H. "Toronto in 1834." *Canadian Geographer* 10 (1966): 172–83.

Bacon, Elizabeth. *Central Asians under Russian Rule: A Study in Culture Change.* Ithaca: Cornell Univ. Press, 1966.

Bailey, Thomas A. *A Diplomatic History of the American People.* 3d ed. New York: F. S. Crofts, 1947.

Baldwin, P. M. "A Short History of the Mesilla Valley." *New Mexico Historical Review* 13 (1938): 314–24.

Bell, David V. J. "The Loyalist Tradition in Canada." *Journal of Canadian Studies* 5 (1970): 22–23.

Berkhofer, Robert F., Jr. *The White Man's Indian: Images of the American Indian from Columbus to the Present.* New York: Random House, 1978.

———. "The North American Frontier as Process and Context." In *The Frontier in History,* ed. Howard Lamar and Leonard Thompson,

43–75. New Haven and London: Yale Univ. Press, 1981.

Bernstein, Harry. "Regionalism in the National History of Mexico." In *Latin American History: Essays on Its Study and Teaching, 1898–1965,* ed. Howard F. Cline, 1:389–94. Austin: Univ. of Texas Press, 1967.

Berry, Mary Frances, and John W. Blassingame. *Long Memory: The Black Experience in America.* New York: Oxford Univ. Press, 1982.

Billington, Ray Allen. *Westward Expansion: A History of the American Frontier.* 4th ed. New York: Macmillan, 1974.

Blouet, Brian W., and Merlin P. Lawson, eds. *Images of the Plains: The Role of Human Nature in Settlement.* Lincoln: Univ. of Nebraska Press, 1975.

Bourne, Kenneth. *Britain and the Balance of Power in North America, 1815–1908.* Berkeley: Univ. of California Press, 1967.

Bowen, William A. *The Willamette Valley: Migration and Settlement on the Oregon Frontier.* Seattle: Univ. of Washington Press, 1978.

Brack, Gene M. *Mexico Views Manifest Destiny, 1821–1846: An Essay on the Origins of the Mexican War.* Albuquerque: Univ. of New Mexico Press, 1975.

Bradley, Harold Whitman. "Hawaii and the American Penetration of the Northeastern Pacific, 1800–1845." *Pacific Historical Review* 12 (1943): 277–86.

Brand, Donald D. *Mexico: Land of Sunshine and Shadow.* New York: Van Nostrand, 1966.

Brebner, John Bartlet. *North Atlantic Triangle: The Interplay of Canada, the United States and Great Britain.* Toronto: McClelland and Stewart, 1966.

Brooks, Philip Coolidge. *Diplomacy and the Borderlands: The Adams-Onís Treaty of 1819.* Univ. of California Publications in History, vol. 24. Berkeley: Univ. of California Press, 1939.

Brown, Charles H. *Agents of Manifest Destiny: The Lives and Times of the Filibusters.* Chapel Hill: Univ. of North Carolina Press, 1980.

Brown, Everett Somerville. *The Constitutional History of the Louisiana Purchase, 1803–1812.* Berkeley: Univ. of California Press, 1920.

Brown, Ralph H. *Historical Geography of the*

United States. New York: Harcourt, Brace, 1948.

Burt, A. L. *The United States, Great Britain, and British North America: From the Revolution to the Establishment of Peace after the War of 1812.* New York: Russell & Russell, 1961.

Caballero, Romeo Flores. *Counterrevolution: The Role of the Spaniards in the Independence of Mexico, 1804–38.* Trans. Jaime E. Rodriguez O. Lincoln: Univ. of Nebraska Press, 1974.

Callahan, James Morton. *American Foreign Policy in Mexican Relations.* Reprint. New York: Cooper Square, 1967.

Campbell, Edna F. "New Orleans at the Time of the Louisiana Purchase." *Geographical Review* 9 (1921): 414–25.

Careless, J. M. S. *The Union of the Canadas: The Growth of Canadian Institutions, 1841–1857.* Toronto: McClelland and Stewart, 1967.

———, ed. *Colonists and Canadiens, 1760–1867.* Toronto: Macmillan, 1971.

Carr, Raymond. *Spain, 1808–1975.* 2d ed. Oxford: Clarendon Press, 1982.

Clark, John G. *New Orleans, 1718–1812: An Economic History.* Baton Rouge: Louisiana State Univ. Press, 1970.

Classen, H. George. *Thrust and Counterthrust: The Genesis of the Canada–United States Boundary.* Don Mills: Longmans Canada, 1965.

Cook, Warren L. *Flood Tide of Empire: Spain and the Pacific Northwest, 1543–1819.* New Haven and London: Yale Univ. Press, 1973.

Corey, Albert B. *The Crisis of 1830–1842 in Canadian-American Relations.* Reissued. New York: Russell & Russell, 1970.

Cornell, Paul G., Jean Hamelin, Fernand Ouellet, and Marcel Trudel. *Canada: Unity in Diversity.* Toronto: Holt, Rinehart and Winston, 1967.

Cotterill, R. S. *The Southern Indians: The Story of the Civilized Tribes before Removal.* Norman: Univ. of Oklahoma Press, 1954.

Cox, Isaac Joslin. *The West Florida Controversy, 1798–1813.* Baltimore: Johns Hopkins Univ. Press, 1912.

Craig, Alan K., and Christopher S. Peebles. "Ethnoecologic Change among the Seminoles, 1740–1840." *Geoscience and Man* 5 (1974): 83–96.

Craig, Béatrice. "Immigrants in a Frontier Community: Madawaska, 1785–1850." *Histoire Sociale/Social History* 19 (November 1986): 277–97.

Craig, Gerald M. *Upper Canada: The Formative Years, 1784–1841.* Toronto: McClelland and Stewart, 1963.

Craton, Michael. *A History of the Bahamas.* London: Collins, 1962.

Creighton, Donald. *The Empire of the St. Lawrence.* Boston: Houghton Mifflin, 1958.

Crété, Liliane. *Daily Life in Louisiana, 1815–1830.* Trans. Patrick Gregory. Baton Rouge: Louisiana State Univ. Press, 1981.

Darby, William. *View of the United States: Historical, Geographical, and Statistical.* Philadelphia: H. S. Tanner, 1828.

Dargo, George. *Jefferson's Louisiana: Politics and the Clash of Legal Traditions.* Cambridge: Harvard Univ. Press, 1975.

Davis, Richard C. *Rupert's Land: A Cultural Tapestry.* Waterloo: Wilfred Laurier Univ. Press, 1988.

Debo, Angie. *The Rise and Fall of the Choctaw Republic.* Norman: Univ. of Oklahoma Press, 1934.

Debouzy, Marianne. "American History in France." *Reviews in American History* 14 (1986): 542–56.

De Bow, J. D. B. *Statistical View of the United States, . . . Being a Compendium of the Seventh Census.* Washington, D.C.: A. O. P. Nicholson, Public Printer, 1854.

DeConde, Alexander. *This Affair of Louisiana.* New York: Charles Scribner's Sons, 1976.

de la Teja, Jesús, and John Wheat. "Bexar: Profile of a Tejano Community, 1820–1832." *Southwestern Historical Quarterly* 89 (1985): 7–34.

DeRosier, Arthur H., Jr. *The Removal of the Choctaw Indians.* Knoxville: Univ. of Tennessee Press, 1970.

"Descriptions of Texas by Stephen F. Austin." *Southwestern Historical Quarterly* 28 (1924): 98–121.

DeVoto, Bernard. *The Course of Empire.* Boston: Houghton Mifflin, 1952.

DeWitt, Howard A. *California Civilization: An Interpretation.* Dubuque: Kendall-Hunt, 1979.

Dicken, Samuel N., and Emily F. Dicken. *The Making of Oregon: A Study in Historical Geog-*

raphy. Portland: Oregon Historical Society, 1979.

"Documents Relating to the Oregon Emigration Movement, 1842–43." *Quarterly, Oregon Historical Society* 4 (1903): 170–77.

[Durham, First Earl of (John George Lambton).] *Lord Durham's Report on the Affairs of British North America.* Vol. 2, *Text of the Report.* Ed. Sir C. P. Lucas. Oxford: Clarendon Press, 1912.

Ellison, William Henry. *A Self-Governing Dominion: California, 1849–1860.* Berkeley: Univ. of California Press, 1950.

Errington, Jane. *The Lion, the Eagle, and Upper Canada: A Developing Colonial Ideology.* Kingston and Montreal: McGill-Queen's Univ. Press, 1987.

Errington, Jane, and George Rawlyk. "The Loyalist-Federalist Alliance of Upper Canada." *American Review of Canadian Studies* 14 (1984): 157–76.

Faulk, Odie B. *Too Far North . . . Too Far South.* Los Angeles: Westernlore Press, 1967.

Foley, William E., and C. David Rice. *The First Choteaus: River Barons of Early St. Louis.* Urbana: Univ. of Illinois Press, 1983.

Foner, Philip S. *A History of Cuba and Its Relations with the United States.* Vol. 1, *1492–1845.* New York: International, 1962

Fried, Morton H. "Land Tenure, Geography and Ecology in the Contact of Cultures." *American Journal of Economics and Sociology* 11 (1952): 391–412.

Friis, Herman R., ed. *The Pacific Basin: A History of Its Geographical Exploration.* New York: American Geographical Society, 1967.

Fuller, John Douglas Pitts. *The Movement for the Acquisition of all Mexico, 1846–1848.* Baltimore: Johns Hopkins Univ. Press, 1936.

Gabriel, Ralph Henry. *The Lure of the Frontier: A Story of Race Conflict.* New Haven: Yale Univ. Press, 1929.

Galbraith, John S. *The Hudson's Bay Company as an Imperial Factor, 1821–1869.* Berkeley: Univ. of California Press, 1957.

Garber, Paul Neff. *The Gadsden Treaty.* Philadelphia: Press of the Univ. of Pennsylvania, 1923.

Garver, John Baltzly, Jr. "The Role of the United States Army in the Colonization of the Trans-Missouri West: Kansas, 1804–1861."

Ph.D. dissertation, Department of Geography, Syracuse Univ., 1981.

Gayarré, Charles. *History of Louisiana: The American Domination.* New York: William J. Widdleton, 1866.

Gentilcore, R. Louis, and C. Grant Head. *Ontario's History in Maps.* Toronto: Univ. of Toronto Press, 1984.

Gibson, A. M. *The Kickapoos: Lords of the Middle Border.* Norman: Univ. of Oklahoma Press, 1963.

Gibson, James R. *Imperial Russia in Frontier America: The Changing Geography of Supply of Russian America, 1784–1867.* New York: Oxford Univ. Press, 1976.

———. *Farming the Frontier: The Agricultural Opening of the Oregon Country, 1786–1846.* Vancouver: Univ. of British Columbia Press, 1985.

Gluek, Alvin C., Jr. *Minnesota and the Manifest Destiny of the Canadian Northwest.* Toronto: Univ. of Toronto Press, 1965.

Goetzmann, William H. *Army Exploration in the American West, 1803–1863.* New Haven: Yale Univ. Press, 1959.

Goodwin, Gary C. *Cherokees in Transition: A Study of Changing Culture and Environment prior to 1775.* Research Paper no. 181. Chicago: Department of Geography, Univ. of Chicago, 1977.

Gough, Barry M. *Distant Dominion: Britain and the Northwest Coast of North America, 1579–1809.* Vancouver: Univ. of British Columbia Press, 1980.

Graebner, Norman A. *Empire on the Pacific: A Study in American Continental Expansion.* New York: Ronald Press, 1955.

Green, Stanley C. *The Mexican Republic: The First Decade, 1823–1832.* Pittsburgh: Univ. of Pittsburgh Press, 1987.

Griswold del Castillo, Richard. "Mexican Views of 1848: The Treaty of Guadalupe Hidalgo through Mexican History." *Journal of Borderlands Studies* 1 (1986): 24–40.

Guyot, Arnold. *The Earth and Man: Lectures on Comparative Physical Geography, in Its Relation to the History of Mankind.* Trans. C. C. Felton. Boston: Gould, Kendall, and Lincoln, 1849.

Hale, Charles A. *Mexican Liberalism in the Age of Mora, 1821–1853.* New Haven: Yale Univ. Press, 1968.

Hamilton, Peter J. *Colonial Mobile: A Study in Southwestern History*. Boston: Houghton Mifflin, 1910.

Hansen, Marcus Lee. *The Mingling of the Canadian and American Peoples*. New Haven: Yale Univ. Press, 1940.

Harmon, George Dewey. *Sixty Years of Indian Affairs, Political, Economic and Diplomatic, 1789–1850*. Chapel Hill: Univ. of North Carolina Press, 1941.

Harris, R. Cole, and John Warkentin. *Canada before Confederation: A Study in Historical Geography*. New York: Oxford Univ. Press, 1974.

Hatcher, Mattie Austin. *The Opening of Texas to Foreign Settlement, 1801–1821*. Univ. of Texas Bulletin no. 2714, April 8, 1927. Austin: Univ. of Texas, 1927.

Heizer, Robert F., and Alan J. Almquist. *The Other Californians: Prejudice and Discrimination under Spain, Mexico, and the United States to 1920*. Berkeley: Univ. of California Press, 1971.

Hewes, Leslie. *Occupying the Cherokee Country of Oklahoma*. Lincoln: Univ. of Nebraska Studies, n.s., no. 57, 1978.

Hietala, Thomas B. *Manifest Design: Anxious Aggrandizement in Late Jacksonian America*. Ithaca: Cornell Univ. Press, 1985.

Horsman, Reginald. *Expansion and American Indian Policy, 1783–1812*. [East Lansing]: Michigan State Univ. Press, 1967.

———. *The Origins of Indian Removal, 1815–1824*. [East Lansing]: Michigan State Univ. Press, 1970.

———. "Recent Trends and New Directions in Native American History." In *The American West: New Perspectives, New Dimensions*, ed. Jerome O. Steffen, 124–51. Norman: Univ. of Oklahoma Press, 1979.

———. *Race and Manifest Destiny: The Origins of American Racial Anglo-Saxonism*. Cambridge: Harvard Univ. Press, 1981.

Howard, Joseph Kinsey. *Strange Empire: A Narrative of the Northwest*. New York: William Morrow, 1952.

Hudson, Charles. *The Southeastern Indians*. Knoxville: Univ. of Tennessee Press, 1976.

Humboldt, Alexander. *The Island of Cuba*. New York: Derby & Jackson, 1856.

Hutchinson, C. Alan. *Frontier Settlement in Mexican California: The Híjar-Padrés Colony, and Its Origins, 1769–1845*. New Haven: Yale Univ. Press, 1969.

Jackson, Andrew. *Correspondence of Andrew Jackson*. Ed. John Spencer Bassett. Publication no. 371, 7 vols. Washington, D.C.: Carnegie Institute of Washington, 1926–35.

Jackson, Donald. *Letters of the Lewis and Clark Expedition, with Related Documents, 1783–1854*. Urbana: Univ. of Illinois Press, 1962.

Jefferson, Thomas. *The Writings of Thomas Jefferson*. Ed. Paul Leicester Ford. Vols. 5–9. New York: G. P. Putnam's Sons, 1895–98.

———. *Writings*. The Library of America. New York: Literary Classics of the United States, 1984.

Johansen, Dorothy O., and Charles M. Gates. *Empire of the Columbia: A History of the Pacific Northwest*. 2d ed. New York: Harper & Row, 1967.

Jones, Howard. *To the Webster-Ashburton Treaty: A Study in Anglo-American Relations, 1783–1843*. Chapel Hill: Univ. of North Carolina Press, 1977.

Juricek, John T. "American Usage of the Word 'Frontier' from Colonial Times to Frederick Jackson Turner." *Proceedings of the American Philosophical Society* 110 (February 1966): 10–34.

Kappler, Charles J., ed. *Indian Affairs: Laws and Treaties*. Vol. 2, *Treaties*. Washington, D.C.: Government Printing Office, 1904.

Kay, Jeanne. "The Fur Trade and Native American Population Growth." *Ethnohistory* 31 (1984): 265–87.

Kicza, John E. "Mexican Demographic History of the Nineteenth Century: Evidence and Approaches." In *Statistical Abstract of Latin America*, ed. James W. Wilkie and Stephen Haber, vol. 21. Los Angeles: UCLA Latin American Center Publications, 1981.

King, Duane H., ed. *The Cherokee Indian Nation: A Troubled History*. Knoxville: Univ. of Tennessee Press, 1979.

Kiple, Kenneth. *Blacks in Colonial Cuba, 1774–1899*. Gainesville: Univ. Presses of Florida, 1976.

Knight, Franklin W. *Slave Society in Cuba during the Nineteenth Century*. Madison: Univ. of Wisconsin Press, 1970.

Kuykendall, Ralph S. *The Hawaiian Kingdom,*

1778–1854: Foundation and Transformation. 1938. Reprint. Honolulu: Univ. of Hawaii Press, 1947.

Lamar, Howard Roberts. *The Far Southwest, 1846–1912: A Territorial History.* New Haven: Yale Univ. Press, 1966.

Landon, Fred. *Western Ontario and the American Frontier.* Toronto: McClelland and Stewart, 1967.

Langley, Lester D. *The Cuban Policy of the United States: A Brief History.* New York: John Wiley & Sons, 1968.

Laurence, Eleanor. "Mexican Trade between Santa Fe and Los Angeles, 1830–1848." *California Historical Society Quarterly* 10 (1931): 27–39.

Lewis, Peirce F. *New Orleans: The Making of an Urban Landscape.* Cambridge, Mass.: Ballinger, 1976.

Lincoln, Abraham. *The Collected Works of Abraham Lincoln.* Ed. Roy P. Basler. New Brunswick, N.J.: Rutgers Univ. Press, 1953.

Lister, Florence C., and Robert H. Lister. *Chihuahua: Storehouse of Storms.* Albuquerque: Univ. of New Mexico Press, 1966.

Loewenberg, Robert J. *Equality on the Oregon Frontier: Jason Lee and the Methodist Mission, 1834–43.* Seattle: Univ. of Washington Press, 1976.

Ludger, Beauregard. "Le Peuplement du Richelieu." *Revue de géographie de Montréal* 19 (1965): 43–74.

McKenney, Thos. L. "Report of the Commissioner of Indian Affairs, 1 Nov. 1828." *New American State Papers: Indian Affairs.* [c. 1972.] 1:69–100.

MacLachlan, Colin M., and Jaime E. Rodriguez O. *The Forging of the Cosmic Race: A Reinterpretation of Colonial Mexico.* Berkeley: Univ. of California Press, 1980.

Malone, Dumas. *Jefferson the President, First Term, 1801–1805.* Vol. 4, *Jefferson and His Time.* Boston: Little, Brown, 1970.

Martin, Calvin, ed. *The American Indian and the Problem of History.* New York: Oxford Univ. Press, 1987.

Martin, Joel Wayne. "Cultural Hermeneutics on the Frontier: Colonialism and the Muscogulge Millenarian Revolt of 1813." Ph.D. dissertation, Department of Religion, Duke Univ., 1988.

Martin, Lawrence. "John Disturnell's Map of the United Mexican States." Ed. and abridged Walter W. Ristow. *A la Carte: Selected Papers on Maps and Atlases.* Comp. Walter W. Ristow. Washington, D.C.: Library of Congress, 1972.

Mason, Philip. *Patterns of Dominance.* London: Oxford Univ. Press, 1970.

Mattes, Merrill J. "The Jumping-Off Places on the Overland Trail." In *The Frontier Reexamined,* ed. John Francis McDermott, 27–39. Urbana: Univ. of Illinois Press, 1967.

May, Robert E. *The Southern Dream of a Caribbean Empire, 1854–1861.* Baton Rouge: Louisiana State Univ. Press, 1973.

Meinig, D. W. *The Great Columbia Plain: A Historical Geography, 1805–1910.* Seattle: Univ. of Washington Press, 1968.

———. *Imperial Texas: An Interpretive Essay in Cultural Geography.* Austin: Univ. of Texas Press, 1969.

———. *Southwest: Three Peoples in Geographic Change, 1600–1970.* New York: Oxford Univ. Press, 1971.

———. "Geographical Analysis of Imperialism." In *Period and Place: Research Methods in Historical Geography,* ed. Alan R. H. Baker and Mark Billinge, 71–78. Cambridge: Cambridge Univ. Press, 1982.

———. *The Shaping of America.* Vol. 1, *Atlantic America, 1492–1800.* New Haven and London: Yale Univ. Press, 1986.

Melish, John. *A Geographical Description of the United States, with the Contiguous British and Spanish Possessions.* Philadelphia: John Melish, 1816.

Merk, Frederick. *Manifest Destiny and Mission in American History, A Reinterpretation.* New York: Alfred A. Knopf, 1963.

———. *The Oregon Question: Essays in Anglo-American Diplomacy and Politics.* Cambridge: Harvard Univ. Press, 1967.

Meyer, Alfred H. "Circulation and Settlement Patterns of the Calumet Region of Northwest Indiana and Northeast Illinois (The First Stage of Occupance—The Pottawatomie and the Fur Trade,—1830)." *Annals, Association of American Geographers* 44 (1954): 245–74.

Mills, David. *The Idea of Loyalty in Upper Canada, 1784–1850.* Kingston and Montreal: McGill-Queen's Univ. Press, 1988.

Miner, H. Craig, and William E. Unrau. *The*

End of Indian Kansas: A Study of Cultural Revolution, 1854–1871. Lawrence: Regents Press of Kansas, 1978.

Monroe, James. *The Writings of James Monroe.* Ed. Stanislaus Murray Hamilton. Vol. 6, *1817–1823.* New York: G. P. Putnam's Sons, 1902.

Mooney, James. *Historical Sketch of the Cherokee.* Chicago: Aldine, 1975.

More, Sir Thomas. *Utopia.* Ed. J. Churton Collins. Oxford: Clarendon Press, 1904.

Morris, John W., and Edwin C. McReynolds. *Historical Atlas of Oklahoma.* Norman: Univ. of Oklahoma Press, 1965.

Morton, Arthur S. *A History of the Canadian West to 1870–71.* London: Thomas Nelson & Sons, 1939.

Morton, Ohland. *Terán and Texas: A Chapter in Texas-Mexican Relations.* Austin: Texas State Historical Association, 1948.

Morton, W. L. *Manitoba: A History.* 2d ed. Toronto: Univ. of Toronto Press, 1967.

———. *Contexts of Canada's Past: Selected Essays.* Ed. A. B. McKillop. Toronto: Macmillan, 1980.

Moseley, Edward H., and Edward D. Terry, eds. *Yucatan: A World Apart.* University: Univ. of Alabama Press, 1980.

Nasatir, Abraham P. *Borderland in Retreat: From Spanish Louisiana to the Far Southwest.* Albuquerque: Univ. of New Mexico Press, 1976.

Nash, Gary B. *Red, White, and Black: The Peoples of Early America.* Englewood Cliffs, N.J.: Prentice-Hall, 1974.

Newton, Milton B., Jr. *Atlas of Louisiana.* Baton Rouge: School of Geoscience, Louisiana State Univ., 1972.

———. "Louisiana Geography: A Syllabus." 3d ed. Baton Rouge: School of Geoscience, Louisiana State Univ., 1976.

Niddrie, David L. "The Caribbean." In *Latin America: Geographical Perspectives,* ed. Harold Blakemore and Clifford T. Smith, 73–120. London: Methuen, 1971.

Olliff, Donathon C. *Reforma Mexico and the United States: A Search for Alternatives to Annexation, 1854–1861.* University: Univ. of Alabama Press, 1981.

Paredes, J. Anthony, and Kenneth J. Plante. "A Re-examination of Creek Indian Population Trends: 1738–1832." *American Indian Culture and Research Journal* 6 (1983): 3–28.

Parkins, Almon Ernest. *The South: Its Economic-Geographic Development.* New York: John Wiley & Sons, 1938.

———. *The Historical Geography of Detroit.* Port Washington, N.Y.: Kennikat Press, 1970.

Perdue, Theda. *Slavery and the Evolution of Cherokee Society, 1540–1866.* Knoxville: Univ. of Tennessee Press, 1979.

Perez, Louis A., Jr. *Cuba and the United States: Ties of Singular Intimacy.* Athens: Univ. of Georgia Press, 1990.

Peters, Virginia Bergman. *The Florida Wars.* Hamden, Conn.: Archon Books, 1979.

Peterson, Jacqueline. "Prelude to Red River: A Social Portrait of the Great Lakes Métis." *Ethnohistory* 25 (1978): 41–67.

Philbrick, Francis S. *The Rise of the West, 1754–1830.* New York: Harper & Row, 1965.

Phillips, Clifton Jackson. *Protestant America and the Pagan World: The First Half Century of the American Board of Commissioners for Foreign Missions, 1810–1860.* Cambridge, Mass.: East Asian Research Center, 1969.

Pike, Douglas. *Paradise of Dissent: South Australia, 1829–1857.* London: Longmans, Green, 1957.

Pillsbury, Richard. "The Europeanization of the Cherokee Settlement Landscape prior to Removal: A Georgia Case Study. *Geoscience and Man* 23 (1983): 59–69.

Pitt, Leonard. *The Decline of the Californios: A Social History of the Spanish-Speaking Californians, 1846–1890.* Berkeley: Univ. of California Press, 1966.

Pletcher, David M. *The Diplomacy of Annexation, Texas, Oregon, and the Mexican War.* Columbia: Univ. of Missouri Press, 1973.

Polk, James K. *The Diary of James K. Polk, during His Presidency, 1845 to 1849.* 4 vols. Ed. Milo Quaife. Chicago: A. C. McClurg, 1910.

Pomeroy, Earl. *The Pacific Slope: A History.* New York: Alfred A. Knopf, 1965.

Powell, Fred Wilbur, ed. *Hall J. Kelley on Oregon.* Princeton: Princeton Univ. Press, 1932.

Pratt, Julius W. *Expansionists of 1812.* Gloucester, Mass.: Peter Smith, 1957.

Prichard, Walter. *Walter Prichard's Outline of Louisiana Studies.* Ed. and expanded Sue Eakin. Gretna, La.: Pelican, 1972.

Pritchett, John Perry. *The Red River Valley, 1811–1849: A Regional Study.* New Haven: Yale Univ. Press, 1942.

Prucha, Francis Paul. *A Guide to the Military Posts of the United States, 1789–1895.* Madison: State Historical Society of Wisconsin, 1964.

———. *American Indian Policy in the Formative Years: The Indian Trade and Intercourse Acts, 1790–1834.* Lincoln: Univ. of Nebraska Press, 1970.

———. *The Great Father: The United States Government and the American Indians.* Vol. 1. Lincoln: Univ. of Nebraska Press, 1984.

———. *Atlas of American Indian Affairs.* Lincoln: Univ. of Nebraska Press, 1990.

Rauch, Basil. *American Interest in Cuba, 1848–1855.* New York: Columbia Univ. Press, 1948.

Ray, Arthur J. *Indians in the Fur Trade: Their Role as Trappers, Hunters, and Middlemen in the Lands Southwest of Hudson Bay, 1600–1870.* Toronto: Univ. of Toronto Press, 1974.

Reeves, Carolyn Keller, ed. *The Choctaw before Removal.* Jackson: Univ. Press of Mississippi, 1985.

Rehder, John B. "Sugar Plantations in Louisiana: Origin, Dispersal, and Responsible Location Factors." *Studies in the Social Sciences, West Georgia College* 12 (1973): 78–93.

Rich, E. E. *The Fur Trade and the Northwest to 1857.* Toronto: McClelland and Stewart, 1967.

———, ed. *The Letters of John McLoughlin: Second Series, 1839–44.* London: Hudson's Bay Record Society, 1943.

Richardson, James D. *A Compilation of the Messages and Papers of the Presidents.* [Washington, D.C.]: Bureau of National Literature and Art, 1910.

Richardson, Rupert Norval. *Texas: The Lone Star State.* Englewood Cliffs, N.J.: Prentice-Hall, 1958.

Roberts, Leslie. *Montreal: From Mission Colony to World City.* Toronto: Macmillan, 1969.

Robertson, James Alexander. *Louisiana under the Rule of Spain, France, and the United States, 1785–1807.* Cleveland: Arthur H. Clark, 1911.

Robinson, David J. "Liberty, Fragile Fraternity and Inequality in Early-Republican Spanish America: Assessing the Impact of French Revolutionary Ideals." *Journal of Historical Geography* 16 (1990): 51–75.

Rogin, Michael Paul. *Fathers and Children: An-drew Jackson and the Subjugation of the American Indian.* New York: Alfred A. Knopf, 1975.

Rollins, Philip Ashton, ed. *The Discovery of the Oregon Trail: Robert Stuart's Narrative of His Overland Trip Eastward from Astoria in 1812–13.* New York: Edward Eberstadt & Sons, 1935.

Royce, Josiah. *California.* [1886] New York: Alfred A. Knopf, 1948.

Russel, Robert R. *Improvement of Communication with the Pacific Coast as an Issue in American Politics, 1783–1864.* Cedar Rapids, Iowa: Torch Press, 1948.

Sartorius, Carl. *Mexico about 1850.* Stuttgart: F. A. Brockhaus, 1961.

Satz, Ronald N. *American Indian Policy in the Jacksonian Era.* Lincoln: Univ. of Nebraska Press, 1975.

Sauer, Carl O. "The Personality of Mexico." *Geographical Review* 31 (1941): 353–64.

Savelle, Max. "The Forty-ninth Degree of North Latitude as an International Boundary, 1719: The Origin of an Idea." *Canadian Historical Review* 38 (1957): 183–201.

Schmidt, Henry C. *The Roots of Lo Mexicano: Self and Society in Mexican Thought, 1900–1934.* College Station: Texas A&M Press, 1978.

Schroeder, Susan. *Cuba: A Handbook of Historical Statistics.* Boston: G. K. Hall, 1982.

Schultz, George A. *An Indian Canaan: Isaac McCoy and the Vision of an Indian State.* Norman: Univ. of Oklahoma Press, 1972.

Sheehan, Bernard W. *Seeds of Extinction: Jeffersonian Philanthropy and the American Indian.* Chapel Hill: Univ. of North Carolina Press, 1973.

Shortridge, James R. "The Expansion of the Settlement Frontier in Missouri." *Missouri Historical Review* 75 (1980): 64–90.

Smelser, Marshal. *The Democratic Republic, 1801–1815.* New York: Harper & Row, 1968.

Smith, Dwight L. "The Land Cession Treaty: A Valid Instrument of Transfer of Indian Title." In *This Land of Ours: The Acquisition and Disposition of the Public Domain,* 87–102. Indianapolis: Indiana Historical Society, 1978.

Smith, Henry Nash. *Virgin Land: The American West as Symbol and Myth.* Cambridge: Harvard Univ. Press, 1950.

Socolofsky, Homer E., and Huber Self. *Historical Atlas of Kansas*. Norman: Univ. of Oklahoma Press, 1972.

Spicer, Edward H. *Cycles of Conquest: The Impact of Spain, Mexico, and the United States on the Indians of the Southwest, 1533–1960*. Tucson: Univ. of Arizona Press, 1962.

———. *A Short History of the Indians of the United States*. New York: Van Nostrand, 1969.

Stagg, J. C. A. *Mr. Madison's War: Politics, Diplomacy, and Warfare in the Early American Republic, 1783–1830*. Princeton: Princeton Univ. Press, 1983.

Stebelsky, I. "The Frontier in Central Asia." In *Studies in Russian Historical Geography*, ed. James H. Bater and R. A. French, 1:143–74. London: Academic Press, 1983.

Sunseri, Alvin R. *Seeds of Discord: New Mexico in the Aftermath of the American Conquest, 1846–1861*. Chicago: Nelson-Hall, 1979.

Swanton, John R. *The Early History of the Creek Indians and Their Neighbors*. Bureau of American Ethnology Bulletin 73. Washington, D.C.: Government Printing Office, 1922.

Tanner, Helen H., ed. *Atlas of Great Lakes Indian History*. Norman: Univ. of Oklahoma Press, 1987.

Tays, George. "Separation in California, 1820–1846." M.A. thesis, Department of History, Univ. of California, Berkeley, 1928.

Tebeau, Charlton W. *A History of Florida*. Coral Gables: Univ. of Miami Press, 1971.

Thomas, David Yancey. *A History of Military Government in Newly Acquired Territory of the United States*. New York: Columbia Univ. Studies in History, Economics, and Public Law, no. 2, 1904.

Thompson, Waddy. *Recollections of Mexico*. New York: Wiley and Putnam, 1846.

Thornton, A. P. *Doctrines of Imperialism*. New York: John Wiley & Sons, 1965.

Thornton, Russell. "Cherokee Population Losses during the Trail of Tears: A New Perspective and an Estimate." *Ethnohistory* 31 (1984): 289–300.

Timmons, Wilbert H. *Tadeo Ortiz: Mexican Colonizer and Reformer*. Southwestern Studies Monograph no. 43. El Paso: Univ. of Texas, 1974.

Tocqueville, Alexis de. *Democracy in America*. The Henry Reeve text as revised by Francis Bowen . . . further corrected and edited . . . by Phillips Bradley. Vol. 1. New York: Alfred A. Knopf, 1945.

Tomkins, George S. "Understanding Ourselves: The Origin and Development of Canadian Studies." In *Interpreting Canada*, ed. Graeme Wynn, 75–94. Vancouver: Tantalus Research, 1986.

Tregle, Joseph G., Jr. "Early New Orleans Society: A Reappraisal." *Journal of Southern History* 18 (1952): 20–36.

Trennert, Robert A., Jr. *Alternative to Extinction: Federal Indian Policy and the Beginnings of the Reservation System, 1846–51*. Philadelphia: Temple Univ. Press, 1975.

Trigger, Bruce G., ed. *Northeast: Handbook of North American Indians*. Vol. 15. General ed., William C. Sturtevant. Washington, D.C.: Smithsonian Institution, 1978.

Tulchinsky, Gerald J. J. *The River Barons: Montreal Businessmen and the Growth of Industry and Transportation, 1837–53*. Toronto: Univ. of Toronto Press, 1977.

U.S. Congress. House. *Country for Indians West of the Mississippi*. 22d Cong., 1st sess., 1832. H. Doc. 172.

———. House. *Regulating the Indian Department*. 23d Cong., 1st sess., 1834. H. Doc. 474.

———. House. *Report of Mr. McCoy, Relative to a Government for the Western Territory*. 25th Cong., 2d sess., 1837–38. H. Doc. 3.

———. House. *Report of the Commissioner of Indian Affairs*. 29th Cong., 1st sess., 1845–46. H. Doc. 2.

———. House. *Report of the Committee on Military Affairs on the Establishment of a Chain of Military Posts from Council Bluffs to the Pacific Ocean*. 27th Cong., 3d sess., 1843. H. Rept. 31.

———. House. *Report of the Secretary of War, Dec. 5, 1857*. 35th Cong., 1st sess., 1857. H. Ex. Doc. 2.

U.S. Congress. Senate. *Memorial of William A. Slacum*. 25th Cong., 2d sess., 1837–38. S. Doc. 2.

Upchurch, John Calhoun. "'Middle Florida': An Historical Geography of the Area between the Apalachicola and Suwanee Rivers." Ph.D. dissertation, Department of Geography, Univ. of Tennessee, 1971.

Vevier, Charles. "American Continentalism: An Idea of Expansion, 1845–1910." *American Historical Review* 65 (1960): 323–35.

von Humboldt, Alexander. *Political Essay on the Kingdom of New Spain.* Trans. John Black. Abridged ed. New York: Alfred A. Knopf, 1972.

Voss, Stuart F. *On the Periphery of Nineteenth-Century Mexico: Sonora and Sinaloa, 1810–1877.* Tucson: Univ. of Arizona Press, 1982.

Warner, Donald F. *The Idea of Continental Union: Agitation for the Annexation of Canada to the United States, 1849–1893.* Lexington: Univ. of Kentucky Press, 1960.

Washburn, Wilcomb E. "Indian Removal Policy: Administrative, Historical and Moral Criteria for Judging Its Success or Failure." *Ethnohistory* 12 (1965): 274–78.

———, ed. *History of Indian-White Relations: Handbook of North American Indians.* Vol. 4. General ed., William C. Sturtevant. Washington, D.C.: Smithsonian Institution, 1988.

Watts, David. *The West Indies: Patterns of Development, Culture and Environmental Change since 1492.* Cambridge: Cambridge Univ. Press, 1987.

Weber, David J. *The Taos Trappers: The Fur Trade in the Far Southwest, 1540–1846.* Norman: Univ. of Oklahoma Press, 1971.

———. *The Mexican Frontier, 1821–1846: The American Southwest under Mexico.* Albuquerque: Univ. of New Mexico Press, 1982.

Weinberg, Albert K. *Manifest Destiny: A Study in Nationalist Expansionism in American History.* Chicago: Quadrangle Books, [1945].

Wells, Samuel J., and Roseanna Tubby, eds. *After Removal: The Choctaw in Mississippi.* Jackson: Univ. Press of Mississippi, 1986.

Wesley, Edgar Bruce. *Guarding the Frontier: A Study of Frontier Defense from 1815 to 1825.* Minneapolis: Univ. of Minnesota Press, 1935.

Wheeler, Geoffrey. "Russian Conquest and Colonization of Central Asia." In *Russian Imperialism from Ivan the Great to the Revolution,* ed. Taras Hunczak, 264–98. New Brunswick, N.J.: Rutgers Univ. Press, 1974.

Whitaker, Arthur Preston. *The Mississippi Question, 1795–1803: A Study in Trade, Politics, and Diplomacy.* New York: D. Appleton-Century, 1934.

White, Richard. *The Roots of Dependency: Subsistence, Environment, and Social Change among the Choctaws, Pawnees, and Navajos.* Lincoln: Univ. of Nebraska Press, 1983.

Wilkes, Charles. *Narrative of the United States Exploring Expedition.* 5 vols. Philadelphia: Lea and Blanchard, 1845.

Williams, Walter L., ed. *Southeastern Indians: Since the Removal Era.* Athens: Univ. of Georgia Press, 1979.

Williamson, Chilton. *Vermont in Quandary, 1763–1825.* Montpelier: Vermont Historical Society, 1949.

Wishart, David. "Cultures in Co-operation and Conflict: Indians in the Fur Trade on the Northern Great Plains, 1807–1840." *Journal of Historical Geography* 2 (1976): 311–28.

Wolf, Eric R. *Europe and the People without History.* Berkeley: Univ. of California Press, 1982.

Woodward, Grace Steele. *The Cherokees.* Norman: Univ. of Oklahoma Press, 1963.

The WPA Guide to New Orleans. The Federal Writers' Project Guide to 1930s New Orleans, with a new introduction. New York: Pantheon Books, 1983.

Wynn, Graeme. "Population Patterns in Pre-Confederation New Brunswick." *Acadiensis* 10 (1981): 124–38.

Zornow, William Frank. *Kansas: A History of the Jayhawk State.* Norman: Univ. of Oklahoma Press, 1957.

PART TWO

Abbott, Carl. *Boosters and Businessmen: Popular Economic Thought and Urban Growth in the Antebellum Middle West.* Westport, Conn.: Greenwood Press, 1981.

———. "Frontiers and Sections: Cities and Regions in American Growth." In *American Urbanism: A Historiographical Review,* ed. Howard Gillette, Jr., and Zane L. Miller, 271–89. Westport, Conn.: Greenwood Press, 1987.

Abernethy, Thomas Perkins. *From Frontier to Plantation in Tennessee: A Study in Frontier*

Democracy. Chapel Hill: Univ. of North Carolina Press, 1932.

———. *The Formative Period in Alabama, 1815–1828.* University: Univ. of Alabama Press, 1965.

Adkins, Howard G. "The Geographic Base of Urban Retardation in Mississippi, 1800–1841." *Studies in the Social Sciences, West Georgia College* 12 (June 1973): 35–49.

Ahlstrom, Sydney E. *A Religious History of the American People.* New Haven and London: Yale Univ. Press, 1972.

Aiken, Charles S. "The Evolution of Cotton Ginning in the Southeastern United States." *Geographical Review* 63 (April 1973): 196–224.

Albion, Robert Greenhalgh. *Square-Riggers on Schedule: The New York Sailing Packets to England, France, and the Cotton Ports.* Princeton: Princeton Univ. Press, 1938.

Ambler, Charles Henry. *A History of Transportation in the Ohio Valley.* Glendale, Calif.: Arthur H. Clark, 1931.

Anderson, Benedict. *Imagined Communities: Reflections on the Origin and Spread of Nationalism.* London: Verso, 1983.

Andrews, Israel D. *Report on the Trade and Commerce of the British North American Colonies and upon the Trade of the Great Lakes and Rivers.* S. Ex. Doc. 112, 32d Cong., 1st sess. Washington, D.C.: Robert Armstrong, 1853.

Angle, Paul M., ed. *Prairie State: Impressions of Illinois, 1673–1967, by Travelers and Other Observers.* Chicago: Univ. of Chicago Press, 1968.

Appleby, Joyce. *Capitalism and a New Social Order: The Republican Vision of the 1790s.* New York: New York Univ. Press, 1984.

Armroyd, George. *A Connected View of the Whole Internal Navigation of the United States.* 2d ed. Philadelphia: Geo. Armroyd, 1830.

Arnold, Ian. *Locomotive, Trolley, and Rail Car Builders: An All-Time Directory.* Los Angeles: Trans-Anglo Books, 1965.

Arnow, Harriette Simpson. *Seedtime on the Cumberland.* New York: Macmillan, 1960.

Baer, Christopher T. *Canals and Railroads of the Mid-Atlantic States, 1800–1860.* Wilmington, Del.: Regional Economic History Research Center, Eleutherian Mills–Hagley Foundation, 1981.

Baltzell, E. Digby. *Puritan Boston and Quaker Philadelphia: Two Protestant Ethics and the Spirit of Class Authority and Leadership.* Boston: Beacon Press, 1982.

Bancroft, Frederic. *Slave Trading in the Old South.* 1931. New York: Frederick Ungar, 1959.

Bancroft, George. *The History of the United States of America from the Discovery of the Continent.* Abridged and ed. Russel B. Nye. Chicago: Univ. of Chicago Press, 1966.

Baron, Dennis. *The English-Only Question: An Official Language for Americans?* New Haven and London: Yale Univ. Press, 1990.

Bateman, Fred, and Thomas Weiss. *A Deplorable Scarcity: The Failure of Industrialization in the Slave Economy.* Chapel Hill: Univ. of North Carolina Press, 1981.

Beecher, Lyman. *A Plea for the West.* 2d ed. Cincinnati: Truman & Smith, 1835.

Belcher, Wyatt Winton. *The Economic Rivalry between St. Louis and Chicago, 1850–1880.* New York: Columbia Univ. Press, 1947.

Bell, Howard H. "Martin Delany and Black Nationalism." In *The Age of Civil War and Reconstruction,* ed. Charles Crowe, 163–67. Homewood, Ill.: Dorsey Press, 1975.

Bender, Thomas. *Toward an Urban Vision: Ideas and Institutions in Nineteenth-Century America.* Baltimore: Johns Hopkins Univ. Press, 1982.

Benson, Lee. *Turner and Beard: American Historical Writing Reconsidered.* New York: Free Press, 1960.

Bergquist, James M. "Tracing the Origins of a Midwestern Culture: The Case of Central Indiana." *Indiana Magazine of History* 77 (March 1981): 1–32.

Berlin, Ira. *Slaves without Masters: The Free Negro in the Antebellum South.* New York: Pantheon Books, 1974.

Berwanger, Eugene H. *The Frontier against Slavery: Western Anti-Negro Prejudice and the Slavery Extension Controversy.* Urbana: Univ. of Illinois Press, 1967.

Bigelow, Bruce Loring. "Ethnic Stratification in a Pedestrian City: A Social Geography of Syracuse, N.Y. in 1860." Ph.D. dissertation, Department of Geography, Syracuse Univ., 1978.

———. "The Disciples of Christ in Antebellum Indiana: Geographical Indicator of the Border South." *Journal of Cultural Geography* 7 (Fall–Winter 1986): 49–58.

Billington, Ray Allen. *America's Frontier Heritage.* New York: Holt, Rinehart and Winston, 1966.

———, ed. *The Frontier Thesis: Valid Interpretation of American History?* New York: Holt, Rinhart and Winston, 1966.

Birkbeck, Morris. *Notes on a Journey in America from the Coast of Virginia to the Territory of Illinois.* 3d ed. London: Severn, 1818.

[Blane, William Newnham]. *An Excursion through the United States and Canada during the Years 1822–23 by an English Gentleman.* 1824. New York: Negro Universities Press, 1969.

Block, Robert H. "Frederick Jackson Turner and American Geography." *Annals, Association of American Geographers* 70 (March 1980): 31–42.

Blodget, Lorin. *Climatology of the United States.* Philadelphia: J. B. Lippincott, 1857.

Blodget, William. *Facts and Arguments Respecting the Great Utility of an Extensive Plan of Inland Navigation in America.* Philadelphia: Wm. Dunne, 1805.

Blouin, Francis X., Jr. *The Boston Region, 1810–1850: A Study in Urbanization.* Ann Arbor, Mich.: UMI Research Press, 1980.

Bogue, Allan G. *From Prairie to Corn Belt: Farming on the Illinois and Iowa Prairies in the Nineteenth Century.* Chicago: Univ. of Chicago Press, 1963.

Boston Looks Seaward: The Story of the Port: 1630–1940. Boston: Bruce Humphries, 1941.

Bourcier, Robert G. "'In Excellent Order': The Gentleman Farmer Views His Fences, 1790–1860." *Agricultural History* 58 (October 1984): 546–64.

Bourgin, Frank. *The Great Challenge: The Myth of Laissez-Faire in the Early Republic.* New York: George Braziller, 1989.

Bratton, Sam T. "Inefficiency of Water Transportation in Missouri—A Geographical Factor in the Development of Railroads." *Missouri Historical Review* 14 (1919): 82–88.

Buley, R. Carlyle. *The Old Northwest: Pioneer Period, 1815–1840.* 2 vols. Bloomington: Indiana Univ. Press, 1950.

Burchard, John, and Albert Bush-Brown. *The Architecture of America: A Social and Cultural History.* Boston: Little, Brown, 1961.

Burghardt, Andrew F. "Transportation in Early Canada." In *The Shaping of Ontario, from Exploration to Confederation,* comp. Nick Mika and Helma Mika, 210–19. Bellevue, Ont.: Mika Publishing, 1985.

Burke, Colin B. *American Collegiate Populations: A Test of the Traditional View.* New York: New York Univ. Press, 1982.

Butler, Jon. *Awash in a Sea of Faith: Christianizing the American People.* Cambridge: Harvard Univ. Press, 1990.

Callcott, George H. *History in the United States, 1800–1860: Its Practice and Purpose.* Baltimore: Johns Hopkins Univ. Press, 1970.

Campbell, Penelope. *Maryland in Africa: The Maryland State Colonization Society, 1831–1857.* Urbana: Univ. of Illinois Press, 1971.

Cayton, Andrew R. L. *The Frontier Republic: Ideology and Politics in the Ohio Country, 1780–1825.* Kent: Kent State Univ. Press, 1986.

Cayton, Andrew R. L., and Peter S. Onuf. *The Midwest and the Nation: Rethinking the History of an American Region.* Bloomington: Indiana Univ. Press, 1990.

Chandler, Alfred D. "Anthracite Coal and the Beginnings of the Industrial Revolution in the United States." *Business History Review* 46 (1972): 141–81.

Chevalier, Michael. *Society, Manners and Politics in the United States: Being a Series of Letters on North America.* Boston: Weeks, Jordan, 1839.

Clark, Victor S. *History of Manufactures in the United States.* Vol. 1, *1607–1860.* New York: McGraw-Hill, 1929.

Clarke, Thomas Curtis, et al. *The American Railway: Its Construction, Development, Management and Appliances.* [1889] Secaucus, N.J.: Castle, 1988.

Cochran, Thomas C. *Frontiers of Change: Early Industrialism in America.* New York: Oxford Univ. Press, 1981.

Cohn, Jan. *The Palace or the Poorhouse: The American House as a Cultural Symbol.* East Lansing: Michigan State Univ. Press, 1979.

Colten, Craig Edward. "The Steeple in the Grid: Landscape Awareness in Nineteenth-Century Ohio." Ph.D. dissertation, Department of Geography, Syracuse Univ., 1984.

Conlin, Mary Lou. *Simon Perkins of the Western*

Reserve. Cleveland: Western Reserve Historical Society, 1968.

Conn, Robert H., with Michael Nickerson. *United Methodists and Their Colleges: Themes in the History of a College-Related Church.* Nashville: United Methodist Board of Higher Education and Ministry, 1989.

Conzen, Kathleen Neils. *Immigrant Milwaukee, 1836–1860: Accommodation and Community in a Frontier City.* Cambridge: Harvard Univ. Press, 1976.

Conzen, Michael P. "A Transport Interpretation of the Growth of Urban Regions: An American Example." *Journal of Historical Geography* 1 (1975): 361–82.

———. "The Maturing Urban System in the United States, 1840–1910." *Annals, Association of American Geographers* 67 (1977): 88–108.

———. "The Morphology of Nineteenth-Century Cities in the United States." In *Urbanization in the Americas: The Background in Comparative Perspective,* ed. W. Borah, J. Hardoy, and G. Stetler, 119–41. Ottawa: National Museum of Man, 1980.

———. "Town-Plan Analysis in an American Setting: Cadastral Processes in Boston and Omaha, 1630–1930." In *The Built Form of Western Cities,* ed. T. R. Slater, 142–70. Essays for M. R. G. Conzen. Leicester: Leicester Univ. Press, 1990.

Coolidge, John. *Mill and Mansion: A Study of Architecture and Society in Lowell, Massachusetts, 1820–1865.* New York: Columbia Univ. Press, 1942.

Cooper, William. *A Guide in the Wilderness.* Dublin: Gilbert & Hodges, 1810.

Coxe, Tench. *A View of the United States of America.* Philadelphia: William Hall and Wrigley & Berriman, 1794.

[Coxe, Tench]. "Essay on the Manufacturing Interest of the United States." Philadelphia: Bartholomew Graves, 1804.

Craig, Lois, and the staff of the Federal Architecture Project. *The Federal Presence: Architecture, Politics, and Symbols in United States Government Buildings.* Cambridge, Mass.: MIT Press, [1984].

Craven, Wesley Frank. *The Legend of the Founding Fathers.* New York: New York Univ. Press, 1956.

Creel, Margaret Washington. *"A Peculiar People": Slave Religion and Community Culture among the Gullahs.* New York: New York Univ. Press, 1987.

Cronon, William. "Revisiting the Vanishing Frontier: The Legacy of Frederick Jackson Turner." *Western Historical Quarterly* 18 (April 1987): 157–76.

Curry, Leonard P. *The Free Black in Urban America, 1800–1850: The Shadow of the Dream.* Chicago: Univ. of Chicago Press, 1981.

Dangerfield, George. *The Awakening of American Nationalism, 1815–1828.* New York: Harper & Row, 1965.

Darlington, James W. "College Graduates on the Frontier: Middlebury Alumni in Illinois, 1820–1860." Unpublished MS.

David, Paul A. "Industrial Labor Market Adjustments in a Region of Recent Settlement: Chicago, 1848–1868." In *Quantity and Quiddity: Essays in U.S. Economic History,* ed. Peter Kilby, 47–97. Middletown, Conn.: Wesleyan Univ. Press, 1987.

Davis, Burke. *The Southern Railway: Road of the Innovators.* Chapel Hill: Univ. of North Carolina Press, 1985.

Davis, James E. *Frontier America, 1800–1840: A Comparative Demographic Analysis of the Frontier Process.* Glendale, Calif.: Arthur H. Clark, 1977.

Dayton, Fred Erving. *Steamboat Days.* New York: Frederick A. Stokes, 1928.

Decker, Leslie E. "The Great Speculation: An Interpretation of Mid-Continent Pioneering." In *The Frontier in American Development: Essays in Honor of Paul Wallace Gates,* ed. David M. Ellis, 357–80. Ithaca: Cornell Univ. Press, 1969.

Delany, Martin Robison. *The Condition, Elevation, Emigration, and Destiny of the Colored People of the United States.* [1852] New York: Arno Press, 1968.

Dew, Charles B. *Ironmaker to the Confederacy: Joseph R. Anderson and the Tredegar Iron Works.* New Haven: Yale Univ. Press, 1966.

Dick, Everett. *The Lure of the Land: A Social History of the Public Lands from the Articles of Confederation to the New Deal.* Lincoln: Univ. of Nebraska Press, 1970.

Doyle, Don Harrison. *The Social Order of a Frontier Community: Jacksonville, Illinois, 1825–70.* Urbana: Univ. of Illinois Press, 1978.

Duden, Gottfried. *Report on a Journey to the Western States of America.* [1824] Columbia: State Historical Society of Missouri, 1980.

Dunn, Richard S. "The English Sugar Islands and the Founding of South Carolina." In *Shaping Southern Society: The Colonial Experience,* ed. T. H. Breen, 48–58. New York: Oxford Univ. Press, 1976.

Dunwell, Steve. *The Run of the Mill: A Pictorial Narrative of the Expansion, Dominion, Decline and Enduring Impact of the New England Textile Industry.* Boston: David R. Godine, 1978.

Dwight, Timothy. *Travels in New England and New York.* 4 vols. Cambridge: Harvard Univ. Press, 1969.

Dykstra, Robert R. *The Cattle Towns.* New York: Alfred A. Knopf, 1968.

Eaton, Clement. *The Growth of Southern Civilization, 1790–1860.* New York: Harper & Row, 1963.

Elazar, Daniel J. *American Federalism: A View from the States.* New York: Thomas Y. Crowell, 1966.

———. *Cities of the Prairie: The Metropolitan Frontier and American Politics.* New York: Basic Books, 1970.

Elson, Ruth Miller. *Guardians of Tradition: American Schoolbooks of the Nineteenth Century.* Lincoln: Univ. of Nebraska Press, 1964.

England, J. Merton. "The Democratic Faith in American Schoolbooks, 1783–1860." *American Quarterly* 15 (1963): 191–99.

Evans, W. A. "Steamboats on the Upper Tombigbee in the Early Days." *Journal of Mississippi History* 4 (1942): 216–24.

Faragher, John Mack. *Sugar Creek: Life on the Illinois Prairie.* New Haven and London: Yale Univ. Press, 1986.

Fein, Albert. *Frederick Law Olmsted and the American Environmental Tradition.* New York: George Braziller, 1972.

Fields, Barbara Jeanne. "Ideology and Race in American History." In *Region, Race, and Reconstruction: Essays in Honor of C. Vann Woodward,* ed. J. Morgan Kousser and James M. McPherson, 143–77. New York: Oxford Univ. Press, 1982.

———. *Slavery and Freedom on the Middle Ground: Maryland during the Nineteenth Century.* New Haven and London: Yale Univ. Press, 1985.

Flint, Timothy. *Recollections of the Last Ten Years, Passed in Occasional Residences and Journeyings in the Valley of the Mississippi.* [Boston, 1826] New York: DaCapo Press, 1968.

Fogel, Robert William. *Without Consent or Contract: The Rise and Fall of American Slavery.* New York: W. W. Norton, 1989.

Fogel, Robert William, and Stanley L. Engerman. *Time on the Cross: The Economics of American Negro Slavery.* Boston: Little, Brown, 1976.

Folsom, Burton W., Jr. *Urban Capitalists: Entrepreneurs and City Growth in Pennsylvania's Lackawanna and Lehigh Regions, 1800–1920.* Baltimore: Johns Hopkins Univ. Press, 1981.

Folsom, Michael Brewster, and Steven D. Lubar, eds. *The Philosophy of Manufactures. Early Debates over Industrialization in the United States.* Cambridge, Mass.: MIT Press, 1982.

Fornell, Earl Wesley. *The Galveston Era: The Texas Crescent on the Eve of Secession.* Austin: Univ. of Texas Press, 1961.

Friedman, Lawrence J. *Inventors of the Promised Land.* New York: Alfred A. Knopf, 1975.

Gaines, Gen. Edmund Pendleton. *To the Young Men of the States of the American Union, Civil and Military.* Ft. Jackson, La. 1838.

———. "In Favor of Memphis, T. as a Place for a Great National Armory . . . " Letter to Secretary of War John Bell, August 31, 1841. *Correspondence and Reports Relating to the Choice of a Site for a Western Armory, 1835–1862.* National Archives RG 156, no. 966.

Gallatin, Albert. *Report of the Secretary of the Treasury on the Subject of Public Roads and Canals.* 1808. New York: Augustus M. Kelley, 1968.

Gates, Paul W. *The Illinois Central Railroad and Its Colonization Work.* Cambridge: Harvard Univ. Press, 1934. New York: Johnson Reprint, 1968.

Gaustad, Edwin Scott. *Historical Atlas of Religion in America.* New York: Harper & Row, 1962.

Genovese, Eugene D. *The Political Economy of Slavery: Studies in the Economy and Society of the Slave South.* New York: Vintage Books, 1967.

———. *Roll Jordan Roll: The World the Slaves Made.* New York: Pantheon Books, 1974.

———. *In Red and Black: Marxian Explorations in Southern and Afro-American History.* Knoxville: Univ. of Tennessee Press, 1984.

Gerlach, Russel L. *Settlement Patterns in Missouri: A Study of Population Origins with a Wall Map.* Columbia: Univ. of Missouri Press, 1986.

Gilmore, James R. *The Advance-Guard of Western Civilization.* New York: D. Appleton, 1888.

Glaab, Charles N. "Visions of Metropolis: William Gilpin and the Theories of City Growth in the American West." *Wisconsin Magazine of History* 45 (1961–62): 21–31.

Glaab, Charles N., and A. Theodore Brown. *A History of Urban America.* New York: Macmillan, 1967.

Glassie, Henry. *Pattern in the Material Folk Culture of the Eastern United States.* Philadelphia: Univ. of Pennsylvania Press, 1968.

Glazebrook, G. P. de T. *A History of Transportation in Canada.* Vol. 1, *Continental Strategy to 1867.* Toronto: McClelland and Stewart, 1964.

Goen, C. C. *Broken Churches, Broken Nation: Denominational Schisms and the Coming of the American Civil War.* Macon, Ga.: Mercer Univ. Press, 1985.

Goff, John H. "The Steamboat Period in Georgia." *Georgia Historical Quarterly* 12 (1928): 236–54.

Goldfield, David R. *Urban Growth in the Age of Sectionalism: Virginia, 1847–1861.* Baton Rouge: Louisiana State Univ. Press, 1977.

Goodstein, Anita Shafer. *Nashville, 1780–1860: From Frontier to City.* Gainesville: Univ. of Florida Press, 1989.

Grattan, Thomas Colley. *Civilized America.* 2 vols. London: Bradbury and Evans, 1859.

Green, Constance McLaughlin. *American Cities in the Growth of the Nation.* New York: Harper & Row, 1965.

Green, Fletcher M. *The Role of the Yankee in the Old South.* Athens: Univ. of Georgia Press, 1972.

Greenfield, Liah, and Michael Martin, eds. *Center: Ideas and Institutions.* Chicago: Univ. of Chicago Press, 1988.

Groves, Paul A. "The Northeast and Regional Integration, 1800–1860." In *North America: The Historical Geography of a Changing Continent,* ed. Robert D. Mitchell and Paul A. Groves, 198–217. Totowa, N.J.: Rowman & Littlefield, 1987.

Gutman, Herbert G. *The Black Family in Slavery and Freedom: 1750–1925.* New York: Pantheon Books, 1976.

Haites, Erik F., James Mak, and Gary M. Walton. *Western River Transportation: The Era of Early Internal Development, 1810–1860.* Baltimore: Johns Hopkins Univ. Press, 1975.

Hall, Peter Dobkin. *The Organization of American Culture, 1700–1900: Private Institutions, Elites, and the Origins of American Nationality.* New York: New York Univ. Press, 1982.

Hamilton, Alexander. *Manufactures.* H. Rept. 31, 2d Cong., 1st sess., December 5, 1791. Reprinted in *American State Papers: Finance,* vol. 5 (1832), 123–44.

———. "Prospectus of the Society for Establishing Useful Manufactures." [1791] In *The Papers of Alexander Hamilton,* ed. Harold C. Syrett, 9:144–53. New York: Columbia Univ. Press, 1987.

Harper, Herbert L. "The Antebellum Courthouses of Tennessee." *Tennessee Historical Quarterly* 30 (Spring 1971): 3–25.

Hatcher, Harlan. *The Western Reserve: The Story of New Connecticut in Ohio.* Indianapolis: Bobbs-Merrill, 1949.

Hatcher, Harlan, and Erick A. Walter. *A Pictorial History of the Great Lakes.* New York: Crown, 1963.

Henlein, Paul C. *Cattle Kingdom in the Ohio Valley, 1783–1860.* Lexington: Univ. of Kentucky Press, 1959.

Hibbard, Benjamin Horace. *A History of the Public Land Policies.* New York: Macmillan, 1924.

Hill, Adelaide Cromwell, and Martin Kilson, eds. *Apropos of Africa: Sentiments of Negro American Leaders on Africa from the 1800s to the 1950s.* London: Frank Cass, 1969.

Hill, Forest G. *Roads, Rails, and Waterways: The Army Engineers and Early Transportation.* Norman: Univ. of Oklahoma Press, 1957.

Hilliard, Sam B. "Pork in the Ante-Bellum South: The Geography of Self-Sufficiency." *Annals, Association of American Geographers* 59 (1969): 461–80.

———. *Atlas of Antebellum Southern Agriculture.* Baton Rouge: Louisiana State Univ. Press, 1984.

Hindle, Brooke, and Steven Lubar. *Engines of Change: The American Industrial Revolution, 1790–1860.* Washington, D.C.: Smithsonian Institution Press, 1986.

Hinsdale, B. A. *The Old Northwest*. 2 vols. New York: Townsend MacCoun, 1891.

Hitchcock, Henry-Russell, and William Seale. *Temples of Democracy: The State Capitols of the USA*. New York: Harcourt, Brace, Jovanovich, 1976.

Holbrook, Stewart H. *The Yankee Exodus: An Account of Migration from New England*. New York: Macmillan, 1950.

Holder, Gerald L. "State Planned Trading Centers in Pioneer Georgia." *Pioneer America* 14 (1982): 115–24.

Holt, Glen E. "St. Louis's Transition Decade, 1819–1830." *Missouri Historical Review* 76 (1982): 365–81.

Hounshell, David A. *From the American System to Mass Production, 1800–1932: The Development of Manufacturing Technology in the United States*. Baltimore: Johns Hopkins Univ. Press, 1984.

Hubbert, Henry Clyde. *The Older Middle West, 1840–1880*. [1936] New York: Russell and Russell, 1963.

Hudson, John C. "North American Origins of Middlewestern Frontier Populations." *Annals, Association of American Geographers* 78 (1988): 395–413.

Hulan, Richard H. "Middle Tennessee and the Dogtrot House." *Pioneer America* 7 (July 1975): 37–46.

Hulbert, Archer Butler. *Where Rolls the Oregon: Prophet and Pessimist Look Northwest, 1825–30*. Colorado Springs: Stewart Commission, 1933.

Hunt, Alfred N. *Haiti's Influence on Antebellum America: Smouldering Volcano in the Caribbean*. Baton Rouge: Louisiana State Univ. Press, 1988.

Hunter, Louis C. *Steamboats of Western Rivers: An Economic and Technological History*. Cambridge: Harvard Univ. Press, 1949.

———. *A History of Industrial Power in the United States, 1780–1930*. Vol. 2, *Steam Power*. Charlottesville: Univ. of Virginia Press, 1985.

Isard, Walter. "Transport Development and Building Cycles." *Quarterly Journal of Economics* 57 (1942–43): 90–112.

Izant, Grace Goulder. *Hudson's Heritage: A Chronicle of the Founding and the Flowering of the Village of Hudson, Ohio*. Kent: Kent State Univ. Press, 1985.

Jakle, John A. *Images of the Ohio Valley*. New York: Oxford Univ. Press, 1977.

Jeremy, David J. *Transatlantic Industrial Revolution: The Diffusion of Textile Technologies between Britain and America, 1790–1830s*. Cambridge, Mass.: MIT Press, 1981.

Johnson, Daniel M., and Rex R. Campbell. *Black Migration in America: A Social Demographic History*. Durham: Duke Univ. Press, 1981.

Johnson, Hildegard Binder. *Order upon the Land: The U.S. Rectangular Land Survey and the Upper Mississippi Country*. New York: Oxford Univ. Press, 1976.

Jordan, Philip D. *The National Road*. Indianapolis: Bobbs-Merrill, 1948.

Jordan, Terry G. "The Imprint of the Upper and Lower South on Mid-Nineteenth Century Texas." *Annals, Association of American Geographers* 57 (1967): 667–90.

———. *Trails to Texas: Southern Roots of Western Cattle Ranching*. Lincoln: Univ. of Nebraska Press, 1981.

———. "Preadaptation and European Colonization in Rural North America." *Annals, Association of American Geographers* 79 (December 1989): 489–500.

Jordan, Terry G., and Matti Kaups. *The American Backwoods Frontier: An Ethnic and Ecological Interpretation*. Baltimore: Johns Hopkins Univ. Press, 1989.

Kaatz, Martin R. "The Black Swamp: A Study in Historical Geography." *Annals, Association of American Geographers* 45 (March 1955): 1–35.

Kaestle, Carl F. *Pillars of the Republic: Common Schools and American Society, 1780–1860*. New York: Hill and Wang, 1983.

Karst, Kenneth L. *Belonging to America: Equal Citizenship and the Constitution*. New Haven and London: Yale Univ. Press, 1989.

Kasson, John F. *Civilizing the Machine: Technology and Republican Values in America, 1776–1900*. New York: Penguin, 1977.

Keir, Malcolm. *The Epic of Industry*. New Haven: Yale Univ. Press, 1926.

Kennedy, Roger G. *Architecture, Men, Women, and Money in America, 1600–1860*. New York: Random House, 1985.

————. *Rediscovering America.* Boston: Houghton Mifflin, 1990.

Kenzer, Robert C. *Kinship and Neighborhood in a Southern Community: Orange County, North Carolina, 1849–1881.* Knoxville: Univ. of Tennessee Press, 1987.

Kettner, James H. *The Development of American Citizenship, 1608–1870.* Chapel Hill: Univ. of North Carolina Press, 1978.

Kielbowicz, Richard B. *News in the Mail: The Press, Post Office, and Public Information, 1700–1860.* Westport, Conn.: Greenwood Press, 1989.

Klein, Benjamin, and Eleanor Klein, eds. *The Ohio River Handbook and Picture Album.* Cincinnati: Young and Klein, 1950.

Kniffen, Fred. "Folk Housing: Key to Diffusion." *Annals, Association of American Geographers* 55 (December 1965): 549–77.

Kouwenhoven, John A. *The Columbia Historical Portrait of New York.* Garden City, N.Y.: Doubleday, 1953.

Kulik, Gary, Roger Parks, and Theodore Z. Penn, eds. *The New England Mill Village, 1790–1860.* Cambridge, Mass.: MIT Press, 1982.

Lang, Marvel. "The Development of Small Towns as a Settlement Process in Mississippi: A Case Study." *Mississippi Geographer* 9 (Spring 1981): 5–14.

Larson, John Lauritz. "'Bind the Republic Together': The National Union and the Struggle for a System of Internal Improvements." *Journal of American History* 74 (1987): 363–87.

Lathrop, Barnes F. "Migration into East Texas, 1835–1860." *Southwestern Historical Quarterly* 52 (1948): 1–31, 184–208, 325–48.

Lawrence, Barbara, and Nedra Branz, eds. *The Flagg Correspondence: Selected Letters, 1816–1854.* Carbondale: Southern Illinois Univ. Press, 1986.

Leblanc, Robert G. *Location of Manufacturing in New England in the Nineteenth Century.* Geography Publications at Dartmouth no. 7. Hanover, N.H., 1969.

Lewis, Peirce F. "Common Houses, Cultural Spoor." *Landscape* 19 (January 1975): 1–22.

Lindstrom, Diane. *Economic Development in the Philadelphia Region, 1810–1850.* New York: Columbia Univ. Press, 1978.

Litwack, Leon F. *North of Slavery: The Negro in the Free States, 1790–1860.* Chicago: Univ. of Chicago Press, 1961.

————. "Trouble in Mind: The Bicentennial and the Afro-American Experience." *Journal of American History* 74 (September 1987): 315–37.

Livingood, James Weston. *The Philadelphia-Baltimore Trade Rivalry, 1780–1860.* Harrisburg: Pennsylvania Historical and Museum Commission, 1947.

Lukermann, Fred. "Empirical Expressions of Nodality and Hierarchy in a Circulation Manifold." *East Lakes Geographer* 2 (1966): 17–44.

Luxon, Norval Neil. "H. Niles, the Man and the Editor." *Mississippi Valley Historical Review* 28 (1941–42): 27–40.

McClelland, Peter D., and Richard J. Zeckhauser. *Demographic Dimensions of the New Republic: American Interregional Migration, Vital Statistics, and Manumissions, 1800–1860.* Cambridge: Cambridge Univ. Press, 1982.

McCoy, Drew R. "James Madison and Visions of American Nationality in the Confederation Period. A Regional Perspective." In *Beyond Confederation: Origins of the Constitution and American National Identity,* ed. Richard Beeman, Stephen Botein, and Edward C. Carter II, 226–58. Chapel Hill: Univ. of North Carolina Press, 1987.

MacGill, Caroline E. *History of Transportation in the United States before 1860.* New York: Peter Smith, 1948.

McLemore, Richard, ed. *A History of Mississippi.* Jackson: Univ. and College Press of Mississippi, 1973.

McManis, Douglas R. *The Initial Evaluation and Utilization of the Illinois Prairies, 1815–1840.* Research Paper no. 94. Chicago: Department of Geography, Univ. of Chicago, 1964.

Mahoney, Thomas R. "Urban History in a Regional Context: River Towns on the Upper Mississippi, 1840–1860." *Journal of American History* 72 (1985): 318–39.

Marks, Bayly Ellen. "Rural Response to Urban Penetration: Baltimore and St. Mary's County, Maryland, 1790–1840." *Journal of Historical Geography* 8 (1982): 113–27.

Marschner, F. J. *Land Use and Its Patterns in the*

United States. Agriculture Handbook no. 153. Washington, D.C.: U.S. Department of Agriculture, 1959.

Marshall, Howard Wight. *Folk Architecture in Little Dixie: A Regional Culture in Missouri.* Columbia: Univ. of Missouri Press, 1981.

Marshall, James M. *Land Fever: Dispossession and the Frontier Myth.* Lexington: Univ. Press of Kentucky, 1986.

Martineau, Harriet. *Society in America.* 3 vols. London: Saunders and Otley, 1837.

Marx, Leo. *The Machine in the Garden: Technology and the Pastoral Ideal in America.* New York: Oxford Univ. Press, 1964.

Mathews, Lois Kimball. *The Expansion of New England: The Spread of New England Settlement and Institutions to the Mississippi River, 1620–1865.* Boston: Houghton Mifflin, 1909.

Mau, Clayton. *The Development of Central and Western New York.* Rochester: DuBois Press, 1944.

Mayer, Grace M. "A Painting of the 'Revulsion' of 1857." *Bulletin, Museum of the City of New York* 3 (May 1940): 68–72.

Meier, August, and Elliott M. Rudwick. *From Plantation to Ghetto: An Interpretive History of American Negroes.* New York: Hill and Wang, 1966.

Merk, Frederick. *Fruits of Propaganda in the Tyler Administration.* Cambridge: Harvard Univ. Press, 1971.

Meyer, David R. *Urban Change in Central Connecticut: From Farm to Factory to Urban Pastoralism.* Cambridge, Mass.: Ballinger, 1976.

———. "A Dynamic Model of the Integration of Frontier Urban Places into the United States System of Cities." *Economic Geography* 56 (1980): 120–40.

———. "Emergence of the American Manufacturing Belt: An Interpretation." *Journal of Historical Geography* 9 (1983): 145–74.

Meyer, Douglas K. "Diffusion of Upland Folk Housing to the Shawnee Hills of Southern Illinois." *Pioneer America* 7 (July 1975): 56–66.

———. "Folk Housing on the Illinois Frontier." *Pioneer America Society Transactions* 1 (1978): 30–42.

Mika, Nick, and Helma Mika. *Railways of Canada: A Pictorial History.* Toronto: McGraw-Hill Ryerson, 1972.

Miller, Cynthia Ann. "The United States Army Logistics Complex: A Case Study of the Northern Frontier, 1818–1845." Ph.D. dissertation, Department of Geography, Syracuse Univ., 1991.

Miller, Donald L., and Richard E. Sharpless. *The Kingdom of Coal: Work, Enterprise, and Ethnic Communities in the Mine Fields.* Philadelphia: Univ. of Pennsylvania Press, 1985.

Mitchell, Brian C. *The Paddy Camps: The Irish of Lowell, 1821–1861.* Chicago: Univ. of Illinois Press, 1988.

Mitchell, Robert D., and Milton B. Newton. "The Appalachian Frontier: Views from the East and the Southwest." *Historical Geography Research Series no. 21* (Institute of British Geographers) (July 1988): 1–64.

Modelski, Andrew M. *Railroad Maps of North America, the First Hundred Years.* Washington, D.C.: Library of Congress, 1984.

Moffatt, Walter. "Transportation in Arkansas, 1819–1840." *Arkansas Historical Quarterly* 15 (1956): 187–201.

Mood, Fulmer. "The Origin, Evolution, and Application of the Sectional Concept, 1750–1900." In *Regionalism in America*, ed. Merrill Jensen, 5–98. Madison: Univ. of Wisconsin Press, 1952.

Moore, John Hebron. "Cotton Breeding in the Old South." *Agricultural History* 30 (July 1956): 95–104.

———. "Two Cotton Kingdoms." *Agricultural History* 60 (Fall 1986): 1–16.

———. *The Emergence of the Cotton Kingdom in the Old Southwest: Mississippi, 1770–1860.* Baton Rouge: Louisiana State Univ. Press, 1988.

Morgan, Philip D. "Work and Culture: The Task System and the World of Lowcountry Blacks, 1700–1880." *William and Mary Quarterly*, 3d ser., 39 (1982): 563–99.

Muller, Edward K. "Selective Urban Growth in the Middle Ohio Valley, 1800–1860." *Geographical Review* 66 (1976): 178–99.

———. "Regional Urbanization and the Selective Growth of Towns in North American Regions." *Journal of Historical Geography* 3 (1977): 21–40.

Mumford, Lewis. *Technics and Civilization.* New York: Harcourt, Brace, 1934.

————. *The City in History: Its Transformations, and Its Prospects.* New York: Harcourt, Brace, 1961.

Murrin, John M. "A Roof without Walls: The Dilemma of American National Identity." In *Beyond Confederation: Origins of the Constitution and American National Identity,* ed. Richard Beeman, Stephen Botein, and Edward C. Carter II, 333–48. Chapel Hill: Univ. of North Carolina Press, 1987.

Nagel, Paul C. *One Nation Indivisible: The Union in American Thought, 1776–1861.* New York: Oxford Univ. Press, 1964.

Nelson, John R., Jr. *Liberty and Property: Political Economy and Policymaking in the New Nation, 1789–1812.* Baltimore: Johns Hopkins Univ. Press, 1987.

Nesbit, Robert. "The Federal Government as Townsite Speculator." *Explorations in Economic History* 7 (Spring 1970): 293–312.

Nettels, Curtis P. *The Emergence of a National Economy, 1775–1815.* New York: Holt, Rinehart and Winston, 1962.

Nevins, Allan. *The Emergence of Lincoln.* 2 vols. New York: Charles Scribner's Sons, 1950.

Newton, Milton B., Jr. "Settlement Patterns as Artifacts of Social Structure." In *The Human Mirror: Material and Spatial Images of Man,* ed. Miles Richardson. Baton Rouge: Louisiana State Univ. Press, 1974.

————. "Cultural Preadaptation and the Upland South." *Geoscience and Man* 5 (June 1974): 143–53.

Nickerson, Michael George. "Sermons, Systems, and Strategies: The Geographic Strategies of the Methodist Episcopal Church in Its Expansion into New York State, 1788–1810." Ph.D. dissertation, Department of Geography, Syracuse Univ., 1988.

Noble, Allen G. *Wood, Brick, and Stone: The North American Settlement Landscape.* Vol. 1, *Houses.* Vol. 2, *Barns and Farm Structures.* Amherst: Univ. of Massachusetts Press, 1984.

North, Douglass C., and Robert Paul Thomas, eds. *The Growth of the American Economy to 1860.* New York: Harper & Row, 1968.

Nye, Russel Blaine. *Society and Culture in America, 1830–1860.* New York: Harper & Row, 1974.

O'Brien, Conor Cruise. *God Land: Reflections on Religion and Nationalism.* Cambridge: Harvard Univ. Press, 1988.

O'Brien, John T. "Factory, Church, and Community: Blacks in Antebellum Richmond." *Journal of Southern History* 44 (November 1978): 509–36.

Olson, Sherry. *Baltimore: The Building of an American City.* Baltimore: Johns Hopkins Univ. Press, 1980.

Owsley, Frank L. "The Pattern of Migration and Settlement on the Southern Frontier." *Journal of Southern History* 11 (May 1945): 147–76.

————. *Plain Folk of the Old South.* Baton Rouge: Louisiana State Univ. Press, 1949.

Parker, William N. "From Northwest to Mid-West: Social Bases of a Regional History." In *Essays in Nineteenth-Century Economic History: The Old Northwest,* ed. David C. Klingaman and Richard K. Vedder. Athens: Ohio Univ. Press, 1975.

————. "New England's Early Industrialization: A Sketch." In *Quantity and Quiddity: Essays in U.S. Economic History,* ed. Peter Kilby, 17–46. Middletown, Conn.: Wesleyan Univ. Press, 1987.

Parkins. A. E. *The South: Its Economic-Geographic Development.* New York: John Wiley & Sons, 1938.

Pattison, William D. *The Beginnings of the American Rectangular Land Survey System, 1784–1800.* Research Paper no. 50. Chicago: Department of Geography, Univ. of Chicago, 1957.

Pease, Jane H., and William H. Pease. *Bound with Them in Chains: A Biographical History of the Antislavery Movement.* Westport, Conn.: Greenwood Press, 1972.

Phillips, Ulrich B. "Transportation in the Ante-Bellum South: An Economic Analysis." *Quarterly Journal of Economics* 19 (1904–5): 434–51.

Porter, Glenn, and Harold C. Livesay. *Merchants and Manufacturers: Studies in the Changing Structure of Nineteenth-Century Marketing.* Baltimore: Johns Hopkins Univ. Press, 1971.

Potter, David M. *The Impending Crisis, 1848–1861.* New York: Harper & Row, 1976.

Pounds, Norman J. G., and Sue Simons Ball. "Core Areas and the Development of the European State System." *Annals, Association of*

American Geographers 54 (March 1964): 24–40.

Power, Richard Lyle. *Planting Corn Belt Culture: The Impress of the Upland Southerner and Yankee in the Old Northwest.* Indianapolis: Indiana Historical Society, 1953.

Pred, Allan. "Some Locational Relationships between Industrial Inventions, Industrial Innovations, and Urban Growth." *East Lakes Geographer* 2 (1966): 45–70.

———. *Urban Growth and the Circulation of Information: The United States System of Cities, 1790–1840.* Cambridge: Harvard Univ. Press, 1973.

Price, Edward T. "A Geographic Analysis of White-Negro-Indian Racial Mixtures in Eastern United States." *Annals, Association of American Geographers* 43 (June 1953): 138–55.

Pulliam, Linda, and M. B. Newton, Jr. "Country and Small-Town Stores of Louisiana. Legacy of the Greek Revival and the Frontier." *Mélanges* (Museum of Geoscience, Louisiana State Univ., Baton Rouge) 7 (April 23, 1973).

Putnam, Jackson K. "The Turner Thesis and the Westward Movement: A Reappraisal." *Western Historical Quarterly* 7 (October 1976): 377–404.

Pyle, G. F. "The Diffusion of Cholera in the United States in the Nineteenth Century." *Geographical Analysis* 1 (January 1969): 59–75.

Radford, John P. "Race, Residence and Ideology: Charleston, South Carolina, in the Mid-Nineteenth Century." *Journal of Historical Geography* 2 (1976): 329–46.

Raitz, Karl B., and Richard Ulack, with Thomas R. Leinbach. *Appalachia: A Regional Geography.* Boulder, Colo.: Westview Press, 1984.

Reed, Merl E. *New Orleans and the Railroads: The Struggle for Commercial Empire, 1830–1860.* Baton Rouge: Louisiana State Univ. Press, 1966.

Reps, John W. *The Making of Urban America: A History of City Planning in the United States.* Princeton: Princeton Univ. Press, 1965.

Rohrbough, Malcolm J. *The Land Office Business: The Settlement and Administration of American Public Lands, 1789–1837.* New York: Oxford Univ. Press, 1968.

———. *The Trans-Appalachian Frontier: People, Societies, and Institutions, 1775–1850.* New York: Oxford Univ. Press, 1978.

Rokkan, Stein. "Nation Building: A Review of Models and Approaches." *Current Sociology* 19 (1971): 7–38.

Rose, Gregory S. "South Central Michigan Yankees." *Michigan History* 70 (March–April 1986): 32–39.

———. "Upland Southerners: The County Origins of Southern Migrants to Indiana by 1850." *Indiana Magazine of History* 82 (September 1986): 242–63.

Rosenberg, Nathan, ed. *The American System of Manufactures: The Report of the Committee on the Machinery of the United States, 1855, and the Special Reports of George Wallis and Joseph Whitworth, 1854.* Edinburgh: Edinburgh Univ. Press, 1969.

Rothstein, Morton. "Antebellum South as a Dual Economy." *Agricultural History* (October 1967): 373–83.

———. "The Cotton Frontier of the Antebellum United States: A Methodological Battleground." *Agricultural History* 44 (January 1970): 149–65.

Rozwenc, Edwin C., ed. *The Causes of the American Civil War.* Lexington, Mass.: D. C. Heath, 1961.

Rudwick, Bracey Meier, ed. *Free Blacks in America, 1800–1860.* Belmont, Calif.: Wadsworth, 1971.

Rugg, Dean S. *Spatial Foundations of Urbanism.* Dubuque: Wm. C. Brown, 1972.

Sadove, Abraham H. "Transport Improvement and the Appalachian Barrier: A Case Study in Economic Innovation." Ph.D. dissertation, Harvard Univ., 1950.

Sale, Randall D., and Edwin D. Karn. *American Expansion: A Book of Maps.* Homewood, Ill.: Dorsey Press, 1962.

Sauer, Carl O. *Land and Life: A Selection from the Writings of Carl Ortwin Sauer.* Ed. John Leighly. Berkeley: Univ. of California Press, 1963.

———. *The Geography of the Ozark Highland of Missouri.* [1920] New York: Greenwood Press, 1968.

———. *Selected Essays, 1963–1975.* Berkeley: Turtle Island Foundation, 1981.

Sayenga, Donald. *Ellet and Roebling.* York, Pa.:

American Canal and Transportation Center, 1983.

Schaper, William. *Sectionalism and Representation in South Carolina.* [1901] New York: DaCapo Press, 1968.

Schein, Richard Huot. "A Historical Geography of Central New York: Patterns and Processes in Colonization on the New Military Tract, 1782–1820." Ph.D. dissertation, Department of Geography, Syracuse Univ., 1989.

Schivelbusch, Wolfgang. *The Railway Journey: The Industrialization of Time and Space in the Nineteenth Century.* Berkeley: Univ. of California Press, 1986.

Schmidt, Louis Bernard. "Internal Commerce and the Development of National Economy before 1860." *Journal of Political Economy* 47 (1939): 798–822.

Schuck, Peter H., and Rogers M. Smith. *Citizenship without Consent: Illegal Aliens in the American Polity.* New Haven and London: Yale Univ. Press, 1985.

Schwab, Eugene L., ed. *Travels in the Old South: Selected from Periodicals of the Time.* 2 vols. Lexington: Univ. Press of Kentucky, 1973.

Scott, Jesup W. "Internal Trade of the United States." *Hunt's Merchant's Magazine* 9 (July 1843): 31–47.

Shaw, Ronald E. "Canals in the Early Republic: A Review of Recent Literature." *Journal of the Early Republic* 4 (1984): 117–42.

Shelton, Cynthia J. *The Mills of Manayunk: Industrialization and Social Conflict in the Philadelphia Region, 1787–1837.* Baltimore: Johns Hopkins Univ. Press, 1986.

Sherwood, Henry N. "Early Negro Deportation Projects." *Mississippi Valley Historical Review* 11 (March 1916): 484–508.

Short, Lloyd Milton. *The Development of National Administrative Organization in the United States.* Baltimore: Johns Hopkins Univ. Press, 1923.

Silver, James W. *Edmund Pendleton Gaines, Frontier General.* Baton Rouge: Louisiana State Univ. Press, 1949.

Stapleton, Darwin H. *The Transfer of Early Industrial Technologies to America.* Philadelphia: American Philosophical Society, 1987.

Staudenraus, P. J. *The African Colonization Movement, 1816–1865.* New York: Columbia Univ. Press, 1961.

Stilgoe, John R. *Common Landscape of America, 1580 to 1845.* New Haven and London: Yale University Press, 1982.

Still, Bayrd. "Patterns of Mid-Nineteenth Century Urbanization in the Middle West." *Mississippi Valley Historical Review* 28 (1941–42): 187–206.

Strauss, Anselm L. *Images of the American City.* New Brunswick, N.J.: Transaction, 1976.

Stuckey, Sterling. *Slave Culture: Nationalist Theory and the Foundations of Black America.* New York: Oxford Univ. Press, 1987.

Swarzlose, Richard A. *The Nation's Newsbrokers.* Vol. 1, *The Formative Years, from Pretelegraph to 1865.* Evanston, Ill.: Northwestern Univ. Press, 1989.

Switzler, Wm. F. *Report on the Internal Commerce of the United States.* 50th Cong., 1st sess., 1888. H. Ex. Doc. 6, Part 2.

Sydnor, Charles. *A Gentleman of the Old Natchez Region.* Durham: Duke Univ. Press, 1938.

Taber, Morris C. "New England Influences in South Central Michigan." *Michigan History* 45 (December 1961): 305–36.

Taylor, George Rogers. *The Transportation Revolution, 1815–1860.* New York: Holt, Rinehart and Winston, 1951.

Tewksbury, Donald G. *The Founding of American Colleges and Universities before the Civil War.* [1932] New York: Archon, 1965.

Thompson, Kenneth. "Wilderness and Health in the Nineteenth Century." *Journal of Historical Geography* 2 (1976): 145–61.

Thompson, Robert Luther. *Wiring a Continent: The History of the Telegraph Industry in the United States, 1832–1866.* Princeton: Princeton Univ. Press, 1947.

Trollope, Frances. *Domestic Manners of the Americans.* Ed. Richard Mullen. 1839. Oxford: Oxford Univ. Press, 1984.

Tucker, Barbara M. *Samuel Slater and the Origins of the American Textile Industry, 1790–1860.* Ithaca: Cornell Univ. Press, 1984.

Tunnard, Christopher, and Henry Hope Reed. *American Skyline: The Growth and Form of Our Cities and Towns.* New York: Mentor Books, 1956.

Turner, Frederick Jackson. *Frontier and Section: Selected Essays.* Englewood Cliffs, N.J.: Prentice-Hall, 1961.

———. *Rise of the New West, 1819–1829.* New York: Crowell-Collier, 1962.

————. *The United States, 1830–1850: The Nation and Its Sections.* [1935] New York: W. W. Norton, 1965.

U.S. Congress. House. *Report of the Committee on Roads and Canals.* Prepared by Mr. Tucker. 15th Cong., 1st sess., December 15, 1817. H. Doc. 435.

————. House. *Report of the Secretary of War on Roads and Canals.* 15th Cong., 2d sess., January 14, 1819. H. Doc. 462.

————. House. *Report of the Committee on Roads and Canals.* Prepared by Mr. Hemphill. 17th Cong., 1st sess., April 20, 1822. H. Doc. 526.

————. *Report of the Committee on Roads and Canals.* Prepared by Mr. Hemphill. 18th Cong., 2d sess. In *Appendix, Gales & Seaton's Register,* vol. 1 (1825), 75–81.

————. *Report . . . upon . . . a National Road from the City of Washington to New Orleans.* 19th Cong., 1st sess., April 12, 1826. H. Doc. 156.

————. *Surveys, with a View of Making Roads & Canals.* Report from the Committee on Roads and Canals. Prepared by Mr. Mercer. 19th Cong., 2d sess., March 2, 1827. H. Rept. 102. In *New American State Papers: Transportation,* vol. 2.

————. *Report from the Committee on Roads and Canals.* Prepared by Mr. Mercer. 20th Cong., 1st sess., May 26, 1828. H. Rept. 270.

————. *Mail—New York to New Orleans Irregularities.* 26th Cong., 1st sess., March 31, 1840. H. Doc. 159.

————. *Commerce, Tonnage, etc., of the Ohio and Other Western Rivers.* Letter from the Secretary of War. 34th Cong., 3d sess., January 23, 1857. H. Ex. Doc. 48.

U.S. Congress. Senate. *Report of the Committee on Roads and Canals.* Prepared by Mr. Morrow. 14th Cong., 1st sess., February 6, 1816. S. Doc. 398.

————. *Report of the Committee on Roads and Canals.* Prepared by Mr. Lacock. 14th Cong., 2d sess., February 14, 1817. S. Doc. 429.

————. *Memorial of the Legislature of Ohio Relative to . . . a National Road from Zanesville, in Ohio, to Florence, in Alabama.* 22d Cong., 1st sess., February 23, 1832. S. Misc. Doc. 69.

————. *Memorial of a Number of Citizens of Cincinnati, Ohio Praying Removal of Obstructions in the Navigation of the Ohio and Mississippi Rivers, March 12, 1844.* 28th Cong., 1st sess., S. Ex. Doc. 179. In *New American State Papers: Transportation,* vol. 7, 379–412.

————. *Report of the Committee on Roads and Canals, . . . to extend the National Road to the City of Alton on the Mississippi River.* 28th Cong., 2d sess., January 15, 1845. S. Doc. 41.

————. *Report on the Steam Marine of the United States.* 32d Cong., 1st sess., 1852. S. Ex. Doc. 42. In *New American State Papers: Transportation,* vol. 7, 487–604.

Upton, Dell. "White and Black Landscapes in Eighteenth-Century Virginia." *Places* 2 (1985): 59–72.

Vance, James E., Jr. *The Merchant's World: The Geography of Wholesaling.* Englewood Cliffs, N.J.: Prentice-Hall, 1970.

————. *This Scene of Man: The Role and Structure of the City in the Geography of Western Civilization.* New York: Harper's College Press, 1977.

————. *Location in a System of Global Extent: A Social Model of Settlement.* Geographical Papers no. 81. Reading: Department of Geography, Univ. of Reading, 1982.

————. *Capturing the Horizon: The Historical Geography of Transportation since the Transportation Revolution of the Sixteenth Century.* New York: Harper & Row, 1986.

————. "Metropolitan America—Evolution of an Ideal." In *Urban Development in the USA and Hungary: First American-Hungarian Geographical Seminar,* ed. Gyorgy Enyedi, 15–45. Budapest: Hungarian Academy of Sciences, 1978.

Wacker, Peter O. "Patterns and Problems in the Historical Geography of the Afro-American Population of New Jersey, 1726–1860." In *Pattern and Process Research in Historical Geography,* ed. Ralph Ehrenberg, 25–72. Washington, D.C.: Howard Univ. Press, 1975.

Wade, Richard C. *The Urban Frontier: Pioneer Life in Early Pittsburgh, Cincinnati, Lexington, Louisville, and St. Louis.* Cambridge: Harvard Univ. Press, 1959. Chicago: Univ. of Chicago Press, 1964.

Walker, Juliet E. K. *Free Frank: A Black Pioneer on the Antebellum Frontier.* Lexington: Univ. Press of Kentucky, 1983.

Wallace, Anthony F. C. *Rockdale: The Growth of an American Village in the Early Industrial Revolution.* New York: W. W. Norton, 1978.

Wallace, David Duncan. *South Carolina: A Short History, 1520–1948.* Chapel Hill: Univ. of North Carolina Press, 1951.

Walsh, Margaret. "The Spatial Evolution of the Mid-Western Pork Industry, 1835–75." *Journal of Historical Geography* 4 (1978): 1–22.

———. *The Rise of the Midwestern Meat Packing Industry.* Lexington: Univ. Press of Kentucky, 1982.

Walters, Vernon. "Migration into Mississippi, 1798–1837." M.A. thesis, Department of History, Mississippi State Univ., 1969.

Ward, David. *Cities and Immigrants: A Geography of Change in Nineteenth-Century America.* New York: Oxford Univ. Press, 1971.

Ward, James A. *Railroads and the Character of America, 1820–1877.* Knoxville: Univ. of Tennessee Press, 1986.

Warner, Sam Bass. *The Private City: Philadelphia in Three Periods of Its Growth.* Philadelphia: Univ. of Pennsylvania Press, 1968.

Warren, Kenneth. *The American Steel Industry, 1850–1970: A Geographical Interpretation.* Oxford: Oxford Univ. Press, 1973.

Wayman, Norbury L. *Life on the River: A Pictorial History of the Mississippi, the Missouri, and the Western River System.* New York: Crown, 1971.

Weaver, David C. "Spatial Strategies in Railroad Planning in Georgia and the Carolinas, 1830–1860." *Studies in the Social Sciences, West Georgia College* 18 (June 1979): 9–23.

Weinstein, Allen, and Frank Otto Gatell. *American Negro Slavery: A Modern Reader.* New York: Oxford Univ. Press, 1968.

Wesley, Charles H. "Manifestos of Slave Shipments along the Waterways, 1808–1864." *Journal of Negro History* 27 (April 1942): 155–74.

Wiebe, Robert H. *The Segmented Society: An Introduction to the Meaning of America.* New York: Oxford Univ. Press, 1975.

———. *The Opening of American Society: From the Adoption of the Constitution to the Eve of Disunion.* New York: Vintage Books, 1985.

Wilkie, Richard W., and Jack Tager, eds. *Historical Atlas of Massachusetts.* Amherst: Univ. of Massachusetts Press, 1991.

Williams, Samuel. *Beginnings of West Tennessee: In the Land of the Chickasaws, 1541–1841.* Johnson City, Tenn.: Watauga Press, 1930.

Williamson, Harold F., ed. *The Growth of the American Economy: An Introduction to the Economic History of the United States.* New York: Prentice-Hall, 1944.

Williamson, Joel. *New People: Miscegenation and Mulattoes in the United States.* New York: Free Press, 1980.

Wilson, Major L. *Space Time and Freedom: The Quest for Nationality and the Irrepressible Conflict, 1815–1861.* Westport, Conn.: Greenwood Press, 1974.

Wood, Joseph S. "Elaboration of a Settlement System: The New England Village in the Federal Period." *Journal of Historical Geography* 10 (October 1984): 331–56.

———. "'Build, Therefore, Your Own World': The New England Village as Settlement Ideal." *Annals, Association of American Geographers* 81 (March 1991): 32–50.

Woods, Sister Frances Jerome. *Marginality and Identity: A Colored Creole Family through Ten Generations.* Baton Rouge: Louisiana State Univ. Press, 1972.

Wooster, Ralph A. *The People in Power. Courthouse and Statehouse in the Lower South, 1850–1860.* Knoxville: Univ. of Tennessee Press, 1970.

Wyckoff, William. *The Developer's Frontier: The Making of the Western New York Landscape.* New Haven and London: Yale Univ. Press, 1988.

Zelinsky, Wilbur. *Nation into State: The Shifting Symbolic Foundations of American Nationalism.* Chapel Hill: Univ. of North Carolina Press, 1988.

PART THREE

Abbott, Carl. "Dimensions of Regional Change in Washington, D.C." *American Historical Review* 95 (December 1990): 1367–93.

Adams, Henry, ed. *Documents Relating to New-England Federalism, 1800–1815.* Boston: Little, Brown, 1877.

Ambler, Charles H., and Festus P. Summers. *West Virginia, the Mountain State.* Englewood Cliffs, N.J.: Prentice-Hall, 1958.

Andrews, J. Cutler. *The South Reports the Civil War*. Princeton: Princeton Univ. Press, 1970.

Ash, Stephen V. *Middle Tennessee Society Transformed, 1860–1870: War and Peace in the Upper South*. Baton Rouge: Louisiana State Univ. Press, 1988.

Barney, William L. *The Secessionist Impulse: Alabama and Mississippi in 1860*. Princeton: Princeton Univ. Press, 1974.

Barnwell, John. *Love of Order: South Carolina's First Secession Crisis*. Chapel Hill: Univ. of North Carolina Press, 1982.

Beecher, Henry Ward. *Patriotic Addresses in America and England, 1850–1885*. Edited by John R. Howard. New York: Fords, Howard, & Hulbert, 1888.

Belz, Herman. "*Twentieth-Century American Historians* and the Old South: A Review Essay." *Civil War History* 31 (June 1985): 171–80.

Bensel, Richard Franklin. *Yankee Leviathan: The Origins of Central State Authority in America, 1859–1877*. Cambridge: Cambridge Univ. Press, 1990.

Berkhofer, Robert F., Jr. "Jefferson, the Ordinance of 1784, and the Origins of the American Territorial System." *William and Mary Quarterly*, 3d ser., 29 (1972): 231–62.

Berlin, Ira, Barbara J. Fields, Thavolia Glymph, Joseph P. Reidy, and Leslie S. Rowland, eds. *Freedom: A Documentary History of Emancipation, 1861–1867*. Series 1, Vol. 1, *The Destruction of Slavery*. Cambridge: Cambridge Univ. Press, 1985.

Blegen, Theodore Christian. *Minnesota: A History of the State*. Minneapolis: Univ. of Minnesota Press, 1975.

The Blockade: Runners and Raiders. Alexandria, Va.: Time-Life Books, 1983.

Bright, Charles C. "The State in the United States during the Nineteenth Century." In *Statemaking and Social Movements: Essays in History and Theory*, ed. Charles Bright and Susan Harding, 121–58. Ann Arbor: Univ. of Michigan Press, 1984.

Bryan, Charles Faulkner, Jr. "The Civil War in East Tennessee: A Social, Political and Economic Study." Ph.D. dissertation, Department of History, Univ. of Tennessee, Knoxville, 1978.

Buck, Solon J. *Illinois in 1818*. 2d ed. Urbana: Univ. of Illinois Press, 1967.

Burns, Lee. *The National Road in Indiana*. Indiana Historical Society Publications, vol. 7, no. 4 (1919).

Callahan, James Morton. *Semi-Centennial History of West Virginia*. [Charleston]: Semi-Centennial Commission of West Virginia, 1913.

Carter, Clarence Edwin, ed. "The Territory of Mississippi 1809–1817." In *The Territorial Papers of the United States*, vol. 6, 593–94, 708–17, 732–35, 765–66. Washington, D.C. Government Printing Office, 1938.

Chittenden, L. E. *A Report of the Debate and Proceedings . . . of the Conference Convention . . . Held at Washington, D.C. in February, a.d. 1861*. New York: D. Appleton, 1864.

Cooper, William J., Jr. *The South and the Politics of Slavery, 1828–1856*. Baton Rouge: Louisiana State Univ. Press, 1978.

Coulter, E. Merton. *The Confederate States of America, 1861–1865*. Baton Rouge: Louisiana State Univ. Press, 1950.

Crofts, Daniel W. *Reluctant Confederates: Upper South Unionists in the Secession Crisis*. Chapel Hill: Univ. of North Carolina Press, 1989.

Curry, Richard Orr. *A House Divided: A Study of Statehood Politics and the Copperhead Movement in West Virginia*. Pittsburgh: Univ. of Pittsburgh Press, 1964.

Davis, Jefferson. *The Rise and Fall of the Confederate Government*. 2 vols. New York: D. Appleton, 1912.

Davis, Kenneth S. *Kansas. A Bicentennial History*. New York: W. W. Norton, 1976.

Degler, Carl N. *The Other South: Southern Dissenters in the Nineteenth Century*. New York: Harper & Row, 1974.

Dumond, Dwight Lowell. *The Secession Movement, 1860–1861*. Reprint. 1931. New York: Negro Universities Press, 1968.

Dumond, Dwight Lowell, ed. *Southern Editorials on Secession*. New York: Century, 1931.

Dunbar, Willis Frederick. *Michigan: A History of the Wolverine State*. Grand Rapids: William B. Eerdmans, 1965.

Eaton, Clement. *A History of the Southern Confederacy*. New York: Free Press, 1954.

Elazar, Daniel J., ed. *Federalism and Political Integration*. Lanham, Md.: Univ. Press of America, 1984.

Escott, Paul D. *After Secession: Jefferson Davis and the Failure of Confederate Nationalism*. Baton Rouge: Louisiana State Univ. Press, 1978.

Evitts, William J. *A Matter of Allegiances: Maryland from 1850 to 1861.* Baltimore: Johns Hopkins Univ. Press, 1974.

Faust, Drew Gilpin. *The Creation of Confederate Nationalism: Ideology and Identity in the Civil War South.* Baton Rouge: Louisiana State Univ. Press, 1988.

Fehrenbacher, Don E. *The South and Three Sectional Crises.* Baton Rouge: Louisiana State Univ. Press, 1980.

Finkelman, Paul. *An Imperfect Union: Slavery, Federalism, and Comity.* Chapel Hill: Univ. of North Carolina Press, 1981.

Fite, Emerson David. *Social and Industrial Conditions in the North during the Civil War.* New York: Macmillan, 1910.

Foner, Eric. *Reconstruction: America's Unfinished Revolution, 1863–1877.* New York: Harper & Row, 1988.

Fowler, William Chauncey. *The Sectional Controversy; or, Passages in the Political History of the United States, Including the Causes of the War between the Sections, with Certain Results.* New York: Charles Scribner, 1868.

Frederickson, George M. *The Inner Civil War: Northern Intellectuals and the Crisis of Union.* New York: Harper & Row, 1965.

Freehling, William W. *Prelude to Civil War: The Nullification Controversy in South Carolina, 1816–1836.* New York: Harper & Row, 1968.

Froncek, Thomas, ed. *An Illustrated History of the City of Washington,* by the Junior League of Washington. New York: Alfred A. Knopf, 1985.

Garraty, John A. *Interpreting American History: Conversations with Historians.* New York: Macmillan, 1970.

Gilchrist, David T., and W. David Lewis, eds. *Economic Change in the Civil War Era.* Greenville, Del.: Eleutherian Mills-Hagley Foundation, 1965.

Green, Constance McLaughlin. *Washington: Village and Capital, 1800–1878.* Princeton: Princeton Univ. Press, 1962.

Haynes, Robert V. "The Road to Statehood." In *A History of Mississippi,* ed. Richard Aubrey McLemore, vol. 1, 217–50. Jackson: Univ. and College Press of Mississippi, 1973.

Hess, Earl J. *Liberty, Virtue, and Progress: North-erners and Their War for the Union.* New York: New York Univ. Press, 1988.

Hesseltine, William B. *Lincoln's Plan of Reconstruction.* Tuscaloosa, Ala.: Confederate, 1960.

Hyman, Harold M., ed. *New Frontiers of the American Reconstruction.* Urbana: Univ. of Illinois Press, 1966.

Indianapolis Remembered: Christian Schrader's Sketches of Early Indianapolis. Indiana Library and Historical Department Occasional Publication no. 3. Indianapolis: Indiana Historical Bureau, 1987.

Jefferson, Thomas. "Plan for Government of the Western Territory" (1784), *The Papers of Thomas Jefferson.* Edited by Julian P. Boyd, vol. 6, 581–617. Princeton: Princeton Univ. Press, 1952.

Johnson, Michael P. *Towards a Patriarchal Republic: The Secession of Georgia.* Baton Rouge: Louisiana State Univ. Press, 1977.

Kennedy, Hon. John P. *The Border States: Their Power and Duty in the Present Disordered Condition of the Country.* Philadelphia: J. B. Lippincott, 1861.

Kenyon, Cecelia M. "Men of Little Faith: The Anti-Federalists on the Nature of Representative Government." *William and Mary Quarterly,* 3d ser., 12 (1955): 3–43.

Kettleborough, Charles. *Constitution Making in Indiana.* Vol. 1, 1780–1851. Indianapolis: Indiana Historical Commission, 1916.

Kincaid, John, ed. *Political Culture, Public Policy and the American States.* Philadelphia: Institute for the Study of Human Issues, 1982.

Klement, Frank L. *The Limits of Dissent: Clement L. Vallandigham and the Civil War.* Lexington: Univ. of Kentucky Press, 1970.

Leonard, Glen M. "Western Boundary-Making: Texas and the Mexican Cession, 1844–1850." Ph.D. dissertation, Department of History, University of Utah, 1970.

McPherson, James M. *Battle Cry of Freedom: The Civil War Era.* New York: Oxford Univ. Press, 1988.

Martin, Asa Earl. *The Anti-Slavery Movement in Kentucky, prior to 1850.* Louisville: Filson Club, 1918.

Matlack, L. C. "The Methodist Episcopal Church in the Southern States." *Methodist Quarterly Review* 54 (January 1872): 103–26.

Memminger, Hon. C. G. *Address [by the] Special Commissioner from the State of South Carolina, before the Assembled Authorities of the State of Virginia, 19 January 1860*. Document 58.

Moore, Glover. *The Missouri Controversy, 1819–1821*. [Lexington]: Univ. of Kentucky Press, 1953.

Moore, Mrs. M. B. *Geographical Reader for the Dixie Children. With Maps*. Raleigh: Branson, Farrar, 1863.

Mosby, John S. *Stuart's Cavalry in the Gettysburg Campaign*. New York: Moffat, Yard, 1908.

Myers, Robert Manson, ed. *The Children of Pride*. New York: Popular Library, 1972.

Norwood, John Nelson. *The Schism in the Methodist Episcopal Church, 1844: A Study of Slavery and Politics*. Alfred, N.Y.: Alfred Press, 1923.

Onuf, Peter S. *Statehood and Union: A History of the Northwest Ordinance*. Bloomington: Indiana Univ. Press, 1987.

Owens, Henry P., and James J. Cooke, eds. *The Old South in the Crucible of War*. Jackson: Univ. of Mississippi Press, 1983.

Perkins, Howard Cecil, ed. *Northern Editorials on Secession*. 2 vols. New York: D. Appleton-Century, 1942.

Potter, David M., and Thomas G. Manning, eds. *Nationalism and Sectionalism in America, 1775–1877: Select Problems in Historical Interpretation*. New York: Holt, Rinehart and Winston, 1949.

Ransom, Roger L. *Conflict and Compromise: The Political Economy of Slavery, Emancipation, and the American Civil War*. Cambridge: Cambridge Univ. Press, 1989.

Richter, Melvin. *The Political Theory of Montesquieu*. Cambridge: Cambridge Univ. Press, 1977.

Rose, Ernestine Bradford. *The Circle, "The Center of the Universe."* Indiana Historical Society Publication, vol. 18, no. 4 (1957).

Rowan, Steven, ed. and trans. *Germans for a Free Missouri: Translations from the St. Louis Radical Press, 1857–1862*. Columbia: Univ. of Missouri Press, 1983.

Schurz, Carl. *Report on the Condition of the South*. 1865. New York: Arno Press and the New York Times, 1969.

Scott, Winfield. "General Scott's Views." *National Intelligencer* (Washington) 49 (January 18, 1861).

Sefton, James E. *The United States Army and Reconstruction, 1865–1877*. Baton Rouge: Louisiana State Univ. Press, 1967.

Shanks, Henry T. *The Secession Movement in Virginia, 1847–1861*. Richmond: Garrett and Massie, 1934.

Shoemaker, Floyd Calvin. *Missouri's Struggle for Statehood, 1804–1821*. 1916. New York: Russell & Russell, 1969.

Sikes, Pressly S. *Indiana State and Local Government*. Bloomington: Bureau of Government Research, Indiana Univ., 1940.

Sitterson, Joseph Carlyle. *The Secession Movement in North Carolina*. Chapel Hill: Univ. of North Carolina Press, 1939.

Smeltzer, William Guy. *The History of United Methodism in Western Pennsylvania*. Nashville: Parthenon Press, 1975.

Smith, Edward Conrad. *The Borderland in the Civil War*. New York: Macmillan, 1927.

Snider, Clyde F. "Township Government in Indiana." *Indiana Studies in Business*, vol. 7, no. 1. Bloomington: Bureau of Business Research, 1932.

Speed, Captain Thomas. *The Union Cause in Kentucky*. New York: G. P. Putnam's Sons, 1907.

Stampp, Kenneth M., and Leon F. Litwack. *Reconstruction: An Anthology of Revisionist Writings*. Baton Rouge: Louisiana State Univ. Press, 1969.

Swaney, Charles Baumer. *Episcopal Methodism and Slavery: With Sidelights on Ecclesiastical Politics*. 1926. New York: Negro Universities Press, 1969.

Sweet, William W. *Methodism in American History*. New York: Abingdon Press, 1953.

Taylor, Robert M., Jr., ed. *The Northwest Ordinance 1787: A Bicentennial Handbook*. Indianapolis: Indiana Historical Society, 1987.

Taylor, William R. *Cavalier and Yankee: The Old South and American National Character*. Garden City, N.Y.: Anchor Books, 1963.

Thomas, Emory M. *The Confederate State of Richmond*. Austin: Univ. of Texas Press, 1971.

———. *The Confederate Nation: 1861–1865*. New York: Harper & Row, 1979.

Thwaites, Reuben G. "The Boundaries of Wisconsin." In *Collections of the State Historical Society of Wisconsin*, vol. 11, 451–501. Madison: Democratic Printing, 1888.

Turner, George Edgar. *Victory Rode the Rails: The Strategic Place of the Railroads in the Civil War.* Indianapolis: Bobbs-Merrill, 1953.

U.S. Congress. *Boundary Line between Land of the United States and Missouri.* 23d Cong., 2d sess., January 28, 1835. H. Doc. 107.

———. *Speech of Mr. Vinton* [on admission of Iowa and Florida]. In *Appendix to the Congressional Globe,* 28th Cong., 2d sess., n.s., February 11, 1845, 330–33.

———. *Admission of Iowa and Florida.* Debate in House of Representatives, February 10, 14, 1845. In *Congressional Globe,* 28th Cong., 2d sess., n.s., 269, 273–75.

———. *The Boundaries of Iowa.* In *Appendix to the Congressional Globe,* 29th Cong., 1st sess., n.s., June 8, 1846, 668–69.

———. House. *Western and Northern Boundary of Iowa.* 34th Cong., 1st sess., August 14, 1856. H. Rept. 347.

———. *Report on Cessions and Divisions of Western Lands.* Ed. John C. Fitzpatrick. In *Journals of the Continental Congress, 1774–1789* 30: 132–33. Washington, D.C.: Government Printing Office, 1934.

Van Deusen, John G. *The Ante-Bellum Southern Commercial Conventions.* Durham: Duke Univ. Press, 1926.

Vandiver, Frank E. *Basic History of the Confederacy.* Princeton: D. Van Nostrand, 1962.

Wall, Joseph Frazier. *Iowa: A Bicentennial History.* New York: W. W. Norton, 1978.

Weber, Thomas. *The Northern Railroads in the Civil War, 1861–1865.* New York: King's Crown Press, Columbia Univ., 1952.

Welles, Gideon. *Diary of Gideon Welles.* 2 vols. Boston: Houghton Mifflin, 1901.

Wender, Herbert. "Southern Commercial Conventions, 1837–1859." *Johns Hopkins University Studies in Historical and Political Science,* vol. 48 (1930), 423–658.

Williams, William Appleman. *The Roots of the Modern American Empire.* New York: Random House, 1969.

Wooster, Ralph A. *The Secession Conventions of the South.* Princeton: Princeton Univ. Press, 1962.

Wright, William C. *The Secession Movement in the Middle Atlantic States.* Cranbury, N.J.: Associated University Presses, 1973.

PART FOUR

Brault, Gerard J. *The French-Canadian Heritage in New England.* Hanover: Univ. Press of New England, 1986.

Carey, Henry C. *Miscellaneous Works.* 2 vols. 1883. New York: Burt Franklin, n.d.

Curtin, Philip D. *Two Jamaicas: The Role of Ideas in a Tropical Colony, 1830–1865.* Cambridge: Harvard Univ. Press, 1955.

Francis, R. Douglas, and Donald B. Smith, eds. *Readings in Canadian History: Post-Confederation.* [Toronto]: Holt, Rinehart and Winston of Canada, 1982.

———. *Readings in Canadian History: Pre-Confederation.* Holt, Rinehart and Winston of Canada, 1982.

Galloway, J. H. *The Sugar Cane Industry: An Historical Geography from Its Origins to 1914.* Cambridge: Cambridge Univ. Press, 1989.

Gibson, James A. "How Ottawa Became the Capital of Canada." *Ontario History* 46 (1954): 213–22.

Goheen, Peter. "The Changing Bias of Inter-Urban Communications in Nineteenth-Century Canada." *Journal of Historical Geography* 16 (1990): 177–96.

Hamshere, Cyril. *The British in the Caribbean.* Cambridge: Harvard Univ. Press, 1972.

Hoetink, H. *The Dominican People, 1850–1900: Notes for a Historical Sociology.* Baltimore: Johns Hopkins Univ. Press, 1982.

Jensen, Ronald J. *The Alaska Purchase and Russian-American Relations.* Seattle: Univ. of Washington Press, 1975.

Johnson, Howard, ed. *After the Crossing: Immigrants and Minorities in Caribbean Creole Society.* London: Frank Cass, 1988.

Kinchen, Oscar A. *Confederate Operations in Canada and the North.* North Quincy, Mass.: Christopher Publishing, 1970.

Knight, David B. *Choosing Canada's Capital: Jealousy and Friction in the Nineteenth Century.* Toronto: McClelland and Stewart, 1977.

Langley, Lester D. *Struggle for the American Mediterranean: United States–European Rivalry in the Gulf-Caribbean, 1776–1904.* Athens: Univ. of Georgia Press, 1976.

Lewis, Gordon K. *Main Currents in Caribbean*

Thought: The Historical Evolution of Caribbean Society in Its Ideological Aspects, 1492–1900. Baltimore: Johns Hopkins Univ. Press, 1983.

Lowenthal, David. West Indian Societies. New York: Oxford Univ. Press, 1972.

Loya, Diego Garcia. Mosaic of Mexican History. Mexico: Editorial CVLTVRA, T.G., S.A., 1958.

MacGillivray, Royce. The Mind of Ontario. Bellevue, Ont.: Mika Publishing, 1985.

Martin, Ged, ed. The Causes of Canadian Confederation. Fredericton, N.B.: Acadiensis Press, 1990.

Meyer, Michael C., and William L. Sherman. The Course of Mexican History. 3d ed. New York: Oxford Univ. Press, 1987.

Mintz, Sidney W., and Sally Price, eds. Caribbean Contours. Baltimore: Johns Hopkins Univ. Press, 1985.

Morton, W. L. The Canadian Identity. Madison: Univ. of Wisconsin Press, 1961.

———. The Critical Years: The Union of British North America, 1857–1873. Toronto: McClelland and Stewart, 1964.

———. "Clio in Canada: The Interpretation of Canadian History." Reprinted in Approaches to Canadian History, ed. Ramsay Cook, Craig Brown, and Carl Berger, 42–49. Toronto: Univ. of Toronto Press, 1967.

Murray, K. A., and D. B. McNeill. The Great Southern and Western Railway. Dublin: Irish Railway Record Society, 1976.

Nelson, William Javier. Almost a Territory: America's Attempt to Annex the Dominican Republic. Newark: Univ. of Delaware Press, 1990.

Nicholls, David. Haiti in Caribbean Context: Ethnicity, Economy and Revolt. New York: St. Martin's Press, 1985.

Poyo, Gerald E. "With All, and for the Good of All": The Emergence of Popular Nationalism in the Cuban Communities of the United States, 1848–1898. Durham: Duke Univ. Press, 1989.

Report of the Commissioner of the General Land Office for the Year 1867. Washington, D.C.: Government Printing Office, 1867.

Rippy, J. Fred. "Mexican Projects of the Confederates." Southwestern Historical Quarterly 22 (1919): 291–317.

Rister, Carl Coke. "Carlota: A Confederate Colony in Mexico." Journal of Southern History 11 (1945): 33–50.

Schoonover, Thomas David. Dollars over Dominion: The Triumph of Liberalism in Mexican–United States Relations, 1861–1867. Baton Rouge: Louisiana State Univ. Press, 1978.

Scott, Rebecca J. Slave Emancipation in Cuba: The Transition to Free Labor, 1860–1889. Princeton: Princeton Univ. Press, 1985.

Spry, Irene M. "The Palliser Expedition. In Rupert's Land: A Cultural Tapestry, ed. Richard C. Davis. Waterloo: Wilfrid Laurier Univ. Press, 1988.

Stevens, G. R. Canadian National Railways. Vol. 1, Sixty Years of Trial and Error. Toronto: Clarke, Irwin, 1960.

Stuart, Reginald C. United States Expansionism and British North America, 1775–1871. Chapel Hill: Univ. of North Carolina Press, 1988.

Tansill, Charles Callin. The Purchase of the West Indies. 1932. New York: Greenwood Press, 1968.

Underhill, Frank H. The Image of Confederation. Toronto: Canadian Broadcasting Corporation, 1964.

Waite, P. B. The Life and Times of Confederation, 1864–1867: Politics, Newspapers, and the Union of British North America. Toronto: Univ. of Toronto Press, 1962.

Winks, Robin W. Canada and the United States: The Civil War Years. Baltimore: John Hopkins Univ. Press, 1960.

INDEX

607